THE BRITISH POLITICAL TRADITION

VOLUME TWO
THE IDEOLOGICAL HERITAGE

THE BRITISH POLITICAL TRADITION
in four volumes

THE BRITISH POLITICAL TRADITION

W.H. GREENLEAF

VOLUME TWO

THE IDEOLOGICAL HERITAGE

METHUEN : LONDON & NEW YORK

First published in 1983 by
Methuen & Co. Ltd
11 New Fetter Lane, London EC4P 4EE
Published in the USA by
Methuen & Co.
in association with Methuen, Inc.
733 Third Avenue, New York, NY 10017

Printed in Great Britain
at the University Press, Cambridge

British Library Cataloguing in Publication Data
Greenleaf, W.H.
The British political tradition.
Vol. 2: The ideological heritage.
1. Great Britain – Politics and government
I. Title
320.941   JN234

ISBN 0-416-34660-X

Library of Congress Cataloging in Publication Data
Greenleaf, W.H.
The British Political tradition.
Includes index.
Contents: v. 1. The rise of collectivism.—v. 2.
The ideological heritage.
    1. Great Britain—Constitutional history. 2. Great
Britain—Politics and government. 3. Great Britain—
Foreign relations. 4. Political science—Great Britain—
History. I. Title.
JN118.G83   1983   320.941   82-18871
ISBN 0-416-15570-7 (v. 1)
ISBN 0-416-34660-X (v. 2)

We construct our world as an interpretation which
attempts to restore the unity which the real has lost by
our making its diversity explicit.
B. Bosanquet, *Logic*, II.ix.1 (i)

CONTENTS

Part Four The Duality of Socialism

ABBREVIATIONS

ASU	Anti-Socialist Union
AUEW	Amalgamated Union of Engineering Workers
BCA	British Constitution Association
BL	British Library
CCO	Conservative Central Office
CDA	Co-operative Development Agency
CPC	Conservative Political Centre
CPS	Centre for Policy Studies
CRD	Conservative Research Department
DNB	*Dictionary of National Biography* (Compact edition, Oxford, 1975)
H.C. Deb.	House of Commons Debates
H.L. Deb.	House of Lords Debates
HLRO	House of Lords Record Office
IEA	Institute of Economic Affairs
ILP	Independent Labour Party
IS	International Socialists
IWC	Institute for Workers' Control
IWW	Industrial Workers of the World
KCA	*Keesing's Contemporary Archives*
LCC	London County Council
LPDL	Liberty and Property Defence League
NAF	National Association for Freedom
NEC	National Executive Committee
NEDC	National Economic Development Council
NGL	National Guilds League
NLF	National Liberal Federation
NU	National Union
NUA	National Unionist Association
NUCA	National Union of Conservative Associations
NUCCA	National Union of Constitutional and Conservative Associations
NUCUA	National Union of Conservative and Unionist Associations
OED	*Oxford English Dictionary* (Compact edition, Oxford, 1971)

Parl. Deb.	Parliamentary Debates
PLP	Parliamentary Labour Party
PRA	Personal Rights Association
PRO	Public Record Office
SDA	Social Democratic Alliance
SDF	Social Democratic Federation
SDP	Social Democratic Party
SLP	Socialist Labour Party
SPGB	Socialist Party of Great Britain
TLS	*The Times Literary Supplement*
Trans. R. Hist. S.	*Transactions of the Royal Historical Society*
UPW	Union of Post Office Workers
USRC	Unionist Social Reform Committee

PREFACE

As explained in the General Preface (see vol. i, *The Rise of Collectivism*, p. xi), this study of the British Political Tradition will be complete in four volumes of which *The Ideological Heritage* is the second. This is an attempt to show how the basic tension between libertarianism and collectivism is reflected in arguments of state; how our three main political doctrines have both stimulated and reacted to the growth of government intervention and the proliferation of public agency; and how they have dealt with the problems of individual liberty involved. The potential range of material is vast and so the case-studies and reviews presented are merely illustrative and (in the context of the whole) might well seem arbitrarily selected. I could have chosen other (and some might say, better) instances, but I am fairly certain that those given are reasonably representative of the most important domestic aspects of the creeds concerned. As it is, a number of specific studies originally undertaken has in the end had to be excluded for reasons of space. I suppose I might have crammed in a wider exemplary array if individual topics, theories, or writers had been more cursorily examined. However, I wanted the great part of what was treated to be dealt with, not of course at definitive length or anything like it, but in a way that gave some scope for more than the baldest summary. This seemed particularly necessary in respect of works at the opposite ends of the scale of political sophistication. With the consciously theoretical polemics (like those of Spencer, Cecil, or Tawney) it is always desirable, or even necessary, to give at least some indication of the general principles intended to provide the explanatory base of the policies presented; while in the case of the brawls and altercations of the ideological hustings, it is important to show how commonplace the themes are and this can only be done at the cost of a certain amount of repetition. Naturally critics could always do it better. Well, let them do so; they will find (oddly enough) a relatively untilled field. For myself, I was always most conscious of having astonishingly few guides to follow at least at the level of generality required in this sort of survey. Perhaps the hint implied by this strange deficiency or neglect should have been taken and the task let severely alone; though this would, in turn, have left an enormous, and wholly indefensible, gap in an account purporting to cover British politics as a whole.

The various debts I owe are as indicated in the General Preface. But I am happy to acknowledge again the particular help given by the Nuffield Foundation; also the permission to cite from documents in the House of Lords Record Office and from Crown copyright material in the Public Record Office.

May 1982   W. H. GREENLEAF
                                                              Swansea

*   *   *

The author and publisher would also like to thank the following for their kind permission to use copyright material:

Bell & Hyman for permission to reproduce extracts from R. H. Tawney, *The Acquisitive Society* (G. Bell, 1921).

Elliot Right Way Books for permission to reproduce extracts from J. E. Powell, *Freedom and Reality*.

George Allen & Unwin for permission to reproduce extracts from G. B. Shaw *et al.*, *Fabian Essays*; R. H. Tawney, *Equality*; and G. Watson (ed.), *The Unservile State*.

The London School of Economics and Political Science for permission to reproduce extracts from B. Webb, *My Apprenticeship* (Pelican Books) and B. Webb, *Our Partnership* (Longman).

PART ONE
THE RANGE OF IDEAS

We hear a great deal of Whig principles, and Tory principles, and Liberal principles, and Mr. Canning's principles; but I confess that I have never seen a definition of any of them, and cannot make to myself a clear idea of what any of them mean.
WELLINGTON, 1828, cited in P. GUEDALLA, *The Duke*, 1931; repr. 1940, p.364

I

DOCTRINE AND
INTERPRETATION

The Spiritual . . . is the parent and first-cause of the Practical. The Spiritual everywhere originates the Practical, models it, makes it: . . . . For as thought is the life-fountain and motive-soul of action, so in all regions of this human world, whatever outward thing offers itself to the eye, is merely the garment or body of a thing which already existed invisibly within; which, striving to give itself expression, has found, in the given circumstances, that it could and would express itself – so. This is everywhere true; and in these times when men's attention is directed outward rather, this deserves far more attention than it will receive.
T. CARLYLE, 'Latter-Day Pamphlets', 1850, in *The Works*, 1871–4, XX.251–2

THE CENTRALITY OF POLITICAL THOUGHT

. . . speculative thought is one of the chief elements of social power. . . .
It is what men think, that determines how they act;. . . .
J. S. MILL, 'Considerations on Representative Government', 1861, in
Collected Works, 1963ff., xix.382

THE DIALECTIC between the growing pressures of collectivism and the opposing libertarian tendency is the one supreme fact of our domestic political life as this has developed over the past century and a half. Of course, the antithesis has displayed itself over a wide range of institutional changes.[1] But it has perhaps been more starkly revealed in the conflict of doctrines, and for this reason alone it is appropriate to begin a detailed examination of our political tradition with a review of the ideological attitudes involved. Certainly no such discussion can be complete without some substantial reference to this theoretical dimension of our heritage. Yet it is curious – very strange indeed – how many works purporting to study our public affairs simply ignore completely this aspect of things. Presumably such concentration of attention is

---

1 See vol.iii, *A Much-Governed Nation*.

premissed on the assumption that politics, being a very down-to-earth and practical (not to say sordid) activity, may most appropriately be regarded as a matter of power centres and pressures, manoeuvre and accommodation, institutions and procedures, ambition and advantage, and that ideas or theories as such do not have much to do with it: 'Ideas! my good sir? There is no occasion for them' as de Quincey wrote on one occasion. If they do come in, it is merely as a sort of rhetorical superficies, a means of persuasion, justification, or concealment, 'a language of representative feelings' (to cite the opium eater again), at worst a way of sustaining interest-begotten prejudice. On these terms the role of ideas, like the utterances of Mr Daubeny in *Phineas Redux*, might be no more than to create confusion and mystery, to be purposely unintelligible.[2] Or, if camouflage and deliberately obfuscatory intent of this sort are not involved, sheer inadvertence may rest at the heart of the matter. As Mallock once wrote (discussing Conservative doctrine), when men are busy with details in 'the heat of party warfare' they have little time to be

> mindful of what seem to be abstract principles. It is true indeed that they have to make constant appeals to these; but they make them in haste, without leisure for calm reflection, and the more eager they grow in their arguments, the less clear they grow as to the final points they are arguing for.[3]

Yet while all this does, of course, point to a vital aspect of the truth, completely to neglect the leading or direct part ideas may none the less play is itself intellectually shallow and may be positively misleading. For it can only result in an abstract and one-sided understanding of what politics is about. Carlyle summed up the matter aptly: 'On the whole', he wrote, 'Institutions are much; but they are not all.' And his contemporary J. S. Mill referred with justice to 'that dullest and most useless of all things, mere facts without ideas'.[4] Indeed the omission is not simply boring or without value, it is impossible: a fact without a framework of perception to give it being, status, and meaning is quite inconceivable.

So far as the study of politics is concerned, then, the error entailed by the neglect of thought is of very considerable moment, and this in respect of both the psychology and the methodology of the matter.

In the first place ideas of one kind or another do sway or determine

2 T. de Quincey, *Confessions of an English Opium Eater* (1821; Penguin, 1981), p.79; A. Trollope, *Phineas Redux* (1874; Panther, 1973), p.60.

3 W. H. Mallock, 'The Philosophy of Conservatism', *The Nineteenth Century*, viii (1880), p.724.

4 T. Carlyle, 'Signs of the Times' (1829), *The Works* (People's edn, 1871–4), vii. 243; J. S. Mill, 'Michelet's History of France' (1844), in *Dissertations and Discussions* (London, 1859), ii. 133.

people's actions. It is sharply evident that men and women are prepared to kill and maim for an ideological cause, a conception, for instance, of a united Ireland or of an Ulster separated from the Catholic republicanism of the south. And short of such harsh extremes, beliefs still have a substantial effect: the notion of a culturally independent Wales free of insidious Saxon influence; of a classless society; of the free enterprise economy; or any of the multitude of opinions of greater or less scope, sense, or absurdity, that appear from time to time in the political market-place. Their very occurrence there indicates a motivating significance. In the end it might seem that, after all, politics is really about nothing but ideas: general notions of right and duty, democracy, authority, power, property, and the like; and also about specific questions in which a strong evaluative element is involved such as, What ought to be the place in our society of the trade unions and should their powers be limited in some way? What can justify a claim to 'fair shares' in the distribution of the national product? Should the object of policy be to maintain or reduce differentials of income or housing? Can special treatment in respect of, say, educational facilities be adequately vindicated? Of course, all this might be put in terms of interests, demands, and claims. But what are these even but conceptions of concern that have to be identified and substantiated? It is significant, too, that even the most blatant *realpolitik* is invariably accompanied by a case made in its behalf, a decent respect being due to the opinions of mankind in this regard. As well, if anything is to be done in politics it is invariably thought best it should be clearly conceived. So for this reason and because, too, others have to be persuaded to support the goals in question, the elaboration of some kind of social philosophy is inevitable to try to give direction and unity to the matter in hand.[5] The significance of theoretical themes is thus substantial, not to say fundamental. Many years ago, Gustave LeBon put the nub of the matter in the broad terms appropriate to historical analysis on the grand scale and gave Marx and the sociologists of knowledge the lie direct:

> Les grands bouleversements qui précèdent les changements de civilisations, semblent, au premier abord, déterminés par des transformations politiques considérables: . . . . Mais une étude attentive de ces événements découvre le plus souvent, comme cause réelle, derrière leurs causes apparentes, une modification profonde dans les idées des peuples. Les véritables bouleversements historiques ne sont pas ceux qui nous étonnent par leur grandeur et leur violence. Les seuls changements importants, ceux d'où le renouvellement des civilisations découle, s'opèrent dans les opinions, les conceptions et les croyances.

5 Cf. L. T. Hobhouse, *Liberalism* (1911; Galaxy Books, 1966), pp. 30–1.

Les événements mémorables sont les effets visibles des invisibles changements de la pensée des hommes.[6]

Then, secondly – a related issue – it is a mistake to study institutions and interests as though they are simply empirical entities. For they are nothing of the kind, as Maitland saw clearly enough when he referred to 'those spiritual things that we call "institutions"'.[7] A political body – such as Parliament, a ministry, a local council, or a public corporation – is a group of people acting in a certain way in accordance with given legal rules, conventions, and the like in order to achieve certain purposes. And roles, rules, and ends are not tangible things like a building or the Speaker's wig: they are conceptions or relations. So it is into these that an institution or an interest dissolves on analysis: a point R. H. Tawney once put succinctly when he wrote that 'social institutions are the visible expression of the scale of moral values which rules the minds of individuals'.[8] And consider the assertion of an infinitely greater and wiser man still. In his essay on the heroic in history Thomas Carlyle wrote:

> It is the *Thought* of Man . . . by which man works all things whatsoever. All that he does, and brings to pass, is the vesture of a Thought. This London City, with all its houses, palaces, steam-engines, cathedrals, and huge immeasurable traffic and tumult, what is it but a Thought, but millions of Thoughts made into One; – a huge immeasurable Spirit of a THOUGHT, embodied in brick, in iron, smoke, dust, Palaces, Parliaments, Hackney Coaches, Katherine Docks, and the rest of it! Not a brick was made but some man had to *think* of the making of that brick.

But, Carlyle adds, 'the *purest* embodiment a Thought of men can have' is the thing we call '"bits of paper with traces of black ink"'.[9] So it is conscious statements of ideas and assumptions to which primary attention is due and which is acknowledged in this present volume.[10]

6 G. LeBon *Psychologie des foules* (1895; Paris, 1912), pp. 1–2. On the practical influence of ideas, see also the famous concluding passage of J. M. Keynes, *The General Theory of Employment, Interest and Money* (1936; London, 1942), pp. 383–4.

7 F. W. Maitland, 'The Survival of Archaic Communities', *Law Quarterly Review*, ix (1893), p. 211.

8 R. H. Tawney, *The Acquisitive Society* (1921; London, 1943), p. 3. Cf. B. Webb, 'The Nature and Classification of Social Institutions', M. Adams (ed.), *The Modern State* (London, 1933), pp. 165ff.

9 T. Carlyle, 'On Heroes, Hero-Worship and the Heroic in History' (1840), *The Works*, xiii. 153, italics and capitalization in original.

10 For a recent and specific example of the analysis of complex organization – local government in Britain – in terms of radical change in the *assumptions* (in this case about levels of public expenditure) of those working in it, see J. D. Stewart, 'From Growth to Standstill', M. Wright (ed.), *Public Spending Decisions: Growth and Restraint in the 1970s* (London, 1980), ch. 2, esp. pp. 11–13.

Nor is a conceptual element of this sort properly to be eliminated by a naturalistic mode of enquiry. Political behaviour cannot satisfactorily or simply be seen from the outside as a series of causes and effects, stimuli and responses; for the way a person categorizes and perceives his experience has to be considered and is fundamental. Moreover where another actor is concerned recognition of intention is involved. And in each case the value or assessment that determines the response is 'structure dependent' (to use the Chomskyan jargon) and has to be attributed to a context of conventions, to a culture, tradition, or way of life, what Professor Bruner called 'the traffic rules' in force in a person's mind. In his Herbert Spencer lecture he concluded that a theory of human behaviour which 'fails to make contact with man's conceptions of his world and his way of knowing', which 'sets these aside as epi-phenomena', will 'neither be an adequate theory of human behaviour nor will it prevail in common sense.'[11]

For this kind of reasons at the least, then, consideration of thought about politics must be granted primacy of attention; and the merely institutional study come along in its proper, that is in second, place. And if it is behaviour that is examined, this is done only to establish the concepts and relationships arising from or implicit in this activity and which are the real object of scrutiny.

IDEOLOGICAL ANALYSIS

> One of the mistakes oftenest committed, and which are the sources of the greatest practical errors in human affairs, is that of supposing that the same name always stands for the same aggregation of ideas.
> J. S. MILL, 'Chapters on Socialism', 1879, in *Collected Works*, 1963ff.,
> v.750

Of specific concern here are the forms of thought usually called ideologies or doctrines. I use these terms very loosely and simply, indeed synonymously, to mean a set of beliefs about political and social arrangements and intended primarily to justify action in respect to this environment, though the fullest statements of this sort additionally constitute a kind of explanation about the growth and structure of that context. Socialism is one such confluence of ideas and policies; Conservatism and Liberalism are others, though these do not, of course, complete the list of exemplary possibilities. But analysis of these entities is not necessarily a straightforward, and may not be an easy, matter, various problems of identification and interpretation being involved.

An initial point is that any political doctrine is not a simple concept: it

---

11   J. Bruner, 'Psychology and the Image of Man', *TLS* (17 December 1976), pp.1590, 1591.

is a collection of aims, arguments, and assumptions. There are the purposes of some kind, a case or conclusion it is sought to establish; there are the techniques of argument used to sustain these ends and to make them as persuasive as possible; and there is the set of beliefs which makes the purpose credible and the arguments cogent and which constitutes the basis of the political views expounded.[12] Of course, these elements may not be kept wholly separate or be well worked-out but in principle they must be present or implicit. And each may be – almost certainly will be – a complex phenomenon in itself manifesting a notable variety of internal differences. For one thing there may be real or apparent disagreement between co-ideologists about the precise nature of the objectives to be sought, the means of their achievement, or the priority of their pursuit. Later chapters will show, for example, the great diversity of emphasis that can exist within a given ideology about the role and office of the state. Again the ideas concerned may be expressed in quite different languages of explanation, justification, and persuasion. The disparate idioms and concepts of religion, the moral life, natural science, the law, history, philosophy, and economics are alike commonly deployed and in no uniform fashion: fellow partisans can urge similar goals in very varied ways, and ideological opponents may make use of the same sort of argumentation drawn from a common world of discourse. Furthermore the level of delivery achieved will fluctuate markedly for not all doctrine is articulated on the same plane of expression. In a moment of frankness Campbell-Bannerman once referred to the rubbish for the groundlings that so often emanates from party platforms. Of the same style is the ephemeral effusion of the party diatribist with his chain of bald assertions. Here one is obviously dealing with the least sophisticated levels of ideological discourse, with (in Orwell's pejorative terms)

> . . . a clique of self-advancers,
> Trained in the tactics of the pamphleteer,
> Where slogans serve for thoughts and sneers for answers. . . .[13]

But all this – the inevitable result of living and working not *in Platonis republica* but *in Romuli faece* – is properly distinguished from a more considered justification of position in which there is reference to, or examination of, some kind of general principles drawn perhaps from conventional norms of political behaviour and assessment, from ethical

---

12 Cf. my *Order, Empiricism and Politics: Two Traditions of English Political Thought, 1500–1700* (London, 1964), pp.1–2.

13 G. Orwell, 'As One Non-Combatant to Another', in P. Larkin (ed.), *The Oxford Book of Twentieth-Century English Verse* (1973; London, 1978), p.517. Campbell-Bannerman's sentiment is expressed in a letter to Garnet Wolseley (1 August 1886), Wolseley papers, cited in J. Wilson, *CB: a Life of Sir Henry Campbell-Bannerman* (London, 1973), p.99.

criteria, or whatever it might be.[14] And this in turn has to be differentiated from the mature exploration of a political creed deliberately set within the framework of a philosophy, a view of things as a whole. And at any level the case can be put with more or less skill and sophistication, systematically or otherwise.

In addition the emphasis of a political doctrine is always changing, continually being modified. Its exposition is subject not only to the spell of intellectual fashion, the current conventions of political debate, and the varied possibilities of different modes of expression, it is also, to an important extent, at the mercy of circumstance, the demands of a particular situation, and all sorts of external pressures. For it may (as already intimated) constitute a kind of rhetoric swayed by all the winds of obliquity to which the hustings are open. Its language is used as a means of action: with Cobden, said John Morley, a speech was a way of accomplishing something and always referred to practical performance of some kind.[15] In political life how else should it be? But this does mean that the performer in that arena may use arguments and ideas that are more indicative of what he thinks will sway his audience than of what he himself deems convincing; and different contexts of blandishment and artifice may suggest a medley of themes not wholly conformable to one another. Unlike Goldsmith's village preacher, the politician will necessarily and properly practise 'to fawn, or seek for power, By doctrines fashion'd to the varying hour'; and Chesterton echoed this expectation when he referred to 'all those delicate difficulties, known to politicians, which beset the public defence of a doctrine which one heartily disbelieves.'[16] Dicey noticed these considerations, too, when he wrote that

> all kind of preaching, whether religious, moral or political, has a certain tendency to produce cant or unreality, because the preacher, in order to bring his doctrine home to his hearers, rouses himself into a state of strong feeling and emphasizes his beliefs more than perhaps represents his ordinary or average feeling. . . .

It is, he added, an oratorical technique like talking more loudly than usual to a large audience and involves 'no real falsity'.[17] So when in 1829

---

14 Cf. the Marxist distinction between 'agitation' and 'propaganda' as described in R. Taylor, *Film Propaganda: Soviet Russia and Nazi Germany* (London, 1979), pp. 44–6.

15 J. Morley, *The Life of Richard Cobden* (London, 1881), ii. 371.

16 O. Goldsmith, *The Deserted Village* (1770), ll. 145–6; G. K. Chesterton, *The Victorian Age in Literature* (1913; London, 1920), p. 8. See also G. Watson, *The English Ideology: Studies in the Language of Victorian Politics* (London, 1973), esp. ch. 7 'Political Oratory'.

17 Dicey to Miss A. Fry (29 November 1905), cited in R. S. Rait (ed.), *Memorials of Albert Venn Dicey Being Chiefly Letters and Diaries* (London, 1925), pp. 191–2. Cf.

O'Connell avowed on the hustings that he was an ardent Benthamite much of what he said 'must be set off as characteristic blarney.'[18] Similarly when Joseph Chamberlain (in the course of expounding his 'unauthorized programme') invoked the necessity of pursuing the greatest happiness of the mass of the people, it might reasonably be asked whether this was to him just a persuasive phrase employed as a device of platform rhetoric merely or whether it involved at least some genuine commitment to the utilitarian paraphernalia even if this was not formally expounded (as, given the occasion, it could hardly be).[19] Again when Lord Rosebery in 1900–1 espoused the cause of national efficiency, did he really accept the bundle of ideas usually involved, or was it to him no more than a popular and timely rallying cry with which to appeal to patriotic men of all parties and of none to give their support to his case for a coalition government?[20] Of little significance perhaps in studying the thought of the consciously intellectual political writer, because he will invariably try to explore his presuppositions, this difficulty or consideration arises progressively in examining the active participant in political life. Yet, of course, the review of any ideology is quite incomplete unless this equivocal and perhaps ephemeral dimension of expression is explored. What Cobbett called 'the principles of Pratt, the principles of Yorke' – referring to two lesser lights of the main parties of his day – have to be treated as well as those of 'the divinised heroes' of each faction.[21] Moreover in examining political ideologies we are dealing not simply with a finished array of ideas but with notions that grow and develop over a period of time; and for this reason alone it would be appropriate to expect a contrariety of themes to emerge. Consequently violence is done to the real diversity of ideas, manner, and attainment involved if these are pressed into the nice conformity of an unchanging system. What is contained within a designated ideological pale is thus not uniform or static and of it can be said what the old Staffordshire poet wrote of fortune: it is always 'full of fresh varietie' and 'Constant in

---

the comments on Crossman's inconsistency of argument and his unpredictable loyalties, J. Morgan (ed.), *The Backbench Diaries of Richard Crossman* (London, 1981), intro., pp.11, 12; also Crossman's own remarks about Aneurin Bevan's 'somersaults', ibid., pp.613–14, 615–16, 629.

18 O. MacDonagh, *Early Victorian Government, 1830–1870* (London, 1977), p.35.

19 J. L. Garvin and J. Amery, *The Life of Joseph Chamberlain* (London, 1932–69), ii. 67, 77. Cf. the case of Lord R. Churchill discussed at pp.219–20 below.

20 G. R. Searle, *The Quest for National Efficiency: a Study in British Politics and Political Thought, 1899–1914* (Oxford, 1971), ch.IV. And for the use of cries such as 'natural selection' and 'the greatest happiness' in the late nineteenth-century debate over school development, see G. Sutherland, *Elementary Education in the Nineteenth Century* (London, 1971), p.37.

21 Cf. Matthew Arnold, 'The Future of Liberalism', *The Nineteenth Century*, viii (1880), p.1.

nothing but inconstancie.'[22] It is not (in a word) monomorphous: it does not – and cannot be expected to – exhibit similarity of form throughout its successive stages of development, its different channels of expression, or in its varying aspects. It is, in the old phrase, a unity in diversity. And the problem of describing and analysing any ideology is one of giving some proper indication of all the varied, even antithetical, aspects of its being and of their connexion.

However, faced with all such dissimilarities of stance and expression, the student of these matters may feel impelled to seek stability amid the chaos by looking for some constant core of ideas which underlies the different versions of theory and policy as, for instance, when L. T. Hobhouse, reviewing the great change in Liberal doctrine that occurred round about the turn of the century, wrote of reaching nevertheless 'the centre and heart', 'the essentials', of the ideology.[23] When achieved, this essence would be taken to constitute a standard of credal identity and purity. Really what is involved in this exercise is a sort of Platonic attempt to transcend the contingency and vagaries of the world of ideological Becoming and to attain the immutable certainty of real Being manifested in the unchanging doctrinal Idea.

But such an enterprise is not without difficulties, problems that, in the end, must lead to a complete rejection of the procedure in view however reasonable it may appear at first sight and however subtle its application. For the truth is that, not only does it prove impossible in practice to achieve an adequate or agreed reduction, any attempt to do so is bound to be misleading. It is found that by no means all the exemplars of the doctrine concerned represent the components of its supposed core in the same way or combination or to the same extent; that it is not easy to reduce to such a denominator the rich variety of personalities and ideas in evidence: too much refuses to fit into the neat pattern of a delimited and unchanging system. Of course, the ideological imprimatur could be refused to those who fail to conform to the established stereotype. But this procedure is all too likely to violate common political usage and to this extent at least to be unsatisfactory. And it would necessarily involve the exaggeration of those aspects of the doctrine insisted on to the damage or denial of other equally important facets of the whole. It is the depiction of a caricature rather than a satisfactory characterization of the ideology in question or, in H. G. Wells's image, like showing a man's skeleton for his portrait.[24] Moreover even if it were feasible to separate

22 Richard Barnfield, 'The Shepherd's Content' (1594), *Poems, 1594–1598*, ed. Arber (Westminster, 1896), p.27.
23 L. T. Hobhouse *Liberalism* (1911; Galaxy Books, 1966), p.29.
24 H. G. Wells, *The Research Magnificent* (London, 1915), pp.3–4. Cf. the remarks in Arnold Bennett's letter to H. G. Wells (24 August 1903), in Harris Wilson (ed.), *Arnold Bennett and H. G. Wells: a Record of a Personal and a Literary Friendship* (London, 1960), pp.95–6.

agreed basic themes of a general kind from other, less noumenal, elements in the doctrine, these could not entail any necessary consequences as to issues of detailed policy or action so that in their application (if not in their theoretical statement) a wide diversity of programmatic possibilities must be reintroduced rather than transcended. Consequently, as one modern commentator observed about the doctrine he was studying, 'there is no formula of faith which can be labeled Liberalism at all times and all places.'[25] Conservatives, of course, have frequently prided themselves on not possessing a systematic theory of things so they at least might be expected to say 'Amen' to the point here suggested; and the variety of Socialisms available is notorious.

Yet though it is thus inappropriate to look for a crucial nucleus of doctrine, the attempt continues to be made. For instance, in a recent, most subtle analysis of this problem, Dr B. C. Parekh discussed how an ideology may be identified and urged (what is undoubtedly true) that too little attention has been given to examining the logical structure of political doctrines. He went on to suggest, unexceptionably, that an ideology should be seen as having a tripartite structure. First there was 'a more or less well articulated metaphysic, a general view of the universe' intended to provide justification for the second element, 'a specific conception of man and society'; then finally there was 'a programmatic content' to indicate how this conception might be realized.[26] It was conceded that the interrelationship of these three components is necessarily contingent; but it was equally urged most strongly that the real identity of an ideology lies in the unchanging view of man and society, the second or central aspect of the threefold structure which thus constitutes its essential character and what distinguishes it from other political creeds. There is here, therefore, a central core of ideas, a set of values and principles, which can be found in all true exponents of the ideology concerned (though they are not exclusively so found).[27]

The argument is succinctly and cogently put though I think it does not in the end save the case. Of course, it starts by allowing enormous divergence of emphasis and exposition in accepting the possibility of a substantial heterogeneity of metaphysic and programme. But, as well, it is by no means apparent why the focal themes envisaged should themselves be beyond the likelihood of substantial variety, for the supposedly central and common principles will consist of general terms and so can encompass a range of meaning, their cash value being by no means constant. They could cover a very wide diversity of emphasis

25 T. P. Neill, *The Rise and Decline of Liberalism* (Milwaukee, Wis., 1953), p.12.
26 B. C. Parekh (ed.), *The Concept of Socialism* (London, 1975), p.2.
27 ibid., pp.2–6, 11–12. Cf. D. J. Manning, *Liberalism* (London, 1976), pp.13, 143, on the three principles which, he believes, characterize the Liberal tradition as a whole; and ibid., ch. 6 for important qualifications.

indeed. In the case in question, Socialism, the principles concerned are said to embrace: a belief in mankind's inherent sociality, a feeling of human brotherhood, that abilities and powers are a social trust; the view that what is fundamental is not self-help or self-interest but a sense of social responsibility for general well-being; the idea that (in consequence) co-operation must replace competition in all areas of life especially the economic; and finally the opinion that planning is crucial as the expression of man's rational and conscious control of his resources and destiny. Yet might there not be different interpretations of the meaning of 'sociality', 'human brotherhood', or 'social trust'? What is entailed by a sense of 'social responsibility' or 'co-operation'? What exactly is involved in a rejection of 'competition'? What is 'rationality' and how and why is this uniquely associated in this context with 'planning'? And so on. The truth is that a substantial dissimilarity will re-emerge within the presumed core ideas, even were it feasible to separate this essence from other aspects of ideological expression. In addition there is a wealth of implication hidden in the admission that the central principles are not exclusive to Socialist writers. This concession invites recognition of what may be called ideological overlap and the impossibility of distinguishing unambiguously the supposed centre of one doctrine from that of another. To steal a phrase, there may (in this world of ideas) be 'underlying affinities' between the apparently contrasting: the kind of resemblance perhaps that, to take but one example, led the young Aldous Huxley to observe similarities in the opinions of two politicians so incongruously different as George Lansbury and Lord Henry Bentinck.[28] And indeed the notion of man and society which Dr Parekh supposes to be essentially Socialist is not uncharacteristic of some Liberal and Conservative writers. It might be said that the latter are, therefore, really Socialists; but what sort of definition is it that secures ideological purity by setting aside personal conviction and common usage? No: to imagine that there is any necessary common denominator to varied forms of ideological expression is an illusion and a mistake. Students of the structure or logical form of political doctrines should not, therefore, try to sustain the possibility of monoideism, that is, the dominance of some intellectual quiddity. Instead they must reckon on and accept multiformity, overlap, divergence, inconsistency, obliquity, and change as features intrinsic to the subject-matter. The basic rule of analysis must be that any ideology is essentially ambivalent in the assumptions, arguments, and aims it

28 Hobhouse, *Liberalism*, p. 31; Huxley's letter (November 1917), cited in S. Bedford, *Aldous Huxley: a Biography* (London, 1973–4), i. 90. Cf. the many similarities between the Socialism of R. MacDonald and Tawney (on the one hand) and the new Liberalism of Hobhouse or Hobson (on the other), as observed by P. F. Clarke, 'The Progressive Movement in England', *Trans. R. Hist. S.*, 5s., xxiv (1974), pp. 171–2.

encompasses. Yet for some reason or other political observers can writhe with anguish or surprise when they note inter-party plagiarism or similarities of viewpoint. One example is a comment in *The Times* that it is remarkable how some observations made by a Labour Cabinet minister 'could easily be voiced in the context of Conservative philosophy'.[29] Similarly a recent academic work on right-wing attitudes and beliefs in British politics, while accepting there is a varied range of opinions involved in Conservative thought and policy, nevertheless insists (somewhat contradictorily) on trying to establish the nuclear elements of a Conservative approach.[30] The myth of ideological purity dies hard. But (it must be repeated) there is no single correct version of any political creed and to assume that there is is a bad and a fundamental error of analysis.

There is in Scottish law a procedure called multiplepoinding which is a form of action by the holder of a fund or property to which there are several claimants and which requires the parties concerned to appear and settle their claims in court. The student of an ideology is rather like such a proprietor. He is, as it were, the possessor of intellectual assets for the ownership of which there is a number of suppliants: for naturally the doctrine appears in many guises and exponents of each assert dominion over the entire estate. Indeed all of the litigants in such an interpleading suit have a legitimate claim and each may reasonably distrain upon some part of their multiform ideological heritage. But none of them may impound it entire. And perhaps the only means whereby their mad jostling for doctrinal place may be confined within due limits is to impose on the omnium gatherum the ordered restraint of academic scrutiny. The justice of the student of these matters consists in trying to represent freely every kind of partiality and to do this by giving different views neither a halter nor a halo but simply a voice.[31] Of course, in the process the ideological expression may well lose something of its immediacy of impact and power to move. But perhaps this is no great sacrifice; and at least what remains should have the virtues of catholicity and quiet understanding and show everything in due condition and proportion: 'Ther were neuer such a company of bedlames driuin wnto ane poyndfauld as wee.'[32]

Instead of nuclear designation, therefore, it is necessary to establish

29 R. Butt, 'Shoring Up the Labour Party', *The Times* (23 February 1978), p.16.
30 N. Nugent and R. King (eds), *The British Right: Conservative and Right Wing Politics in Britain* (Farnborough, Hants., 1977), esp. pp.5–6, 8–10, 13–14, 22–3.
31 Cf. G. K. Chesterton's interesting remarks in *Robert Browning* (1903; London, 1919), pp.170–5.
32 The rueful but apt comment of Captain John Spottiswoode reflecting, under sentence of death, on the traitorous associates he had had, cited in J. Maidment (ed.), *The Spottiswoode Miscellany* (Edinburgh, 1844–5), i. 211.

the character of an ideology by, first, admitting the inevitability of diversity and change and then, secondly, by delimiting this variety through observation of the extreme and opposing manifestations between which the point of view appears to be confined. An ideology is identified by describing the cardinal antitheses of the political disposition it reveals. For Liberalism extends from Spencer and Cobden on the one hand to Lloyd George and the doctrines of the 'Yellow Book' on the other; the concept of Conservatism has to include not only Disraeli and Macmillan but also Lord Hugh Cecil and Sir Keith Joseph, the 'Drys' as well as the 'Wets'; while Socialism has to be seen encompassing the collectivism of the Fabians and the contrasting ideas of the Guildsmen, the Christian moralism of Tawney, and the Trotskyite Marxism of the 'Militant Tendency'. Nor are these major doctrines distinct in the sense of not having common ground.

Fortunately an overall framework of consideration is to hand in the perspective provided by the rise of collectivism and its opposition to libertarianism. The range of reaction to be discerned within each ideology reflects this basic tension of our age. Each doctrine thus nurtures two conflicting or contrasting modes of thought; and the history of modern ideological opinion in Britain is generally 'an oscillation between these extremes.'[33] The following chapters are intended to illustrate this contention. The coverage is not, of course, anything like complete but nor (I like to think) is it untypical of the different forms and levels of ideological thinking involved. And I should perhaps add that no sort of priority is intended in the order of presentation of these doctrines. Because Socialism is reviewed last does not mean I wish to imply it is in any sense a completion or culmination of ideological development: though this is not to deny that it is Socialism of the statist kind which with its 'importunate chink' has for long made the most noise in the political field of modern Britain.

Let us, then, with Malvolio, read politic authors and our tongues tang arguments of state.

---

33 The phrase cited is J. S. Mill's, taken from a comment on a key intellectual antithesis of his own day, 'Coleridge' (1840), Collected Works, ed. J. M. Robson et al. (London, 1963ff.), x. 124.

PART TWO
THE AMBIVALENCE OF LIBERALISM

. . . we fell into a discussion of the changing qualities of Liberalism.
H. G. WELLS, *The New Machiavelli*, 1911, repr. 1946, p.200

2

INTRODUCTORY THEMES

No man can be a collectivist alone or an individualist alone. He must be
both. . . .
W. S. CHURCHILL, *The People's Rights*, 1909, repr. 1970, p. 153

IN HAROLD LASKI's view Liberalism has been, over the last four
centuries, 'the outstanding doctrine of Western Civilization'.[1] One sees
what he had in mind and, of course, he used the term in a special way; but
unless carefully qualified the judgement may be rather misleading not
only in terms of the time-scale envisaged but in respect of not giving due
acknowledgement to the range of meaning which can be attached to the
word. The epithet 'liberal' was indeed in general if ambiguous use for a
long while before it acquired a strictly political sense. Thus it might refer
approvingly to a certain manner or habit of thought especially that
indicative of a spirit of spacious tolerance or generosity, as in the phrases
'a liberal offer' or 'a liberal education'. Chesterton suggested that a
liberal-minded man was one who, if he could stop forever the mouths of
all the deceivers of mankind simply by waving his hand in a dark room,
would not do so.[2] At the same time, by a kind of linguistic inversion, the
word could also express opprobrium suggesting licence, lack of restraint,
or some unseemly indulgence, as when Desdemona refers to Iago as 'a
most profane and liberal counsellor'.[3] A tendency to be captious might
also be implied, reproach on this account being not unrelated to that
sense of critical open-mindedness invariably taken to be crucial to the
liberal attitude. For the stance entailed an inclination to commit for trial
any institution or belief brought before it, a willingness to question
anything, especially the merely orthodox or conventional, and to assess it
only on its apparent merits. All sorts of radical possibilities were thereby

1 H. J. Laski, *The Rise of European Liberalism: an Essay in Interpretation* (1936; Unwin
Books, 1962), p. 5.
2 G. K. Chesterton, *Robert Browning* (1903; London, 1919), pp. 86–7.
3 *Othello*, II. i. 163–4. Similarly there is a reference in *Much Ado About Nothing*, IV. i.
92–3, to 'a liberal villain' as a ruffian prone to secret and vile encounters; cf. *Hamlet*, IV.
vii. 171. There is a like ambivalence about the cognate term 'liberty' which can mean
both freedom and licentiousness.

intimated; and this perhaps negative or sceptical aspect of the liberal point of view was indeed long dominant. In this sense there was always (in G. M. Young's phrase) 'something rather explosive' about it.[4]

However, a specific political meaning appears not to have emerged in this country until the early nineteenth century. 'Liberal' seems first to have been current as an adjective in France after the Revolution to refer to open and unstinting principles of politics and was certainly used in this sense by Napoleon himself on the occasion of his *coup d'état* on 18 *Brumaire*. Subsequently it indicated those who supported the radical spirit of the day. However the substantive (with a definite party or factional reference) did not appear for another decade and in another country: it was employed in Cadiz towards the end of 1810 or the beginning of the following year to describe, probably pejoratively, those members of the Cortes and their supporters who were in favour of liberty of the press and more widely of the proposed anti-clerical constitution modelled on the revolutionary French system of 1791. From the outset, therefore, the association of the political term with reformist views, popular liberty, and the overthrow of established privilege was clear. It was probably introduced into the British political vocabulary a few years later and (as in Spain) was initially used in a polemical way, in this case to refer to the more extreme members of the Whig opposition. The Spanish or French form of the word was usually employed to suggest an exotic and undesirable connexion with extreme revolutionary tendencies. But because of the conventionally laudatory associations of the term (and the existence of another word 'radical' to refer to the less desirable propensity) the description was adopted without much difficulty or rancour by those thus denominated; and in due course (by the late 1840s) it had become the official designation of an entire party.[5]

Naturally, although the name was new in this sense, the constellation of political themes presented was not. The ideology was woven of diverse but related strands of thought, many of them long-standing and drawn from a number of sources and contexts.[6] Nor could Liberalism be a static

4 Cf. L. T. Hobhouse, *Liberalism* (1911; Galaxy Books, 1966), p.14; H. G. Wells, 'The Past and the Great State', Lady Warwick *et al.*, *The Great State: Essays in Construction* (London, 1912), p.14. For G. M. Young's remark, see his 'The Liberal Mind in Victorian England', H. Grisewood *et al.*, *Ideas and Beliefs of the Victorians: an Historic Revaluation of the Victorian Age* (1949; Dutton, 1966), p.335.
5 The best account of the origins of the term is J. Marichal, 'España y las raíces semánticas del liberalismo', *Cuadernos* (Congreso por la libertad de la cultura; March–April 1955), pp. 53–60. See also: *OED*; T. P. Neill, *The Rise and Decline of Liberalism* (Milwaukee, Wis., 1953), p.7; and E. Halévy, *A History of the English People in the Nineteenth Century* (1913–46; 2nd trans. edn, London, 1961), ii. 81 and n. 3; ibid., iii.180 n.1. Examples of the early use of the word are cited in Ramsay Muir's article on the 'Liberal Party' in *Ency. Brit.*, 14th edn (Chicago, 1947), xiii.999.
6 There is a most admirable survey of these matters with ample exemplification in E. K.

and unchanging doctrine. And in fact it has in this country passed through two main phases in a development which nicely reflects the antithesis between libertarianism and collectivism, between two contrasting views of freedom, personal fulfilment, and the proper place of government in society.

The first of these phases, during which the so-called 'classical' form of the doctrine prevailed, is one easily compatible with the conventional significance of the term liberal as already described. It clave to a view of the individual as ideally subject to as little external restraint as possible whether this derived from custom or from the overt action of public authority in either church or state. It is a creed distrustful of the powers of government because their use might become arbitrary, partial, or overweening; and to prevent the preponderance of privilege and sinister interest, substantial change is thus urged in the law governing traditional and established forms in both the secular and the ecclesiastical spheres. It is believed, too, that progress and the general welfare depend substantially on private initiative. To achieve the optimum in this regard, while it may be necessary for the state to create a framework of security within which commercial and other energies should find their full release, in economic life generally the principle is to sustain so far as possible free trade at home and abroad. Thus the main purpose of classical Liberalism was the emancipation of the individual from public control; and the corollary of this basic tenet was a repudiation of any authority, person, procedure, or institution which seemed to obstruct its implementation.[7]

This position was supported by various sorts of argument which may briefly be exemplified as follows.

There was first a certain picture of British constitutional development, a view that underlay much of the so-called Whig interpretation of history. It rested on the belief that the political system of this country derived from the institutions of our Saxon or Gothic ancestors, a mixed polity in which the power of the executive was always strictly limited. It was held, too, that in all essentials this ancient constitution of the realm had continued in being ever since those distant days surviving even the impact of the Norman Conquest. It had also withstood the assaults of unscrupulous monarchs (such as King John and Charles I) who had wished to undermine it in the interests of a royalist predominance; and its principles and liberties had from time to time been reasserted as in

Bramsted and K. J. Melhuish (eds), *Western Liberalism: a History in Documents from Locke to Croce* (London, 1978). A brief official acknowledgement of these eclectic origins is to be found in the report of the Liberal Party Commission, *Liberals Look Ahead* (London, n.d. [1969]), p.9.
7 Cf. Laski, *The Rise of European Liberalism*, p.22; and his 'The Decline of Liberalism' (1940), pp.7–10, in *Hobhouse Memorial Lectures, 1930–1940* (London, 1948).

Magna Carta, the Petition of Right, and, climactically, the revolution settlement of the late seventeenth century. In the following years these ideas survived strongly in certain circles and were still being deployed after 1800 to sustain hostility to the Crown and its executive government and to support reform proposals of various kinds designed to complete, extend, or restore traditional freedoms.[8] When in the crisis of 1848 *The Economist* wrote 'Thank God we are Saxons!' it was this array of political ideas and virtues that was invoked; as similarly in 1855 when the doctrine of the ancient constitution was used in its propaganda by the Administrative Reform Association.[9]

Two of the themes crucial to this point of view – the concept of a fundamental constitutional law and a stress on the traditional rights of Englishmen – often assumed a more general form, appearing (and this indicates the second type of argument) in the abstract guise of a doctrine of natural law and natural rights. For the modern world John Locke presented a paradigmatic statement of this theory in his second treatise *Of Civil Government*. Drawing on the Stoic-medieval notion of the eternal law of God which was also the law of reason, a theme powerfully exemplified by the works of St Thomas Aquinas and of the Elizabethan divine Richard Hooker, Locke postulated such a 'law of nature' as the main source of moral guidance in respect of human affairs. It was the foundation of man's rights to life, liberty, and property for the better protection of which civil society and government were created. It followed that the executive arm was neither absolute in its power nor unlimited in its scope but restricted to those purposes concerning the maintenance of these basic claims for which it was originally established; and if it transgressed these limits or frustrated those ends it might properly be cashiered. Locke's analysis of these ideas is not indeed without ambiguity or hiatus; but through his substantial influence they

8 For the genesis and development of these notions, see Professor J. G. A. Pocock's definitive *The Ancient Constitution and the Feudal Law: a Study of English Historical Thought in the Seventeenth Century* (Cambridge, 1957); also his 'Burke and the Ancient Constitution: a Problem in the History of Ideas' (1960), in *Politics, Language and Time: Essays on Political Thought and History* (London, 1972), ch.6. For the later manifestations, see also S. Kliger, *The Goths in England: a Study in Seventeenth and Eighteenth Century Political Thought* (Cambridge, Mass., 1952), pp.101–6; C. Robbins, *The Eighteenth-Century Commonwealthman: Studies in the Transmission, Development and Circumstance of English Liberal Thought from the Restoration of Charles II until the War with the Thirteen Colonies* (Cambridge, Mass., 1959), *passim*; J. W. Burrow, *A Liberal Descent: Victorian Historians and the English Past* (Cambridge, 1981), *passim*.

9 *The Economist* (28 April 1848), p.447, cited in Halévy, op. cit., iv.244 n.3; O. Anderson, 'The Janus Face of Mid-Nineteenth-Century English Radicalism: The Administrative Reform Association of 1855', *Victorian Studies*, viii (1964–5), pp.232, 240.

were majestically transmitted to later generations, joining in this regard those classical authorities (such as Cicero, Livy, and Tacitus) who had always been associated with hostility to absolute or arbitrary power.[10] The idea of natural rights as a limitation on established authority in society was indeed powerfully reinforced by such pamphleteers as Paine and by manifestoes like the US Declaration of Independence and the French Declaration of the Rights of Man and the Citizen.[11] Thus in an extreme statement of the case Paine argued that government was a negative thing, required simply because man was capable of being wicked or vicious: its existence was 'the badge of lost innocence', and, even in its best form, it was merely 'a necessary evil'.[12] Consequently it must always be confined, as by the forms of a written constitution designed, like society itself, to sustain the equal rights of man against its depredations.[13]

Thirdly, a concept of natural or divine harmony was involved. It was widely believed that, in economic affairs in particular, optimum progress could be achieved only by letting rational individuals pursue their own ends as untrammelled as may be by official rules and interference. After all they knew their own interests better than anyone else and would seek them more ardently and skilfully. Moreover intervention entailed the disutilities of taxation and compulsion.[14] A related consideration was simply the manifest corruption and incompetence of the public agencies of the day: if they did intervene it would only be to some venal or partisan end or with inefficient and untoward result. But in terms of theoretical rationalization the most important factor in this context was that it was broadly accepted that God had so arranged the world that the best collective advantage was attained by leaving people alone, allowing their purposes and initiatives to proceed under the benevolent guidance of the tutelary deity or natural order. Shaw later summarized the idea by saying that in England Liberalism conquered the traditional autocracy 'and then left industry to make what it could of the new political conditions by the unregulated action of competition between individuals.' 'Briefly', he went on, 'the Liberal Plan was to cut off the King's head, and leave the

---

10 See Z. S. Fink, *The Classical Republicans: an Essay in the Recovery of a Pattern of Thought in Seventeenth Century England* (1945; 2nd edn, [Evanston, Ill.], 1962), for an account of these influences. Halévy, op. cit., iv.209, suggests their effect on two outstanding Liberal figures of the mid-century, Lord John Russell and Macaulay.

11 For such subsequent statements, see Bramsted and Melhuish op. cit., pp.9–12, 146–62.

12 T. Paine, *Common Sense* (1776; Penguin, 1976), p.65.

13 T. Paine, *Rights of Man: Being an Answer to Mr. Burke's Attack on the French Revolution* (1791–2; Thinker's Library, 1944), pp.29ff.

14 Cf. J. Viner, 'Bentham and J. S. Mill: the Utilitarian Background', *American Economic Review*, xxxix (1949), p.370.

rest to Nature, which was supposed to gravitate towards economic harmonies when not restrained by tyrannical governments.'[15]

There were many expressions of these topics or themes during the eighteenth century, that of Adam Smith being the most well-known. His statement in various works was intended to constitute a complete system of thought, the understanding of economic life and the proper office of government being an important part of this whole.[16] So far as human conduct is concerned Smith's assumption is a kind of self-preference principle. As he said in *The Theory of Moral Sentiments*, every man is by nature 'first and principally recommended to his own care'.[17] But it so happens, fortunately for mankind, that as the individual thus follows his own purposes he is under the protection of a 'great, benevolent, and all-wise Being' who sustains in the universe at all times 'the greatest possible quantity of happiness.'[18] In so satisfying his own wants and seeking his own gain, a man is thus 'led by an invisible hand to promote an end which was no part of his intention.'[19] And Smith is clear that the general interest is thus more effectively achieved, albeit indirectly, than by its specific pursuit. 'I have never', he says sarcastically, 'known much good done by those who affected to trade for the public good.'[20] Given, then, Smith's belief in a natural order of this kind, watched over by a power of beneficent omnipotence, it is hardly surprising that he was so often an opponent of state regulation or provision. He held that, save in the rare case of something that cannot be secured by the market mechanism – such as defence, justice, the provision of roads, bridges, and canals – intervention can only cause harm.

> The uniform, constant and uninterrupted effort of every man to better his condition, the principle from which public and national, as well as private opulence is originally derived, is frequently powerful enough to maintain the natural progress of things towards improvement, in spite both of the extravagance of government, and of the greatest errors of administration.[21]

Of course, the belief in what S. G. Checkland once called 'the optimism

15 G. B. Shaw *et al.*, *Fabian Essays* (1889; Jubilee edn, London, 1950), 'Preface to the 1908 Reprint', p. xxix.
16 For a short, recent account of the overall design, see B. A. Reisman, *Adam Smith's Sociological Economics* (London, 1976).
17 A. Smith, *The Theory of Moral Sentiments* (1759; ed. Bohn, London, 1853), VI.ii.1, p.321.
18 ibid., VI.ii.3, p.345.
19 A. Smith, *An Inquiry into the Nature and Causes of the Wealth of Nations* (1776; World's Classics, 1904), IV.ii, p.33). Cf. *The Theory of Moral Sentiments*, IV.i.1, pp.264–5.
20 Smith, *Wealth of Nations*, ibid.
21 ibid., II.iii (vol. i, p.383).

of automatic equilibrium' was never complete.[22] As was noted in the previous volume, each economist in the so-called classical school made various qualifications to the pure doctrine; and they differed among themselves about its application.[23] As for Smith in particular, Harold Laski once commented that there was much less of *laissez faire* in *The Wealth of Nations* than one was tempted to assume. Nevertheless progress and achievement were, by and large, attributed in the Smithian mode just described to the unhindered activity of self-seeking individuals: as Keynes once put it, 'free competition built London.'[24] This belief that collective interference would inhibit the natural process of self-regulation and so progress itself is reflected in the growing use of the term *laissez faire* after it first appeared in 1751. As intimated, the association was not wholly accurate or just, but the idea became fixed in the general mind as a cardinal truth of classical political economy and for a long time was accepted as such by Liberals.[25] Bentham urged this view in what became typical terms:

> The practical questions, therefore, are . . . how far the end in view is best promoted by individuals acting for themselves? and in what cases these ends may be promoted by the hands of government? . . . .
>
> With the view of causing an increase to take place in the mass of national wealth, or with a view to increase of the means either of subsistence or enjoyment, without some special reason, the general rule is, that nothing ought to be done or attempted by government. The motto, or watchword of government, on these occasions, ought to be – *Be quiet.* . . . The art, therefore, is reduced within a small compass . . . . The request which agriculture, manufactures, and commerce present to governments, is modest and reasonable as that which Diogenes made to Alexander: '*Stand out of my sunshine.*'[26]

After the great symbolic victory of Corn Law repeal in 1846, *laissez faire* assumed for Liberals (as with others) the form almost of a religion, what Halévy christened 'Nonconformist Neo-Liberalism'.[27] The domestic ideal was non-intervention, the international goal an extending free trade. Above all perhaps the development of mutual commercial dependence would (it was hoped) eliminate even war itself so that in this

22 S. G. Checkland, 'The Ricardo Years', *TLS* (27 May 1977), p.654.
23 See *The Rise of Collectivism*, pp.124–7.
24 Laski to Holmes (25 February 1922), M. de W. Howe (ed.), *Holmes-Laski Letters: the Correspondence of Mr. Justice Holmes and Harold J. Laski, 1916–1935* (London, 1953), i. 407; J. M. Keynes, *The End of Laissez-Faire* (London, 1926), p. 14.
25 Keynes, op. cit., pp.18–19, 21–5.
26 J. Bentham, 'A Manual of Political Economy' (1798), J. Bowring (ed.), *The Works of Jeremy Bentham* (1838–43; New York, 1962), iii.33–5, italics in original.
27 Halévy, *A History of the English People in the Nineteenth Century*, iv.184.

respect the major coercive function of government would wither away. The poetic vision of Tennyson's *Locksley Hall* reflected this Liberal dream of universal peace, when

> . . . the war-drum throbb'd no longer, and the battle-flags were furl'd
> In the Parliament of man, the Federation of the world.[28]

The metaphysical idea of a harmonious order was invariably based on some sort of religious belief which was, therefore, yet another strand in the formation of Liberalism. Of particular significance (as Halévy's phrase, just cited, implied) were the various forms of Protestant dissent. Of course, it is not suggested that no Liberals were Anglicans or Catholics; nor that the Nonconformist propensity was not associated with other political ideologies. It is simply that historically there is a strong association between Liberalism in politics, with its air of toleration and its defence of the civil rights of the individual against the various forms of authority, and the beliefs and moral rigour of the Dissenting churches and sects, in particular their assertion of liberty of conscience and of individual responsibility. Liberals, wrote Gilbert Murray, 'are politically the descendants of the Puritans' for they combine (just as Milton did) 'the search for righteousness and the belief in freedom'; while Chesterton (an ardent Catholic) noted the same characteristic when he referred to Liberalism's 'zest for heresies' and its tendency to carry religious toleration to the point of eccentricity.[29] The specific link with radicalism was simply that opposition to Anglican dominance meant also a repudiation of that political and social framework by which the religious establishment was sustained. Herbert Spencer for one took great pride in linking his own anti-authoritarian Liberalism with the pronounced Nonconformity of his ancestors; and it is clear in his case how the religious opinions are related to his hostility to the aristocracy and landed gentry. T. H. Green similarly saw in Liberalism the fulfilment and correction of Puritanism.[30] And, on the practical rather than the theoretical level of politics, an example of the connexion is that the traditional strength of Liberalism in Wales was closely linked to a popular repudiation of what was seen as an alien ascendancy in both church and state.

Yet as time wore on free trade and limited government seemed panaceas all too defective, inappropriate to the growing mass of problems being faced in economic and social life. During the late nineteenth

28 Lord Tennyson, 'Locksley Hall', *The Works* (London, 1894), p.101.
29 G. Murray, 'What Liberalism Stands For', H. L. Nathan and H. H. Williams (eds), *Liberal Points of View* (London, 1927), p.21; Chesterton, *Robert Browning*, pp.86, 91, 93.
30 H. Spencer, *An Autobiography* (London, 1904), i.6–8, 11–13, 41–2; M. Richter, *The Politics of Conscience: T. H. Green and his Age* (London, 1964), p.41.

century Liberalism began to reveal a change in the hitherto dominant emphasis of its ideas, in particular with respect to the role of political agencies. The state (itself, of course, by then much changed) was increasingly seen less as a necessary evil and more as a vital instrument of reform. Liberalism was still formally concerned with countering tyranny and maintaining freedom but the specific objects involved were being radically transformed. The external restraints which had now to be removed were not the cramping effects of arbitrary authority and outmoded privilege but those conditions which inhibited the full life for the mass of citizens, the poverty and distress brought about by unregulated economic growth and technological change. To the under-privileged majority living in a hostile world, 'peace, retrenchment, and reform' might seem a very empty slogan. Writing in 1881, John Morley said that his biography of Richard Cobden (which came out in that year) appeared at a time when there was a glaring tendency to subject the principles for which Cobden had stood to hostile criticism. A few years later Sidney Webb could refer to the anti-statist views of some Liberals as 'old-fashioned'. And Dicey noted that by the turn of the century Liberalism had 'learned to place no small confidence in the beneficent effects of State control', adding that 'this trust, whether well-founded or not, is utterly foreign to the liberalism of 1832.' And (a final instance) in 1909, Winston Churchill, then a Liberal Cabinet minister, said, 'The whole tendency of civilization is . . . towards the multiplication of the collective functions of society. The ever growing complications of civilization create for us new services which have to be undertaken by the State, and create for us an expansion of the existing services.' And he clearly wanted to see government embark on further novel and adventurous experiments of the same sort.[31]

In the view of this new Liberalism, therefore, government had not merely to provide a framework of legal order and security within which individual advantage might be pursued and the general interest emerge; it had not only to prevent abuse of power by 'sinister interests', to constrain political privilege, and the like. It had to do something more than create the negative conditions for the liberation of individualist forces, to go beyond this to a more positive view of freedom involving increased intervention on its part in the details of social and economic life. It had to ensure that people have (in T. H. Green's phrase) 'a positive power or capacity of doing or enjoying something worth doing or

---

31 J. Morley, *The Life of Richard Cobden* (London, 1881), vol. i, p. [vii]; S. Webb, 'The Basis of Socialism: Historic', Shaw *et al., Fabian Essays*, p. 49; A. V. Dicey, *Lectures on the Relation between Law & Public Opinion in England during the Nineteenth Century* (1905; 2nd edn, London, 1920), p. 39; W. S. Churchill, *The People's Rights* (1909; London, 1970), p. 154.

enjoying'.[32] Society had the duty to see, that is, that its citizens were in a social and economic position to take advantage of the opportunities for fulfilment that a reformed political and legal order provided. As D. L. George put it in 1908, the new Liberalism must devote its endeavour to removing 'the immediate causes of discontent.'[33]

It is a nice question whether this shift of emphasis involves a betrayal of classical Liberalism or whether it is a wider application and development of its themes. What is witnessed in this change? A decline into statism or a deeper understanding of the needs of individuality? Herbert Spencer contrasted, of course, genuine Liberalism which seeks to extend men's freedom, and its other, perverted, form which, while giving men 'nominal liberties in the shape of votes (which are but a means to an end) is busily decreasing their liberties, both by the multiplication of restraints and commands, and by taking away larger parts of their incomes to be spent not as they individually like, but as public officials like.'[34] And in a characteristic passage he contrasted the new statist tendency (which, in his opinion, could only lead to disaster) with the older notions (which were the sole recipe for progress and success):

> The average legislator, equally with the average citizen, has no faith whatever in the beneficent working of social forces, notwithstanding the almost infinite illustrations of this beneficent working. He persists in thinking of a society as a manufacture and not as a growth: blind to the fact that the vast and complex organization by which its life is carried on, has resulted from the spontaneous co-operations of men pursuing their private ends. Though, when he asks how the surface of the Earth has been cleared and made fertile, how towns have grown up, how manufactures of all kinds have arisen, how the arts have been developed, how knowledge has been accumulated, how literature has been produced, he is forced to recognize the fact that none of these are of governmental origin, but have many of them suffered from governmental obstruction; yet, ignoring all this, he assumes that if a good is to be achieved or an evil prevented, Parliament must be invoked. He has unlimited faith in the agency which has achieved multitudinous failures, and has no faith in the agency which has achieved multitudinous successes.[35]

32 T. H. Green, 'Lecture on Liberal Legislation and Freedom of Contract' (1881), *Works*, ed. Nettleship (London, 1885–8), iii. 371.
33 Speech at Swansea (1 October 1908), in *Better Times* (1910), cited in A. Bullock and M. Shock (eds), *The Liberal Tradition from Fox to Keynes* (1956; Oxford, 1967), p. 212.
34 Spencer, *An Autobiography*, i. 421.
35 Spencer, *The Principles of Ethics* (London, 1892–3), ii. 247.

It was indeed true, as Halévy later observed though less pejoratively, that the new democratic Liberalism of the twentieth century had little in common with the Liberalism of Gladstone.[36] Of course, this antithesis in Liberal ideology has long been remarked. For instance, in 1940 in his Hobhouse Memorial Lecture on the decline of Liberalism, Laski commented on the extraordinary complexity of the doctrine's roots and suggested that what he saw as its contemporary eclipse was associated with just such an internal contradiction.[37] This had indeed been present from the beginning, being signalled, for instance, by the apparently inconsistent emphasis in the thought of John Locke between the rights and freedom of the individual on the one hand and the emphasis on the other that he gives to the consideration of the 'public good' which might legitimately override the more specific claims and interests.[38]

What immediately follows is a more or less detailed review within this general context of the major aspects or forms of Liberalism so that its full range of character may be discerned. Richard Cobden and Herbert Spencer are taken to embody two versions of extreme classical Liberalism; John Stuart Mill and T. H. Green are then discussed as showing (in their varied ways) the beginning of the shift in Liberal thought from individuality to collectivism; finally the end of *laissez faire* is signalled by reference to a range of subsequent and more recent Liberal utterance of one kind or another.

---

36 Halévy, *A History of the English People in the Nineteenth Century*, vi.287.
37 Laski, 'The Decline of Liberalism', loc. cit., pp.6–7.
38 See e.g. Locke, *Two Treatises of Government*, ed. Laslett (Cambridge, 1960), II.3, 37, 131; and on the problem of consent involved, ibid., II.95, 138, 140, 193. For commentary cf. W. Kendall, *John Locke and the Doctrine of Majority-Rule* (1941; 2nd edn, Urbana, Ill., 1959).

3

COBDEN AND SPENCER VERSUS THE STATE

... there has always been an element in the Liberal party which has
regarded with deep-rooted suspicion every measure involving State
interference with industry as an invasion of liberty. This element has
sometimes been very powerful. ...

R. MUIR, *Politics and Progress*, 1923, p.99

PERFECT LIBERTY

How small, of all that human hearts endure,
That part which laws or kings can cause or cure,
Still to ourselves in every place consign'd,
Our own felicity we make or find: . . . .

O. GOLDSMITH, 'The Traveller, or a Prospect of Society', 1765, *ad fin*.

IN THE speech he made in 1847 on Fielden's Factories Bill, Joseph Hume
was characteristically blunt. The principles of political economy, he said,
were quite clear that 'Government should interfere as little as possible'
and that such action was never justified except 'to remove prohibitions
and protections.' If the best interests of the community were to be
properly regarded, Parliament had no right to meddle 'either with labour
or capital'. For his part, he concluded, 'he was prepared to sweep away
every restriction that now remained, and to let one general and uniform
principle of perfect liberty pervade our legislation.'[1] It is a view (or
vision) that was widely shared and (as later chapters of this volume will
show) not only by Liberals. Two among a multitude of possible instances
must suffice to confirm the stance involved. Consider, for example, the
conclusion of Macaulay's essay of 1830 on Southey's *Colloquies*. It is true
that Macaulay was not always so unambiguous but he does in this
context offer a very clear statement of the libertarian attitude; and it is
one which was much quoted, later in the century, by supporters of *laissez
faire*. Southey had defended, in Tory terms, the patriarchal role of
government and this Macaulay repudiates:

1 89 Parl. Deb. 3s., 10 February 1847, cols 1074–80.

It is not by the intermeddling of Mr. Southey's idol, the omniscient and omnipotent State, but by the prudence and energy of the people, that England has hitherto been carried forward in civilisation; and it is to the same prudence and the same energy that we now look with comfort and good hope. Our rulers will best promote the improvement of the nation by strictly confining themselves to their own legitimate duties, by leaving capital to find its most lucrative course, commodities their fair price, industry and intelligence their natural reward, idleness and folly their natural punishment, by maintaining peace, by defending property, by diminishing the price of law, and by observing strict economy in every department of the state. Let the Government do this: the People will assuredly do the rest.[2]

The second example is the famous opening passage of *Self-Help*, the most celebrated work of 'that modern Plutarch, Mr. Samuel Smiles'.[3] It is a typical and one of the most well-known reflections of the major themes at issue:

'Heaven helps those who help themselves' is a well-tried maxim, embodying in a small compass the results of vast human experience. The spirit of self-help is the root of all genuine growth in the individual; and, exhibited in the lives of many, it constitutes the true source of national vigour and strength. Help from without is often enfeebling in its effects, but help from within invariably invigorates. Whatever is done *for* men or classes, to a certain extent takes away the stimulus and necessity of doing for themselves; and where men are subjected to over-guidance or over-government, the inevitable tendency is to render them comparatively helpless.

Even the best institutions can give to man no active help [and] the value of legislation as an agent in human advancement has usually been much over-estimated. . . . Moreover, it is every day becoming more clearly understood, that the function of Government is negative and restrictive, rather than positive and active; being resolvable, principally into protection – protection of life, liberty, and property. . . .

National progress is the sum of individual industry, energy, and uprightness, as national decay is of individual idleness, selfishness, and

---

2 Lord Macaulay, *Essays* (London, 1889), p.122. For the contrasting emphasis, see Macaulay's speech on the Ten Hours Bill in 1846 in which he stressed that while intervention could never be accepted for economic reasons it might be very necessary on social grounds, *The Miscellaneous Writings and Speeches* (London, 1889), pp.719–20.
3 The description is Shaw's: see G. B. Shaw *et al.*, *Fabian Essays* (1889; Jubilee edn, London, 1950), p.9.

vice. . . . The highest patriotism and philanthropy consist, not so much in altering laws and modifying institutions, as in helping and stimulating men to elevate and improve themselves by their own free and independent individual action.[4]

As with Macaulay, Smiles was nevertheless prepared to accept state action in certain fields such as public health.[5] He was aware, too, of the baser aspects of economic competition; and he always stressed duty, character, and knowledge rather than mere material success.[6] But the emphasis of opinions like those cited is clear and it entailed a hostility to over-legislation, officialism, the growth of public expenditure, militancy in external policy, and all the other bugbears of those who adhered to the classical Liberal doctrine.

The notion of limited and economical government was a commonplace ideal, then. However, I must here be content with giving a detailed account of only a couple of the many Liberal statements of the creed, though these are in fact most important exemplars and show, in their different form and manner, a good part of what the stance involved. One instance is Richard Cobden, a markedly independent and influential politician, who has reasonably been described as the real author of the middle-class Liberalism which dominated Britain for more than a generation.[7] The other is Herbert Spencer, a writer whose work constituted not simply a very full and extreme version of this kind of Liberalism but also (as I have come to believe) one of the ablest intellectual achievements in British thought and letters of the Victorian age. The chapter concludes with a fragmentary survey of some of the subsequent expressions of Liberal opposition to the collectivist state.

COBDEN AND THE MANCHESTER SCHOOL

. . . the unquestionably greatest Englishman whom the present century
has produced. . . .
J. TOULMIN SMITH's tribute in *The Parliamentary Remembrancer*, vii,
1865, p.61

In Smiles's *Self-Help* there are only a couple of brief references to Richard Cobden but his early career embodies many of the qualities that book

4 S. Smiles, *Self-Help with Illustrations of Conduct and Perserverance* (1859; 4th edn, London, 1908), pp.1–3, italics in original.
5 S. Smiles, *Thrift* (1875; London, 1897), pp.337ff.
6 Smiles, *Self-Help*, preface, pp.vii–viii. Cf. K. Fielden, 'Samuel Smiles and Self-Help', *Victorian Studies*, xii (1968–9), pp.155–76. For the general background to Smiles's ideas, see J. F. C. Harrison, 'The Victorian Gospel of Success', ibid., i (1957–8), pp.155–64.
7 W. F. Monypenny and G. E. Buckle, *The Life of Benjamin Disraeli, Earl of Beaconsfield* (1910–20; rev. edn, London, 1929), i.503.

was written to praise. Born in Sussex in 1804 into an impoverished family of yeomen farmers and starting thus from pretty well nothing, he built up in time a prosperous textile firm so that to a notable degree he was the completely self-made man basing success on his energy and confidence in his own abilities. He was, too, largely self-educated: he learned little at school but much more later from very wide reading and the lessons of his own experience and travels. And quite early he established a consistent attitude to affairs and realized he had done so, with the result that he was easily able subsequently to absorb within this intellectual and moral framework all the facts and ideas he later acquired and with it to confront the problems he faced in both economic and political life. By his death in 1865 he had become, on one modern judgement, 'the complete democratic Radical'.[8] And if his main concern was with the international harmony to be anticipated from the spread of free trade and disarmament, he did not hesitate to draw out the domestic implications of his opinions. These made him a powerful and influential exponent of a point of view hostile to extensive state intervention in economic and social affairs. A later Liberal (and then Unionist) politician, Joseph Chamberlain, whose ideas differed markedly from those of Cobden, summed up the latter's beliefs in this way:

> The doctrine of Mr. Cobden was a consistent doctrine. His view was that there should be no interference by the State in our domestic concerns. He believed that individuals should be left to themselves to make the best of their abilities and circumstances, and that there should be no attempt to equalise the conditions of life and happiness. To him, accordingly, protection of labour was quite as bad as protection of trade. To him a trade union was worse than a landlord. To him all factory legislation was as bad as the institution of tariffs.[9]

What follows now is an indication of the way in which Cobden worked out and justified this position and then, more briefly, an account of the so-called Manchester School of thought that emerged on a similar basis.

The principles of free exchange

Cobden came from traditional rural England and always said that, had there been any choice, he would have preferred its 'pastoral charms' to the environment of cotton-mill and manufactory; and indeed after the triumph of the anti-Corn Law campaign in 1846 he returned to live in the Sussex countryside. But for the nation as a whole he believed there was no option: the great fact of the age was the development and spread of

8 D. Read, *Cobden and Bright: a Victorian Political Partnership* (London, 1967), p. ix.
9 C. W. Boyd (ed.), *Mr. Chamberlain's Speeches* (London, 1914), ii.258–9.

industrialism and the question to be faced was both how to mitigate its evil consequences and to take advantage of the prosperity and opportunities for progress which it offered.[10] In this unprecedented situation, brought about by the growth of towns and factories, conventional views and policies were inappropriate and new criteria of action were demanded: 'at certain periods in the history of a nation, it becomes necessary to review its principles of domestic policy, for the purpose of adapting the government to the changing and improving condition of its people'.[11] So Cobden sought to establish a range of consistent general themes appropriate to the new circumstances and issues faced.

In examining these beliefs it is important to recognize that Cobden had deep religious feelings which underpinned his political and economic arguments and infused them with a high degree of moral zeal. His biographer John Morley (perhaps because he was himself an agnostic) did not adequately credit the importance of this kind of motivation and he has been followed by others in this; thus more recently Dr Kitson Clark seemed to feel that Cobden's religious fervour was perhaps a rather contrived aspect of his political propaganda.[12] But this judgement is both odd and unfair, one which gives too little weight to views so often expressed in both public and private life and which were so clearly compatible with the common predisposition of the day. There can be no doubt, for instance, that in Cobden's opinion protective legislation (such as that establishing duties on corn and other imports) was not simply inexpedient but sinful and contrary to God's Law and Order.[13] The Corn Laws imposed an unjust tax on the poor, they unnaturally limited the supply of food, and they prevented the nations of the world from developing through free exchange the particular resources with which God through nature had endowed them. Sir Louis Mallet, who worked as Cobden's assistant during the French treaty negotiations in 1860 and who knew him well, stressed his master's belief in the moral as well as the empirical truth of economic laws and his understanding that the advance of civilization depended on a dutiful obedience to their dictates.[14] In a speech he made in 1843 Cobden denied the Corn Laws could bring any prosperity to either agriculture or industry because they were 'unnatural'

10 F. W. Chesson (ed.), *The Political Writings of Richard Cobden* (1867; 4th edn, London, 1903), i.108–9.
11 ibid., i.122.
12 J. Morley, *The Life of Richard Cobden* (London, 1881); G. K. Clark, 'The Repeal of the Corn Laws and the Politics of the Forties', *Economic History Review*, 2nd series, iv (1951–2), pp.5–6.
13 Cf. Read, op. cit., pp.30–2.
14 Sir Louis Mallet, 'The Political Opinions of Richard Cobden', *North British Review* (1867) repr. in *Political Writings*, vol.i, p.xxiv. And see the justification in religious terms of buying in the cheapest market and selling in the dearest in Cobden's *Speeches on Questions of Public Policy*, ed. J. Bright and J. E. T. Rogers (London, 1878), p.198.

and interfered 'with the wisdom of the Divine Providence' substituting 'the law of wicked men for the law of nature'.[15] There is no evidence that such sentiments were mere platform religiosity; and much indeed to the contrary. In addition probably the main secular inspiration of Cobden's ideas about universal moral law was a book called *The Constitution of Man* published in 1828. Its author was George Combe, the phrenologist and writer on ethics, whom Cobden knew well: they corresponded on these matters for many years. The main theme of Combe's extremely popular work was that natural laws reflect a benevolent design and embody a retributive power; the importance of self-help was stressed, as was the need for personal and social flexibility of response; and the pseudo-scientific basis of the analysis provided an important link between conventional religious morality and the idea of material improvement. These notions, so hostile to human legislation, influenced a range of opinion and were an important part of the intellectual armament of the contemporary *avant-garde*. Nor was this sort of attitudes new, being found, for instance, in the writings of Bentham and Hodgskin.[16] But, of course, presuppositions of this sort, although crucial, were liable to be cast in general and abstract terms; and they needed to be filled out with the detail of concrete argument to clarify their bearing on particular practical issues. This applicative elaboration was Cobden's task.

The case assumes that man is placed on earth by God to possess and subdue it. To fulfil this destiny, indeed to live, he must labour (though advances of science and industry may lighten the task enormously). Thus the law of labour lies at the root of human life, its rights are sacred and must be safeguarded. The argument is very like that of Locke or Adam Smith, and Cobden probably derived it from the latter. For instance, on one occasion he cited *The Wealth of Nations* to urge that

'The property which every man has in his own labour, as it is the original foundation of all other property, so it is the most sacred and inviolable. The patrimony of a poor man lies in the strength and dexterity of his hands, and to hinder him from employing this strength and dexterity in what manner he thinks proper without injury to his neighbour, is a plain violation of the most sacred property. It is a manifest encroachment upon the just liberty both of the workman and of those who might be disposed to employ him.'[17]

15 Speech of 28 September 1843, cited in C. R. Fay, *Life and Labour in the Nineteenth Century* (1920; 2nd edn, Cambridge, 1933), p.153.
16 See e.g. the discussion in E. Halévy, *Thomas Hodgskin* (1903; trans. edn, London, 1956), pp.50–5.
17 *Speeches*, p.45 citing, accurately, Smith's *Wealth of Nations*, I.x.II (World's Classics, 1904, i.137).

Hence the rights of labour include the right of personal liberty (which implies the free use of a man's powers and faculties) and the right of property (an inalienable title to the products of his labour in use or exchange).[18] Where these rights are violated or suppressed there is injustice and inhumanity. As with Locke or Smith, the doctrine does not imply any notion of egalitarian levelling but it does embrace the idea that some inequalities that actually exist are unnecessary or unnatural. These arise where laws or social arrangements infringe the basic rights of possession and freedom. Cobden particularized all this by an attack on exclusiveness, monopoly, and restriction, wherever and in whatever form this occurred, as being incompatible with a genuine moral liberty. Specifically he was hostile to merely traditional privilege, to what he often described as the 'feudal' elements in government and economic life. Instead of rule by an aristocracy there should be the 'antagonist principle' of constitutionalism; and in place of restriction there should be 'Free Exchange', a principle through which the apparently divergent interests of individuals and nations become identified in accordance with the dictates of morality. Under this aegis peaceful rivalry would prove to be the way to progress and civilization. 'The more I reflect on such matters', he wrote to John Bright during the Crimean War, 'the greater importance do I attach to that principle of competition which God has set up in this wicked world as the silent arbiter of our fate, rewarding the industrious, frugal, and honest, and punishing . . . the wasteful and the wicked.' He added that 'this law operates in nations as well as individuals.'[19]

In one way Cobden was always concerned above all with relations between the peoples of the world. The doctrine of free trade was in this respect crucial to him both as means to and portent of international peace. And he denied that his assertion of this principle was merely a matter of the economic advantages it would bring; its basic appeal lay clearly in the ethical progress that would ensue from its recognition and implementation:

> . . . I have been accused of looking too much to material interests. Nevertheless I can say that I have taken as large and great a view of the effects of this mighty principle as ever did any man who dreamt over it in his own study. I believe that the physical gain will be the smallest gain to humanity from the success of this principle. I look farther; I see in the Free-trade principle that which shall act on the moral world as the principle of gravitation in the universe, – drawing men together,

18 Speeches, p.181; Mallett, in Political Writings, vol.i., pp.xxxvi–xxxvii. Cf. the passage cited in Read, op. cit., pp.24–5; also E. Wallace, 'The Political Ideas of the Manchester School', University of Toronto Quarterly, xxix (1959–60), p.126.
19 Cited in Read, op. cit., p.114.

thrusting aside the antagonism of race, and creed, and language, and uniting us in the bonds of eternal peace.[20]

Of course, with the advantages of hindsight Cobden might be accused of naïvety, of failing to recognize that increased commercial intercourse on the international scale could lead rather to trade rivalry and thus to war than to the outcome he envisaged: but this is not to deny his fervour and sincerity.[21]

Within this moral framework he made a detailed economic case for the abolition of protective tariffs, greater international specialization, and so on. It was not the most complete case of the kind possible – that of his French associate and disciple, Frédéric Bastiat, was, for example, notably more systematic.[22] But in his fashion Cobden expounded most effectively the belief that free trade would stimulate commerce and domestic industry alike, lower the cost of living, reduce unemployment, free resources for further development, and in many other ways bring economic and social improvement. There would also be specific political advantages not least in respect of the limitation of armaments and so the reduction of military expenditure. Cobden was never a pacifist and accepted that appropriate measures of defence were proper. But equally he never condoned adventurism in foreign policy, the pursuit of the balance of power, or the maintenance of the force such objectives might entail; and he completely rejected colonialism as involving an artificial system of trade that had to be expensively protected and sustained. Commerce, he believed, was 'the grand panacea' that would inoculate all the nations of the world against these follies.[23] Referring in one place to 'the desire and the motive for large and mighty empires', 'for gigantic armies and great navies', indeed for all 'those materials which are used for the destruction of life and the desolation of the rewards of labour', he said he believed that 'such things will cease to be necessary, or to be used, when man becomes one family, and freely exchanges the fruits of his labour with his brother man.'[24] These diplomatic and military changes would themselves have a substantial domestic effect: the reduction that would become possible in taxation and the national debt would sustain a more useful deployment of resources and stimulate economic effort. This in turn would create a framework of affairs in which a lasting improvement might prove possible in respect of such matters as

20 *Speeches*, p.187. Cf. the similar passages, ibid., pp.201, 234, and those cited in Read, op. cit., pp.33, 146.
21 Cf. the comments in G. L. Dickinson, *Letters from John Chinaman* (London, 1901), p.15.
22 e.g. Bastiat's *Economic Sophisms* (1845, 1848; trans. edn, New York, 1964).
23 *Political Writings*, i.36.
24 *Speeches*, p.187. Cf. ibid., p.343; also Cobden's first pamphlet, *England, Ireland and America* (1835) on the need to cut back military expenditure.

education, temperance, criminal reform, health care, and the like. All this was of major significance in the decline of militancy.[25]

This, then, is the broad context of ideas and policies in which Cobden's views about specifically domestic issues are to be seen, in particular his attack on economic and political privilege and his general opinion of government intervention. For he was the foe of both the traditional aristocracy and gentry and the paternalistic attitude with which they approached contemporary problems.

He was, of course, a leading figure in the campaign against the Corn Laws, a commitment which revealed not merely the class interest with which he associated himself but also his stance on the broadest issues arising from the condition of England question.[26] He saw this legislation as constituting a restrictive economic monopoly that ought to be 'utterly extirpated' like the similar privileges of Tudor and Stuart times.[27] The Corn Laws dated from the Middle Ages and so were not new; but they had latterly acquired a fresh significance which is why in 1815 they had been strengthened. The contemporary growth in population meant an increased need for food; but, although domestic agricultural production was increasing, it could not meet the intensifying demand. Hence the importation of corn from abroad much of it coming at that time from Prussia and Poland. However, the landlord and farming interests dominated the unreformed House of Commons and, of course, the upper chamber as well and were thus able to resist proposals to facilitate a larger inflow of foreign produce. In times of economic stress the consequences of this restriction were particularly hard. These matters were, of course, the focus of the well-known agitation of the Anti-Corn Law League, ultimately successful in 1846 when a repealing statute was passed. As Morley said, this was not just a battle about a customs duty but rather a political and social conflict of a fundamental kind between traditional landed interests and the new industrial and commercial forces. It was even more than the symbol of a new spirit of self-assertion in a great social order: in Cobden's eyes it was a moral crusade.[28]

Nor was the attack on the Corn Laws the only reflection of his hostility to the traditional feudal classes. He also believed that the concentration of land ownership in a few hands was one of the great evils contributing to national impoverishment, making it imperative to liberate the land by subjecting it to economic principle: there should be free trade in land as in corn. This goal could be approached, for instance, by repealing the laws which kept land off the market (those concerning entail, settlement, transfer, and so on) and in particular by abolishing the system of

25 e.g. Cobden to G. Combe (14 July 1846), cited in *Life*, i. 410–11.
26 On the admission of the distinct class interest involved, see *Speeches*, p. 49.
27 ibid., pp. 58–9.
28 *Life*, i. 141–3, 187. Cf. ibid., ii. 396–7, 481–2.

primogeniture.[29] Short of confiscation – which he never advocated – this was the only way to break up the great estates and spread ownership more widely. Similarly Cobden's activity in the campaign to secure the incorporation of Manchester is best seen as a repudiation of what he regarded as the outdated and ineffective feudal rule of the manorial Court leet.[30] Again, his criticism of excessive military expenditure and warlike foreign policies is a rejection of the pre-eminence in these spheres of the members and manner of the traditional aristocracy, embodied for him most of all perhaps in the person of Lord Palmerston. Like Herbert Spencer, Cobden was much concerned with the apparent development of militarism and war spirit in the 1850s which he felt could only foster aristocratic dominance.[31] His usual attitude to the existing political system was reflected in a letter he wrote to his brother in 1838 where he referred (in almost Bentham-like phrases) to 'that great juggle of the "*English Constitution*" – a thing of monopolies, and Church-craft, and sinecures, armorial hocus-pocus, primogeniture, and Pageantry!'[32]

Cobden also objected on the whole to the paternalism involved in attempts at legislative or other public supervision of economic and social life. And though his expressions of opinion about this invariably emerged as judgements on particular issues, the general theme is also clearly stated. Thus he asserted in 1846 that it was essential to leave the industry and intelligence of the people to develop as they will:

> If you attempt by legislation to give any direction to trade or industry, it is a thousand to one that you are doing wrong; and if you happen to be right, it is a work of supererogation, for the parties for whom you legislate would go right without you, and better than with you.[33]

And two years later, in a debate on monetary policy, he urged that 'it was a most dangerous doctrine to advance, that it was the duty of the Government, under all circumstances, to find employment for all who were able to work, and of good character.'[34] He believed, too, it was quite impossible effectively to control wages and prices by legislation and that the attempt to do this would only create on the one hand an artificial

---

29 ibid., ii. 215–16, 456; *Speeches*, p.493.
30 See *Speeches*, p.348. Cobden's part in the agitation in Manchester is described in detail by J. A. Williams, *Manchester and the Manchester School, 1830–1857* (unpublished MA thesis, Leeds University, 1966), ch. xi.
31 e.g. *Life*, ii.114–15, 119–20, 143, 169; *Political Writings, passim*. See also the passages cited in E. Hughes, 'The Development of Cobden's Economic Doctrines and His Methods of Propaganda: Some Unpublished Correspondence', *Bulletin of the John Rylands Library*, xxii (1938), pp.405–6, 416–16.
32 R. Cobden to F. Cobden (11 September 1838), cited in *Life*, i.130.
33 *Speeches*, p.197.
34 101 H.C. Deb. 3s., 29 August 1848, col. 649.

scarcity and on the other a 'monstrous' despotism.[35] Quite early in his political career he had developed his position on a cognate theme in a statement issued during his unsuccessful campaign to get elected at Stockport in 1837. A Ten Hour Bill was then under discussion and Cobden published a letter on factory legislation in which he rejected regulation of labour as he did that of markets and commodities. He freely conceded that Parliament might, on medical and physical grounds, forbid the employment in factories of children of thirteen years and under and also regulate the hours of labour of young persons, and he later widened this category, again on medical grounds, to include women workers. But as a matter of principle he believed the 'legislature of a free country' ought not to interfere in such a feudal manner with 'the freedom of adult labour'.[36] The improvement of the condition of the working classes, in itself highly desirable, must come not from the law but from their own efforts and self-reliance: 'I say to them, *Look not to Parliament, look only to yourselves.*'[37] There might, therefore, be some humanitarian grounds for public action here but only to a limited extent. Cobden was also opposed – it was the subject, in fact, of his last speech in Parliament in July 1864 – to the government undertaking the manufacture of things for its own use that might be purchased elsewhere. He was most perturbed that, while for twenty years the country had in commercial policy 'been acting on the principle of unrestricted competition, believing that that is the only way to secure excellence and stability of production' and while private industry was more than equal to the demands of government, the departments had none the less 'been allowed to raise up these gigantic Government monopolies'. He had in mind in particular the array of ordnance factories that had developed since the Crimean War and the deficient arms situation that had resulted therefrom; though he also instanced the factories set up to make military uniforms, and the royal dockyards which had been spending millions in building valueless wooden vessels.[38] In his view the reason these untoward consequences had occurred was the lack of effective Treasury control; and it was no answer to suggest that the legislature should try to supervise the administration more, and in more detail, for instance by committee investigation. The only proper course was to backtrack from the false path which had come to be followed and to adhere scrupulously to the principle that 'the Government should not be allowed to manufacture for itself any article which can be obtained from private producers in a competitive market'.[39] And he put his finger on a point that has worried

35 *Speeches*, pp.11–13, 60–1, 70–1, 176–7; Read, op. cit., pp.34–5.
36 Cobden to W. C. Hunt (21 October 1836), *Life*, i.464–5.
37 ibid., i. 297ff., 467, italics in original.
38 *Speeches*, pp.294–5; for an earlier criticism of public works and manufactories, ibid., pp.429–32.
39 ibid., p.295.

anti-collectivists ever since public functions began to expand noticeably. I find, he said, that you can never make the people that run government establishments understand that the capital they handle is 'really money.' 'How should it be real money to them ?' he asked: 'It costs them nothing, and, whether they make a profit or a loss, they never find their way into' bankruptcy. The reality comes home 'only to the taxpayers.'[40]

Despite such firm assertions of anti-statist principle, Cobden was, however, prepared to make exceptions where there were special reasons of a technical or humanitarian kind. The former is witnessed by his approval of control of railway construction so as to enforce a standard gauge.[41] The latter is evidenced not only by the example already given about the control of hours of labour but above all by his attitude to state involvement in education. He considered it so important that the people should be properly educated that he supported the establishment of a compulsory national system on a secular basis and financed through the rates. The reason was simply that, given the sectarian and other difficulties involved, the task was only likely to be accomplished in this way.[42] But, however compelling, this view caused Cobden considerable difficulty with some of his Liberal constituents who favoured a voluntaryist solution; and his colleague John Bright, who shared a dislike of state interference with manufacturing, felt it was inconsistent with the principles of individualism for Cobden to accept the idea of state aid in this sphere.[43]

But apart from these few exceptions, important though they were, the general thrust of Cobden's case was undoubted: that government should never meddle with the productive sphere in which its servants are not competent and its organization not appropriate. And he was confident that under a system of international free trade, prosperity for all would ensue to such an extent indeed that the need or call for such government intervention must diminish.[44] Equally his continual stress on retrenchment and the reduction of state expenditure was in any case incompatible with the substantial extension of public action.

Manchesterism

It was Disraeli who in 1848 referred to supporters of Cobden's policy as 'the School of Manchester', and the title became generally associated with the belief in free trade, self-interest, and *laissez faire*. The salient

40 ibid., p.301.
41 But cf. the sarcastic account of legislative meddling in *Political Writings*, i. 93–4.
42 Morley, *Life*, i.410; *Speeches*, pp.589–617.
43 N. McCord, 'Cobden and Bright in Politics, 1846–1857', R. Robson (ed.), *Ideas and Institutions of Victorian Britain* (London, 1967), pp.97–8; E. L. Woodward, *The Age of Reform 1815–1870* (1938; Oxford, 1958), pp.115–16.
44 Read, op. cit., p.4.

doctrine was (as Benjamin Kidd saw it) that if left alone any economic or social evil would cure itself; and the term is still in use to describe such a point of view.[45] Yet there was not really a school at all in the strict sense of there being a comprehensive theory or consistent set of opinions which received authoritative statement and exemplification. As one adherent freely admitted there was 'plenty of room . . . for differences of opinion on particular questions, and for varieties of degree in the application of the general principles which were held in common.'[46] Nor is this surprising because in origin the movement consisted of a number of different groups which were united (and then not in every respect) only on the issue of repealing the Corn Laws. This apart, the people concerned had indeed different economic, social, and intellectual interests. There were the businessmen, the humanitarians, those concerned with the prospects of international peace, the economists, the middle-class radicals, and no doubt others: a diverse collection of individuals which, concentrating on the particular political goal, saw no reason on the whole to go beyond the practical campaign to sound a general *laissez faire* note.[47] At the same time a good number of free-traders undoubtedly shared a rather negative attitude to substantive public action: they were not necessarily hostile to it as such but thought that any particular proposal for intervention had to have a very strong case made out before it could be approved. As Goldwin Smith put it, in one of the best brief summaries of what Manchesterism involved, 'It thought that man having, after centuries of struggle, shaken himself free from the paternal control of autocrats or aristocracy, and got a chance of self-development, ought to be allowed to make what he could of that chance, and not thrust again under a despotic yoke', even if this be that of 'a paternal Government'. As to the specific limits of state action, he went on,

> I am not aware that the Manchester School ever attempted exactly to fix them. They must be fixed largely by circumstance, and by the stage of social progress at which any community has arrived. . . . What

45 97 H.C. Deb. 3s., 10 March 1848, col. 417; B. Kidd, *Principles of Western Civilisation: A Sociological Study* (1902; rev. edn, London, 1908), p.405. For a recent usage, see the reference of Professor M. Friedman, specifically citing Cobden and Bright, in P. H. Douglas and J. E. Powell, *How Big Should Government Be?* (Washington, DC, 1968), p.211.

46 Goldwin Smith, 'The Manchester School', *The Contemporary Review*, lxvii (1895), p.379.

47 W. D. Grampp, *The Manchester School of Economics* (London, 1960), ch.1. F. W. Hirst (ed.), *Free Trade and Other Fundamental Doctrines of the Manchester School* . . . (London, 1903), intro., pp.xi–xiii. On the varied motives involved, see Grampp, op. cit., ch.5. The leading members of the School have been listed as Cobden, Bright, W. J. Fox, T. Milner Gibson, L. Mallet, T. B. Potter, Goldwin Smith, H. Ashworth, and A. Prentice: see E. Wallace, 'The Political Ideas of the Manchester School', *University of Toronto Quarterly*, xxix (1959–60), pp.124–5.

services Government should undertake, whether it should own the railways as well as the high roads, and the telegraph as well as the post; whether it should build in private yards or in yards of its own, is not a question of principle; nor am I aware that the Manchester School ever enunciated any dogma on the subject, though no doubt it always leant decidedly in favour of the spontaneous agencies against the official.

In these terms state assistance for education or in respect of sanitary regulation and other major questions of public health was not ruled out; though the notion that the state has in general 'rights transcending those of the individual citizen' and a 'duty to regulate our industries and lives' is treated with notable suspicion.[48] On the whole, free-traders were most likely to stress urgently and continuously the need for economy in public spending which certainly implied a diffidence about government inter-vention.[49] And it is manifestly true that the subsequent reputation of the School was closely associated with the doctrine of economic freedom and the limited state. Bright at least was consistent in his attitude to state interference: his slogan was always 'Hands Off!' whether the question was one of factory legislation, fixing wages, or temperance reform.[50]

Manchesterism was undoubtedly widespread, the 'philosophy in office' so to say. Its ideas were ventilated in Parliament and were extremely important in official circles.[51] One instance to hand must suffice as specific illustration. Sir Charles Trevelyan was assistant secretary at (that is, permanent head of) the Treasury from 1840 to 1859. He conducted a considerable correspondence much of which survives in his letter-books; and the material concerning the Irish and Scottish famines is particularly relevant here.[52] A great deal of it consists of what Mrs Hart describes as 'long sermons . . . to government officials and organizers of private charitable funds on the demoralizing effect of getting something for nothing, whether the recipient was a landlord or a peasant.' Trevelyan himself wrote: 'To give to those who are not in want

48 G. Smith, art. cit., pp. 385–6.
49 Hirst, op. cit., pp. ix, xi–xiii. The School's links with the cause of financial reform are described in J. A. Williams, op. cit., ch. ix.
50 A. Briggs, *Victorian People: a Reassessment of Persons and Themes, 1851–67* (1954; Penguin, 1970), pp. 218–19.
51 A. J. Taylor, *Laissez-faire and State Intervention in Nineteenth-century Britain* (London, 1972), pp. 30–1 and the references there given.
52 J. Hart, 'Sir Charles Trevelyan at the Treasury', *English Historical Review*, lxxv (1960), p. 99 from which the citations in the text are taken. See also R. D. Edwards and T. D. Williams (eds), *The Great Famine* (Dublin, 1956), esp. pp. 151, 223–4, 257–9. Mrs C. Woodham-Smith's *The Great Hunger* (London, 1962), should only be cited after careful independent check as she was a complete stranger to the canons of exact scholarship: on which see my 'Biography and the "Amateur" Historian: Mrs. Woodham-Smith's *Florence Nightingale*', *Victorian Studies*, iii (1959–60), pp. 190–202.

must do unmixed harm' (30 March 1847); 'The bolstering and cockering system has been carried to the utmost – people under it have grown worse rather than better' (28 May 1847); dependence on others was a 'moral disease' and must be eradicated (15 January 1848). He seems to have believed that the Irish famine was God's judgement on an undeserving and indolent people that showed too little self-reliance, His way of teaching them a lesson. It followed that the calamity 'must not be too much mitigated'. The lazy and selfish must learn the error of their ways so that they might improve and a better state of affairs arise. Trevelyan thus regarded death by starvation as a painful but necessary 'discipline' essential to secure a greater good (11 February 1848). The tone is positively Spencerian.[53] This is also true of his attitude to the poor and to the social system generally.[54]

The flavour of the Manchester doctrine may be further indicated by reference to some expressions of opinion in the press, in particular *The Economist* under the inaugural editorship of James Wilson which, with its circulation of some 3000 copies, was 'the most important vehicle of laissez faire newspaper journalism.'[55] Wilson had been involved in the public debate about free trade and had brought out a couple of influential pamphlets in 1839 and 1840 to show that not even the landed and agricultural classes benefited from the Corn Laws. He founded *The Economist* in 1843 not as a League paper simply but to expound the 'pure *principles*' underlying the free-trade cause and to apply them to all the questions of the day. He had a great and basic faith in the beneficent harmony of a free economy and it was this belief that coloured his many journalistic contributions.[56] With this has to be associated, too, the rather anarchist approach to government of the Ricardian Socialist, Thomas Hodgskin, who also wrote extensively for the paper in its early days, as did Nassau Senior. Herbert Spencer was also on its staff for a few years, serving as sub-editor from 1848 to 1853; and he certainly found the editorial line very congenial even if he contributed little himself.[57]

The pedigree of the paper's themes at that time was by Bastiat out of Adam Smith, the general idea being that the main social lesson to be learned was that 'our greatest social inconveniences, though caused by

53 Cf. Spencer's sentiments as indicated at pp.76–8 below.
54 Hart, art. cit., pp.109–10.
55 S. Gordon, 'The London *Economist* and the High Tide of Laissez Faire', *Journal of Political Economy*, lxiii (1955), p.462. Cf. Grampp, op. cit., pp.13–14. The following paragraphs are largely based on Gordon, art. cit.
56 Gordon, art. cit., pp. 462–3.
57 ibid., pp. 469–76; J. D. Y. Peel, *Herbert Spencer: the Evolution of a Sociologist* (London, 1971), p.77; D. Wiltshire, *The Social and Political Thought of Herbert Spencer* (Oxford, 1978), pp.47–51. Hodgskin's opinions during his time on *The Economist* are reviewed in Halévy, *Thomas Hodgskin* pp.130ff.

laws, are to be cured only by an utter absence of legislation.'[58] The approach is also reflected in the following passage:

> The *Economist* has long taken in politics a very decided part, founded mainly on the principle 'that self-love and social are the same;' that private interest is the best guide to individual happiness; and that the happiness of the community is nothing but the happiness of the individuals . . . . On these principles we have contended for freedom of trade, being convinced that every merchant and dealer, capitalist and artisan, is the best judge of his own interest; and that what he finds . . . to be advantageous to him, will be for the advantage of the state. On these principles we have contended for self government . . . . On these principles we have continually insisted that *laissez faire* is the true and only policy . . . . Individuals should be freed as much as possible, and as quickly as possible, from any restraints on their actions as individuals . . . . Nature has provided for the whole order of society. She has evidently not enabled the most gigantic intellect to accomplish social order by regulations . . . . The more we give or allow scope to the free exercise of self-love, the more complete will be the social order.[59]

It is not the let-alone policy which is properly to be described as anarchy but the interference of governments. This view was premeditated partly on the basis of some understanding of what was later to be developed as the theory of perfect competition; but more importantly and fundamentally there was the natural-law faith in the rational order of the universe, an order which, if allowed to prevail, would not only maximize national wealth but also ensure its optimum distribution.[60] The whole metaphysic of *laissez faire* – it was never merely an economic doctrine – was in fact well summed up in a series of five articles which *The Economist* published in 1846 dealing with the question, Who is to blame for the condition of the people? The answer given is – the people themselves: they have come to rely too much on state aid and have thus eschewed the only possible route to improvement, that is, self-help and the complete acceptance of personal responsibility. The last article sums up the matter as follows:

> The state, because it assumes to provide for the welfare of the people . . . makes itself unwisely responsible for it. The collateral and permanent effects of legislation . . . are so very complicated, and very often so much more important than the direct and temporary effects, that to make good laws seems a work fit rather for God than man. One

58 *The Economist* (20 April 1844), p.716.
59 ibid., vi (22 April 1848), pp.451–2.
60 ibid., vii (1 September 1849), pp.965–6.

of those collateral effects . . . is the general helplessness of the masses, which is sure to be induced by the state undertaking to provide for their welfare . . . . They come to rely on it and take no care for themselves . . . .

The desire for happiness, or what is called self-interest is universal. It is not confined to man – it pervades the whole animal kingdom. It is the law of nature, and if the pursuit of self-interest, left equally free for all, do not lead to the general welfare, no systems of government can accomplish it.[61]

Civil society was natural and arose from divinely implanted instincts; and if left untrammelled it would manifest the signs of inevitable progress. But government was an artificial institution and should be limited to the protection of life and property; anything more interfered with the divine plan of advance. In deployment of these themes, Locke and Burke seem to have been major sources of inspiration.[62]

By reference to this sort of standard, *The Economist* assessed issues of contemporary policy. It was, for instance, against special measures to assist the lower classes because these would interfere with the natural laws of political economy and so inhibit the progress of society; moreover they would not really help those concerned but would rather increase the dependence of the poor on others and hamper their sense of personal initiative which alone can stimulate development. On such a basis *The Economist* attacked Ashley's Ten Hour Bill.[63] Likewise opposition was expressed to state or municipal responsibility for water supply or urban sanitation; and hostility characterized the paper's attitude to proposals for a Board of Health.[64] The attitude was very bluntly put. In a book review in 1850 *The Economist* stated that poor housing and high urban death rates sprang from two causes.

The first is the poverty of the masses, which, if possible, will be increased by the taxation inflicted by the new laws. The second is that the people have never been allowed to take care of themselves. They have always been treated as serfs or children, and they have to a great extent become in respect to those objects which the government has undertaken to perform for them, imbecile. . . . There is a worse evil than typhus or cholera or impure water, and that is mental imbecility, which the perpetual interference with the business of individuals by legislation occasions.[65]

61 ibid., iv (21 November 1846), pp. 1517–18.
62 Gordon, art. cit., p. 481.
63 ibid., pp. 483–4, and the references there cited. Cf. the examples of other Liberal opposition to factory legislation, cited in H. Samuel, *Liberalism* (London, 1902), p. 21.
64 Gordon, art. cit., p. 484.
65 *The Economist*, viii (13 July 1850), p. 773.

Thus Chadwick and that ilk were anathema. State education was, too, a disservice to those for whom it was provided and an interference with the principle of free trade.[66] Likewise scientific research should not be state supported even though it might in the short run seem to benefit industry and commerce: the long-term price of such dependence is too high. In the same vein the patent law was held to be an unjust interference and copyright protection to be untoward in its effects.[67] Somewhat inconsistently the penny post was ardently supported and, on one aberrant occasion, the paper actually came out in favour of government-imposed safety regulations in mines.[68]

Although thus extreme *The Economist* was hardly unique in the political stance it adopted. A number of provincial newspapers expressed a similar point of view among them the *Leeds Mercury*. Under the editorship of Edward Baines and then of W. Reid, it emphasized (like its London contemporary) the power of the market. As late as 1876 one of its leader-writers was impugning 'the old fallacious faith in the power of political institutions to arrest the action of natural laws'.[69] It is true the *Mercury* was only a local newspaper of limited circulation but it had a considerable standing and influence among provincial journals of its kind. Like *The Economist* in the capital it provided an outlet for, and gave rationality and coherence to, opinions widely held among the industrial middle classes.[70]

Crane Brinton once suggested that the relatively elementary or unformed notions of Cobden and the Manchester School were a much better index to the mind of the ordinary Liberal than the more systematic ideas of writers like J. S. Mill.[71] Perhaps this is true; but it is also clear that after the climactic success of 1846, Cobden, Bright, and the others were not able to keep the ear of the country as they had over the Corn Law question, perhaps because they were too rigid or rationalistic in their perception of affairs.[72] This is not to say, of course, that the extreme libertarian message was not continually purveyed; and, in Manchester itself, even free trade would be sacrificed if it was too closely associated with an unpalatable degree of state intervention in the welfare field (as it was when the so-called new Liberalism developed).[73] And the fact remains that Cobden and his like were practical men of business and

66 Gordon, art. cit., pp.484–5.
67 ibid., p.485.
68 ibid., p.486 and n.87.
69 *Leeds Mercury* (23 September 1876), cited in Taylor, op. cit., pp.28–9.
70 ibid., p.29.
71 C. Brinton, *English Political Thought in the 19th Century* (1933; Harper Torchbooks, 1962), p.104.
72 McCord, loc. cit., ch.4; N. C. Masterman's introduction to J. A. Hobson, *Richard Cobden: the International Man* (1918; London, 1968), p.2.
73 Cobden's *Political Writings*, vol.i, p.xxiii; P. F. Clarke, 'The End of Laissez Faire and the Politics of Cotton', *Historical Journal*, xv (1972), pp.493–512.

politics hardly concerned with the extended and consistent exposition of a theory in all its variety and fullness. They produced pamphlets and speeches for particular occasions rather than anything that resembled a coherent treatise. However, a very complex and sophisticated statement of the themes involved was expounded by Herbert Spencer who not only deployed the specific and familiar ideas about rights, freedom of exchange, criticism of the landed interest, hostility to a spirit of militancy, opposition to government interference, and so on but also presented these matters as part of a fully worked-out doctrine, one based moreover on an elaborate naturalistic metaphysic. It is the range and systematic nature of his point of view, together with his very considerable influence on doctrinaires of all parties, that justifies an extensive review of his ideas here.

HERBERT SPENCER: A PHILOSOPHY OF ANTI-STATISM

Individualism rests its foundations in natural science, and particularly
that part of it known under the name of Evolution
E. KELLY, *Government or Human Evolution*, 1900–1, ii.10

Herbert Spencer was a very remarkable man and at one time widely recognized as such. J. S. Mill expressed the view that he was 'one of the most vigorous as well as boldest thinkers that English speculation has yet produced, full of the true scientific spirit'; and across the Atlantic Mr Justice Holmes wrote that he doubted 'if any writer of English except Darwin' had 'done so much to affect our whole way of thinking about the universe.'[74] An ardent disciple, Auberon Herbert, claimed that Spencer had 'connected all human knowledge', taught us to see that 'everything in the world' is part of the same 'great growth', and had thus helped mankind to grasp 'the reason that governs the whole'. In similar vein Leslie Stephen compared Spencer with Hobbes (who 'may be called a Herbert Spencer of the seventeenth century') in that both aimed at 'exhibiting a complete system in which the results of the physical sciences will be co-ordinated with ethical and political theory.'[75] A. R. Wallace,

74 J. S. Mill, 'Auguste Comte and Positivism' (1865), *Collected Works*, ed. J. M. Robson *et al.* (London, 1963ff.), x. 301; Mr Justice Holmes to Lady Pollock (2 July 1895), in M. de W. Howe (ed.), *The Pollock-Holmes Letters: Correspondence of Sir Frederick Pollock and Mr. Justice Holmes 1874–1932* (Cambridge, 1942), i. 57–8. On the stimulating effect Spencer and his ideas could have, see the comments of G. H. Lewes, cited in G. S. Haight, *George Eliot: a Biography* (Oxford, 1968), pp.271–2. For Spencer's impact in the USA, see e.g. S. Fine, *Laissez-Faire and the General-Welfare State: a Study of Conflict in American Thought, 1865–1901* (1956; Ann Arbor Paperbacks, 1964), esp. ch. II; B. Crick, *The American Science of Politics: its Origins and Conditions* (London, 1959), ch. III; and H. J. Laski, *The American Democracy: a Commentary and an Interpretation* (London, 1949), pp.56, 231, 745.
75 A. Herbert, *A Politician in Trouble about his Soul* (London, 1884), pp.223–4; L.

the great naturalist, was immensely impressed with and indebted to Spencer's work and drew it to Darwin's attention in terms of high praise. He rated it far above the contribution of J. S. Mill.[76] And so on and so forth. Yet during most of the present century there has been little appreciation of Spencer's ability and importance. It is not too much to say that since his death in 1903 he has been little read or discussed and invariably dismissed in disparaging words. He became one of the forgotten mentors of the day before yesterday; at least until quite recently when there has been some revival of interest. A few swallows do not make a summer but some of his writings have lately been reprinted (either complete or in the form of edited selections) and critical reassessment has begun.[77] However despite this long neglect what is clear is that, because Spencer's influence was at one time so considerable, his ideas were one of the main channels through which many of the characteristic themes, both of the Enlightenment and of his own time, were systematized and perpetuated. Moreover he might reasonably claim to be regarded as one of the founding fathers of sociology in this country for (as Mill's and Stephen's remarks suggested) he was much concerned with the meaning of scientific method and the way it might be applied to the study of man and society. What is of particular relevance in the present context is that he was a most powerful champion of the contemporary attack on the growing powers and role of the state. As both scholar and publicist he asserted in an extreme form the claims of individuality against all kinds of external control. For he was convinced that the best political and social arrangements were those that offered the fullest possible freedom of personal choice and endeavour. He believed that, however well-meaning the intention involved, limitations on individual conduct imposed by public agency were invariably destructive of the common good. As he told Henry Sidgwick in the course of a discussion of these issues, 'the accumulation of experiences by the individual, suffering and benefiting by his own conduct, and checking himself by his own judgments (wise or foolish as the case may be), will work out a beneficial adaption more certainly than will the enforcing of

Stephen, *Hobbes* (London, 1904), p.73. For similar recognition by Liberal opponents, see the opinions of Hobhouse and Hobson, cited in M. Freeden, *The New Liberalism: an Ideology of Social Reform* (Oxford, 1978), pp.78–9; and, for an instance of Conservative admiration, Sir H. Maine, *Popular Government: Four Essays* (1885; 2nd edn, London, 1886), p.49.

76 J. R. Durant, 'Scientific Naturalism and Social Reform in the Thought of Alfred Russel Wallace', *British Journal for the History of Science*, xii (1979), pp. 32, 42, 55–6 n.61.

77 For the latter, see in particular J. W. Burrow, *Evolution and Society: a Study in Victorian Social Theory* (1966; Cambridge, 1970); J. D. Y. Peel, *Herbert Spencer: the Evolution of a Sociologist* (London, 1971); and D. Wiltshire, *The Social and Political Thought of Herbert Spencer* (Oxford, 1978).

additional restraints by the *reason of society* as embodied in *law*'.[78] Of course, this sort of opinion was hardly unusual. But what makes Spencer's exploration of the matter especially interesting is precisely the universalizing and purportedly scientific habit of mind already mentioned. Spencer did not simply assert the anti-statist point of view in a polemical manner, he expounded it in the context of an explicit and systematic view of things as a whole and one premeditated on a naturalistic basis. He is indeed an excellent example of both the crucial and the subsidiary nature of a general philosophy to political ideology. The importance is shown by the need Spencer clearly felt to elaborate as complete an intellectual structure as possible. But at the same time it is obvious that, although this broad dimension of thought has a momentum and significance of its own, the reason he embarked on this wide-ranging exercise, its real purpose, lay in a sense outside itself: it was part of the process of trying to provide a rationale for a set of political opinions through detailed empirical reference and general argument. It seems to me quite clear that, in Spencer's case, chronologically these opinions came first and were always uppermost in his mind; all the rest of it, the complex and sophisticated paraphernalia of the 'Synthetic Philosophy', is in some vital respects no more than a highly wrought underpinning and justification of the original prejudice or insight, whichever it is. One reviewer, at the time of Spencer's death, noted that the array of his works was simply the principles of 'the Spencer family' philosophized; another commentator observed that what Spencer aimed at was the creation of a 'Cobdenite universe', the whole vast rational machinery being intended to give sanction to the Manchester doctrine.[79] This is surely correct. Yet to observe it is by no means to depreciate Spencer's achievement which, indeed, constituted a very fine and considerable intellectual effort. But it is necessary in this way and in all honesty to get the perspective and priorities right at the outset, even if his procedure in this respect is merely commonplace.[80]

Spencer wrote his own account of his life and it is in many respects a fascinating and appealing work. The central figure and narrator of one of H. G. Wells's novels writes, 'I disliked Herbert Spencer all my life until I read his autobiography, and then I laughed a little and loved him.'[81] He

78 H. Spencer to H. Sidgwick (12 January 1875), in D. Duncan, *The Life and Letters of Herbert Spencer* (London, 1908), p.176, italics in original.
79 A. S. Pringle-Patterson, 'The Life and Philosophy of Herbert Spencer', *Quarterly Review*, cc (1904), p.251; E. Wingfield-Stratford, *The History of English Patriotism* (London, 1913), ii.475. Cf. Spencer's own remarks in the original preface to 'The Data of Ethics', repr. in *The Principles of Ethics* (London, 1892–3), vol. i, p.vii, and in *The Study of Sociology* (1873; Ann Arbor Paperbacks, 1961), p.135.
80 Cf. the general comment in J. Morgan (ed.), *The Backbench Diaries of Richard Crossman* (London, 1981), p.36.
81 H. G. Wells, *The New Machiavelli* (1911; Penguin, 1946), p.86. The following

was born into a lower middle-class household in Derby in 1820. As a young man, as a boy even, he became much interested in social, political, and religious issues. His home background stimulated this sort of concern but probably the most important influence was that of his uncle, the Reverend Thomas Spencer, who had for a while looked after and educated him. Thomas Spencer was something of a radical in politics being, for example, an advocate of disestablishment, a supporter of franchise reform and of the repeal of the Corn Laws. He devoted much time and energy to philanthropic acts but was very hostile to any form of compulsory public charity as being vicious in its effects. He produced a number of popular pamphlets on these topics including one on *Legislative Meddling*. He was a leading member of a group of like-minded reformers who maintained links with the Chartist and anti-Corn Law movements and whose views were reflected in *The Nonconformist* newspaper. This had been founded by some Birmingham radicals to aid the campaign for democratic principles and universal suffrage; and its general sentiments were of an extreme libertarian type rejecting government in excess and the way the limbs of the nation were increasingly pinioned by Parliamentary regulation.

In the political context of the day it was thus not particularly moderate company in which Herbert Spencer passed his youth.[82] He waxed most indignant about the swindling and tyranny of the aristocracy, eagerly anticipated fundamental change in the entire system of government as a means of overthrowing that oppression, and (not least) abused the propensity to over-legislation which he believed was paralysing initiative and energy in society. Given their hostility to the social privilege of the traditional landed classes and to the dominance of the Anglican establishment and, too, given their acceptance of *laissez faire* political economy, those with whom Spencer was connected were indeed 'shrewd enemies' of government.[83] He was an angry young man. A significant aspect of this repudiation of the conventional was the heterodox religious views which he formed early and retained to the end of his days. Partly this attitude derived from the challenge to established belief required by Nonconformity; partly it was related to his early interest in the physical sciences and mathematics which he probably got from his father (who was a teacher) and which entailed, for him, a kind of secular naturalism. Spencer once said of himself that the consciousness of the

---

biographical details are based mainly on Spencer, *An Autobiography* (London, 1904), Duncan, op. cit., and Wiltshire, op. cit., chs 1–5, the last being an account which is both concise and full.

82 For descriptions of this background of political radicalism, religious dissent, and scientific naturalism, see Peel, op. cit., chs 2–3, and Wiltshire, op. cit., ch. 1.

83 The phrase cited is from Sir Ernest Barker's 'The Discredited State', *Political Quarterly*, no. 5 (February 1915), p.105.

universality and uniformity of physical causation had always been deeply rooted in him. He had, too, come across the concept of evolution in his early twenties and been much impressed.[84] And these principles meant that the universe and everything in it will have reached its present form 'through successive stages physically necessitated.'[85]

These two strands, the political and the naturalistic, which appear in more extensive form throughout the works of Spencer's mature years, were clearly expressed as early as 1842 (when he was 22 years old) in a series of letters which he wrote for *The Nonconformist* and which were soon reprinted as a pamphlet. There he argued (much as Malthus, for instance, had done before him) that man and society are just as much subject to law as inanimate nature and that these social principles are such that any evils are self-rectifying through a process of organic adaptation to environment. The inference followed, he thought, that, in order to optimize this process of development, the function of government should be strictly limited.[86] The basic political point was made as well in an unpublished paper he also wrote in his early twenties in which he summed up 'the cause of our national distress' in the following terms:

> We conceive that the great family of ills that have been for so long preying upon the national prosperity, wasting the resources and paralyzing the energies of the people, are all the offspring of the one primary and hitherto almost unsuspected evil – over-legislation. . . . We can discover no radical remedy for our social maladies but a stringent regulation which shall confine our governors to the performance of their primitive duty – the protection of person and property.[87]

As a young man Spencer went through a period of lack of aim and irregular employment – including a formative spell on *The Economist* – before finally settling down to a literary and journalistic career that, in due course and amid protracted financial and other difficulties, proved not wholly unsuccessful: he never became rich but nor was he ever in dire straits. Initially he produced essays on miscellaneous topics ranging from 'The Sources of Architectural Types' and 'Reciprocal Dependence

84 On the likely sources of this idea of development, see Peel, op. cit., ch. 6; J. W. Burrow, *Evolution and Society*, pp. 187–90; Wiltshire, op. cit., pp. 60–6. See also e.g. *Autobiography*, i. 351; Spencer's *Essays: Scientific, Political & Speculative* (1857–74; rev. edn, London, 1891), i. 9, 35, 96; Spencer's 'The Filiation of Ideas' (1899), in Duncan, op. cit., pp. 536, 541, 546; and E. Barker, *Political Thought in England, 1848–1914* (1915; 2nd edn, rev., London, 1947), p. 74.

85 *Autobiography*, ii. 6. On Spencer as the heir of the eighteenth-century tradition of provincial science and radicalism, see Peel, op. cit., esp. p. 43, and Wiltshire, op. cit., pp. 10–11.

86 H. Spencer, *The Proper Sphere of Government* (London, 1843), pp. 3–5, 24–5, 34–5; *Autobiography*, i. 209, 211. Cf. *The Study of Sociology*, pp. 5–6.

87 Cited in Duncan, op. cit., p. 37.

in the Animal and Vegetable Creations' to 'A Theory of Tears and Laughter'. Among these early papers was one on 'The Development Hypothesis' and another on the 'Theory of Population' in which the concept of the preservation of the select (or the survival of the fittest as Spencer called it in the latter essay) was first intimated, albeit not effectively pursued, seven years before the publication of Darwin's *The Origin of Species*. In fact this sort of idea was in the air. Darwin and Wallace reached it independently: the former sketched the notion as early as 1837 and admitted he found it confirmed in Malthus's *Essay on Population* (1798). There is, too, a remarkably clear anticipation in James Hutton's unpublished manuscript on the principles of agriculture which was composed a year or so before Malthus's essay appeared.[88] It is in many ways not surprising that an acute and knowledgeable young man with marked scientific interests like Spencer should have grasped the concept even before Darwin's work came out. At the same time Spencer readily admitted he did not discern the specific mechanisms of evolutionary change systematically studied by Darwin.[89]

Spencer's first book was published in 1851 with the title of *Social Statics*: it is a work of considerable moment in the history of his thought. He then wrote a study of psychology which, he hoped, would 'ultimately stand beside Newton's *Principia*.'[90] Appearing in 1855 it was not, however, particularly well received though J. S. Mill seems to have been impressed. Meanwhile Spencer continued to make his living by a varied literary activity, turned his hand (as ever) to inventions of different kinds, moved about in this country and abroad (he was always rather restless), worried about his health (he was a considerable valetudinarian), and was generally still somewhat unsettled or even aimless. He later acquired something of a reputation for an eccentric personal manner: hardly surprising given, for instance, his practice of dictating the text of a work to a secretary while rowing on the Serpentine or in intervals of playing squash rackets or billiards (at which he was an expert).[91]

There then occurred a crucial moment of intellectual enlightenment. In January 1858, towards the end of his first authorial decade, he realized (rather suddenly it would seem) that all his hitherto sporadic ideas hung together and might be expounded in 'something like a consolidated system of thought'. He perceived that he had come to form certain leading themes or conceptions and had worked out a method of looking at problems that was fundamentally uniform regardless of its area of

---

88 On the importance of Hutton's work, see Sir E. Bailey, *Charles Lyell* (London, 1962), pp. 83–4.
89 *Essays*, i. 53n., 91.
90 Letter cited in Duncan, op. cit., p. 75.
91 And see e.g. the curious and amusing procedure described in K. Muggeridge and R. Adam, *Beatrice Webb: a Life, 1858–1943* (London, 1967), p. 40.

application.[92] Pursuing this inspiration he was enthused with the purpose of treating all aspects of human life 'after the spirit and methods of physical science'.[93] He then proceeded to draw up a detailed programme for a complete and unified body of doctrine conceived in this style in which 'all the higher sciences' were reduced to a rational form. The whole scheme is outlined in the famous prospectus 'A System of Philosophy' issued in 1860.[94] Unlike Bacon, his spiritual ancestor in more ways than one, he actually carried through this project for a renewal of learning on scientific lines. His *First Principles* (1862) was followed two years later by the *Principles of Biology* a work based on considerable experiment and observation. There subsequently appeared, at intervals, new editions of the *Principles of Psychology*; similar works (also frequently later revised) on the principles of sociology and ethics; and as well the multi-volumed *Descriptive Sociology* which contained information about many different races and societies illustrative of the theories of social evolution elsewhere expounded. In this connexion it is important to recall that, although (so to say) an amateur scientist – like the seventeenth-century 'virtuoso' he so much resembled – Spencer was a practising experimentalist of some skill and reputation whose work attracted the admiring attention of Darwin, Alfred Wallace, Ray Lankester, and others; and he long had a close association with T. H. Huxley whose advice he sought on biological matters. At the same time it would not be correct to suggest that his research procedures in the sphere of social studies were more than industrious. He had, for instance, a somewhat haphazard and indirect method of acquiring data about primitive societies. Thus his secretary was instructed, when they were dealing with a given tribe, to read three 'trustworthy authors' and abstract the relevant material, this being any matter that confirmed the thesis under review.[95] But at least Spencer's intention is quite clear. It was to expound a systematic sociology based inductively on as wide a range of material as could be acquired from the comfort of a study chair and using for its organizing themes the fundamental principles of science. And he called his comprehensive system the 'Synthetic Philosophy' because it purported to bring together on this intendedly naturalistic basis all the knowledge available about man and society and which he believed could be deduced from first principles. His works often give the

92 *Autobiography*, ii.5–14.
93 Letter to J. D. Hooker (13 December 1858), cited in Duncan, op. cit., p.89.
94 Letter to J. S. Mill (29 July 1858), cited in *Autobiography*, ii.23. The prospectus is reprinted e.g. ibid., ii.479–83 and in *First Principles* (1862; 6th edn, 1900, Thinker's Library, 1945), pp. xv–xx. In one of his last essays, Spencer gave a summary of his leading concepts, 'The Filiation of Ideas' (1899), appendix B, Duncan, op. cit., pp.533–76. Cf. *Autobiography*, ii.165–70.
95 Duncan, op. cit., pp.141–2.

impression of an extreme form of theoretical abstraction. There is Huxley's famous quip that Spencer's idea of a tragedy was a deduction killed by a fact.[96] And Mrs Webb (who knew Spencer very well) commented in her diary on his methodological naïvety, writing that there was 'something pathetic in the isolation of his mind, a sort of spider-like existence; sitting alone in the centre of his theoretical web, catching facts, and weaving them again into theory.'[97] Spencer himself, however, often liked to assert the purely empirical or inductive character of his work.[98]

The remainder of this section will consist of an outline of Spencer's system of thought to show how its major themes bear on the question of the relation of man to the state and how these ideas are intended to support an extreme libertarian opinion on that issue. Spencer was always really concerned to state a moral principle. Like many other Victorians he saw orthodox religious belief as more and more in decline, ebbing away like the tide of traditional faith in Arnold's 'Dover Beach'.[99] Although not himself requiring the psychological support of firm religious belief, Spencer realized that the great contemporary need was nevertheless to provide some practical alternative to what he called the old 'code of supernatural ethics', a view he shared with many positivists.[100] What was needed was 'a compass':

> 'Give us a guide,' cry men to the philosopher. 'We would escape from these miseries in which we are entangled. A better state is ever present to our imaginations, and we yearn after it; but all our efforts to realize it are fruitless. We are weary of perpetual failures; tell us by what rule we may attain our desire.'[101]

In response to this supposed plea Spencer creates the picture of a perfect libertarian society, a sort of ideal by which to judge the actual state of

96 A possibly apocryphal application of a more general phrase, cited in *The Oxford Dictionary of Quotations*, 2nd edn (London, 1974), p.266 §19.

97 B. Webb, *My Apprenticeship* (Penguin, 1938), i. 48 (entry for 5 May 1884). Cf. Spencer's own comments on his mental processes, *Autobiography*, i. 242, 304–5, 399–404.

98 See the conversation reported in H. Macpherson, *Herbert Spencer: the Man and his Work* (London, 1900), p.42; also ibid., pp.43–7.

99 For a good example of the 'reluctant and very sad' unbelief created by scientific advance, see D. Hudson, *Munby: Man of Two Worlds. The Life and Diaries of Arthur J. Munby 1828–1910* (1972; Abacus, 1974), pp.64–5 (diary entry for 1 July 1860).

100 Cf. S. Eisen, 'Frederic Harrison and Herbert Spencer: Embattled Unbelievers', *Victorian Studies*, xii (1968–9), pp.33–56; also the passages cited in Burrow, op. cit., pp.93–4.

101 H. Spencer, *Social Statics: Or, The Conditions Essential to Human Happiness Specified, and the First of Them Developed* (1851; Farnborough, Hants., 1970), pp.1, 8. Cf. *Facts and Comments* (London, 1902), pp.206–9.

affairs and in terms of which collectivist development stands condemned.[102] The rationale of this vision is found in the theory of evolution and this in turn is rooted in a scientific metaphysic: for it is the ineluctable implications for social conduct (derived from natural science) that are to replace the fading dogmas of Christianity in Spencer's scheme of things.[103]

Basic principles

Fideism is a doctrine well embedded in the British empirical tradition.[104] Its practical significance was that by separating the spheres of faith and reason not only were the truths of religion made independent of the advance of natural knowledge but also that the latter was freed from the trammels imposed by the requirements of spiritual belief and theological dogma. There is a sense in which in this mode Spencer agreed with Milton who had written in *Paradise Lost*,

> Heaven is for thee too high
> To know what passes there. Be lowly wise. . . .[105]

For he undoubtedly believed that there were limits to the reach of human knowledge, holding (in an argument somewhat similar to Hume's) that it is impossible to know things in themselves; all we have is our impression of things.[106] It is true that we also have the consciousness of an 'Actuality lying behind Appearances' but its nature necessarily defies our understanding: it is the 'Unknowable'.[107] In this nescience, however, even religion and science were reconciled as they both sought, necessarily in vain, to grasp the 'ultimate mystery'. It was indeed an 'Absolute' which Spencer himself seemed sometimes to hold in awe.[108] But, on this convenient basis, he was able to deny accusations of irreligion for he did not say firmly there was no spiritual reality. Similarly he could repudiate the charge of materialism. He just did not see how a decided view could be established one way or the other about the nature of this unreachable noumenon.

Nevertheless a great deal remained effectively within the frame of

102 On the status of Spencer's account as constituting a description of perfection, cf. *Social Statics*, p.409 and *Autobiography*, i. 359, 416.
103 Spencer, 'The Filiation of Ideas', in Duncan, op. cit., pp. 575–6.
104 See e.g. my *Order, Empiricism and Politics: Two Traditions of English Political Thought 1500–1700* (London, 1964), esp. pp.158ff.
105 Milton, *Paradise Lost*, viii. 172–3.
106 e.g. *First Principles*, p.55. Cf. Hume, *A Treatise of Human Nature* (Everyman, 1940), I. ii, §vi (i. 71–2).
107 *First Principles*, p.80; *Essays*, i. 35.
108 *Facts and Comments*, p.213; *Essays on Education and Kindred Subjects* (1854–9; Everyman, 1966), pp.40–2.

comprehension; and this knowable universe was not a chaos but an order the basic form of which could be established by philosophical inquiry.

Philosophy Spencer defined as completely unified knowledge, as the mode of thought which operates at the highest level of generality.[109] It stands, therefore, at the peak (or at the base) of the family of special sciences, dealing with the principles or propositions common to all classes of phenomena: it is their universal synthesis. The concept resembles very much Bacon's notion of 'First Philosophy'.[110] Spencer further held that all the fundamental ideas involved were to be thought of in terms of various forms of 'force' or 'energy'. This was indeed the basic concept of the knowable realm, 'the ultimate of ultimates', of which such categories as space, time, matter, and motion are simply diverse expressions.[111] And he supposed that the amount of force must be fixed: matter must be indestructible and motion continuous for if energy could come into or go out of existence at any time then, so far as it was thus liable to sudden creation or arbitrary annihilation, the universe would be irregular and confused. Without some such assumption, an 'incalculable element, fatal to all positive conclusions' would be introduced and knowledge would be impossible.[112]

Thus there can only be changes of state of a constant amount of energy, a basic principle Spencer called 'the persistence of force', the term he preferred to the more usual 'conservation of energy'. This was really the immediate axiom of all his thought, the necessary truth which, although it transcends demonstration, is the effective foundation on which he builds his natural and social theories alike.[113] There was also an important corollary to the effect that these changes of state proceeded according to law: there was a 'persistence of relations among forces'. And this 'unvaryingness' took the form of necessary and universal connexions of cause and effect, every manifestation of force being preceded and succeeded by an equivalent occurrence.[114]

Foremost among these causal relations was the law of evolution and dissolution which Spencer regarded as the formula that most clearly governed or revealed the continuous redistribution of matter and

---

109 *First Principles*, pp.113, 115, 484–6.
110 ibid., pp.121–3, 244. Cf. Bacon's *Works*, ed. Spedding *et al.* (London, 1877–87), iv. 337 and *The Advancement of Learning*, ed. Wright (1868; 5th edn, Oxford, 1926), p.105 (II. v. 2).
111 *First Principles*, pp.140–6.
112 ibid., II. iv, v (citation at p.148).
113 ibid., pp.165, 168–71, 241.
114 ibid., p.174; *Social Statics*, p.40; *The Proper Sphere of Government*, pp.3–4. On the importance Spencer attributed to the concept of causation, see *Autobiography*, ii. 5–7; *Essays*, i. 35ff.; *Social Statics*, p.40; *Principles of Ethics* (London, 1892–3), i. 47–9, 61–3.

motion. It was the one great fact of the observable universe and all phenomena were merely aspects of it of more or less complexity:

> Whether it be in the development of the Earth, in the development of Life upon its surface, in the development of Society, of Government, of Manufactures, of Commerce, of Language, Literature, Science, Art, this same evolution . . . holds throughout. From the earliest traceable cosmical changes down to the latest results of civilization, we shall find that [this] transformation . . . is that in which progress essentially consists.[115]

And this evolutionary process reveals important general features or aspects. Thus greater size appears through increasing integration or aggregation; the homogeneous is transformed into the heterogeneous; there is more coherence or consolidation of the parts of any entity; also growing definiteness. Broadly, the simple evolves into the complex through successive differentiations, a process Spencer examines at length in the work called *First Principles*.[116] The reason for this nature and direction of events is that every active force produces more than one change, every cause more than one effect.[117] The result, for instance, is that the diffuse gaseous nebulae evolve into complex stellar and planetary systems; the simple, undifferentiated cells of primeval life are elaborated into all the different forms of creature that have subsequently appeared; the primitive tribe gives way to the sophisticated civilizations of the modern world. Social causation was indeed particularly 'fructifying' in this way.[118] As to what lay ahead, although Spencer did sometimes speculate about the long-term future, he invariably concluded that it was a meaningless incursion into what was really beyond the stretch of thought.[119]

The central purpose of the great range of discussion comprising the 'Synthetic Philosophy' was to trace this causal and evolutionary process through the varied forms of things and events examined and thus to interpret and unify them. It is in these terms that the evolution of life is explored in the *Principles of Biology* and of mind in the *Principles of Psychology*. And, of course, the 'Super-organic' sphere, the evolution of man in his social and political relationships, must be analysed in a like fashion.

---

115 *Essays*, i. 10. Cf. ibid., i. 35.
116 See also the useful summary, ibid., ii. 140–2. That 'differentiation' became a fashionable philosophical term of wide application, see F. W. Maitland, *The Constitutional History of England* (1908; Cambridge, 1974), p.105.
117 *Essays*, i. 37–8; *First Principles*, chs xx–xxii.
118 *The Man Versus the State* (1884; Penguin, 1969), p.132; *The Study of Sociology*, pp.294–7; *Facts and Comments*, pp.97ff.; *Essays*, iii. 242–5, 401–2.
119 *First Principles*, pp. 473–4, 481, 494–5.

Social evolution

Spencer was convinced, then, that 'social evolution forms a part of evolution at large', that the various arrangements of society were the outcome of natural causes and revealed 'a normal order of growth.'[120] In order to demonstrate this he undertook a lengthy review of the structure and function of the family, ecclesiastical and ceremonial institutions, professional and economic activity, political organization, and so on.[121] And their development clearly revealed, he thought, the basic features of the evolutionary process as shown in the natural world. Thus increasing integration or aggregation is indicated by the tendency of societies to grow in size even to the possibility of supranational federation.[122] The transition from homogeneity to heterogeneity is exemplified by the way in which 'the simple tribe, alike in all its parts' gives way 'to the civilized nation, full of structural and functional unlikenesses.'[123] Increasing coherence is observed too:

> We see the wandering group dispersing, dividing, held together by no bonds; the tribe with parts made more coherent by subordination to a dominant man; the cluster of tribes united in a political plexus under a chief with sub-chiefs; and so on up to the civilized nation, consolidated enough to hold together for a thousand years or more.[124]

There is also increasing definiteness as social arrangements become more settled and precise. Class divisions emerge and become more distinct; custom passes into law which itself establishes more fixed and specific forms; institutions separate and specialize, developing their own structures as with the various offices that have, in time, emerged from a single original such as the Privy Council or the Secretaryship of State.[125] Thus, concludes Spencer, the formula of evolution is fulfilled in this social context 'in all respects'. There is a general direction of change 'from societies which are small, loose, uniform, and vague in structure' to those 'which are large, compact, multiform, and distinct'.[126]

---

120 *Autobiography*, ii. 8; *Principles of Ethics*, i. 47–9, 61–3; *Essays on Education*, p. 30; *The Principles of Sociology*, i. 584–5. This last work was published in three volumes in various editions and reprints from 1876 on. Those available to me and to which reference is made here are: vol. i, 3rd and enlarged edn, 1885; vol. ii, 1902; vol. iii, 1896. In each case the place of publication was London.

121 There is a brief, general summary of the whole scheme in *Principles of Sociology*, i. 426–32.

122 ibid., ii. 614–5; *First Principles*, p. 282.

123 *Principles of Sociology*, i. 584–5; *First Principles*, pp. 295, 301, 307–24; *Essays*, iii. 439.

124 *Principles of Sociology*, i. 584–5; cf. ibid., ii. 265–87, 643–4.

125 *First Principles*, pp. 283–4, 335ff.; *Principles of Sociology*, ii. 288–310, 645–6.

126 *Principles of Sociology*, ii. 646. Cf. ibid., i. 581–2, 585; *First Principles*, pp. 356–7. The detailed process of social development envisaged is summarized in many passages e.g. *Essays*, i. 19–23.

Naturally this is a very long and complex process; and equally
extensive and complicated is the social typology which Spencer works
out partly on the basis of an analogy between the social and the natural
organisms.[127] But he also suggests a broader perspective that, in fact, has
a close affinity to the general theme of this study of the British political
tradition. This is his famous distinction between two fundamental forms
of social organization which he calls 'militant' and 'industrial', 'a
sociological Ahriman and Ormuz'.[128] The idea is that any actual society
at a particular stage of its development will constitute a 'ratio' between
the two types or tendencies, reflecting the specific factors or causes
operating in its case. Nor need the character and rate of change of the
balance be the same in all its parts, and in this respect a continual 'social
metamorphosis' is always under way.[129]

To appreciate Spencer's libertarian attack on over-legislation, it is
necessary to explain what he had in mind in respect of these two
antithetical types of social ethos and arrangement. The categories if not
the specific terms were present even in his earliest published work though
it is not clear whether he thought the concepts were his own invention.[130]
But even if others should have this distinction it was certainly Spencer
who gave these notions world-wide popularity.[131]

A society in which militant tendencies[132] dominate is one in which its
members are regarded as existing 'for the benefit of the whole' and not
for their own sakes; in such places there is scarcely any concept or
assertion of personal rights in opposition to the ruling power.[133] As

127 For the use of the parallel, see e.g. *Principles of Sociology*, part II *passim*, esp.
i.437–50; also *The Study of Sociology*, pp.301–6; and *Essays*, i. 101–7, 265–307. As
this is a common point of criticism it is important to note that Spencer himself was
fully aware of the limitations of these comparisons e.g. *Principles of Sociology*, i.
449–50, 578–81; *The Study of Sociology*, p.52; *Social Statics*, p.238; *Essays*, i. 272–7.
Unfortunately commentators have not always observed his prudent reservations
about the correspondence.
128 This last phrase is from Wingfield-Stratford, *The History of English Patriotism*, ii.
479.
129 *Principles of Sociology*, i. 544–5, 557–62; ii. 244–8, 263, 568–9, 646; *The Study of
Sociology*, pp.316–17. Cf. Spencer's letter cited in S. H. Harris, *Auberon Herbert:
Crusader for Liberty* (London, 1943), p.215.
130 *The Proper Sphere of Government*, letter v on war.
131 E. Halévy, *The Era of Tyrannies: Essays on Socialism and War* (1938; trans. edn,
London, 1967), pp.22–6, 58–60, suggests the idea passed from St-Simon to Comte to
Buckle and so to Spencer. For Comte's use of the theme, see the extracts in J. H.
Abraham, *The Origins and Growth of Sociology* (Penguin, 1973), pp.138ff.; J. S.
Mill used it in *The Principles of Political Economy* (1848), *Collected Works*, iii.890.
For a recent example of the distinction, see M. Friedman, *Capitalism and Freedom*
(Chicago, 1962), p.13. There are numerous similarities between Spencer's and
Friedman's doctrines.
132 The phrase is not intended to have any contemporary reference, that is, to the present
day, but its implications may not be inapt in this regard. See below pp.494–5.
133 *Principles of Sociology*, i. 551–2; ii. 571–8; *Principles of Ethics*, ii. 217–19.

Spencer analyses it, the notion (in its extreme form) comes to resemble the more recent concept of totalitarianism in which the public encroaches extensively and increasingly on the private sphere.

> Thus the trait characterizing the militant structure throughout, is that its units are coerced into their various combined actions. As the soldier's will is so suspended that he becomes in everything the agent of his officer's will; so is the will of the citizen in all transactions, private and public, overruled by that of the government. The co-operation by which the life of the militant society is maintained, is a *compulsory* co-operation.[134]

As the term 'militant' implies, the origins of this type of society may be traced to the need for leadership and control in war. In the conditions of hostility that existed among primitive peoples there emerged a hierarchical social structure infused with a regimental subordination, economic activity being seen simply as a kind of commissariat existing 'solely to supply the needs of the governmental-military structures, and having left over for itself only enough for bare maintenance'; and there is extensive official regulation of life at large not excluding personal conduct.[135] Spencer was, of course, aware that the extent of such control has varied and that the stringent discipline of ancient or primitive societies of this militant sort had not (at least up to his day) been attained in recent times. Yet he asks his reader to recall modern laws which have regulated food or dress, prevented movement, prohibited some games or dictated others. And he cites contemporary France as a place where there is 'peremptory control of journals and suppression of meetings', a centralized uniformity of education, official administration of the fine arts, and the like: the 'characteristic regulating system ramifies everywhere.'[136] Czarist Russia and the German Empire, he thought, provided similar exemplification.[137] Nor – a matter he shrilly deplored – were signs of militancy absent from contemporary Britain.[138]

Industrial society is quite different, is indeed a completely contrasting social form, one in which government is not only democratic and representative (in contrast to the 'despotic' controlling agency of militant society) but is also limited in its scope and action and, as well, 'uncentralized' and diffused. There is great stress on individuality and minimal supervision of personal conduct.[139] Free associations flourish; a

---

134 *Principles of Sociology*, i.552, italics in original. Cf. the discussion of Socialism, ibid., iii. 565–79, 585–6.
135 ibid., i.549. Cf. ibid., i.550, 583–4; ii. 569–71.
136 ibid., i.550–1.
137 ibid., ii.257, 584–6, 588–90; iii.584–6; *Principles of Ethics*, ii.44.
138 *Principles of Sociology*, ii.590–2; iii.589–92.
139 ibid., i.557, 583–4; ii.607–40; and see *The Study of Sociology*, p.81 on free institutions as a means of preventing abuse of power.

diversity of opinion is tolerated especially in religion; the government (being subordinate to the will of the citizens) is, in particular, 'not allowed to dictate modes of production nor to regulate trade.' Its purpose is simply to maintain the conditions in which people themselves may pursue the 'highest individual life'. It is a régime of '*voluntary* cooperation' so that contract, the mutual and unforced 'rendering of services', is the key and not status backed by a system of compulsion.[140] One of the main features of industrial society is 'plasticity'. Because it is not controlled by a central authority rigidly and in detail, it is pluralistic, enterprising, more able flexibly and quickly to respond to the demands made on it by varying pressures and circumstances: an important matter because, as with any other form of being, effective adaptation to environment is crucial to the process of natural selection.[141] All this meant that, in evolutionary terms, industrial society was more advanced and would, therefore, emerge as the increasingly dominant form unless (through, for instance, a greater intensity of war) a Neanderthal regression to militancy supervened.[142] Spencer also envisaged (in a few passages) an even more advanced social type in which activity was dedicated to cultural and intellectual purposes.[143] But he realized that there had been in history few instances of non-militant societies which had evolved on the large scale.[144] And he feared, as time wore on, that many influences of an increasingly powerful kind were creating circumstances in which it was more and more difficult for the industrial form to flourish. Nevertheless his life's task (as he saw it) was to describe what was involved in this ideal, a picture of which he had presented 'in its highest conceivable perfection' in his first major work *Social Statics*.[145]

He always realized that change in the desired direction depended, above all, on an elevation of the character, manner, and beliefs of individuals. Constitutional or social tinkering was superficial by comparison and might be dangerous.[146] It was the achievement of the more advanced moral ethos of industrial society that was crucial.

Evolutionary ethics

Spencer's doctrine was nothing if not an ethical one, the attack on the growth of government being premised on the belief that over-legislation

---

140 *Principles of Sociology*, i.555–7, italics in original; ii.613; *Principles of Ethics*, ii.228–9; *Essays*, iii.450ff.; *The Man Versus the State*, p.63.
141 *Principles of Sociology*, ii.613–14.
142 ibid., vol. ii, part v, ch.xix.
143 ibid., i.563; *Essays on Education*, pp.30–1.
144 *Principles of Sociology*, i.553.
145 *Social Statics*, p.15. Cf. ibid., pp.38, 55–6.
146 e.g. *Principles of Sociology*, ii.661–3.

was immoral. If people cried out to the philosophers for a guide as to what they should do, Spencer aimed to provide it.[147] And, of course, in an age of declining religious faith, the old 'code of supernatural ethics' had to be replaced by principles of right and wrong resting on a secular and 'scientific' basis.[148] There were indeed natural rules of conduct in human society as there were laws throughout the universe: 'As well might we seek to light a fire with ice, feed cattle on stones, hang our hats on cobwebs, or otherwise disregard the physical laws of the world, as go contrary to its equally imperative ethical laws.'[149] This 'strictly scientific morality' would necessarily be composed of deductions from the 'primary law of man' and the basic principles of evolution. A society not modelled on this inevitable frame will, he was certain, assuredly tumble to pieces.[150]

Spencer had begun to sketch an outline of this 'scientific' moral ideal in the early essays on *The Proper Sphere of Government* and subsequently elaborated it in numerous other works but most fully in *The Principles of Ethics* published in various volumes brought out between 1879 and 1892. And the main inspiration of his doctrine was utilitarianism, his often harsh criticism of the creed notwithstanding. He said he found its key concepts vague and its consideration of means imprecise. As well, the assumption of many supporters of the school that the achievement of the greatest happiness required an extensive agenda for government was naturally quite unacceptable to him.[151] Yet Spencer did not so much completely repudiate utilitarianism as try to build on it and improve it by making it (as he claimed) more scientific. Bentham had wanted to be the Newton of the moral sciences but his achievement had been flawed; Spencer had the ambition to succeed as 'the moral Euclid' where his predecessor had failed. Specifically this would entail a more adequate analysis of the causes which produce good or evil results seen in hedonistic terms. He hoped in this way to be able to indicate more concretely and effectively than Bentham which kinds of action and situation lead to happiness and which do not.[152]

Now the standard of happiness or welfare is 'infinitely variable'

147 See the passage from *Social Statics* cited above p.55.
148 *Principles of Ethics*, vol.i, pp.vii–viii.
149 *Social Statics*, pp.41–2. Cf. Hodgskin's *Travels in the North of Germany* (1820), ii.465, cited in E. Halévy, *Thomas Hodgskin* (1903; trans. edn, London, 1956), p.51. For Hodgskin's probably considerable influence on Spencer, ibid, pp.142, 171.
150 *Social Statics*, pp.3, 30, 40–2, 50–1, 71–2.
151 ibid., 'The Doctrine of Expediency', pp.1–16; also ibid., pp.19–21, 28; *Principles of Ethics*, vol.i, I. ix, xiii; ibid., ii.239–40; *Autobiography*, ii.87–90; *The Man Versus the State*, pp.180–3. See also his letter to J. S. Mill, in *Principles of Ethics*, i. 56–8 and cf. Mill's *Collected Works*, x.258n.
152 *Principles of Ethics*, vol. i, I. iii, iv, esp. pp. 57–8, 61–3; *The Man Versus the State*, pp.180–1; *The Proper Sphere of Government*, pp.3–7.

according to persons and circumstances.[153] But it is basically a matter of meeting bodily needs, fulfilling desired purposes, and exercising faculties in as complete and harmonious a way as possible not least in respect of self-preservation as an individual and of ensuring the continuation of the species. For all these ends, as much liberty of personal choice and action is desirable as inevitable social relationships and restraints permit. Thus:

> Man cannot exercise his faculties without certain scope. He must have liberty to go and to come, to see, to feel, to speak, to work; to get food, raiment, shelter, and to provide for each and all of the needs of his nature. He must be free to do everything which is directly or indirectly requisite for the due satisfaction of every mental and bodily want. . . . He has a *right* to that liberty.[154]

A fundamental corollary is what Spencer calls 'the law of equal freedom', the rule that 'Every man is free to do that which he wills, provided he infringes not the equal freedom of any other man.'[155] But not only is the maximum amount of liberty thus required, it is also entailed by the demands of the evolutionary process. The following passage illustrates the connexion between the idea of natural selection and Spencer's views on ethics and political control:

> Of man, as of all inferior creatures, the law by conformity to which the species is preserved, is that among adults the individuals best adapted to the conditions of their existence shall prosper most, and that individuals least adapted to the conditions of their existence shall prosper least – a law which, if uninterfered with, entails survival of the fittest, and spread of the most adapted varieties. And . . . so . . . we see that, ethically considered, this law implies that each individual ought to receive the benefits and the evils of his own nature and consequent conduct: neither being prevented from having whatever good his actions normally bring to him, nor allowed to shoulder off on to other persons whatever ill is brought to him by his actions.[156]

There should, therefore, be no attempt to interfere with individuals in their free pursuit of faculty gratification. Only thus can people find optimum happiness; only thus can 'fitness' to survive be tested.

What specific conditions does all this indicate? Spencer's initial answer to this question signals one of his departures from utilitarian orthodoxy, for it takes the form of a doctrine of 'rights', a concept of which Bentham

153 *Social Statics*, p. 3. On the nature of goodness seen in utilitarian terms, see *Principles of Ethics*, i. 30, 45–6, 448; and *The Proper Sphere of Government*, pp. 14–15.
154 *Social Statics*, pp. 76–7, italics in original.
155 *Principles of Ethics*, ii. 46, 155–6; *Social Statics*, pp. 76–8, 87–8, 103; Spencer's letter to Henry Sidgwick (1875) cited above pp. 49–50.
156 *Principles of Ethics*, ii. 17. Cf. *Essays on Education*, p. 23.

had been very critical. For Spencer these 'particular freedoms' constituted a statement of the conditions required by the general demand for liberty to exercise the faculties and achieve gratification. They included the right to life and 'physical integrity', to 'free-motion and locomotion', to the use of the natural media (light, air, and land), to various claims concerning property, and to free speech and publication including religious worship and profession. His view of these matters was not always consistent with the extreme libertarian reputation he later acquired. For instance, in the first, full flush of hostility to the land-owning classes, he regards all individual ownership of land as aggression and urges that life-maintaining activities are best sustained where 'the surface of the Earth' belongs to 'society at large'.[157] Equally he was quite capable of demanding action by the authorities to prevent pollution of the environment by noise, smoke, or other unwholesome mischiefs detrimental to the individual's pursuit of his well-being.[158] However his more characteristic line of argument emerges in consideration of the bundle of rights concerning property, bequest, and exchange. In this regard he argued that the law of equal freedom implied the assertion that 'each is free to keep for himself all those gratifications and sources of gratification which he procures' without trespassing on his neighbour's spheres of action. If someone is stronger, more ingenious, or hard-working than another person then he is, by this rule, assigned 'exclusive possession' of the greater return to his efforts; and no one can properly deprive him of this 'without claiming for themselves greater liberty of action than he claims'.[159] What is proper is not that each shall have an equal share but, what is quite different, a like freedom to pursue those things which would gratify the faculties. Only in these conditions, too, can a social and civic degeneration be prevented; otherwise the inferior will subsist by robbing or holding back those less unfit than themselves.[160] The argument is clearly a restatement by Spencer of the conventional utilitarian (or, indeed, common law) case that happiness is maximized by ensuring to each person the greatest amount of the product of his labour.[161] Thus far indeed all is broadly in accordance with

157 *Principles of Ethics*, vol. ii, IV. ix, esp. p. 81; app. B, ii. 440–4; *Social Statics*, chs ix–x. Sidney Webb commented that few of those who followed Spencer along his libertarian paths realized that he accepted land nationalization 'as a necessary condition of an Individualist community', in G. B. Shaw *et al.*, *Fabian Essays* (1889; Jubilee edn, London, 1950), p. 38 n. 1. In fact, Spencer later changed his tune and was less prepared to condemn individual land-ownership outright.

158 *Principles of Ethics*, vol. ii, IV. ix and p. 137.

159 ibid., ii. 100; *Social Statics*, pp. 130–5.

160 *Principles of Ethics*, vol. ii, IV. xii, xiii. On gift and bequest, ibid., IV. xiv; free exchange and contract, ibid., IV. xv and *Social Statics*, pp. 146–7; and 'free industry', *Principles of Ethics*, vol. ii, IV. xvi.

161 See e.g. J. S. Mill, 'Essay on Government' (1821), J. Lively and J. Rees (eds),

the array of radical ideas usual at the time. But in respect of so-called political rights Spencer takes a firm and decisive stand that gives a characteristic form and emphasis to his position. For he will not admit that most of these political claims are rights in the true sense at all, on a par with those already listed.

His point is that particular political institutions and practices are not themselves rights but appliances or instrumentalities, means merely, used to secure the conditions involved in these other rights. And, as such, they may or may not be effective in establishing or maintaining that liberty of individual action that the pursuit of happiness and the evolution of the species alike require. Though, Spencer wrote, 'the so-called political rights may be used for the maintenance of liberties, they may fail to be so used, and may even be used for the establishment of tyrannies.'[162] An incursion into the realm of individual freedom stands condemned whether it is undertaken by a despotic monarchy or a representative democracy. So, to take a particular instance, giving every adult the vote may have a morally untoward effect if it leads a popularly-based government to invade the rights of property, taking from one person what he has earned to give it to another who is less diligent or capable.[163] Spencer waxed increasingly vituperative about 'the great political superstition of the day', 'the baseless belief in the unlimited power of a majority'; and specifically he complained more and more shrilly about the 'miserable assumption' that 'a body elected by the greater number of citizens has the right to take from citizens at large any amount of money for any purpose it pleases!'[164]

What evolutionary ethics required, as the condition alike of optimum individual satisfaction and social progress, was in truth a rigorous limitation of government the function of which is to protect the individual against aggression and otherwise to uphold the law of equal freedom, to sustain the genuine rights to which this law gives rise. Only thus can it be said to administer justice.[165]

Utilitarian Logic and Politics (Oxford, 1978), p. 57; D. Hume, *A Treatise of Human Nature* (Everyman, 1949), III.ii.2 (ii.195); and J. Locke, *Two Treatises of Government*, ed. Laslett (Cambridge, 1960), I.42 (p.188).

162 *Autobiography*, i.439–40. Cf. the papers on 'Representative Government – What Is It Good For?' (1857) and 'Parliamentary Reform: the Dangers and the Safeguards' (1860), *Essays*, iii.283–325, 358–86. The former is also reprinted in *The Man Versus the State*, pp.234–72.

163 *Principles of Ethics*, ii.176–80, 192; *Social Statics*, pp.209ff.; *The Man Versus the State*, p.79; *Autobiography*, ii.367–9. Spencer's views on electoral reform changed quite radically during the course of his life: see *Autobiography*, ii.466, and the discussion in Wiltshire, op. cit., esp. pp.110–19.

164 *The Man Versus the State*, p.125n. Cf. ibid., pp.155, 157–8, 164–79. See also *Principles of Ethics*, ii.190–2; ibid., vol.ii, VI.ix; *Principles of Sociology*, ii.661–3; *Facts and Comments*, pp.117–18; *Autobiography*, ii.367–9.

165 *Social Statics*, pp.253–4.

How may this be effectively done? What political arrangements will most conduce to this end? And what, specifically, is the proper role and office of government seen in concrete detail? To explore these issues, Spencer analyses the nature and constitution of the state.

The diminishing state

By the state Spencer means not only central government but all other public agencies as well. And he believes that, because like anything else, the political reflects the evolutionary process, there is not only one constant conception of a proper polity. Like so many things in the organic or inorganic worlds, the nature of the state must change quite substantially as circumstances and times alter and as the motives or ends which men seek by social aggregation vary also.[166] The extremes of governmental character are, in fact, set in terms of the contrasting political styles of militant and industrial society. The kind of public regulation in any particular community will be a combination of these limiting forms, somewhere in the spectrum of possibilities between them.[167]

In the militant type of society, largely concerned with 'efficient external action . . . against other societies', there will be autocratic centralization and suspension of rights; generally a 'coercive constitution' will be required.[168] All large services necessarily devolve on the state and slave-power or some cognate form of conscription is the means used to build roads, canals, and the like and to provide public services generally. Given the situation of such a society and its purpose, all this is 'relatively right'. But, at the more advanced evolutionary stage represented by the industrial type of community, a completely different form of political arrangement is appropriate. Government will not be autocratic but be representative, not in the sense of embodying a principle of majority rule simply (which will only lead to the greater number exploiting power to its own ends) but in some form of the representation of interests, functions, or communities.[169] And, so far as the duty of the state in industrial society is concerned, it is simply to uphold the law of equal freedom, that is, to create the conditions which maintain the right of men freely to seek gratification by the exercise of their faculties. In this sense government is 'a national institution for preventing one man from infringing upon the rights of another'.[170] Its basic task is, therefore, the protection of the individual from aggression at

166 *Principles of Ethics*, ii.181–3, 187.
167 ibid., ii.183–7; *Social Statics*, p.287.
168 *Principles of Ethics*, ii.188–9; *Principles of Sociology*, vol.ii, §§547–61; *The Man Versus the State*, pp.112–13.
169 *Principles of Ethics*, ii.192–3.
170 *Social Statics*, pp.251–4; *Autobiography*, i. 197. Cf. ibid., i. 209, 210.

home and from abroad.[171] And Spencer believed (in the Cobdenite manner) that, as the forms of industrial society became more widespread, the incidence of both sorts of threat, and so the role of government, would decrease. Furthermore, in industrial society with its heterogeneous social structure and a growing diversity of activities, tasks which had previously fallen to some public agency would be discharged by 'multitudinous voluntary associations' of citizens.[172] He said in *Social Statics* that, as civilization advances, so does government decay.[173] As compared with militant society,

> ways of living are no longer dictated; dress ceases to be prescribed; the rules of class-subordination lose their peremptoriness; religious beliefs and observances are not insisted upon; modes of cultivating the land and carrying on manufactures are no longer fixed by law; and the exchange of commodities, both within the community and with other communities, becomes gradually unshackled.[174]

Yet, in Spencer's own day, even in Britain, arguably the most advanced industrial society which had yet emerged, considerable elements of militancy still existed. He came to fear indeed (as we shall see) that they were on the increase. But the following passage gives some indication of where they were to be discerned and points the basic contrast Spencer has in mind:

> Those who are forced to send their children to this or that school, those who have, directly or indirectly, to help in supporting a State priesthood, those from whom rates are demanded that parish officers may administer public charity, those who are taxed to provide gratis reading for people who will not save money for library subscriptions, those whose businesses are carried on under regulation by inspectors, those who have to pay the costs of State science-and-art-teaching, State emigration, &c., all have their individualities trenched upon, either by compelling them to do what they would not spontaneously do, or by taking away money which else would have furthered their private ends. Coercive arrangements of such kinds, consistent with the militant type, are inconsistent with the industrial type.[175]

And the reason they are inconsistent is not only that, as indicated, the degree of public control involved is incompatible with free individuality, it is also that such government regulation means rigidity and uniformity;

---

171   *Principles of Ethics*, vol. ii, IV. xxv.
172   ibid., ii. 228–9. Cf. *Principles of Sociology*, ii. 661; *Social Statics*, pp. 13–14.
173   *Social Statics*, p. 14. See also *Principles of Ethics*, ii. 229.
174   *Principles of Sociology*, ii. 659.
175   *Principles of Sociology*, ii. 612–13. Cf. *Principles of Ethics*, ii. 222–3; *The Man Versus the State*, p. 182.

and, of course, without variety and flexibility, response to a changing environment is less easy and evolutionary advance less likely.

Yet if the task of the state is to be severely restricted, is this not the prescription of a soulless society in which everyone is for himself and the devil takes the hindmost? Spencer's answer is, in effect, an unrepentant and hardly qualified affirmative in the sense that he believes it is vital to leave individuals to reap the advantages and disadvantages resulting from their actions in pursuit of the gratification of their faculties. For only in this way, in the competition for satisfaction, will society as a whole prosper and a superior type of human being emerge. Naturally he does not completely exclude the exercise of altruism on the part of individuals. It is true that indiscriminate corporate charity administered by the state (and financed through a compulsory redistribution of wealth) can, in his view, only result in 'a slow degeneracy'.[176] But private beneficence has an important transitional role to play in society and may in some cases properly mitigate the full rigours of the competitive struggle.[177] This may be the case, with due care and discrimination, in helping the sick and poor; and it is proper above all in family life where positive beneficence is justified and necessary in order that the species should survive.[178] Never one to inhibit the play of prejudice or idiosyncrasy Spencer, who objected to tipping railway porters, explained how untoward this practice was and how, if it continued, dire evolutionary consequences were to be anticipated!

On the specific question of *laissez faire*, Spencer holds that more than merely economic questions are involved: it is a principle that may be applied to people's conduct in general. At the same time, and quite logically, he objects to individuals being made to suffer (as well as claiming benefits) due to the acts of others and holds that it is the duty of government to intervene if necessary to ensure that every person bears the consequences only of his own actions. This was what he called negative, in contrast to (what he opposed) positive, regulation. On this basis he was prepared to refer to a concept of *laissez faire* that was quite 'disastrous' because it tolerated action by some people to interfere with the freedom of others, action which (he held) government should regulate.[179] But there was a clear limit in principle to this kind of supervision: it was one thing 'to secure to each man the unhindered

176 *Principles of Ethics*, vol. ii, v. i; *Principles of Sociology*, ii 610–11. Cf. J. S. Mill's 'Principles of Political Economy', *Collected Works*, ii. 114–115, 215–17.
177 *Principles of Ethics*, vol. ii, v. ii–vii, vi. x; *Principles of Sociology*, ii. 610.
178 *Principles of Ethics*, vol. ii, vi. i–viii; *Principles of Sociology*, i. 707–9.
179 Among many such references, see e.g. *The Study of Sociology*, pp. 320–2; *Essays*, iii. 417–20, 438, 479; *Social Statics*, ch. xii; *Various Fragments* (London, 1897), p. 100; also Spencer's letter to J. E. Cairnes (21 March 1873), in Duncan, op. cit., p. 161.

power to pursue his own good'; it was quite another 'to pursue the good for him.'[180]

It would be inaccurate to say that Spencer's views on the proper sphere of the state showed no alteration or inconsistency at all, though he often denied they did.[181] Early on he saw things much more narrowly in respect of positive regulation than he did in his later years when he was even prepared to concede, for example, that in towns the care of roads and pavements might be undertaken by public authority and probably also the disposal of sewage: though he cautiously added, 'Doubtless it is difficult to draw the line.'[182] Nevertheless the general thrust of his view is clear and is summed up in one of the chapter titles of Social Statics, 'The Right to Ignore the State'.[183] The real, or ideal, freedom a citizen should enjoy is ultimately 'the absence of all external checks to whatever actions the will prompts'; and, in a social context, the only legitimate restrictions are those 'arising from the presence of other men who have like claims to do what their wills prompt.'[184] In truth, it is a sort of anarchism which Spencer expounds in his doctrine of the withering away of the state as industrial society advances.[185]

The attack on 'legislative aggression'

What all this intellectual paraphernalia comes to, what indeed is its purpose or foundation, is an attack on the positive or teleocratic state, on 'over-legislation' or 'legislative aggression' as Spencer variously termed the feature of modern politics he most disliked. This is the rationale of the whole exercise in 'synthetic philosophy', what it all leads up to. As the most recent study of Spencer's thought quite rightly suggests, state intervention (or rather hostility to it) was 'the fixed criterion of his judgement on all issues; all else is variable, and is adjusted in conformity with its dictates.'[186] Reflections relating to this preoccupation are naturally scattered broadcast throughout the many studies Spencer produced during his long life; but the concern is clearest and most elaborated in Social Statics and The Man Versus the State.[187] The earlier work of 1851

180 Essays, iii.235.
181 e.g. Various Fragments, pp.196–201.
182 Facts and Comments, p.157.
183 Social Statics, ch.xix.
184 Autobiography, i.439.
185 For recognition of this point, see e.g. P. Kropotkin, Anarchist Communism: its Basis and Principles (Freedom Publications no.4, London, n.d.), pp.7–8; S. Webb, in Fabian Essays, p.49; G. K. Chesterton, The Victorian Age in Literature (1913; rev. edn, London, 1920), pp.233–4; Peel, op. cit., pp.49–50, 58; Wiltshire, op. cit., pp.160, 202, 212–13.
186 Wiltshire, op. cit., p.117.
187 See also, among many other papers, those on 'Over-Legislation' (1853), 'Political

has an air of optimistic expectation about it. It is as though with all the certainty of an intelligent young man Spencer feels his case to be so obvious that it has only to be forcefully and rationally stated to be widely accepted. Thirty or more years on, however, more worldly-wise and pessimistic, he has seen the tendency towards militancy nevertheless survive and even intensify as in the growth of public charity and the development of imperialism and war-mindedness.[188] The mood of despair is reflected in a poem written, ten years before Spencer's death, by his disciple Auberon Herbert and in which a youth sets forth with an alluring message for humankind which he is sure must be heeded but who, long years later, realizes its impotence to move men:

'I have spoken my word, and none has heard,
And the great world rolls as before.'[189]

In consequence Spencer's later diatribe is commensurately more shrill and also more narrowly political. 'All Socialism', he says (and by this he means what is here called collectivism), 'involves slavery', a slave being a person who is compelled to work for the benefit of someone else. If, without an option, a man has to labour for a society (through the payment of taxes) then, to the degree he has to do this, he is a slave.[190] The 'welfare of the many' has been more and more accepted as the aim of public policy and, together with the resurgence of warlike propensities, has led to 'Dictatorial measures, rapidly multiplied' which have cumulatively narrowed the liberties and infringed the rights of individuals.[191] The 'tacit assumption', he says, too easily accepted, is that 'Government should step in whenever anything is not going right.'[192] There is thus

an unhesitating faith in State-judgment. . . . Bodily welfare and mental welfare are consigned to it without the least doubt of its capacity. Having by struggles through centuries deposed a power which, for their alleged eternal good, forced on men its teachings, we invoke another power to force its teachings on men for their alleged temporal good. The compulsion once supposed to be justified in

Fetichism' (1865), 'Specialized Administration' (1871), and 'From Freedom to Bondage' (1891), all in *Essays*, vol. iii. The last two are also reprinted in *The Man Versus the State*, pp. 273–335. The early letters on *The Proper Sphere of Government* (1843) are equally relevant.

188 See e.g. the essays on 'Imperialism and Slavery', 'Re-Barbarization', and 'Regimentation', in *Facts and Comments*, pp. 112–41.

189 'Morning and Evening' from Herbert's *Windfall and Waterdrift*, cited in S. H. Harris, *Auberon Herbert*, p. 359.

190 *The Man Versus the State*, pp. 100–1.

191 ibid., pp. 59, 70. See also the letters cited in Duncan, op. cit., pp. 238, 301.

192 *The Man Versus the State*, p. 93.

religious instruction by the infallible judgment of a Pope, is now supposed to be justified in secular instruction by the infallible judgment of a Parliament. . . .[193]

An instance of the mischief he saw afoot is revealed in the following passage:

> Instead of extending the principle proper to the industrial type [of society], of providing quick and costless remedies for injuries, minor as well as major, which citizens inflict on one another, legislators extend the principle of preventing them by inspection. The arrangements in mines, factories, ships, lodging-houses, bakehouses, down even to water-closets in private dwellings, are prescribed by laws carried out by officials. Not by quick and certain penalty for breach of contract is adulteration to be remedied, but by public analyzers. Benefits are not to be bought by men with the money their efficient work brings them . . . , but benefits are given irrespective of effort expended: without regard to their deserts, men shall be provided at the public cost with free libraries, free local museums, etc.; and from the savings of the more worthy shall be taken by the tax-gatherer means of supplying the less worthy who have not saved.[194]

The gravamen of the criticism was, of course, that the extension of government responsibility involved in all this was contrary to the evolutionary process and incompatible with justice as expressed in the law of equal freedom. But in addition there was a series of other detailed arguments purporting to show the 'immense mischiefs' wrought by 'ill-considered legislation' and state action.[195]

There was the assertion that legislative interference was ineffectual because it was difficult or even impossible to foresee all the consequences of a particular policy or statute.[196] The principle at work here is the one noted on an earlier page that social causes above all produce a multiplicity of effects.[197] And there are, Spencer urges, so many recorded instances of schemes, intendedly for the general welfare, producing consequences which are both unexpected and untoward, cumulatively so. One instance arising from the Malthusian concerns of the day, has its amusing side:

> When it was enacted in Bavaria that no marriage should be allowed between parties without capital, unless certain authorities could 'see a reasonable prospect of the parties being able to provide for their

193   *Principles of Sociology*, i.572–3. Cf. *The Man Versus the State*, pp.130–1.
194   *Principles of Sociology*, i.572. Cf. ibid., ii.612–13 cited above p.68.
195   ibid., ii.653.
196   *The Man Versus the State*, pp.88–91.
197   See above p.58.

children', it was doubtless intended to advance the public weal by checking improvident unions and redundant population; a purpose most politicians will consider praiseworthy, and a provision which many will think well adapted to secure it. Nevertheless this apparently sagacious measure has by no means answered its end; the fact being that in Munich, the capital of the kingdom, half the births are illegitimate![198]

Then there is the point that legislative interference can often cause positive mischief and suffering: 'Acts of Parliament do not simply fail; they frequently make worse.'[199] Spencer thinks, for instance, that government attempts to control interest rates or prices by law simply prevent the productive use of spare capital and cause a dearth of the commodities concerned.[200] Almost the entire essay on 'The Sins of Legislators' is devoted to showing how in various fields – for instance, working-class housing, or quality control and inspection – government intervention has only intensified the problem addressed. State protection of existing interests also introduces economic and technological rigidity inhibiting desirable change: if government had owned and operated the stage-coach industry, he asked, would the railway have been allowed to develop? Pointedly he goes on to attack, too, the notion of a legislative science of reform based on Benthamite principles, one of the dominant intellectual themes of the time:

> Does not the experience of all nations testify to the futility of these empirical attempts at the acquisition of happiness? What is the statute-book but a record of such unhappy guesses? or history but a narrative of their unsuccessful issues? . . . Nearly every parliamentary proceeding is a tacit confession of incompetency. There is scarcely a bill introduced but is entitled 'An Act to amend an Act.' The 'Whereas' of almost every preamble heralds an account of the miscarriage of previous legislation. Alteration, explanation, and repeal, form the staple employment of every session. . . . The history of one scheme is the history of all. First comes enactment, then probation, then failure; next an amendment and another failure; and, after many alternate tinkerings and abortive trials, arrives at length repeal, followed by the substitution of some fresh plan, doomed to run the same course, and share a like fate.[201]

Spencer's account clearly constitutes a hostile attack on 'incrementa-

198 *Social Statics*, p.8. There is a similar example cited from British experience in *The Man Versus the State*, p.88.
199 *Essays*, iii.240–2. Cf. *The Man Versus the State*, pp.116, 118.
200 *The Man Versus the State*, pp.116–17.
201 *Social Statics*, pp.10–11. Cf. *Principles of Ethics*, ii.240–7; *Essays*, iii.399; *The Study of Sociology*, pp.145–57, 245–8; *The Man Versus the State*, pp.118–19, 149–50.

lism', the process of administrative growth already described in the previous volume.[202] And his complaint is that continual failure of state action does not at all destroy faith in the value of public intervention. 'Daily we castigate the political idol with a hundred pens, and daily pray to it with a thousand tongues.' 'State-agency' is always doing wrong, but the remedy is always more officialism of the same kind; the plea, when some problem arises, is still, Let government deal with it. There is 'an irrational confidence in all the paraphernalia . . . of State-action.'[203]

There is, further, the sheer administrative inefficiency of officialdom: the 'vices', confusions, and delays of 'red-tape routine', and the like.[204] Throughout his works, Spencer gives a very large number of contemporary instances of official short-sightedness and incompetence, from the failure of the Admiralty to deal with scurvy among sailors long after an effective preventive was known to the utter carelessness that prevailed in looking after official documents.[205] In a vituperative essay on 'Over-legislation', bureaucracy is accused of being: habitually slow (in the absence usually of any competing or alternative service); stupid (because – Spencer is writing in 1853 – merit is not the basis of selection); extravagant in its numbers and costs; obstructive; and unadaptable (being fitted only for average requirements). 'Society, a living growing organism, placed within apparatuses of dead, rigid, mechanical formulas, cannot fail to be hampered and pinched. The only agencies which can efficiently serve it, are those through which its pulsations hourly flow, and which change as it changes.'[206] Moreover there is the continual possibility of corruption.[207] It is quite foolish to suppose that officials are the most intelligent of mortals; rather they merely reflect the usual range of ability to be found in any group of citizens. Nor are these fundamental defects likely to be remedied by mere administrative reform in the absence of a complete change in the character of all those concerned.[208] Of course, this sort of attack was not in itself new and had for long been a constant theme of radicals like Joseph Hume and Richard Cobden; but this simply added the power of the habitual to the intrinsic force of Spencer's assertions.

Moreover, from the economic and financial point of view, Spencer argues that government expenditure actually impedes social and economic advance. It deprives some people (who are taxed) of means on

202 See vol.i, *The Rise of Collectivism*, ch.4, pp.221–8.
203 *The Study of Sociology*, pp.153–5. See also *Essays*, iii.231–2, 394–5; *The Man Versus the State*, pp.92–3; *Principles of Sociology*, i.572–3.
204 *The Man Versus the State*, pp.126–7; *Social Statics*, p.294.
205 See e.g. *The Study of Sociology*, pp.2–3, 5, 145–54. *Essays*, iii.231–59.
206 *Essays*, iii.250. Cf. the comments of J. E. Powell, cited below pp.321–2.
207 *Essays*, iii.250–2.
208 *The Study of Sociology*, pp.248, 250, 255–6; *Essays*, iii.474–5.

which their faculties depend for their gratification and exercise.[209] Also state action inculcates the habit of relying on public aid and so produces an inability or disinclination to do things for oneself: 'State-superintendence' produces 'national enervation'; it transforms every citizen 'into a grown-up baby "with bib and pap-spoon"'.[210] Spencer accepts that the position of the family requires prolonged aid to be given to its young and immature members; were this not so 'the species would disappear in a generation.' But the matter is quite otherwise outside the family group. The beneficence appropriate there cannot indiscriminately be applied to the corporate situation without the danger of species degeneration and the decay of social vitality.[211] What is required is not more paternal government but, on the contrary, the creation of conditions which stimulate men and press and strain their faculties to the utmost. Economic and social growth is not otherwise possible.

No one can need reminding that demand and supply is the law of life as well as the law of trade – that strength will show itself only where strength is called for – that an undeveloped capability can be developed only under the stern discipline of necessity. Would you draw out and increase some too feeble sentiment? Then you must set it to do, as well as it can, the work required of it. It must be kept ever active, ever strained, ever inconvenienced by its incompetency. Under this treatment it will, in the slow lapse of generations, attain to efficiency; and what was once its impossible task will become the source of a healthy, pleasurable, and desired excitement. But let a state-instrumentality be thrust between such faculty and its work, and the process of adaptation is at once suspended. Growth ceases; and in its place commences retrogression. The embryo agency now super-seded by some commission – some board and staff of officers, straightway dwindles; for power is as inevitably lost by inactivity as it is gained by activity. Hence, humanity no longer goes on moulding itself into harmony with the natural requirements of the social state; but begins, instead, to assume a form fitting these artificial require-ments. It is consequently stopped in its progress toward that self-sufficingness characteristic of the complete man; or, in other words, is prevented from fulfilling the conditions essential to complete happi-ness. And thus . . . not only does a government reverse its function by taking away more property than is needful for protective purposes, but even what it gives, in return for the excess so taken, is in essence a loss.[212]

209 *Social Statics*, p.281; *Principles of Sociology*, ii. 262.
210 *Essays*, iii.276–80; *Principles of Ethics*, vol.ii, v. i; *Social Statics*, p.287.
211 *The Man Versus the State*, pp.136–8, 182; *Principles of Sociology*, i.707–9.
212 *Social Statics*, pp.281–2. Cf. *The Study of Sociology*, pp.309ff.; *The Man Versus the State*, pp.132–3; and *Principles of Ethics*, vol.ii, IV. xxix.

Finally, because the state illegitimately tries to do so much (as well as doing it badly and to untoward effect), it necessarily neglects its proper job of protecting the citizen from aggression. What it ought to do (instead of meddling with so much that is not its concern) is, for instance, to concentrate on improving the efficiency and cheapness of the judicial system so that a quick, simple, and inexpensive process is available for the investigation and redress of grievances. Thus to deal with bad house-building it ought not to pass a Building Act providing for inspectors, supervision of materials, regulation of practice, and the like but instead be sure that there is a prompt and easy legal remedy within the reach of all so that builders who default or do a bad job can be taken to court by those aggrieved.[213]

The kind of detailed argument Spencer deployed in such matters as these may be illustrated by reference to his discussion of the Poor Laws, a topic in which he was interested from his young days.[214] He was wholly hostile, of course, to 'schemes of a coercive philanthropy', any public provision for the indigent.[215] No one has a right to claim such aid. The only right in this context is to use whatever powers or abilities a person has in whatever opportunities present themselves. If, however, government does intervene and taxes some people to benefit others by giving them public charity then the state has violated its duty towards the person taxed (which duty is to protect him in the enjoyment of the results of his efforts) to do more than its duty (which is the same) to the person receiving the dole concerned. This has particular point when, as must occur, the hard-working artisan is mulcted to benefit a more apathetic and less deserving fellow-citizen. In any case such liberality is short-sighted; to indulge in it is to overlook the 'mercy of severity' and the necessity of suffering in the scheme of things. There are some passages in *Social Statics* which reflect most succinctly the unyielding nature of Spencer's views and their rationale in an evolutionary context. For instance:

> the well-being of existing humanity, and the unfolding of it into . . .
> ultimate perfection, are both secured by that same beneficent, though
> severe discipline, to which the animate creation at large is subject: a
> discipline which is pitiless in the working out of good: a felicity-
> pursuing law which never swerves for the avoidance of partial and
> temporary suffering. The poverty of the incapable, the distresses that

213 *Essays*, iii.270–6. This was a not uncommon view: see e.g. Toulmin Smith's *To the Electors of the Borough of Sheffield* (Sheffield, 1852), p.3.
214 See the summary of the case against such public charity in his early *The Proper Sphere of Government*, p.12.
215 *Principles of Sociology*, i.572; *Social Statics*, pp.328–9; *Principles of Ethics*, vol.ii, VI. vii; *The Proper Sphere of Government*, pp.7–16. The following account is based largely on *Social Statics*, ch. xxv.

come upon the imprudent, the starvation of the idle, and those shoulderings aside of the weak by the strong, which leave so many 'in shallows and in miseries', are the decrees of a large, far-seeing benevolence. It seems hard that an unskilfulness which with all his efforts he cannot overcome, should entail hunger upon the artizan. It seems hard that a labourer incapacitated by sickness from competing with his stronger fellows, should have to bear the resulting privations. It seems hard that widows and orphans should be left to struggle for life or death. Nevertheless, when regarded not separately, but in connection with the interests of universal humanity, these harsh fatalities are seen to be full of the highest beneficence – the same beneficence which brings to early graves the children of diseased parents, and singles out the low-spirited, the intemperate, and the debilitated as the victims of an epidemic.[216]

Many sympathetic and amiable persons (he goes on) cannot look this situation in the face and, seeking to remedy it, pursue a course which is in the final analysis injudicious and even cruel: they try to ameliorate things by a munificence which is none the less spurious because in the end, and considering future generations, it causes greater misery than it alleviates.

Blind to the fact, that under the natural order of things society is constantly excreting its unhealthy, imbecile, slow, vacillating, faithless members, these unthinking, though well-meaning, men advocate an interference which not only stops the purifying process, but even increases the vitiation – absolutely encourages the multiplication of the reckless and incompetent by offering them unfailing provision, and *dis*courages the multiplication of the competent and provident by heightening the prospective difficulty of maintaining a family. And thus, in their eagerness to prevent the really salutary sufferings that surround us, these sigh-wise and groan-foolish people bequeath to posterity a continually increasing curse.[217]

Communally provided charity, therefore, like that offered by the Poor Laws, hinders evolutionary progress not least because it causes a retrogression of character on the part of its recipients. The more numerous such 'public instrumentalities' become, the more there is generated in citizens the notion that things will be done for them and each generation becomes less familiar with doing things for itself either through individual action or private combination. In the face of any need, it feels that action by a government agency provides the only possible solution.[218] As well, Spencer is very scathing about the moral

216 *Social Statics*, pp. 322–3.
217 ibid., p. 324, italics in original.
218 *The Man Versus the State*, pp. 95–6.

stature of those who are content to do good by official proxy and never do any themselves. In a similar way, he rejects the idea that the state should embark on an extensive programme of sanitary supervision: it may not (in his opinion) properly establish a public sewage system, control rabies, vaccinate compulsorily, or the like. Nor is it government's job to provide an educational system, run the post, supervise the currency, or manufacture coin. It may not even intervene to prevent cruelty to children.[219]

It is thus a very restricted view, indeed, of the role of government which lies behind Spencer's attack on legislative aggression. It is, too, a stern and uncompromising doctrine. He repeatedly says this kind of thing:

> The forces which are working out the great scheme of perfect happiness, taking no account of incidental suffering, exterminate such sections of mankind as stand in their way, with the same sternness that they exterminate beasts of prey and herds of useless ruminants. Be he human being, or be he brute, the hindrance must be got rid of.[220]

This is the law of the jungle, of nature red in tooth and claw, applied with pitiless logic to the human scene with the 'herds of useless ruminants' being replaced by the weak, the poor, and the indigent. It is easy to understand (if not to condone) Wingfield-Stratford's sarcastic remark that 'while a Benthamite might glean a certain amount of reflected pleasure from feeding a starving man, a Spencerian would with cheerful conscience let him die in a ditch, in order to encourage thrift and keep down the rates.'[221] Opponents quickly recognized the harsh significance of Spencer's views. Joseph Chamberlain, a great collectivist, once told Beatrice Webb, 'Happily, for the majority of the world, his [Spencer's] writing is unintelligible, otherwise his life would have been spent in doing harm.'[222] But Spencer insisted that, however brutal his doctrine might seem, it was more humane in the end.[223] To impose too great a degree of political direction was to make progress impossible: it was to freeze society, to condemn it to a less advanced and, therefore, more undesirable stage of development than it might otherwise achieve. It was necessary always to recall that it was not government which had secured the great intellectual and commercial advances of which men commonly boasted but society, groups and individuals moving to attain their own ends without official aid or interference.[224] To neglect such considerations could mean, for example, unfortunate consequences for some

219 He did later qualify this particular opinion, *Autobiography*, i. 361.
220 *Social Statics*, p. 416.
221 Wingfield-Stratford, op. cit., ii. 480.
222 B. Webb, *My Apprenticeship*, i. 146 (diary entry, June 1883).
223 *The Study of Sociology*, p, 372.
224 *Essays*, iii. 234–5. Cf. the remark of Lord Keynes cited above, p. 25.

communities on the international scene given 'the industrial struggle for existence' between them. Those nations will survive and prosper which produce the best individuals, those most adapted to the modes of economic and commercial competition. 'Suppose', Spencer goes on,

> two societies, otherwise equal, in one of which the superior are allowed to retain, for their own benefit and the benefit of their offspring, the entire proceeds of their labour; but in the other of which the superior have taken from them part of these proceeds for the benefit of the inferior and their offspring. Evidently the superior will thrive and multiply more in the first than in the second.[225]

Accumulated small infractions of the vital conditions of life spell disaster at home and overseas. As he put it in a lapidary sentence cited in his *Autobiography*: 'The ultimate result of shielding men from the effects of their folly is to fill the world with fools'.[226]

At the same time Spencer recognizes that in practice the institutions of any given age will 'exhibit the compromise made by these contending moral forces' of freedom and authority 'at the signing of their last truce'.[227] He sees, that is, that the character of British society is constituted by a certain tension between the twin tendencies of libertarianism and collectivism.[228] None the less, in his severe view, the ideal future can only lie with the dominance of the former, though a mixed system may continue so long as men's nature is only 'partially-adapted' and developed; there may even be phases of retrogression. But in the end, he believes, 'individuation' must triumph; and the law of equal freedom is the law under which this process will become perfect.[229]

It is the extensive exploration of this antithesis of tendencies, coupled with the extreme, libertarian ideal which Spencer himself favours and feels inevitable, that make his works so important here.

Spencer and the 'new Liberalism'

Spencer was invariably an incurable optimist about the march of inevitable progress towards the ideal, industrial society he described. He seems to have thought, for instance, that the essays comprising *The Man Versus the State* would reinvigorate traditional Liberalism and that there were good prospects of 'ending . . . the present retrograde movement' towards state intervention.[230] Yet he could not but be aware of the

225 *Principles of Sociology*, ii.610. Cf. *The Man Versus the State*, pp.136–8.
226 *Autobiography*, ii.5. Cf. *The Man Versus the State*, p.182.
227 *Social Statics*, p.428.
228 See e.g. the specific reference, ibid., pp.469–70.
229 ibid., pp.429, 440–1.
230 *Letters*, cited in Duncan, op. cit., p.243; *Principles of Sociology*, ii.660.

growing manifestations of a contrary tendency, of a sense that the transition from militant to libertarian society might well be prolonged or, worse, that the process of change might be reversed and 're-barbarization' ensue.[231] The broad historical sweep within which he envisaged the occurrence of these events and ideas is revealed in an interesting passage from *The Principles of Ethics*. This indicates first of all the long growth of government interference in Britain; secondly the diminution of this militancy or collectivism which he believed the nineteenth century to have witnessed; and thirdly the recent revival on an international scale of tendencies which he so deplored:

> how great and persistent were the restraints on industrial liberty among European peoples during the supremacy of that militant organization which in all ways subordinates individual wills. In Old-English days, the lord of the manor in Court-leet inspected industrial products; and, after the establishment of kingship, there came directions for cropping of lands, times of shearing, mode of ploughing. After the Conquest regulations for dyeing were enacted. From Edward III onwards to the time of James I, official searchers had to see that various wares were properly made. Certain traders were told how many assistants they should have; the growing of particular plants was made compulsory; tanners had to keep their hides in the pits for specified periods; and there were officers for the assize of bread and ale. With the development of institutions characterizing the industrial type, these restrictions on industrial freedom diminished; and, at the time George III began to reign, five-sixths of them had disappeared. Increasing though they did during the war-period brought on by the French revolution, they again diminished subsequently; until there had been abolished nearly all State-interferences with modes of production. Significantly enough, however, the recent revival of militancy here, consequent on the immense re-development of it on the Continent (set going, for the second time, by that greatest of all modern curses the Bonaparte family) has been accompanied by a reaction towards industrial regulations; so that during the last 30 years there have been numerous acts saying how businesses shall be carried on: ranging from the interdict on taking meals in match factories except in certain parts, to directions for the building and cleaning of artizans' dwellings – from orders for the painting of bakehouses to acts punishing farmers if they employ uneducated children.[232]

He recognized this reaction as being manifested within Liberalism

---

231 See e.g. the letters cited in Duncan, op. cit., pp. 238, 301–2, 420; the postscript to *The Man Versus the State*, pp. 184–9; and *Autobiography*, ii. 369, 373–4.
232 *Principles of Ethics*, ii. 133–4. Cf. ibid., ii. 154–5, 241–2.

itself. The doctrine had at one time simply meant the achievement of the general happiness through the abolition of restraint wherever this occurred. It had thus involved the pursuit of greater freedom in religious belief and practice, in the expression of opinion, and in social and economic activity. It was broadly concerned, therefore, with diminishing the range of governmental action and authority and with increasing the area of voluntary co-operation. Yet in his own day the thing had changed: it was coming to mean the search for the public good or 'the welfare of the many' as an end in itself regardless almost of the degree of state coercion that might be involved. As he put it in one place, referring to the paternalistic ethos of certain kinds of Conservatism, 'Most of those who now pass as Liberals, are Tories of a new type.'[233] Again, in 1900, he wrote:

> I do not desire to be classed among those who are in these days called Liberals. In the days when the name came into use, the Liberals were those who aimed to extend the freedom of the individual *versus* the power of the State, whereas now (prompted though they are by desire for popular welfare), Liberals as a body are continually extending the power of the State and restricting the freedom of the individual. Everywhere and always I have protested against this policy, and cannot now let it be inferred that I have receded from my opinion.[234]

In the past, the function of 'true liberalism' was to limit royal power: now and in the future, Spencer believes, its task will be to limit the powers of a Parliament based on the popular voice and to challenge the assumption that 'a majority has powers which have no bounds.'[235] In terms of the key theoretical concepts involved, what was happening (Spencer thought) was that liberty was being forgotten in the wake of the cry for equality.[236] He was not opposed to certain kinds of equality but rejected notions of uniformity and levelling. He wrote to W. H. Hudson in 1903 that his principle had all along been 'Not the equality of men, but the equality of their claims to make the best of themselves within the limits mutually produced'.[237]

Of course, Spencer's ideological opponents condemned him as an anachronism, as a general without an army. Frederic Harrison, the positivist, said in the 1880s, 'Mr. Spencer has . . . just published a very remarkable work, "the Man *versus* the State;" to which he hardly

233 *The Man Versus the State*, p. 63.
234 Letter to A. M. Scott (26 July 1900), in Duncan, op. cit., p. 449, italics in original. Cf. *Autobiography*, ii. 365–9.
235 *The Man Versus the State*, pp. 78–9, 155, 183.
236 *Principles of Ethics*, ii. 179–80.
237 Spencer to W. H. Hudson (7 January 1903), cited in Duncan, op. cit., p. 466.

expects to make a convert except here and there, and about which an unfriendly critic might say that it might be entitled "Mr. Spencer against all England."[238] John Rae suggested that the doctrine of *laissez faire* had never been held by any English thinker 'unless, perhaps, Mr. Herbert Spencer.'[239] And a little later William Clarke, the Fabian, urged on an American audience the view that

> *Laissez-faire* individualist political philosophy is dead. In vain does poor Mr. Herbert Spencer endeavor to stem the torrent. His political ideas are already as antiquated as Noah's ark. I do not know a single one of the younger men in England who is influenced by them in the slightest degree, though one hears of one occasionally, just as one hears of a freak in a dime museum.[240]

Of course, this is partisan exaggeration and goes much too far; though it is the case that, looking back, one can see that a long drawn-out rearguard action was beginning; and it was to prove a defence in which Conservatives rather than Liberals were perhaps to play the larger part. Yet the classical Liberal creed itself was not without a variety of support during the time when the advanced state was gathering more and more momentum.

THE CONTINUING OPPOSITION

> Nothing is more certain to destroy the happiness and stop the progress of a civilised nation than the idea, now so fashionable, that it is the duty of Government departments to 'plan' and to formulate schemes under which the bureaucrats, paid servants of the people, will become their masters . . . .
> F. W. HIRST, *Liberty and Tyranny*, 1935, p.288

Spencer's was not a lone voice and (as already suggested) his influence was at one time considerable. His message was trumpeted for those who would listen by numerous commentators of varying political affiliation. A number of these writers and the groups with which they were associated tended to become adjuncts of Conservatism.[241] Some disciples took his arguments even further along the anti-statist road than he did himself or cast them in a rather different mould. The identity of connexion, purpose, and theme among this continuing opposition to collectivism was not exact, therefore. And, after a limited exploration of

238 F. Harrison, 'Agnostic Metaphysics', *The Nineteenth Century*, xvi (1884), p.366.
239 J. Rae, *Contemporary Socialism* (1884; 2nd edn, London, 1891), p.352.
240 W. Clarke, 'The Fabian Society and its Work', in *Socialism: the Fabian Essays* (Boston, Mass., 1894), p.xxxiii. Cf. S. Webb, *Socialism in England* (London, 1890), p.27.
241 See below ch.8, esp. pp.265–87.

the material, I must confess to a strong suspicion that there is a much more substantial literature of this kind than has so far been recovered during the period of neglect engendered by the dominance of collectivist ideas. But something of what was involved for Liberals may be indicated by the examples briefly reviewed in the remainder of this chapter.

The 'pattern nation' and other instances

Spencer's theories and reputation were widely invoked by those who were opposed to what was often pejoratively described as 'creeping Socialism'. For instance, a pamphlet on individual liberty issued by the Anti-Socialist Union urged the undiluted Spencerian doctrine that the duty of the state should be limited to the protection of individual rights and freedom from the aggression of others and that the great danger of the day was the undesirable consequences of over-legislation and paternalism coupled with the inefficiency of officials.[242] The doctrine was equally widely acknowledged on the continent, being continually deployed by such publicists as the French academic and journalist, Paul Leroy-Beaulieu, many of whose anti-statist tracts were translated and published in this country.[243] In the scientific world, too, Spencer's ideas received support as in the case of F. W. Headley, a prominent zoologist, who maintained the view that Darwinism fully understood made Socialism impossible because the well-being of any civilized community required 'the continuance of competition and Natural Selection'.[244] Similarly undoubted echoes of Spencerian argument may be detected in the writings of J. H. Levy who, bewailing the tendency for the tide of events to flow in a collectivist direction, stressed instead the fundamental rights of individuals and the basic principle that liberty depends upon property: for him government was no more than an evil.[245] Frederick Millar (a great admirer of Spencer and his more extreme disciple Auberon Herbert) put forward the familiar points about freeing the individual and all economic activity from public control, about the evils

242 *Individual Liberty* (ASU no. 67, London, n.d.), pp. 1–4.
243 e.g. P. Leroy-Beaulieu, *The Modern State in Relation to Society and the Individual* (1890; trans. edn, London, 1891), some extracts from which are reprinted in E. K. Bramsted and K. J. Melhuish, *Western Liberalism: a History in Documents from Locke to Croce* (London, 1978), pp. 643–52. For discussion, see ibid., pp. 67–70, 587–9 and, for a brief biography, pp. 767–8. See also Leroy-Beaulieu's *Collectivism: a Study of Some of the Leading Social Questions of the Day* (London, 1908).
244 F. W. Headley, *Darwinism and Modern Socialism* (London, 1909), p. v.
245 J. H. Levy, *The Outcome of Individualism* (1890; 2nd ed., London, n.d. [1890]), pp. 4–5, 11–13, 31–2. On Levy, who was associated with the Vigilance Association, see E. J. Bristow, *The Defence of Liberty and Property in Britain, 1880–1914* (unpublished PhD thesis, Yale University, 1970), pp. 75–6.

of bureaucracy, the danger of endowing the incompetent, and so on.[246] Thus Spencer's voice was not the only one to be heard in this chorus of protest though its particular tones were often the most strident.

There were also, of course, many Liberal politicians who at the end of the century held views hostile to the development of intervention. Goschen, while recognizing, somewhat reluctantly, the inevitability of more state control, nevertheless accepted that there would be substantial dangers and costs involved in moving away from *laissez faire*; and his review of these untoward possibilities is clearly of Spencerian type.[247] Lord Morley's adherence to classical Liberalism is well-known. It is not without significance that he wrote biographies of both Cobden and Gladstone; and he much admired Spencer himself as the encomium in his *Recollections* shows.[248] And, of course, he declared (when a candidate for Newcastle in 1892) that he would rather not be elected than concede the right of government to regulate hours of labour.[249] As F. W. Hirst said, Morley remained to the end of his life 'a liberal, and an individualist'; though by 1920 Harold Laski felt that this meant no more than that Morley had somewhat 'outlived his generation, in the sense that the pure milk of the Cobdenite word remains pure even in the midst of changes.'[250]

One most interesting libertarian tract which appeared in the period immediately before the Great War was called *The Province of the State*, its author being Sir Roland Wilson, Fellow of King's College, Cambridge, and Reader in Indian Law in the University from 1878 to 1892. He was a noted individualist and prominent in the Personal Rights Association, a body which grew out of the campaign against the Contagious Diseases Acts and which stood for a challenge to the state wherever it infringed personal liberty or freedom of contract.[251] In 1875

246 See e.g. the account of his debate with Mrs Besant in *Socialism v. Individualism. . .* (Nottingham, 1890), pp. 2–7, 27; also the series of papers in the various editions of his *Socialism: its Fallacies and Dangers* (1900; 5th edn rev., London, 1923). On Millar, see N. Soldon, 'Laissez-Faire as Dogma: the Liberty and Property Defence League, 1882–1914', K. D. Brown (ed.), *Essays in Anti-Labour History: Responses to the Rise of Labour in Britain* (London, 1974), esp. pp. 219–20.

247 G. J. Goschen, . . . *Laissez-Faire and Government Interference* (London, 1883), pp. 25ff.

248 J. Morley, *Recollections* (London, 1917), i. 110–16. On Cobden, see ibid., i. 134–44.

249 Cf. Y. Guyot, *The Tyranny of Socialism* (London, 1894), p. xxv. But see the acceptance of some state protection for those who could not help themselves (as opposed to insistent meddling) in the letter cited in S. Harris, *Auberon Herbert: Crusader for Liberty* (London, 1943), p. 223.

250 F. W. Hirst, 'John Morley', *DNB*, ii. 2803; Laski to Holmes (8 September 1920), in M. de W. Howe (ed.), *Holmes-Laski Letters: the Correspondence of Mr. Justice Holmes and Harold J. Laski, 1916–1935* (London, 1953), i. 278.

251 See the statement of PRA objectives in R. K. Wilson, *Individualism and the Land Question: a Discussion* (PRA, London, n.d. [1912]), pp. 117–20.

Wilson had published a history of modern English law with which Dicey was greatly impressed because it detected clearly the contrast between the Blackstonian age of relative legislative quiescence and the subsequent 'Benthamite era of scientific law reform'. Dicey wondered, too, whether at some time Wilson might not bring his treatise up to date by taking account of the more recent surge of state interference.[252] In fact Wilson was already engaged on the cognate task of trying to settle the principles which should be used to judge this growth of collectivism. His book on the role of the state was the outcome of this consideration.[253] He had stated his position in principle some decades before when he wrote that the 'true Liberal' must necessarily 'be in favour of the maximum of *liberty*, in other words, of the minimum of legal commands and prohibitions which is compatible with the protection of members of the community from mutual injuries and from foreign hostility'. Such a Liberal, he added, must also be in favour of '*equal liberty*' which was simply another name for 'justice'.[254] So, in the later work, he asserted that the 'Libertarian State', seen in the barest terms, is basically 'a justice-enforcing association' concerned to protect the prior rights of individuals. As such it is not charged with 'a general commission for the improvement of human affairs' but rather with 'the specific duty of preventing or redressing wrongs.'[255] Its tasks might include elements of municipal trading and some degree of supervision of major public utilities such as the railways; and nationalization of the land could not entirely be ruled out.[256] But equally there is no general right to act in public health matters, to relieve destitution, to impose compulsory education, or to use the tax power to redistribute wealth.[257] As Wilson said himself, the approach, though diverging in some respects, is 'very largely Spencerian'.[258] The tone and theme of the following passage illustrate this:

252 A. V. Dicey, *Lectures on the Relation between Law & Public Opinion in England during the Nineteenth Century* (1905; 2nd ed. repr., London, 1920), preface to 1st edn, pp. ix–x.

253 Sir R. K. Wilson, Bt, *The Province of the State* (London, 1911), pp. v–vi.

254 In Sir G. C. Lewis, *Remarks on the Use and Abuse of Some Political Terms* (1832; ed. R. K. Wilson, Oxford, 1877), p.188 note a, italics in original.

255 Wilson, *The Province of the State*, pp.49, 90; *Individualism and the Land Question*, pp.1–2.

256 On the land, see Wilson, *The Province of the State*, pp.254–7, 307–9; and *Individualism and the Land Question*, pp.4–7, where it is argued that the state holds land for the common benefit but lets it to others to exploit and improve.

257 Wilson, *The Province of the State*, chs IV, XI-XII, esp. pp.174, 192, 241; also his *The First and Last Fight for the Voluntary Principle in Education (1846–1858)* (London, n.d. [1916]).

258 Wilson, *The Province of the State*, p.254. The specific divergences are discussed, ibid., pp.254–69.

We spend millions on inspectors of various kinds, in order to enforce the ever-growing mass of sanitary and other regulations, and we are assured that they are still far too few to do the work properly; whereas many of these regulations would enforce themselves automatically if we had everywhere gratuitous tribunals ready to award damages to the actual sufferers on their own complaint. Gratuitous civil justice is far from being the only extension, or rather intensification, of State activity in its primary sphere which [my] theory demands; but I deem it on the whole the most important. . . .[259]

As with Spencer himself, the point of this remark is that the proper tasks of the state are neglected for the sake of other, illegitimate, functions in the field of social reform and economic control.

Another analysis of the collectivist tendency, which appeared a few years before Wilson's study, was written by Sir Henry Wrixon, a lawyer of Irish origin who subsequently made a political and academic career for himself in Australia. This book, called *The Pattern Nation*, is an extremely perceptive review of the consequences of political democracy and is full of prophetic insight. It appeared shortly after the 1906 general election which confirmed for Wrixon that 'the mass of the people . . . are the new king' and that the domination of the class of wage-earners 'will be the great fact of our age.'[260] Inevitably the pressures will grow to apply the principles of democracy and equality at work in political life to industry and society at large.[261] What Wrixon fears will happen in these circumstances is the development of what he calls 'semi-Socialism', a condition of paternalist regulation in some ways not dissimilar to the concept of the 'Servile State' which Belloc popularized a little later.[262] Wrixon describes the process he has in mind in terms of an exemplary state of affairs occurring in 'the pattern nation', an advanced European country not unlike Great Britain. The beginning lies in piecemeal attempts to mitigate the hardships of the poor and underprivileged. But dealing with such problems reveals a further dimension of difficulty to be tackled and in addition stimulates fresh wants. Clearly Wrixon is here describing that process of empirical legislation which so concerned libertarian critics like Toulmin Smith and Spencer, the incremental growth in administration that acquired an inner dynamic of its own.[263] He also observed, as they did, that social reform of this kind has to be paid for and creates indeed a new and lavish attitude to public spending

259 ibid., pp. 306–7.
260 Sir H. Wrixon, *The Pattern Nation or Socialism, its Source, Drift, and Outcome* (1906; 2nd edn, London, 1907), pp. 12, 33, 48.
261 ibid., pp. 1–2, 69–70, and ch. 1 *passim*.
262 See below pp. 91–3.
263 Cf. the review of 'administrative momentum' in vol. i, *The Rise of Collectivism*, ch. 4, pp. 221–8.

and consequently higher levels of taxation to meet the cost of the paternalist schemes involved. 'During the uncertain semi-Socialist period in our pattern nation', he says, 'the lot of the wealthy will not be a happy one.'[264] Increasingly, too, the role of the private employer becomes more difficult as his costs are increased not only by higher taxation but as well by expensive improvements in conditions of work which he is required to meet by legislation or by union action. Also state intervention in or control of industry will grow.[265] And here is the rub, in Wrixon's view: in these circumstances the comforts of collectivism, though without its discipline, are combined with the formal freedom of individualism, though without its effective spur, real competition.[266] People

> glory in the beneficence of the Socialistic state, but do not face its responsibilities; and denounce the tyrannical capitalist system, while they live on the fruits of its industry. For, in this transition state, things will be kept going by drawing on the accumulated wealth of the community, and by the impetus of the habits of industry and thrift that have grown up under the centuries of freedom and self-help.

Yet after a generation or so of this semi-collectivism, Wrixon prophesies,

> a falling off in production will become manifest, and a stationary condition of industry will set in. The decay of the spirit of private enterprise, and the growth of a national habit of mingled extravagance and dependence upon others, which government paternalism natur-ally leads to, will be a general predisposing cause of the decline. There will be an all-round falling off in the productivity of labour.[267]

This will be reflected in the publicly owned industries, too.[268]

The problems of the pattern nation in this semi-Socialist stage are, therefore, stark and clear. The principle of self-help is being lost or paralysed; the gospel of hard work becomes unfashionable and effort is discredited.[269] The circle of government aid widens; but this assistance has to be paid for by those still working for themselves. The productive class or section is, therefore, more and more squeezed and inevitably it gradually becomes 'less strenuous, less saving, less able', less venture-some, and there is a weakening of industrial vigour and productiveness. A period of slow economic decline sets in.[270] At this point there may, if the crisis is properly grasped, be a choice between two paths, Wrixon

264 Wrixon, *The Pattern Nation*, p. 124.
265 See e.g. ibid., pp. 131–2.
266 ibid., p. 141.
267 ibid., pp. 141–2.
268 ibid., pp. 142–6.
269 ibid., pp. 152, 157.
270 ibid., pp. 154, 157–8.

suggests: either towards more collectivism or to restore the conditions of individualism.[271] He hopes himself – but then in 1906 he could perhaps still be optimistic without being naïve – that the more people experience 'semi-Socialism', the more they will realize that to move further in a collectivist direction will mean more subordination and control. Yet if they do not choose freedom and individuality, it will be clear the course of our civilization has run into the sands: 'Things move quickly in our time, and the present century will see either Socialism discredited or Europe declining. A social system, the foundation of which is the sacrifice of freedom for ease, contains within itself the conditions of decay.'[272]

This is indeed a most interesting and perceptive polemic; but it is perhaps also important and symptomatic that, after having run into a second edition within a year of its original publication, it has since not been heard of (at least so far as I know). Perhaps it should now be reprinted to be read by collectivists of all parties and of none so that they may reflect on the analysis it presents in the context of our recent history and present position. But if Wrixon's discussion was subsequently little known, this has certainly not been true of the doctrine known as Distributism which is associated above all with Chesterton and Belloc.

The Chesterbelloc and the servile state

The Distributist circle was a mixed one politically and embraced high Tories, Guild Socialists, and wayward Liberals; many were Catholics.[273] They drew substantial inspiration from the ideals of the pre-industrial age and specifically from the social themes of the old Thomist canon as well as from its more recent expression in the papal encyclical of 1891 *De rerum novarum*. Because of this ethos a certain air of anachronism or quaint irrelevance has always seemed to hang about these people and their views; and it is not implausible to suggest that they represent 'the end of a tradition'.[274] But the verdict may none the less be a little misleading because their anti-statism has lingered on in various ideological guises as with the ideas of a property-owning democracy, profit-sharing schemes, small land-ownership, the co-operative, and forms of

271 ibid., pp.158–61.
272 ibid., pp.184–97, citation at p.197.
273 See e.g. J. P. Corrin, 'The Formation of the Distributist Circle', *The Chesterton Review*, i (1974–5), pp.52–83; G. Macdonald, 'The Other Face: that Distributist Decade', ibid., pp.84–99; and B. Sewell, 'Father Vincent McNabb: a Great Distributist', ibid., iv (1977–8), pp.75–88.
274 R. S. Barker, *Political Ideas in Modern Britain* (London, 1978), p.90. Cf. H. G. Wells's discussion of these 'Conservators', 'The Past and the Great State', Lady Warwick *et al.*, *The Great State: Essays in Construction* (London, 1912), pp.16–18; also Wells, *The World of William Clissold* (1926; London, 1933), i.120–3; and *Mr. Britling Sees It Through* (1916; London, 1933), p.17.

worker participation and control. Nor is it unreasonable to detect affinities in, say, the Welsh nationalism of Saunders Lewis or E. F. Schumacher's theme that 'small is beautiful'. However it is undoubtedly the case that contrary tendencies of thought and action have become more and more dominant. Certainly as time wore on (and like Spencer before them) both Chesterton and Belloc, the leading exponents of the group, saw that their view of how the world should be ordered was increasingly being disregarded.

They were both Liberal radicals with a growing concern about the way modern society was developing and about the part being played, in particular, by the Liberal Party after the reformist triumph of 1906 not least because of the growing state interference its policies required. Maurice Reckitt was convinced that the Chesterbelloc thesis was sufficiently explosive to blow the new Liberalism sky-high.[275] Chesterton was (so to say) a Liberal by inheritance and continued to believe in the principles of the creed as much as or more than he ever did despite the untoward emphasis involved in the official programme.[276] He met Belloc while working on the Liberal journal *The Speaker*. Belloc himself had given some indication of social commitment by his involvement in the famous London dock strike of 1889 and had also made his mark as a contributor to the Oxford *Essays in Liberalism* in which *inter alia* he expressed his hostility to the contemporary growth in the power of the state and stressed instead the cause of the free individual and a tradition of self-government.[277] For four years after 1906 Belloc was a Liberal MP but as a result of this experience he became heartily sick of what he took to be the unreality of party warfare and the corruption of the ruling plutocracy. And he felt that fundamental freedoms were being exchanged for state-provided security. Certainly his attack on the 'servile state' together with other aspects of the Chesterbelloc political doctrine constituted a potent form of Liberal anti-collectivism. They and their followers rejected both the idols of their day. Old-style capitalism was repudiated because of its material values, its concern with efficiency and quantity simply, and its association with the evils of industrialism, mechanization, and mass production which were destructive of real individuality. In any case the principles of feral competition and the free market were increasingly impossible to realize in practice: as Chesterton said in one place, the England of Cobden was as dead as the England of

275 M. B. Reckitt, *As It Happened: An Autobiography* (London, 1941), p. 108.
276 M. Ward, *Gilbert Keith Chesterton* (London, 1944), pp. 254, 256, 470–1.
277 H. Belloc, 'The Liberal Tradition', Six Oxford Men, *Essays in Liberalism* (London, 1897), pp. 4–5. Cf. the letter from H. H. Asquith to another contributor (29 December 1896), acknowledging the anti-collectivist emphasis of the essays, cited in F. W. Hirst, *In the Golden Days* (London, 1947), p. 157.

Canute.[278] Equally they abhorred Fabianism and all it stood for: state control (which was what contemporary Socialism entailed) meant the end of any real freedom. There was undoubtedly a crisis of capitalism but to impose an extensive collectivism was no answer being both irrelevant to the real problems and disastrous in the consequences entailed. Man is thereby offered a fully-planned, future utopia when he only wants a house: while the distinction between public and private spheres is continually undermined. The result is that 'piece by piece and quite silently, personal liberty is being stolen from Englishmen'. The manifest need is to counteract these oppressive centralizing trends.[279] Yet they were so strong that resistance to them might seem no more than a hopeless gesture. However Chesterton believed the task was not an impossible one. There were, he said optimistically, a hundred tales of human history 'to show that tendencies can be turned back, and that one stumbling-block can be the turning-point.' The smallest prick will shrivel the biggest balloon.[280]

The whole point, therefore, of the Chesterbelloc position was that both capitalism and collectivism led to unfree individuals; the former because of the growing concentration of ownership and wage-slavery which it entailed; the latter because it placed economic power in the hands of a few political leaders ruling through a centralized bureaucracy. What was needed was for formal constitutional equality to be supplemented and sustained by economic equality.[281] This meant a revolutionary transformation of industrial and commercial life and the subordination of that sphere to a proper 'moral gospel', distributing property to restore liberty.[282] The essence of Distributism was thus described by one apostle as

> the demand for the expression and embodiment in social organisation and relationship of the vital truth of individual Free Will. Negatively, we demand that the family, or . . . the individual, shall have such measure of economic resources as will give him the power to resist oppressive systems, official or unofficial, bureaucratic or plutocratic. Positively, we affirm that not only will personality be truly released, but that society will best be served where every citizen finds, through

278 G. K. Chesterton, *The Outline of Sanity* (London, 1926), p. 32; *idem, Autobiography* (1936; London, 1937), p.26. For a recent brief analysis, see G. A. Smith, 'Distributism and Conventional Economic Theory', *The Chesterton Review*, v (1978–9), pp.232–52.

279 G. K. Chesterton, *What's Wrong with the World* (London, 1910), pp.73–5, 267–8; *The Outline of Sanity*, p.56.

280 Chesterton, *The Outline of Sanity*, pp.72, 94–5.

281 Chesterton, 'An Explanation in Brackets', *G. K.'s Weekly*, iv (15 January 1927), p.197.

282 W. R. Titterton, 'In Defence of Distributism', ibid., v (25 June 1927), p.464.

some experience of property, the opportunity for the exercise of initiative, for the acceptance of responsibility, for the freedom of choice.[283]

The most systematic analysis, from this point of view, of how the modern dilemma had arisen is presented in Hilaire Belloc's *The Servile State*. This was first published in 1912 but grew out of some articles he had previously written for the *New Age* and also from a speech he had made in an ILP debate with Ramsay MacDonald about the significance of the Liberal social reform programme in particular the National Insurance Bill then being put through Parliament.[284] Belloc believed that change of this sort was a great mistake.[285] It would lead not (as some of its supporters expected) to fulfilment or (which many of them believed was the same thing) Socialism but to a new form of slavery, a condition of affairs he described as the 'Servile State'. This is not exactly the same as the collectivism against which, say, Spencer's onslaught was directed. But Belloc's attack was equally against many aspects of these extensions of public control and may thus also be deemed libertarian in nature.

The general perspective of the argument is a picture of European historical development. 'Pagan' or classical civilization was based on slavery, with society divided into two clearly marked groups: free citizens owning property, and 'a mass dispossessed of the means of production and compelled by positive law to labour at command.'[286] But over the long years between, roughly, 600 and 1600 AD this servile class disappeared, the slave being transformed first into a serf then into a peasant. Belloc believed this change was 'the big economic phenomenon of Western Europe' constituting the appearance of the 'Distributive State' of the Middle Ages, a condition of things so called because of the wide dispersion of property which characterized it and through which men were 'economically free through the possession of capital and of land.'[287] Then a kind of reversion to the previous state of things occurred, the Reformation being seen as a major factor in this undesirable retrogression: for the wealth released by the dissolution of the monasteries and the disposal of Church property which followed went to enrich still further an already affluent section of the community.[288] Thus a

283 M. B. Reckitt, 'Distributism As I See It', ibid., v (9 April 1927), p. 332.
284 For a verbatim account of the debate, see H. Morrison (ed.), *Socialism and the Servile State* (SW London Federation of the ILP; London, 1911).
285 For his growing anti-statism, see e.g. R. Speaight, *The Life of Hilaire Belloc* (London, 1957), pp. 266–9.
286 H. Belloc, *The Servile State* (1912; 3rd edn, London, 1927), pp. 34–7.
287 Morrison (ed.), *Socialism and the Servile State*, p. 9; Belloc, *The Servile State*, pp. 50–1.
288 This process is described in Belloc, *The Servile State*, section IV, 'How The Distributive State Failed'. For an earlier summary, see his 'The Liberal Tradition',

powerful landowning oligarchy was created and, in time, small estates tended to be swallowed up and the independent peasantry to disappear.[289] Belloc believed that by the end of the seventeenth century more than half the population had been dispossessed of capital and land, and the subsequent process of industrialization simply reinforced that tendency of affairs. Control of the means of production was in the hands of a very small group, and the mass of the people, though it became politically free in a formal sense, was in economic terms little more than a propertyless proletariat whose life was in so many ways insecure and insufficient.[290] So unstable was this 'Capitalist State' that from its inception it had been found necessary to mitigate the harshness of its competitive principles, an interference that, in its cumulative impact, intimated its inevitable supersession by some other form of society.

In theory it might be assumed that the easiest and most likely succession was a transformation into the Socialist state. This would seem a natural extension simply of that pattern of public provision which had grown up even in the hey-day of capitalism (as with the municipal ownership of public utilities) and which might seem appropriate, too, as a means of securing the responsible operation of large organizations such as trusts, combines, and monopolies. Moreover Socialism bid fair to promise a notable improvement in the condition of the masses. And yet, Belloc argued, this apparently natural, even inevitable, transition to the classless society was not taking place. Instead something quite unanticipated was occurring: the emergence of the 'Servile State', that is, a society in which the mass of men are 'constrained *by law* to labour to the profit of a minority' though, as compensation for such restraint, they 'enjoy a security which the Old Capitalism did not give them.'[291] The workers thus nestle contentedly in the arms of a collectivism which gives them a stability and level of care such as they have never before known as through statutes concerning employers' liability, health and unemployment insurance, guaranteed wage rates, and so forth. They prefer this security to the arduous responsibilities of independence, and are thus segregated as a passive, benefit-receiving class.[292] More than this, there will become attached to the receipt of these advantages a series of penalties or sanctions such that in due course, Belloc believes, the

---

Six Oxford Men, *Essays in Liberalism*, esp. pp.18ff. This is a theme found in many places. For two widely varying examples, see B. Disraeli, 'Sybil' (1845), I.v., *Collected Edition of the Novels and Tales* (London, 1878–81), iii. 70ff.; and A. J. Penty, *A Guildsman's Interpretation of History* (London, 1920), chs xi–xii.

289 A. H. Johnson's famous study, *The Disappearance of the Small Landowner*, had first appeared in 1909.
290 Belloc, *The Servile State*, pp. 57–8, 81–3, 98, and section v *passim*.
291 ibid., p.116, italics in original.
292 Cf. Chesterton's comments in *Autobiography*, pp.273–4, 297.

arrangements involved will come to constitute a condition of 'compulsory labour'. Meanwhile the capitalist who has been bought out is, through the compensation received, confirmed in the privileged possession of the 'surplus value' produced. In sum:

> The future of industrial society, and in particular of English society, left to its own direction, is a future in which subsistence and security shall be guaranteed for the Proletariat, but shall be guaranteed at the expense of the old political freedom and by the establishment of that Proletariat in a status really, though not nominally, servile. At the same time, the Owners will be guaranteed in their profits, the whole machinery of production in the smoothness of its working, and that stability which has been lost under the Capitalist phase of society will be found once more.[293]

In order to escape this drift towards the 'Servile State' (which is clearly not unlike Wrixon's slightly earlier concept of 'semi-Socialism') Chesterton and Belloc urged the establishment of a Distributive State in which political and social freedoms are alike secured by a wide dispersion of property.[294] Belloc's book was prefaced by this epigraph: '. . . If we do not restore the Institution of Property we cannot escape restoring the Institution of Slavery; there is no third course.'[295] This was the only way ahead, though Belloc himself became more pessimistic about the prospect of success as time went by and the chains of servility tightened: by the mid-1930s he believed that the restoration of the 'proprietary state' had become 'a task *almost* impossible of achievement.'[296] Chesterton's attitude (as indicated earlier) was more robust and buoyant.[297] He was always prepared to 'fight the whole world', to try to turn the tide of the whole time we live in, and so to believe in the possibility of the revolution in social arrangements and attitudes that was necessary to prevent a mere uniformity – the 'indiscriminate' mass – and to secure a reversion to the ideals of the past: the small-scale, the domesticity of the ideal house and happy family, and (beyond this) the truly local community and a nation of peasant proprietors, craftsmen, and small tradesmen.[298] And the general principle of recovery was that a healthy society rests on a

293 Belloc, *The Servile State*, p. 183. Cf. Belloc's remarks in Morrison (ed.), *Socialism and the Servile State*, pp. 10–11.
294 e.g. Belloc, *The Servile State*, pp. 187–9.
295 ibid., title page. Cf. Belloc, *An Essay on the Restoration of Property* (London, 1936), p. 6.
296 Belloc, *An Essay on the Restoration of Property*, pp. 4, 5–6, italics in original.
297 See above p. 90.
298 Chesterton, *What's Wrong with the World*, pp. 33–4, 45–6, 278; *idem*, 'The Issue of the Indiscriminate', *G.K.'s Weekly*, viii (9 March 1929), p. 411. Cf. Belloc, *An Essay on the Restoration of Property*, pp. 21, 40–1, and ch. III *passim*.

diffusion of private property so that every man can own something basic that is his and that will enable him to choose effectively, to shape things in his own image. Only thus will he be meaningfully free and able to express his creative urges.[299] Solely in this way could there be revived a sense of belonging and a solution to the primary problem achieved: 'how men could be made to realise the wonder and splendour of being alive' instead of merely existing in an environment 'which their imagination had left for dead.' He thus yearned for a 'visionary revolt against the prosaic flatness of a nineteenth-century city and civilisation'.[300] Nor were specific proposals lacking that might help set events on the right road. Chesterton suggested that, at the purely personal level, we should stop patronizing the big shop and use instead the facilities of the small tradesman. The quality of goods and genuine craftsmanship must be prized. And it was recognized that the role of government itself must be crucial in aiding the transition in view. It might discourage the sale of small property to large owners by the heavy taxation of contracts and stimulate the break-up and dispersion of large properties by appropriate changes in testamentary law and the abolition of primogeniture. Equally the law could protect experiments in small land-ownership by subsidies and tariffs; and where large capital nevertheless remained it could promote the introduction of profit-sharing, joint control, and the like. As well the state might improve the judicial system so that the poor had easier access to the law to defend their property and interests against the great and the powerful.[301] The crucial question of the machine is treated at some length though hardly effectively. Chesterton recognizes it is in many ways vital to human well-being; and he cannot condemn it as such. But all he has to suggest as to its control is that where it must exist it should, together with the profits of its operation, be in the charge of some local guild.[302] Above all a start must be made in thus revolutionizing society and on any occasion or at any opening that appeared. Any appropriate expedient would do, for the last thing to be pursued was a mere uniformity:

> even my Utopia would contain different things of different types holding on different tenures; . . . as in a medieval state there were some peasants, some monasteries, some common land, some private land, some town guilds, and so on, so in my modern state there would be some things nationalized, some machines owned corporately, some guilds sharing common profits, and so on, as well as many absolute

299 Chesterton, *What's Wrong with the World*, pp. 47–8, 57–60; *The Outline of Sanity*, p. 52.
300 Chesterton, *Autobiography*, pp. 134, 137.
301 Chesterton, *The Outline of Sanity*, pp. 67–9, 78, 80, 88, 125, 225.
302 ibid., part IV *passim*, and p. 58..

individual owners [who] give ... the standard and tone of the society.[303]

It was necessary, then, to restore man to himself and to the possibilities of fulfilment by subjecting the economic process to a moral purpose. Collectivism was not a solution but a most perilous danger; and while the aid of the law would (as indicated) be essential, there was an utter denial of any 'complete confidence in the State.'[304]

Liberalism and the decline of liberty

The Servile State was dedicated to E. S. P. Haynes who specifically acknowledged Belloc's influence and who was himself no mean crusader in the old Liberal cause of individual freedom. He inveighed against such tendencies as the tyrannical growth of a 'vast and irresponsible bureaucracy' and the decline in respect for private life and personal rights by politicians, officials, press, and public opinion. At the same time he was not opposed to the existence of a strong central power as such which he believed to be necessary to sustain liberty; and he admitted the need for public control of the social services.[305] But he did not hesitate to repudiate the way in which 'from modern Berlin Mr Lloyd George and his friends have imported their experiments in establishing the Servile State.'[306] The brief humorous anecdote with which his book on the decline of English liberty ends is horrifying in its view of the collectivist future.[307] Haynes wished rather to see a prospect of genuine individual involvement in a localized system of administration in which all could participate, an echo not simply (as it explicitly was) of the Athenian model but also of the Saxon tradition of local self-government and of the Chesterbelloc sense of community.[308]

Liberal expression of anti-statist doctrine did not end there however. There are other late examples of the twin themes of free trade and domestic libertarianism. One is provided by Harold Cox.[309] He was secretary of the Cobden Club in 1899 and strongly opposed to the tariff

---

303 ibid., p.108.
304 Chesterton, Autobiography, p.269. Interestingly G. Orwell, always strongly suspicious of any government tendency to 'oligarchical collectivism', said (in the late 1930s) that what England needed was to follow the policies of G.K.'s Weekly: see B. Crick, George Orwell: a Life (London, 1980), p.175.
305 E. S. P. Haynes, The Decline of Liberty in England (London, 1916), pp.206–7; also his essay on 'Law and the Great State', Lady Warwick et al., The Great State, p.191.
306 Haynes, The Decline of Liberty in England, pp.18, 219, 223.
307 ibid., appendix, pp.227–30.
308 Haynes, 'Law and the Great State', loc. cit., pp.187–8. Cf. his later The Enemies of Liberty (London, 1923).
309 For biographical details, see DNB, ii.2583.

reform campaign. In 1906 he became a Liberal MP committed to free trade and found the principles and implications of George's financial and social policies quite unacceptable as he did the advent of the Labour Party. He explained in his *Socialism in the House of Commons* (1907) that he objected to the undermining of individual and group responsibility involved. On this basis he fought, more or less single-handed, a campaign against his party's old age pension proposals, the plan to give meals to needy schoolchildren, and a money grant to provide work for the unemployed.[310] G. P. Gooch, a Liberal supporter of such reforms, said that Cox 'was the only man on the Liberal side who clung to the doctrines of *laissez-faire* in their unadulterated form. While we saw in the state an indispensable instrument for establishing a minimum standard of life for the common man, he dreaded the slackening of moral fibre as a result of getting "something for nothing".' It was, Gooch added, 'a delight to listen to his lucid expositions of an unpopular creed', though (Gooch also thought) Cox gave too little weight to the maladjustments of the economic system and too much to the prospects of improvement open to the ordinary person by his own efforts.[311] This ideological rift led to Cox's withdrawal from Parliament. Subsequently as journalist and editor he continued to be a strong opponent of bureaucracy and the growth of public expenditure.[312] His beliefs are most fully expounded in a series of essays which he published in 1920 which were concerned 'to defend economic liberty against the attacks made on it' by those 'who think that they can secure progress by various schemes for curtailing freedom'; whereas it can be attained only by enterprise which is the outcome of liberty.[313] The power of the state can properly be used to maintain public order or prevent fraud but its methods can never be appropriate 'to deal with the ever-varying complexities of social life', and 'it is better to endure some evil that may result from the absence of regulation rather than lose the boons that liberty brings.'[314] Specifically it is not possible to get rid of the institution of property (including a right of inheritance) without doing violence to man's natural instincts and without destroying both the main cause of material progress and the foundation of liberty itself.[315] All the paraphernalia of libertarian politics are present in Cox's book: free trade; the stress on the negative concept of freedom; the rejection of growing state intervention in the form of

310 H. Cox, *Socialism in the House of Commons* (London, 1907), pp.7–8.
311 G. P. Gooch, *Under Six Reigns* (London, 1958), p.147.
312 See e.g. his attack on excessive state control in *The Basis and Ethics of Socialism* (ASU, n.s. no.88; London, n.d. [1924]), esp. pp.5–8.
313 H. Cox, *Economic Liberty* (London, 1920), p.v. For the specific conditions of economic liberty, see ibid., p.2 and chs I–II *passim*.
314 ibid., pp.v–vi.
315 ibid., p.25.

nationalization and of unemployment insurance and other welfare
schemes; concern, therefore, about the increase of public expenditure
(and taxation) and of the army of officials with its waste and
incompetence; the tyrannical propensities of democracy in pursuit of 'the
delusion of equality'. Spencer's name is not mentioned at all; but his
spirit is ubiquitous throughout Cox's post-war exposition of traditional
Liberalism. Of similar persuasion there was the so-called 'Holt Cave'
described by Richard Holt himself as a 'combined remonstrance by
business men and some survivors of the Cobden-Bright school of thought
against the ill-considered and socialistic tendencies of the Government
finance'.[316]

Another such instance is F. W. Hirst, the Liberal scholar, publicist, and
man of letters, one of the most powerful journalists of Liberalism as he
has recently been called.[317] He was a strong and consistent protagonist of
the classical Liberal tradition, was indeed 'the archetype of the stern and
unbending Cobdenite', though he represented as well the model of 'late-
Victorian grace and cultivation': 'Intellectually tough, morally hard, he
was courteous and lovable, kindly and gay.'[318] He was early associated
with the Liberal cause, for example as joint editor of a well-known and
influential symposium on the subject which appeared in 1897, his own
contribution being on the topic of Liberalism and wealth. The basic
point he made there was the crucial importance of relying on the well-
tried principles of political economy, that is, free trade and the spirit of
individual enterprise based on private property.[319] He had a lifelong
interest in public finance. Maurice Bowra who knew Hirst well said that
for him the 'expenditure of public money was a moral activity which
should be governed by the highest principles and never prostituted to
electoral or party needs.'[320] Perhaps because the tide of events was
running in an uncongenial direction, he was unbending, even intolerant,
in the expression of his views. MacCallum Scott noted in his diary in 1916
that Hirst was convinced that everyone who differed from him was
'either a rogue, or a time-server or a weakling. His political ideal seems
summed up in Peace and Retrenchment. If he adds "Reform" it is only in
the sense of constitutional reform – the extension of the franchise. His
creed is intensely individualist and opposed to all State interference.'[321]

316 Holt Diary (19 July 1914), Holt MSS, Liverpool Central Library, cited in M. Bentley,
   The Liberal Mind, 1914–1929 (Cambridge, 1977), p.15.
317 ibid., p.184. Dr Bentley's reference there to Hirst's 'perverse and antiquated
   individualism' is a curiously unhistorical judgement.
318 A. F. Thompson, in G. Murray et al., F. W. Hirst By His Friends (London, 1958),
   pp.35–6, 39.
319 Six Oxford Men, Essays in Liberalism, ch.II, esp. pp.54–7, 63.
320 Bowra, in Murray et al., op. cit., p.32.
321 MacCallum Scott diary (15 January 1916) cited in Bentley, op. cit., p.184.

Hirst early came under Morley's influence and helped him write his *Life of Gladstone*; he was also involved in the Cobden Club response in 1904 to the protectionist campaign then under way. In 1907 he became editor of *The Economist* and sustained in that paper the traditional principles of peace, economy, and individual liberty, though he resigned in 1916 because he could not support the war and the policy of conscription, the latter being (as he later put it) a 'horrible institution' and the cause through which, more than any other, military tyranny has developed and popular liberty declined in Europe in our time.[322] He naturally had no use for 'Mr. George' and the kind of Liberalism he stood for. Hirst's opinions about current tendencies on the domestic scene were reflected in his long-standing hostility to government spending and in his view that the welfare state was a 'Beveridge Hoax'. He was always little convinced of the capacity of government action to increase happiness and well-being though he did not, it is true, oppose every measure concerning public health and education. Likewise he objected to the budget being used as a means of redistributing wealth and he was strongly, even harshly, critical of Keynesian economics.[323] He was for long connected with Sir Ernest Benn and the Individualist Movement but parted company in the 1940s because of its growing Conservative connexions: he certainly always believed in the right of personal decision against superior authority.[324] He was, too, naturally completely out of sympathy with developments in the Liberal Party after 1945. Looking back, towards the close of his life, over the events and trends of the period since 1900, he said that the conflict with the Boers

> was a prelude to the first Great War and to the second, which have left the country shorn of its liberties in a state of bankruptcy and serfdom, oppressed by ruinous taxation, overwhelming debt, and conscription, menaced by more and more inflation, entangled in new alliances . . . , and with military commitments in all parts of the world.[325]

He was, ideologically and otherwise, a Manchester man to the end; in his later years (he died in 1953) he lived in Cobden's old house, a fine act of symbolism.

Hirst's firm and unyielding adherence to the tenets of individual liberty and personal responsibility and his refusal to compromise these principles by considerations of expediency are thus revealed throughout his long life. His explanation of their meaning is best summarized in two complementary studies he published in 1935. One, *Liberty and Tyranny*,

322 F. W. Hirst, *Liberty and Tyranny* (London, 1935), p.73. Cf. ibid., pp.203–7.
323 J. E. Allen, in Murray *et al.*, op. cit., pp.16–17; A. F. Thompson, ibid., p.37; F. W. Hirst, *In the Golden Days* (London, 1947), p.48.
324 Hirst, *In the Golden Days*, p.64. For Benn, see ch.8, pp.295–306 below.
325 Hirst, *In the Golden Days*, p.202.

dealt with the political and constitutional features of his position; the other, *Economic Freedom and Private Property*, examined a distinct but closely related and equally crucial side of the articles of political faith involved.

The first of the two books mentioned is – deliberately – not so much an abstract treatise expounding the nature and implications of liberty as a series of historical essays on various institutional and theoretical aspects of the subject. Hirst intended to show by this range of experience (which stretches, rather in the style of Machiavelli and for similar purpose, from ancient to modern times) how the various forms of liberty – political, legal or civil, religious, and the like – are essential for the achievement of happiness and progress.[326] The message is that liberty is a natural right that flourishes only in an ordered democratic environment where all enjoy equal rights under equal laws.[327] Of course, the freedom of the individual must be restricted to prevent his becoming a nuisance to others; but no precise delimitation is possible of the boundaries between the proper sphere of government and that of the citizen: the matter will necessarily vary and quite widely from place to place and time to time.[328] Yet Hirst is typically sure of one thing: that (as stated in the epigraph which stands at the head of this section) nothing is more likely to inhibit progress and the achievement of happiness than the idea, then coming into vogue, that government must plan economic and social life. The result (the passage cited continues) can only be that officials will direct every man's occupation or business, force all industry into approved 'grooves', restrict free markets, obstruct the laws of supply and demand, and otherwise force a harmful pattern on affairs.[329] This topic, introduced as one among a series of final comments in the first study, becomes the main theme of the other work on economic liberty – 'a department of the larger subject of political liberty' – which was published as a companion volume in the same year.[330]

The point of departure is that property, liberty, and security go together and that the possibility of free and competitive economic life is essential to the achievement of happiness and progress.[331] Complete *laissez faire* was never feasible and there are necessarily some limitations imposed by the state, for instance to prevent monopoly or other restrictions, deal with nuisances, safeguard safety and health, and so on.[332] However, the great contemporary danger (under the influence of

326 Hirst, *Liberty and Tyranny*, pp.9, 15–16, 36–7, 40.
327 ibid., pp.23, 190.
328 ibid., pp.286–7, 293.
329 ibid., p.288.
330 F. W. Hirst, *Economic Freedom and Private Property* (London, 1935), p. 9. It is really a further section simply of the other book.
331 ibid., pp.13, 30, 58.
332 ibid., pp.9–10, 51–3, 60ff.

theories of Socialism and of protection) is that government may go too far. The risk is of too much interference not too little. In western-type democracies like Great Britain, Hirst wrote, the most insidious danger to economic liberty was 'the extension of bureaucracy'.[333] Socialism – co-operation is different, rather a Liberal idea, he thinks – means the confiscation of private property, the elimination of competition, and 'seeks the complete subordination of the individual to the State.'[334] Liberalism, in contrast, recognizes 'the importance of private property as an essential element of freedom. Without it a modern State will sink into anarchy or servitude to an all-powerful bureaucracy.'[335] In fine, this collectivist prospect must be distinguished from the classical Liberal tradition to which Hirst adheres and which has so proud a record: the practitioners of the latter

> reformed the franchise, set up our admirable system of local government, created a first-class civil service, established free trade and economic liberty, promoted international peace by arbitration and reduction of armaments, and instituted a superlatively efficient system of national finance.

The doctrine has to its credit too (Hirst urges) all the great progress the nation achieved during the nineteenth century.[336] Is this fact, he seems to ask, to be weighed and found wanting as against a mere theory, and one with such undesirable implications?

The surge of collectivism that has occurred in the decades since Hirst's two studies appeared made the sort of Liberalism he stood for appear irrelevant or uncongenial (at least until quite recently). But the old-fashioned doctrine was not wholly without expression. It was, for instance, expounded in an extreme and curious little book published during the last war by a Dr W. C. Ross of the Indian Medical Service. It is an analysis of the political situation that had developed up to that time with a view to learning from the mistakes committed and, during the interval provided by the war, ensuring that they are avoided in the future. There is a whole series of evils which comes under attack: the growth of officialdom, decline in standards of conduct in both public and private life, the preaching of class antagonism, and so forth.[337] The key point is that the 'control of trade and industry exercised by Government and the bureaucracy which it has created must be stopped.'[338] And here all three

333 ibid., pp.10, 24. Cf. ibid., p.27.
334 ibid., p.103. On co-operation, see esp. pp.111–12.
335 ibid., pp.67–8.
336 ibid., pp.116–17.
337 W. C. Ross, *Despotism or Democracy? Britain at the Crossroads* (Edinburgh, 1942), pp.5–7.
338 ibid., p.19.

parties are to blame, each of them in their different ways and according to their opportunities having pursued policies leading to the creation of 'an authoritarian form of government'.[339] Liberalism, in particular, has unfortunately failed to challenge these developments, contrary to its old tradition of liberty, free trade, cutting public expenditure, and so on.[340] It is not a well-argued book; whatever importance it has lies in the despairing classical Liberal cry it represents.

At a quite different level of discussion is the economic Liberalism of writers such as Professor F. A. Hayek and Lord Robbins and other similar theorists of the *Rechtsstaat*. Hayek's very extensive discussion might be said to be the most profound analysis of these matters to have appeared in English since the days of Spencer.[341] Nor has this sort of theme lacked exponents in the United States.[342] Alas, these crucial expositions can only be thus weakly mentioned here.

What is of notable significance is that, for a long time now, no major Liberal politicians have, except as a formality or as rhetoric, espoused what Spencer once called the 'old, true Liberalism'.[343] Practical pressures to the contrary have been too great. The cause has been left to the publicists and economists; or it has migrated to the Conservative side of things. Tawney effectively described in 1921 a situation that has continued to prevail:

> When . . . Liberalism triumphed in England . . . , it carried without criticism into the new world of capitalist industry categories of private property and freedom of contract which had been forged in the simpler economic environment of the pre-industrial era. In England these categories are being bent and twisted till they are no longer recognizable, and will, in time, be made harmless. . . . This doctrine has been qualified in practice by particular limitations to avert particular evils and to meet exceptional emergencies.

339 ibid., chs IV, VII, IX.
340 ibid., p.228.
341 Hayek's most important works in this context are *The Road to Serfdom* (1944), *The Constitution of Liberty* (1960), *Studies in Philosophy, Politics and Economics* (1967), and *Law, Legislation and Liberty* (3 vols, 1973–9). For Robbins, see e.g. the comments in his *Autobiography of an Economist* (London, 1971), pp.106–9, 162, 224–5. For a recent, pessimistic analysis of the political future in Britain by a Liberal economist, see C. K. Rowley, 'Liberalism and Collective Choice', *National Westminster Bank Quarterly Review* (May 1979), pp.11–22.
342 One of the most interesting and wayward of these is the late Ayn Rand who became a sort of cult figure: see e.g. her *The Virtue of Selfishness* (1961), and the series of novels, esp. *The Fountainhead* (1943) and *Atlas Shrugged* (1957). One useful, and committed, study is N. Branden, *Who is Ayn Rand?* (New York, 1962). But the most generally influential is Professor M. Friedman, on whom see vol. i, *The Rise of Collectivism*, ch. 3, pp.155–61.
343 Spencer, *The Man Versus the State*, p.79. For one partial instance, see the speech of the then Chairman of the Liberal Party, in *The Times* (24 November 1971), p.2.

Nevertheless, although thus limited in special instances, 'its general validity' was broadly 'regarded as beyond controversy' and up to 1914 at least 'it was the working faith of modern economic civilization.'[344]

The story of modern Liberalism, then, is of a libertarian doctrine increasingly affected by collectivist elements until, by the time of the Great War, the old themes had, in many ways, come to seem anachronistic. It remains to describe this transformation. In the late nineteenth century Spencer himself had noticed the ambivalence of the creed and this was reflected in the exemplary figures reviewed in the next chapter, writers who shared Spencer's concern about individual freedom and his fear of social and political tyranny. Yet in their different ways they made concessions in the direction of the controlling and welfare roles of public agencies and originated and reflected an emphasis in Liberal thought that subsequently led to the end of *laissez faire*.

344 R. H. Tawney, *The Acquisitive Society* (1921; London, 1943), pp.21–3.

4
THE TRANSITION TO COLLECTIVISM

The main reason for desiring more State action is in order to give the
individual a greater chance of developing all his activities in a healthy
way. The State and the individual are not sides of an antithesis between
which we must choose; . . . .

D. G. RITCHIE, *The Principles of State Interference*, 1891, p.64

J. S. MILL: 'WEAVING IT ANEW'

. . . in his single person he spans the interval between the old and the new
Liberalism.

L. T. HOBHOUSE, *Liberalism*, 1911, repr. 1966, p.58

PROFESSOR TAWNEY once referred to John Stuart Mill as 'the last and
the greatest of Liberal thinkers'.[1] It is a flattering assessment and is, too, a
good indication of the respect and even the awe with which Mill and his
work are customarily regarded. Yet the terms of the encomium are
hardly accurate or acceptable. If it means that Mill represents the
quintessence or climacteric of traditional Liberal doctrine then it is not
really true, for in some vital respects he was to be a major instrument of
its betrayal: in 1843, during a conversation about Bentham's surviving
disciples, Mill smilingly – though not in jest – made the remark that he
himself was Peter who denied his Master.[2] And if it is being urged that
nevertheless he provided the fullest or most systematic and sophisticated
statement of classical Liberal doctrine, it must be suggested that perhaps
the palm should be bestowed elsewhere. Yet there is certainly no
doubting the enormous influence of his work; and in the present context

1 R. H. Tawney, *The Acquisitive Society* (1921; London, 1943), p.102.
2 D. Masson, 'Memories of London in the "Forties"', *Blackwood's*, clxxxiii (1908),
p.553, cited in J. Viner, 'Bentham and J. S. Mill: the Utilitarian Background', *American
Economic Review*, xxxix (1949), p.376.

his ideas are very significant because they display a notable ambivalence of attitude that nicely reflects the transition from a sternly individualist to a more collectivist form of Liberal ideology. Mill himself recognized this co-existence of opposites in his thought and so did others. For instance, he described in the *Autobiography* how he found the fabric of his 'old and taught opinions' giving way in many places and how, while he never allowed it to fall to pieces, he was 'incessantly occupied in weaving it anew.' Equally, the French libertarian publicist, Paul Leroy-Beaulieu, whose works were widely read in translation in this country, wrote in the early 1890s that the world had never known 'a more persevering or more persuasive defender of liberty' than Mill even though he had at bottom an inclination towards collectivism that it was difficult to suppress and which tended at times to carry him away. 'We find it again and again in many parts of his writings: but he never yields to it finally or without a struggle.'³ Others were less tolerant or compromising in their judgement: Dicey was a great admirer of Mill's defence of individuality but believed, too, that certain aspects and implications of Mill's social thought completely reneged this commitment.⁴

J. S. Mill was the son of James Mill who was both the friend of Jeremy Bentham (the virtual founder of the utilitarian school in this country) and a major exponent of his ideas adding to them indeed not a little of his own. Born in 1806 John Stuart was brought up to be the strict exemplar and embodiment of the principles of this most intellectual creed. Nevertheless the sensibility of his nature led him to be aware of other, not necessarily compatible, themes and pressures: art, music, poetry, and the role in life, and the intrinsic worth, of feeling or sentiment, for instance. He read deeply in such authors as Wordsworth, Coleridge, Carlyle, and de Tocqueville; and many of the ideas he thus imbibed were barely congenial to the hard and formal naturalism of the Benthamite point of view. The outcome was a tension of mind and spirit that at one stage contributed to a period of mental depression Mill movingly if restrainedly described in his autobiography. This phase – which subsequently recurred – and the circumstances surrounding it constitute an incident of some note in the intellectual history of the last century. It is important here as a kind of symbol indicating that Mill's state of mind and ideas were always something of an amalgam of manifestly contrary forces. He explicitly and formally championed the standard utilitarian proposition that the supreme goal of human action was and should be the greatest happiness of the greatest number; yet he seems often to write as

3 J. S. Mill, *Autobiography* (1873; World's Classics, 1963), p.132; P. Leroy-Beaulieu, *The Modern State in Relation to Society and the Individual* (1890; trans. edn, London, 1891), pp.17–18.
4 R. A. Cosgrove, *The Rule of Law: Albert Venn Dicey, Victorian Jurist* (London, 1980), pp.12–13. Cf. the opinion of J. H. Levy cited below, p.119.

though there were other ultimate values than utility, those associated with virtue, liberty, and individuality, for instance, and which he treats as if they have an independent significance of their own. The implications of this apparent antithesis of standards have long provided the occasion for extensive exegesis and critical comment. Here interest must centre on one aspect of the ambivalence, reflected in a single question: If the greatest happiness principle indicates the purpose that must be pursued then, given that this is a general and abstract notion, how may it best be realized in terms of practical policy and, especially, what is the type and manner of government most appropriate to its achievement? In particular, is a growing degree of public intervention indicated and, if so, how far is this compatible with the maintenance of that freedom of individual spirit and decision that Mill regarded so highly?

Though lacking perhaps any great degree of rhetorical power, Mill's consideration of these matters probes deeply and is expressed in prose of apparently limpid clarity. Moreover his work both shaped and reflected an increasingly dominant view about the limits of state supervision and social interference: in an important way he moulded the form in which much discussion of these topics was subsequently cast. As Dicey suggested, the

> changes or fluctuations in Mill's . . . convictions, bearing as they do in many points upon legislative opinion, are at once the sign, and were in England, to a great extent, the cause, of the transition from . . . individualism . . . to . . . collectivism. . . . His teaching specially affected the men who were just entering on public life towards 1870. It prepared them at any rate to accept, if not to welcome, the collectivism which from that time onwards has gained increasing strength.[5]

Here first of all some indication will be given of the way in which Mill justified the traditional notion of individuality; then it will be explained how he nevertheless advanced various considerations that, in themselves or by implication, were hardly compatible with this libertarian concept.

The protection of individuality

In his autobiography Spencer referred to 'genuine Liberalism – the Liberalism which seeks to extend men's liberties'.[6] This was the kind of concern so often associated with Benthamism in its attack on sinister

5 A. V. Dicey, *Lectures on the Relation between Law & Public Opinion in England during the Nineteenth Century* (1905; 2nd edn, London, 1920), p.432. Cf. George Lichtheim's remark that Mill was the 'crucial figure' in the movement towards collectivism, *Marxism: an Historical and Critical Study* (1961; 2nd edn, London, 1964), p.26.
6 H. Spencer, *An Autobiography* (London, 1904), i.421.

interests and in its support for political reform and the 'stand-out-of-my-sunshine' view of economic life. It was a cause particularly espoused by Mill who was always greatly concerned about any political and social threat to 'the sovereignty of the individual' because the integrity of personality was in his view the basic element of well-being.[7] As early as 1836 he had written that the most remarkable consequence of the advance of civilization, 'which the state of the world is now forcing upon the attention of thinking minds, is this: that power passes more and more from individuals, and small knots of individuals, to masses: that the importance of the masses becomes constantly greater, that of individuals less.'[8] And this irresistible advance of public opinion is not without threatening consequence, in particular that 'the individual is lost and becomes impotent in the crowd, and that the individual character itself becomes relaxed and enervated'.[9] This is also a major concern of the later essay On Liberty (1859) which explores 'the nature and limits of the power which can be legitimately exercised by society over the individual'; and, too, of the discussion of the problems of representative government which emphasizes the need to ensure that the individual can develop his faculties to the fullest possible extent in conditions of minimum external restraint.[10] The tone of the passages in which such sentiments are expressed is often not unlike that of Spencer or Samuel Smiles.

Mill believed that, at one time, governments had been restricted either by the recognition of certain immunities (for instance, by so-called political liberties or rights) or by the existence of constitutional checks. But with the development of representative systems in which those who ruled were supposed to be identified with the general interest and responsible to the community, it began to be suggested that too much importance could be attached to the limitation of political power in these traditional ways. 'The nation did not need to be protected against its own will' for (it was urged) it would not tyrannize over itself. Mill, however, believed this to be a profound mistake and that the 'limitation . . . of the power of government over individuals loses none of its importance' simply because 'the holders of power are regularly accountable to the community'.[11] He felt rather that the potential for social and political tyranny in a democracy was greater than under any aristocracy or monarchy. In a popular régime, freedom of action and opinion would be

7 For the phrase cited, see Mill's Autobiography, p.217.
8 J. S. Mill, 'Civilization' (1836), Collected Works, ed. J. M. Robson et al. (London, 1963ff.), xviii.121.
9 ibid., xviii.126–7, 136.
10 'On Liberty' (1859), ibid., xviii.217; 'Representative Government' (1861), ch.III, esp. ibid., xix, 409–12.
11 ibid., xviii.218–19.

increasingly subject to 'a hostile and dreaded censorship', to 'the tyranny of the majority'. There would be a natural and inevitable tendency towards 'collective mediocrity', and 'individual spontaneity' would not be recognized as having 'any intrinsic worth'. The greater part of the people, 'being satisfied with the ways of mankind as they now are', is unable, he felt, to understand why those ways should not be good enough for everybody: 'conformity is the first thing thought of'.[12] The basic reason for this kind of development was the increasing homogeneity of the condition of life of all classes of people, a growing lack of diversity which the spread of education, in itself desirable, helped to reinforce. There were indeed so many contemporary 'influences hostile to Individuality, that it is not easy to see how it can stand its ground' against the popular 'despotism' that threatens it.[13] The 'greatness of England is now all collective'; and so with the rise of democracy the problem of protecting liberty had become more not less acute.[14]

This concern (which, of course, Spencer acutely shared) explains why Mill's attention focused on the need to formulate a rule to distinguish those matters in which the public may reasonably interfere with individual conduct and those in which it may not. In the *Principles of Political Economy* he states as his premiss the belief that 'there is a circle around every individual human being, which no government . . . ought to be permitted to overstep'.[15] The problem is where to draw the line. Similarly at the beginning of *On Liberty*, he writes:

> The object of this Essay is to assert one very simple principle, as entitled to govern absolutely the dealings of society with the individual in the way of compulsion and control, whether the means used be physical force in the form of legal penalties, or the moral coercion of public opinion. That principle is, that the sole end for which mankind are warranted, individually or collectively, in interfering with the liberty of action of any of their number, is self-protection. That the only purpose for which power can be rightfully exercised over any member of a civilized community, against his will, is to prevent harm to others. His own good, either physical or moral, is not a sufficient warrant.[16]

On this basis Mill went on to elaborate the famous Benthamite terminology involving a distinction between 'self-regarding' and 'other-

---

12 ibid., xviii. 219–20, 261, 264–5, 268; xix. 457.
13 ibid., xviii. 261, 272–5. Cf. ibid., iii. 979; and Mill, *Autobiography*, p.215.
14 *Collected Works*, xviii. 227, 272. See also J. C. Rees, *Mill and His Early Critics* (Leicester, 1956), pp.5–6, 56 n.13 for reference to the genesis and formation of this concern.
15 *Collected Works*, iii.938.
16 ibid., xviii. 223. Cf. ibid., xviii. 220.

regarding' action.[17] The precise details of this distinction and the difficulties involved in its expression need not be explored here.[18] It is sufficient for the present purpose to note Mill's attempt, in the name of individuality, to limit the extent of communal interference and to get clear the existence of a sphere of action – self-regarding action – in which a person is not subject to external authority. What must be further observed, however, is that in his concern for individual freedom Mill goes further still. He suggests that even where, on the basis of this distinction, social or political intervention might be legitimate (because concerned with other-regarding action), it may well be proper and expedient that nevertheless it should not always ensue. Thus – to take the example of interference by government itself – it ought not to act where what is to be done would be in many respects better effected by individuals or voluntary groups. A business, for instance, is best conducted by those concerned and there ought to be no interference with trade or 'the ordinary processes of industry'. In terms of the distinction proposed it would be quite reasonable to enforce on employers appropriate sanitary precautions or arrangements to protect workpeople in dangerous occupations: but generally, Mill believes, it is better not to do this and to leave people to themselves rather than to control them. Again, even where individuals do not do a thing so well as the government and its officials, it is often desirable to let private persons alone so they may gain experience, extend their social education and understanding, learn to exercise judgement, and so on. This is not only an essential means to a proper diversity; it is also one of the justifications for jury trial, local self-government, voluntary associations, and the like. The task of the state is thus, not to tolerate no experiments or institutions other than its own, but to act as the emollient of any difficulties that arise through allowing people to tackle their own problems. Finally, Mill is concerned about the dangers of excessive concentration of power in government especially if its administration is conducted as efficiently as it should be.[19]

In sum the main thrust of Mill's argument seems indisputably libertarian and his statement of its essence is often like Spencer's law of equal freedom: 'The only freedom which deserves the name', he says, 'is that of pursuing our own good in our own way, so long as we do not attempt to deprive others of theirs'.[20] And although Mill does not generally put the case in Spencer's rigorous and extensive fashion, his

17 'On Liberty', chs iv–v, esp. ibid., xviii.276, 280–2, 292–3. See also ibid., ii.205; iii.938, 978.
18 For scholarly discussion of the problem, see e.g. J. C. Rees, 'A Re-Reading of Mill on Liberty', *Political Studies*, viii (1960), pp.113–29.
19 *Collected Works*, xviii. 293, 305–10.
20 ibid., xviii. 226.

basic concern is undoubtedly well epitomized in this sentence: 'There is a limit to the legitimate interference of collective opinion with individual independence: and to find that limit, and maintain it against encroachment, is as indispensable to a good condition of human affairs, as protection against political despotism.'[21]

And yet there are features of Mill's defence of the libertarian position that appear to point in a quite different direction. He always recognized there were in principle two possible modes of social existence for human beings: they might be left to the natural consequences of their mistakes in life; or society might protect them in this regard either by prevention or punishment.[22] He formally opted for the first; though in his *Autobiography* he wrote that there was a moment in his mental progress when he 'might easily have fallen into a tendency towards over-government, both social and political'.[23] Perhaps he did incline this way more than he thought.

Collectivist propensities

Those aspects of Mill's attitude that seem to point in a collectivist direction appear in various places and in different ways.

Ambiguity of language

First of all it is partly a question of the vagueness or ambiguity of the language in which he expounds and illustrates the distinction between self- and other-regarding action and cognate matters. The apparent confusions here (what actions which are not trivial *are* purely self-regarding?) for long led commentators to reject Mill's explicit formulation though, of course, this involved a considerable weakening of his libertarian stand. For if (despite the apparent linguistic ambivalence) a close textual exegesis may render his position more cogent and consistent, the reformulation involves nevertheless the admission that Mill's principle 'can yield no clear directive' about state interference where the interests of others are involved.[24] Thus there is present a margin of manoeuvre and discretion in which, it might seem, the power of control could legitimately grow.[25]

The kind of problem involved is illustrated by the famous matter of the bridge. Mill had said, at the outset of the essay *On Liberty*, that his principle required freedom

21 ibid., xviii. 220.
22 Mill, 'The Claims of Labour' (1845), ibid., iv. 374.
23 Mill, *Autobiography*, p.214.
24 Rees, 'A Re-Reading of Mill on Liberty', loc. cit., pp.127–9.
25 Cf. M. Cowling, *Mill and Liberalism* (Cambridge, 1963), p.100.

of tastes and pursuits; of framing the plan of our life to suit our own character; of doing as we like, subject to such consequences as may follow: without impediment from our fellow-creatures, so long as what we do does not harm them, even though they should think our conduct foolish, perverse, or wrong.[26]

And yet, later in the text, one of the cases Mill used to illustrate his principle is put as follows:

> ... it is a proper office of public authority to guard against accidents. If either a public officer or anyone else saw a person attempting to cross a bridge which had been ascertained to be unsafe, and there were no time to warn him of his danger, they might seize him and turn him back, without any real infringement of his liberty; for liberty consists in doing what one desires, and he does not desire to fall into the river.[27]

Critics soon fastened on the problems raised by this example. The basic issue is one concerning the meaning of the word 'liberty'. As stated, Mill is above all anxious to create an area of freedom for the individual in which he may act as he sees fit. Such liberty is (as the term goes) 'negative', that is, it consists in the absence of external restraint so that a person may do as he pleases; and this is clearly the notion of freedom ostensibly defined in the first passage cited above. Yet, in the illustration, though what the person obviously intends is to cross the bridge, he is stopped, and properly so hindered in Mill's view. A distinction is thus made between what the person seems to want to do (to cross the bridge) and what, so to say, he really wants to do or what it is in his best interests to do (not to cross the bridge if it is unsafe). The implication is that liberty is doing, not simply what one seemingly intends or wishes, but what one ought to want to do. Here a different or 'positive' conception of freedom is involved and, as Bosanquet pointed out, there is implied the 'real will' doctrine of Rousseau and the philosophical idealists.[28] And this doctrine may not be so libertarian in implication as Mill intended and might possibly be taken to justify incursions into the area of individual choice. An inquisitor might say to the heretic he was torturing: 'You desire salvation in your way (to cross over the bridge); but I, in the certainty of my knowledge, am seeking to prevent your being damned (it is unsafe, you will fall and be killed), and this you cannot really want.' And the same inference emerges from Mill's discussion of slavery: an agreement freely made by a man to sell himself into slavery is void because (despite

26 *Collected Works*, xviii. 226. Cf. ibid., xviii. 277; xix. 405–6.
27 ibid., xviii. 294.
28 B. Bosanquet, *The Philosophical Theory of the State* (1899; 4th edn, London, 1958), pp. 64–5.

his explicit intention) it is not really in his interest that he should be allowed to do so.[29]

There may, as well, be a certain looseness of implication revealed in Mill's attitude to despotic rule. He says the 'backward states of society' will be likely to require firm government:

> Despotism is a legitimate mode of government in dealing with barbarians, provided the end be their improvement, and the means justified by actually effecting that end. Liberty, as a principle, has no application to any state of things anterior to the time when mankind have become capable of being improved by free and equal discussion. Until then, there is nothing for them but implicit obedience to an Akbar or a Charlemagne, if they are so fortunate as to find one.[30]

This is positively Carlyleian in its possibilities; and Dicey for one did not fail to stress that the concession may go farther than Mill seems to perceive, for in principle the maxim might reasonably be applied 'to every case where a government is far more intelligent than the governed.'[31] As presumably the Guardians (or, perhaps more appropriately, the *moguls*) of India House had the right to authority over the ignorant millions of the sub-continent.

The functions of government

A further ambiguity arises in connexion with Mill's discussion of the 'necessary' and 'optional' functions of government. In principle, of course, he does not wish to extend the scope of political authority without due cause preferring to rely instead on voluntary action where this is forthcoming or may be prompted. In this frame of mind he makes at length a series of objections to government intervention very similar to those advanced by people such as Spencer, Toulmin Smith, and de Tocqueville, and which are, therefore, familiar enough. Thus he urges that intervention is undesirable because it involves the use of compulsory powers and so restricts the freedom of choice of the individuals affected; it always involves taxation the imposition of which may cramp initiative and which offends the fundamental tenet that each person is to be rewarded according to his own efforts; it increases the power and influence of government and public pressure and may entail the tyranny of the majority; government offices are often inefficient and their work is frequently defective and badly organized as compared with private

---

29 *Collected Works*, xviii. 299–300. The example about the inquisitor is based on D. G. Ritchie, *The Principles of State Interference: Four Essays on the Political Philosophy of Mr. Herbert Spencer, J. S. Mill, and T. H. Green* (London, 1891), pp. 86–7.
30 *Collected Works*, xviii. 224. Cf. ibid., xix. 377–8, 393–6, 413–21.
31 Dicey, *Law & Public Opinion*, p. 147 n. 2.

agencies which have a stronger direct interest in or knowledge of the work concerned; and it inhibits the habit of voluntary action by groups of individuals.[32] Bringing this array of considerations to bear on a particular point he said, in a paper on London's water supply written in 1851, that he conceived the 'jealousy which prevails in this country of any extension of the coercive and compulsory powers of the general government' to be 'on the whole, a most salutary sentiment'. It is indeed one of the chief points in which British habits and arrangements are superior to those of such other governments as there may happen to be.[33] And he does not hesitate to say that the basic rule should broadly be one of *laissez faire*. A case of this sort is put firmly and unequivocally in the *Principles of Political Economy*; and there must be some significance to the fact that this blunt statement was never – unlike many others – subsequently amended in the various later editions of that work. Yet the qualifications have to be noted: non-intervention is to be the rule on the whole only; practice should conform to the *laissez faire* principle merely in general.[34] And it transpires that the exceptions admitted are more considerable than the initial formulation of the premiss might appear to permit. For in detailed discussion Mill concedes the need to accept a notable degree of government action that in fact amounts to a very formidable agenda indeed. The range of tasks he reviews under the heading of 'necessary' and 'optional' public functions is, he admits, 'considerably more multifarious' than most people imagine; and it is certainly not possible to draw round them 'very definite lines of demarcation'.[35] He states openly that government cannot be limited to the role of night-watchman simply: on the contrary its ends 'are as comprehensive as those of the social union.'[36]

What specifically does Mill think this array of public activity involves? Some of the matters he reviews are those that would largely have been accepted even by anti-statists like Spencer: defence and the maintenance of internal order; the establishment of a system of courts; the enforcement of contract and the prevention of fraud; the administration of the land as a vital, limited resource; and the control of inheritance and bequest.[37] At the same time he also gives some aspects of these matters a rather wider scope as when he accepts that the law might regulate contracts involving unfavourable terms for one of the parties.[38] And he goes quite beyond the conventional emphasis of classical Liberalism

32 See e.g. *Collected Works*, iii. 882–3, 913–44, 955.
33 ibid., v.435.
34 ibid., iii. 944–5. Cf. 'Auguste Comte and Positivism' (1865), ibid., x. 303.
35 ibid., iii. 800.
36 ibid., iii. 800, 807; xix. 383.
37 ibid., ii. 218–32; iii. 800–3, 887, 959–60, 971.
38 ibid., iii. 802.

when (following Coleridge) he urges that, in the case of people who cannot effectively care for themselves, the *laissez faire* principle breaks down and government as a sort of trustee must assume the broad, hydra-headed task involved.[39] Here Mill clearly looks to the sort of public philanthropy that Spencer so much deplored. It is true that in one context he restricts the application of this supervisory rule to infants, lunatics, and the lower animals and specifically excludes from this provision the conditions of employment of women and *a fortiori* of men. Even so a considerable degree of intervention in economic and social life may be warranted by this *in loco parentis* role.[40] Moreover there are passages in which Mill provides for a still wider application of this task, urging other cases in which the persons concerned are 'incompetent judges' of their needs and situation. In particular he asserts that the 'uncultivated' masses fall into this category and in this regard a more active part for public authority than that formerly permitted by the non-interference principle must result.[41] In these terms he is in the end prepared to accept intervention in such matters as education; the supervision and even public ownership of certain utilities and monopolies including gas, water, and railways; aid to voluntary bodies (such as trade unions); the provision of a minimum of subsistence to those in want; government assisted schemes of emigration; and responsibility for a number of services of 'general convenience' ranging from paving, lighting, and cleaning of streets to subsidizing scientific research, running the Post Office, and building lighthouses.[42] In thus outlining such a substantial agenda for public agencies Mill goes in principle quite a way on the collectivist road. While the interference of government is not to be accepted lightly it must, he believes, be firmly admitted where arguments of general expediency in its favour are strong.[43] He says clearly that

> the intervention of government cannot always practically stop short at the limit which defines the cases intrinsically suitable for it. In particular circumstances of a given age or nation, there is scarcely anything really important to the general interest, which it may not be desirable, or even necessary, that the government should take upon itself, not because private individuals cannot effectually perform it, but because they will not.[44]

He can, therefore, envisage that without state action there may be 'no

39 Cf. ibid., x. 156.
40 ibid., iii. 803, 951–3.
41 ibid., iii. 947–8.
42 For all these functions, see ibid., ii.132–3, 141–2; iii.803–4, 948–50, 955–71; v.433–7, 672, 690; xviii. 301–4.
43 ibid., iii. 804.
44 ibid., iii. 970.

roads, docks, harbours, canals, works of irrigation, hospitals, schools, colleges, printing presses'; and though he thought he had nicely steered between the opposing poles of centralization and independent activity, he none the less opens the way in this fashion for a range of collectivist enterprise of an order calculated to make the strict libertarian blench.[45] It is more than possible that Mill's *Political Economy* was the target Spencer had in mind in his *Social Statics* and elsewhere. And it is no wonder that the Fabians and their like owed perhaps more to Mill than any other mentor.[46]

A tendency to élitism

Furthermore it is by no means clear that Mill would in reality have placed limits on the role of authority where it was cultured and rational. He stresses the desirability of liberty in the context of a society dominated by oppressive forces; but where rule is not so obscurantist the claims of utility might demand its wider application to the detriment of a merely negative freedom. Cowling puts the point thus: '*On Liberty* does not offer safeguards for *individuality*; it is designed to propagate the individuality of the elevated by protecting *them* against the mediocrity of opinion as a whole.'[47] Indeed another aspect of Mill's ideas which bears certain collectivist implications concerns his favourable view of élitism, his thought being deeply touched in this regard by a variety of influences: Plato, a Calvinist belief in the elect, and an array of similar notions derived from people like Carlyle, Coleridge, and St-Simon. His worry about the pressures of public opinion and popular government suggested a crucial role for a kind of secular clerisy (to adopt Coleridge's term).[48] This had a twofold function: to provide leadership and instruction for the uneducated masses who, though increasing in political power, were hardly capable of the rational pursuit of even their own interest; and to maintain secure the lamp of intellectual and moral culture against the enveloping darkness of popular philistinism.[49]

Mill invariably expressed deep concern about the existing character of the labouring masses and the likely consequences of their accession to a major role in the community's life. He mentioned their low level of probity, their lack of a spirit of industry, their deficiency of practical good sense, the improvidence of their breeding habits.[50] He feared, too, that the effects of social advance and of a redistribution of wealth might not necessarily be advantageous, believing, for instance, that as 'soon as

45 ibid., iii. 970; *Autobiography*, pp. 163–4.
46 See e.g. G. B. Shaw *et al.*, *Fabian Essays* (1889; Jubilee edn, London, 1950), pp. 52, 54–5; S. Webb, *Socialism in England* (London, 1890), pp. 19, 85.
47 Cowling, op. cit., p. 100, italics in original.
48 *Collected Works*, x. 123–40, 313–15, 326–7, 344ff.
49 ibid., ii. 104 n.*f–f*; iii. 948 n.*.
50 ibid., ii. 107, 110, 281–2, 351–2, 357–8; xviii. 286–7.

any idea of equality enters the mind of an uneducated English working man, his head is turned by it. When he ceases to be servile, he becomes insolent.'[51] Equally the effects of well-intentioned reform might be unwelcome. He felt, for instance, that government attempts to control prices in the interest of labourers or otherwise to subsidize them might merely achieve their conversion into 'unworking classes'.[52] It was this sort of estimate of the mass of the people, together with similar unflattering appreciations of the intolerance, indolence, unthoughtful-ness, and selfishness of the English as a whole, that led Mill to stress the social and political role of a superior intellectual caste.[53] In *The Spirit of the Age* (1831) he wrote that men should always follow reason so far as that faculty will carry them and should, therefore, cultivate it 'as highly as possible.' But, he went on, reason itself will teach that most men 'must, in the last resort, fall back upon the authority of still more cultivated minds. . . . Society may be said to be in its *natural* state, when worldly power, and moral influence, are habitually and undisputably exercised by the fittest persons whom the existing state of society affords.'[54] Mill also wrote of the need for political questions to be decided not by appeal to 'an uninstructed mass' but by 'a select body, . . . a comparatively few, specially educated for the task.' This will not in itself guarantee good government; but 'good government cannot be had without it.'[55] The specific reference here is to the role of professional civil servants, people like Mill and his father, of course.[56] But this matter of the place and task of an élite is one which notably affects Mill's whole attitude to democracy.

Reflecting on one occasion on de Tocqueville's views, Mill wrote in summary, and in seeming agreement, that in the modern world democracy (which entailed a tendency to equality) was both inevitable and on the whole desirable: but, he added, 'only under certain conditions'.[57] Being convinced that men were not equally endowed with the qualities that make for sound political judgement, he believed it was unwise in the extreme to accept without qualification a system of government in which the majority would have a claim to some kind of ultimate control.[58] A popular assembly was only too likely to reflect,

51 ibid., ii. 109.
52 ibid., iii. 926.
53 ibid., ii.104n., 105; iii.935; xviii.268–9.
54 J. S. Mill, *The Spirit of the Age*, ed. Hayek (Chicago, 1942), pp. 31, 35. Cf. the passage from an article in the *Examiner* (4 July 1832), p. 417, cited in J. H. Burns, 'J. S. Mill and Democracy, 1829–61', J. B. Schneewind (ed.), *Mill: a Collection of Critical Essays* (1968; London, 1969), p.284.
55 'Rationale of Representation' (1835), *Collected Works*, xviii.23–4.
56 Cf. Burns, loc. cit., p.292.
57 *Collected Works*, xviii.158, 159.
58 J. H. Burns, 'Utilitarianism and Democracy', *Philosophical Quarterly*, ix(1959), p.168.

indeed itself to contain, a low grade of opinion and intelligence; it would not be able to function effectively as a legislature or as a body of administrative control; and it will be prone to act despotically and to indulge in 'class legislation' on behalf of the numerical majority instead of attending to the national interest.[59] The practical problem is how to abate these evils without destroying the benefits of democratic government. It was necessary to recognize the ultimate control of the representative assembly but at the same time to secure an appropriate degree of 'deference to' even 'reverence for' the 'superiority of cultivated intelligence' as represented by the executive, 'the acquired knowledge and practised intelligence of a specially trained and experienced Few.'[60]

This sort of concern found expression, of course, in a number of the institutional provisions discussed in the essays on Parliamentary reform and representative government. It was in this context of consideration that Mill supported a system of proportional voting as a way of ensuring the presence in a popular assembly of representatives of minorities and also of what he called 'first' or 'instructed minds', persons of superior intellect, character, and moral power, 'the very *élite* of the country'.[61] The 'function of Antagonism' would be likewise secured. He also would have considered limiting the right to vote in various ways to ensure a high quality electorate, for instance by the use of educational tests, grant of the vote only to taxpayers and those not in receipt of poor relief, and the use of weighted or plural voting based on grades of presumed intelligence.[62] Nor was this an emphasis without its counterpart in other aspects of Mill's thought. For instance, in the ethical theory expounded in the essay on utilitarianism, a concept of qualitative differentiation in pleasure and experience was urged, the 'more valuable' being discerned by 'instructed' persons of 'higher faculties'.[63] Even the essay *On Liberty* has been seen as 'one of the most aristocratic books ever written'.[64] Certainly Mill does urge there the importance of the man of genius and individuality even if he concedes that such a man can only point out the way and cannot make people follow him.[65] There is, too, a brief passage in the original version of the *Political Economy* which suggests perhaps

59 *Collected Works*, xix. 424ff., 434, 448.
60 ibid., x. 109 and n. *l–l*; xix. 432–4, 438–9. It is not without significance that Mill's argument was seized by the Committee on Ministers' Powers to sustain in its report the case for the delegation of legislative and judicial functions to the executive, Ministers' Powers Cttee Rep., 1931–2 (vol. xii), Cmd. 4060, §5, p. 5 n. 4.
61 *Collected Works*, xix. 456–7, 459–60, 468.
62 ibid., xix. 470–9. Burns, in Schneewind, op. cit., reviews the changes and developments in Mill's views on these and cognate matters of political machinery and institutions.
63 *Collected Works*, x. 211–13.
64 R. J. White, intro. to J. F. Stephen, *Liberty, Equality, Fraternity* (1873; Cambridge, 1967), p. 2.
65 *Collected Works*, xviii. 269.

the possible connexion in Mill's mind between this élitism and his growing conviction about the virtues of Socialism (a point to which attention must next be directed). He observes that Owenism at least supposes the democratic control of industry and social wealth and an equal division of their fruits. But he adds that, in 'a more refined and elaborate form of the same scheme' which is associated with St-Simon, 'the administering authority was supposed to be a monarchy or aristocracy, not of birth but of capacity'.[66]

Mill never hankered after rule by an élitist autocracy and did not accept the kind of spiritual despotism that people like Comte seemed to urge. Yet some ghost of these sentiments appears in his views. He was sure no society could progress culturally or otherwise where there was not a group of superior minds who could lead and whose authority would be accepted.[67] Perhaps it is for them that he pleads so persuasively on behalf of liberty of thought and expression and of the sphere of self-regarding independence? What is certain is that for the rest of the populace they will provide tutorial guidance which, while beneficent and far-seeing, is nevertheless a form of social and political direction of a substantive kind.

Conversion to Socialism
There has to be added to these other matters the force of Mill's conversion to 'a qualified Socialism', the doctrine that had (he said in one place) 'become irrevocably one of the leading elements in European politics'. It was, he told Mrs Taylor, *'inextinguishable'*.[68] Once Mill had thought something through and made up his mind, he was willing to adopt the opinion or position achieved however radical or unpopular it might be. His early anti-Malthusianism and his involvement in the movement to spread ideas about birth-control (which on one occasion nearly cost him his career) provide a good instance of this. His attitude to the French revolution of 1830 is another. Effective efforts at Parliamentary and other reforms at home were hardly yet in sight and Mill (then a young man of 24) began, like so many other political observers, to wonder whether change by constitutional means was, in fact, likely or possible. In October 1831 he wrote to his friend John Sterling that

> until the whole of the existing institutions are levelled with the ground, there will be nothing for a wise man to do. . . . I should not care though a revolution were to exterminate every person in Great Britain

66 ibid., ii. 202 n.g–g.
67 e.g. *Autobiography*, p.179.
68 ibid., p.161; *Collected Works*, iii.1007; Mill to Mrs Taylor (c. 31 March 1849), ibid., iii.1031, italics in original.

& Ireland who has £500 a year. Many very amiable persons would perish, but what is the world the better for such amiable persons ?[69]

As Mill's biographer observes, at that time Mill 'was an uncompromising intellectual red.'[70] Certainly he was capable, in his published works as well, of criticism, often outspoken, of existing injustices in society.[71] Of course, many of the ideas that Mill expounded then and later and which have a Socialistic air could have been premeditated on quite orthodox utilitarian or other strictly non-Socialist premises. As noted in the previous volume, Benthamism could bear substantial collectivist implications and did not necessarily entail the view that state intervention was always unacceptable.[72] Moreover Bentham's idea of utility presupposed a notion of equality that might be seen to involve a radical reapportionment of property; this was certainly true of the so-called inequality-minimizing principle.[73] So in this regard Mill's rejection of an absolute right of inheritance and of an unlimited right to property in land were, while radical, not necessarily associated with Socialist tendencies.[74] Bentham, Ricardo, St-Simon, and other non-Socialists had their contribution to make in the formation of such views which are, in any case, also very like those associated with so extreme a libertarian as Herbert Spencer.[75] Likewise Mill's belief that important general services, such as the Post Office and the railways, and basic resources, like coal and iron, should be publicly supervised or owned could be equally founded on utilitarian considerations about the most appropriate way of achieving efficiency and so the greatest happiness.[76]

Nevertheless Sir Leslie Stephen's remark to the effect that in the *Political Economy* Mill was at least on the way to state Socialism is not without foundation.[77] And it is certainly true that, in the later editions of that work, Mill's treatment of Communism and Socialism becomes more sympathetic, in particular in respect of his assessment of the prospect of meeting the difficulties which these systems of economic organization

69 Mill to J. Sterling (20 October 1831), *Collected Works*, xii.78, 84.
70 M. St J. Packe, *The Life of J. S. Mill* (London, 1954), p.104.
71 Among many such passages, see e.g. *Collected Works*, ii.54, 88–9, 207, 367; *Autobiography*, p.145.
72 Vol. i, *The Rise of Collectivism*, ch.5, pp.247–55.
73 e.g. *Collected Works*, x.257–9. And cf. Spencer's comment in *The Principles of Ethics* (London, 1892–3), ii.41.
74 *Collected Works*, ii.218–32; iii.800–1, 887. Cf. ibid., v.450–2, 672, 689–95; x.157–8.
75 On the specific influence of the St-Simonians, see *Autobiography*, pp.141–2, 146.
76 e.g. *Collected Works*, ii.132–3, 141–2.
77 Sir L. Stephen, *The English Utilitarians* (1900; London, 1950), esp. iii.230. See also Lord Robbins, *The Theory of Economic Policy in English Classical Political Economy* (1952; London, 1965), lecture v, and his intro. to vols iv. and v. of Mill's *Collected Works*, esp. vol. iv, pp.xxxviii–xli, where the phases and varying stress of Mill's views on Socialism are outlined.

might be thought to entail.[78] Certainly his conciliatory attitude is clear elsewhere, too, in the study of 'Newman's Political Economy' (1851) for instance.[79] And it is manifest above all perhaps in the posthumously published 'Chapters on Socialism' (1879). His review there of Socialist objections to the existing order of society is both full and concordant: he is clearly not writing a merely descriptive account of the evils of competition and the like, but is himself persuaded of the iniquity, vicious folly, and wastefulness of the existing arrangements. To be sure he admits the Socialist case is often exaggerated or based on ignorance of clear economic fact. But equally he is convinced that much of the criticism is valid and concludes that in many respects the intellectual and moral grounds of Socialism afford the best guiding principles available as to the way in which the present economic system might be improved especially in regard to the rules about property and its distribution.[80] Mill's views on these matters were undoubtedly effective, too, in Socialist circles: the Christian Socialists more than once had it in mind to reprint as propaganda the chapter in the *Political Economy* 'On the Probable Futurity of the Labouring Classes'; and Sidney Webb affirmed that Mill's influence was of great importance in preparing the public mind for change of a Socialist sort.[81] More extreme or persistent individualists equally acknowledged the impact of Mill's concessions on these points: for instance, J. H. Levy (the collaborator of Auberon Herbert) believed that Mill had done more to propagate Socialism 'than any writer of our generation, Karl Marx not excepted', essentially because he had fudged the importance of the principle that liberty and private property 'are inseparable'.[82]

In fact Mill hovers a little uncertainly between the claims of a system based on private property and competition and one based more on common ownership and co-operation: he can see the strengths of each. Yet, while as concerned as anyone about the dangers of paternalism and merely charitable government, the degree of reform he thinks necessary in existing arrangements must undoubtedly enhance the part public agencies have to play in the process of improvement.

Mill held that whereas the laws governing the production of wealth derive from the nature of things and are ineluctable, the distribution of what is produced is 'a matter of human institution solely' and depends, therefore, on 'the laws and customs of society.' So, while not a purely

78 Cf. esp. book II, ch. i, §§3–6 in the earlier and later versions, *Collected Works*, ii.203–14; and app. A, ibid., iii.975–87.
79 ibid., v.441–7.
80 ibid., v.736, 745–6, 748–50, 753.
81 ibid., iii.1026 n.5, 1032; for S. Webb see the references at p.114 n.46 above.
82 J. H. Levy, *The Outcome of Individualism* (1890; 2nd edn, London, n.d. [1890]), pp.4, 11.

arbitrary matter, the property system might take varied forms.[83] The question was what choice to make between the possibilities. Apart from the continuation of the existing system Mill thought there were two, Communism and Socialism, both of which were reactions 'from the miseries and iniquities of a state of much inequality of wealth'.[84] The former doctrine was associated not with Marx but with Owen and his followers.[85] It meant 'the entire abolition of private property' and 'absolute equality in the distribution of the physical means of life and enjoyment'.[86] Socialism, which Mill preferred, did not go this far though it did entail the ownership of land and the instruments of production by communities, associations, or government. Mill believed, in fact, that for the foreseeable future the concepts of private property and competition would continue to prevail with such mitigation of their practical defects as might be possible, in particular by ensuring that more people participated in the benefits of production.[87] The role of Socialist ideas and experiments was in the first instance to act as a stimulus in this respect. In the final outcome the choice between the two systems would, Mill held, depend on which was 'consistent with the greatest amount of human liberty and spontaneity.'[88] His concern for individuality comes through here in the way in which he favoured schemes calculated to aid the development of independence, initiative, and a sense of responsibility by the labouring classes. In agriculture such purposes were to be achieved by a system of peasant proprietorship and small landed properties: not only was the small farm not incompatible with agricultural improvement, it would stimulate hard work, train intelligence, promote forethought and self-control, and so on.[89] In supporting this direction of change Mill was aligning himself with a well-established radical nostrum that had, for instance, also been strongly urged by the Chartist, Feargus O'Connor.[90] With respect to industry, however, the advantages of the large-scale made similar arrangements inappropriate. Nevertheless Mill was of the opinion that the same ends would be achieved by the growth of partnership schemes in the form of either profit-sharing arrangements or the establishment of workers' co-operatives.[91] Later Socialist reaction

83 *Collected Works*, ii.199–200.
84 ibid., ii.202.
85 Mill seems not to have been directly familiar with Marx but only with some Marxist ideas, about which he expressed concern: see L. S. Feuer, 'J. S. Mill and Marxian Socialism', *Journal of the History of Ideas*, x (1949), pp.297–303.
86 *Collected Works*, ii.203.
87 ibid., ii.207–8, 214; v.746–7, 750.
88. ibid., ii.208.
89 ibid., ii.142–52, 278–96; iii.767–8; iv.387–9 n.*n*; v.681–5.
90 M. Beer, *A History of British Socialism* (1919; rev. edn, London, 1953), ii.155–6.
91 *Collected Works*, iii.769–94; iv.382, 385–6; v.743.

to this sort of proposal was on the whole critical if not hostile.[92] But Mill firmly believed that if mankind continued to improve its condition then, in the end, the form of association that would predominate was that 'of the labourers themselves on terms of equality, collectively owning the capital with which they carry on their operations, and working under managers elected and removable by themselves.'[93] There was thus a 'brilliant future reserved for the principle of co-operation' and already it had achieved much practical success.[94] And its main advantage or purpose was not simply the economic development it would sustain but especially the 'moral revolution' it would entail, realizing in industrial life for the first time 'the best aspirations of the democratic spirit'.[95]

In fact what Mill wanted was to retain the virtues and advantages of competition and the sense of responsibility that private ownership at its best could foster together with the elimination of the untoward consequences of inequality, poverty, and ignorance.[96] He believed that the claims of individuality demanded this, as they required in effect change in a Socialist direction that would also sustain them. He wished, therefore, to ensure the multiform development of human nature; but embarking on the reforms necessary must require the action of government: peasant proprietorship and industrial co-operatives will not spring up spontaneously. There is indeed, as Sir Isaiah Berlin once said, a 'very peculiar relationship' between Mill's Socialist and his individualist convictions.[97]

The implications of scientism
Finally there is the matter of Mill's scientism. He reflected a good many of the positivist attitudes of his day: specifically he believed that 'the methods of physical science' were 'the proper models' for political explanation.[98] This was, of course, part of the syndrome of ideas inherited from Bacon and Hobbes and their successors; though, most oddly, Mill seemed to believe it was Bentham who had invented the idea of applying scientific concepts and manners of thinking to matters of morals and politics.[99] All this constitutes, of course, a powerful framework of analysis. Yet it seemed to involve for Mill two difficulties

92 E. Bristow, 'Profit-Sharing, Socialism and Labour Unrest', K. D. Brown (ed.), *Essays in Anti-Labour History: Responses to the Rise of Labour in Britain* (London, 1974), p.263.
93 *Collected Works*, iii.775. Cf. ibid., iii.903–4.
94 ibid, iii.776ff., 785, 895–6, 905–6; iv.382–3 n.*a*.
95 ibid., iii.791–3, 903, 906.
96 On the advantages of competition, see e.g., ibid., iii.794–5.
97 Sir I. Berlin, *John Stuart Mill and the Ends of Life* (London, n.d. [1960?]), p.12 n.1.
98 *Autobiography*, p.140.
99 *Collected Works*, x.83, 87.

in connexion with his libertarian sense of the fundamental significance of individuality and freedom.

For one thing if, through a proper conception of scientific method, the laws of human character and behaviour are elicited then it may seem that, like anything else, human action is predictable. It is thereby determined and the realm of freedom of choice is to all intents and purposes eliminated, human beings becoming no more than things. Mill's own concern at this prospect revealed by the implications of the naturalistic view was one of the factors involved in the recurrence of his mental perturbation:

> . . . during the later returns of my dejection, the doctrine of what is called Philosophical Necessity weighed on my existence like an incubus. I felt as if I was scientifically proved to be the helpless slave of antecedent circumstances; as if my character and that of all others had been formed for us by agencies beyond our control, and was wholly out of our own power.[100]

Of course, this is a problem only if there is a single, unique mode of thought and analysis, that modelled on the determinism of the natural sciences. If, however, this is simply one framework of reference among a number of equipollent perspectives then the difficulty disappears: what is causally determined from the scientific point of view is seen quite differently, and equally legitimately, in terms of choice from the moral or practical standpoint. The full realization of this way out lay with the philosophical idealists; though Mill had indeed a sufficient inkling of the issue to realize that a means of escape from the dilemma which worried him was to suggest a radical discontinuity of some kind between 'conformity to nature' and questions of 'right and wrong'.[101] Nevertheless to the extent that the problem remained it constituted a standing threat to the reality of individual freedom.

Then there is the implication of the cognate suggestion he makes in the *Logic* that, despite the deterministic corollaries of his method, the will may be conceived as rising in some cases above the causal pressure of circumstance and habit.[102] But the point relates here to the élitist possibilities of Mill's thought mentioned earlier. Like Hobbes, who had a vision of some men of magnanimity to whom the all-motivating fear of death was less significant than honour, Mill conceives of persons of superior mind and energy who equally rise above the common herd.[103] And they, in Benthamite mode, may tutorially mould society on the

---

100 *Autobiography*, p.143. See the discussion of Mill's attempt to avoid the determinist position in A. Ryan, *J. S. Mill* (London, 1974), pp.84–7.
101 *Collected Works*, x.400. Cf. ibid., x.459.
102 ibid., viii. 836ff.; *Autobiography*, pp.144–5.
103 *Collected Works*, x.393–7.

proper principles of 'philosophical legislation'.[104] The 'scientific' politician, he says in an early paper, as opposed to the quack or mere empiric, knows and applies the general principles of cause and effect by which the phenomena of human society are regulated.[105] But what then of individual freedom, that of the puppet-master apart?

The tension

In Mill's writings there is thus to be found a stress on individuality, on self-development, and a cognate fear of excessive external authority that might hinder this process of improvement; but, as well, side by side with this libertarian emphasis, there is recognition of the necessary limits of individual freedom and especially of a need for enhanced elements of collective action. The presence in his thought of this latter strand of ideas marks his position as potentially very different indeed from that of his younger contemporary Herbert Spencer who would never have made so many concessions of this statist kind. Undoubtedly Mill's basic sympathies are of a libertarian sort, but equally clearly he looks to a more 'mixed' or intermediate situation than Spencer would have found palatable or, indeed, regarded as possible if the evolutionary process was to be sustained.

The dimension of doubt or ambiguity in Mill's mind is brought out in the following passage, taken from the preface to the third edition (1852) of the *Principles of Political Economy*:

> It appears to me that the great end of social improvement should be to fit mankind by cultivation, for a state of society combining the greatest personal freedom with that just distribution of the fruits of labour, which the present laws of property do not profess to aim at. Whether, when this state of mental and moral cultivation shall be attained, individual property in some form (though a form very remote from the present) or community of ownership in the instruments of production and a regulated division of the produce, will afford the circumstances most favourable to happiness, and best calculated to bring human nature to its greatest perfection, is a question which must be left, as it safely may, to the people of that time to decide. Those of the present are not competent to decide it.[106]

Clearly the goal Mill envisages is in principle the same as Spencer's: the greatest possible happiness of human kind and the swiftest possible progress to this desired end. But the means implied by Mill as perhaps

104 ibid., x.9–10.
105 ibid., iv.111.
106 ibid., vol.ii, p.xciii. Cf. *Autobiography*, p.196.

necessary to this purpose are, in the last resort, in complete and utter contrast. Indeed the only real, albeit important, reservation Mill has to what he understood as Socialism, 'regarded as an ultimate result of human progress', was 'the unprepared state of mankind in general, and of the labouring classes in particular' for this consummation.[107] With Mill, then, Liberalism and Socialism (in H. O. Pappe's phrase) 'entered into a peculiar marriage'; as, to be just, Mill's individualism undoubtedly sobered and tempered the radical utopianism that Socialist doctrine in Britain might otherwise have become.[108]

A similar and perhaps equally hesitant step was taken in a collectivist direction by other and rather different nineteenth-century Liberals, by T. H. Green and some of his fellow Idealists.

T. H. GREEN AND POSITIVE FREEDOM

It is not true to say that Green gave a new content to liberalism; events themselves had of necessity done that. But it is, I think, true to say that he gave to the idea of positive liberalism its letters of credit.
H. J. LASKI, *The Decline of Liberalism*, 1940, p.11

Although by trade an academic Green was one of those curious members of the breed who feel prompted to be practically involved in politics: he lived for questions affecting citizenship.[109] And these concerns, though different, were by no means unconnected in his mind. His preoccupation with the need to lead a useful life was stimulated, or at least justified, by his philosophical thought as this, in turn, was permeated and sustained by his strong sense of moral and political duty. His beliefs and reputation in this regard provided the model for the Rev. Mr Grey, a character whose omnipresent influence presides over the course of events recounted in Mrs Humphry Ward's novel *Robert Elsmere* and through which he became more widely known perhaps than through his own works.[110] He is described as 'an eager politician' who indulged in 'a good deal of talk about politics' and showed great interest 'in the needs and training of that broadening democracy on which the future of England rests'. He was a thinker who never shirked action in the name of thought and for whom conduct was always 'the first reality.' Green was indeed one of those to whom the book was dedicated in the 'love of God and the

107　*Collected Works*, vol.ii, p.xciii.
108　H. O. Pappe, *John Stuart Mill and the Harriet Taylor Myth* (Melbourne, 1960), p.43.
109　Cf. Mrs Humphry Ward, *A Writer's Recollections* (London, 1918), pp.132–3; B. Bosanquet, preface to Green's *Lectures on the Principles of Political Obligation* (1882; London, 1948), p.vi.
110　W. S. Peterson, *Victorian Heretic: Mrs Humphry Ward's 'Robert Elsmere'* (Leicester, 1976), p.134.

service of man'.[111]

So far as party allegiance was concerned Green was a fervent Liberal and an active one. He appeared on political platforms to support the cause and was concerned in particular with two of the major social issues of the day, educational improvement and temperance reform. He was an elected member of Oxford City Council and the local school board; and his standing was such that at one time he was under considerable pressure to become a Liberal candidate in the Parliamentary elections. His opinions were of the radical kind and always had been. In his younger days he had thought nothing of travelling a long way to attend meetings of a congenial political flavour and he admired many of the policies of Bright and Cobden. Dicey, who knew Green well, commented on this affinity of ideas while properly stressing the notably different process of argument involved.[112] Given this sort of context, the range and nature of his opinions are hardly surprising, therefore: acceptance of free trade, an inclination to pacifism and internationalism, hostility towards the traditional land-owning classes, an assertion of the case for extending the franchise and cognate political reform, a strong belief in the importance of individual self-development, and a stress on the possession of private property as a means essential to the growth of character. And although he was the son of an Anglican clergyman there was, too, much in Green that marked the influence of religious dissent, a spirit which has so often been important in the development of Liberal thinking. As Professor Richter says, Green always displayed 'a persistent sympathy for the Puritans and their Nonconformist posterity'; J. A. Symonds had called him a 'philosophical Puritan'.[113]

But in two important respects Green departed from the then dominant syndrome of Liberal ideas and in so doing symbolized, perhaps more than any other thinker of his day, a turning away from the old individualism.[114] First of all he envisaged a role for the state that

111 Mrs H. Ward, *Robert Elsmere* (1888; London, 1889), dedication and pp. 60, 535. Green's lay sermons are specifically cited, ibid., pp. 58, 330, 355–6. According to E. H. Jones, *Mrs. Humphry Ward* (New York, 1973), pp. 158–9, Green also appears as 'the wise Sorell' in Mrs Ward's *Lady Connie* (1916) but I have not read that novel.

112 On this affinity, especially with Bright, see R. L. Nettleship, *Memoir of Thomas Hill Green* (London, 1906), pp. 23–4, 57, 169–70; also M. Richter, *The Politics of Conscience: T. H. Green and His Age* (London, 1964), pp. 79, 269–73, 276, 362–5. Dicey's remark is in R. S. Rait (ed.), *Memorials of Albert Venn Dicey Being Chiefly Letters and Diaries* (London, 1925), pp. 37–8.

113 Richter, op. cit., p. 41; J. A. Symonds to Mrs T. H. Green (3 November 1886) in H. M. Schueller and R. L. Peters (eds), *Letters of John Addington Symonds* (Detroit, 1969), iii. 176. Cf. E. Barker, 'The Discredited State', *Political Quarterly*, (no. 5, February 1915), p. 104.

114 H. J. Laski, 'The Leaders of Collectivist Thought', H. Grisewood *et al.*, *Ideas and Beliefs of the Victorians: an Historic Revaluation of the Victorian Age* (1949; Dutton Paperbacks, 1966), p. 421.

potentially went far beyond that normally conceded and helped, therefore, to destroy the idea that government intervention is an evil thing. For instance, not long before he died in 1882 he made a speech to the Oxford North Ward Liberal Association in which he said that his idea of a true Liberal programme was 'the removal of all obstructions which the law can remove to the free development of English citizens': a wide invitation indeed. And he indicated the link between this view and traditional radical doctrine when he added that, so long as Parliament was merely 'a sort of club of rich men', it would have no interest, as it should, in helping 'the struggling and suffering classes of society.'[115] Then secondly the rationale of the wider function thus attributed to public authority was founded on a positive hostility to utilitarianism which was dismissed, so to say, as a mere insular anachronism in the oecumenical history of thought.[116] In this important way Green differed formally and substantially from both Spencer and Mill, the reigning saints of Liberalism at the time, who, for all the differences between them, were alike apostles of the greatest happiness principle. In *Robert Elsmere* Mrs Ward comments on this reaction against the 'overdriven rationalism' which had long dominated the intellectual scene. It was, she said, beginning to be recognized 'with a great burst of enthusiasm and astonishment' that, after all, Mill and Spencer 'had not said the last word on all things in heaven and earth.'[117]

The ground of Green's repudiation of these Liberal orthodoxies was that they were narrow and incomplete in two vital respects: philosophically they were based on a mere empirical naturalism; and ethically they reflected an unsatisfactory hedonism. Basically, and like so many of his contemporaries, what Green was trying to do was save the essentials of Christian-based moral belief from the sceptical and undermining effects of developments in the natural sciences, Biblical criticism, and other scholarship. Much of this learning, rationally unassailable as it seemed, cast substantial doubt on many of the traditional elements of faith especially so far as these either depended on revelation, miracle, or other supernatural agency of merely quondam occurrence, or were associated with particular theological doctrines or ecclesiastical institutions that appeared increasingly indefensible or of diminishing appeal.[118] Spencer (as already noted) had felt the same tension or hiatus. But whereas he was content to sweep ultimate questions into that limbo he called 'the

---

115 Nettleship, op. cit., pp. 183–4. Cf. H. J. Laski, 'The State in the New Social Order' (1922), *Studies in Law and Politics* (London, 1932), p. 132.
116 I take this phrase from W. F. Monypenny and G. E. Buckle, *The Life of Benjamin Disraeli* (1910–20; new edn, London, 1929), i. 312.
117 Mrs H. Ward, *Robert Elsmere*, pp. 62–3.
118 R. L. Nettleship (ed.), *Works of Thomas Hill Green* (London, 1885–8), iii. 240–3,

Unknowable' and, for the rest, to rely for understanding (or at least justification) on the procedures and concepts of natural science, Green for his part had in view no less than a restoration of the essential, that is the ethical, principles of Christianity but on rational grounds. Mrs Ward, in a letter to Gladstone, told how after a 'long intellectual travail' Green found 'the miraculous Christian story was untenable'; but equally it was with great difficulty that he gave it up and he continued to cling 'to all the forms and associations of the old belief with a wonderful affection.'[119] And Green himself described to a friend, Henry Scott Holland, his faith in 'the new Christianity' in which God spoke not authoritatively through the priest but 'rationally thro' the educated conscience'.[120] This form of religion which was intended, in Jowett's phrase, to be 'independent of the accidents of time and space', was explored through a surrogate theology elaborated within the framework of Idealist philosophy which was indeed admirably suited for the purpose.[121] For this philosophy, while recognizing the great importance of science, did not allow it to dominate the entire scene. Instead reason was reconciled with traditional morality and in a context of thought which emphasized the positive role of society in the process of individual fulfilment. By the exploration and development of these philosophical themes Green was able, therefore, to attempt the rational combination of the ethos of Christian morality and the duties and possibilities of full and expanding citizenship under the aegis of an active public agency. In this sense his political ideas and the framework of philosophical theology within which they were premeditated are closely linked. The latter indeed gives the political thought its intellectual life and character.[122] Here attention must naturally concentrate on the more programmatic aspects of Green's views especially that concerning the extent of state intervention he envisaged and promoted, though enough will be said of the other matters to give some indication of the broad tendency of theological and philosophical argument underlying the political prescription or, at least, associated with it by way of justification.

256–60, 263–4; T. H. Green, *Prolegomena to Ethics* (1883; 4th edn, Oxford, 1899), §1 (p.2).

119 Mrs H. Ward to W. E. Gladstone (17 April 1888), cited in J. P. Trevelyan, *The Life of Mrs. Humphry Ward* (London, 1923), p.63.

120 Green to H. S. Holland (9 January 1869), in S. Paget (ed.), *Henry Scott Holland . . . , Memoir and Letters* (London, 1921), p.32. Cf. the remarks in Mrs Ward's *Robert Elsmere*, pp.408–11, 532; also Mrs Ward's own 'Unbelief and Sin' (1881), cited in Jones, *Mrs. Humphry Ward*, p.54.

121 For Jowett's remark, see E. Abbott and L. Campbell, *The Life and Letters of Benjamin Jowett* (London, 1897), ii.77.

122 Nettleship, *Memoir*, pp.1–2, 24–34.

The moral basis

For Green God did not reveal himself in the ways conventionally understood and accepted. Instead, an alternative perspective of a rather Burkeian (or Hegelian) kind was proposed:

> God is for ever reason; and his communication, his revelation, is reason; not, however, abstract reason, but reason as taking a body from, and giving life to, the whole system of experience which makes the history of man. The revelation, therefore, is not made in a day, or a generation, or a century. The divine mind touches, modifies, becomes the mind of man, through a process of which mere intellectual conception is only the beginning, but of which the gradual complement is an unexhausted series of spiritual discipline through all the agencies of social life.[123]

God is thus immanent in the world, in all forms of human experience and expression, and His nature is, therefore, more fully unfolded as time goes by: revelation involves the concept of potential and of progress towards it. And from the ethical point of view (entailing questions of personal conduct and decision) the key notion is the similar one of development by which God makes himself manifest in the individual. 'Moral action . . . is an expression at once of conscious contrast between an actual and possible self, and of an impulse to make that possible self real; . . . it is a process of self-realisation, ...'[124] Such transformation of man and so of his world is the highest Christian duty. Nor can the improved self be achieved either by some kind of monastic withdrawal or through the pursuit of merely selfish goals. Morality can never be a matter simply of doing what one likes or satisfying momentary wants and desires; man needs to be delivered from self-seeking and sensuous judgement.[125] Consequently Green was a harsh critic of utilitarianism.[126]

But granted that moral life rests on the notion of a continuing perfectibility, how can what is involved be made concrete or particularized? A first approximation to the detailed specification of good conduct is to be found in the mores of society itself which is 'the condition of all development of our personality'.[127] Human consciousness has created all those institutions by which 'our elementary moralisation is brought about' and through which the will is initially transformed: society is thus 'a complex organisation of life, with laws

123 *Works*, iii.239–40. Cf. *Prolegomena to Ethics*, §180 (pp.213–14).
124 *Works*, iii.224.
125 ibid., iii.234, 269–70; *Prolegomena to Ethics*, IV.ii.
126 See the admirable summary in A. J. M. Milne, 'The Idealist Criticism of Utilitarian Social Philosophy', *European Journal of Sociology*, viii (1967), pp.319–31.
127 *Prolegomena to Ethics*, §183 (p.217). Cf. ibid., §§190 (pp.225–6), 217 (p.260).

and institutions, with relationships, courtesies, and charities, with arts and graces through which the perfection is to be attained.'[128] Again:

> So long as a man presents himself to himself as possibly existing in some better state than that in which he actually is – and that he does so is implied even in his denial that the possibility can be realised – there is something in him to respond to whatever moralising influences society in any of its forms or institutions, themselves the gradual outcome through the ages of man's free effort to better himself, may bring to bear on him. The claims of the family, the call of country, the pleading of the preacher, the appeal of the Church . . . , may at any time awaken in him that which we call (in one sense, truly) a new life, but which is yet the continued working of the spirit which has never ceased to work in, upon, and about him.[129]

Green continually refers in this way to the formative influence of 'the organic life of custom and institution'.[130] And it follows, he believes, that a sense of active, social duty is a vital part of the process not simply of communal improvement but also of self-realization: 'citizenship only makes the moral man'.[131] As he wrote to his friend Henry Scott Holland: 'True citizenship "as unto the Lord" (which includes all morality) I reckon higher than "saintliness" in the technical sense.'[132]

This transformation of the will of the individual in a social context is a continuing and variable matter. Reading Green's works one has no sense that he expects to establish a certain or mistake-proof direction of moral advance. But he gives guidance enough about 'what is of permanent moral value in the institutions of civil life, as established in Europe' and how these institutions contribute to 'the possibility of morality in the higher sense of the term'.[133] This viewpoint rests initially on a positive concept of 'freedom' and emerges in a compatible view of law and its function.

Freedom and the province of law

Green tackles head-on the issue how to sustain a proper conception of freedom (and so of self-development) in the face of a range of state activity being increased in response to the social and other problems of the day. Following Kant and Rousseau he makes an important distinction between two types or notions of liberty. He rejects as

128 *Works*, iii. 270; ii. 329 (§23).
129 *Prolegomena to Ethics*, §112 (pp. 131–2).
130 e.g. ibid., §§180 (pp. 213–14), 183 (pp. 216–17); *Works*, iii. 277.
131 From a speech on Parliamentary reform (1868), cited in Nettleship, *Memoir*, p. 170.
132 Green to H. S. Holland (29 December 1868), cited in Paget, op. cit., p. 29.
133 *Works*, ii. 337 (§5).

incomplete the negative view (as held, for instance, by Spencer and, for much of the time, by most of the utilitarians) that freedom is simply the absence of external impediment or restraint.[134] The deficiency in this notion is that it says nothing about the character of the objects sought. In the unconfined circumstances envisaged, a man might (says Green) will either the 'satisfaction of animal appetite or an act of heroic self-sacrifice'. Properly, real freedom depends on the purpose of activity: not the satiation of desire but rather the gradual realization of a better self.[135]

> . . . when we . . . speak of freedom, we . . . do not mean merely freedom from restraint or compulsion. We do not mean merely freedom to do as we like irrespectively of what it is that we like. We do not mean a freedom that can be enjoyed by one man or one set of men at the cost of a loss of freedom to others. When we speak of freedom as something to be so highly prized, we mean a positive power or capacity of doing or enjoying something worth doing or enjoying, and that, too, something that we do or enjoy in common with others.[136]

In Green's view, then, the mere removal of external restraint or compulsion – as required by the pursuit of maximum freedom of contract or general *laissez faire* – constitutes an inadequate policy because there is no guarantee that the opportunities created will be used for purposes that are worthwhile. Social and legal restraint of 'the momentary inclinations of the individual' may thereby be implied.[137] For instance, in discussing the temperance question Green wished to recommend 'a large inter-ference with the liberty of the individual to do as he likes in the matter of buying and selling alcohol.' And he would justify this intervention

> on the simple ground of the recognised right on the part of society to prevent men from doing as they like, if, in the exercise of their peculiar tastes in doing as they like, they create a social nuisance. There is no right to freedom in the purchase and sale of a particular commodity, if the general result of allowing such freedom is to detract from freedom in the higher sense, from the general power of men to make the best of themselves.[138]

Of course, not all restraint is morally beneficial; and, in some social and political circumstances, existing laws and institutions may positively

---

134 This rejection of the negative conception of freedom was implicit in some of the contemporary criticisms of Mill's *On Liberty*: see J. C. Rees, *Mill and His Early Critics* (Leicester, 1956), pp. 14–16.

135 *Works*, ii. 321–6 (§§15–20). Cf. the contrast Green draws between 'the carnal interests of the world' and 'the universal spiritual force', ibid., iii. 364.

136 ibid., iii. 370–1.

137 ibid., ii. 428–30 (§§114–16). Cf. ibid., iii. 371.

138 ibid., iii. 383.

inhibit the possibility of personal realization to such a degree indeed that substantial, even revolutionary, change might be required to remedy or improve the prevailing state of affairs.[139] Similarly excessive supervision of a paternalistic kind might well hamper individual self-development because it could stultify the sense of initiative and responsibility. It has always to be recognized that ethical fulfilment is an internal or personal matter and that society and government cannot in the end make people moral.[140] Social and legal controls can make men do things; but not necessarily for the right reasons. These limitations notwithstanding, society can at least create an environment in which it is more feasible for its citizens to pursue a proper course of action and, so far as it does this, it is morally justified.[141] Thus the province of law concerns whatever 'is really necessary to the maintenance of the material conditions essential to the existence and perfection of human personality.'[142] In urging this positive view of freedom Green was not introducing a major departure of either thought or practice. The idea was certainly not unprecedented and had been familiar from the Greeks on; moreover, it had come into common use not least in respect of the agitation against the slave-trade and in favour of its prohibition. As it has (in this context) been observed, 'if there had ever been any doubt whether it was within the province of the state to outlaw any commercial activity, the anti-slave trade movement had dispelled it'.[143] To this extent, Green was simply following existing opinion rather than creating or leading it.[144]

Green develops his theme about the function of law through the elaboration of a doctrine of rights, these being the mutually recognized conditions of realizing a moral end in society; the ways, that is, in which an individual finds God through the fulfilment of his personality. The manner in which this doctrine bears on the matter of government intervention may be exemplified by reference to Green's discussion of the right of the state in regard to property.[145]

Green accepts the institution of private property because the acquisition of goods by the individual is an important way in which he

139 ibid., ii. 339–40 (§9), 416ff. (§§100ff.), 442–3 (§132).
140 ibid., ii. 345–6 (§18).
141 ibid., ii. 338–9 (§7).
142 ibid., ii. 341 n.1 (§11) citing the German jurist Henrici.
143 B. Harrison, *Drink and the Victorians: The Temperance Question in England, 1815–1872* (London, 1971), p. 200.
144 Cf. ibid., pp. 202–10 on the way Green, in effect, gave theoretical expression to ideas already in common use. I owe this and the previous reference to Mr P. Nicholson of the University of York who also drew my attention to *Prolegomena to Ethics*, §327, in which Green makes clear that the role of the philosopher is not to supply a moral dynamic but to analyse and understand the implications of an actual, already declared, spiritual nature in man.
145 *Works*, ii. 517–35 (§§211–32).

extends his personality, gives reality to his ideas and wishes, and develops a sense of responsibility. Moreover appropriation of this kind is in principle recognized by others because they, too, wish to hold similar means of self-satisfaction. There arises in society, therefore, a common consciousness of the conditions of this realization and a mutual recognition of the right to property and its regulation by custom and law.[146] As an aid (one supposes) to their own fulfilment, Green and his wife both owned investments: for instance, the schedule of property held by the trustees of their marriage settlement was valued at over £17,000 and produced an income of more than £700 a year.[147]

There was, however, a considerable problem in the fact that property is very unequally distributed and that very many people own hardly anything at all:

> . . . the actual result of the development of rights of property in Europe, as part of its general political development, has so far been a state of things in which all indeed *may* have property, but great numbers in fact cannot have it in that sense in which alone it is of value, viz. as a permanent apparatus for carrying out a plan of life, for expressing ideas of what is beautiful, or giving effect to benevolent wishes. In the eye of the law they have rights of appropriation, but in fact they have not the chance of providing means for a free moral life, of developing and giving reality or expression to a good will, an interest in social well-being. A man who possesses nothing but his powers of labour and who has to sell these to a capitalist for bare daily maintenance, might as well, in respect of the ethical purposes which the possession of property should serve, be denied rights of property altogether.[148]

Now Green is prepared to accept that there must be some inequality in the distribution of property (because of differences of ability, assiduity, and need); and if men are to exploit their faculties and opportunities there has to be freedom of trade and bequest as well.[149] He is convinced that if there is indeed 'an impoverished and reckless proletariate' with only its labour power to sell, this is not simply because private property as such exists or because the accumulation of wealth occurs. On the contrary the indirect benefits of this latter process may be substantial (as with increased employment opportunities); and even the 'large masses of

146 ibid., ii. 518–23 (§§213–17), 526 (§221).
147 See the list abstracted from the Green papers at Balliol College, Oxford, in C. Harvie et al. (eds), *Industrialisation and Culture, 1830–1914* (London, 1970), pp. 86–7. Allowing for changes in the purchasing power of the pound since 1869, the current equivalent of this income would be over £11,000 p.a.
148 *Works*, ii. 525 (§220), italics in original.
149 ibid., ii. 527–30 (§§223–5).

hired labourers' may find possibilities of social and moral advancement through saving, the activities of co-operative and benefit societies, and acquiring at least some possessions of their own.[150] Other factors than private property as such or the legal and social paraphernalia of capitalism must, therefore, be the cause of the terrible conditions in which many people lived. And Green's examination of this matter has an intriguing air of old-fashioned radicalism about it. It is indeed an historical argument which Green now introduced into the process of abstract moral discussion, specifically an attack on the landed aristocracy and gentry cast in terms very like those deployed in many quarters during the early modern period and after, and associated in particular with the concept of the 'Norman Yoke'. No doubt these themes are not unrelated to his considerable interest in the English Revolution of the seventeenth century: he was certainly familiar, for instance, with the anti-Normanism of the Diggers.[151]

In Green's view, then, the root material cause of contemporary social and economic difficulties was not the right to private property as such but the particular distribution of it that prevailed. Land was the one resource that was limited and could not be increased. The cause of the trouble was its ownership by that plutocracy in feudal form which governed modern England. The descendants of the Norman invaders still held the kingdom in thrall, the labouring classes being trained in habits of serfdom, to a life of forced labour relieved only by charity, and with little opportunity to develop any sense of personal fulfilment or family responsibility.[152]

It is difficult to summarise the influences to which is due the fact that in all the chief seats of population in Europe the labour-market is constantly thronged with men who are too badly reared and fed to be efficient labourers; who for this reason, and from the competition for employment with each other, have to sell their labour very cheap; who have thus seldom the means to save, and whose standard of living and social expectation is so low that, if they have the opportunity of saving, they do not use it, and keep bringing children into the world at a rate which perpetuates the evil. It is certain, however, that these influences have no necessary connection with the maintenance of the right of individual property and consequent unlimited accumulation of capital, though they no doubt are connected with that régime of

---

150 ibid., ii. 530–1 (§§226–7).
151 ibid., iii. 341. The fullest history of these particular political notions is to be found in C. Hill's 'The Norman Yoke' (1954), *Puritanism and Revolution: Studies in Interpretation of the English Revolution of the 17th Century* (London, 1958), ch. 3. For Green's abhorrence of class privilege (despite his own substantial unearned income), see E. Caird, preface to the 5th edn (1906), *Prolegomena*, p. vii.
152 Cf. *Works*, iii. 364.

force and conquest by which existing governments have been established, – governments which do not indeed create the rights of individual property, any more than any other rights, but which serve to maintain them. It must always be borne in mind that the appropriation of land by individuals has in most countries – probably in all where it approaches completeness – been originally effected, not by the expenditure of labour or the results of labour on the land, but by force. The original landlords have been conquerors.[153]

The only justification for the appropriation of the earth by proprietors is that it contributes more substantially than any other arrangement to social well-being than if it were held in common. But the landlords have exploited their privileges to the detriment of others, have turned fertile land into forest, evicted tenants and even depopulated whole areas, built houses that were bad or erected in unhealthy places, stopped up means of communication, and the like. The necessary restraints on the use of land which the public interest requires have been pretty much ignored.[154]

Thus the whole history of the ownership of land in Europe has been of a kind to lead to the agglomeration of a proletariate, neither holding nor seeking property, wherever a sudden demand has arisen for labour in mines or manufactures. This at any rate was the case down to the epoch of the French Revolution; and this, which brought to other countries deliverance from feudalism, left England, where feudalism had previously passed into unrestrained landlordism, almost untouched. And while those influences of feudalism and landlordism which tend to throw a shiftless population upon the centres of industry have been left unchecked, nothing till quite lately was done to give such a population a chance of bettering itself, when it had been brought together. Their health, housing, and schooling were unprovided for. They were left to be freely victimised by deleterious employments, foul air, and consequent craving for deleterious drinks. When we consider all this, we shall see the unfairness of laying on capitalism or the free development of individual wealth the blame which is really due to the arbitrary and violent manner in which rights over land have been acquired and exercised, and to the failure of the state to fulfil those functions which under a system of unlimited private ownership are necessary to maintain the conditions of a free life.[155]

Because of such considerations Green believed that there ought to be a

153 ibid., ii. 531–2 (§228). Cf. the interesting parallel provided by the passages cited in E. Halévy, *Thomas Hodgskin* (1903; trans. edn, London, 1956), pp. 121–2.
154 *Works*, ii. 532–3 (§229).
155 ibid., ii. 533–4 (§230).

special degree of public control over rights of property in land.[156] In a speech on the implications of Parliamentary reform which he made in February 1868, he said a change in the land laws ought to be one of the main tasks of any new legislature:

> Our present system of great estates, as I believe, gives a false set to society from top to bottom. It causes exaggerated luxury at the top, flunkeyism in the middle, poverty and recklessness at the bottom. There is no remedy for this poverty and recklessness as long as those who live on the land have no real and permanent interest in it. . . . It is this debased population that gluts the labour-market, and constantly threatens to infect the class of superior workmen, who can only secure themselves, as I believe, by such a system of protection as is implied in the better sort of trades-union. This is an evil which no individual benevolence can cure. Ten thousand soup-kitchens are unavailing against it. It can only be cured by such legislation as will give the agricultural labourer some real interest in the soil.[157]

Yet Green was not only concerned with questions concerning the accumulation and distribution of landed property crucial though these matters were. The 'power of class-interests' had kept the operation of the law too cribbed and confined whereas it was obvious that state intervention was required on a wider basis.[158] Thus he welcomed the emergence of a broad spirit of reform, of a 'great system' of legislation that necessarily interfered with the freedom of individuals to do as they would with their own in the course of providing a wider range of positive opportunities for all.[159] It is doubtless, he said, 'a prime business of government' to uphold the sanctity of contracts, 'but it is no less its business to provide against contracts being made, which, from the helplessness of one of the parties to them, instead of being a security for freedom, become an instrument of disguised oppression.'[160] In this context Green goes on to indicate a range of circumstances in which society is 'plainly within its right' to restrain people's actions in the interests not merely of the present but also of future generations. For instance it ought to regulate conditions of work in factories and mines to prevent circumstances fatal to health or otherwise inimical to personal fulfilment and the making of a free contribution to social good. Equally the law must interfere with contracts to buy or rent 'unwholesome

---

156 ibid., ii. 534–5 (§231). He was, however, dubious about the idea that 'unearned increment' should accrue to the state, ibid., ii. 535 (§232).
157 Cited in Nettleship, *Memoir*, p.171.
158 *Works*, ii. 515–16 (§210); iii. 377ff.
159 ibid., iii. 368–72.
160 ibid., iii. 382.

dwellings' and with such matters as the 'traffic in deleterious commodities'. Society must obviously be interested, too, in 'the growth of
population relatively to the means of subsistence'.[161] Dicey commented
on Green's intense preoccupation with 'the evil of pauperism' and the
'sufferings of the poor' and his continual stress on the capacity for
growth of all persons, including those in the labouring classes, and the
need to develop this.[162] Perhaps the key for Green in this connexion was
the provision of adequate educational facilities. A person cannot be held
to be free to develop his faculties without 'a command of certain
elementary arts and knowledge' so that the state may legitimately, and
must, 'prevent children from growing up in that kind of ignorance which
practically excludes them from a free career in life'.[163] Green was
convinced the existing educational system in Britain was defective
because it was organized on class lines and that a solution required action
in behalf of the community as a whole.[164] He had been an assistant
commissioner to the Schools Inquiry from 1864; and he was a supporter
of the National Education League and spoke for it in favour of
compulsory attendance, unsectarian instruction, and the maintenance of
schools out of public funds.

In sum:

> Our modern legislation . . . with reference to labour, and edu-
> cation, and health, involving as it does manifold interference with
> freedom of contract, is justified on the ground that it is the business of
> the state, not indeed directly to promote moral goodness, for that,
> from the very nature of moral goodness, it cannot do, but to maintain
> the conditions without which a free exercise of the human faculties is
> impossible.[165]

It followed that Green had little sympathy for those Liberals who were
always carping about 'over-legislation' though he might have joined in
complaints about excessive centralizing tendencies.[166] This would
perhaps have satisfied critics like Toulmin Smith at least to some degree;
but not Herbert Spencer and his extreme libertarian followers. Green's
complete rejection of their point of view is clearly revealed in his concern
for the condition of the 'untaught and under-fed denizen of a London
yard with gin-shops on the right hand and on the left'; and is indicated, as

161 ibid., ii. 515–16 (§210); iii. 368–9, 373.
162 A. V. Dicey to Mrs Green (17 September 1882), cited in Richter, op. cit., pp. 81–2;
     ibid., p. 77. Cf. *Prolegomena*, §217 *ad fin.* (p. 260), and *Works*, iii. 372.
163 *Works*, iii. 373–4. Cf. Nettleship, *Memoir*, pp. 62, 174.
164 *Works*, iii. 390, 403, 432, 458.
165 ibid., iii. 374.
166 ibid., iii. 374–5.

well, in the following passage from his lecture on 'Liberal Legislation and Freedom of Contract' (1881):

> Sometimes it was the argument that the state had no business to interfere with liberties of the individual. Sometimes it was the dilatory plea that the better nature of man would in time assert itself, and that meanwhile it would be lowered by compulsion. Happily a sense of the facts and necessities of the case got the better of the delusive cry of liberty. Act after act was passed preventing master and workman, parent and child, house-builder and householder, from doing as they pleased, with the result of a great addition to the real freedom of society. The spirit of self-reliance and independence was not weakened by those acts. Rather it received a new development. The dead weight of ignorance and unhealthy surroundings, with which it would otherwise have had to struggle, being partially removed by law, it was more free to exert itself for higher objects.[167]

Influence

Clearly in many respects Green's conclusions about the role of the state and the province and function of law were not too dissimilar from those of J. S. Mill, though he largely reached these conclusions as a result of a very different kind of argumentation. Green was not a philosophic radical but a radical philosopher. It may be that it was because his discussion was more akin to the moral considerations urged by conventional religion (though without many of its trappings) that the influence of his doctrine was in diverse ways so substantial. His stress on the Christian responsibilities of citizenship was well caught in the notions of Bishop Gore and other socially aware ecclesiastics and in the work of such organizations as the Christian Social Union, Lux Mundi, the London Ethical Society, and the temperance movement.[168] His particular effect on affairs is often difficult to establish though Professor Richter adds his authority to the suggestion that Green 'converted Philosophical Idealism . . . into something close to a practical programme for the left wing of the Liberal Party.'[169] Perhaps this is not, however, quite the right sort of emphasis to give: and Dr Freeden has recently warned against attributing too great and formative a role in the development of the new Liberalism to Green and his associates. The

---

167 ibid., ii. 314; iii. 385–6.
168 e.g. Richter, op. cit., pp. 118ff., 281, 293–7, 360–1.
169 ibid., p. 13. Cf. S. Collini, 'Hobhouse, Bosanquet and the State: Philosophical Idealism and Political Argument in England, 1880–1918', *Past and Present* (no. 72, 1976), esp. pp. 110–11.

ideology would have been transformed without the aid of Idealism in any case, but no doubt it derived substantial intellectual support through the compatible ideas it was able to assimilate from that philosophical quarter.[170] Even so, advanced radicals of the next generation were by no means all admirers. Lowes Dickinson, for instance, thought Green's *Lectures* a bad book, 'long and tedious' with a theme never clearly stated. 'The "philosophy"', he added, 'is that of a tired Oxford whig, not of a good, solid English Liberalism.'[171] However, anti-collectivists did hold Green responsible for some of the directions taken by the new Liberalism. For instance, in 1896 Dicey wrote to John St Loe Strachey (Green's nephew) that the '"unnatural" and at any rate quite unusual meaning' Green gave to the concept of liberty was lending support to the current growth of state intervention and 'social despotism'.[172] Arnold Toynbee certainly claimed that Green and he had routed the forces of the old Liberalism at Oxford, a claim sustained by L. T. Hobhouse and S. Webb alike who further urged the wider impact still of these ideas.[173] Toynbee himself used his analysis of recent English history to sustain the view that civilization meant interference with the 'brute struggle' of economic life through 'wise regulation' by positive laws and institutions.[174] Certainly a number of major public figures such as Campbell-Bannerman, Asquith, and Haldane, did acknowledge an intellectual debt to Green.[175] And the so-called 'inner ring' of young dons and undergraduates that gathered around Arthur Acland at Oxford was deeply affected by Green's Idealism and subsequently not uninfluential in public life.[176] Acland himself became a Cabinet minister with responsibility for

170 M. Freeden, *The New Liberalism: an Ideology of Social Reform* (Oxford, 1978), pp. 16–18, 55–60.
171 Dickinson's annotations on Green's *Lectures*, cited in M. Bentley, *The Liberal Mind, 1914–1929* (Cambridge, 1977), p. 164.
172 Dicey to Strachey (26 December 1895 and 30 January 1896), Strachey MSS, HLRO, cited in E. J. Bristow, *The Defence of Liberty and Property in Britain, 1880–1914* (unpublished PhD thesis, Yale University, 1970), p. 56.
173 A. Toynbee, *Lectures on the Industrial Revolution of the Eighteenth Century in England*... (1884; London, 1908), p. xxv; L. T. Hobhouse, *Liberalism* (1911; Galaxy Books, 1966), p. 112; S. Webb, *Socialism in England* (London, 1980), p. 75.
174 T. S. Ashton (ed.), *Toynbee's Industrial Revolution* (Newton Abbot, 1969), pp. 19–22, 86–7.
175 Richter, op. cit., pp. 294–5 on Asquith. Cf. Asquith's recognition of the 'positive' conception of freedom and its policy implications in his intro. to H. Samuel, *Liberalism: an Attempt to State the Principles and Proposals of Contemporary Liberalism in England* (London, 1902), p. x. Perhaps a little more of Green's influence was apparent than Asquith himself liked to admit? Contrast the passage cited in Freeden, op cit., p. 18 n. 41.
176 P. Gordon and J. White, *Philosophers as Educational Reformers. The Influence of Idealism on British Educational Thought and Practice* (London, 1979), part 2; W. S. Fowler, 'The Influence of Idealism upon State Provision of Education', *Victorian*

education; other members of the group included J. A. Spender, the Liberal journalist, and Michael Sadler who became one of the most well-known educational administrators of his time. An equally powerful influence on such matters was Sir Robert Morant who, as a student at Oxford, had been much interested in Green's lay sermons and moral theory. Beveridge was also affected by Green's ideas at least to some degree.[177]

There have been suggestions, as well, that Green's ideas provided the philosophical foundations of English Socialism.[178] Certainly Tawney's Christian-based doctrine owed a lot to Caird and Gore, both Green's disciples. Sidney Ball, the Fabian don, said that Green was probably the most formative intellectual influence in his life, a continual stimulus to work in the field of working-class education.[179] The degree of general Idealist influence on the Fabian circle is not clear, however. A number of its members were at Oxford during Green's time and D. G. Ritchie was, no doubt, a powerful reinforcement in this regard though on the whole it seems pretty certain that Fabian doctrine was set by other influences than this.[180] On the other hand it is very obvious how much Laski took over from Green's ideas (either directly or via the influence of Sir Ernest Barker) especially his doctrine of the positive functions of the state as an aid to the fulfilment of individual personality, and also the associated theory of rights.[181]

Of course, Green had an indirect influence, too, through other Idealists. Professionally his impact was substantial even on such a remarkably independent mind as F. H. Bradley's whose political prejudices, in fact, differed sharply from Green's. More obvious and direct was the effect on, say, Bernard Bosanquet who was also taught by Green and imbibed much of his style of thought.[182] It is hardly surprising,

Studies, iv (1960–1), pp.343–4; Richter, op. cit., p.325; N. Masterman, The Forerunner: the Dilemmas of Tom Ellis, 1859–1899 (Llandybie, 1972), p.115; P. F. Clarke, Liberals and Social Democrats (Cambridge, 1978), pp.23–4.

177 J. Harris, William Beveridge: a Biography (Oxford, 1977), pp.2, 312, 472.
178 e.g. A. B. Ulam, Philosophical Foundations of English Socialism (Cambridge, Mass., 1951); Fowler, art. cit.; J. H. Randall Jr, 'T. H. Green: the Development of English Thought from J. S. Mill to F. H. Bradley', Journal of the History of Ideas, xxvii (1966), p.218; R. Barker, Education and Politics, 1900–1951: a Study of the Labour Party (Oxford, 1972), p.11; J. H. Hallowell, Main Currents in Modern Political Thought (New York, 1963), p.286.
179 O. H. Ball (ed.), Sidney Ball: Memories & Impressions of 'An Ideal Don' (Oxford, 1923), pp.224–5, 241–2, 254.
180 A. M. McBriar, Fabian Socialism and English Politics, 1884–1918 (1962; Cambridge, 1966), p.74.
181 Cf. my 'Laski and British Socialism', History of Political Thought, ii (1981), §IV.
182 H. Bosanquet, Bernard Bosanquet: a Short Account of His Life (London, 1924), pp.24, 28.

therefore, that in his own writings Bosanquet should have stressed the importance of enlightened state action to create the conditions of morality. The famous phrase about the role of the state as hindering hindrances to the good life is his rendering of the Kantian (and Greenian) doctrine.[183] And while fully aware that excessive government aid might inhibit the growth of a sense of initiative and responsibility in citizens, he was prepared to accept public action to relieve a housing shortage, to overcome illiteracy, or to prevent intemperance; equally he was fully capable of such radical sentiments as welcoming the most extensive increments of workers' ownership and control of the means of production.[184] In his later days, too, Bosanquet became sympathetic to the ideals of the Labour Party.[185] And the reason for this kind of political emphasis is simple: it is that Bosanquet believed the doctrinaire individualist to be fundamentally mistaken about the social conditions of effective choice. If liberty means 'freedom from felt coercion, and power to do what you please' then it does not follow that 'increased liberty means decreased restriction.'[186] On the contrary the liberty of the citizen 'in the common, straight-forward sense of doing what he pleases' becomes 'greater and greater' as the range of possible actions presented for his choice is augmented by social authority: a 'compulsory enactment' may in this fashion be 'the very organ of an enlarged liberty'. This is because coercive regulation can bring an immense increase in the range of possible action.[187] It thus does not appear as restraint or coercion at all, is 'not felt as compulsion.'[188] In sum, 'liberty, in the plainest and simplest sense of the word, does not depend on the absence of legislation, but on the comprehensiveness and reasonableness of life.'[189] Of course, extreme libertarians such as Spencer would have urged that the debilitating effect and waste of public provision is always greater than its supposed advantages: but the drift of Bosanquet's argument is clear and its invitation (or, at least, absence of necessary hostility) to state interference equally obvious. Nor has Green's reputation declined in Liberal circles. As recently as 1969 an official party inquiry into the principles of the

183 B. Bosanquet, *The Philosophical Theory of the State* (1899; 4th edn, London, 1958), p.178; Kant, *The Metaphysics of Morals*, intro., §D in H. Reiss (ed.), *Kant's Political Writings* (Cambridge, 1971), p.134.
184 Bosanquet, *The Philosophical Theory of the State*, pp.xxxix n.1, 178, 185 n.1; and his *Essays and Addresses* (1889; 2nd edn, London, 1891), pp.45–6.
185 J. H. Muirhead (ed.), *Bernard Bosanquet and his Friends: Letters Illustrating the Sources and the Development of his Philosophical Opinions* (London, 1935), pp.217–18; H. Bosanquet, op. cit., pp.97–8.
186 Bosanquet, 'Liberty and Legislation', *The Civilization of Christendom and Other Essays* (London, 1893), pp.360, 367.
187 ibid., pp.368–70.
188 ibid., pp.374–5.
189 ibid., p.379.

creed and their programmatic implications began its chapter on 'Planning and Forecasting in a Free Society' by citing Green to the effect that will, not force, is the basis of the state and by asserting that this principle had particular relevance to the question at issue in that planning had not to be detailed and inflexible but a framework in which freedom of choice and the achievement of excellence may flourish.[190]

By the end of the last century, then, there was emerging in the Liberal context a conflict between the traditional libertarianism of the faith and the fresh emphasis on social action. And, as the examples which have been reviewed show, it was a debate conducted at the highest intellectual level, at a pitch indeed that was hardly later sustained in Liberal circles (or often achieved at all in the other ideological contexts). But something more of the antithesis and of the eventual triumph of the collectivist aspect of Liberalism will be reviewed in the next chapter.

190 The Liberal Commission, *Liberals Look Ahead* (London, n.d. [1969]), p. 66.

5

THE END OF *LAISSEZ FAIRE*

> Those wistful misgivings about the undue extension of the State's
> prerogative which were natural enough in Mr. Gladstone at eighty seem
> strangely out of place in men who have got the Twentieth Century
> before them. To us, who occupy an intermediate station between the
> octogenarian Onlooker and the Young Lions, the cause of Collectivism
> seems to be the cause of Social Progress. It is the new and better
> Revolution.
>
> G. W. E. RUSSELL, *Collections and Recollections*, series II, 1909, p.72

THE CHANGING FACE OF LIBERALISM

> ... with the statesman rests the responsibility to devise ... those
> reforms by which ... there may be compassed for our people a wider
> diffusion of physical comfort, and thus a loftier standard of national
> morality. This is the new Liberalism.
>
> L. A. ATHERLEY-JONES, 'The New Liberalism', *The Nineteenth
> Century*, xxvi, 1889, p.192

TOWARDS the end of the nineteenth century, as Spencer for one
recognized only too well, Liberalism began to change its form and
emphasis. There was a growing feeling that, as C. P. Scott said, the 'older
libertarian Liberalism had done its work'.[1] In particular this was because
some response had to be made to the demands of the increasingly
articulate and organized mass of the people in respect of such matters as
employment, housing, and pensions. A few instances of this growing
concern are easily cited. In 1883 it was declared on behalf of the radical
wing of the Liberal Party that the legislative machinery of the democratic
state must be used to achieve practical reforms of this kind.[2] Twelve
years later the *Manchester Guardian* expressed the similar conviction
that 'the world must be made a better place for the underprivileged
many'.[3] And on crossing the floor of the Commons early in the present

---

1 J. A. Hobson and M. Ginsberg, *L. T. Hobhouse: His Life and Work* (London, 1931),
  intro., p.7. For Spencer's views, see above pp.79–82.
2 'The Future of the Radical Party', *Fortnightly Review*, xxxiv (1883), p.4.
3 Cited in C. B. Cox and A. E. Dyson (eds), *The Twentieth-Century Mind: History, Ideas
  and Literature in Britain* (London, 1972), i. 3.

century to join the Liberal benches, Winston Churchill said he hoped to see his new party's policy based on 'the cause of the left-out millions'.[4] Observing the contemporary scene in 1906 Beatrice Webb commented in her diary that she and Sidney felt 'in better spirits as to the course of political affairs' than they had for some years. For whatever the deficiencies of the current wave of Liberal enthusiasm 'it looms as progressive in its direction and all the active factors are collectivist.'[5] It is a point that has become increasingly clear and which has been convincingly demonstrated with impressive historical scholarship in particular by Dr P. Clarke and Dr M. Freeden.[6] If the prevailing view used to be that the Labour movement became the driving force behind progressive radicalism it is now necessary to see this impetus as deriving in substantial part from the intimations of Liberalism itself while Labour as a whole tended to concentrate on narrower trade union concerns. It is clear there was a small network of friends and collaborators – Hobhouse, Hobson, Wallas, and the two Hammonds in particular – who explored and propagated the new Liberal doctrines much as the Fabians (whom they closely resembled and indeed overlapped) did for Labourism.

So much indeed did Liberals increasingly invite positive action by the state that there was a growing number of references in the literature to what one continental observer called 'the Socialism of the Liberal School'.[7] But the emerging point of view was more often described as the 'modern' or 'progressive' or (most usually) the 'new' Liberalism to distinguish it from the conventional doctrine which was libertarian or anti-statist in nature. These terms began to appear in the mid- or late 1880s and became common thereafter.[8] It was not so much that the old stress on individual self-help and freedom of choice and action was discarded as that it was overlaid or overtaken by the new policy emphases. The traditional claims had to be adjusted to collectivist pressures and made more appropriate to the conditions and problems of the day.[9] The development was consciously undertaken. For instance in 1897 the young John Simon wrote that side by side with 'the idea of individuality as secure *from* legislative interference there has grown up,

4 ibid., i.2–3.
5 B. Webb, *Our Partnership* (London, 1948), pp.330–1.
6 See especially P. F. Clarke, *Lancashire and the New Liberalism* (Cambridge, 1971); idem, *Liberals and Social Democrats* (Cambridge, 1978); and M. Freeden, *The New Liberalism: an Ideology of Social Reform* (Oxford, 1978). See also Dr Clarke's 'The Progressive Movement in England', *Trans. R. Hist. S.*, 5s., xxiv (1974), pp.159–81.
7 A. Naquet, *Collectivism and the Socialism of the Liberal School* (1890; trans. edn, London, 1891), book IV.
8 L. A. Atherley-Jones, 'The New Liberalism', *The Nineteenth Century*, xxvi (1889), pp.186–93. A few years before this G. W. Russell had referred to 'Modern Liberalism' as a doctrine stressing an increased role for the state: see the reference in his 'The New Liberalism: a Response', ibid., xxvi (1889), p.496.
9 Cf. Clarke, 'The Progressive Movement in England', loc. cit., p.170.

in apparent contradiction, the idea of individuality as secured *by* legislative interference.' Liberal principles are, he went on, not at all sacrificed by legislation which redresses inequality of condition in contractual relations.[10] Similarly another contributor to the same volume of essays asserted it was more and more recognized that the view of the state entailed by Liberal policy is of an authority whose purpose is 'to promote the growth of individual character' by developing 'the conditions of civic activity'.[11] A few years later another Liberal publicist stressed in the same vein the constructive role the state could play (as a matter both of social justice and of prudence) in helping to clear away difficulties and in offering judicious assistance to the efforts of individuals and voluntary associations alike to achieve their aims and fulfilment.[12]

Naturally there was considerable debate in Liberal circles about the appropriate nature of the creed in an age that seemed to invite or require these more active policies of social reform. There was a range of warring elements from those completely loyal to the old tradition to those urging various increments of collectivist change, some even wanting to start with a completely clean slate.[13] In fact a period of controversy and upheaval accompanied the emergence of the new ideological emphasis, hinging not least on the nice question how the transformed doctrine was to be distinguished from certain kinds of Socialism and Conservatism. Some aspects of the transition have already been revealed as they were manifest at the level of theoretical discussion. In the present chapter the growing Liberal pressure for social reform will be indicated in respect both of politicians and others concerned with the practical level of activity and of various more formal justifications of this tendency.

SOCIAL REFORM AND THE STATE

> Whether we look to the events of successive years, to the acts of successive Parliaments, or to the publication of successive books, we see narrower and narrower limits assigned to the application of the principle of 'Laissez faire,' while the sphere of Government control and interference is expanding in ever widening circles.
>
> G. J. GOSCHEN, *Laissez-Faire and Government Interference*, 1883, p. 3

10 J. A. Simon, 'Liberals and Labour', Six Oxford Men, *Essays in Liberalism* (London, 1897), pp. 109, italics in original, 114.
11 J. L. Hammond, 'A Liberal View of Education', ibid., p. 176.
12 'B. Villiers' [F. J. Shaw], *The Opportunity of Liberalism* (London, 1904), pp. 15–16, 30–1. For a summary of the growth of Liberal concern with social justice and state intervention (in alliance with Labour), see P. F. Clarke, *Lancashire and the New Liberalism*, esp. ch. 15 'Edwardian Progressivism'.
13 See e.g. the account in H. C. G. Matthew, *The Liberal Imperialists: the Ideas and Politics of a Post-Gladstonian Elite* (Oxford, 1973), ch. IV; and for policy details, ibid., ch. VII.

Goschen himself was a political piebald. He began as a Liberal and served in government under Gladstone but gradually became disenchanted with the direction of Liberal policy in particular as regards electoral reform and Home Rule. He subsequently took office in Conservative administrations. And the comment cited immediately above as epigraph to this section reflects in fact a worried observation made by many libertarians in both parties. So far as the Liberals are concerned, growing acceptance of the tendency described may be indicated by reference both to those active in the Parliamentary arena itself and to perhaps more detached observers of the passing scene.

Praxis

Of course, the actual extension of state agency entailed by the new Liberalism could only occur through the actions and with the support of politicians especially those holding office in government. Yet many of them were diffident about if not hostile to this direction of affairs and their resistance was only gradually overcome.

Gladstone was one who expressed qualms about the tendency among Liberals to support what he called 'construction' by which he meant 'taking into the hands of the State the business of the individual man.' It involved whole 'vistas of social quackery'.[14] His view was reflected in the warm admiration he expressed for Spencer's introduction to a volume of extreme libertarian essays published in 1893 under the title *A Plea for Liberty*.[15] A little later he wrote specifically of his firm opposition to 'Collectivism' and of his support for 'individual freedom and independence'.[16] Mrs Webb commented on his 'policy of diminishing the function of government' and his lack of sympathy with 'the collectivist trend of the new democracy'.[17]

Nor was he alone in this view, of course. Goschen shared the Gladstonian prejudice and always remained an ardent individualist and free-trader objecting to the dethronement of political economy and its replacement in the public counsels by 'Philanthropy'.[18] It was not that he deplored all state regulation and action. He recognized indeed the

14 Gladstone to Lord Acton (11 February 1885), in J. Morley, *The Life of William Ewart Gladstone* (London, 1903), iii.172–3; B. Webb, *My Apprenticeship* (Penguin, 1938), i.203.

15 D. Duncan, *The Life and Letters of Herbert Spencer* (London, 1908), p.302.

16 Gladstone to F. W. Hirst (2 January 1897), in F. W. Hirst, *In the Golden Days* (London, 1947), p.158.

17 Diary entry of 3 November 1903, cited in B. Webb, *Our Partnership* (London, 1948), p.275. On Gladstonian hostility to the state, cf. S. Webb, 'Lord Rosebery's Escape from Houndsditch', *The Nineteenth Century*, l (1901), pp.366, 369–71.

18 A. D. Elliot, *Life of George Joachim Goschen, First Viscount Goschen, 1831–1907* (London, 1911), i.163.

pressing nature of the causes which had dictated the various forms and increments of intervention. But he also had the deepest suspicion of these departures from the principles of individual freedom and stressed rather the difficulties and dangers involved than the possible advantages. His pamphlet on *Laissez-Faire and Government Interference* is, although brief, a key document in Liberal discussion of these matters. This is not least because his conclusion nicely reflects both the diffidence and ambivalence with which the growing collectivism was regarded in many Liberal quarters:

> The dangers in the road of social reconstruction under Government control are so grave that they can scarcely be exaggerated; dangers arising, not only from the serious chance of inefficiency in the methods chosen, but from the transfer of responsibilities, from the establish-ment of national law in the place of individual duty, from the withdrawal of confidence in the qualities of men in order to bestow it on the merits of administrations, from the growing tendency to invoke the aid of the State, and the declining belief in individual power. . . . We cannot see universal state action enthroned as a new principle of government without grave misgivings. . . .
>
> Let us hope that in the State Socialism of the future, to which some thinkers suggest we are drifting at no slow pace, room will still be left for that self-reliance and independence and natural liberty, which, if history has taught us anything, are the main conditions on which depend the strength of the State, the prosperity of the community, and the greatness of nations.[19]

Some Liberals, however, were simply prepared to accept the new propensity and to try to marry it happily with the old by making distinctions between the areas of policy concerned, some appropriate to intervention, some not. This was the case with that fascinating polymath George Campbell, 8th Duke of Argyll, who held office in Gladstone's first two governments. His interests ranged from poetry and geology to evolution and philosophy; politically he travelled the spectrum from Peelite to Liberal Unionist while being known, too, as the 'Radical Duke'. Perhaps not surprisingly his attitude to the role of the state was equally eclectic – he always said he had a cross-bench mind – for he was both a free-trader and an interventionist. He believed the role proper to government depended on the questions at issue. During the nineteenth century, he wrote in one place,

> two great discoveries have been made in the Science of Government: the one is the immense advantage of abolishing restrictions upon Trade; the other is the absolute necessity of imposing restrictions upon

19 G. J. Goschen, *Laissez-Faire and Government Interference* (London, 1883), pp. 35–6.

Labour. . . . And so the Factory Acts instead of being excused as exceptional, and pleaded for as justified only under extraordinary conditions, ought to be recognised as in truth the first Legislative recognition of a great Natural Law, quite as important as Freedom of Trade, and which like this last, was yet destined to claim for itself wider and wider application.[20]

There was also, of course, the radicalism of Chamberlain's 'unauthorized programme' developed when he was still a leading Liberal.[21]

No obvious basis of unity existed in the Liberal Party on these domestic questions, the various wings ranging from Nonconformists and land reformers to London progressives and organized Labour.[22] The Newcastle programme of 1891 was an early attempt to fuse some of the varied demands involved though (as already indicated) Gladstone himself was diffident about proposals of collectivist intent. But in 1894 he finally left the political scene and, with less concentration on the Irish question, the more radical elements were able to push to the fore demands entailing not a little interference with property rights. These proposals included the removal of Church endowments, the expropriation of liquor licences, the establishment of secure tenures, taxation of the unearned increment, municipal housing, public ownership of certain utilities, employers' liability, and other items of a like kind. In the circumstances of the day these proposals, taken together, undoubtedly constituted a notable collectivist emphasis.[23] And given this sort of pressure the Liberal governments of 1892–5 had inevitably gone some way in this general direction to tackle social problems. There were the Acts giving local authorities power to acquire land (compulsorily if necessary) to provide allotments, to repair or close unhealthy houses and build new ones, to establish libraries and public baths. There was legislation to check excessive hours of work on the railways; to extend the factory regulations and make inspection more stringent; and so on and so forth. Listing these and other legislative achievements Herbert Samuel concluded that 'No more complete abandonment of the old theory of negation can be imagined than is shown by this governmental activity, so extensive and so minute.' The catalogue of policies he describes is not unlike that in Morley's biography of Cobden with the difference that Samuel clearly approves what has been happening.[24]

20 Duke of Argyll, *The Reign of Law* (1867; 5th edn, London, 1870), pp. 334–5, 360–1. Cf. Tennyson's comment in *The Works* (London, 1894), p. 575.
21 For Chamberlain, see below ch. 7, pp. 223–31.
22 K. O. Morgan (ed.), *The Age of Lloyd George* (London, 1971), pp. 21–3.
23 ibid., pp. 23–5, 36. Cf. R. C. K. Ensor, *England 1870–1914* (1936; Oxford, 1968), pp. 207–8.
24 H. Samuel, *Liberalism: an Attempt to State the Principles and Proposals of Contemporary Liberalism in England* (London, 1902), pp. 22–3. For Morley's account, see vol. i, *The Rise of Collectivism*, pp. 87–8.

Equally the Anglo-Boer War of 1899–1902 generated a concern with some social questions especially those concerning the physical state of the people. One group of progressive Liberals published during that war an overall indictment of *laissez faire* capitalism and insisted on a systematic and comprehensive approach to social reform that recognized the interrelated nature of all the many aspects of the condition of the poor, unemployment, housing, and malnutrition alike.[25]

At the beginning of the new century, then, Liberals were still divided on these domestic questions. Halévy has described the two main groups into which in this respect the party leaders broadly fell. On the one side, he said, were those who remained faithful to the Gladstonian tradition, 'convinced opponents of expenditure and war, of bureaucracy and state socialism.' On the other were 'the younger men' who vied with the Conservatives in imperialist zeal and who, in deliberate contrast with the old-fashioned Liberalism, emphasized their progressiveness by displaying 'leanings towards collectivism', albeit these were indefinite and moderate inclinations.[26] Nor were the intentions of the radical wing itself at all homogeneous.[27] It is hardly surprising that many of those in the senior ranks of the party accepted a programme of social reform only with some reluctance. This was certainly true, for instance, of Sir Henry Campbell-Bannerman who was Prime Minister of the new Liberal government from its accession to office in December 1905 until shortly before his death just over two years later. As a young man he had gone against his family by becoming a Liberal. It is not clear why he did this though it may have been a matter of intellectual conviction. He had read and been impressed by Herbert Spencer and certainly always retained a belief in the importance of individual freedom and enterprise and as a result invariably had a rather negative conception of the functions of the state.[28] In 1900 he wrote to a close friend and colleague that as time went on he was 'more and more confirmed in the old advanced Liberal principles' with which he had entered Parliament thirty years before.[29]

25 C. F. G. Masterman *et al.*, *The Heart of the Empire: Discussions of Problems of Modern City Life in England* ... (London, 1901); and see vol.i, *The Rise of Collectivism*, pp.68–9.
26 E. Halévy, *A History of the English People in the Nineteenth Century* (1913–46; 2nd trans. edn, London, 1961), v.6–8. Cf. ibid., v.100–3; vi.47–8. On this diversity of Liberal attitudes to social reform, see also J. Harris, *Unemployment and Politics: a Study in English Social Policy, 1886–1914* (Oxford, 1972), pp.212–35, 264–72.
27 J. F. Harris and C. Hazelhurst, 'Campbell-Bannerman as Prime Minister', *History*, lv (1970), pp.372, 375–6.
28 ibid., pp.370, 377; J. Wilson, *CB: a Life of Sir Henry Campbell-Bannerman* (London, 1973), pp.38, 148, 394; P. Magnus, 'Another Unknown Prime Minister', *The Spectator* (3 February 1973), p. [137].
29 Campbell-Bannerman to 5th Earl Spencer (19 February 1900), Spencer Papers, cited in Wilson, op. cit., p.326. Cf. ibid., pp.394, 634.

He was, too, mistrustful of the Webbs and what they stood for, thus resisting their attempts at 'permeation'.[30] Yet pragmatically he was prepared to accept interference in some respects if there were a proper and worthwhile public advantage to be gained. In a speech he made in 1898, the year in which he became Leader of the Opposition, he described what he took Liberalism to mean and in so doing indicated the ambivalent attitude involved. The doctrine was, he said, based on acknowledgement of the truth that in practical life 'men are best governed who govern themselves', that 'the general sense of mankind, if left alone, will make for righteousness'; it followed that 'artificial privileges and restraints upon freedom' are 'hurtful'. But then there is the admission: 'so far as they are not required in the interests of the community'. In this regard, he added that while laws could not be expected to equalize conditions they might at least help to avoid 'aggravating inequalities'; and they could have as their legitimate object 'the securing to every man the best chance he can have of a good and useful life.'[31] Of course all this was mere generality and might mean much or little. But there was undoubtedly increasing pressure from radical elements in the party, from Sir John Brunner for instance, who with others increasingly urged the need for a policy of strenuous development of Britain's resources especially in respect of transport and communications.[32] Certainly it was increasingly apparent that British industry and commerce needed help to make them more efficient and to face the consequences of trade depression. In addition there was the political need to secure or retain the support of the enfranchised working class and, as well, to offset the appeal of Chamberlain's tariff reform policy. Campbell-Bannerman and the party leadership generally were rather lukewarm and slow to react. Nevertheless, social reform was emphasized more and more as an important part of the Liberal programme and was given as much weight as this sort of diffidence and the adherence to free-trade policy would admit.[33] Among the first steps the Campbell-Bannerman government took in 1905 were decisions to consider education and unemployment; the following year it took over the Labour-sponsored Trades Disputes Bill. The Prime Minister was personally aware, too, of the need to tackle the problems of urban life; though, typically, he was opposed to proposals to establish state control

30 e.g. ibid., pp. 347, 360, 371, 394, 635. For the Webb policy of 'permeation', see below pp. 380–1, 389, 401–2.
31 Report in *The Liberal Magazine* (January 1898), p. 530, cited in Wilson, op. cit., p. 232.
32 See the detailed proposals cited in Harris, *Unemployment and Politics*, pp. 217–18.
33 Wilson, op. cit., pp. 407, 410, 413, 635; Harris and Hazlehurst, art. cit., pp. 367, 372–3; Harris, *Unemployment and Politics*, pp. 212–15.

of railways and canals.[34] Yet though he genuinely wanted a better deal for the poor and, for instance, supported compulsory education, he really remained an old-fashioned Cobdenite and had no time for anything that smacked of too much state interference.[35]

Consequently it was not until Campbell-Bannerman had left the political stage that the forces of the new Liberalism began fully to be felt, mainly through the impact of D. L. George and W. S. Churchill though naturally their influence depended on the existence of a not insubstantial radicalism in the ranks of the party as a whole.[36] This was represented, for instance, by the views of Sir Francis Channing, a Northamptonshire MP, who stressed how much there was in common between Labour and the Liberals on many subjects from the rights of the working man in respect of hours and wages to graduated taxation, land reform, and school meals.[37] Such views had equally received early support from R. B. Haldane who was, of course, an important member of Liberal Cabinets from 1905 until 1915 (and who later became Lord Chancellor in the first Labour administration). He early wrote a clear confession of his collectivist faith. He affirmed that 'what was the truth for the last generation is not necessarily the truth for this', and said that he belonged to a rapidly growing school of thought 'the leading tenet of which is that the problem of today' – this was written in 1893 – 'is distribution and not production, and that better distribution requires the active intervention of the state at every turn.' He continued:

> The disciples of this school believe that society is more than a mere aggregate of individuals, and see in it a living whole, which not only does control the lives of its component parts, but must do so if these parts are to remain healthy. . . . Such a general control they say is natural, and while they agree that the members must have scope for free development as individuals, they say that such development takes place most healthily when it is kept in consistency with the equally real life of the common whole. They point to the success of the Factory Acts, of the Mines and Merchant Shipping and Truck Acts, and to many other illustrations of their principles, and they demand that this principle shall receive in the future the more extended application which they think its past history justifies.[38]

34 Wilson, op. cit., pp.469–70, 587–8; Harris, op. cit., pp.218–19, 224–5.
35 Wilson, op. cit., p.641; cf. Harris and Hazlehurst, art. cit., pp.361, 372, 377.
36 On the factors that made this 'Liberal Volte-Face' both feasible and politically desirable, see Harris, *Unemployment and Politics*, pp.264–72.
37 K. O. Morgan (ed.), *The Age of Lloyd George*, pp.35, 140–2, citing F. A. Channing, *Memories of Midland Politics, 1885–1910* (1918), pp.308–10.
38 R. B. Haldane, preface to L. T. Hobhouse, *The Labour Movement* (London, 1893), pp. x, xi.

Naturally George and Churchill could not have achieved what they did without the support of such colleagues as Haldane and, in particular, without that of Asquith who had in 1908 succeeded Campbell-Bannerman as Prime Minister. He, too, had long been on record as believing that 'the collective action of the community' should be used in a positive way to enhance the real freedom of the individual.[39] And perhaps the first outward evidence of a new trend was Asquith's public commitment to an old age pension scheme early in 1907.[40] But the palm (if such it is) was theirs: for they were perhaps the real founders of the modern welfare state.

Churchill had first entered the House in 1900 as a Conservative and was later, of course, to revert to that allegiance. He was an ardent free-trader and supporter of individual effort and, even before he became an MP, declared he was really a Liberal 'in all but name'. It was because of Home Rule that (as he wrote to his mother in 1897) he decided to range himself under the banner of the Tory Democracy. And his description of the domestic aspects of this creed demonstrates the sort of policy he espoused and would expect to find, too, in Liberalism.[41] It embraced a wide range of political and social reform: extension of the franchise to every adult male; the provision of universal education; wide measures of local self-government; the eight-hour day; a progressive income tax; and the like. 'I will', he wrote, 'vote for them all'.[42] And if he would not then countenance public interference with 'private trade', he was quite clear that the improvement of the condition of the people and raising the position of labour were, or should be, the main aim of modern government.[43] In a speech made during the general election of 1906 (which he fought as a junior member of the Liberal government) he spoke of the state's 'embarking on various novel and adventurous experiments' and stated by way of conclusion:

> I do not want to impair the vigour of competition, but we can do much to mitigate the consequences of failure. We want to draw a line below which we will not allow persons to live and labour yet above which they may compete with all the strength of their manhood. We

39 See e.g. Asquith's 1892 election address, cited in his *Memories and Reflections, 1852–1927* (London, 1928), i. 113. Yet see also the rather different view expressed in a letter (29 December 1896), cited in F. W. Hirst, *In the Golden Days*, p. 157.

40 Harris, *Unemployment and Politics*, p. 265.

41 R. S. Churchill *et al.*, *Winston S. Churchill* (London, 1966 ff.), ii. 276. Something of the wider framework of images and ideas deployed is described in P. Addison, 'The Political Beliefs of Winston Churchill', *Trans. R. Hist. S.*, 5s., xxx (1980), pp. 23–47.

42 W. S. Churchill to Lady R. Churchill (6 April 1897), R. S. Churchill, op. cit., i. 318. On the free-trade question, ibid., ii. 62ff.

43 ibid., i. 280–1, 335, 344, 422, 445.

do not want to pull down the structure of science and civilisation – but to spread a net over the abyss.[44]

In other places in the following years he spoke of avoiding the impoverishment of 'the great left-out labour interest', developing the educational system, improving technical instruction and apprenticeship, mitigating 'the sorrows of old age', and redistributing the burden of taxation.[45] In January 1909 he proclaimed that in Britain, where the organization of industrial conditions 'urgently demands attention', the 'social field lies open' and the reformer is 'confronted with a mass of largely preventable and even curable suffering' which he must tackle.[46]

One systematic statement of Churchill's attitude was contained in a long letter published in *The Nation* in 1908 when he was Under-Secretary of State at the Colonial Office and soon to be translated to the Cabinet as President of the Board of Trade. It was headed 'The Untrodden Field of Politics'.[47] Churchill commented on the important change which had been taking place 'in the internal conception of the Liberal Party'. The party had not, he went on, in any respect abandoned

> its historic championship of Liberty, in all its forms under every sky; but it has become acutely conscious of the fact that political freedom, however precious, is utterly incomplete without a measure at least of social and economic independence. . . . All over the world the lines of cleavage are ceasing to be purely political, and are becoming social and economic.

In this mood and context the movement to achieve 'a Minimum Standard' will take form. And there are, he believes, two clear lines of advance ahead: one 'corrective', to assert 'the just precedence' of public over private interests; the other 'constructive', to make good 'the patent inadequacy of existing social machinery'. 'Science, physical and political alike', he argued, 'revolts at the disorganization which glares at us in so many aspects of modern life'. The 'riddles of unemployment and under-employment' were 'quite unsolved'; and he deplored the acceptance of 'a labour surplus', the consequences of dead-end jobs, the undernourishment of children, the effects of intemperance, and so on. There was opposition to tackling these problems. But it

> is false and base to say that these evils, and others like them, . . . are

44 Cited ibid., ii.277.
45 ibid., ii.277–8.
46 Cited ibid., ii.279.
47 *The Nation* (7 November 1908), pp.812–13, cited in K. O. Morgan, *The Age of Lloyd George*, pp.144–8, from which the extracts in the text are taken. Mrs Webb claimed that Churchill had taken the ideas in the article from her husband and herself, *Our Partnership*, p.404.

inherent in the nature of things, that their remedy is beyond the wit of man, that experiment is foolhardy, that all is for the best in 'Merrie England'. No one will believe it any more. . . . The nation . . . demands the application of drastic corrective and curative processes. . . .

Stern labours lie ahead, therefore, and the tasks include 'the serious undertaking by the State of the elimination of casual employment', the 'scientific treatment' of any unabsorbed residuum of labour, the extension of the wage board system, and the search for means to counterbalance fluctuations in world trade by the state acquisition of railways and canals and by the development of certain national industries. There has to be 'an altogether unprecedented expansion' in educational facilities especially those concerned with technical training. There must be, too, adequate provision for the aged. And in this pursuit of the minimum standard all classes must be prepared to make sacrifices especially those whose wealth is unearned. These are the 'untrodden fields of British politics' towards which Churchill beckons. Clearly, as his biographer said recently, he 'had no dogmatic inhibitions against government intervention to deal with the social and economic problems caused by a free market economy'; and Mrs Webb commented at the time that Churchill was 'definitely casting in his lot with the constructive state action.'[48] As a Liberal Cabinet minister Churchill was subsequently to be involved in a number of important legislative items and administrative occasions reflecting just this sort of incursion by government: the Coal Mines (Eight Hours) Bill; another bill to provide for safety measures in mines; proposals to deal with sweated labour; the establishment of labour exchanges; coping with industrial conciliation cases and other aspects of trade disputes.[49] But perhaps the main project of this kind in which Churchill was involved was the scheme to introduce compulsory unemployment insurance, subsequently merged in David Lloyd George's National Insurance Act of 1911.[50]

In the period after 1908 George was (in K. O. Morgan's phrase) 'the supreme tribune of the new liberalism'.[51] He was certainly a political force in his own right although an outsider: as George Dangerfield once wrote, before the Great War the Liberal Party was a strange mixture of 'whig aristocrats, industrialists, dissenters, reformers, trade unionists,

48 R. S. Churchill, op. cit., ii. 278; B. Webb, *Our Partnership*, diary entry (16 October 1908), p. 417.
49 For examples, see R. S. Churchill, op. cit., ii. 284–8, 296–300, 423–4.
50 See the account, ibid., ii. 300–15.
51 K. O. Morgan, 'The New Liberalism and the Challenge of Labour: the Welsh Experience, 1885–1929' (1973), in K. D. Brown (ed.), *Essays in Anti-Labour History: Responses to the Rise of Labour in Britain* (London, 1974), p. 169.

quacks and Mr. Lloyd-George'.[52] Whatever his other political preoccupations he had early gone on record as supporting a collectivist view of
government: thus he was reported as saying in 1896 that 'the state . . .
recognises that it is possessed of a conscience, the combined consciences
of all, and the state now, therefore, meddles with everything'.[53] It was not
by any means that he dispensed with 'the old panaceas of rural
radicalism'; but a number of his actions as President of the Board of
Trade after 1905 showed he could treat ideological shibboleths in a most
cavalier way: his Acts dealing with Patents and Merchant Shipping were
'a striking breach' of free-trade doctrine; and his intervention in the 1907
railway strike and the imposition of conciliation procedures hardly
reflected a policy of leaving trade matters to themselves.[54] And, always
the pragmatist, the apparent decline in Liberal fortunes (as shown by the
loss of by-elections) and the impact of his visit to Germany in 1908 led
him as Chancellor of the Exchequer in the reconstituted government of
that year to infuse it with a new spirit of reform. Between 1908 and 1910
he became 'the tribune for a new social concern' being aided in this by the
energy and advocacy of Churchill at the Board of Trade: for they now –
the Welsh outsider and the renegade Tory – viewed traditional
Liberalism with some scepticism.[55] The key to the whole package was the
'People's Budget' of 1909 calculated to provide a financial basis for
expensive social reform (and a programme of naval building) by tapping
fresh sources of revenue: new licensing duties; taxes on unearned
increment, underdeveloped land, mining royalties, and so on; and this
while not infringing free-trade principles as the alternative policy of tariff
reform would have done.[56] It had the advantage, too, of being (like its
successor of 1914) an attack on traditional Liberal enemies – landlords,
brewers, and the like – although the schemes to be supported, for
example, old age pensions and national insurance, were relatively novel.
Even at the height of the controversy over the Lords' veto George stressed
in one memorandum the importance of obtaining all-party support to
make possible a constructive policy on critical social issues such as
housing, education, drink, unemployment, inland transport, land
reform, and poor law.[57] In each case it was the action of government that

52 G. Dangerfield, *The Strange Death of Liberal England* (London, 1936), p.68.
53 *North Wales Observer* (18 December 1896), cited in Brown, op. cit., intro., p.2.
54 Morgan, *The Age of Lloyd George*, p.41. Cf. Brown, op. cit., pp.169–70, on the
    traditional perspective of George's early social views.
55 The rest of this paragraph is mainly based on the superb summary in Morgan, op. cit.,
    pp.41–8, 51–2.
56 Cf. H. V. Emy, 'The Land Campaign: Lloyd George as a Social Reformer, 1909–14',
    A. J. P. Taylor, *Lloyd George: Twelve Essays* (London, 1971), ch.11.
57 'Memorandum on the Formation of a Coalition' (1910), in C. Petrie, *The Life and
    Letters of the Right Hon. Austen Chamberlain* (London, 1939–40), i.381–8.

was called for; and in its general scope this document is not unlike an outline of the famous inter-war 'Yellow Book'.[58]

Two other politicians who expounded the new Liberalism also deserve some attention: C. F. G. Masterman and H. Samuel.

Because Masterman's political career was sadly foreshortened his significance has perhaps been unduly diminished; for in the social reform wing of the Liberal Party he played an important if, in political terms, ancillary role in the period before the Great War.[59] While always opposed to the 'insect state' of Socialism Masterman was early prepared to accept and urge the reconstruction of society 'on a Collectivist basis'. He entered political life, in Chesterton's phrase, 'from the noblest bitterness on behalf of the poor', being in particular affected by his knowledge and experience of the miseries of life in overcrowded cities, bringing to these questions, too, the zeal of a sensitive Christian conscience.[60] In numerous books and articles he wrote about such problems as housing, poverty, sweating, and unemployment. A good instance of this is the symposium called *The Heart of the Empire* which appeared in 1901 and which stressed the need for a real and effective social policy if the appeal of Liberalism was to be sustained.[61] Basically what most impressed him was the contrast between the squalor of the slums and the luxury of Mayfair or even suburbia, and in his most well-known tract *The Condition of England* (1909) he writes fervently of the social dangers this state of affairs involved in particular that of the likely boiling over of the forces of the abyss.[62] He continued to urge a progressive social policy to deal with these questions after his election to Parliament in 1906 and he was critical of the absence of sufficiently strong reform proposals in the programme of the Campbell-Bannerman government. For instance, on one occasion he put forward not simply a series of palliatives but a comprehensive scheme involving 'an active campaign against insanitary housing; decasualisation of labour; state wages boards to fix minimum wage rates; unskilled work for the unemployed; migration and emigration schemes for surplus casual labour; a land colony; and efficient operation of statutory legislation

---

58 It seems that these pre-war collectivist proposals were not uncongenial to much of the Conservative leadership at least, according to George's own account in his *War Memoirs* (1933–6; new edn, London, n.d. [1938]), i.22–3. On the 'Yellow Book', see below pp.175–8.

59 E. David, 'The New Liberalism of C. F. G. Masterman, 1873–1927', K. D. Brown (ed.), *Essays in Anti-Labour History*, ch. 2, esp. p.27. My brief account of Masterman's ideas is largely based on this source. See also L. Masterman, *C. F. G. Masterman: a Biography* (London, 1939).

60 Chesterton's remark is in his *Autobiography* (1936; London, 1937), p.123.

61 C. F. G. Masterman *et al.*, *The Heart of the Empire*, also referred to at p.148 above. And cf. L. Masterman, op. cit., pp.40–3.

62 See the passage cited in vol.i, *The Rise of Collectivism*, p.290.

relating to the medical inspection of schoolchildren to prevent the "manufacture of the unemployed".'[63] In junior office he was subsequently very closely involved in various legislative proposals: at the Home Department measures to extend state control over working conditions in shops and mines; and in the formulation of the health insurance schemes sponsored by George. He was also amongst those urging a complete programme of land reform under government aegis in the period before 1914. Nor did Masterman cease to be a stimulus to radical Liberal thinking in the brief post-war years before his death in 1927.[64] His general attitude is perhaps summed up in some passages from a speech he made early in 1924 shortly after being returned again to the House of Commons. The report in the press said:

> Liberalism had never been committed to individualism pure and simple, never. It had been engaged during the long historic course of its great triumphs in the last century in trying to reconcile individual liberty with the intervention of the community. . . . The new Liberalism was prepared to go a long distance . . . in the intervention of the State for the general advantage, especially that of the poorest of the community. . . .

And he added that the Liberal Party, while not prepared to work for 'a Socialist State', is quite open to arguments in favour of industrial control and rationalization, the nationalization of monopolies, and the extension of the democratic ideal from the political into the economic field.[65]

Herbert Samuel was Masterman's contemporary but achieved political preferment slightly earlier entering the Liberal Cabinet in 1909. And, of course, he was at the centre of political affairs over a much longer period and led the Liberal Party in the early 1930s, though he last held office, briefly, in the National government from 1931 to 1932. He died in 1963. He was a man of many interests outside domestic politics and wrote widely on questions ranging from moral philosophy to Zionism. In the present context, notice must be taken of a long study he published in 1902 which attempted to state the principles and programme of contemporary Liberalism in a coherent and extensive way.

As someone long interested in the problems of ethics and philosophy, Samuel properly asserted the primacy of the moral law which, he assumed, provides the basis for any consideration of political matters: 'The trunk of the tree of Liberalism is rooted in the soil of ethics.' And if the duty of man is himself to lead (and to help others, too, to lead) the

63 Masterman, 'Causes and Cures of Poverty', *Albany Review*, ii (February 1908), pp. 531–47, summarized in Brown, op. cit., p. 25.
64 Cf. L. Masterman, op. cit., chs 12–14. And see below p. 172.
65 L. Masterman, op. cit., pp. 335–6.

good life, then this precept conditions the role of society and government.[66] It is thus 'the duty of the State to secure to all its members . . . the fullest possible opportunity to lead the best life.'[67] This is, says Samuel, the basis of policies of social reform which have become increasingly characteristic of the Liberal Party in recent times.[68] But he is bound to recognize that the Liberal tradition was one which stressed a rather different, much more negative, view of public policy; and his main initial task in the book is to justify the switch of emphasis which has occurred and which has his full approval. This he does by examining the three main types of objection that (as he sees it) classical Liberalism had to the extension of state action. Samuel's account is a key example of the kind of rationale that lay behind the emergence of the new Liberalism.

The first type of objection rests on the assertion that, despite the continuing existence of distress, the condition of the people has latterly been greatly improved, the implication being that forces are at work that will carry this progress even farther and which render the intervention of the state unnecessary. Samuel admits the general tendency but suggests both that considerable difficulties still exist and that in any case a great deal of the gain already achieved has been due to state action and cannot be attributed merely to some general evolution of society that is beyond control.[69] The second type of objection is specifically laid at the door of Herbert Spencer. It is that the process of evolution requires the elimination of the unfit and that, in social terms, only the harsh conditions of stringent competition in the struggle for survival are compatible with this end. 'There is little doubt', says Samuel, in acknowledgement of the influence of the Spencerian doctrine, that this sort of argument, 'applied to politics, furnishes an intellectual basis for much of the opposition to social reform.'[70] But he goes on to deny that the poor are necessarily the unfit or that harsh social conditions will 'crush out the inferior types'. Experience shows rather that, despite all the difficulties they may face, the weak, idle, and imprudent survive and propagate. Moreover civilization both forbids such harshness and provides an alternative: penalties there must be but they may be accompanied by help.

> To extend education, to bring powerful moral influences to bear, to make surroundings better, to remove the causes that lower the physical type, to give a stimulus to self-improvement by making it easy for men to rise, these, experience proves, are the most powerful means

66 H. Samuel, *Liberalism*, pp. 5–6.
67 ibid., p. 4.
68 ibid., pp. 8–9, 11.
69 ibid., pp. 13–17.
70 ibid., p. 17.

for raising the standard of life and character. That such methods are possible makes the Spencerian policy as unnecessary as it is cruel.[71]

And he goes on, in repudiation of the doctrine of 'these political Darwinians':

> When men say, therefore, that we need not vex our minds too much at the sight of the evils that fester at the base of our society, for after all the fittest must survive and the unfit go to the wall, reformers answer that you are driving against the wall many who are not unfit, but only unfortunate; that the unfit are not by these means removed, they still survive as well as the fittest; that you are taking the surest means of producing fresh generations of weak and incapable; and that progress can be made by methods more humane, by using the powerful agencies within our reach that tend not to kill but to cure, not to destroy but to raise, that would enlarge the opportunities for becoming fit rather than overwhelm with penalties those who fail.

The evolutionary argument, he thus concludes, need not 'stay the hand of reform.'[72]

The third point is one that rests on the assertion that the state is incompetent and that its interference 'always fails'; that men, left alone, will find their own way out of difficulties, and that social reform weakens self-reliance and causes more evils than it cures. 'This was the view in the main of the older school of Liberals. Recent years have brought a striking change.'[73] There follows a clear statement of the contrast between the old Liberalism and the new and of the transition between them now well under way:

> To many among the fathers of modern Liberalism, government action was anathema. They held, as we hold, that the first and final object of the State is to develop the capacities and raise the standard of living of its citizens; but they held also that the best means towards this object was the self-effacement of the State. Liberty is of supreme importance, and legal regulation is the opposite of liberty. Let governments abstain from war, let them practise economy, let them provide proper protection against violence and fraud, let them repeal restrictive laws, and then the free enterprise of commerce will bring prosperity to all classes, while their natural ambitions on the one hand, the pressure of need on the other, will stimulate the hindmost to seek and to attain their own well-being: such was their doctrine.

This was the creed of non-interference which inspired 'in large measure' the politics of a century. In this guise,

71 ibid., pp. 18–20.
72 ibid., pp. 19, 20.
73 ibid., p. 20.

Liberalism became a negative policy, opposing foreign enterprises and
entanglements, attacking the laws regulating trade, opinion, combination, land tenure, which had been inherited from a previous
generation; its positive proposals were constitutional, aiming at a
democratic State structure, and they were constitutional only. If,
especially, proposals were made for interfering with the conditions of
employment, the Liberals of that generation heard them with
suspicion and accepted them, if acceptance was forced by events, with
reluctance. . . . In the same spirit every proposal of the same character
was received, and State interference as a whole was condemned as
injurious to commerce and relaxing to character.[74]

This attitude has to be contrasted with, for example, 'the measures of
social reform that were the distinctive work of the Liberal Government
of 1892 to 1895' and which entailed a great deal of state intervention in
economic and social life.[75] There are, Samuel goes on, numerous reasons
for the change of emphasis that has occurred: the machinery of
government has become both more efficient and responsible; circumstances have altered radically; the good effects of state action have been
seen; the social conscience has been awakened; a new concept of liberty
has emerged which recognizes that regulation is often a help rather than
a hindrance to fulfilment; and so on.[76] So while it is clear that the state
cannot do everything and there are boundaries beyond which its action
cannot or should not go, it is an acceptable general rule (if a vague one)
that it is entitled to act in any way which, in Jevons's words, '"adds to the
sum-total of human happiness"'.[77] Consequently as government becomes more efficient and new wants arise, 'the province of State action is
gradually enlarged' at both central and local level. And this is the kind of
process that, as Samuel saw it, lay behind the new and very different
Liberal platform of the day.[78] It is on this basis that he then goes on to
consider in detail a wide range of policies in many fields of domestic and
foreign policy.[79] The book is thus, in the Liberal context, a unique *tour de
force*: I think there is no similarly comprehensive review until the
Georgeite policy statements of the 1920s. It is also a work that makes very
clear the extensive and radical nature of the programme being urged by
the advanced Liberals. The Fabians themselves could show nothing quite
like this; and even allowing for the diffidence of Campbell-Bannerman
and some other party leaders, it is enough to scotch all the suggestions
that the Liberals were unable to set out a policy that would be attractive
to the reformist inclinations of the growing Labour movement.

74 ibid., pp.20–21.
75 ibid., pp.21–2. The exemplary measures concerned are listed ibid., pp.22–3.
76 ibid., pp.23–9.
77 ibid., pp.29–30, citing W. S. Jevons, *The State in Relation to Labour*, p.13.
78 Samuel, *Liberalism*, pp.24 n.1, 31.
79 ibid., parts II–IV.

This is a view reinforced by one other similar work which must be very briefly mentioned here, *The Meaning of Liberalism* published in 1912 by the scholar, journalist, and Liberal politician, J. M. Robertson. He urged that the basic feature of the doctrine had always been a concern with the underprivileged and that, in modern circumstances, this meant above all attention must be given to the social and other disabilities of the wage-earning classes. The Liberal, Robertson wrote, 'is the man who realizes that the growing demand of the mass for equity of treatment ought not to be refused on grounds of mere apprehension.'[80] And recognition of these claims, which was a moral matter, necessarily entailed public action: *laissez faire* was a perfectly reasonable maxim to follow when state interference was motivated by the interest of a privileged class; but this is not the case when the interference is 'scientifically planned' and motivated by the wish to serve 'the well-being of the entire community.'[81]

Theory

What was afoot in the transformation of Liberal doctrine was made clear not only by those active in the political arena in the decade before the Great War but also in the writings of various publicists and theorists who sought to provide a perhaps more systematic account of the nature and implications of the new emphasis and the intellectual factors at work in its development. These factors were, of course, extremely numerous and varied in nature: positivism, evolution, eugenics, changes in economic thought, utilitarianism, Idealism, and so on; all had a contribution to make to the emergence of the new Liberalism as it appeared in the context of the practical pressure for change.[82] This context with its schemes for old age pensions, dealing with unemployment, accepting public responsibility for feeding schoolchildren, and for establishing national insurance arrangements presented a climacteric in the growth of what John Rae called 'the English doctrine of social politics'. This theory of practical action undoubtedly gave the state a major role in the process of ameliorating conditions of life and work, of securing for the weaker classes 'the essentials of all rational and humane living'.[83] It involved a new concept of the community and its responsibility; but at the same time there was also concern about the protection of the individual. The theoretical problem hinged on the appropriate balance to be achieved between these two considerations.

What was clear was that the idea of the minimal state was more and

80 J. M. Robertson, *The Meaning of Liberalism* (London, 1912), pp. 24ff., 44.
81 ibid., pp. 54–5.
82 M. Freeden, *The New Liberalism: an Ideology of Social Reform* (Oxford, 1978) is a crucial survey.
83 J. Rae, 'State Socialism and Social Reform', *Contemporary Review*, lviii (1890), pp. 435, 436.

more being abandoned by the Liberal mainstream. During the 1870s and 1880s Dicey (then a Liberal supporter) might inveigh in an outburst of journalism about the dangers of centralization, the growth of executive power, Parliamentary weakness, and such like tokens of (as he saw it) undesirable collectivist advance.[84] But the new and contrasting position was increasingly urged and was, for instance, reflected in an editorial of 1903 in the new Liberal journal, the *Independent Review*, which argued that the 'gospel of freedom' as traditionally conceived had proved incapable of coping with the social evils of the day. A better answer was offered by 'the direct intervention of the State'. This passage continues:

> Let the community as a whole control what concerns the community; let the sources of production be worked by the State in the general interest. That is the answer given by the modern movement. . . . The future lies with those who can elicit and apply to actual life what is fruitful in the new ideas, and can combine it with those elements in our past inheritance that are still living and productive of good; who can, as occasion calls, determine the limits within which the community may interfere with advantage; who can discern the directions in which it may be to the interest of all for the corporate action of State or municipality to replace private initiative; and who can, at the same time, both safeguard and extend each man's full freedom of action where it does not clash with the common welfare, and can ensure that individual enterprise is neither thwarted nor impaired, but merely guided into those channels in which it can produce its best results.[85]

What Spencer had foreseen and feared would happen occurred: 'the welfare of the many came to be conceived . . . as the aim of Liberalism', the 'popular good has come to be sought by Liberals, not as an end to be indirectly gained by relaxations of restraints, but as the end to be directly gained.'[86] Or as John Rae said, in the article already cited, the function of government was 'to promote the mental and moral elevation of the people'; and so it had to look not to liberty alone but as well to 'every other necessary security for rational progress.'[87] There were qualms about bureaucratic mismanagement and paternalist despotism, the need to guard and preserve individual choice.[88] But from the point of view of the traditional doctrine the pass was sold. Something of the emphasis given by new Liberals in favour of the state is further exemplified in the

---

84 T. H. Ford, 'Dicey as a Political Journalist', *Political Studies*, xviii (1970), pp. 224–5, 227, 229, 234.
85 'A Plea for a Programme', *Independent Review*, i (1903–4), pp. 3–4.
86 H. Spencer, *The Man Versus the State* (1884; Penguin, 1969), p. 70.
87 Rae, art. cit., p. 436.
88 See the passage from F. V. Fisher, 'Social Democracy and Liberty', *Westminster Review*, cxli (1894), p. 651, cited in Freeden, op. cit., p. 61.

prospectus of the so-called 'Rainbow Circle'. This group – which met regularly from 1894 until 1920 – consisted of such people as Samuel, Rae, C. P. Trevelyan, Robertson, Hirst, and Hobson. Its aim was

> to provide a rational and comprehensive view of political and social progress, leading up to a consistent body of political and economic doctrine which could be ultimately formulated in a programme of action, and in that form provide a rallying point for social reformers. . . . It is proposed to deal with: (1) the reasons why the old Philosophic Radicalism and the Manchester School of Economics can no longer furnish a ground of action in the political sphere; (2) the transition from this school of thought to the so-called 'New Radicalism' or Collectivist politics of today; (3) the bases, ethical, economic and political, of the newer politics, together with the practical applications and inferences arising therefrom in the actual problems before us at the present time.[89]

But the fullest exposition of such ideas was reflected in the writings of L. T. Hobhouse and J. A. Hobson. The former died in 1929, the latter as recently as 1940, but their main, formative work in the establishment of collectivist Liberalism was really already done by the time the Great War occurred.

Hobhouse and 'Liberal Socialism'
It is an interesting paradox that part at least of Hobhouse's contemporary reputation rests on his criticism of Bosanquet's political theory as involving too large a role for the state. Yet, in fact, it is Hobhouse who urges a greater degree of public intervention in welfare and other fields.[90] It is the case, too, that while critical of Idealism his own view of things was much closer to the conceptual world of that philosophy than either his formal commitment to an empiricist rationalism should allow or than his *Metaphysical Theory of the State* might suggest.[91] He said himself that his philosophical inquiries in the end took him back 'into unexpected contact with Idealism' and he specifically admitted a debt to the work of both Green and Bosanquet.[92] In many

89 Samuel Papers, A/10, cited ibid., pp.256–7. On the collectivism of this circle, cf. P. F. Clarke, *Liberals and Social Democrats* (Cambridge, 1978), pp.54ff., esp. pp.56, 58–9.

90 S. Collini, 'Hobhouse, Bosanquet and the State: Philosophical Idealism and Political Argument in England 1880–1918', *Past and Present* (no.72, August 1976), p.87.

91 See M. Ginsberg, 'The Contribution of Professor Hobhouse to Philosophy and Sociology' (1929), in *Reason and Unreason in Society* (1947; London, 1965), ch.2, esp. pp.45–6, 58.

92 L. T. Hobhouse, *Liberalism* (1911; Galaxy Books, 1966), pp.67–9; biographical note preceding Hobhouse's 'The Philosophy of Development', J. H. Muirhead (ed.), *Contemporary British Philosophy: Personal Statements*, First Series (1924; London, 1953), p.150. Cf. Clarke, *Liberalism and Social Democrats*, pp.25–7.

ways this affinity is hardly surprising. As in the case of Green, the severe religious discipline of Hobhouse's home inculcated a strong moral sense which never left him; he came into close contact with the dominant Idealism of the day when he was at Oxford; and he early developed a commitment to practical work in the cause of social reform, becoming a zealous and advanced Liberal, one who was active, too, on the fringes of the Labour movement (which was, in fact, the subject of his first book in 1893). At the same time, he was open to other influences as well. His interest in philosophy was much affected by a Realist direction of thought as was indicated in the work on the theory of knowledge he published in 1896. He was equally fascinated by developments in the physical sciences, psychology, and sociology – in particular the writings of Spencer and Comte – and this reflects and helps to explain the empiricist bent of his mind. In this mode he was seized with a Baconian or Spencerian sense of the unity of all knowledge and the prospects of human progress. Hence his lifelong concern with nothing less than a synoptic view of human relations in all their aspects so as to reveal the laws or principles of social evolution, in particular the growth in the historical process of a social mentality, a sort of rational collective mind, in terms of which individuals progressively recognize their mutual involvement in the common good.[93] It was, as one recent commentator said, a 'rather unusual derivation of idealist conclusions from empiricist premises.'[94] Hobhouse's whole career showed that his interests were never merely academic and (as one of his pupils wrote) 'he longed to use his powers in the world of action.'[95] So he left Oxford and for some years worked on the *Manchester Guardian* whose editor C. P. Scott was then campaigning vigorously for a programme of social reform. Yet even in the midst of a prodigious journalistic output Hobhouse continued his philosophical and social studies; and in 1907 he returned to university life as holder of the new chair of Sociology at London though again without subsequently neglecting his political interests. He always believed that the intellectual and the practical must interrelate, that general principles must be brought to bear on and inform political judgement and involvement. J. A. Hobson believed that no one more than Hobhouse so well vindicated 'the unity that underlies theory and practice.'[96]

So far as the theory was concerned, Hobhouse presented a kind of fusion of Spencer and Green. In a form of hyper-Darwinism he uses the

93 e.g. Hobhouse, 'The Ethical Basis of Collectivism', *International Journal of Ethics*, viii (1897–8), pp.150–1, 154–5; Ginsberg, op. cit., p.53.
94 P. Weiler, 'The New Liberalism of L. T. Hobhouse', *Victorian Studies*, xvi (1972–3), p.143.
95 Mrs Barbara Hammond, cited in J. A. Hobson and M. Ginsberg, *L. T. Hobhouse: His Life and Work* (London, 1931), p.36.
96 ibid., p.61.

idea of evolutionary growth to underpin an ethic of individual fulfilment that entails a substantial degree of control over the social environment. For Hobhouse any valid theory had to rest on a scientific basis and, in his day, this meant the idea of evolution. 'I was convinced', he said in one place, 'that a philosophy that was to possess more than a speculative interest must rest on a synthesis of experience as interpreted by science, and that to such a synthesis the general conception of evolution offered a key.'[97] And if the process of evolution had been automatic in the natural world and even in the early stages of human development, there came a point where the mind began to acquire an increasingly conscious mastery over material factors and physical handicaps. It is in this way that civilization has emerged: science has begun to regulate man's environment, and ethics and religion have begun to form 'ideas of the unity of the race, and of the subordination of law, morals and social constitutions generally to the needs of human development which are the conditions of the control that is required.'[98] Evolution is, therefore, the story of the development of consciousness and self-consciousness and the resultant domination of mind over the conditions of life to ensure that human existence is increasingly pervaded by harmony, co-ordination, and adjustment.[99] Specifically social progress may be seen as the emergence of these features in human relationships.[100] It is thus the development of mind that enables the individual to grasp the importance of the communal framework within which he exists and the need for its rational, that is, conscious regulation: 'harmony . . . is something which does not come of itself, but is achieved in greater or less degree by effort, that is to say, by intelligence and will.'[101] The most highly evolved society, therefore, is one 'in which the efforts of its members are most completely coördinated to common ends, in which discord is most fully subdued to harmony.'[102] In general terms, of course, this is not incompatible with Spencer's near anarchist view. But the drift and conclusion of Hobhouse's use of these themes is of a contrasting kind; for he urges that the moral position established in such a sophisticated society involves a substantial regulatory role for various associations including above all the state. 'The evolutionist argument . . . correctly understood', he says, 'makes straight for collectivist control' as embodied for instance in the Factory Acts, sanitary regulations, and the Poor Laws.[103]

97 L. T. Hobhouse, *Development and Purpose: An Essay towards a Philosophy of Evolution* (London, 1913), p.xviii.
98 ibid., pp.xxii–xxiii.
99 ibid., pp.xxviii–xxix.
100 Hobhouse, *Social Evolution and Political Theory* (New York, 1911), pp.127, 185.
101 ibid., pp.93, 100–1.
102 ibid., p.23. Cf. ibid., pp.155–6.
103 L. T. Hobhouse, *The Labour Movement*, p.93; 'The Ethical Basis of Collectivism', loc. cit., p.155.

The detailed political discussion is deliberately put in the context of the transformation under way from the old to the new Liberalism. Hobhouse was fully aware of the great achievements of the classical doctrine in asserting the varied and numerous claims of individual freedom against arbitrary government and cramping restriction.[104] In its critical way, the old creed was a powerful 'movement of liberation, a clearance of obstructions, an opening of channels for the flow of free spontaneous vital activity.'[105] He was well seized, too, of the intellectual force of the many arguments by which this movement was justified, a dialectical array ranging from concepts of natural right to those associated with the utilitarian case for the maximization of human happiness; and all to sustain a plea for 'the unfettered action of the individual' as 'the mainspring of all progress' and thus the sole basis of particular and general welfare.[106] Yet he believed this doctrine was neither unassailable in theoretical terms nor, in the changing circumstances of the day, relevant or helpful. It had 'done its work' and 'had the air of a creed that is becoming fossilized as an extinct form'.[107] The need was, therefore, to revive Liberalism by giving it a fresh emphasis and impetus more appropriate to contemporary problems, and so restoring its fortunes and popularity. This meant above all dealing with the needs of the underprivileged, with all the terrible questions of poverty that still remained; and such purposes necessarily entailed a growing role for collective action. The case for this new emphasis was built on a 'more concrete' and 'positive' conception of freedom; and was encapsulated in the oft-quoted epigram: 'liberty without equality is a name of noble sound and squalid result.'[108]

As Hobhouse put it in one place, there is a distinction (of a clearly Millite kind) between 'social' and 'unsocial' freedom. The latter is 'the right of a man to use his powers without regard to the wishes or interests of any one but himself' and is obviously 'antithetic to all public control.' 'Social freedom' on the other hand rests on restraint and is the 'freedom to choose among those lines of activity which do not involve injury to others'; it is a 'liberty which can be enjoyed by all who dwell together' and it is 'measured by the completeness with which by law, custom, or their own feelings' people are 'restrained from mutual injury.' Naturally, as the experience of the social consequences of action widens, so the social conscience is awakened and the area of restraint increased.[109] Now classical Liberalism, though affirming in principle a doctrine of (in these terms) 'unsocial freedom', invariably conceded on moral and social

104 Hobhouse, *Liberalism*, pp.14–15 and ch.II *passim*.
105 ibid., p.28.
106 ibid., chs III–IV. The phrases cited are at p.44.
107 ibid., p.110. Cf. Hobhouse, *Democracy and Reaction* (London, 1904), pp.209–10.
108 Hobhouse, *Liberalism*, p.48.
109 ibid., pp.50–1.

grounds the need for certain exceptions to the general rule of non-interference. But these cases admitted of great extension: 'If the child was helpless, was the grown-up person . . . in a much better position?'[110] Hobhouse intended to press this intimation of the old doctrine in an increasingly collectivist direction.

The 'foundation of Liberty', he wrote, 'is the idea of growth', the ethical belief that the prime good is the fulfilment of the individual. So the kind of society to be sought is one that sustains this improvement to the highest possible degree: the 'best social life consists precisely in the harmonious working out to their fullest possible development of the best capacities of all members of the community.' True freedom (following Green) is properly said to be found 'when each man has the greatest possible opportunity for making the best of himself.' Society has to ensure such possibilities even though this necessarily involves some curtailment of freedom of action.[111] Thus 'the theory of collective action' is 'no less fundamental than the theory of personal freedom.'[112]

These opportunities for individual fulfilment are assisted by social agency of various kinds, that of the trade unions and co-operatives for instance, but above all perhaps by the effect of law at both national and local level. It is not that character and its development can be forced from without – on the contrary, personality 'grows from within' – but political fiat can help create the most suitable conditions for this growth. Therefore, the object of state action and of any compulsion this entails is 'to secure the most favourable external conditions of inward growth and happiness so far as these conditions depend on combined action and uniform observance'; or, as he put it elsewhere, to provide 'the material requisites for a good and full life for all members of the community.' And Hobhouse is prepared to accept the name of 'Liberal Socialism' for what this view entails.[113] And the sort of programme of social and economic reform required is (in the context of the day) not inconsiderable and involves vesting the state with a kind of overlordship in respect of property in general and of industrial assets in particular, covering such matters as control of the land, transfer to the community of socially created value, the ownership and operation of public utilities and key industries, the maintenance of a living wage for all, supervision of conditions of work, the elimination of functionless reward, extensive graduated taxation, limiting the possibilities of inheritance, generally ensuring a better distribution of the products of industry, and, in terms of welfare, the creation of a vast organization of state aid from old age

110 ibid., p.46. Cf. ibid., p.23.
111 ibid., p.66; *The Labour Movement*, pp.93–4.
112 Hobhouse, *Liberalism*, p.67.
113 ibid., pp.76, 78, 87; *The Labour Movement*, pp.3–4. Cf. *Liberalism*, p.91.

pensions and adequate housing to educational and insurance schemes.[114] Nor did his views on these questions moderate with time at all. In what is possibly his last paper he considers the role of the state in terms much like those he had used nearly forty years earlier and, for example, looks forward to 'an extension of public ownership and management in a variety of forms and degrees'.[115]

This is the great point of contrast between the old Liberalism and the new 'civic state'.[116] It is the notion that the individual is not to be seen as opposed to the state but as working through and with it, seeing it as a means essential to his own moral ends; that liberty in the full and proper sense requires restraint or control. Here, too, lies the possibility of danger to what is valuable in the old tradition; and so Hobhouse is careful to assert the need for tolerance of all forms of discussion and belief and for democratic forms and safeguards, urging for instance the decentralization of authority wherever feasible. With all its faults, actual and potential, democracy 'is the necessary basis of the Liberal idea.'[117] There are here all the possibilities of popular despotism and perhaps something of this element may be discerned in Hobhouse's harsh reference to idleness as 'a social pest, to be stamped out like crime'; a view little different in essence perhaps from Spencer's relegation of the 'unfit' to extinction in the struggle for existence.[118] Yet the general freedom of spirit of Hobhouse's argument may be found reflected in the concluding (and somewhat elaborate) passage of his early study of the Labour movement:

> The duty of having convictions is correlative and supplementary to the duty of tolerance and open-mindedness.
>
> Both duties may be recognised in our public action, and the due balance of both can alone secure a continuous forward movement of mankind, and in it lies the solution of the old question between liberty and authority. Using every available means of obtaining true ideas of what is necessary as the fundamental condition of social health, it is our right and duty to enforce that by any and every form of collective authority, legally or voluntarily constituted. It is equally right and good to leave a fair field of discussion open to all who consider themselves aggrieved, or who think we are in the wrong path. And, finally, collective control has not so much to make people good and happy, as to establish the necessary conditions of goodness and

114 Hobhouse, *Liberalism*, ch.VIII; *The Labour Movement*, pp.10, 51–3.
115 Hobhouse, 'Industry and the State' (1929), in *Sociology and Philosophy: a Centenary Collection of Essays and Articles* (London, 1966), p.232.
116 For this phrase, see *Liberalism*, p.9.
117 ibid., p.116. Cf. ibid., pp.90–1; *The Labour Movement*, pp.95–6.
118 *The Labour Movement*, p.13.

happiness, leaving it to individual effort and voluntary association to develop freely and spontaneously all the fair flower and fruit of human intercourse and knowledge and beauty. . . .[119]

It is this attitude, Hobhouse believed, which distinguished a Liberal from other forms of 'Socialism' whether Marxist or Fabian, both of which he repudiated.[120] And, above all, he always recognized (as did R. H. Tawney for the Socialists) that mere change of machinery can do nothing, it is 'worthless unless it is the expression of a change of spirit and feeling.'[121]

Hobson and the crisis of Liberalism

In his recent scholarly study of the new Liberalism, Dr Freeden suggests that it was J. A. Hobson who, more than most, recognized the great value of action through the state; also that he was 'by far the most original and penetrating of the new liberal theorists'.[122] This is certainly a judgement that the reading of Hobson's works is likely to favour.

Hobson was impressed and influenced by the writings of both Spencer and Ruskin. The latter made him see that economics is a branch of ethics and that matters of production and distribution cannot be viewed in disregard of their effect on the quality of life. The former persuaded him that social conduct has to be seen scientifically in the context of biology, society being an organic whole.[123] Hobson early came to the conclusion that capitalism was quite unacceptable as the economic basis of social organization. It caused waste, as in unemployment, and war; and the distribution of wealth it entailed was both deleterious in its economic effects (because it led to underconsumption) and morally quite unacceptable (because it deprived so many people of the chance of leading a full life). From this foundation Hobson was led to urge a whole range of social reforms to be achieved by redistributive taxation and extensive public provision and control. These themes he pursued through a series of influential works that appeared in the last years of the nineteenth century and the beginning of this. They included *The Physiology of Industry* (1889), *The Social Problem* (1901), *The Industrial System* (1909), and *Work and Wealth* (1914). The nature of the analysis and its specific application to the ideological change of emphasis in question here is, however, best revealed in *The Crisis of Liberalism* which

---

119 ibid., p.98.
120 For his rejection of 'Mechanical' and 'Official' Socialism, see *Liberalism*, pp.88–90.
121 Hobhouse, *The Labour Movement*, p.4. On Tawney, see ch.12 below, esp. pp.444–6.
122 M. Freeden, *The New Liberalism*, pp.66, 253. I have drawn freely on Dr Freeden's account, esp. pp.70–5, 99–116.
123 On these twin influences, see H. N. Brailsford, *The Life-Work of J. A. Hobson* (London, 1948), pp.5, 7.

appeared in 1909 two years before Hobhouse's more well-known review of these matters.

Hobson begins with the assumption that *laissez faire* Liberalism is dead in so far as it is a quite inappropriate framework of ideas with which to approach the major questions of the new century. But despite this, too many Liberals (he believed) still clung to its outmoded and extreme individualism.[124] It is true that a new Liberal viewpoint had been emerging but it had done so in a piecemeal or opportunistic way. What was necessary was to create instead a comprehensive and systematic policy of social reform. This was the test that contemporary Liberalism faced. And it was a crisis of traumatic proportions in that although the old individualism had long been dying it was still psychologically powerful, a major shibboleth difficult to abandon. Yet the key to success of the organic and progressive policy proposed was 'a new attitude to the functions of the State.'[125] Hobson specifically rejects a merely negative view of liberty and urges instead a positive conception of freedom involving the creation of conditions of fulfilment. This meant the establishment in various ways of equality of opportunity in particular through adequate educational provision.[126] A notable extension of public control of industry will be required, especially where its processes are of a 'routine' or socially 'necessary' character.[127] This might well entail public ownership of the railways, of electricity and other sources of energy, the provision of state insurance schemes, more equitable access to the courts, and so on.[128] Hobson summarizes the demands involved in a context that indicates the change of view required:

> It is true that the attainment of this practical equalisation of opportunities involves a larger use of the State and legislation than Liberals of an older school recognised as necessary or desirable. But the needs of our day are different from theirs, and the modern State is a different instrument. There is nothing in Liberalism to preclude a self-governing people from using the instrument of self-government for any of the measures I have named: on the contrary, to refuse to do so is to furnish the mere forms of liberty and to deny the substance. . . . Free land, free travel, free power, free credit, security, justice and education, no man is 'free' for the full purposes of civilised life to-day unless he has all these liberties.[129]

124 J. A. Hobson, *The Crisis of Liberalism: New Issues of Democracy* (London, 1909), pp. vii–viii, 3–4.
125 ibid., p. xi.
126 ibid., pp. 93–4 and II.ii *passim*.
127 ibid., II.iii, esp. pp. 131–2.
128 ibid., pp. 99–108. Cf. the 'new People's Charter', pp. 171–2.
129 ibid., p. 113.

In his various works Hobson spelled out in almost Fabian detail the requirements of the minimum standard of life to be provided by public agencies. It included 'Good air, large sanitary houses, plenty of wholesome, well-cooked food, adequate changes of clothing for our climate, ample opportunities for recreation' and, as well, 'art, music, travel, education', and so forth.[130] He was very much aware of the resistance to these advances that existed in established arrangements; but he felt that unless Liberalism was prepared to grasp the nettle of social reform and engage in the radical change required it would be doomed.[131] Of course, Hobson keenly appreciated the dangers of excessive bureaucracy and other barriers to the individual development of character and moral understanding.[132] But the need to create the possibility of spiritual and cultural advance was crucial. The main deficiency of the industrial system was a 'failure of central control' and this had to be remedied above all else.[133] Hobson believed that a reformed Liberalism could undertake the task. And if later he was not so sure and associated himself with the ILP and the Labour Party, it is also true that he never really felt at home there. It is in a Liberal context that his best work was done.

THE YELLOW BOOK AND ALL THAT

Do you see this square old yellow Book, . . .?
A book in shape but, really, pure crude fact
Secreted from man's life when hearts beat hard,
And brains, high-blooded, ticked two centuries since.
Give it me back! The thing's restorative
I' the touch and sight.
R. BROWNING, *The Ring and the Book*, 1868–9, I. 33, 86–90

It is undoubtedly the case that the Liberal Party and its cause were severely damaged by the crisis unleashed by the Great War.[134] The issues arising from the formation of the coalition with the Conservatives in 1915, the introduction of conscription, and finally, of course, the split in the party leadership were traumatic. To a traditional Liberal like Richard Holt, it seemed that 'All the old principles . . . have been

130 J. A. Hobson, *The Social Problem: Life and Work* (1901; 2nd edn, London, 1909), p.79.
131 Hobson, *The Crisis of Liberalism*, II.iv (pp.133–8).
132 e.g. Hobson, *John Ruskin, Social Reformer* (London, 1899), pp.204–5.
133 Hobson, *The Crisis of Liberalism*, pp.265–6.
134 For recent discussion of the decline and its possible causes, see T. Wilson, *The Downfall of the Liberal Party, 1914–1935* (1966; Fontana, 1968); K. O. Morgan (ed.), *The Age of Lloyd George* (London, 1971), pp.38–9 and ch. 3 *passim*; M. Bentley, *The Liberal Mind, 1914–1929* (Cambridge, 1977), ch.1. There is a brief summary of the different views in the introduction to K. D. Brown (ed.), *Essays in Anti-Labour History: Responses to the Rise of Labour in Britain* (London, 1974), pp.8–10.

virtually abandoned'; he felt that Liberalism could not live in the atmosphere of war.[135] It was not simply the Liberal Party which was regarded as having been routed; the 'death of Liberalism' itself was seen to have occurred.[136] Of course, George survived; and he continued the belief in state intervention in order (as he told Lord Riddell in 1918) 'to secure that everyone has a fair chance and that there is no unnecessary want and poverty.'[137] And there was something still of the progressive social spirit of the new Liberalism in the coalition manifesto for the election of that year as also in the 1923 campaign after the *rapprochement* with Asquith.[138] And despite the variations of emphasis manifest in George's views during the mid-1920s, this theme continued to emerge clearly in the major policy inquiries he sponsored. Of course, the emphasis on social reform did not appear uniquely there but the stimulus he gave was considerable: C. F. G. Masterman told his wife that although he often disagreed greatly with George he had to confess that when he 'came back to the party, ideas came back to the party' too.[139]

Beatrice Webb confided to her diary at the end of 1916 that radicals should have high hopes of the new coalition government. The Asquith administration had been too Whiggish and was on the whole opposed in principle to state control even for war purposes. Its successor would, she thought, 'be boldly and even brutally interventionist' where necessary, breaking all conventions and controlling all inconvenient vested interests.[140] And during the following year one of the Liberal ministers in the new Cabinet, C. Addison, believed that by 1917 the country was 'ready for a bold move forward under State inspiration.'[141] Certainly it was necessary to accommodate the new social forces the war had released. The so-called 'Manchester wing' of the party, which included such people as Ernest Simon and which was very different from the earlier 'Manchester School', wanted to pursue a radical industrial policy involving increased state responsibility including even nationalization in some cases such as railways and mines. This kind of programme would, it was hoped, help retain the support of some who might otherwise adhere to the Labour Party. The object was to enable capitalism to work

135   Holt diary (6 August 1916), Holt MSS, Liverpool Central Library, cited in Bentley, op. cit., p.41.
136   S. McKenna, *While I Remember* (London, 1921), p.186. This phrase appears in a chapter entitled 'At the Liberal Graveside'.
137   Lord Riddell, *War Diary 1914–1918* (London, n.d. [1933]), p.324.
138   Morgan, op. cit., pp.74, 192–3.
139   L. Masterman, *C.F.G. Masterman: a Biography* (London, 1939), pp.345–6.
140   M. Cole (ed.), *Beatrice Webb's Diaries, 1912–1924* (London, 1952), p.74. For earlier unfavourable comments about Asquith's lukewarm attitude to intervention, cf. B. Webb, *Our Partnership* (London, 1948), pp.112, 224.
141   C. Addison, *Four and a Half Years: a Personal Diary from June 1914 to January 1919* (London, 1934), ii.459.

better and ensure fair play in industry and see its benefits were more widely spread and to do this without destroying the basis of competitive private enterprise. Socialism would simply put economic man in a strait-jacket and frustrate initiative. But there was opposition to these views from more traditionally minded Liberals who in 1920 formed the 'Liberal Anti-Nationalization Committee' to fight these suggestions.[142] Thus the split in the party at the personal and organizational level was reflected in ideological terms.

In 1920 C. F. G. Masterman published a survey of the new Liberalism as it appeared in its application to the affairs of the post-war world.[143] He himself described the account as 'pretty sketchy and thin.'[144] And so it is in many respects and prone to a rather flowery rhetoric too: but through it all the message is clear. Both the dominant state run by 'Samurai' and the night-watchman state are firmly rejected.[145] What is crucial is (within those extremes) the enlargement of freedom seen in positive terms: the goal of Liberalism in home affairs is to achieve both 'the triumph of liberty' and 'the destruction of poverty'.[146] And inevitably, therefore, the role of public authority must be greater than old-fashioned Liberals would have accepted.[147] More increments of state ownership will be necessary, of great natural resources and monopolies such as coal, transport, and the land; equally government must act to secure an adequate level of wages, limited hours of work, proper and reasonable housing, and provision against unemployment.[148] A not dissimilar kind of emphasis was visible in the papers presented to the Liberal Summer School in 1922: a general attempt to steer between the claims of liberty and the need for state provision and control is here worked out in a number of fields and in some specific detail.[149] Professor Henry Clay of Manchester University espoused the same cause of moderation and the middle way. In an interesting paper published in mid-1926 he urged that a reformulation of Liberal principles was necessary if the party was to be held together and the demands of a widening electorate met, and this on a basis distinct from those of the other two parties. The sticking-point he seized on was free trade and the problem was to find a domestic policy compatible with it that would serve the purposes in view and that would

142 Bentley, op. cit., pp. 142, 143.
143 C. F. G. Masterman, *The New Liberalism* (London, 1920), preface, pp. vii–ix.
144 Letter (18 June 1920), cited in L. Masterman, *C. F. G. Masterman*, p. 316.
145 Masterman, *The New Liberalism*, pp. 28, 105.
146 ibid., pp. 26, 29–30, 36–7.
147 ibid., p. 134.
148 ibid., chs v–vii.
149 Lord Robert Cecil *et al.*, *Essays in Liberalism* (London, 1922): see esp. pp. viii, 146–7 on the 'Liberal Bias'; pp. 157–8, 165–8 on a state-enforced minimum wage; pp. 149–50 on extended financial control; and pp. 154–5, 199ff. on the state and the coal-mines and railways.

as well keep business and government distinct, a fundamental point.[150] The answer could not be a pure or simple *laissez faire*. Certainly the objective must be free enterprise and free competition; but this did not mean the absence of state regulation of any kind; nor did it entail tolerating the degree of economic inequality that had grown up in our society. Clay was in fact prepared to accept the large inheritance of an effective industrial code to supervise conditions of work and prevent 'the grosser forms of exploitation'. Similarly he condoned 'a reasonable minimum of free education and of provision for all cases of invalidity and unemployment'. And, in Benthamite fashion, inequality should be minimized by various devices such as the heavier taxation of higher incomes and 'the repartition by inheritance of large aggregations of capital in every generation' so as to secure a wider diffusion of property.[151] He believed, too, that some key economic functions that for efficiency required a monopolistic organization – the railways, electricity supply, or banking, for instance – might be operated as public utilities: not as government departments, however, but rather as corporations on the model of the Port of London Authority.[152] He urged that in this way the essentials of private enterprise would be sustained and the economic and social demands of a popular democracy be met more effectively than through any other means. He accepted indeed that private enterprise was the most efficient way of producing goods and feared the excessive growth of government economic activities as a threat to the freedom of the individual.[153]

Of greatest importance, however, in the attempt to make Liberalism the medium of a new social critique were the ideas emanating from George's wing of the party. In an attempt to recast the Liberal point of view he collected around him a staff of advisers and produced a series of new programmes. Foremost among those connected with this enterprise was J. M. Keynes who, in a celebrated lecture given in 1926, sounded the death-knell of the traditional doctrine of a series of crisp negative assertions:

> Let us clear from the ground the metaphysical or general principles upon which from time to time, *laissez-faire* has been founded. It is *not* true that individuals possess a prescriptive 'natural liberty' in their economic activities. There is *no* 'compact' conferring perpetual rights on those who Have or those who Acquire. The world is *not* so governed from above that private and social interest always coincide.

150 H. Clay, 'Liberalism, Laissez Faire and Present Industrial Conditions', *Hibbert Journal*, xxiv (1925–6), pp.731–3.
151 ibid., p.738.
152 ibid., p.739.
153 'Sir Henry Clay', in *DNB*, ii.2570. He was later concerned, too, about the consequences e.g. in respect of inflation, of Keynesian full employment policies, ibid.

It is *not* so managed here below that in practice they coincide. It is *not* a correct deduction from the Principles of Economics that enlightened self-interest always operates in the public interest. Nor is it true that self-interest generally *is* enlightened; more often individuals acting separately to promote their own ends are too ignorant or too weak to attain even these. Experience does *not* show that individuals, when they make up a social unit, are always less clear-sighted than when they act separately.[154]

It is impossible, Keynes continued, to settle the proper role of public action on abstract grounds: it is a matter of particular merit and specific consideration. Possibly the main job of economists is, in neo-Benthamite fashion, 'to distinguish afresh the *Agenda* of Government from the *Non-Agenda*', while the cognate task of students of politics is 'to devise forms of Government within a Democracy which shall be capable of accomplishing the *Agenda*.'[155] In this context Keynes looked to the ongoing development of the semi-autonomous corporation as a promising institutional device; and suggested that the proper role of government itself was to do, not what individuals were already doing, but what no one would do if the state did not. Examples were dealing with the currency, unemployment, or population problems by central action.[156] It is not so much a question of replacing capitalism but of managing it wisely; if this is done, a greater economic efficiency will be achieved than under any alternative system yet in sight.[157]

What was involved in terms of detailed policy was spelled out in a series of programmatic statements that appeared in the 1920s. A portent of things to come was the brief survey of Liberalism and industry produced in 1920 by Professor Ramsay Muir summarizing the conclusions of a series of meetings of Manchester businessmen held the previous year under the aegis of Sir Ernest Simon.[158] Then there were the addresses and papers, subsequently published, that were originally given as lectures to meetings of the London Liberal Candidates Association and the Liberal Summer Schools. These schools had begun in 1922 and constituted a major focus of discussion of Britain's economic and other difficulties. The object was to transcend the level of normal party propaganda and to attempt a systematic restatement of 'Liberal philosophy in its application to the major problems of the day.'[159] Partly,

154 J. M. Keynes, *The End of Laissez-Faire* (London, 1926), pp. 39–40, italics in original.
155 ibid., pp. 40–1.
156 ibid., pp. 41–9.
157 ibid., pp. 52–3.
158 R. Muir, *Liberalism and Industry* (London, 1920). See also the remarks of Sir E. Simon, in S. Hodgson (ed.), *Ramsay Muir: an Autobiography and Some Essays* (London, 1943), pp. 181–4.
159 H. L. Nathan and H. H. Williams (eds), *Liberal Points of View* (London, 1927), and

of course, the exercise was concerned with showing how Liberalism had a distinctive approach, in particular the extent to which there was and was not an affinity with the policies of the Labour movement. And while there was no commitment to state intervention for itself simply, it was broadly recognized that circumstances demanded its extension both generally to create more equality of opportunity and in particular to cope with specific problems such as unemployment.[160] In one lecture on 'Liberalism and Industry' Keynes stressed the changing nature of the doctrine, the way it was varying in response to the rise of democracy, the claims of the wage-earning classes, and the new economic problems of the day; and he indicated that it was altering in such a manner that the fulfilment by government of certain crucial tasks was necessarily entailed. In this context he refers to a range of responsibilities from the reform of company law to the supervision of labour and its conditions of work; but most interestingly there is no mention at all of the role government might play in regulating the level of economic activity by fiscal manipulation.[161] And, of course, in the later volume there is substantial reference to the proposals of the Industrial Inquiry which are said indeed by one enthusiast to constitute the details of a Liberal Utopia.[162] Certainly this inquiry was the most extensive and well-known of these studies in Liberal policy: the famous 'Yellow Book' of 1928 entitled *Britain's Industrial Future*. This volume was the work of a committee which, as well as George himself, included Hubert Henderson, Keynes, Ramsay Muir, B. S. Rowntree, Herbert Samuel, and Sir John Simon: clearly a high-powered and authoritative body from the world of Liberalism whose influence in later years was very considerable and not by any means only on their own party. This investigation had been set to work and financed by George.

In the introduction to the detailed programme the inquiry established in general terms what it took to be the genuine and proper Liberal point of view and, in so doing, it repudiated both an extreme individualism and a doctrinaire Socialism. The conditions which made the idea of *laissez faire* feasible had passed away. Political democracy had been established and its devices were properly being used to remedy the grievances of the people arising from the defects of the existing industrial system, to create

---

    Liberalism and Some Problems of Today (London, 1929). The phrase cited is from the introductory note to the former volume at p.11.

160 e.g. T. E. Gregory, 'The Production and Distribution of Wealth', Nathan and Williams (eds), *Liberal Points of View*, esp. pp.48–9, 69; and H. D. Henderson, Nathan and Williams (eds), *Liberalism and Some Problems of Today*, pp.464ff.

161 J. M. Keynes, 'Liberalism and Industry', Nathan and Williams (eds), *Liberal Points of View*, ch.VIII, esp. pp.205–7, 212ff.

162 See esp. E. H. Gilpin, 'Liberal Industrial Policy', and W. T. Layton, 'The Liberal Utopia', Nathan and Williams (eds), *Liberalism and Some Problems of Today*.

the conditions necessary to their welfare, to see that no member of the community was denied 'the opportunity to live a full and free life.' This was to a great degree a matter of achieving justice and efficiency in the economic realm.[163] Given, however, that Liberalism stands for liberty it was wrong to suppose that it must, therefore, involve the negative doctrine that the greatest freedom is obtained when government does least. A more positive view of the matter is necessary: 'Often more law may mean more liberty.'[164] This does not mean at all that the functions of the state should be increased as much as possible: there should be no commitment to state intervention for its own sake simply. Nevertheless, Herbert Spencer and classical Liberalism are firmly repudiated:

> We are not with those who say that, whatever may be our present difficulties, the intervention of the State would only increase them. . . . The scope of useful intervention by the whole Society, whether by constructive action of its own or by regulating or assisting private action, is seen to be much larger than was formerly supposed. . . . [There] is much positive work that the State can do which is not merely consistent with liberty, but essential to it. The idea of the extreme individualist, that in proportion as State action expands freedom contracts, is false.

In this light, the inquiry approved the progressive assumption by the state over the previous hundred years of 'a vast range of functions that closely affect industry and commerce.'[165] Its aim was to show how the further pursuit of a wider freedom could be carried through in the conditions of the mid-twentieth century. In this context the committee went on to elaborate its perception of the main contemporary problems facing the British economy and how it thought these might most effectively be tackled. And, in the terms indicated, the role of public authority was a considerable and increasing one. This was quite explicitly acknowledged when, for instance, it was stated that the greater part of the proposals made 'will be found to demand legislation or administrative action from Parliament or the Government of the day'.[166]

On this basis, then, the inquiry recommended a wide range of measures: a more effective (though not more extensive) role for the various forms of 'Public Concern';[167] an increasing control by government over private industry especially where monopoly prevailed and in

163 *Britain's Industrial Future being the Report of the Liberal Industrial Inquiry* (London, 1928), pp. xvii, xxi.
164 ibid., p. xix.
165 ibid., pp. xix–xxi.
166 ibid., p. vi.
167 ibid., pp. 61, 63ff., 456–8.

connexion with the flow of investment;[168] the establishment of better machinery of government supervision as through a Committee of National Development, a Ministry for Industry (in which should be centralized the whole system of state regulation), an Economic General Staff, and improved statistical data as a basis for state guidance of industry;[169] the stimulation by state action of management skills and the rationalization of industry;[170] provision for a system of compulsory arbitration in the settlement of industrial disputes;[171] a programme (under state stimulation and regulation) of industrial co-operation and conciliation by the setting up of Trade Boards, Joint Industrial Councils, Works Councils, a representative Council of Industry, the encouragement of various forms of profit-sharing, and the like.[172] There should also be increasing state concern with the problem of unemployment and the alleviation of the suffering and waste it causes through a vigorous policy of national reconstruction to achieve planned development in many important fields such as roads, housing and slum clearance, electricity, docks and waterways, agriculture and mining, and the development of educational facilities.[173] In addition the diffusion of property ownership should be more deliberately pursued through taxation policy and control of inheritance, and the encouragement of saving and investment on a wide and popular scale.[174] In broad principle and in each case the matter was one of harmonizing the respective claims of individual liberty and the general good, personal initiative and a common plan.[175]

In fine it all added up to a programme of advance towards 'a new industrial order', one which was essentially 'a system of industrial self-government under the regulation and encouragement of the State.' And it was 'the business of statesmanship to perceive the direction of this movement, and to guide and assist it.'[176]

Not all reaction to the Yellow Book was favourable. MacCallum Scott wrote in his diary not long after the proposals were published:

> The mind of the man in the street simply refuses to digest this mass of dry intellectual chaff. Few even of the most hardened politicians will digest it. It is a mass of detailed proposals, comments and exhortations

168 ibid., pp.61, 110–15, 458–61.
169 ibid., pp.116–25, 220ff., 286, 461–2.
170 ibid., p.132.
171 ibid., chs xv, xvii; pp.465–6.
172 ibid., book 3 *passim*; pp.468–74.
173 ibid., book 4 *passim*; pp.476–80.
174 ibid., ch. xix.
175 ibid., p.63.
176 ibid., p.205.

but absolutely no general idea of political principle emerges. It will not be a life-belt but a sodden sack of straw for the unfortunate Liberal candidates in the next election.[177]

This was not only unfair as an analysis but as a prophecy was not borne out by events: the Liberal vote nearly doubled in the 1929 election. George's programme promised to reduce the number of those out of work to a normal level within one year and without any increase in taxation. The centrepiece of the policy was a massive programme of 'works of national utility and development' in such areas as 'electricity, telephones, housing, roads, and railways'. The scheme was, George claimed, the result of the earlier inquiry, 'the only thorough and consistent study which has been given to our national problems during the last few years'.[178]

Nor did subsequent reviews of Liberal policy in the period before the Second World War differ very much in emphasis. There was, for instance, the survey published in 1934 under the aegis of the National Liberal Federation, a document which, while repudiating a merely doctrinaire adherence to planning for its own sake, accepted as a basic premiss the view that in certain crucial aspects of economic life government regulation was vital: in the fields of money, transport, and power; in the use of land and in respect of afforestation; for the provision of schools and houses; to secure industrial peace; and, by social services, to protect the weaker elements of the community, prevent poverty and unemployment, and conduct a war against unhealthy living conditions.[179] The detailed elaboration of these themes is little more than a more general or popular version of the programme of the Yellow Book of 1928.[180] But, perhaps more than in the earlier statement, there is a concern both to repudiate the extreme versions of classical Liberalism and to deny that the growing acceptance of state interference by Liberals necessarily meant there was no difference between them and the Socialists and Tories who (in their varied ways) also stressed the economic role of government.[181] Rejecting the policy of leaving things alone did not mean accepting a complete system of 'state-management': the middle way of 'state-regulation' of the free enterprise system and not its abolition was the properly Liberal theme, for it is

177 MacCallum Scott Diary (3 February 1928), cited in Bentley, *The Liberal Mind, 1914–1929*, p.113.
178 F. W. S. Craig, *British General Election Manifestos, 1918–1966* (Chichester, 1970), p.61.
179 National Liberal Federation, *The Liberal Way: a Survey of Liberal Policy* . . . (London, 1934), pp.127–35, 182, 188ff.
180 ibid., parts V–VI.
181 See esp. ibid., pp.169–72.

merely the expression, in the economic sphere, of the essential function of the State in relation to its citizens, a function which it can never abdicate – that of securing for them all, and especially for the weaker among them, peace, justice, and liberty, and the opportunity of using their own powers to the best advantage, and of living the best kind of life of which they are capable.[182]

This ethos was reflected, too, in George's campaign during 1935 for a 'new deal' for 'Peace and Reconstruction' based on a massive programme of government expenditure to combat unemployment and the creation of more effective machinery, like a general staff, for economic planning. But in the political context of the day it all had little direct political effect.[183] Yet obviously, if this Yellow-Book Liberalism fell short of an extreme state Socialism, it was nevertheless a very different doctrine from that which Cobden or Spencer or Morley would have accepted. Even so fervent an individualist as Ramsay Muir, hostile to the growth of bureaucratic power, recognized as inevitable a substantial degree of state intervention in the economic sphere and that this role would even expand still further.[184] And Beveridge's social ideas, though they veered between an almost total commitment to the free market and an equally strong advocacy of an authoritarian administrative state, had by the 1930s come round to accepting comprehensive government planning for large-scale social reform.[185] As the second war intensified, so this propensity was strongly reinforced not least as a means of securing an effective programme of post-war reconstruction.[186] So far on this road did he travel that Mrs Webb believed he had in effect become a Socialist.[187]

AN UNSERVILE STATE – AND COMMUNITY POLITICS

. . . we propose that the existing Welfare State should be transformed
. . . into a Welfare Society.
E. DODDS in G. Watson (ed.), *The Unservile State*, 1957, p.20

182 ibid., p.171. Cf. ibid., pp.181, 185.
183 Morgan, *The Age of Lloyd George*, p.105; F. Owen, *Tempestuous Journey: Lloyd George, his Life and Times* (London, 1954), pp.729–30; I. Macleod, *Neville Chamberlain* (London, 1961), pp.171–2.
184 R. Muir, *How Britain Is Governed: a Critical Analysis of Modern Developments in the British System of Government* (London, 1930), pp.302, 304.
185 J. Harris, *William Beveridge: a Biography* (Oxford, 1977), pp.2, 311–12, 324, 328; for the phases of thought involved, see *idem*, 'The Social Thought of William Beveridge', *Bulletin of the Society for the Study of Labour History* (no. 31, Autumn 1975), pp.8–10.
186 Harris, *William Beveridge*, pp.365–6. Cf. Beveridge's *Full Employment in a Free Society: a Summary* (London, 1944), pp.39–40.
187 Cited in Harris, op. cit., p.366.

The Liberal balance

The Liberal case as developed in the post-war period has reflected the varied emphasis already described though, as with the later Beveridge, there has been some tendency to stress a need to move away from state provision. The ambivalence is clear. One publicist, writing a few years ago in *The Times* newspaper, argued that a competitive economic system based on private enterprise ought to be sustained not only as being more efficient than any alternative but also as in practice 'a prerequisite of freedom'. Yet at the same time he urged the need to secure greater public support for the social services and for other areas of communal value.[188] Similarly a popular statement of Liberal ideology and programme that appeared in the late 1950s bore a like imprint. The change in the doctrine at the turn of the century is accepted; and the idea of state intervention and the inspiration of the Yellow Book run throughout.[189] Yet a free economy is stressed albeit distinguished from *laissez faire* in that government regulation will be required to ensure its efficient functioning and to provide as well substantial welfare and similar services.[190]

A key reflection of the Liberal search for identity in the post-war era was the symposium on the so-called 'Unservile State' which appeared in 1957: significantly the book was sub-titled 'Essays in Liberty *and* Welfare'.[191] It was the work of a group of interested persons which had been formed in Oxford in 1953 with the object of developing and propagating Liberal ideas. Together with a supplementary series of essays issued a few years later by the Oxford Liberal Group and entitled *Radical Alternative* (1962) and with an accompanying array of pamphlets, all this constituted the first full-scale exploration of Liberal attitudes and policies since the Yellow Book of 1928. The basic theme is the need to rely on the state for crucial provision; while the underlying hope is the possibility of replacing government action by that of individuals and groups themselves. Thus in an introductory essay Elliott Dodds (then editor of the *Huddersfield Examiner* and vice-president of the Liberal Party) urged that Liberalism repudiated any antithesis between liberty and welfare, regarding them rather as complementary means to the same basic end: the creation of opportunities for men and women to become self-directing, responsible persons. Fulfilment sometimes requires absence of restraint; sometimes – where social conditions unduly narrow possibilities or frustrate choice – it entails positive measures. And, while the state must often be involved, it was to be hoped

188 J. Grimond, 'The Two Dilemmas of Democracy', *The Times* (4 July 1970), p. 9.
189 R. Fulford, *The Liberal Case* (Penguin, 1959), esp. pp. 150–1, 153–8.
190 ibid., pp. 98–9.
191 My italics. See G. Watson (ed.), *The Unservile State: Essays in Liberty and Welfare* (London, 1957).

that this role would diminish and the area of private endeavour, voluntary service, and mutual aid be correspondingly enlarged. The goal is a welfare society rather than a welfare state.[192] It followed that, in order to stimulate any tendencies in this direction, Liberals should be distributist, wanting to spread wealth, ownership, power, and responsibility as much as possible and to create greater equality of opportunity. And if it was necessary to plan the economy in certain central points this was basically to preserve the freedom of economic life as a whole.[193] The Liberal position is summarized elsewhere in this volume as follows:

> The root of Liberalism is belief in the intrinsic value of the individual. From this belief springs the demand for freedom and the fear of concentration of power, since this concentration is seen to lead to an inevitable limitation of opportunities for the individual to make responsible choices and to the probable abuse of power, with wanton restrictions on individual freedom.
>
> In applying these principles to industrial affairs, Liberals normally favour the system of free enterprise with a large number of competing firms, and oppose the growth of State-owned industry and of private monopolies. Free enterprise gives a wider range of choice to the consumer enabling him to spend his money as he sees fit; greater scope for the entrepreneur to develop his ideas, his capital and his energies to the best advantage; and greater opportunity for the worker to choose his employer and his job. But while we must logically be supporters of free enterprise we do not deny that the State has rights and duties in the economic and industrial sphere, and it will be a major problem for the Liberal society of the future to decide what action the State should take to ensure that relationships within industry, and between industry and the State, are in accordance with Liberal ideas.[194]

This kind of belief could be seen as a comment on the recession of collectivist ideas it might have been reasonable to discern at a time when setting the people free of controls was a popular slogan.[195] In fact Liberal

192 E. Dodds, 'Liberty and Welfare', in Watson (ed.), *The Unservile State*, pp.15–19.
193 ibid., pp.20–2. For a more detailed review of the Liberal concept of equality, see P. Wiles, 'Property and Equality', ibid., ch.IV. G. Watson, *Is Socialism Left?* (Unservile State Paper no.14; 1967; rev. edn, London, 1972) is an attack on the dominant statist elements in Socialism. Cf. a recent persuasive plea in behalf of individuality in M. Cranston, *The Right to Privacy* (Unservile State Paper no.21; n.p. [London], n.d. [1974]).
194 N. Sear, 'Relations in Industry', in Watson (ed.), *The Unservile State*, p.187. The case for co-operation is then developed from this premiss. On the crucial role of the free market mechanism, see also W. Eltis, 'Growth Without Inflation', in G. Watson (ed.), *Radical Alternative: Studies in Liberalism by the Oxford Liberal Group* (London, 1962), pp.84–5.
195 Cf. N. Micklem, in Watson (ed.), *The Unservile State*, pp.314–15.

programmes themselves often bore a decidedly interventionist imprint urging, for instance, the need for 'a national plan for economic growth', government playing 'a far more positive role in the export drive', more effective transport and housing policies within a framework of population and regional planning, control over incomes, government stimulation of scientific development, and the like.[196] The 1966 manifesto closed with a call for a 'plan for the best interest of all individuals' and for 'positive action to create a closer partnership between all sections of the community'.[197]

A typical amalgam of libertarian and collectivist tendencies in the 1960s is the review of Liberalism by Donald Wade (for a brief period Deputy Leader of the Parliamentary party) entitled *Our Aim and Purpose*. There is the ritual stress on freedom and the value of individual personality, on the importance of encouraging initiative and participation, on private property as a means of enlarging personal liberty, on shared ownership in industry, on the maximization of choice, and so on. At the same time it is denied that Liberalism entails *laissez faire* and freely acknowledged that there must be a substantial role played by the central government and other public agencies of direction and regulation in creating the framework of a free society.[198] The state must 'prevent exploitation and . . . limit privilege'; it must plan to ensure full employment, the proper allocation of resources and, therefore, control prices and wages to some degree; it has major though not unique responsibilities in the provision of social welfare concerning health, education, and housing.[199] A more extensive analysis on broadly the same lines was provided shortly afterwards by the report of a Liberal Party inquiry under the chairmanship of Lord Wade (as he had then become), resting on the twin pillars of liberty, participation, and diversity on the one hand and of the duty of the state to create the conditions of fulfilment on the other.[200] It is pretty clear, however, that the modern Liberal Party has, since the century's beginning, gone a long way on the statist road and, in the pursuit of positive freedoms, has endorsed numerous 'coercive interventions' to this end.[201]

But one fresh – and yet old – version of a more libertarian balance

196 See e.g. the programmes for the 1964 and 1966 elections, in F. W. S. Craig (ed.), *British General Election Manifestos, 1918–1966* (Chichester, 1970), pp.247–54, 286–97.
197 ibid., p.297.
198 D. Wade, *Our Aim and Purpose* (Liberal Publication Dept, 1961; 4th edn, London, 1967), pp.8, 9.
199 ibid., pp.20, 24–25, 28ff.
200 The Liberal Commission, *Liberals Look Ahead* (Liberal Publication Dept, London, n.d. [1969]), esp. p.8.
201 Cf. C. K. Rowley, 'Liberalism and Collective Choice', *National Westminster Bank Quarterly Review* (May 1979), pp.12–13.

between individual and public forces has taken the form of a new Liberal radicalism frequently associated with so-called 'youth politics'.

Radical Liberalism and participatory democracy

This development arises partly out of a sense of the bigness and remoteness of our social institutions and the insolubility of contemporary political problems; partly out of a, perhaps consequential, sense of alienation and ineffectiveness on the part of many groups and individuals. And though these questions, of size, decentralization, and participation, for instance, have not been unrecognized by the party leadership,[202] the activity and pressure to explore this new perspective or dimension of Liberalism has largely come from younger members and the grass-roots. Foremost among those expounding the themes involved has been P. Hain. And although he later switched his political allegiance to the Labour Party – a little oddly perhaps in view of what he had so recently said about it – it was nevertheless in the Liberal context that his ideas for the regeneration of radicalism were first formulated, so they may not inappropriately be considered here (even though he sometimes called the point of view 'libertarian socialism').

The basic thrust of the criticism of contemporary society is that it is dominated socially and economically by great gulfs of inequality arising from the capitalist system. It is also warped by technology and the curse of bigness as exemplified by the multinational corporation and the public bureaucracy alike. It has created, too, a soulless environment in which large numbers of people are alienated and unfulfilled, disillusioned in addition with the orthodox style of politics and its often meaningless Parliamentary charade. What is required is 'direct action' to help create an alternative state of affairs, a classless, participatory democracy based on the more or less self-governing commune in which ownership is shared. Though never named, the brooding omnipresence that presides over the exploration of these themes is Rousseau. But this, and similar exotic influences apart, the links with yesteryear that most often come to mind when reading, say, Hain's *Radical Regeneration*, are advocates of local self-government like Toulmin Smith, opponents of centralized collectivism such as Spencer and the Guild Socialists and even, in some respects, the Distributists: that is, the pluralists and decentralizers of one kind or another.

Hain believes that Liberalism has lost its identity because of the

202 See e.g. D. Steel, *The Liberal Way Forward* (Liberal Publication Dept, London, n.d. [1975]), pp. 3–4, 10–12; A. Fergusson, 'The Liberal Challenge', *The Times* (13–14 August 1969), p. 9 on each date; J. Grimond, 'Four Reasons Why The Morals of the Left Must Prevail', ibid. (22 December 1972), p. 12.

ambivalence in the past about its meaning: whether it stands against state interference as in the classical tradition or acted as the forerunner of big government as with the new Liberalism of George and Keynes. The doctrine must, he argues, break loose from this context of ideas and embrace a genuinely distinctive and relevant alternative to the concentrations of power that characterize the modern state.[203] The Young Liberal movement intended to help provide the necessary impetus within the party. One of its first statements was the so-called *Harle Syke Declaration*, a brief four-page pamphlet constituting an affirmation by the officers of the movement as to what it stood for; and to which in many respects little was later added.[204] What is anticipated or hoped for through the process of 'participation' and 'community politics' is nothing less than the transformation of human nature. At present power is divorced from the people, being held by 'an élite of technocrats, civil servants, Party Managers and bureaucrats'; modern technology is dehumanizing; individuals feel powerless before the forces that control their lives. There must be a radical redistribution of wealth and income; pollution and other problems of the environment must be controlled; education reformed on comprehensive and democratic lines; and so on. What Hain adds to this brief statement is, first, a detailed account of the recent context of the movement's development, seeing it in the background of the whole array of recent radical protest, the 'youth politics' of the 1960s and such outbursts as those of CND, the 'Squatters' and strikers, the Claimants' Unions, the anti-Vietnam war protests, the Stop the Seventy Tour campaign, and the like.[205] Secondly he reveals an acute awareness of the importance of practical tactics to the success (or otherwise) of a policy of non-violent direct action.[206] And finally he has a sense, however vague and abstract the actual formulation, of the strategic need to keep clear the moral nature of the goal in view, the so-called alternative society. The ethos or manner involved is exemplified in the following two passages:

> Community politics is a style of political action through which people gain the confidence to mobilize for their rights and the ability to control their lives. It involves cultivating in each individual a habit of participation. It also involves a willingness to take direct action. Community politics is essentially an alternative form of politics,

203 P. Hain, *Radical Regeneration* (Quartet Books, 1975), pp. 93–4. Cf. his *Radical Liberalism and Youth Politics* (Liberal Publication Dept, London, n.d. [1973]), pp. 9, 14.
204 The Young Liberals, *The Harle Syke Declaration* (London, 1971).
205 On the last, see Hain's own detailed account, in *Don't Play with Apartheid: the Background to the Stop the Seventy Tour Campaign* (London, 1971).
206 Hain, *Radical Regeneration*, esp. chs 7–8, and *Don't Play with Apartheid, passim*.

bursting out from within the community and involving people in the experience of taking and using power on their own behalf, and on their community's behalf. . . . It is not content to rest at the level of a series of one-off local projects. Instead, it is the strategy of a movement which takes action on the whole range of issues and at every level of society.[207]

And the final goal is lightly sketched in these terms:

> The march towards a participatory democracy is a march towards a society based on a series of self-managed communities which will gradually federate upwards into free associations. The aim is to create a society with an infinity of centres of power, expressing the principles of mutual aid and mutual co-operation, rather than competition and authoritarianism. The central characteristic of a participatory democracy is its emphasis on decentralized decision making and control of resources. . . . The overall principle is the abolition of private capital and the vesting of ownership co-operatively in the hands of the workers and the communities in which they reside.

And these 'self-managed communities' would be 'as economically self-sufficient as is possible', and put the quality of life before material consumption and people before profit.[208] Hain's enthusiasm leads him into manifest absurdities as with his remarks about the democratic control of schools and universities through all those involved having an equal say in the educational process – what, one wonders, does a plumber who happens to work in a school for the mentally retarded know about the pedagogic problems of the institution? But this sort of nonsense apart and allowing for the air of moral dubiety that hangs over the characteristically self-righteous assertions of the radical in love with his cause, the statement is a powerful and relevant revival of the old grass-roots libertarianism of days gone by and a clear repudiation of collectivism and centralization. And it is a good instance of the ambivalence or vagueness of our political ideologies that for a time it found a home in the Liberal Party rather than any other quarter of the contemporary ideological scene. It is the sort of theme, too, which has been much stressed of late by the publicists of the Social Democratic Party now in alliance with the Liberals.[209]

207 Hain, *Radical Regeneration*, pp.155–6.
208 ibid., pp.61, 165, 167.
209 On the SDP, see below, pp.533–9.

PART THREE
CONSERVATISM AND ITS MODES

In the course of its history the Tory Party has fulfilled two distinct and apparently opposite rôles. . . . It strongly advocated . . . a state-controlled economy [or] the merits of a free economy.
T. E. UTLEY, *Essays in Conservatism*, 1949, p.17

6

CONSERVATISM: THE TWIN INHERITANCE

Shall the main consideration be the individual. . . ? Or shall it be the
collectivity?
R. NORTHAM, *Conservatism, the Only Way*, 1939, p. 3

SOCIALISTS and Liberals alike tend perhaps to be ideologically assertive making a great virtue of the possession of a well-articulated doctrine and a systematized programme. Conservative exhibitionism has on the contrary often taken the form of veiling such matters in a decent obscurity. Taking pride in the rejection they deny that there is any such settled body of beliefs and concepts to which they owe allegiance: 'No British Conservative has produced a system of abstract political ideas or an ideology'; the 'Tory party has always mistrusted theories or blueprints'; 'Conservatives reject the shallowness of doctrinaire reasoning'.[1] Disraeli is said to have concluded advice given to the editor of a new party journal, 'Above all no programme'; and in *Coningsby* his hero described the Conservative cause as the first public association of men to work for an avowed end without enunciating an embarrassing array of principles.[2] Acknowledging the deficiency (if, of course, it be such) the Earl of Derby wrote to Disraeli that Conservatives 'are weakest among the intellectual classes' adding 'as is natural'. Walter Elliot said in the 1920s that 'Toryism is not and cannot be a creed of logic.'[3] Nor are other similar expressions of opinion wanting.[4] And, of course, commentators

1 I. Gilmour, *Inside Right: a Study of Conservatism* (London, 1977), p. 111. Cf. ibid., p. 132; P. Dean, 'Tory Principles Today', P. Dean *et al.*, *Conservative Points of View* (CPC no. 306; London, 1964), p. 5; P. Goldman, *Some Principles of Conservatism* (CPC no. 161; 1956, rev. edn, London, 1961), p. 6.
2 R. B. McDowell, *British Conservatism, 1832–1914* (London, 1959), p. 9; B. Disraeli, *Collected Edition of the Novels and Tales* (London, 1879–81), ii. 263, 351.
3 Derby to Disraeli (18 February 1875), Disraeli Papers B/XX/S 968, cited in P. Smith, *Disraelian Conservatism and Social Reform* (London, 1967), p. 301 n. 2; W. Elliot, *Toryism and the Twentieth Century* (London, 1927), p. 45.
4 e.g. F. J. C. Hearnshaw, *Conservatism in England: an Analytical, Historical, and*

(especially those that have a mind to be critical) have not been slow to play upon this supposed characteristic asserting that Conservatism has 'no rational philosophy', that it 'defies the intellect', and is thus, in speculative or deliberative terms, 'poverty stricken'.[5]

On the other hand, while formally eschewing abstract doctrine and the policy blueprint, Conservatives have usually been prepared to admit to a certain perhaps instinctive approach to politics, a rather vaguely formed disposition or 'mode of feeling'. As R. A. Butler saw it, Conservatism 'is no mere collection of catchpenny slogans and ephemeral theories; it is an abiding attitude of mind, a code of values, a way of life.'[6] And Conservative publicists have from time to time sought to explore this manner and to explain something of its style and implication.[7] Nor has the Conservative agenda of the moment been without explanation or defence often expressed at length or in great detail. With this consideration and this sort of material in mind, therefore, the more perceptive observers have refused to take at face value the usual Conservative protestation of ideological innocence and have discerned in the mass of writings, speeches, and actions before them a set of ideas more or less coherent which (albeit implicit rather than deliberately and fully worked-out or systematized) may be said to constitute the nucleus of a quite elaborate doctrine.[8] As Professor E. Kedourie cautiously put it:

Political Survey (London, 1933), pp. 6–10; R. Northam, 'The Conservative Approach', *Swinton Journal*, vol. viii (no. 2 October 1962), p. 37; C. J. M. Alport, *About Conservative Principles* (London, 1946), p. 3; T. Szamuely, *Unique Conservative* (CPC no. 531; London, 1973), p. 19.

5 H. Glickman, 'The Toryness of English Conservatism', *Journal of British Studies*, i (1961–2), pp. 112–14. Cf. G. K. Lewis, 'The Present Condition of British Political Parties', *Western Political Quarterly*, v (1952), pp. 231, 245. M. Woods, *A History of the Tory Party in the Seventeenth and Eighteenth Centuries with a Sketch of its Development in the Nineteenth Century* (London, 1924), p. 364.

6 R. J. White (ed.), *The Conservative Tradition* (1950; 2nd edn, London, 1964), intro., p. 1; *The New Conservatism: an Anthology of Post-War Thought* (CPC no. 150; London, 1955), pp. [7]–[8]. Cf. Goldman, op. cit., p. 13.

7 Among the tracts of this kind are e.g. Lord Hugh Cecil, *Conservatism* (London, 1912); G. Butler, *The Tory Tradition* (1914; new edn., London, 1957); W. Elliot, op. cit.; A. Bryant, *The Spirit of Conservatism* (1929; 2nd edn, Ashridge, 1932); R. Northam, *Conservatism: the Only Way* (London, 1939); Q. Hogg, *The Case for Conservatism* (1947; rev. edn, Penguin, 1959); B. Patterson, *The Character of Conservatism* (London, 1973); P. Goldman, op. cit.; Gilmour, op. cit., esp. pp. 109ff.; W. Waldegrave, *The Binding of Leviathan: Conservatism and the Future* (London, 1978), esp. pp. 41–6; and for the latest attempt to establish a principled dogma, see R. Scruton, *The Meaning of Conservatism* (Penguin, 1980).

8 e.g. S. P. Huntington, 'Conservatism as an Ideology', *American Political Science Review*, li (1957), pp. 456, 469; L. Savastano, *Contemporary British Conservatism* (n.p. [London], n.d. [1961]); R. T. McKenzie and A. Silver, *Angels in Marble: Working Class Conservatives in Urban England* (London, 1968), esp. ch. 2; R. Lewis, *Principles to Conserve* (CPC no. 417; London, 1968).

Conservatism . . . is the outcome of activity in various circumstances and over a long period of the Conservative party, an abridgement, and so to speak a codification, of this activity. Conservatism follows and does not precede the existence of a Conservative party. It is a natural attempt by a body with a long continuous existence to articulate and make intelligible to itself its own character.

But it should not be supposed, he adds, that the doctrine thus articulated, simply because it takes the form of a theory, governs the action of the party or explains its operations.[9]

Inevitably, because of the diverse cross-currents of circumstance and business involved, the themes thus perceived have varied in form and combination. But the traditional or basic Conservative doctrine has (in this way) been said to rest on: a sense of religion and divine order coupled with a veneration of Christian virtues; a rather pessimistic view of human nature combined with a scepticism about rationalist possibilities; an organic and hierarchical conception of society founded on the family as the basic social unit and on the importance of private property; a sense of empire; an acceptance of political and spiritual authority; a stress on tradition and prescriptive experience and thus on slowly mediated change; and the understanding that the realm of politics is essentially limited. Thus, in his recent exposition of the Conservative attitude, Sir Ian Gilmour, while rejecting in the usual way the view that there is any systematic ideology involved, nevertheless suggests (after a review of some major Conservative thinkers) that certain common themes emerge: trimming against extremes, the avoidance of factionalism, scepticism about utopian and rationalist schemes, 'the instinct for enjoyment', a stress on prescription and moderate or limited reform, on 'one nation' and its interests, and so on.[10] And something of the rhetoric characteristic of the creed is revealed in the following extract from a speech made at Edinburgh in December 1875 by the 15th Earl of Derby, then Foreign Secretary in Disraeli's government:

A Conservative policy, as it seems to me, tells its own story – to distrust loud professions and large promises; to place no confidence in theories for the regeneration of mankind, however brilliant and ingenious, to believe only in that improvement which is steady and gradual, and accomplished step by step; to compare our actual condition, not with the ideal world which thinkers may have sketched out, but with the condition of other countries at the present day, and with our country

9 E. Kedourie, 'Conservatism and the Conservative Party', *Solon*, vol. i (no. 4, October 1970), pp. 44–5.
10 Gilmour, op. cit., pp. 109–11, and see ibid., part three, ch. 3 for a detailed review of the 'Tory Themes'.

at other times; to hold fast what we have till we are quite sure that we
have got hold of something better instead.[11]

In any event the upshot is the view that a 'history of conservative thinkers
. . . necessarily involves the repetition over and over again of the same
ideas.'[12] In this vein A. Quinton has recently suggested (in an analysis
both mellifluous and learned) that resting on the assumption of man's
intellectual and moral imperfection are the three Conservative principles
of 'traditionalism', 'organicism', and 'political scepticism'.[13]

In a large sense this sort of conclusion is clearly true. Yet it is an insight
that may be very misleading if it persuades the student of Conservatism
to anticipate the discovery of a nuclear corpus of ideas constituting the
essence of the doctrine. For these generalities have to be cashed in terms
of current issues and when this is done then Conservatism, like any other
contemporary political stance, reveals a notable degree of diversity.
Harold Macmillan cites a letter written in 1950 saying, 'Our Party . . .
includes men holding varying views on many topics, and he would be a
bold spirit who would dogmatically proclaim himself a custodian of the
undefiled well of Conservatism.'[14] This is why it is invariably accepted
that the the emphasis of Conservative ideas and policy will inevitably and
properly fluctuate according to needs and circumstances.[15] Yet, as with
the other two political doctrines here examined, there is none the less a
certain unity to be observed amid the variety of Conservative expression,
not in the form of common and essential themes but in the existence of
opposing views about the role and office of the state.

This is a dualism which has been perceived at least from the time of W.
H. Mallock.[16] The existence of two antithetical ideals, one 'Tory', the
other 'Neo-Liberal', was noticed in a very thorough study of

11 T. H. Sanderson and E. S. Roscoe (eds), *Speeches and Addresses of Edward Henry
XVth Earl of Derby K.G.* (London, 1894), i.267.

12 Huntington, art. cit., p.469.

13 A. Quinton, *The Politics of Imperfection: the Religious and Secular Traditions of
Conservative Thought in England from Hooker to Oakeshott* (London, 1978),
pp.16–17.

14 H. Macmillan, 'The Middle Way: 20 Years After' (1958), *The Middle Way: a Study of
the Problem of Economic and Social Progress in a Free and Democratic Society* (1938;
London, 1966), p.xiii.

15 e.g. P. Dean, loc. cit., p.7; A Maude, *The Common Problem* (London, 1969), p.287.
And on the 'contradictory elements' in Conservative rhetoric, cf. N. Harris,
*Competition and the Corporate Society: British Conservatives, the State and
Industry, 1945–1964* (London, 1972), pp.14–18.

16 On whom see A. V. Tucker, 'W. H. Mallock and late Victorian Conservatism',
University of Toronto Quarterly, xxxi (1961–2), pp.233–41; and D. J. Ford, 'W. H.
Mallock and Socialism in England, 1880–1918', in K. D. Brown (ed.), *Essays in Anti-
Labour History: Responses to the Rise of Labour in Britain* (London, 1974),
pp.317–42.

Conservative views and policies during the early 1940s.[17] At this time, too, an ardent opponent remarked on the 'two sections' in the Tory Party, to him each equally obnoxious.[18] The same sort of contrast has been detected in respect of more recent times also. In the last volume of his autobiography, Harold Macmillan describes how he (as Prime Minister) and the Chancellor of the Exchequer were working on a proposal to create a 'National Economic Development Council, drawn from trade unions, management and government' and which would 'participate in central planning advice.' The establishment of this body was ultimately agreed by the Cabinet but only after two long meetings, discussion in which revealed, Mr Macmillan says, 'a rather interesting and quite deep divergence of view between Ministers, really corresponding to whether they had old Whig, Liberal, *laissez-faire* traditions, or Tory opinions, paternalists and not afraid of a little *dirigisme*'.[19] And a few days earlier, he had written in his diary that some critics in the party demanded '*more* planning' while others urged that the '"Liberal" economy' had never been given a chance.[20] Subsequently Professor Maurice Peston noted that the 'economic philosophy of the Conservative Party' has latterly been 'dominated by two, largely contradictory, themes.' On the one hand there has been 'a benevolent paternalism and a recognition that the Government must govern'; on the other 'there has been right-wing radicalism, . . . seeing a minimal role for government.' One might quarrel with Professor Peston's odd and unhistorical contention that the latter is not really a Conservative view at all: but the fundamental antithesis is undoubtedly properly observed.[21] Nor has the existence of these two contrasting wings of the Conservative Party been otherwise unremarked.[22] And does not the current division between 'Wets' and 'Drys' reveal similar dichotomy?

A range of contrasting positions is possible, therefore, each of them

17 H. Kopsch, *The Approach of the Conservative Party to Social Policy during World War II* (PhD, London University, 1970), ch. 1, esp. pp. 22–3.
18 'Celticus' [A. Bevan], *Why Not Trust the Tories?* (London, 1944), p. 86.
19 Macmillan's diary (21 September 1961), cited in *At the End of the Day, 1961–1963* (London, 1973), p. 37.
20 Entry for 16 September 1961, cited ibid., p. 39. Cf. the incident described ibid., pp. 391–2; and on the compatibility of some degree of state interference and 'traditional Tory philosophy', ibid., pp. 398–9.
21 M. Peston, 'Conservative Economic Policy and Philosophy', *Political Quarterly*, xliv (1973), p. 411.
22 J. Biffen, 'Intellectuals and Conservatism: a Symposium', *Swinton Journal*, vol. xiv (no. 2, Summer 1968), pp. 9–10; R. Blake *et al.*, *Conservatism Today* (CPC no. 350; London, 1966), p. 57; R. H. S. Crossman, *The Diaries of a Cabinet Minister* (London, 1975–7), i. 422; T. E. Utley, 'The Signifiance of Mrs. Thatcher', M. Cowling (ed.), *Conservative Essays* (London, 1978), pp. 41–4; A. Budd, *The Politics of Economic Planning* (Fontana, 1978), pp. 48–50.

equally at home in the Conservative tradition and available according to personal predilection or the demands of circumstance. The motives involved extend widely from simple humanitarian sentiment to administrative necessity, from the desire for radical political reform to the need to grapple with economic crisis. Similarly the arguments and idioms used to sustain this variety of viewpoint are also diverse and embrace the languages of social evolutionism, Christian theology, constitutional history, economic theory, and more. And, of course, what bulks largest is discussion of specific economic developments and of particular social and political problems. There is not, if truth be told, a great deal of conscious theoretical elaboration and (except in the case of Oakeshott who is, however, hardly more than mentioned in the following account) not much that deserves the name of political philosophy. Naturally, in the short review of Conservatism that follows, many writers and publicists of some or even great importance have been omitted: there is little or nothing on Mallock, Maine, Balfour, Eustace Percy, Amery, and a host of others, all of whom had a great deal to say. But the general framework of analysis would happily accommodate them and the examples which have been given are (I believe) broadly representative of the range of party opinion.

It might be urged, however, that while the ideological ambivalence which has been suggested may be real, it must nevertheless be true that Conservatism differs in crucial respects from other doctrines such as Socialism and Liberalism. On this point two things might be conceded.

The first is that however much a collectivist Conservative might be prepared, for instance, to admit or encourage state intervention, he would always do so with certain important reservations in mind, the most significant of which would be that, in principle, the rights of property must be respected. Yet the extent to which many Conservatives have been prepared to entrench on private rights in the general interest (through redistributive taxation, for instance) has in practice been considerable. So much so that, on a wide range of issues, the views of many Conservatives are well-nigh indistinguishable from those of their opponents, Liberals and even a good many people who call themselves Socialists. Hence the way in which, at the beginning of the century, one ardent libertarian lumped together, as his adversaries, 'spurious Liberals, Tory Democrats, and other vote-cadging popularity-hunters'.[23] Hence, too, the existence of such figures of journalistic fun as 'Butskell' and 'Heathkins'. Then again, libertarian Conservatives share many other theories and ideas with their counterparts elsewhere. There is, for example, a great deal of common ground in the Christian moralism deployed before the Great War by Lord Hugh Cecil and the kind of sentiments set down in Tawney's *Commonplace Book*; and it is not

23 F. Millar (ed.), *Socialism: its Fallacies and Dangers* (1906; 3rd edn, London, 1907) pp. 20-1.

merely accident that many free-trade Liberals were able easily to find a congenial home in Conservative ranks. Thus, too, the degree of compatibility to be observed between, on the one hand, union leaders calling for free collective bargaining and, on the other, those on the Tory side urging the case for a free market, the mutual interest being hostility to state intervention in these crucial respects.

Then, secondly, there is the point that the Conservative case (whether collectivist or libertarian) is usually expressed in its own special idiom. Conservatives traditionally speak the language of authority, continuity, appeal to the nation (rather than to the people), hierarchy, and the like. Yet these concepts are abstract and not a little vague, and are thus capable of widely differing use or interpretation. So that when their emptiness is filled out concretely, when they are programmatically cashed, the basic antinomy easily re-enters.

There remains the continuing assertion that there *must* be common characteristics in Conservatism (or any other ideology) of a meaningful and distinguishing kind. But, whatever its superficial appeal, this claim must be denied, and the counter-question asked: What *are* the aims, arguments, and assumptions that are shared by Stafford Northcote and R. A. Butler, Joseph Chamberlain and Enoch Powell, Mallock and Macmillan, a Central Office pamphlet issued in (say) 1927 and the notions of Sir Keith Joseph? They do not even necessarily oppose the same things. The conclusion must be the rather Namierite one that a party's identity – if it can be established in a unified sense at all – must be found elsewhere than in its doctrines. 'I do not mind', said 'a well-born Tory' in 1946, 'what the Labour Government are doing . . . but I do mind that *they* and not *we* should be doing it.'[24] Moreover, given the range of oppugnant attitudes of which Conservatism consists and also given the cognate variety of posture to be found embraced by other political creeds as well, it is not surprising that genuine ideological opposition between parties – as opposed to convenient tactical bickering – is often no stronger, or less harsh, than it is within them.

Conservatives have not infrequently levelled an accusation of inconsistency and variety at their opponents without necessarily observing that they, too, reveal the same feature; it is as though to depart from a mere uniformity were to do something intellectually or politically shameful.[25] However in the following three chapters it will be shown how, in common with the other two ideologies, the modes of Conservatism reflect the same twin inheritance of ideas in respect of the tension in our political life between libertarian and collectivist tendencies.

24 Cited by S. H. Beer, 'Two Kinds of Conservatism', *The Observer* (8 May 1955), p. 10, italics in original.
25 For a nice if rather old example, see *The Case against Radicalism, 1909: a Fighting Brief for Unionist Candidates, Agents, and Speakers* (London, n.d. [1910?]), pp. 26–7, 33–4.

7

TORY PATERNALISM AND THE WELFARE STATE

In the long run it was mainly the Conservatives who introduced
socialism into Britain.
C. N. PARKINSON, *Left Luggage*, 1967, Penguin, 1970, p.70

TORYISM AND THE STATE

Conservatives have always been ready to use the power of the State.
R. A. BUTLER, *Our Way Ahead*, 1956, p.10

IN A FAMOUS essay Herbert Spencer described the Liberalism of his day
(he was writing in the 1880s) as 'The New Toryism'.[1] His intention was,
of course, to stress the increasingly collectivist tendency of Liberal ideas
and policies and to highlight the system of compulsory co-operation they
involved. But in the present context it is significant that he does this by
pointing to an important aspect of Conservatism. For it is true that
traditionally Toryism has invariably stressed the role and responsibilities
of established authority. Partly this is simply a practical matter of
effective government or of reverence for the Crown. But it is often
associated as well with a disbelief in social views based on any kind of
atomic individualism and in the associated doctrine of natural rights, a
sense that more important than the recognition of any particular or
personal claims is the achievement of stability and well-being through
properly constituted control. Sentiments of this sort are often associated,
too, with the view that levelling is undesirable, or rather impossible,
because society is an organic hierarchy in which a sort of natural
aristocracy should and must rule. 'The Tory believes in the *Samurai*
leading' as one discussion had it.[2] It is partly a matter also of the concept

---

1 H. Spencer, *The Man Versus the State* (1884; Penguin, 1969), pp. 63–81. Among many
other passages in Spencer's works observing the association of Toryism with state
control, see *The Principles of Sociology* (London, 1876ff.), i. 573; *First Principles* (1862;
6th edn, Thinker's Library, 1945), pp. 460–1.
2 Viscount Lymington, *Ich Dien: the Tory Path* (London, 1931), p. 17, italics in original.

of human nature frequently held by Conservatives (though not, of course, only by them), one which stresses not so much the primacy of reason as the likely dominance of passion. And while we may be indebted to this motivating force for what Disraeli called 'the great achievements which are the landmarks of human action and human progress', men's emotions need not always be thus fruitful or noble.[3] Consequently if the Conservative should have a strong and pessimistic sense of original sin, he might well fear the worst of his race and deem it no more than prudent if the mark of authority were strongly imprinted on society so that the worst possible effects of man's nature might be averted or held in check.

As so often in the Conservative canon, Burke is the paradigm frequently cited on these matters. He is well-known for his remarks about 'the fallible and feeble contrivances of our reason' and for the belief that 'Society cannot exist unless a controlling power upon will and appetite be placed somewhere'.[4] Nor have these somewhat Hobbesian sentiments been subsequently neglected by Conservative politicians and publicists. A. J. Balfour, who had philosophical interests to indulge, put the same sort of point in one of his theological works as follows:

> it is Authority rather than Reason to which, in the main, we owe, not religion only, but ethics and politics; . . . it is Authority which supplies us with the essential elements in the premises of science; . . . it is Authority rather than Reason which lays the deep foundations of social life [and] which cements its superstructure. And though it may seem to savour of paradox, it is yet no exaggeration to say, that if we would find the quality in which we most notably excel the brute creation, we should look for it, not so much in our faculty for convincing and being convinced by the exercise of reasoning, as in our capacity for influencing and being influenced through the action of Authority.[5]

In a Tory textbook of the early 1930s, Arthur Bryant repeated the same general lesson: men are naturally 'covetous and acquisitive', he wrote, and only with difficulty can these characteristics 'be prevented from plunging society into anarchy.'[6] Nor are these themes which have fallen out of fashion in recent years. Just after the last war Aubrey Jones remarked that authority, property, power, and such-like features of the human situation are based on 'the unchanging elements' in man's nature

---

The reference to the Samurai is presumably to the ruling élite of that name in H. G. Wells, *A Modern Utopia* (1905), ch. ix.

3 B. Disraeli, *Coningsby*, IV. xiii, *Collected Edition of the Novels and Tales* (London, 1879–81), ii. 240.

4 E. Burke, *The Works* (World's Classics, 1925), iv. 37, 319. Cf. ibid., iv. 95; also K. Feiling, *Toryism: a Political Dialogue* (London, 1913), pp. 37–8.

5 A. J. Balfour, *The Foundations of Belief: Being Notes Introductory to the Study of Theology* (London, 1895), pp. 229–30.

6 A. Bryant, *The Spirit of Conservatism* (1929; 2nd edn, Ashridge, 1932), p. 12.

and will, therefore, always be with us. Every institution, from what
period of history soever, embodies authority: it is an 'inner truth and
principle' which will never be obsolete. The Conservative, he goes on, is a
person who understands this and sees that 'the abiding problem of
politics is the suppression of evil' which can only be done 'through
authority and force'.[7] Shortly afterwards T. E. Utley put the same point,
in a rather extreme de Maistreian way, when he urged that basically
politics was a matter of the application of public power, and added:
'Human nature is violent and predatory and can be held in check only by
three forces, the Grace of God, the fear of the gallows, and the pressure of
a social tradition, subtly and unconsciously operating as a brake on
human instinct'.[8] And so on.[9]

There is thus ample warrant for the suggestion that an authoritarian
strand exists in Conservative doctrine. It is, however, misleading to urge
that this aspect of Conservatism is the feature which uniquely charac-
terizes the ideology and which marks it as that of a dominant social and
political group.[10] Of course, there is or may be a sociological element of
this sort involved. But at the same time élitism of this kind is also to be
found elsewhere: it is clearly discernible, for instance, in the ideas and
interests of Fabians like the Webbs, Shaw, or Wells. In addition (as the
present chapters will show) there are other, contrary, aspects of the
Conservative creed to which attention must be paid. Nevertheless it is
undoubtedly the case that, in the brand of Conservatism now under
review, it is assumed or argued that there is, or should be, a proper caste
of light and leading in the community whether it be a territorial gentry, a
successful bourgeoisie, or a meritocracy of talent. But, it is invariably
added, the power thus possessed will not be irresponsible; it must not be
abused or intemperately employed. So the character of the political
leadership and its devotion to public service and the general welfare is a
matter of the utmost significance. The authoritarianism is moral and
paternalistic; it has duties to those it commands. As good an example of
this as any is the remark of George Wyndham: 'The State ought to launch
the young, and provide a haven for the old. Between youth and age the
State should say that a good man deserves a living.'[11]

In this general way, then, what Spencer called 'altruistic Toryism' has

7 A. Jones, *The Pendulum of Politics* (London, 1946), pp.158–9.
8 T. E. Utley, *Essays in Conservatism* (CPC no.45; London, 1949), pp.1–2, 12.
9 For another more recent instance, see R. Scruton, *The Meaning of Conservatism*
   (Penguin, 1980), esp. chs1–2.
10 For such an assertion, see e.g. R. Eccleshall, 'English Conservatism as Ideology',
   Political Studies, xxv (1977), pp.62–83.
11 Cited in J. Biggs-Davison, *George Wyndham: a Study in Toryism* (London, 1951),
   p.238. For another contemporary example of similar paternalist sentiment, see the
   Earl of Portsmouth's *A Knot of Roots: an Autobiography* (London, 1965), pp.122–3.

never in principle been averse to the use of power as a means of achieving the aims of social welfare and the general good. There has thus always been an 'inherent collectivism' in British Conservatism.[12] This was what Marx and Engels must have had in mind when they referred to the 'feudal socialism' of the Young England movement; and what Cobden wrote of when, during the struggle over Ashley's factory legislation, he alluded slightingly to 'the Socialist doctrines of the fools' on the Tory back-benches.[13] Sidney Webb also noted the close connexion between the Conservative Party and the use of the state for social and industrial reform; and another, though more wayward, Fabian, H. G. Wells, equally acknowledged that, subject to certain limits, that party was indeed 'as constructive and collectivist as any other'.[14] At the beginning of the century, one Conservative, who did not in fact find this tendency in his colleagues wholly congenial, wrote that they were less averse 'than the earlier Liberals from invoking the hand of authority' and 'outstripped their opponents in the endeavour to remedy the distresses of the poorer classes by legislation.'[15] The French historian Elie Halévy, an old-fashioned Liberal, acknowledged this 'Tory socialism' or philanthropy as he called it; and in 1934 Ramsay Muir (from a similar standpoint) confirmed that in practice Conservatives had been notably prepared to go 'farther than any Socialist Government has ever dared to do in bringing industry, and still more agriculture, under the rigid and sterilising control of the State.'[16] Much more recently still, it has been said that 'A good Tory has never been in history afraid of the use of the State' and that 'Toryism has always been a form of paternal socialism'.[17] Expressions of this Conservative form of statism crop up in unexpected places. For instance, Dorothy L. Sayers (the creator of Lord Peter

12 The phrase cited is taken from H. Glickman, 'The Toryness of English Conservatism', *The Journal of British Studies*, i (1961–2), p.111.
13 K. Marx and F. Engels, *Manifesto of the Communist Party* (1848; ed. Laski, London, 1948), p.147; J. Morley, *The Life of Richard Cobden* (London, 1881), i. 302. Morley agreed with this judgement, ibid., i. 302–3.
14 S. Webb, *Socialism in England* (London, 1890), p.3; H. G. Wells, *The New Machiavelli* (1911; Penguin, 1946), pp.236–7. See also S. Webb's *The Basis and Policy of Socialism* (Fabian Socialist Series, no. 4; London, 1908), p. 53. Tories often worked with radicals, as when they co-operated with Fabians and others in the 'progressive' movement in London: see R. C. K. Ensor, *England 1870–1914* (1936; Oxford, 1968), p.296 and n.3.
15 Lord Hugh Cecil, *Conservatism* (1912; London, 1928), p.72. Cf. ibid., pp.169–70, 195–6, 247.
16 E. Halévy, *A History of the English People in the Nineteenth Century* (1913–46; 2nd trans. edn, London, 1961), ii.283; v.227–8, 279; R. Muir, foreword to National Liberal Federation, *The Liberal Way: a Survey of Liberal Policy* ... (London, 1934), p.17.
17 These remarks are attributed to R. A. Butler and H. Macmillan by Glickman, art. cit., pp.134, 137.

Wimsey and translator of Dante) always insisted she was 'the bluest of
Tories'. Yet – or therefore – in January 1940 she published an essay
entitled *Begin Here* which, rejecting 'sheer individualism', invoked the
need for some form of organized society, indeed for adequate control and
planning to eliminate shortages in and maldistribution of this world's
goods.[18] Certainly the amount of social and economic legislation that
Conservatives have sponsored for one reason or another since 1800 is not
inconsiderable; and they have often based their propaganda on this
'fruitage of Tory Democracy'.[19] For instance, immediately after the
passing of the 1867 Act which extended the franchise to the urban male
householder, the National Union issued a statement about 'Conservative
Legislation for the Working Classes'.[20] In one form or another this
pamphlet and its progeny have been in print for most of the time ever
since, consisting of a detailed review of Tory Bills put on the statute book
to improve the condition of the working man and his family and to aid
the trade unions.[21] It is a formidable account and a useful electoral
weapon. Naturally the story told is hardly surprising when it is recalled
that the Conservatives have been in office longer than any other party
over the past century and a half and so have had more opportunity to
initiate or sustain the course of economic and social reform. The
cumulative effect of this Conservative effort has been very substantial
indeed. In war and out of it the Conservatives have done more than any
other political group to achieve the collectivist state we now enjoy (or
suffer under).[22] What is odd in the light of this record is the defensive
attitude Conservatives have often adopted in the face of accusations of
hard-heartedness and *laissez faire*. Even more singular is the success of
the radical myth that social improvement only comes from non-

18 D. L. Sayers, *Begin Here: a War-Time Essay* (London, 1940), e.g. pp. 34, 57–8.
19 See the extensive review of this legislation, in W. J. Wilkinson, *Tory Democracy*
    (New York, 1925), chs v–vi. On the electoral appeal, see R. T. McKenzie and A.
    Silver, *Angels in Marble: Working Class Conservatives in Urban England* (London,
    1968), pp. 42–7. Asa Briggs comments on working-class support for Tory radicalism
    in Leeds and Bradford over a long period, *Victorian Cities* (1963; Penguin, 1968),
    pp. 142–3.
20 National Union Pamphlets, British Library collection, vol. 1 (1868–77), no. vi.
21 Among many such examples are e.g. *The Rights of Labour – a Word to Working Men*
    (CCO no. 12; London, 1896); *Recent Conservative Legislation for the Miners* (CCO
    no. 14; London, 1897); *Working-Class Legislation Passed By Conservatives &
    Unionists* (NU no. 315; London, 1904); *Why Working Men Should Support the
    Unionist Government* (NU no. 357; London, 1905); *What Conservatives Have Done
    for British Workers* (NU no. 2812; London, 1928); *How Conservatives Have Helped
    the British People* (10th edn, London, 1963). For the latest version, see C. E. Bellairs,
    *Conservative Social and Industrial Reform: a Record of Conservative Legislation
    between 1800 and 1974* (CPC no. 600; rev. edn, London, 1977).
22 In addition to the comment cited as epigraph to this chapter, see the remarks of M.
    and R. Friedman, *Free to Choose: a Personal Statement* (Penguin, 1980), p. 128.

Conservative pressure and activity. This belief is, of course, very important politically because it is widely held; but it is none the less curious being hardly sustained by an historical review of the legislative record. Perhaps the crucial reason is suggested by a remark of Philip Guedalla's that, by 'a peculiar division of labour British History, quite considerable parts of which have been made by Tories, has been very largely written by Whigs; and Whig historians are a little apt to dispose summarily of Tory reputations.'[23] One need only add to the Whigs, intellectualist radicals and Socialists to bring the point up-to-date.

This catalogue of Tory reputation and intent, not to mention achievement, may have seemed laboured. But it is necessary because so many unhistorically minded critics persist in seeing the Conservative record anachronistically in terms of some misleading legend based on ideological hostility, or in the exclusive context perhaps of the other, very different and anti-statist, strand in the Conservative tradition. Whether one approves of it or not, the Tory Party effort and effect in this collectivist regard has been very substantial indeed.

However, it is not altogether easy to bring together and express the scope and chronology of this Conservative interventionism and the range of motives and reasons involved. Yet, while it may not be an exclusive categorization, the aspects reviewed in the rest of this chapter are clear in their significance and well illustrate the development of Conservatism in its collectivist mode.

ASPECTS OF CONSERVATIVE COLLECTIVISM

> . . . any candid person, who takes a comprehensive view of our position, must admit that in some respects the intervention of the Government is much more necessary now than it used to be in former times; and that social questions are assuming such large dimensions that they cannot be adequately dealt with except by the employment of the central administrative machinery.
>
> SIR STAFFORD NORTHCOTE, 'Opening Address', *Trans. of the Nat. Assoc. for the Promotion of Social Science*, 1869, p.4

Reviewing nineteenth-century political developments, A. V. Dicey commented that 'Ancient toryism died hard' and, too, that it 'lived long enough to leave time for the rise of a new toryism in which democratic sentiment deeply tinged with socialism, blends with that faith in the paternal despotism of the State which formed part of the old Tory creed.'[24] In this doctrine various elements or motives were blended.

---

23 P. Guedalla, *The Duke* (1931; London, 1940), p.viii.
24 A. V. Dicey, *Lectures on the Relation between Law & Public Opinion in England during the Nineteenth Century* (1905; 2nd edn, London, 1920), p.39.

Humanitarianism

In 1841 Richard Cobden wrote to his brother that he 'had observed an evident disposition on the Tory side to set up as philanthropists.'[25] The tone of mockery or surprise is hardly apt: Conservatives have been at least as sensitive to social evil and human suffering as most people. Probably what Cobden was objecting to was their tendency to do something about it because this involved the use of the state power in a way he disapproved. Certainly at the very outset of the period relevant here the humanitarian sentiment found expression in a doctrine of responsibility towards the underprivileged. There might be those like the Earl of Abingdon who believed that humanity was a private feeling and 'not a public principle to act upon'.[26] But this was not true of the men who were prompted to abolish the slave-trade. Nor was it reflected in the radicalism of Tories such as Richard Oastler and Thomas Sadler or in the crusades of Tory evangelists like Wilberforce and Shaftesbury, the latter urging that state regulation need not limit but could enhance men's freedom and multiply opportunities for the enjoyment of rights.[27] Conservative romanticists, such as Coleridge and Southey, stressed the positive ends of the state over and above the basic protection of persons and property, the need for the magistrate to deal, for instance, with all the cruelties of the factory towns. To such an extent was this kind of sentiment urged indeed that Dicey called Southey the 'preacher of Tory philanthropy' who was 'the prophetic precursor of modern collectivism.'[28] On the more workaday side of Tory politics, humanitarian social reform of various kinds was suggested by, for instance, the lawyers Archibald Alison and R. S. Sowler.[29] The sort of practical goals pursued included banning night-work in factories, the provision of family allowances, the creation of allotments for the urban labourer, the humanizing of the new Poor Law, and legislation to enforce decent standards of working-class housing. Sir Robert Peel's attitude to the Corn Laws was deeply affected by the sufferings of the poorer classes.[30]

25 R. Cobden to F. Cobden (27 September 1841), in J. Morley, *The Life of Richard Cobden* (London, 1881), i.185.

26 *Parl. Hist.*, xxx.657, cited in E. M. Howse, *Saints in Politics: the 'Clapham Sect' and the Growth of Freedom* (1953; London, 1971), p.31.

27 See e.g. the comments in A. Toynbee, *Lectures on the Industrial Revolution in England* . . . (1884; Newton Abbot, 1969) who refers to this 'Tory Socialism', pp.18–19, 103, 207–9, 214–15; J. W. Bready, *Lord Shaftesbury and Social-Industrial Progress* (London, 1926), p.40; and see the references cited in R. M. Gutchen, 'Local Improvements and Centralization in Nineteenth-Century England', *Historical Journal*, iv (1961), p.85.

28 Dicey, *Law & Public Opinion*, p.225.

29 R. B. McDowell, *British Conservatism, 1832–1914* (London, 1959), pp.30–1.

30 G. K. Clark, 'The Repeal of the Corn Laws and the Politics of the Forties', *Economic History Review*, 2s., iv (1951–2), p.2.

And at the mid-century the record shows the efforts at social reform of such Conservative politicians as Sir John Packington and Charles Adderley.[31]

Perhaps the flavour of what this kind of humanitarian radicalism could involve may best be indicated by a particular example taken from the Tory grass-roots.[32] The Rev. J. R. Stephens was a Conservative of a traditionalist kind: he believed in the ordered, hierarchical society which looked after the welfare of the labouring classes. But their conditions of life and future prospects were being outraged by the factory system and by the abolition of the old Poor Law which was a denial of their long-standing right to assistance. As with Oastler and Shaftesbury the basis of Stephens's social views was religious, his theological beliefs providing the foundation for a political crusade. 'Unless', he said, 'a priest of the living God be a politician in the pulpit, he has no business there at all. Law and Religion can never be separated . . . politics without religion is dead, religion without politics is dead'.[33] At one time he considered standing for Parliament as a Conservative candidate; but his main activity was as a political leader pressing for particular changes, often indeed in association with the Chartists. In pursuit of his aim of 'a full, sufficient and comfortable maintenance' for the working man 'according to the will and commandment of God', he was prepared to recommend very extreme action and indeed went to prison for his views.[34] It was not a Communist revolutionary but a Tory preacher who declared in 1837 that there 'was not a mill in England that had not been built with gold coined out of the blood and bones of the operatives'; and until their grievances were redressed the social question could not be regarded as settled.[35] This was the sort of impassioned militancy that so often underlay the rejection by Tory humanitarians of the existing state of affairs, and equally the activities of the Operative Conservative Societies formed to combat the new Poor Law.[36] It is no wonder that, in the light of the activities of agitators like Stephens, it was easy for Conservatives to claim that their tradition represented a concern for the working man. And there is no reason to suppose that this kind of benevolence, 'hesitating' as it often was no doubt, has ever ceased to exert some moral influence in Conservative ranks and to find its practical outlet in personal

31 P. Smith, *Disraelian Conservatism and Social Reform* (London, 1967), pp.20–1.
32 This paragraph is based on J. T. Ward, 'Revolutionary Tory: the Life of Joseph Rayner Stephens of Ashton-under-Lyne (1805–1879)', *Trans. of Lancs. and Cheshire Antiquarian Soc.*, lxviii (1958), pp.93–116.
33 J. R. Stephens, *Sermon . . . Charlestown, Jan.* 6 (London, 1839), p.4, cited ibid., p.105. Cf. the citations, ibid., p.109.
34 ibid., p.107.
35 *Report of Proceedings . . .* (Leeds, 1837), p.14, cited ibid., p.100.
36 ibid., p.99.

philanthropy and remedial legislation.[37] Stanley Baldwin, who himself gave a good proportion of his wealth to the state, stressed in one speech this record of Tory humanitarianism and claimed on its behalf, 'We have been in the forefront of the battle to help the people of this country to raise themselves, more than a generation before the word Socialism was coined.'[38]

Noblesse oblige *and piecemeal concession*

Privilege and riches entail responsibility; and the duties of class leadership, reflected in what Dicey called 'the paternal despotism of the State', have (as already suggested) always bulked large in the Tory tradition.[39] In this connexion attention has recently been drawn to the continuance in the period after 1815 of the 'aristocratic ideal' as in Sadler's exposition of the 'Paternal System' and in the attacks in *Blackwood's Edinburgh Review*, a high Tory journal, on classical political economy and the concept of limited government. True Tory principles, it was urged in one place, would, while maintaining a due hierarchical order in society, sustain also the right of all to protection and support. The Tory motto should be: 'govern the people, and govern them strictly, but see that they are fed', for it is 'the duty of those set in authority to protect those who are placed below them.'[40] What this attitude implies in the present context is exemplified in classic form by the social and political ideas of Disraeli.

Disraeli and the 'Tory Idea'
Although like all politicians subject to the pressure of changing events, Disraeli invariably expressed a consistent view of the English polity and its leaders' duty of social amelioration. It was an attitude that in fact owed much to the policies and ideas of Sir Robert Peel.[41]

Disraeli began his political career in the guise of a popular or philanthropic (as opposed to a Benthamite or philosophic) radical of a

37   McDowell, op. cit., pp. 138, 145.
38   Cited in *Looking Ahead: a Re-statement of Unionist Principles and Aims . . .* (London, 1924), p. 33. For a later expression of a similar sentiment, see Lord Kilmuir, 'The Shaftesbury Tradition in Conservative Politics', *Journal of Law and Economics*, iii (1960), pp. 70–4.
39   Dicey, *Law & Public Opinion*, p. 39.
40   [W. Johnstone], 'Our Domestic Policy No. 1', *Blackwood's*, xxvi (1829), p. 768, cited in H. Perkin, *The Origins of Modern English Society, 1780–1880* (1969; London, 1972), p. 250. On Sadler and the *Blackwood's* economists generally, ibid., pp. 237–9, 241–51, 263.
41   For a superb summary of Peel's position, see N. Gash, 'The Founder of Modern Conservatism', *Solon*, vol. i (no. 2, January 1970), pp. 11–18.

sort best represented perhaps by Cobbett, Burdett, or Sadler.[42] It is not, therefore, surprising to find in his early pronouncements some indication of the need to improve the condition of the lower orders of society. Thus in the *Vindication* he makes brief reference to 'the compulsory provision for the poor' as a vital part of the English constitution and to the right of 'the meanest subject' to 'an honest and decorous maintenance' as a result of his labours.[43] This was indeed the traditional common-law doctrine.[44] But while such statements were undoubtedly sincere, the place of social reform in his general idea of politics is as yet incidental and only realized incompletely.[45] He was, however, formulating a view of politics which would provide a rationale for a larger understanding of the needs of the populace.

The basic and constant premiss of all his ideas and actions in respect of domestic policy was a stress on the preponderance, in what he called 'the Territorial Constitution of England', of the landed and agricultural interest, an interest which he did not define at all narrowly but considered to embrace 'the vast majority' of the nation. It was the feudal and local values of this predial tradition by which he set so much store, for it was 'the best and surest foundation for popular rights and public liberty, imperial power and social happiness.' And this belief explains the importance he attached to the maintenance of the country's agriculture as 'the necessary condition' of 'the enjoyment of that Constitution'.[46] In these terms the responsibility of the realm rested on the shoulders of the socially superior persons living in each county and parish. 'The proper leaders of the people', he told the House of Commons in 1848, 'are the gentlemen of England. If they are not the leaders of the people, I do not see why there should be gentlemen.'[47] And the responsibility of this class should be a real one. The basic principle of this long-standing polity is

42 He was strongly and perceptively critical of abstract utilitarianism: see his *Vindication of the English Constitution* (1835), ch.II, in W. Hutcheon (ed.), *Whigs and Whiggism: Political Writings by Benjamin Disraeli* (London, 1913), pp.114–18.

43 Hutcheon, *Whigs and Whiggism*, pp.150, 229. Cf. W. F. Monypenny and G. E. Buckle, *The Life of Benjamin Disraeli* (1910–20; new edn rev., London, 1929), i.378.

44 See e.g. W. Blackstone, *Commentaries on the Laws of England* (1765–9; 6th edn, Dublin, 1775), i.131, 359ff.; also Blackstone's *Reports* (Dublin, 1781), indexes *sub* 'Poor'.

45 For Dicey's unfavourable opinion, see his letter to Lady Farrer (5 November 1920), in R. S. Rait (ed.), *Memorials of A. V. Dicey Being Chiefly Letters and Diaries* (London, 1925), pp.273–4.

46 See Disraeli's Buckingham election address (1847), cited in Monypenny and Buckle, op. cit., i.836–8; T. E. Kebbel (ed.), *Selected Speeches of the Late Right Honourable the Earl of Beaconsfield* (London, 1882), i.48–9, 53, 55, 142, 264, 266–7.

47 99 Parl. Deb., 3s., 20 June 1848, col.964. Cf. Carlyle's references in *Chartism* (1839) to the old aristocracy which used to be the governors and guides of the lower classes, *Works* (People's edn, London, 1871–4), xi.146ff.

that 'the tenure of all property shall be the performance of its duties.'[48]

These were the sentiments of the coterie (it was hardly a party) called Young England. Disraeli was one of its leading spirits; and its romanticist ideals – Morley's 'childish bathos' is rather hard[49] – embracing a sort of feudal paternalism are expressed in the trilogy of political novels which were written in the 1840s, of course to make money but also as a sort of manifestoes to influence opinion.[50] For instance, at one of the climaxes of the plot of *Coningsby*, when the hero of the story defies his grandfather and tells that formidable and rather unpleasant old man that he cannot agree to stand for Parliament on this patriarch's terms, he justifies himself by reference to the ideas mentioned and thus states the doctrine of Conservatism as the 'new generation' of Young England understood it.

> 'What we want, sir, is . . . to establish great principles which may maintain the realm and secure the happiness of the people. Let me see authority once more honoured; a solemn reverence again the habit of our lives; let me see property acknowledging, as in the old days of faith, that labour is his twin brother, and that the essence of all tenure is the performance of duty. . . .'[51]

What was then lacking in Britain – this is the lesson – was a sense of community. There was only association or gregariousness, two nations instead of one, and this because the propertied class was not meeting its obligations.[52] Many years later, Disraeli summarized the ideas which had been at work in the 1840s and the course that lay before 'a reconstructed Tory party' as Young England understood it in these terms: they involved *inter alia* changing back 'the oligarchy into a generous aristocracy round a real throne', infusing 'life and vigour' into the Church as 'the trainer of the nation', elevating 'the physical as well as the moral condition of the people' by establishing that labour as well as property required regulation and protection; 'and all this rather by the use of ancient forms and the restoration of the past than by political revolutions founded on abstract ideas'.[53] Nor was Disraeli's expression

---

48 Kebbel, *Speeches*, i. 50–2; General preface (1870) to *Collected Edition of the Novels and Tales* (London, 1879–81), vol. i, p. ix. On the traditional 'obligation to serve' and moral responsibilities of property ownership, cf. S. and B. Webb, *The Development of English Local Government, 1689–1835* (London, 1963), pp. 8ff., and R. H. Tawney, *The Acquisitive Society* (1921; London, 1943), pp. 62–4.

49 J. Morley, *The Life of Richard Cobden*, i. 297.

50 See e.g. preface to 5th edn of *Coningsby*, in *Novels*, vol. ii, pp. vii–viii.

51 *Coningsby*, VIII. iii, in *Novels*, ii. 411.

52 *Sybil*, II. v, ibid., iii. 70–7.

53 'General Preface' (1870), ibid., vol. i, pp. x–xi. Cf. the eulogy of the ideal Tory Party in *Sybil*, IV. xiv, ibid., iii. 314–15. There is an excellent account of the broad historical

of such opinions unique: they were, for instance, shared by J. B. Bernard, a Fellow of King's College, Cambridge, who in a tract published in 1835 urged the restoration of the traditional rights of the working people through the aid of the Conservative nobility and gentry.[54]

These views constituted the theoretical rationale of Disraeli's opposition to Peel over the Corn Laws: their repeal was a step that would strike at the heart of the landed interest and, therefore, at the ancient constitution of the kingdom itself.[55] This was why, after the deed was accomplished in 1846, Disraeli continually supported policies designed to protect agriculture and the people dependent on it. This explains as well his diagnosis of the major contemporary political and social problems. Not only were some of the traditional landed classes (like Lord Marney in *Sybil*) not fulfilling the duties of their position − Disraeli's sarcastic and vituperative criticisms in this respect are bitter and telling − but, further, a new group of wealthy men was emerging in commerce and manufacture many of whom likewise showed no proper sense of the duty their property involved: *richesse*, and not only *noblesse*, *oblige*. They had obtained important political and social station without observing the conditions that ought to be associated with the possession of such privileges. Labour, he said in a speech at Shrewsbury in 1843,

> also has its rights as well as its duties; and when I see masses of property raised in this country which do not recognise that principle; when I find men making fortunes by a method which permits them (very often in a very few years) to purchase the lands of the old territorial aristocracy of the country, I cannot help remembering that those millions are accumulated by a mode which does not recognize it as a duty 'to endow the Church, to feed the poor, to guard the land, and to execute justice for nothing.' And I cannot help asking myself, when I hear of all this misery, and of all this suffering; when I know that evidence exists . . . of a state of demoralisation in the once happy

perspective envisaged in Monypenny and Buckle, *Life*, i. 311−20, and ii. x *passim* on 'The Tory Idea'; the context of religious beliefs is treated, ibid., i. 848−82. One of the main influences on Young England was Frederick Faber, a product of the Oxford Movement and hostile to Liberalism in all its guises and, therefore, to *laissez faire*. He appears in *Sybil* as Aubrey St Lys.

54 J. B. Bernard, *Appeal to the Conservatives, on the Imminent Danger to which the Nation is Exposed from the Democratic Propensities of the House of Commons . . .* (London, 1835).

55 e.g. Kebbel, *Speeches*, i. 57. For an expression of this opinion before the crisis with Peel supervened, see the passage from the Shrewsbury speech of May 1843 (not cited by Kebbel) in Monypenny and Buckle, *Life*, i. 538−9. The alternative Disraeli would have preferred to general free trade was what he called the policy of Bolingbroke and Pitt, i.e. a series of reciprocal treaties with individual countries, on which see Kebbel, op. cit., i. 45, 210, 338−9.

population of this land, which is not equalled in the most barbarous countries . . . – I cannot help suspecting that this has arisen because property has been permitted to be created and held without the performance of its duties.[56]

However, if the country was to be 'turned into a spinning-jenny machine kind of nation',[57] Disraeli's ideal was embodied, for example, in the figure of Mr Millbank, the capitalist who in *Coningsby* – his counterpart in *Sybil* is Mr Trafford the mill-owner – is described not only as an extremely efficient entrepreneur but also as one who cares for the good reputation of his order and for the health and welfare of his work-people.[58] And the factory town over which Mr Millbank paternalistically presides is in the sharpest possible contrast to the dirt and misery prevailing in Wodgate that the spuriously ennobled Mowbrays have negligently allowed to grow up and fester under their aegis. It contrasts, too, with the misery of the decayed rural town of Marney.[59]

It is, then, in this context of an almost feudal sense of the social responsibilities of property, which Disraeli believed was the ethos of traditional England, that he sees the condition of the people question which was for him undoubtedly a crucial matter. There is no subject, he said in 1844, in which he had taken a deeper interest. 'I had', he claimed,

long been aware that there was something rotten in the core of our social system. I had seen that while immense fortunes were accumulating, while wealth was increasing to a superabundance, and while Great Britain was cited throughout Europe as the most prosperous nation in the world, the working classes, the creators of wealth, were steeped in the most abject poverty and gradually sinking into the deepest degradation.[60]

In his address to the electors of Buckinghamshire in 1847 Disraeli stated it was hardly necessary for him to say he would 'support all those measures, the object of which is to elevate the moral and social condition of the Working Classes, by lessening their hours of toil – by improving their means of health – and by cultivating their intelligence.'[61] Certainly Disraeli had, too, a considerable knowledge of the situation. He had familiarized himself with the problem of urban and rural poverty not least because he was involved in the Poor Law and Factory Bill debates in

---

56 Kebbel, *Speeches*, i. 52.
57 ibid., i. 54.
58 *Coningsby*, IV. iii–iv; *Sybil*, III. viii.
59 *Sybil*, II. iii; III. iv.
60 *Shropshire Conservative* (31 August 1844), cited in Monypenny and Buckle, *Life*, i. 629. Cf. the passage in *Sybil*, III. v, about the degraded brute condition of industrial serfdom prevailing in England, *Novels*, iii. 198.
61 Monypenny and Buckle, *Life*, i. 838.

Parliament; he was a supporter of Lord Ashley in his struggle to pass legislation ameliorating conditions of work in factory and mine. And when writing *Sybil* (the place in which, perhaps, his main reflections on the social problems of the day are most fully to be found) he thoroughly immersed himself in the reports of the Children's Employment Commission, obtained access to and studied the complete correspondence of Feargus O'Connor, one of the Chartist leaders, and personally visited a number of northern industrial towns for specific purposes of investigation.[62] So it was not without foundation that he claimed the pages of this novel might 'be consulted with confidence' as 'an accurate and never exaggerated picture' of the times.[63] Lord Morley, who was certainly no disciple, felt that the author of *Sybil* had grasped 'the real magnitude and even the nature of the social crisis' brought about by rapid industrialization.[64]

All this constituted a theme publicized most elaborately and effectively perhaps in his famous speeches at Manchester and at the Crystal Palace in 1872 towards the end of his long political career in which, as leader of his party, he committed Toryism to a policy of sanitary and other social reform, a policy which had many aspects and was very wide-ranging:

> It involves the state of the dwellings of the people, the moral consequences of which are not less considerable than the physical. It involves their enjoyment of some of the chief elements of nature – air, light, and water. It involves the regulation of their industry, the inspection of their toil. It involves the purity of their provisions, and it touches upon all the means by which you may wean them from habits of excess and of brutality.[65]

This sort of attitude expressed over many years might seem to invite a substantial degree of central government action. Yet, reflecting a powerful contemporary fashion, Disraeli's position expresses a certain ambivalence about 'centralisation'. Explicitly indeed his point of view required a stress on the diffusion of initiative and responsibility. It was our local institutions, he held, which had made us a free people and alone can keep us so, and this

> by the bulwark which they offer to the insidious encroachments of a convenient, yet enervating, system of centralisation, which, if left unchecked, will prove fatal to the national character. Therefore, I have

62 See e.g. his description of the plight of the handloom weavers, *Sybil*, II, xiii, and of the 'tommy-shop', ibid., III. iii.
63 General Preface, *Novels*, vol. i, p. xiii.
64 Morley, *The Life of Richard Cobden*, i. 297.
65 Kebbel, *Speeches*, ii. 507–12, 531–2. The citation is at ii. 532.

> ever endeavoured to cherish our happy habit of self-government, as sustained by a prudent distribution of local authority.[66]

It followed, then, that the amelioration of conditions was (as intimated above) the duty of social leaders in the localities: England should be governed by England, not by London.[67] Reform would thus be conducted within the framework of the territorial constitution and the traditional 'disposition of property'.[68] It was not the case, therefore, that Disraeli felt the state of the people necessarily required continual intervention and legislation by the central government. Indeed he believed that the demand for such action was often little more than a cheap and unworthy device by which the new ruling class tried to avoid the proper social duties of their station as these appeared in the areas where they lived and worked. So when, for instance, in 1839 he supported the idea of a national system of education he distinguished what he had in mind from a system run from the centre.[69] Similarly Disraeli's support for the Corn Laws was basically on the ground that their existence sustained the territorial constitution as a security for local self-government and a barrier to 'that system of centralisation which has taken root and enslaved the energies of surrounding nations.'[70] In this mode he preferred (if there had to be legislation) law that gave permissive powers rather than compelled.[71] And, in the last resort even, it is 'not so much to the action of laws as to the influence of manners that we must look'.[72]

Yet it would be true to say that, this formal localist emphasis notwithstanding, Disraeli's ideas and actions assisted to a degree the opposing tendency. He invariably looked to a flourishing throne as a crucial element in the community of his dreams, a stress easily compatible with an emphasis on the role of the Crown as its powers came to be exercised by ministers in the popular behalf. Similarly there were at least two important contexts in which Disraeli always conceded the right and duty of central government to act extensively and deeply and both might be seen as precedents for further centralized development.

One will be obvious: government must lead in the protection of the landed interest and in that sense always be concerned with major economic questions. On this basis Disraeli defended the Corn Laws. And although after their repeal in 1846, he felt that protectionists like himself

---

66 Buckingham election address, 1847, in Monypenny and Buckle, *Life*, i.837. Cf. Kebbel, *Speeches*, i.14.
67 Monypenny and Buckle, *Life*, i.839.
68 *The Spirit of Whiggism* (1836), in *Whigs and Whiggism* (edn cit.), p.349.
69 Monypenny and Buckle, *Life*, i.460–1. On Disraeli's views about educational administration and reform, see also e.g. ibid., ii.313–15, 386–7, 461–2.
70 ibid., i.766.
71 225 Parl. Deb. 3s., 24 June 1875, col.525.
72 Monypenny and Buckle, *Life*, i.646.

should accept the free-trade position (in the sense that the laws regulating a great industry should not be the subject of continual partisan alteration or repealed as a result of a chance Parliamentary situation and without a major shift in opinion), at the same time he continually pressed on behalf of the Country Party the urgent necessity of doing something to compensate the land in its new situation so as to relieve agricultural distress, for instance by a readjustment of taxation.[73] Implicit indeed in this whole controversy is the belief, accepted by all parties, that government had the duty and right to regulate these important aspects of the nation's economic life. For instance, Disraeli's election address of June 1852 and subsequent speeches recurred to the need to treat the agricultural interest fairly, given that the free-trade system had come to stay, and stated it was the duty of the legislature to help cut down production costs.[74] The other context was that of Ireland, always a special case and recognized to be in a quite different stage of economic and social development from the rest of the United Kingdom. Disraeli frequently declared that in Ireland strong control by central authority was essential. And, for instance, in the crisis of 1846–7, he supported a policy of extensive public works there on the ground that in Ireland the normal 'commercial principle' was unable to cope with the situation.[75] There were, too, some occasions at home on which Disraeli was, for various reasons, prepared to support government intervention in the field of private interests and business activity. For instance, he agreed in 1866 that government should take over the private telegraph offices and that a subsidy should be granted to railway companies which were in financial difficulties.[76] And earlier, in 1858, as Chancellor of the Exchequer in Lord Derby's second administration, Disraeli was personally responsible for the passage into law of a bill to purify the Thames by a system of main drainage to be carried out under the supervision of the Metropolitan Board of Works and with a Treasury guarantee.[77]

But it is indeed to a consideration of the significance of Disraeli's achievement when he was in government that it is now appropriate to turn.

The record in office
In the hagiography of Tory paternalism Disraeli takes pride of place. The

73 e.g., ibid., i. 1098–100, 1116, 1233–6. For the proposals in his own abortive budget of 1852, see ibid., i. 1241ff. And cf. Kebbel, *Speeches*, i. 208–39, 258ff.
74 Monypenny and Buckle, *Life*, i. 1185–6, 1193–4. The whole controversy over free trade and protection was settled for nearly half a century by the defeat of Villiers's motion in 1852, ibid., i. 1237–8.
75 ibid., i. 831–3.
76 ibid., ii. 212–13, 386.
77 ibid., i. 1570.

doctrine just described has undoubtedly been a potent influence of almost mythical impact on the later development of the Conservative mind. And one major element in this influence has been the belief that when in office and especially when, as Prime Minister from 1874–80, Disraeli finally achieved effective Parliamentary power, he acted on and carried through the programmatic implications of the ideology he had long expounded: 'The aspirations of *Sybil* and "Young England", the doctrines in which Disraeli had "educated" his party for thirty years, the principles laid down in the great speeches of 1872, were translated into legislative form; it was Tory Democracy in action.'[78] Yet it is now clear that considerable care may be necessary in the assessment of this traditional picture. What is involved is a fascinating case-study of the relation in political life between theory and practice. Moreover what recent historical inquiry has revealed about the genesis and working out of the policies of the administrations with which Disraeli was connected shows, too, what is meant by the third significant aspect of Conservative interventionism, piecemeal concession: that is, *ad hoc* recognition of political or administrative necessity.[79]

It is not, of course, to be denied that considered as a whole the social and reformist measures implemented by Derby's administration of 1866–8 (in which Disraeli served as Chancellor of the Exchequer) and of Disraeli's own government were considerable. The achievement of the latter alone constituted the largest instalment of constructive legislation passed by any one government in the nineteenth century. It was the first time Parliament had devoted so much attention to social and welfare matters. And Shaftesbury noted in his diary that these questions had thus become established as subjects of 'Imperial' concern.[80] Ministers were often preoccupied with proposals intended to improve the condition of the people especially during the busy second session of Parliament in 1874–5. For instance, on 15 November 1874, Disraeli wrote to the Queen: 'The Cabinet was engaged yesterday in considering the measure for the

78 ibid., ii.709. Cf. the account in R. C. K. Ensor, *England 1870–1914* (1936; Oxford, 1968), pp.35–7, 39–40.

79 The work I have mainly in mind here is, of course, Professor Paul Smith's superb study *Disraelian Conservatism and Social Reform* (London, 1967) to which this subsection is heavily indebted. There is an intriguing parallel to be observed in the development of the social reforms of the Asquith government before the Great War, Dr José Harris having shown, in a similarly magisterial work, how Liberal unemployment policy was the outcome not of a consistent plan of social reform but of an array of personal, departmental, and tactical considerations: see her *Unemployment and Politics: a Study in English Social Policy, 1886–1914* (Oxford, 1972), esp. p.351.

80 Smith, op. cit., pp.2–3, 202, 322; R. Blake, *Disraeli* (London, 1960), p.553. H. E. Gorst, *The Fourth Party* (London, 1906), p.73. Shaftesbury's diary (11 January 1875), in E. Hodder, *The Life and Work of the Seventh Earl of Shaftesbury, K.G.* (London, 1887), iii.355. On the work of the Derby administration, see Smith, op. cit., esp. ch.1.

Improvement of the Dwellings of the People. . . . This, and some other measures completing the code of sanitary legislation, took up the whole sitting. . . .'[81] So under Disraeli's premiership many important measures of reform were passed into law. These included, as well as the Artizans' Dwellings Act, statutes to promote Friendly Societies and secure small savings; to make labour contracts more equitable and to remove trade union activity from the operation of the conspiracy law (and incidentally to legalize peaceful picketing); to improve the position of agricultural tenants in regard to 'unexhausted improvements'; to protect the working conditions of merchant seamen in particular from the dangers of unseaworthy ships; to deal with the sale of food and drugs; to inspect and regulate canal boats; to extend the Truck Acts; to consolidate existing public health legislation; to codify the Factory Acts (a bill highly praised by Shaftesbury); to prevent the enclosure of common land for private gain; to prevent the pollution of rivers by untreated sewage and industrial waste; and to improve educational facilities as by extending elementary education. Significant departures of principle were often involved. For instance, although the Artizans' Dwellings Act (1875) was not in fact a wholly effective measure, it was a major attempt to tackle the problem of urban working-class housing as a whole and the first time public authorities were given the responsibility for remedying defects in privately owned dwellings by compulsory purchase if necessary. And the substantial use to which the powers it gave could be put was shown by what happened, a few years after its passage, in Birmingham during Joseph Chamberlain's mayoralty.

Yet it may be that a simple review of all this legislation tends to give an exaggerated impression of its practical significance. Lord Morley was convinced that when power fell into Disraeli's hands 'he made no single move of solid effect for either social reform or imperial unity.' Similarly a modern American commentary suggests that in practice Conservatives then did little to support intervention to remedy the problems of industrial society.[82]

Certainly it would be misleading to regard the commitment and activity of Disraeli and his ministers simply as the implementation of a philosophy, of the views on social reform the Prime Minister had long espoused. There was undoubtedly an element of political expediency involved, for example. After the Reform Act of 1867 many politicians quickly realized the growing electoral importance of social issues and of the need to have a firm policy that would appeal to the new working-class

81 Cited in Monypenny and Buckle, *Life*, ii.701.
82 Smith, op. cit., p.259; J. Morley, *The Life of William Ewart Gladstone* (London, 1903), ii.392; D. Roberts, 'Tory Paternalism and Social Reform in Early Victorian England', *American Historical Review*, lxiii (1957–8), pp.323–37.

voters. It was an opportunity to end the period of a quarter of a century during which the Conservatives had been in a minority. Hence the interest expressed by some of them during the years of opposition (1868–74) in the so-called New Social Movement of 1871 and the pressure on Disraeli to give the party a more positive platform than he himself sometimes felt it was wise to adopt.[83] None the less there was good reason for him to turn to social reform as questions of this sort were topical and he thought it tactically wise not to let the Liberal administration monopolize them. Moreover he wanted to divert attention from proposals to extend the household franchise to the counties.[84] Hence his major speeches at Manchester and the Crystal Palace in the spring of 1872 and the appeal on issues both of imperial policy and social improvement particularly sanitary reform and the regulation of labour. No doubt none of the themes was ideologically uncongenial to Disraeli but the need to restore his party position and to gain the political initiative were factors more immediately important.[85] Further there is the point that this legislation is not to be seen as the required practical outcome of ideological predisposition but as having been promulgated in an unplanned way as a series of rather reluctant concessions made necessary by the pressing demand of circumstances. Indeed the attitude of Disraeli's ministers (as now revealed by the archives) was, far from being congenial to paternalistic regulation, rather conditioned by the still predominant anti-interventionism of the day. They dealt as they did with slum clearance, the over-insurance of merchant shipping, and the like because of specific political necessity, because a particular investigation and report seemed to demand action, because of the special interests of a minister or the exigencies of party politics, because, that is, of a practical – and rather confused – empiricism, and not because they saw themselves as implementing a Conservative philosophy of paternalistic concern.[86] As for Disraeli himself, it now appears that on assuming office he had no concrete proposals of his own and even showed little interest in these domestic matters choosing to rely instead on suggestions put forward by colleagues, in particular R. A. Cross the Home Secretary, who referred indeed to his leader's lack of initiative and legislative forethought.[87] Part of the problem may have been that of getting interventionist policies accepted by a party many quarters of which found them, not to mention

83 Smith, op. cit., pp. 36–7, 133, 148–56, 218.
84 ibid., pp. 2–3, 157–8; Monypenny and Buckle, *Life*, ii. 650–1.
85 Smith, op. cit., pp. 158–61.
86 ibid. e.g. pp. 34–5, 206, 218, 223, 257–8, 299.
87 ibid., pp. 199–200; Blake, *Disraeli*, pp. 476, 543, 549, 553–6, 652, 762; C. J. Lewis, 'Theory and Expediency in the Policy of Disraeli', *Victorian Studies*, iv (1960–1), pp. 251–3, 255–6. Cf. Monypenny and Buckle, *Life*, ii. 699.

their leader, quite uncongenial.[88] To take but one instance albeit an important one: in January 1872 the Earl of Derby made a speech on the policy of the Conservative Party in which he dealt *inter alia* with the legislative projects in view. His attitude was revealed when he considered the prospect of sanitary improvement. He approved of the objects of this but wondered whether they might not be better achieved not by more lawnmaking but by more effective enforcement of existing powers. Then follows a criticism of the habit of relying too much on state agency and too little on personal initiative, the expression of these sentiments being concluded with the following passage:

> I don't tell you in so many words that the State should take on itself no functions except those which it actually performs; but I do tell you that the tendency to enlarge indefinitely the scope of its operations is one to be watched with great jealousy. There is risk of extravagance and jobbery; there is discouragement of individual enterprise; there is loss of individual self-reliance; there is the inevitable discontent caused by the disappointment of unreasonable expectations, ...[89]

Whatever the reason, in the general elections of the time there was little sign, save in some constituencies, of a commitment to a general programme of Tory reform.[90] Some quite extreme criticisms of Disraeli, impinging in effect on his integrity, have been penned because he was (in office) less assertive of the need for change than his previously expressed ideas demanded.[91]

Perhaps, persuasive as it is, this depreciatory view of Disraeli's achievement goes rather too far. There is some contrary evidence: for instance, he had been giving the labour laws close personal study and, when the Cabinet hesitated over policy on this issue, it was he who converted the doubters and saw the thing through because he was convinced of its importance.[92] It is true that he followed the practice of ministerial delegation in which he had long believed: this was natural, too, given his age and failing health and his preoccupation, as leader of

88 E. J. Feuchtwanger, *Disraeli, Democracy and the Tory Party: Conservative Leadership and Organization after the Second Reform Bill* (Oxford, 1968), ch.1, esp. pp.16–17; F. E. Smith's comments in the introduction to K. Feiling, *Toryism: a Political Dialogue* (London, 1913), p.ix.
89 *The Policy of the Conservative Party: Speech of the Earl of Derby . . . Jan. 9th 1872* (London, 1872), pp.9, 11–12.
90 Blake, op. cit., p.512; Smith, op. cit., pp.119–21. Cf. R. Blake *et al.*, *Conservatism Today* (CPC no.350; London, 1966), pp.10–11.
91 Lord Rosebery, *Lord Randolph Churchill* (London, 1906), pp.129–30, 148–50; Smith, op. cit., pp.12–13, 16–17, 161, 181, 200, etc.; D. Roberts, art. cit.
92 See Disraeli to Lady Bradford (29 June 1875), and to the Queen (same date), cited in Monypenny and Buckle, *Life*, ii.711–12.

the government, with many other matters demanding attention. But there is no reason to suppose that the weight of his general approval was not vital to the development of his ministry's reforming efforts.[93] At the very least, it may be said that, when circumstances pressed, neither the Premier himself nor his views stood in the way of legislative intervention. Shaftesbury confided to his diary that in the 1860s he still found Disraeli, 'as I always found him in the House of Commons, decided and true to the cause'.[94] And Alexander Macdonald, one of the first trade union MPs, was in no doubt about what had been done. He told the miners of Stafford in 1879 that they had 'gained more from the Conservatives in respect to matters effecting [sic] the working-men than the Liberals would ever dare have granted.'[95]

The Disraelian heritage

Lord Hugh Cecil reflected a common opinion when he wrote that Disraeli was not only an able political tactician but quite as much a man of theory or ideas.[96] He was able, therefore, through this means to influence others, contemporaries and those who came after him. And his doctrinal effect has indeed been considerable. Lord Blake noted recently in his Ford Lectures how 'so many modern Conservatives look back on Disraeli as their prophet, high priest and philosopher rolled into one.'[97]

In the latter part of the nineteenth century, many rather different wings of the Conservative Party reflected or were affected by the paternalism or social reformism with which Disraeli, rightly or not, was associated. The landed interest was taught that country gentlemen should not be averse (through public action and the fulfilment of the traditional duties of their station) to seeking the welfare of the people so long as excessive centralization or too large a rate burden were avoided. The 'new Conservatism of the boroughs', reflecting the ideas of the major centres of population and the commercial and professional middle classes, was often persuaded to accept reform as with such representatives as Cross, Sandon, and W. H. Smith.[98] One relevant aspect of this (which has already been mentioned) was the New Social Movement of the 1870s which was designed to bring Tories together with Labour representatives in a programme to secure the improvement of the working classes. Encouraged by Disraeli himself it envisaged, among other things, a large slum clearance and housing scheme, a programme for the land little short

93 Smith, op. cit., p. 322; cf. ibid., pp. 200, 215.
94 Diary entry (9 August 1866), cited in Hodder, op. cit., iii.214.
95 *Staffordshire Sentinel* (18 January 1879), p.6, cited in W. J. Wilkinson, *Tory Democracy* (New York, 1925), p.162.
96 Lord Hugh Cecil, *Conservatism* (1912; London, 1928), p.70.
97 R. Blake, *The Conservative Party from Peel to Churchill* (1970; Fontana, 1972), p. 3.
98 Feuchtwanger, op. cit., p.47.

of nationalization, extensive local government reform, an eight-hour day, and the development of technical education, all with state aid.[99] Then there was the image of the so-called Fourth Party of Lord Randolph Churchill and his three associates. The former at least was a great admirer of Disraeli and consciously sought to follow in Elijah's footsteps. What this was taken to mean is explained in a famous letter J. E. Gorst wrote to *The Times* in 1907 in which he described the domestic policy of his 'ancient master':

> The principle of Tory democracy is that all government exists solely for the good of the governed; that Church and King, Lords and Commons, and all other public institutions are to be maintained so far, and so far only, as they promote the happiness and welfare of the common people; that all who are entrusted with any public function are trustees, not for their own class, but for the nation at large; and that the mass of the people may be trusted so to use electoral power, which should be freely conceded to them, as to support those who are promoting their interests. It is democratic because the welfare of the people is its supreme end; it is Tory because the institutions of the country are the means by which the end is to be attained.[100]

And, given such elements of Conservative thought and action, it was not (in this respect) too difficult to absorb Joseph Chamberlain and his unauthorized programme which could easily be seen as reinforcing the reformism sponsored by Disraeli.

By the beginning of the present century, therefore, a paternalism of this sort had become part of the traditional wisdom of the Conservative creed. In 1913, the 2nd Earl of Selborne, addressing a dinner at the Junior Constitutional Club, said:

> Nor could there be a shadow of doubt what should be the message they should deliver to the well-to-do classes. 'Noblesse Oblige. To you much has been given, from you much is required. All that you possess and enjoy is the direct result of the conditions bequeathed to you by the England of the past. It is for you to shoulder the task of making a better England for the future.'[101]

Consequently it has since been quite usual for Disraeli's name and the themes conventionally associated with him to be ritually invoked by Conservative writers and pamphleteers of all kinds.[102] Sometimes,

99 See the accounts, ibid., pp. 91–4, and Smith, op. cit., pp. 149–54.
100 *The Times* (6 February 1907), cited in Monypenny and Buckle, *Life*, ii. 709.
101 Reported in *The Times* (26 June 1913), p. 6. I owe this reference to Dr D. G. Boyce who has edited the Selborne papers.
102 Some more or less latter-day examples are: L. H. Lang, 'The Young Conservative', *National Review*, lxxxiii (1924), pp. 73–4; R. V. Jenner, *Will Conservatism Survive?*

indeed, this element has been seen as by far the most crucial in the Conservative tradition. For instance, writing in 1905, one publicist saw it as a vanished dream that nothing – not even the various injections of Tory radicalism – had replaced: hence the hiatus then being felt in party attitudes and thinking. 'The early Conservative reformers', he wrote,

> were kept from 'political' Democracy by a definite political theory of their own. They dreamt of a transformed England – happy and prosperous through the beneficence of those called to high estate, – which would, under new conditions, reproduce, and continue through helpful charity, the old dependence, half feudal and half patriarchal, of class upon class.[103]

There was thus no place for what has since become increasingly dominant, some form of popular control; and not even the 'hesitant Radicalism' adopted by the Tories had really met that tendency of the day.[104]

One interesting exposition of Conservative principles that (despite a certain eccentricity) showed not a few similarities with the Disraelian position was that of A. M. Ludovici.[105] Originally an artist and illustrator he was for a time secretary to the sculptor, Auguste Rodin, and later translated a number of the volumes of Nietzsche's works. After service in the Great War he turned to a more literary career, publishing a series of books on social and political doctrine written from a point of view at once defensive of the role of an aristocracy or propertied élite and critical of the canons of Liberalism. Among these volumes is one on Conservatism which is directly relevant here.[106] The argument is that

---

(London, 1944); E. S. Riley, *Our Cause: a Handbook of Conservatism* (1938; 2nd edn, Exmouth, 1948), pp. 7, 14–15, 28–32, 43; I. Macleod and A. Maude (eds), *One Nation: a Tory Approach to Social Problems* (CPC no. 86; London, 1950), p. 13; Sir E. Boyle, in *Great Conservatives* (CPC no. 125; London, 1953), p. 29; *This Is To Welcome You . . .* (PY 4242; 1953), pp. 5–6; R. A. Butler *et al.*, *Tradition and Change* (CPC no. 138; London, 1954), p. 11; H. Macmillan, *Winds of Change: 1914–1939* (London, 1966), p. 44; *Tides of Fortune 1945–1955* (London, 1969), pp. 306, 451. For a very recent partisan use of Disraeli's interventionist reputation, see T. Russel, *The Tory Party: its Policies, Divisions and Future* (Penguin, 1978), pp. 8, 11. And for a fascinating suggestion of Conservative disenchantment with the Disraelian image, M. Foot, 'The Tory as Hero', *TLS* (18 April 1980), pp. 493–4.

103 'Hakluyt Egerton' [Arthur Boutwood], *Patriotism: an Essay Towards a Constructive Theory of Politics* (London, 1905), app. II, 'Conservatism and Social Democracy', pp. 309–10.

104 ibid., pp. 310–12.

105 I am grateful to Dr D. J. Manning of Durham University for first drawing my attention to Ludovici's work.

106 A. M. Ludovici, *A Defence of Conservatism: a Further Text-book for Tories* (London, 1927). See also *A Defence of Aristocracy: a Textbook for Tories* (1915; rev. edn, London, 1933), and *The False Assumptions of 'Democracy'* (London, [1921]).

Conservative thinking depends upon such concepts as hierarchy, order, subordination, and discipline, and asserts the propriety of a kind of feudal social structure based on the land which sustains a responsible gentry with patriarchal duties in regard to the protection of those who depend on them.[107] And Ludovici believes this position was betrayed by those who permitted modern industry to develop in a quite unregulated fashion: the Conservatives of the day shirked the issues raised by industrialization and so lost their opportunity to control the future. Modern Conservatism now has to confront the consequences of this disastrous error. The social solution envisaged, a widespread diffusion of landed property, is in some ways not unlike that of Distributism while the attitude to industrial organization has a close resemblance to some of the proposals of the Guild Socialists.[108] And although Ludovici is hostile to the growth of the large, centralized state he accepts that public authorities must exercise a substantial array of functions for the good of the labouring masses, tasks concerning the health of the nation, education, the promotion of agriculture, procuring economic security for wage earners, and so forth.[109] Politics is indeed no less than a science of enlightened interference to preserve national life.[110]

There was, then, in these various forms a continuing Disraelian inheritance; and the kind of intervention it entailed was indeed – and here the next factor emerges – easily married to the various forms of political radicalism that appeared among some leading Conservatives in the last years of the nineteenth century. Here one thinks, of course, of the Tory Democracy of Lord Randolph Churchill and the considerably more important body of ideas associated with Joseph Chamberlain, the ethos of which he took over to the Conservative benches when he broke with Gladstone over Home Rule. Fittingly perhaps, the continuation into a later period of the same concepts of social reform may be exemplified by reference to the policies of Joseph Chamberlain's son, Neville.

Conservative radicalism

Randolph Churchill and the Tory Democracy
As with so many politicians it is difficult to assess Lord Randolph Churchill's sincerity in the expression of his views. He had to react to a wide range of different events, problems, and pressures and had little time for or interest in leisurely reflection of a systematic kind.[111] And, in

107 e.g. *A Defence of Conservatism*, pp. 33–4, 36, 55, 58–9, etc.
108 ibid., pp. 161–7.
109 ibid., pp. 216ff.
110 ibid., p. 15.
111 Cf. Churchill's own comments, in L. J. Jennings (ed.), *Speeches of the Right Honourable Lord Randolph Churchill, M.P., 1880–1888* (London, 1889), i. 255–6.

pursuit of his policy of harassing not only Gladstone but also his own party leaders, whose conduct and policy he deemed inadequate, he would as part of the tactics involved take up issues and press points he did not necessarily think really significant. But, of course, to someone active in the political field principle is always thus liable to be 'the slave of opportunity'. He was, too, personally impetuous and volatile, as mercurial as his political career: Rosebery, his lifelong friend, called him 'the shooting star of politics'; *The Spectator* (which supported the party leadership he treated with contumely) referred to him as 'this horrid young mutineer'.[112] None the less there are some themes to which he recurred so very often and at such length that it would obviously be misleading and almost certainly unjust, even amid the undoubted political opportunism, not to suppose they reflect the carefully formed and firmly held opinions of one of the most formidable and shrewd, if ultimately unsuccessful, Tory politicians of his day. Mandell Creighton wrote to Churchill in 1883 that it is easy to be either a doctrinaire or a purely party politician but not at all easy to combine the two in a distinct line of policy. It is not too naïve to suppose that this is what Churchill tried to do through his version of progressive Conservatism.

'Tory Democracy' was a set of ideas about the role, structure, and policies of the Conservative Party in an age of increasing popular tendency, a time that was less and less committed to the dominance of what Sir John Gorst called 'the Old Identity', that is, the traditional ruling classes especially the magic circle of great landowners. It was necessary to obtain a wider basis of support for the principles of the party, specifically to help sustain established institutions that might otherwise come under threat like the monarchy, the House of Lords, and the Church.[113] The policy that Churchill envisaged as a means to this end had two main aspects. The first was organizational being the use of the National Union and the formation of Tory working-men's clubs which he proposed as a way of bringing a larger number of people within the fold and, too, of creating a power base from which to move to an assault on the party leadership. The second, which is the aspect of the matter most relevant in this context, was the formulation of a policy designed to appeal both to the rising middle ranks of society and, more importantly, to the recently enfranchised members of the labouring class so as to grapple them close to the Conservative Party.[114] Its themes were consciously elaborated on the received Disraelian model as Churchill's

---

112 Lord Rosebery, *Lord Randolph Churchill*, p.180; 'The New Split in the Tory Ranks', *The Spectator*, lvii (24 May 1884), p.672.

113 Jennings, *Speeches*, i.116–17, 296–8, 331–2.

114 Cf. T. H. S. Escott, *Randolph Spencer-Churchill as a Product of His Age*. . . . (London, 1895), p.158; Blake, *The Conservative Party from Peel to Churchill*, pp.147–8.

famous article 'Elijah's Mantle' makes clear.[115] It was not spelled out in any particularly systematic or detailed way but broadly what it all added up to was a Tory version of the old radical cry for peace, retrenchment, and reform with the difference that the last item meant not constitutional change but dealing with social issues.[116]

Despite his aristocratic origin and background, Churchill was something of a natural rebel, a radical of the old type in Tory clothing.[117] In terms made familiar by Joseph Hume and J. A. Roebuck, he was scathing about the inefficiency and waste of government departments especially the military and naval offices where he believed it was important to secure reductions of expenditure (a matter over which he resigned as Chancellor of the Exchequer in 1886). Given this sort of view he was not disposed to believe that Parliament or the Executive should continually interfere in matters of trade and commerce and meddle with freedom of contract.[118] But he was quite clear about the practical limits of his diffidence:

> I recognise that the democracy of Britain is continually making fresh demands on the State, that the democracy expects the State to perform duties which in former days the State was allowed to leave to private enterprise, and I recognise that the tendency of modern social reform must tend to check any hopes of large decrease in our civil expenditure.[119]

The social progress of the 'Commons of England', he said, achieved by measures of legislative reform, 'must be the policy of the Tory Party.'[120] In consequence he was prepared not simply to accept but to advocate government action to deal with a large number of contemporary problems ranging from the control of railway rates and the extension of employers' liability to the provision of free elementary education and the establishment of the eight-hour day. He was also an advocate of the reform of county government and of measures to promote the cause of the small landowner; and he recognized that much would have to be

---

115 Randolph S. Churchill, 'Elijah's Mantle; April 19th, 1883', *The Fortnightly Review*, n.s. xxxiii (1883), pp. 612–21. Cf. Jennings, *Speeches*, i. 140. Also Wilkinson, op. cit., pp. 62–6, 79; Gorst, op. cit., p. v.
116 Jennings, *Speeches*, ii. 139. However for a recent suggestion that Churchill's association with progressive Conservatism was much more fitful and slight than usually supposed, see R. E. Quinault, 'Lord Randolph Churchill and Tory Democracy, 1880–1885', *Historical Journal*, xxii (1979), pp. 141–65, esp. pp. 163–5.
117 Cf. Sir J. E. Gorst's preface to H. E. Gorst, *The Fourth Party*, pp. v–vi; and J. B. Crozier in his critical *Lord Randolph Churchill: a Study of English Democracy* (London, 1887), pp. 145–6.
118 Jennings, *Speeches*, ii. 79–80, 227.
119 ibid., ii. 179.
120 ibid., i. 138–9.

conceded to the growing strength of the 'Labour interest'. There were further areas, too, which he thought cried aloud for legislative attention and these, like the other issues which he wanted to 'occupy the future time' of governments, were not necessarily careful of the usual Tory concerns. Thus while he followed (in an orthodox way enough) Disraeli's maxim that sanitation and health were among the great objects of public interest, he was prepared to tackle questions arising from the multiplication of establishments for the sale of drink and the vast amount of money people spent on it each year. This was 'ruining both the health and the morals of a large portion of our urban population' and was 'the direct parent' of the great part of the crime, poverty, disease, and other misery that afflicted and tarnished the English scene. He was quite sure that 'a strong despotic administration with regard to the number of liquor-shops would be attended with the most unmixed and un-adulterated good.' He would, in effect, rather see England sober than England free. He referred also to other urgent matters which needed to be dealt with. One was the

> overcrowded state of large portions of our great towns. . . . Recent very appalling atrocities have sharply drawn the attention of the metropolis to the East of London; and we must remember that terrible condition is by no means peculiar to the metropolis. We shall find it repeated in all its wretched phases in many of our large towns in this country; and it cannot possibly be denied that we have a prolific parent of vice, misery, and crime in the condition of the dwellings of a great portion of our labouring population. Closely allied with that subject is a question which excites much attention in London – the immigration of foreign paupers: how to check the undue flow into this country of people who have no means to subsist upon, no means by which they can maintain themselves, and who clearly add by their influx to the evils arising from the overcrowded state of our towns. Again I say that the laws of health imperatively call upon the Legislature to deal with the question. . . . I call attention to one other object . . . – a subject of immense importance – the question of cheap labour, better known as the sweating system. . . . The State cannot regulate the price of labour, but the State can insist that labour in the mass shall not be carried on under conditions which violate all the principles of cleanliness, all the principles of health, all the principles of decency, and all the principles of morality.[121]

If in many ways Churchill's general attitude and his rhetoric were merely vague and untutored, his position was manifestly not unfavourable to the

121 ibid., ii. 370–3.

extension of state activity in important respects. Lord Rosebery, in his short and perceptive, though sometimes misleading, study of Churchill, observed correctly that 'Randolph found himself on the verge of collectivism'.[122]

Of course, many of the ideas of Tory Democracy hardly aroused widespread support in Conservative circles. And, under the rather sceptical aegis of Lord Salisbury, perhaps little was to be anticipated, for his attitude was a sort of pale and negative Disraelism: not hostile to innovation or state intervention where it was absolutely necessary but concerned to delay concessions and, when they had to be made, to assimilate them with the least possible trouble.[123] Yet after Lord Randolph's departure the radical spirit continued strong as in the activities of bodies like the Tory Reform League. Committees were also set up to develop Unionist policy in such fields as social reform (especially in respect of health and housing), social insurance, and small ownership; and there was substantial support in the party for schemes intended to encourage the small farmer, promote industrial co-partnership, and the like. Propaganda in the style of Churchillian Tory Democracy also appeared: for instance, Sir John Gorst, the disciple of Disraeli and friend of Churchill, published some papers of this sort.[124] Nor was the actual legislative achievement during Tory years of office unimpressive with statutes on such matters as the abolition of school fees, the reform of county government, further factory legislation, improvement of the tithe law in favour of the tenant farmer, a married woman's property act, the adoption of the eight-hour day in government establishments, and so on.

But undoubtedly a most important impetus behind this continuing radicalism was the injection of Chamberlainism which, though much more developed, was in many ways not unlike Churchill's doctrine.[125] Hence, no doubt, the ease with which it was absorbed by the Tory Party.

Joseph Chamberlain: social and economic radicalism
Chamberlain's political frame of mind was formed by a number of

122 Rosebery, op. cit., p.154. Cf. W. S. Churchill, *Lord Randolph Churchill* (1906; new edn, London [1952]), pp.564, 717. What Rosebery fails to make clear is that Tory collectivism is not a contradiction in terms, op. cit., pp.139–40.
123 Cf. M. Pinto-Duschinsky, *The Political Thought of Lord Salisbury, 1854–1868* (London, 1967), a study of the early political writings.
124 Gorst, 'Social Reform: the Obligation of the Tory Party', *Nineteenth Century*, liii (1903), pp.519–33; *idem*, 'Governments and Social Reform', *Fortnightly Review*, lxxvii (1905), pp.843–55; also other references in Wilkinson, op. cit., p.76 n.3.
125 Cf. *The Radical Programme* (London, 1885), pp.17–18; Morley, *Life of Gladstone*, iii.200–1. On the impact of Chamberlain's ideas, see J. L. Garvin and J. Amery, *The Life of Joseph Chamberlain* (London, 1932–69), vi.994–5; Sir Charles Petrie, *The Chamberlain Tradition* (London, 1938), p.276; I. Macleod and A. Maude (eds), *One Nation*, p.14.

influences and motives. Part of his apprenticeship to the family business had involved a period at the workbench and he found himself not unsympathetic to the Chartists with whom he then mingled. The atmosphere of Protestant dissent in which he was brought up led to a strong feeling that all religious disabilities and the environment of ecclesiastical privilege which sustained them should be attacked and removed. His political interest was much stimulated, too, by the reform agitation of 1866-7 and he became concerned in particular with the need to educate the newly-enfranchised electorate. He had been involved for some time with voluntary teaching at secular Sunday schools and at night school but now he was convinced that nothing less than compulsory education for all would answer. And this in turn directed his attention to related problems such as housing and squalid living conditions, for if these were not tackled the educational effort would surely fail.[126] To deal with these matters national legislation was necessary; so Chamberlain became heavily involved in the campaign for the creation of educational provision that was unsectarian, compulsory, and free.[127] He was a leader of the dissenting agitation against Forster's elementary education Bill of 1870 and then, after the passage of the Act, of the attempt to rally Nonconformist strength throughout the country in the school board elections which ensued and in which the detailed organization of the vote was crucial.[128]

Being thus committed to a political career Chamberlain quickly became a man of more than this one issue. For example, in 1872 he championed the 'rural' revolt of Joseph Arch and the agricultural labourers.[129] The following year, in a famous article in the *Fortnightly Review*, he attacked the Liberal leaders for failing to see that social reform was the question that must dominate contemporary politics.[130] This agitation was an important step in the transformation of Liberalism at this period; Chamberlain was, in effect, envisaging the formation of a new Radical party with an advanced programme to replace the old Liberalism, one capable of dealing with the social issues occasioned by the development of industrialization and democracy.[131]

But, most important of all, he had (in John Morley's phrase) become

---

126 Garvin and Amery, *Life*, i.146; C. W. Boyd (ed.), *Mr. Chamberlain's Speeches* (London, 1914), i.51, 55-6; Petrie, op. cit., p.50.

127 Garvin and Amery, *Life*, i.90-3, 96, 100; Boyd, *Speeches*, i.6.

128 The caucus method Chamberlain developed is described in Garvin and Amery, *Life*, i.186ff.

129 e.g. Boyd, *Speeches*, i.25-6.

130 J. Chamberlain, 'The Liberal Party and its Leaders', *Fortnightly Review*, xiv (1873), pp.287-302. Cf. a later article, 'The Next Page of the Liberal Programme', ibid., xvi (1874), pp.405-29.

131 See his letter to Morley (12 August 1873), cited in Garvin and Amery, *Life*, i.161; also ibid., i.218-19.

'King of Birmingham'. He entered the council in 1869 and was three times mayor (1873–6). Winston Churchill believed that no greater municipal officer had ever adorned English local government, adding that, if radicalism was his war-horse, municipal politics was the stirrup by which he mounted to the saddle.[132] He introduced many changes to deal with contemporary social problems, in particular those concerning health and the conditions of living, which he believed could only be tackled by active public authority: the abatement of nuisances, such as smoke; the establishment of a new sewage system and the arrangement of a main drainage union with other towns. He believed, too, that monopolies of general interest should be run by public representatives; so the Birmingham corporation acquired control of the town's gasworks and water supply. And the profits which accrued were used (under the powers which had recently been given by Disraeli's government in the Artizans' Dwellings Act) to finance extensive slum clearance and rebuilding in an improvement scheme which transformed the town centre. Further, cultural amenities were improved and enlarged. The effects of all this activity, packed into a mayoralty of only two and a half years, was considerable constituting in effect a new 'civic gospel': among the specific consequences was a dramatic fall in the average death-rate, for example.[133] Sir Keith Feiling urged that in this fashion Chamberlain 'made Birmingham the pioneer of a planned city'; while Chamberlain's own later summary of the work was to describe it as 'municipal socialism' achieved by 'popular representative local government'.[134] The collectivist tendency was clear: extensive action by public authority was involved, compulsory powers were used, organization centralized, private interests superseded, and all in the name of the public good. Nor was the example unnoticed as a precedent for similar municipal development elsewhere or for action on a national scale.[135] In London, Fabians and other progressives were certainly most impressed.

Chamberlain's focus of attention now shifted. Commercial success and ample means had come to him as a quite young man and he was thus able to contemplate virtual retirement from business to devote himself more fully to politics. This he did in 1874 at the age of thirty-eight. Two years later he was elected Liberal MP for Birmingham. Nor was he long in making his mark on the national political scene: after less than four years in the Commons and with no previous experience of office he joined Gladstone's Cabinet; this was preferment of a then unusual kind.

At this political eminence his collectivist propensities came quickly to

132 W. S. Churchill, *Great Contemporaries* (1937; rev. edn, London, 1938), pp.64–5.
133 Garvin and Amery, *Life*, i.199; A. Briggs, *Victorian Cities* (1963; Penguin, 1968), ch. 5.
134 K. Feiling, *The Life of Neville Chamberlain* (London, 1946), p.2; J. Chamberlain, 'Favorable Aspects of State Socialism', *North American Review*, clii (1891), p.538.
135 Garvin and Amery, *Life*, i.213.

the fore. He proposed extensive schemes for relief and public works in Ireland deliberately modelling his proposals on the work he had done at Birmingham: as his biographer put it, this was 'planning on a national scale'.[136] He had in view an array of legislation on various social issues including the public control of the London water companies, the taxation of the development value of urban property, bettering the conditions of work and employment of merchant seamen, an improved scheme of accident compensation for workers; and other matters. And to get the necessary Bills through Parliament he was prepared to back substantial changes in procedure.[137] At this time he wrote to a friend: 'The politics of the future are social politics, and the problem is still how to secure the greatest happiness of the greatest number and especially those whom all previous legislation and reform seem to have left very much where they were before.'[138] He soon came into conflict with the Whigs in the Cabinet over his vehement campaign for what he called 'constructive Radicalism'.[139] A famous Tenniel cartoon in *Punch* entitled 'The Daring Duckling' shows the Prime Minister (the 'Grand Old Hen'), feathers ruffled, watching with concern one of her perky young offspring, seemingly a different sort of bird completely, swimming out on a pond marked 'Radicalism': 'Come back!', she cackles, 'Goodness gracious – wherever *is* he going to?' Chamberlain himself thought this drawing 'hit off the situation with admirable felicity.'[140]

He had been conducting very vigorously his campaign to win Liberals and others over to a radical solution to the problems of the under-privileged. Partly he did this through his speeches, partly through the publication of a series of papers, produced by different hands but under his detailed supervision, to provide a systematic survey of what in his view a democratic politics involved.[141] Appearing between 1883 and 1885 these articles were in the latter year republished in that little red book of the day *The Radical Programme*. General policy statements had been made before by party leaders sometimes at length; but a doctrinal discussion of this scope by an active participant was unprecedented.[142] It was the basis of Chamberlain's campaign for the so-called 'unauthorized programme' which he further expounded in a series of famous speeches and which stood in contrast to the official policy of the party embodied in Gladstone's Midlothian address.

136 ibid., i. 323, 359, 366 n. 1; Boyd, *Speeches*, i. 307; J. Chamberlain, *A Political Memoir, 1880–92*, ed. Howard (London, 1953), pp. 7–8.
137 Garvin and Amery, *Life*, i. 377–8; Chamberlain, *A Political Memoir*, pp. 4–5.
138 Chamberlain to Sir E. Russell (22 January 1883), in Garvin and Amery, *Life*, i. 384–5.
139 ibid., i. 391–8.
140 *Punch* (30 June 1883), repr. ibid., opp. p. 398. Chamberlain, *A Political Memoir*, p. 87
141 See e.g. the address at Bristol in 1883 which foreshadowed and summarized his policies, in Boyd, *Speeches*, i. 111–14; Garvin and Amery, *Life*, ii. 57.
142 Garvin and Amery, *Life*, i. 547; McDowell, *British Conservatism, 1832–1914*, p. 131.

Chamberlain stressed the importance of recognizing the need to deal with the problems of the day especially given the situation created by the recent extension of the franchise. For the first time, he said, 'the toilers and spinners will have a majority of votes' and thus, if they wish, will control the government of the country. 'The centre of power has been shifted, and the old order is giving place to the new'.[143] This must mean that policy will have to be directed much more than in the past to 'social subjects'. The promotion of the greater happiness of the people and the increase of their enjoyment of life is the problem of the future. Property must recognize its obligations to those whom it has exploited and pay its 'ransom' or 'insurance' to secure the necessary improvement in the general conditions of life. The legislation required would thus be financed through extensive and progressive taxation.[144] Like many others who observed Chamberlain's activities with alarm, Gladstone was in no doubt what it all meant: 'Its pet idea is what they call construction, – that is to say, taking into the hands of the state the business of the individual man.' The Queen, too, was horrified by the programme; and Lord Iddesleigh referred to Chamberlain as Jack Cade.[145]

Chamberlain himself was well aware of the collectivism deliberately involved in his policies for 'a comprehensive scheme of legislative action'.[146] He specifically repudiated the doctrines of Herbert Spencer (with which he was very familiar) and refused to treat social evils as 'the inevitable incidents of the struggle for existence'. Far from regarding these features of our life as 'the natural concomitants of our complex civilization', they should be tackled by government acting on behalf of the community as a whole. This is the only way these misfortunes can be dealt with and provision made for people who cannot cope merely 'by their solitary and separate efforts.'[147] 'Government is the organised expression of the wishes and the wants of the people, and under these circumstances let us cease to regard it with suspicion. . . . Now it is our business to extend its functions, and to see in what way its operations can be usefully enlarged.'[148] These new conceptions of public duty and the developments of social enterprise involved, reflected an explicitly non-libertarian attitude to the state:

> They sound the death-knell of the *laissez-faire* system; . . . . The goal towards which the advance will probably be made at an accelerated pace, is that in the direction of which the legislation of the last quarter

143 Boyd, *Speeches*, i.131.
144 ibid., i.137–60 *passim*. Cf. Chamberlain's letter to Gladstone (7 February 1885) summarizing his position, in Garvin and Amery, *Life*, i.563–4.
145 Gladstone to Lord Acton (11 February 1885) in J. Morley, *Life of Gladstone* (London, 1903), iii.173; R. C. K. Ensor, *England 1870–1914*, p.92.
146 *The Radical Programme*, p.25.
147 Boyd, *Speeches*, i.163–4.
148 ibid., i.164. Cf. ibid., i.165–6.

of a century has been tending – the intervention . . . of the State on behalf of the weak against the strong, in the interests of labour against capital, of want and suffering against luxury and ease.[149]

At the same time, however, that Chamberlain called in these terms for an extensive legislative programme he did not envisage that its implementation need necessarily be highly centralized. On the contrary there is some reason to suppose he believed much of these schemes should rather be administered by elected local authorities as a sort of municipal Socialism than directly through the agency of central government.[150] But it was undoubtedly the sense of public responsibility for social issues and the consequent need for government action as such that constituted the main impact of his radical doctrine. Other coming politicians of similar persuasion, such as D. L. George and R. MacDonald, enthused over the Chamberlain programme.[151]

But this political ethos was shortly to be grafted onto the cognate heritage of Tory paternalism and this is the relevance of the doctrine here and why it has been described at some length. For Chamberlain was soon to break with Gladstone over Home Rule and to throw in his lot with the Unionists. Nor did he feel that his radicalism was in any real way abated or frustrated by this change even after the fall and early death of Randolph Churchill whom Chamberlain and his friends naturally regarded as the most 'sound' of the Conservative leaders.[152] He had long held the belief, even when associated with the Liberals, that something in the way of reform could be looked for from the Tories.[153] And the support they gave to proposals to change Irish local government, to reform the land system even by compulsory purchase, and to undertake public works of various kinds encouraged him to believe that many of them might be cast in his own mould.[154] Nor was this belief without foundation however fragile it might sometimes be. For instance, the Tory leader, Lord Salisbury, said in 1891 that the 'Conservative Party has always leaned, perhaps somewhat unduly leaned, to the use of the State, so far as it could be properly used for improving the physical, moral and intellectual condition of our people, and I hope that that mission the Conservative Party will never renounce.'[155] And while like many of his

149 *The Radical Programme*, pp.vi, 16, 21. Cf. ibid., pp.61 ff.; also Chamberlain's 'Favorable Aspects of State Socialism', loc. cit., pp.546–7.
150 See the speech cited by C. D. H. Howard, 'Joseph Chamberlain and the "Unauthorized Programme"', *English Historical Review*, lxv (1950), p.489.
151 Garvin and Amery, *Life*, ii.82–3.
152 Boyd, *Speeches*, i.76–7; Garvin and Amery, *Life*, ii.271, 275.
153 Garvin and Amery, *Life*, i.88, 94, 202, 212–13, 234. Cf. Wilkinson, op. cit., pp.115, 160.
154 Garvin and Amery, *Life*, ii.350, 411–12, 417–19, 421–2; also Chamberlain, *A Political Memoir*, p.277.
155 Salisbury's speech of 15 July 1891, cited in NUCCA, *The Case Against Radicalism,*

colleagues Salisbury was sometimes hesitant about state promoted benevolence he was certainly prepared to concede its necessity in principle.[156] Looking back several years later Chamberlain stressed the interventionist side of Conservatism to which, as he saw it in 1904, he had added his own radical convictions:

> We now no longer think that we ought to leave human beings like ourselves ... to struggle against the overpowering pressure of circumstances. We do not believe in the theory of every one for himself and the devil take the hindmost. Accordingly, we have for years been engaged in considering – I think I may say without conceit no one more seriously than myself – these questions of social reform. Now, note something. During the last thirty or fifty years there has been a great deal of what is called social legislation. By whom has it been promoted? By the Conservative party, and latterly by the Unionist party. You owe all your factory legislation to Lord Shaftesbury as its originator. You owe to the Unionist party free education, and that provision for allotments and small holdings which has, at all events, secured for the labourers in the country something like 100,000 holdings which they had not before. You owe to us compensation for workmen in the case of accidents during the course of their business. Now, why is that? I do not pretend that the Liberal or Radical party ... are or have been less anxious to do good – less philanthropic, or less considerate for the poor than we are; but they have been prevented from taking this course by the theories by which they have been governed. All this legislation is inconsistent with what they call Free Trade. You must no more interfere to raise the standard of living, to raise the wages of working men, than you must interfere to raise the price of goods or the profits of manufacturers.[157]

It was in this spirit that during his long association with the Conservatives Chamberlain continually urged the positive role of the state to achieve social reform. It was a kind of new unauthorized programme and ranged from proposals for labour exchanges and municipal control of the drink trade to supporting a state mortgage system and the idea of industrial arbitration courts; from cheap train fares for workers and the extension of smallholdings to improved

---

    1909: a Fighting Brief for Unionist Candidates, Agents, and Speakers (London, n.d. [1910?]), p.273.

156 Cf. the speech of 30 October 1894 in which, while the role of the state is admitted, fairly firm limits to government action are asserted as well, cited *National Union Gleanings*, iii (July–December 1894), pp.302–3; also speech of 30 October 1895, ibid., v (July–December 1895), pp.262–3. McDowell, op. cit., pp.136–8 brings out the 'hesitant benevolence' involved in Salisbury's attitude.

157 Boyd, *Speeches*, ii.259–60. Cf. Garvin and Amery, *Life*, ii.608, citing an article Chamberlain wrote in 1892 for the *Nineteenth Century*.

insurance schemes and stronger housing legislation.[158] In respect of a proposal for the introduction of old age pensions, 'I desire', he said, 'the intervention of the Government and the assistance of the State'; and in support of the miners' eight hour Bill he asserted that 'the State is justified in passing any law, or even in doing any single act, which in its ulterior consequences added to the sum of human happiness.' Even as Colonial Secretary – in which office Chamberlain naturally stressed the import-ance of government aided development – he was largely responsible for steering a major Workman's Compensation Bill through the Commons, a piece of legislation that was typically collectivist in that it replaced a right to legal action by individuals by a statutory duty and imposed to this end a charge on a particular class of citizens, the employers.[159]

Julian Amery once suggested that Chamberlain was 'the destroyer of *laissez-faire* and the founder . . . of the Welfare State.'[160] If this is hyperbole it is at least plausible. Certainly he firmly reinforced the Conservative radical tradition with his antipathy to the idea of limited government and his corollary belief that political power should be used to shape the pattern of social life at all levels.[161] Sidney Webb commented in the *Fabian Essays* that 'Mr. Chamberlain and the younger Conservatives openly advocate far reaching projects of social reform through State and municipal agency'.[162] It is very much worth quoting, too, the perhaps lengthy comments on Chamberlain's character and purpose that appear in Mrs Webb's diary. She knew him well, at one time was in love with him, almost married him, but refused to accept the subordinate place he thought proper in a wife.[163] In June 1883 she wrote:

> Interesting dinner here on the 18th. A Whig Peer on one side of me – Joseph Chamberlain on the other. Whig Peer talked of his own possessions; Chamberlain passionately of getting hold of other people's – *for the masses!* Curious and interesting character, domi-nated by intellectual passions, with little self-control but with any amount of purpose. Herbert Spencer on Chamberlain: 'A man who may mean well, but who does, and will do, an incalculable amount of mischief.' Chamberlain on Herbert Spencer: 'Happily, for the majority of the world, his writing is unintelligible, otherwise his life would have

158 On his campaign during the 1892 general election, see Garvin and Amery, *Life*, ii. 544; and for the proposals he made before taking office in Salisbury's Cabinet in 1895, ibid., ii. 615–16. Cf. MacDowell, *British Conservatism*, pp. 163–4.

159 Garvin and Amery, op. cit., ii. 511–12, 534; iii. 19–20, 23–5, 155–7. Cf. Ensor, *England 1870–1914*, pp. 237–8.

160 In J. Gill *et al.*, *Great Conservatives* (CPC no. 125; London, 1953), p. 50. Cf. Garvin and Amery, *Life*, ii. 511–12, 533–4, 618.

161 Cf. Garvin and Amery, *Life*, vi. 994–5.

162 G. B. Shaw *et al.*, *Fabian Essays* (1889; Jubilee edn, London, 1950), p. 49.

163 M. Cole (ed.), *Beatrice Webb's Diaries, 1924–1932* (London, 1956), app., pp. 311–16.

been spent in doing harm.' No personal animus between them, but a fundamental antipathy of mind.[164]

Six months later the following entry occurs: Chamberlain

told me the history of his political career; how his creed grew up on a basis of experience and sympathy; how his desire to benefit the many had become gradually a passion absorbing within itself his whole nature. 'Hitherto, the well-to-do have governed this country for their own interest; and I will do them this credit – they have achieved their object. Now I trust the time is approaching for those who work and have not. My aim in life is to make life pleasanter for the great majority; I do not care if it becomes in the process less pleasant for the well-to-do minority. . . .'

The political creed is the whole man – the outcome of his peculiar physical and mental temperament. He is neither a reasoner, nor an observer in the scientific sense. He does not deduce his opinions by the aid of certain well-thought-out principles, from certain carefully ascertained facts. He aims, rather, at being the organ to express the *desires* – or what he considers the desires – of the majority of his countrymen. His power rests on his intuitive knowledge of the wishes of a certain class of his countrymen; on his faculty of formulating the same, and of reimpressing them forcibly on a mass of indifferent-minded men, who, because these desires are co-extensive with their real or apparent interests, have these desires latent in them. . . . Chamberlain is an organ of great individual force; the extent of his influence will depend on the relative power of the class he is adapted to represent.

By temperament he is an enthusiast and a despot. A deep sympathy with the misery and incompleteness of most men's lives, and an ear desire to right this, transform political action into a religious crusade; but running alongside this genuine enthusiasm is a passionate desire to crush opposition to his will. . . .[165]

Yet after 1895 Chamberlain became less directly concerned with domestic change as such; and, of course, he left the government in 1903 resigning on the issue of tariff reform. This is a matter which has considerable bearing on the growth of Conservative collectivism and further reference will be made to it shortly. At this point, however, it is appropriate to notice how the commitment to social reform through state action was fully shared after his departure by others including his son Neville.

164 B. Webb, *My Apprenticeship* (Penguin, 1938), i.146, italics in original.
165 ibid., i.146–7, italics in original; ibid., at pp.147–51, Mrs Webb gives a most vivid description of the way Chamberlain dominated a public meeting.

The continuators: Neville Chamberlain and others

The great Tory defeat of 1906 led in some quarters of the party to what
would nowadays probably be called a period of rethinking. There had
been, one party critic suggested, a century's abstention from thought by
Conservatives, a failure to deal constructively and imaginatively with the
problems created by the rise of democracy.[166] The electoral failure was
widely attributed to neglect of issues of social welfare and reform. The
Morning Post ran a series of articles proposing a number of changes
Conservatives ought to support; some Conservative politicians like Lord
Henry Bentinck consciously thought of themselves as refurbishing the
radical heritage of the Tory Democracy.[167] Typical of the pamphlet
literature of the time urging this emphasis was a tract by a one-time ILP
member turned Conservative who suggested the need for what he called
a national policy to secure general well-being and greater efficiency and
which involved such steps as the extension of the trade boards system, a
national minimum wage, an agricultural tariff, educational reform, and
the like, a 'bold and thorough policy' of 'national reconstruction.'[168]
Similarly an official party handbook, while putting the case against
'radicalism', nevertheless recognized and approved the identification of
Conservative policy and the use of state power to better the general
condition of the mass of the people.[169] Lord Milner frequently spoke of
the importance to Conservatives of their tradition of social reform and
recognized the way in which this had led them to make the largest
contribution to the development of 'socialism' over the previous half
century. Equally the mainspring of imperial strength was a happy and
contented people so that a concern with welfare was vital from this point
of view too.[170] Sir Sidney Low, the Tory historian, rejected 'old-
fashioned individualism' as out-of-date and urged that the state must
have an important, if not overwhelming, role in supervising industry and
providing social services.[171] In the early years of the century a group of

---

166 Anon. [A. Boutwood], *National Revival: a Re-statement of Tory Principles* (1911;
      2nd edn, London, 1913), pp.1–15. Cf. J. M. Kennedy, *Tory Democracy* (London,
      1911), pp.5–6. Interestingly, the prescription urged here is a kind of fusion of social
      reform, localism, and Guild ideas.
167 Wilkinson, *Tory Democracy*, pp.245–53.
168 H. Roberts, *Constructive Conservatism* (London, 1913), pp.18ff. Cf. L. S. Amery's
      introduction, ibid., pp.4–5.
169 NUCCA, *The Case Against Radicalism*, 1909, pp.272–3. See also the citation at
      p.228 above.
170 Alfred, Lord Milner, *The Nation and the Empire: Being a Collection of Speeches and
      Addresses* (London, 1913): 'A Constructive Policy' (29 October 1907), pp.214–16;
      'Unionists and Social Reform' (19 November 1907), p.245; 'The Two Nations' (9
      December 1912), pp.494–500.
171 See e.g. the three letters of 1908 and 1910, cited in D. Chapman-Huston, *The Lost
      Historian: a Memoir of Sir Sidney Low* (London, 1936), pp.222, 224, 237.

Tory MPs from London called the 'Young Forwards' argued the case for social reform – pensions schemes, for example – as a means essential to combat Socialism. In the same style they sought Fabian support for their ideas and themselves aided the Webbs during the Poor Law campaign.[172] There was also an influential body called the Unionist Social Reform Committee which was founded by F. E. Smith to arouse interest among Conservative MPs in social questions. For instance, it published in 1914 an inquiry into industrial unrest recommending that the state should not remain indifferent to these problems.[173] Smith himself in his *Unionist Policy and Other Essays* had firmly rejected a *laissez faire* attitude to these matters and expounded an earlier version of the 'middle way'.[174] He had also asked Samuel Hoare to be chairman of the group's sub-committee on education and this produced proposals for school reform.[175] In similar vein another publicist, Pierse Loftus, discussed the Tory conception of society as a reconciliation of individualism (the claims of which the Manchester radicals and Whigs over-exaggerated) with the necessary degree of control by the state representing the general interest. Bureaucracy was to be avoided as much as the let-alone ethos but government had a duty to carry through social reform by providing good houses, maintaining a prosperous agricultural population, and through other carefully planned schemes to improve the condition of the people. Nor, Loftus stated, in a remark directed at Tory apostles of Spencer, should talk of the 'survival of the fittest' inhibit this.[176] Often, of course, the need for public action was accepted with some reluctance: thus a symposium on Unionist policy issued in 1908 recognized the need to adjust to new conditions but was very cautious in its acceptance of 'Collectivist legislation' and, while noting its advantages, referred also to its constituting a 'deadly menace'.[177]

Some quite sophisticated theoretical statements were produced of what was involved in this regeneration of 'Constructive Toryism'. For instance, in 1911 Arthur Boutwood published anonymously a restatement of Tory principles that seems to have drawn on the Idealist

172 E. J. Bristow, *The Defence of Liberty and Property in Britain, 1880–1914* (unpublished PhD thesis, Yale University, 1970), pp. 318–19. Cf. H. Bentinck, *Tory Democracy* (London, 1918), pp. 77ff.; also Dr Bristow's 'Profit-Sharing, Socialism and Labour Unrest', in K. D. Brown (ed.), *Essays in Anti-Labour History: Responses to the Rise of Labour in Britain* (London, 1974), pp. 282–4.
173 J. W. Hills *et al.*, *Industrial Unrest: a Practical Solution* (London, 1914).
174 F. E. Smith, 'State Toryism and Social Reform', *Unionist Policy and Other Essays* (London, 1913), pp. 20–46.
175 J. A. Cross, *Sir Samuel Hoare, a Political Biography* (London, 1977), p. 30.
176 P. Loftus, *The Conservative Party and the Future: a Programme for Tory Democracy* (London, n.d. [1912]), pp. 23–4, 30, 35, 110–12.
177 Lord Malmesbury (ed.), *The New Order: Studies in Unionist Policy* (London, 1908), e.g. pp. 3, 10, 12, 20, 327–8.

tradition in important respects.[178] The argument depends on a doctrine of rights which are taken to depend on the will of God and the objective moral order. They inhere in man as such, therefore, and variously express the fundamental need for the opportunity to live and grow. These rights are discovered through, though not derived from, society.[179] Man gradually realizes and takes account of the needs of others and there thus grows up a 'national conscience' or system of claims constituting a concept of social justice. The state has a general duty to safeguard these rights impartially and make them effective and is thus to be conceived as the instrument of the general good. Consequently it must sustain these requirements against inequities in the social order and this may involve altering the existing distribution of wealth and influence. The power of the state is only authoritative so far as this duty is fulfilled; and when the aim is so pursued its demands are superior to any particularist claims or freedoms. And while state Socialism is eschewed, state help of a not inextensive order is implied (though detailed specification is, in this particular account, noticeably lacking).[180] Boutwood was quite clear, however, that the organization of British political and social life was no longer adequate to the demands being made on it since the working classes discovered themselves. Hence the need for the elimination of social inequity and the eleemosynary extension of state provision.

For the decade or so following 1906 there is in fact ample evidence of discussion in Conservative circles of reform policies and of the need for government aid and action in respect of town planning, housing, and a good many other matters not excluding industrial questions such as the right of workers to a share in management.[181] The Great War itself sustained this tendency of ideas, as the activity of the Unionist Social Reform Committee and of the 1918 'Group' led by Earl Winterton showed.[182] For instance, young Conservative MPs like Sir Oswald Mosley and Lord Robert Cecil held quite advanced views and spoke of the need for the state to intervene to improve working-class housing, to extend the wage-board system, and to 'socialize' certain basic industries. Cecil continually stressed the importance of giving labour a position of respect and of recognizing its rights through, for instance, co-partnership schemes and even workers' control.[183] One commentator summed up

178 [A. Boutwood], *National Revival*. The contemporary value of Green's ideas is noted, and Hegel is specifically cited ibid., pp. 4–5, 127. The phrase 'Constructive Toryism' is at p. 38.
179 ibid., pp. 29–34.
180 ibid., pp. 93–4 on state help; and on partnership in industry, ibid., p. 112.
181 Wilkinson, op. cit., pp. 260, 266–7, 270–3.
182 On the USRC, see e.g. P. R. Wilding, 'The Genesis of the Ministry of Health', *Public Administration*, xlv (1967), p. 154.
183 Wilkinson, op. cit., ibid., where detailed references are given. Cf. Sir Oswald Mosley, *My Life* (1968; London, 1970), pp. 90–1, 136.

this sort of views by asserting that 'State aid has probably come to stay. It is difficult to see how industry can resume its normal course without direction and assistance from the State.'[184] Many Conservatives realized or accepted this. During the war, for example, it was the Unionist leaders who, against Asquith's diffidence, insisted on the need for mobilization of the nation's resources under a vigorous war directorate and in this way accepted more easily the spirit of mercantilism that the demands of war entailed.[185] In a more minor key W. C. Dampier Whetham urged in 1917 that *laissez faire* was an inadequate guide and that increasing collective action was what the age required: 'The true Tory is one who regards the State . . . as a living complex organism, ever developing to meet the growing needs of a changing time, and working . . . for the good of all'.[186] Nor were proselytizing scientists the only publicists of this persuasion: Lord Rothermere was told in 1925 by an MP friend that half Baldwin's government were 'Socialists'.[187]

It is, in fact, possible and appropriate to see this aspect of Conservatism reflected and continued, so far as social questions are concerned, in the work and policies of Joseph Chamberlain's son Neville, a born social reformer and a 'very Radical sort of Conservative' as Feiling called him.[188] His political life followed the pattern of his father's and specifically imitated his example.[189] And in a like fashion the commitment to change important aspects of communal life necessarily had a collectivist impact. Of course, in the present context it is important to see Neville Chamberlain in a perspective different from the usual (and normally critical) concentration on his later preoccupation with foreign policy. It is certainly ironical that Chamberlain, who by background, ability, and interest was equipped to lead a reforming Conservative government, should have spent the brief years of his premiership so much involved with matters of diplomacy and war.[190] Even so it can be said that he might properly claim to be one of the most important reforming ministers of the early twentieth century. Iain Macleod wrote that from the study he made (in the late 1950s) of Chamberlain's social legislation he began to form of this man he never knew a mental picture that seemed utterly different from his general public image.[191]

184 H. Bentinck, *Tory Democracy* (London, 1918), p.97.
185 P. Fraser, 'The Impact of the War of 1914–18 on the British Political System', M. R. D. Foot (ed.), *War and Society* (London, 1973), esp. pp.127–8, 136–7.
186 W. C. Dampier Whetham, *The War and the Nation: a Study in Constructive Politics* (London, 1917), pp.iv, 9, 36.
187 Rothermere to Croft (9 August 1925), Croft MSS, Churchill College, Cambridge, cited in M. Bentley, *The Liberal Mind, 1914–1929* (Cambridge, 1977), p.120.
188 K. Feiling, *The Life of Neville Chamberlain*, pp.13, 81. Cf. Iain Macleod, *Neville Chamberlain* (London, 1961), pp.203ff.
189 Feiling, *Life*, p.120.
190 Cf. ibid., p.303.
191 Macleod, op. cit., p.13. Cf. the fascinating character study in Feiling, *Life*, ch.x.

In the family tradition Neville Chamberlain showed a substantial interest in voluntary public service and in the welfare side of his business activities; and, as a means of securing good industrial relations, he even advocated that there should be at least a partial workers' voice in management.[192] When he formally entered local politics in Birmingham in 1911 his attitude to the many problems of a growing city was like that revealed in his father's improvement schemes. He believed there should be an overall town plan embracing the interrelated matters of health, housing, slum clearance, employment, and transport. Birmingham was, under his aegis, the first local authority in the country to put forward schemes made possible by the latest Housing and Planning Act; and he was responsible for establishing municipal control of the new bus services he had sponsored.[193] But although he became Lord Mayor in 1915 at the age of forty-six, the war prevented the implementation of his most ambitious plans of reform. Like his father, too, he then entered national politics. A brief and, in the circumstances, inevitably unsuccessful tenure of office in the National Service Department was followed by entry into Parliament in 1918. In his election campaign he put forward views typical of what Professor Mowat called the 'Tory Socialism' of the time.[194] He was far from hostile to the social claims of organized labour and so he supported such policies as 'a great programme of national housing', the extension of state pension schemes, a minimum wage, and more expenditure on health and welfare.[195] After he was elected he served on a number of committees notably that on slum clearance in unhealthy areas whose reports he wrote and which were an important source of later legislation on the subject. He expressed a belief, too, in the need for greater state control over, maybe the nationalization of, major industries like coal and railways.[196]

In March 1923 he entered the Cabinet as Minister of Health, the office (as Feiling says) 'for which all his life had prepared him.'[197] There he stayed until 1929 apart from a short interlude at the Treasury and the brief period of opposition during the first Labour government. The Ministry of Health had been created in 1919 out of the old Local Government Board and other bodies. It had a wide range of duties from health in the strict sense (hospitals, nursing, and disease) to Poor Law matters, old age pensions, housing, and health insurance. It was, therefore, necessarily concerned with many of the activities of local

192 Macleod, op. cit., pp. 52–3, 79.
193 Feiling, *Life*, pp. 53–5; Macleod, op. cit., p. 46.
194 C. L. Mowat, *Britain Between the Wars 1918–1940* (1955; London, 1968), p. 338. Cf. ibid., p. 43 on 'Socialism by the Back Door'.
195 Feiling, *Life*, p. 81; Macleod, op. cit., p. 79.
196 Feiling, *Life*, pp. 89–90; Macleod, op. cit., pp. 79–81.
197 Feiling, *Life*, p. 102.

government of which it was the main supervisory department. On assuming office Chamberlain submitted to the Cabinet twenty-five measures he wanted to pass into law. Macleod, who had later experience in the field himself, called this 'one of the most far-reaching and complicated programmes of legislation any Minister had attempted before or since.'[198] All but four of these proposals were on the statute book when Chamberlain left the Ministry of Health and this remainder was embodied in later legislation.[199] Taken as a whole they manifestly indicate a belief not simply in the importance of state assistance to voluntary effort already under way but also in the necessity of using the power of government to achieve social reform and to create the administrative arrangements appropriate to the efficient conduct of these tasks. Among the measures involved were the following: the Housing Act (1923) mainly of benefit to the lower middle classes which Mowat described as 'perhaps the most lasting monument of the period, another step by the Conservatives along the road to collectivism';[200] the Rating and Valuation Act (1925) to help the local authorities deal with their increasing burden of responsibilities; the Widows, Orphans and Old Age Pensions Act (1926) which imposed a compulsory contributory scheme and was, in fact, part of a wider budgetary strategy; the National Health Insurance scheme introduced in 1928; and, of course, the massive Local Government Act (1929) which dealt with the Poor Law, local finance, and much else and which, though greatly changed at Treasury insistence from what Chamberlain had envisaged, was none the less in itself an outstanding legislative achievement. There were also various minor Bills on such matters as smoke abatement and the sale of proprietary medicines. All this constituted a wide-ranging coherent strategy of change that made for one of the outstanding legislative achievements in the field of social reform.[201] Under Conservative rule there thus occurred a notable consolidation and development of social policy such that by 1939 the social services in Britain were (as one recent commentator suggested) 'taken all in all, . . . the most advanced in the world.'[202] And

---

198 Macleod, op. cit., pp.113–14. The Bills are listed in Chamberlain's Cabinet memorandum of November 1924, in Feiling, *Life*, app. A, pp.459–62.
199 Feiling, *Life*, p.129.
200 Mowat, op. cit., p.164.
201 For some assessments, see D. Thomson, *England in the Twentieth Century (1914–63)* (Penguin, 1966), pp.100–1; B. Keith-Lucas, 'Epilogue' to Redlich and Hirst, *The History of Local Government in England*, 2nd edn (London, 1971), pp.227–33; Lord Morrison of Lambeth, *Herbert Morrison: an Autobiography* (London, 1960), p.175; B. Donoghue and G. Jones, *Herbert Morrison: Portrait of a Politician* (London, 1973), p.70; H. Macmillan, *Winds of Change: 1914–1939*, pp.172–4.
202 P. Addison, *The Road to 1945: British Politics and the Second World War* (London, 1975), p.33.

in this advance Chamberlain's role was clearly substantial. As he wrote in a private letter shortly before he died in 1940, 'It was the hope of doing something to improve the conditions of life for the poorer people that brought me at past middle life into politics and it is some satisfaction to me to know that I was able to carry out some part of my ambition'.[203]

THE ECONOMIC CRISIS AND AFTER

> Amid the post-war ruins of our half-bankrupt industry one fact has emerged clearly, . . . – the need for reorganisation. . . . In this anarchy . . . some guiding hand and principle is needed. And as to Cincinnatus at his plough, men to-day turn to the State. . . .
>
> A. BRYANT, *The Spirit of Conservatism*, 2nd edn, 1932, pp. 126–7

The last major factor in the development of Conservative interventionism before the Second World War was the vital series of reactions to the decline in Britain's economic position brought about by increasing foreign competition and the gradual passing of this country's commercial hegemony, by technological change, and by the impact of depression and mass unemployment. In the minds of many Conservatives these problems invited an extension of state activity of an important kind. Social legislation was one thing; and *ad hoc* treatment of specific industrial problems was another. But the deliberate and considerable use of the authority of government to regulate the general pattern of the country's economic life as a whole was an altogether different proposition; and its necessity was not unacknowledged as reference to the campaign for tariff reform and to the policy of the 'middle way' will show.

Tariff reform

Here again Joseph Chamberlain was an important figure in the development of this new ethos of Conservative thought about economic control. Interestingly enough Chamberlain was first converted to the protectionist position by the leader of the Tory Democracy. The economic depression of the 1870s led some Conservatives to be critical of free trade and hark back to the position that had prevailed before 1846, or at least to urge some kind of partial protection to ensure 'fair trade' or the possibility of reciprocity in commercial agreements. By 1882 the Fourth Party had begun to attack *laissez faire* and to move in this direction. Chamberlain, as Gladstone's President of the Board of Trade, was put up by the free-trade Liberals to answer these arguments and he followed Lord Randolph Churchill around the country to rebut his

203 N. Chamberlain to Sir J. Simon (6 October 1940), Simon Papers, cited ibid., p. 33.

speeches. In the process Chamberlain was himself converted and thus got the idea of wholesale tariff reform.[204] But he did not begin to assert the policy in any fervent way for more than a decade, that is, until after his experience at the Colonial Office and until the growing economic and social pressures of the time had declared themselves more acutely.

There were three aspects or purposes to the tariff reform policy Chamberlain put forward.

First he held it would strengthen imperial ties. His time at the Colonial Office had persuaded him it was necessary to take positive steps to secure the unity of Britain's world-wide possessions and associates in the Empire. One way of achieving this would be to create closer economic links by granting commercial privileges to the dominions and colonies. This would also, it was hoped, sustain the flow of raw materials and secure the markets on which British industry depended. A policy of reciprocal fiscal preferences was strongly urged by the colonial premiers themselves at the conference of 1902. But all this would require the end of free trade and of a purely revenue concept of customs duty. To grant an effective drawback to the colonies meant that a genuinely protective tariff had to be raised against other countries in the first place. Secondly Chamberlain believed the policy of protection would aid, what had been in Disraeli's time associated with imperialism, the progress of social reform.[205] This was being held up at least in part by financial problems. There was opposition from Conservative interests that disliked the redistribution of wealth entailed and which held, too, that the burden would cause a relative deterioration in the competitive position of British industry and at a time of already acute labour difficulties. There was the feeling as well that the expenditure of government was already too high and the limits of taxation had been reached. Those were innocent days: income tax stood at about 1/– (or 5p) in the £; but the feeling was strong that, far from general taxation being allowed to rise, retrenchment was necessary. Yet the Conservative government was committed in many ways to increasing expenditure not least, for instance, in respect of the programme of educational improvement required by Balfour's Act of 1902. Not only this, many Conservatives of whom Chamberlain was one were quite clear that in order to hold the working classes to a Conservative allegiance it was necessary to outbid other parties in constructive social improvements.[206] Tariff reform seemed to offer a way

204 R. R. James, *Lord Randolph Churchill* (London, 1959), pp. 117–18; J. L. Garvin and J. Amery, *The Life of Joseph Chamberlain* (London, 1932–69), v. 209–10.
205 Garvin and Amery, *Life*, iv. 391, citing J. P. Smith, 'Memories of Joseph Chamberlain', *National Review*, May 1932.
206 See e.g. Chamberlain's comments on the 'Labour earthquake' of the 1906 election, Garvin and Amery, *Life*, vi. 792; also the entry in Beatrice Webb's diary (9 February 1906), in *Our Partnership* (London, 1948), p. 331.

out of this dilemma. The revenue needed to finance expensive social amenities like schools and old age pensions would be obtained from customs duties; at the most the burden would thus be spread over the whole community and not hit particular interests too hard and, at the best, the cost would be transferred to the foreigner.[207] Finally – and this is the most important point of reference in the present context – there was the need to sustain British industry against growing competition. As early as 1898 Chamberlain had invoked Bolingbroke on the need not only to hearten the colonies but also ' "to give ease and encouragement to manufactury at home" '.[208] The long delayed effects of 1846 were being felt and agriculture needed help against the inflow of cheap foreign produce. Particular industries were also suffering from the effects of depression and unemployment caused by trade regarded as unfair. This arose because competitors were often themselves sheltered by tariff barriers, received subsidies, employed lower paid workers, and were not required by law to maintain so high a standard of working conditions. Looking after the interests of labour in industry meant higher costs and so was in the circumstances incompatible with free trade. The answer was protection if only as a means of securing reciprocal concessions in commercial negotiation.[209]

For such reasons, then, Chamberlain invited government, not to stand aside as free-trade doctrine demanded, but continuously to intervene for political and economic purpose. It was a kind of reversion to the mercantilism under which Britain had taken the vital steps to economic take-off in the two centuries before 1846.[210]

The collectivist implications of the programme were clear. Government would have to decide which interests to safeguard, what level of tariff to impose, and when to grant a drawback and for what reasons. To embark on a policy of protection necessarily involved, to this extent, the regulation of the economy and the attempt to determine in important respects the level, direction, and rate of its activity. Mrs Webb wrote in her diary in 1903 that one result of Chamberlain's raising the tariff issue would be to advertise enormously 'the need for investigation and the desirability of deliberate collective regulation'. She added that 'All this is to the good and makes towards . . . collectivism of the best sort.' It committed the Conservatives to state control of the economy.[211] Nor was it without a kind of symbolic significance that the advisers, a sort of professional brains trust, on whom Chamberlain came to rely a

207 Garvin and Amery, *Life*, iv.400; v.231–5, 267–8; vi.726, 823–4.
208 ibid., v.215.
209 ibid., iv.405; v.184–92; vi.488–93, 742, 892; C. W. Boyd, *Mr. Chamberlain's Speeches* (London, 1914), ii.125–40, 206–7, 218–26, 260–2, 266–70, 317–26, 368–9.
210 Cf. Garvin and Amery, *Life*, vi.994–5.
211 B. Webb, *Our Partnership*, pp.267, 332.

great deal during his tariff reform campaign came from a group originally set up by Sidney Webb to further Fabian ideas.[212]

It was certainly realized by the protagonists in the disputes that ensued that a major conflict of doctrines was involved. This is made clear in a letter the Prime Minister, A. J. Balfour, wrote in 1903 to the Duke of Devonshire, a free-trader whose resignation from the government he was trying, vainly as it happened, to prevent:

> My own view, perhaps, can be put most clearly by drawing a comparison between my theories upon fiscal questions and my theories upon social questions. The old free-traders were consistent advocates of the *laissez-faire* principle in both departments of policy. Their advocacy of Free Trade and their objection to factory legislation sprang from the same root-principle – the principle of *laissez-faire* and individualism. The movement of thought and the pressure of events have compelled us (in my opinion, rightly compelled us) to abandon these principles in their extreme form. But this does not mean that you or I are Socialists. It does mean that we now feel bound to consider many proposals on their merits, which the Manchester school of sixty years since would summarily have dismissed on (what they called) 'principle'.
>
> My attitude upon fiscal questions is precisely the same.[213]

Chamberlain himself understood very clearly, of course, that a great debate about principles was involved: the 'Birmingham school' was contesting with that of Manchester and Cobden.[214] This came through in a speech he made in July 1906. In fact in this, his last public utterance before his final illness, a sort of political testament, the collectivist basis of his ideas is clearly brought out:

> In domestic politics we, of every class and of every section of the Unionist party, have supported every constructive proposal for bettering the condition of the masses of the people, and for raising the standard of life amongst the great majority. . . . In a democratic State such as ours, with a Government which in our time has been made truly representative, we together have held the belief that advantage ought to be taken of the machinery which has thus been created to do for the people at large, for the whole community, what no individual can do for himself.

He went on to list the achievements:

212 Garvin and Amery, *Life*, v.286.
213 Cited in Garvin and Amery, *Life*, v.376–7. Cf. the views of another tariff reform imperialist, recorded in J. Biggs-Davison, *George Wyndham: A Study in Toryism* (London, 1951), pp.221–2.
214 Boyd, *Speeches*, ii.367–8. Cf. ibid., ii.205–7.

The extension of local government, the provision of free education, the facilities given for the creation of allotments and small ownerships, the great development of factory legislation, the compensation provided for accidents in the course of employment – these constitute only a small part of the practical social reforms which have been carried by Conservative and by Unionist governments during the generation to which I am referring.

And always, he said, the main opposition came from the Whig free-traders:

. . . these gentlemen, Free Traders as they are, were quite right in opposing the proposals of social reform, as they are right now in opposing proposals for fiscal reform. The same principles are involved. The Free Traders were against all State interference of any kind. They were against the Factory Acts; they were opposed to the laws to prevent fraud and adulteration, especially in the interests of the working classes; they were against trade unions, they were in favour of unlimited competition, they would buy everything in the cheapest market, and especially labour.

Much had already been achieved yet one major task remained: to 'secure for the masses of the industrial population in this country constant employment at fair wages.' The remedy was to hand, he said; and it was, of course, protection and imperial preference.[215]

Free-trade doctrine remained very strong however, often being seen, not altogether justly, as the basis of Britain's long prosperity. In consequence many people found it impossible to accept tariff reform especially as it might lead to 'dear food' or invite commercial retaliation. The stability of the Conservative Party and so of the government for most of the 1920s was much affected by these controversies. Winston Churchill, an ex-Liberal Cabinet minister and in a key position as Chancellor of the Exchequer from 1924 to 1929, was a free-trader and did not lack support in his view. Neville Chamberlain was, like his father before him, a tariff reformer and had been so since his early days in politics; so in their different ways were Amery and Beaverbrook. The dispute was shrill and prolonged especially in view of previous election pledges to eschew food taxes. Meanwhile the economic situation did not improve. The General Strike of 1926 seemed to indicate something was radically wrong with the state of British industry. Rising unemployment and the long slump, the apparently ineradicable problem of the depressed areas, argued that the economy was fundamentally ill. How to deal with all this?

215 ibid., ii. 364–6, 368–9.

While still in opposition, in March 1930, Neville Chamberlain became chairman of a new party research department and he set it to work at once to examine the problems of unemployment and out-relief, over-production, thrift and co-partnership schemes in industry, and agriculture.[216] He felt, as it were in the family tradition, that mass unemployment had finally killed the doctrines of Cobden and the Manchester School and that Britain's strength could only be restored and sustained by a policy of imperial protection.[217] In April 1931, during the debate on the budget which had been presented by the Labour Chancellor, Philip Snowden, who was ardently orthodox in matters of public finance, Chamberlain reflected to himself that here was the last Chancellor who would ever introduce a free-trade budget in the Commons: '"it will remain a mark to show the end of an obsolete and worn-out system and the beginning of something more adaptable to the needs of modern industrial civilization."'[218]

When the crash came not many weeks later and with it the fall of the minority Labour administration, Chamberlain played a major part in the formation of the National Government in which, after a further very brief tenure at the Ministry of Health, he went to the Treasury remaining in that office until he became Prime Minister in 1937. He therefore bore a major responsibility in trying to determine or control the course of economic events during these crucial years. His main remedy was a full policy of protection. In February 1932 he introduced a general 10 per cent duty on all goods not already charged or on a free list (such staple items as wheat, meat, cotton, and wool). He set up an independent tariff board – the Import Duties Advisory Committee – to recommend additional duties. Colonial produce would enter duty free; but the Board of Trade was empowered to retaliate against foreign discrimination or to lower tariffs by reciprocal treaty. Joseph Chamberlain had thus triumphed two decades after his death; government had intervened decisively in the vital sphere of international commerce; and the era of free trade was at an end.

Measures of various kinds were also taken to ease the unemployment position and its consequences. The Chancellor could not be persuaded to embark on the then unorthodox course of budgeting for a deficit to stimulate trade though this was pressed on him, for instance, by the group of 'young Tory intellectuals' and 'planners' which included Harold Macmillan and Eustace Percy. But he did initiate a limited programme of public works and investment, the reason for the limitation being simply that he believed government intervention of this kind, while sometimes useful, had only a restricted impact on employment levels. It

216 K. Feiling, *The Life of Neville Chamberlain* (London, 1946), p.177.
217 ibid., pp.181–2.
218 I. Macleod, *Neville Chamberlain* (London, 1961), p.146.

was, he thought, an ineffective and circuitous way of reducing the number out of work; a much quicker solution would be to try to create conditions in which ordinary trade itself would be stimulated.[219] But he did initiate plans of the public works kind and especially for the distressed or special areas.[220] He co-operated closely with the departments concerned to develop agricultural policy and regulate the market and provided a range of subsidies such as those to fisheries and beef production. He put forward a suggestion for an Unemployment Assistance Board to remove the grant of relief from local political pressure; extended insurance to new classes; developed the proposals and arranged the finance for slum clearance and the elimination of overcrowding that were contained in the Housing Act of 1935 (though this was aborted in its full effect by the second war). As well, aid was given for the modernization of the iron and steel industry; subsidies were granted, for instance, for tramp shipping and the building of the great Cunard liner that became the *Queen Mary*; money was injected into the telephone service; a comprehensive Factory Act substantially improving working hours and conditions was put on the statute book in 1937; the Physical Training and Recreation Act of the same year was a major step in the improvement of facilities and aid in this important social area. Moreover much else was on the stocks. In the years immediately before the war it was proposed to raise the school leaving age, to subsidize air transport, to develop trunk roads, to improve the cattle trade, and to increase aid to the special areas in various respects (for instance by an increase in block grants and the direction of armament contracts), to nationalize coal royalties, and to permit compulsory amalgamation of pits. A lot more was also in view. Shortly before the Munich crisis, for example, Chamberlain was revolving in his mind a scheme for 'a central authority to act at once as an information bureau, with special regard to the location of industry, and as a central planning body for the country as a whole'.[221]

All this constitutes a not unenterprising programme of collectivist reconstruction even though there were others who would have pushed on faster and farther and more systematically. It is rather strange, therefore, that Chamberlain's public image even at the time, let alone since, has not been one to allow credit for what was attempted in this regard. He wrote on one occasion to his sister: 'There are some who think I am over-cautious, − timid, Amery calls it − humdrum, commonplace, and unenterprising. But I know that charge is groundless'.[222] And were it not

219 ibid., pp.172–3; Sir C. Petrie, *The Chamberlain Tradition* (London, 1938), pp.264–6.
220 Feiling, *Life*, p.266; Macleod, op. cit., pp.170–1.
221 Cited in Feiling, *Life*, p.307.
222 Cited ibid., p.235.

for the foreign policy preoccupations which beset his premiership and the vituperation to which he has been subject because of the so-called appeasement policy (whether justly or not is not here in question) he might well be recognized as one of the greatest ministers in the field of social and economic reform in the first half of this century: as perhaps he was. The most cautious judgement must concede at least that 'the European imbroglio' to which Chamberlain was heir 'has masked the degree to which he was a radical democrat', one who shared a compassionate understanding of the people and their needs.[223] Certainly government intervention grew apace under his tutelage. Even so, there were those in the Conservative ranks who thought more should have been done in respect of state provision and supervision as Harold Macmillan and his conception of the 'middle way' indicate. Macmillan was indeed someone in whom all the various Tory themes so far reviewed appear to come together as the basis of a policy with which to face the crisis of Britain in the present century.

The middle way

To see Macmillan as belonging to and sustaining the tradition of Tory paternalism is wholly appropriate given the form of his career and the nature of the views he held. Nor is it even at odds with the languid manner or image he acquired or fostered in later years or incompatible with his background of wealth, service in the Guards, and marriage into the aristocracy: political radicalism founded on the duties of social station was equally part of the family heritage. His grandfather, who built up the successful publishing house, had been involved with the Christian Socialist movement and was influenced by Charles Kingsley and William Morris; one of this grandfather's brothers established a working men's club and wrote a tract on 'British Industry and Socialism'. This sort of interest endured and Macmillan knew of it and consciously followed it.[224] In a newspaper interview printed in 1936 he said he thought the Conservative Party had become too much dominated by the City and other monied interests and by *laissez faire* ideas. He on the contrary adhered to the 'paternal socialism' of his forbears which had always been one of the major forms of Toryism.[225] Other influences in his younger days included Ronald Knox, his tutor at Eton, and A. D. Lindsay, an Oxford don who pursued the reformist implications of Idealist philosophy. But his hero was Disraeli and he read as much as

223 A. Jones and M. Bentley, 'Salisbury and Baldwin', M. Cowling (ed.), *Conservative Essays* (London, 1978), p. 37.
224 A. Sampson, *Macmillan: a Study in Ambiguity* (1967; Penguin, 1968), pp. 11–12; H. Macmillan, *Winds of Change, 1914–1939* (London, 1966), p. 51.
225 *The Star* newspaper (25 June 1936), cited in Sampson, op. cit., p. 48. Cf. ibid., p. 39.

possible about him.[226] Referring to one of his own early speeches, he later
commented it was hardly remarkable being simply 'a mixture of
Disraeli's "Young England", Shaftesbury, Joe Chamberlain, and all the
rest.'[227] When he was about to resign as Prime Minister he would have
preferred to be succeeded by either Hailsham or Macleod because he
thought these were the two most able men in the party who best
represented 'the Disraeli tradition of Tory Radicalism, which I had
preached all my life.'[228] The conscious pedigree of his ideas is clear,
therefore, and was the basis of his attitude to contemporary economic
and social difficulties. As well when the problem of unemployment
originally developed on a massive scale specific direction was given to his
propensity towards state intervention by the influence of Maynard
Keynes whom he knew: when Macmillan spoke in the Commons on the
Finance Bill in 1936 he simply set out to give a popular version of some of
Keynes's ideas.[229]

In 1924 Macmillan was elected MP for Stockton-on-Tees, one of the
depressed areas hard hit by economic troubles. It was at Stockton, he
wrote half a century later, that his political career had begun and where
he had gone through the 'terrible years' of the slump 'which left indelible
marks' on his 'mind and heart'.[230] He soon associated himself with a
group of other young Conservative Members of similar interests
including Oliver Stanley, R. S. Hudson, Robert Boothby, John Loder,
Anthony Eden, and Duff Cooper. They had all served in the trenches and
emerged from the war imbued with that *Grabenkameradschaft* which (as
Professor Michael Howard has suggested) was so important to the
generation of men that survived.[231] They shared a strong sense of social
responsibility towards the men who had soldiered with them and who
were now out of work, suffering from bad housing, and the like. The
thinly fictional George Sherston, marching with his regiment up the line
to the Battle of Arras, describes how he was learning that 'life, for the
majority of the population, is an unlovely struggle against unfair odds,
culminating in a cheap funeral.'[232] In this way the general radical
commitment received focus and point, and the 'YMCA' (as this group of
young Members was called because of its eager earnestness to get things

226 Macmillan, *Winds of Change*, pp.43, 44.
227 ibid., p.210.
228 Macmillan, *At the End of the Day, 1961–1963* (London, 1973), p.496.
229 Macmillan, *Winds of Change*, pp.9, 490.
230 Macmillan, *At the End of the Day*, p.61.
231 M. Howard, Introduction to F. Manning, *The Middle Parts of Fortune* (1929; Mayflower, 1977), p.vi.
232 S. Sassoon, *The Complete Memoirs of George Sherston* (1937; London, 1940), p.425. On this sort of social confrontation during the war and its effects, cf. J. Keegan, *The Face of Battle* (London, 1976), pp. 220–1; P. Fussell, *The Great War and Modern Memory* (1975; London, 1977), pp.164–5.

done in a hurry) urged from the outset that state intervention was necessary to help industry and bring work to the unemployed.[133] It was presumably to this group that Harold Laski referred when he wrote in 1927 that one of a number of young Conservative MPs 'was a Disraelite Tory who was nearer to me in sympathies than many of my own party. . . . They were most pleasant lads who still retain a good deal of that *noblesse oblige* which is so very attractive at its best.'[234] These young MPs were indeed dedicated to the proposition that the idealism of Disraeli and the impetus of Tory Democracy had been lost and needed to be revived in which view they were encouraged by some of their elders especially Winston Churchill.[235] Their sentiments were those expressed in a short book (one of whose authors was later to become Lord Halifax, Governor-General of India and, nearly, Prime Minister) which laid on the state a wide obligation ' to ensure that individuals may live their lives under conditions of reasonable security and content', a duty which is clearly placed in the context of the war and the problems it created.[236] But according to Macmillan the foremost figure and intellectual leader of this 'little company' was Noel Skelton, MP for Perth. It was he who developed the philosophy of the new Toryism and publicized its doctrine 'in short but intensely interesting pamphlets'. For example in September 1924 Skelton published a brochure on *Constructive Conservatism* which, it seems, had a great effect on the younger members of the party.[237] Many years later Lord Boothby, too, still wrote in the very highest terms of Skelton's teaching, his brilliance, originality, and influence.[238] The last must be allowed, at least because so many of those concerned refer to it. As to the rest it may, to the uncommitted reader of these slight publications today, smack somewhat of retrospective hyperbole.

Skelton argued that inevitably an era dominated by an educated political democracy would be particularly concerned with and perceptive about issues of social conscience.[239] And in order to meet the challenge of Socialism, so powerful and appealing because it presents a comprehensive view of life and politics, Conservatism had to be thought out afresh and promulgated anew. Specifically it had to get beyond the traditional caretaker view of the state with which it was associated (or so Skelton

233 Macmillan, *Winds of Change*, pp.177–8; Sampson, op. cit., pp.29–30.
234 Laski to Holmes (28 June 1927), in M. de W. Howe (ed.), *Holmes-Laski Letters: the Correspondence of Mr. Justice Holmes and Harold J. Laski, 1916–1935* (London, 1953), ii.957.
235 L. H. Lang, 'The Young Conservative', *National Review*, lxxxiii (1924), pp.73–4; *The Spectator*, cxxxiii (1924), pp.149, 152, 158–9, 163; Macmillan, *Winds of Change*, p.176.
236 Sir G. Lloyd and Major E. Wood, *The Great Opportunity* (London, 1918), pp.1–3.
237 Macmillan, *Winds of Change*, pp.177–8. Cf. ibid., pp.171, 256.
238 R. Boothby, *My Yesterday, Your Tomorrow* (London, 1962), pp.138, 204.
239 Noel Skelton, *Constructive Conservatism* (Edinburgh, 1924), pp.10–12.

asserted) and to realize that an attitude resting on a concept of restricted government action and a belief in the limitations of politics could not appeal to the mass of the people.[240] For them the key contemporary issue was economic status: they had political rights and educational opportunities but the régime of industry and commerce, by which they lived, granted them little in the way of recognition, initiative, or responsibility. The structure of society had thus become lopsided and unstable. To restore the balance was the master-problem of the new era and the Conservative solution should be to extend property ownership more widely – it was Skelton who coined the phrase 'property owning democracy' – to encourage co-partnership and profit-sharing in industry, and co-operation and smallholding in agriculture.[241] There was hardly anything new in all this and, in fact, Skelton's emphasis was sometimes rather more libertarian than the views Macmillan himself came to expound.[242] Here Skelton's attitude was perhaps rather more reflective of group opinion than Macmillan's. For instance Duff Cooper, while recognizing the baleful effect of *laissez faire* and the need to sustain the Conservative tradition of social reform, urged at the same time the clear financial limits to state intervention, the frequent ineffectiveness of economic regulation, and the danger of excessive control over individual rights and liberties: altogether a rather lukewarm indication of collectivist intent.[243] It was not unusual in the party during those years to distinguish between 'social reform' (desirable and fully in the Disraelian tradition) and 'socialism' (undesirable because it meant an extension of government power over the economy and a trammelling of personal freedom and of that mainspring of individualism, private enterprise).[244] All this shows how much more radical than the norm Macmillan's own views were. Certainly the key lesson he took from Skelton was of the need for Conservatism to apply itself firmly and consistently to the problems of economic life which were so important to the mass democracy that had been created.

Macmillan himself early began to write on topics of contemporary political interest. In 1925, for instance, he produced a series of articles in the provincial press and elsewhere on such matters as slum clearance,

240 ibid., pp.13–16.
241 ibid., pp.17, 23–4, 25–30. Cf. Skelton's *The Cause and Cure of Socialism* (ASU no.112; London, n.d. [1927]), pp.6–10.
242 See e.g. the insistence on limiting state action to helping the individual help himself simply, *Constructive Conservatism*, p.22.
243 A. Duff Cooper, *The Conservative Point of View* (NUCUA no.2616; London, 1926), pp.16, 32–3; and his *The Impossibility of Socialism* (ASU no.106; London, n.d. [1927]).
244 NUCUA, *The Conservative Past and the Conservative Future* (no.2606; London, 1925), pp.4, 6; H. M. Adam, *The Fallacies of Socialism* (NUCUA no.2613; London, 1926), pp.6–7, 10.

building methods, and rating reform.[245] But the major issue, especially after the General Strike of 1926, was the condition of industry and the proper role of the state in attempting a remedy. An important reflection of this concern in political circles was the appearance in 1927 in book form of a series of essays and addresses called *Industry and Politics* whose author was Sir Alfred Mond, later Lord Melchett. Mond, who had previously published a similar volume concerned with industrial problems,[246] was especially experienced in these matters after a legal and commercial career of some success. He had been a Liberal MP who achieved ministerial and Cabinet office in the coalition governments of 1916–22. But in 1926, after a disagreement with D. L. George over land policy, he joined the Conservative Party. His new book repudiated both state Socialism and *laissez faire* and looked instead to a *via media* in which government had a vital interventionist role in securing industrial peace and co-operation, stimulating technological progress, and dealing with 'the crime of unemployment'.[247] Nor was this view uninfluential. For instance, the sections of a contemporary, and semi-official, survey of Conservative doctrine which deal with the relations between industry and government are explicitly indebted to Mond's views.[248] Recognition of the need for a notable amount of state activity was indeed not at all unusual in Tory circles in the decade after the war.[249]

In this fashion Macmillan and three of his associates produced a similar manifesto on industrial problems.[250] They hoped through this means to help wean the Conservative Party away from the old allegiance to unadulterated private enterprise which seemed (in the authors' view) to dominate it. They also wished to rebut the suggestion that 'safeguarding', that is, the policy of limited protection which was increasingly favourably received in the party, would by itself be adequate to deal with contemporary economic problems though at least it indicated the abandonment of the old policy of free trade.[251] Macmillan followed up this statement with many other speeches, articles, and books.[252] The

245 Macmillan, *Winds of Change*, pp. 209–10, 237–9.
246 A. Mond, *Questions of To-day and To-morrow* (London, 1912).
247 A. Mond, *Industry and Politics* (London, 1927), e.g. pp. 50–1. For a slightly earlier statement by Mond about the need for state intervention to regulate the economic system and control its consequences, see his contribution to the debate on Snowden's motion condemning capitalism, 161 H.C. Deb. 5s., 20 March 1923, esp. cols 2502–3.
248 A. Bryant, *The Spirit of Conservatism* (1929; 2nd edn, Ashridge, 1932), esp. part III.
249 Sir Reginald M. Banks, *The Conservative Outlook* (London, 1929), esp. pp. 273–6.
250 R. Boothby *et al.*, *Industry & The State: a Conservative View* (London, 1927).
251 Macmillan, *Winds of Change*, pp. 222–4, 283–5, 355–7.
252 See the array of publications for 1932–3 alone described ibid., pp. 357–68. One particularly good instance of the collectivist tendency involved is a memorandum Macmillan produced for private circulation called 'The State and Industry in 1932'. The increasing 'agenda' of government are reviewed, ibid., pp. 7ff.

most important of these discussions were his own *Reconstruction* (1933) subtitled 'A Plea for a National Policy', two collaborative publications issued in 1935, *Planning for Employment* and *The Next Five Years*, – the latter also the title given to the Conservative election manifesto in 1959 when he was party leader – and, of course, his study *The Middle Way* (1938) which became quite well-known and indeed a sort of symbol of a revised Conservatism. In what was urged in all this Macmillan saw himself not as a doctrinaire innovator but as building on tendencies long under way.[253]

The deep-seated nature of the problem was frankly recognized: the slump indicated a widespread industrial malaise. Immediate and bold action was necessary to reorganize and stimulate industry and to enable it to develop to the full and cope with the technical possibilities revealed by modern science and invention. As well effective aid had to be offered to the depressed areas; and at least a minimum level of social provision had to be achieved to avoid the terrible conditions of poverty, malnutrition, and insecurity in which many people lived. Of course, to meet these objectives meant producing resources which could be used to raise the standard of living (in respect of food, clothing, housing, and so on) of the large number of people existing at or below the margin of subsistence. 'Economic reconstruction', Macmillan wrote, 'has today become the only possible or sound basis for social reform.'[254] And – this is the key point in the present context – all this required substantial government action both to initiate and co-ordinate the required changes. For instance, in a speech in the House of Commons in 1934 he said, 'we shall have to take great power in the hands of the State to direct in what localities and areas fresh industrial development will be allowed'.[255] Yet although more direct state involvement with public utilities might be needed, it was not the object of the whole exercise to eliminate private enterprise: on the contrary the express purpose of the proposed government action was rather to sustain and stimulate it. But to do this did require a wide strategic intervention by public authority and something in the nature of a national plan through which economic life could be revived and radical social reform accommodated by the resources thus created. To this end Macmillan envisaged a varied range of policies. Public control of some key industries such as fuel and transport would be essential.[256] Government aid would have to be

253 Macmillan, *The Middle Way: a Study of the Problem of Economic and Social Progress in a Free and Democratic Society* (1938; London, 1966), pp. 119–20, 173–4, ch. viii. On the Next Five Years Group, see T. A. Smith, *The Politics of the Corporate Economy* (London, 1979), pp. 37–9.
254 Macmillan, *The Middle Way*, p. 37. Cf. ibid., pp. 14, 21–30.
255 287 H.C. Deb. 5s., 22 March 1934, col. 1523.
256 A party pamphlet *Cheap Electricity for Everybody* (NU no. 2904; London, 1929) emphasized the great advantages to be expected from the complete reorganization

available to assist industrial combination so that advantage could be taken of the economies of scale. Centralized supervisory boards (or National Industrial Councils) should be created for each major product to ensure output was not in excess of market demand and to encourage efficient co-ordination of purchasing, production, marketing, and research. Industrial development would be directed to especially hard pressed areas. Encouragement should be given (by legislation if necessary) to establish in industry arrangements for the conciliation of disputes and machinery for collective bargaining as through the extension of joint industrial councils, trade boards, co-partnership, and profit-sharing schemes.[257] A minimum wage or security payment should be enforced by law; credit and taxation policy be used to control fluctuation of currency and prices; and schemes of public investment created to help meet industrial needs. All this was to be supervised by an Investment and Development Board (or Central Economic Council) set up by government. Macmillan also wrote of the need to ensure a wider extension of property ownership. And, of course, the augmented regulatory role of the state would require administrative improvements in the government machine: a rational rearrangement of departmental organization, the creation of an economic general staff, and provision to obtain adequate statistical data as a basis for policy making.[258] And the whole was seen to constitute 'a middle way' between the extremes of *laissez faire* and state Socialism, a way in which nevertheless new and greater responsibilities were thrust on government to improve the general economic and social condition of the nation. In one place Macmillan called this a 'mixed system' of 'planned capitalism'.[259] Once minimum human needs had been achieved and the basic degree of economic control assured it was necessary to preserve deliberately the sphere of private enterprise for not only was this more efficient economically (in ensuring initiative, adoption of new methods, exploration of market possibilities, and the like) but also its retention in this crucial sphere was vital to the general preservation of freedom elsewhere.[260]

The tone of these policies as well as many of the detailed prescriptions were not, of course, unique: not even the term 'middle way' was new. Macmillan popularized it but the idea was already in common use especially in Liberal circles which had long been looking for an emphasis

---

of the power industry under the 1926 Conservative legislation which created the Central Electricity Board.

257 These were common Conservative themes at this time; for another instance, see Viscount Lymington, *Ich Dien: the Tory Path* (London, 1931), p.65.

258 R. Boothby *et al.*, *Industry & the State*, pp.55–65; app., pp.231–45.

259 Macmillan, *The Middle Way*, pp.176–87.

260 ibid., p.102.

different from that of their party rivals. In 1922 Liberal propaganda referred to such 'a *via media*'; and four years later Philip Kerr, trying to work out a distinctively Liberal style of tackling post-war problems, produced 'a proposal for a middle way such as the Liberals ought to be able to make their own'.[261] The phrase was also used in a similar sense by Mrs Webb in 1925.[262] And the concept had been envisaged, if not the actual words, by C. F. G. Masterman a few years earlier still.[263] In terms of the policies considered by Macmillan there was a close parallel with the themes of the Liberal Yellow Book with much of which Macmillan sympathized.[264] Indeed not long before, the National Liberal Federation had noted how over recent years the idea of economic planning had been enthusiastically taken up by young Tories.[265] For some time, too, though in the end he remained aloof, Macmillan found much that was congenial in Mosley's New Party and its proposals to deal with unemployment by a properly planned economy.[266] However, critics saw it all as a new unauthorized programme and as 'thinly-veiled Socialism'.[267] Certainly economic orthodoxy was bluntly repudiated in favour of the new doctrine of the middle way and of the belief that men were not the prisoners of ineluctable natural law but might impose their will on the economic process.[268]

Macmillan's propensities in this direction were reinforced by wartime experience at the Ministry of Supply from 1940 to 1942 where he was able to try out in practice some of the ideas he had previously premeditated in theory about the control and direction of industrial production and organization. Then, after the traumatic Conservative defeat in the 1945 election, he was able to play some part in the reformation of party policy, attempting to bring it up to date to suit the new political and economic circumstances. The ideas he urged in this context showed he was still the apostle of the middle way that he had expounded before the war. His

261 *Lloyd George Liberal Magazine*, June 1922; Kerr to George (23 July 1926), Lothian MSS, GD40/17/223/231, Scottish Record Office. Both cited in M. Bentley, *The Liberal Mind, 1914–1929* (Cambridge, 1977), p.158.

262 B. Webb, *Diaries, 1924–32*, pp.70, 73. It is misleading, therefore, to attribute the first use of the term to Sir A. Salter's *Recovery: the Second Effort* (London, 1932), p.21, as in T. A. Smith, op. cit., pp.32–3.

263 C. F. G. Masterman, *The New Liberalism* (London, 1920), pp.30–1.

264 Macmillan, *Winds of Change*, p.165.

265 NLF, *The Liberal Way: a Survey of Liberal Policies . . .* (London, 1934), p.127.

266 Sampson, op. cit., pp.35–7; H. Nicolson, *Diaries and Letters, 1930–1939* (1966; London, 1969), pp.72–5. For a good account of Mosleyite policies and their collectivist implications, see N. Nugent, 'The Ideas of the British Union of Fascists', N. Nugent and R. King (eds), *The British Right: Conservative and Right Wing Politics in Britain* (Farnborough, Hants., 1977), ch.6, esp. pp.135–48.

267 Macmillan, *Winds of Change*, p.224.

268 Macmillan, *The Middle Way*, pp.7–13; ibid., ch. VII on 'Past Theories and Present Needs'.

own election address in 1945 clearly manifested the same themes.[269] He was a member of the party committee which drafted the *Industrial Charter* (1946) which one commentator referred to as a second edition of *The Middle Way*.[270] He recognized that his views on nationalization were not unlike those of the moderates in the Labour government.[271] And he continually reasserted his pre-war policies based on a large degree of government intervention and strategic management of the economy as a whole. Indeed at the 1946 party conference he went so far as to criticize the Labour administration for not carrying this task through as fully and as systematically as circumstances required. And by the end of that year he believed that the Conservative Party as such had (like the Labour government) come to accept the doctrine of the mixed economy in which there was a crucial role for the state.[272] As Minister of Housing from 1951 to 1954 he early realized the need for efficient organization and firm central direction on the wartime model – the parallel is significant – if the building target was to be achieved.[273] Then, of course, the ideas of the middle way came into their own when Macmillan became Prime Minister. From 1957 to 1963 he set his stamp on the Conservative Party and on national affairs with an impress that is likely to endure a long time. To symptomize the event, it is worth recalling that while from 1951 to 1958 the state's share in the national income had shown a tendency to decline, in the latter year it began, albeit slowly, to rise again. This was the corollary of the middle way with its advocacy of public intervention. As a critical Cabinet colleague has observed with only some degree of partisan exaggeration:

In the great decision Macmillan took with him his Government, his party and the country. From that moment onwards the whole range of policies which he had espoused 20 years before was adopted by the Conservative Party.

Conservatives in 1955 would have been more incredulous than indignant had anyone told them that in seven year's time their political platform would consist of national economic planning, regional economic planning, planning of incomes ('incomes policy'), rationalization of industries by state intervention, more subsidised housing, and higher public expenditure generally.

269 H. Macmillan, *Tides of Fortune, 1945–1955* (London, 1969), p.35. See the citation from the address in Sampson, op. cit., p.79.
270 Macmillan, *Tides of Fortune*, pp.302ff. Cf. Sampson op. cit., p.84; Lord Butler, *The Art of the Possible* (London, 1971), p.144.
271 Macmillan, *Tides of Fortune*, pp.54, 74.
272 ibid., pp.81–2, 304–7; KCA (1946–8), p.8179. Cf. his speech *The Conservative Approach to Modern Politics* (London, 1946), pp.7–8.
273 *Tides of Fortune*, p.395, and ch. xiii *passim*.

Similarly in the crisis of 1962, Powell suggests, the Premier prescribed more of the same medicine and there was an intensification of measures of the kind just listed: redundancy payments, contracts of service, training schemes and boards, differential tax benefits for depressed areas, NEDC, and so on.[274] From the pages in Macmillan's autobiography dealing with these matters it would seem – to take one crucial instance – it was he himself who initiated the plan for an incomes policy and the idea of a permanent commission to administer it.[275]

It is an interesting paradox that Harold Macmillan, who cultivated the reputation of being Edwardian and old-fashioned, foppish and aristocratic, was in fact one of the main personalities concerned in the adaptation of his party's paternalistic tradition to the age of economic planning and the positive state.[276] His views were formed early in the mould of Tory radicalism and reform and they were in principle consistent and unchanged throughout his political career. Nor since the war has he alone expounded such views.

THE 'NEW CONSERVATISM' SINCE 1940

The Conservative of today stands in the line of this tradition – this antipathy to laisser-faire, this recognition of the State as an arbitrating and guiding force.
A. JONES, *Right and Left*, 1944, p.17

During the earlier part of his political life Winston Churchill had, like his father, been much associated with schemes of social and administrative reform. And although his later career was largely involved with wider issues he never completely lost his interest in these domestic matters after he became Prime Minister in 1940. It was he who, during the war years, instructed R. A. Butler to improve the education of the people and who accepted and sponsored the idea of a four-year plan for national development and the commitment to sustain full employment in the post-war period. As well he approved proposals to establish a national insurance scheme, services for housing and health, and was prepared to accept a broadening field of state enterprise.[277] It was because of this coalition policy that Enoch Powell referred to the veritable social revolution which occurred in the years 1942–4.[278] Aims of this kind were

274 J. E. Powell on Macmillan's *Winds of Change, Glasgow Herald* (5 September 1966), pp.8–9.
275 Macmillan, *At the End of the Day*, pp.91, 106.
276 Cf. his farewell message to the Conservative annual conference, cited in Macmillan, *At the End of the Day*, pp.506–7.
277 See the summary of Churchill's broadcast of March 1943, in P. Addison, *The Road to 1945: British Politics and the Second World War* (London, 1975), p.227–8.
278 E. Powell, *The Welfare State* (CPC no.245; London, 1961), p.7.

embodied in the Conservative declaration of policy issued by the Premier before the 1945 general election.[279] The aims were also compatible with the inclinations of many of his party colleagues though not all. For instance, Lord Selborne (who was Minister for Economic Warfare from 1942 to 1945) indicated to the Prime Minister towards the end of the war that one reason he wished to leave office as soon as possible was his increasing disagreement with much of the government's 'domestic policy, not only in Town Planning, but also on other semi-Socialist extravagances'.[280] Macmillan was on the contrary obviously one who concurred with the growing tendency though in the later stages of the war his then ministerial post took his main interests in another direction. But during the war years the ideas of the middle way continued to be reasserted as by Robert Boothby (one of Macmillan's authorial colleagues of the 1920s) who in a study called *The New Economy* urged that the state should bring unused factors of production into play through capital expenditure and taxation policy, should exercise control over the volume of credit, basic monopolies, external trade, and so on. For such purposes it should create new institutions, too, such as a National Development Board and an Economic General Staff.[281]

There was also a wartime equivalent of the old YMCA ginger group. In 1943 a number of Conservative MPs, forty or so of them including H. Molson, P. Thorneycroft, Lord Winterton, D. Gammans, Q. Hogg, and Lord Hinchingbrooke (who was in fact the prime mover), formed the Tory Reform Committee. One august older associate was Lord Hankey.[282] Members of the group issued pamphlets and booklets to support their views which were also expressed in the party journal *Onlooker*. These Tory Reformers were anxious to repudiate much of what they took to be the inter-war image of the party and wanted to identify it whole-heartedly with the wartime changes. Lord Hinchingbrooke wrote in 1944:

> True Conservative opinion is horrified at the damage done to this country since the last war by 'individualist' business-men, financiers, and speculators ranging freely in a *laissez-faire* economy and creeping unnoticed into the fold of Conservatism to insult the Party with their votes at elections, to cast a slur over responsible Government through influence exerted on Parliament, and to injure the character of our

279 F. W. S. Craig (ed.), *British General Election Manifestos, 1918–1966* (Chichester, 1970), pp. 89–97.
280 Selborne to Prime Minister (31 October 1944) in PRO, PREM 4, 35/2A.
281 R. Boothby, *The New Economy* (London, 1943), pp. 47, 65, 67–8, 132–3.
282 Cf. S. Roskill, *Hankey: Man of Secrets* (London, 1970–4), iii. 576–7. On the Tory Reform Committee generally, see H. Kopsch, *The Approach of the Conservative Party to Social Policy During World War II* (unpublished PhD thesis, London University, 1970), pp. 46–63, 138ff.

people. It would wish nothing better than that these men should collect their baggage and depart. True Conservatism has nothing whatever to do with them and their obnoxious policies.[283]

The group's specific purpose initially was to press the government 'to take constructive action on the lines of the Beveridge Scheme' (including the provision of a comprehensive health service) but it subsequently tried to influence coalition policy more generally not only on matters of social reform but also on the need for state management of the economy as a means of developing the national resources, and so forth.[284] Thus the Committee urged in Keynesian fashion the maintenance of full employment as 'an essential and urgent task of government.' For this purpose it was necessary that the volume and timing of capital expenditure should be influenced or, if necessary, controlled by government so as to ensure an adequate level of demand; equally government would be involved in the securing of industrial diversification and increased training facilities; similarly there would be supervision of agriculture and other essential aspects of economic life.[285] In modern conditions state ownership and enterprise is inevitable and, as government cannot be indifferent to the way private industry is run, so is state planning of the economic framework: *laissez faire* and free trade are alike anachronisms that must be abandoned.[286]

The party had also set up in 1941 a Central Committee on Post-War Reconstruction which in the following years issued a series of interim reports for discussion on such subjects as demobilization and resettlement, labour, agriculture, education, housing, and other post-war problem areas.[287] So, given this sort of background of collectivist thinking within the Conservative Party, it was not really surprising that when in 1942 Sir Stafford Cripps was turning his thoughts towards the post-war world and its problems and coming to the conclusion that a new centre party was needed to bring about planned production and consumption, he insisted that there were more Conservative than Labour MPs ready to act on these lines.[288] And, of course, after the 1945 defeat there were intensified moves to refurbish and strengthen the inter-

---

283 Hinchingbrooke, *Full Speed Ahead! Essays in Tory Reform* (London, n.d. [1944]), p.21.
284 Tory Reform Committee, *Forward – By the Right!* (London, 1943), pp.1, 13, 15–16; H. E. Molson, 'The Tory Reform Committee', *New English Review*, xi (1945), pp.245, 247; Addison, *The Road to 1945*, pp.232–3.
285 *Forward – By the Right!* pp.8, 9–12; Molson, art. cit., pp.247–8.
286 Molson, art. cit., pp.249–50. For some second thoughts in changed circumstances, see V. Montagu, *The Conservative Dilemma* (Monday Club; London, 1970), pp.14–16, 18–23.
287 On the work of this body, see Kopsch, op. cit., p.42 and sections II–IV *passim*.
288 B. Webb diary (23 July 1942), cited in P. Addison, *The Road to 1945*, p.205.

ventionist aspects of party doctrine. In 1945 L. D. Gammans (who later held minor office in government) wrote a booklet on party principles. While naturally rejecting any conception of an overweening state and stressing the need for economy in public life, he indicated in various ways that Conservatives were quite prepared to envisage a substantial role for government in respect of the economy and social welfare. For instance, he denied the accusation of the Labour Party that Conservatives were against economic controls as such; this could, he affirmed, be seen to be untrue simply by examining the record:

> This country was not exactly a jungle before the War. Our economic life was controlled to a far greater extent than any other country except Russia and Nazi Germany. By income tax, super tax and death duties, incomes were redistributed on a scale which by American standards would be regarded almost as confiscation. Hours and conditions of labour were regulated. Farming was organised in Marketing Boards. State monopolies had been created in broadcasting, London Transport, and in the production of electricity. Municipalities were taking an increasing part in housing, transport, gas, water and electricity.[289]

There was also the policy of protection. And Conservatives would accept regulation, and nationalization even, where it was deemed necessary.[290] The following year 1946, in a discussion of party principles, C. J. M. Alport, while recognizing the importance of the free development of individual personality and the limitations of political action, nevertheless asserted (in phrases that were continually used) that the Conservative

> has never been frightened of using the power of the State to improve social conditions, to organise economic effort and to provide collective services such as defence, education and health. From its factory and health acts of the nineteenth century to the Education Act of 1944, the Conservative Party has been responsible for a mass of legislation dealing with social, industrial, economic and financial subjects and designed to improve conditions of work and living, to guide industrial enterprise and to provide increased opportunities for brains and energy.[291]

Although it is not called that, it is the 'middle way' which is here explored and commended. Similarly Quintin Hogg wrote to R. A. Butler, who was

289 L. D. Gammans, *Facing the Facts* (NUCUA no. 3787; London, 1945), pp. 18–19.
290 ibid., pp. 21–2. It is none the less true that after 1945 the Conservatives mounted a substantial campaign against the nationalization proposals of the Labour Party.
291 C. J. M. Alport, *About Conservative Principles* (London, 1946), pp. 12–14 (citation at p. 14). Cf. ibid., pp. 15–16; also L. S. Amery, *The Conservative Future: an Outline of Policy* (n.p., n.d. [1946]), pp. 5, 10–11, 15.

so centrally involved in this process of policy formulation, that what the party needed was a new Tamworth Manifesto; and Butler agreed saying that 'As in the days of Peel, the Conservatives must be seen to have accommodated themselves to a social revolution.'[292] It is curious, looking back, to see how defensive in many ways Conservatives' attitudes were at this time. As has been seen, their party had a long tradition and record of social and economic reform. Yet its contemporary image seemed to underplay this important element in its history and ideology and it was felt necessary not simply to re-emphasize it but almost to reinvent it. Butler himself urged the need for the party to accept redistributive taxation to help reduce extremes of poverty and wealth, to repudiate let-alone economics in favour of a system of 'humanized capitalism' in which the state acted as 'a trustee for the interests of the community and a balancing force between different interests'.[293] The party established or revived a series of committees and research bodies to set on foot examination of these matters. The outcome was a series of policy and discussion documents of which the *Industrial Charter* (1946) was among the earliest and most well-known. Macmillan's doctrines of *The Middle Way* were, as already noted, a crucial influence on the thinking embodied in this paper. Its main purpose was to stress that Conservatism was not the party of 'industrial go-as-you-please' and that full employment and the welfare state were safe in Conservative hands. Thus in economic matters the vital functions of government were insisted on in Keynesian terms. As Butler, the main architect of the Charter, put it, it was first and foremost 'an assurance that, in the interests of efficiency, full employment and social security, modern Conservatism would maintain strong central guidance over the operation of the economy.'[294] This was followed by exercises of a similar kind including the many and wide-ranging publications of the Conservative Political Centre.[295] The general style of this 'new conservatism' was reflected in a speech made at the party conference in 1947 by Anthony Eden who had (it will be recalled) been a member of the group of radical young MPs to which Macmillan had adhered in the 1920s. Eden was proposing the adoption of the newly formulated industrial policy: 'We are not', he said, 'a Party of unbridled, brutal capitalism, and never have been. Although we believe in personal responsibility and

292 Lord Butler, *The Art of the Possible* (London, 1971), p.133.
293 Butler, op. cit., pp.133–4, citing a speech of March 1946.
294 ibid., p.146. Cf. Blake, *The Conservative Party from Peel to Churchill* (1970; Fontana, 1972), p.259.
295 e.g. G. M. Young *et al.*, *The Good Society* (CPC no.122; London, 1953); R. A. Butler *et al.*, *Tradition and Change* (CPC no.138; London, 1954); P. Goldman *et al.*, *The Future of the Welfare State* (CPC no.178; London, 1958); and the other pamphlets listed in G. D. M. Block, *A Source Book of Conservatism* (CPC no.305; London, 1964), §VI.

personal initiative in business, we are not the political children of the "laissez-faire" school. We opposed them decade after decade.' And, as Eden went on to assert, Conservatives were never averse to the use of legislation to deal with industrial and social problems.[296] These are the genuine accents of orthodox Tory collectivism; and they have been heard increasingly since (though never uniquely). In 1946 R. A. Butler warned that, in considering the major question of the state and its functions, it was impossible to hope to return to the nineteenth-century view of uncontrolled economic life:

> We must recognise that the absolutely free working of such a system cannot now be accepted. We are living in too closely knit a structure of society in which the very complication of our immense programme of social reform and industrial development necessitates strong powers being retained at the centre. It will be necessary to use the organising power and majesty of the State in a variety of ways. The State will have to be the grand arbiter between competing interests.[297]

At the same time it should nurture and not destroy the creative energies of individuals though its substantial role in society and the economy was inevitable and proper.[298] The following year, too, in another pamphlet about the Industrial Charter (which he had done so much to sponsor) Butler provided a good example of the view that the collectivist state should be regarded as the norm. *Laissez faire*, he suggests, is to be seen as a mere interlude between earlier and later periods of considerable state intervention. In the early modern age much industrial and commercial activity had been subject to government regulation; and by the end of the nineteenth century 'Tories and others set about the task of dealing with the social consequences of the Industrial Revolution by calling upon the power of Government to redress injustice' so that once again the state 'assumed the functions of protecting the common interest and safeguarding the interests of the weaker members of society.'[299] Equally, in between the two world wars, public action was again foremost in fostering industrial and commercial advance: indeed during these years 'the partnership of Government and industry became closer than it had been in peace at any time since the Age of Mercantilism.' The second war, of course, much hastened this tendency especially in the way it fostered the idea of 'planning'.[300] He goes on: 'The term "planning" is a new word for coherent and positive policy. The conception of strong Government policy in economic matters is, I believe, in the very centre of

296 Cited in *The New Conservatism* (CPC no.150; London, 1955), pp.11–12.
297 R. A. Butler, *Fundamental Issues* (CPC no.3837; London, 1946), p.7.
298 ibid., pp.7–8.
299 Butler, *About the Industrial Charter* (CPC no.17; London, 1947), pp.4–5.
300 ibid., pp.4, 5–6.

the Conservative tradition. We have never been a party of *laissez-faire*.'[301] And he exemplified this by reference to the party's history, in particular its support of tariff reform which was a policy very like that of national planning in that both were built on the principle of 'the conscious guidance of the national economy into predetermined channels.' 'Conservatives', he claimed, 'were planning before the word entered the vocabulary of political jargon' though, of course, he deplored the extreme use of controls and the like as being unnecessary to effective 'National Housekeeping'.[302] This guidance involved, again, a sort of middle way with government taking 'the grand strategic decisions' and setting the economic framework within which industry would then freely operate: neither '*laissez faire*' nor 'Socialism', he said.[303] In 1950 Butler wrote that it was the task of the present generation of Conservatives to build on the two ineluctable features of the age, 'the existence of universal adult suffrage' and what this implies, 'the acceptance by authority of the responsibility for ensuring a certain standard of living, of employment, and of security for all.'[304] He repeated in 1956 that 'Conservatives have always been ready to use the power of the State' though, at the same time, sounded a warning note about the excessive restrictions that could arise in a planned economy.[305] By the 1960s the government formally announced a commitment to planning. In July 1961 S. Lloyd presented some new measures to deal with a current sterling crisis using these terms:

> I shall deal, first, with growth in the economy. The controversial matter of planning at once arises. I am not frightened of the word. . . . I think that the time has come for a better co-ordination of these various activities. I intend to discuss urgently with both sides of industry procedures for pulling together these various processes of consultation and forecasting with a view to better co-ordination of ideas and plans.[306]

This was followed up by a letter to the TUC and employers' organizations urging the same development and led in due course to the establishment of the NEDC which itself produced a long term plan for the economy and helped spawn a whole series of neo-mercantilist devices.[307] Likewise the Bow Group accepted that in complex industrial

301 ibid., p.6.
302 ibid., pp.6–7, 10ff.
303 ibid., p.16.
304 R. A. Butler, Introduction to *Conservatism, 1945–1950* (CPC no.90; London, 1950), p.3.
305 R. A. Butler, *Our Way Ahead* (CPC no.169; London, 1956), pp.10–13.
306 645 H.C. Deb. 5s., 25 July 1961, col.220.
307 A. Budd, *The Politics of Economic Planning* (Fontana, 1978), pp.80, 92–3. Cf. J. T. Winkler, in R. Skidelsky (ed.), *The End of the Keynesian Era: Essays on the Disintegration of the Keynesian Political Economy* (London, 1977), p.80.

society it was necessary for the state to plan and otherwise extend its role to make capitalism work.[308] One CPC booklet said in 1960 that town planning, though 'an autocratic process', is now 'a function of government as essential as the maintenance of law and order.'[309] In 1964 G. Johnson Smith reflected the party acceptance of the high level of public expenditure involved and observed that Tories would enter the forthcoming election 'not as the latter-day apostles of Gladstonian economic principles but as the party which can best use the nation's resources to modernise the country.' Professor Esmond Wright accepted, in a party pamphlet appearing in 1968, that a quite large civil service and a substantial degree of state activity were necessary.[310] The Monday Club is dedicated rather more to the cause of free enterprise but even so in its publications there can be a recognition of the positive role of the state. For instance, in 1966, and reflecting an updated echo of the middle way, J. Biggs-Davison urged the claims of Toryism to be 'a centre force' which has 'taken post between unfettered capitalism and excessive collectivism.' He added that 'Tories must nowadays be concerned to check and control the excesses of bureaucratic and technocratic power. At the same time they will recognise the need of State intervention . . . to correct . . . injustices . . . and new forms of material, moral, mental and spiritual poverty.'[311] In the aftermath of the October 1974 election defeat, Sir Ian Gilmour repudiated 'Selsdon man' and warned of the dangers to the party of accepting an easy identification with the cause of the unbridled individualism of the free market.[312] His later study of Conservative thought is indeed a very good instance of the rejection of free-trade and free-market ideas as merely neo-Liberal and not Conservative at all. At the same time there is the belief that today government has become perhaps rather excessive; and the Conservative aim should always be to achieve an appropriate balance between these antithetical claims as circumstances dictate from time to time.[313] Nevertheless it must be

---

308 See e.g. the citations from *Crossbow*, in A. Gamble, *The Conservative Nation* (London, 1974), pp. 76–7. For a similar view from the provinces, cf. the Birmingham Bow Group's *Reform or Regret?* (Birmingham, n.d. [1965]), pp. 2–3, 6, 8 urging a market economy made more effective by a framework of rising public provision.

309 T. Knight *et al.*, *Let Our Cities Live* (CPC no. 221; London, 1960), p. 28.

310 G. J. Smith, 'National Equities?', *Crossbow*, vol. 7, no. 27 (April–June 1964), p. 33; E. Wright, *Freedom and Technology* (CPC no. 398; London, 1968), pp. 10–11. Cf. R. Lewis, *Principles To Conserve* (CPC no. 417; London, 1968), p. 8; and Gamble, op. cit., pp. 139–42.

311 J. Biggs-Davison, *Antecedents: the Story of the Conservative Party* (Monday Club paper no. 1; London, 1966), p. 13.

312 I. Gilmour, in *The Times* (22 November 1974), p. 16. Cf. the remarks of P. Walker reported ibid. (4 November 1974), pp. 1–2. These were presumably responses to the speech of Sir Keith Joseph calling for a radical re-emphasis in Conservative policy, ibid. (21 October 1974), p. 3 (on which see below ch. 9, pp. 341–4).

313 I. Gilmour, *Inside Right: a Study of Conservatism* (London, 1977), pp. 38, 130, 152–4, 168.

recognized that in today's conditions 'the state is bound to play an important part in the economy' (which will, therefore, be mixed) as well as in the provision of welfare and other amenities which are essential ingredients in a humane society.[314] The policies adopted by the Conservative government between 1970 and 1974 – and despite previous protestations to the contrary – and not least in respect of the compulsory prices and incomes policy, are a good reflection of this as, too, is the reminder that there is an unacceptable face of capitalism which the party will not condone and must move to remould.

*   *   *

These diverse strands of thought, policy, and interest have, then, contributed to form a brand of Conservatism that has, increasingly, found both necessary and proper the intervention of government in the nation's economic and social life. Of course, anything like totalitarian control or the deliberate repudiation of property rights as such has always been repudiated and, except in war, largely eschewed. Nevertheless the trammels that this kind of Conservatism has been prepared to envisage or actually to impose on the free enterprise or competitive system and on private property have been very considerable indeed.

Yet there has always been another and sometimes very different aspect of Conservative ideology. In 1955 Professor S. H. Beer wrote in *The Observer* newspaper, 'The Tories have never been the party of *laissez-faire*, and they justly lay claim to a large part in founding the Welfare State.'[315] The latter observation is true; but the former part of the Professor's opinion may certainly be rather misleading as the next two chapters will suggest.

314 ibid., pp.19–20. Cf. the summary of a speech reported in *The Times* (12 February 1980), p.12.
315 'Two Kinds of Conservatism', loc. cit., 8 May 1955, p.10.

8

THE LIBERTARIAN STRAND

... if the present drift of things continues, it may by and by really happen
that the Tories will be defenders of liberties which the Liberals, in pursuit
of what they think popular welfare, trample under foot.
H. SPENCER, *The Man Versus the State*, 1884, Penguin, 1969, p.81n.

LIBERTARIAN CONSERVATISM

One sometimes feels ... that the laissez-faire Liberal party of the
nineteenth century never really died, but instead took over sections of the
Conservative party.
PATRICK COSGRAVE, in *The Spectator*, 22 January 1972, p.130

IN THE mid-1920s the group of young Conservatives who, as noted
in the previous chapter, were themselves busily advocating a policy of
extending state responsibility, observed in one of the commentaries they
sponsored that the

> Individualist view ... clings ... to the 'laissez-faire' policy of mid-
> Victorian Liberalism. It insists, with varying degrees of success, that
> there shall be no Government interference in industry whatever. The
> only part it allots to the Government is what is popularly called
> 'holding the ring'.... This view, which, since the Conservative party
> from 1886 onwards has been so strongly infected with Whig and
> Liberal doctrine, has made much progress and commands honourable
> adherents in many quarters of the party....[1]

A later passage in the same work referred to the 'Die-hard section of the
Conservative party, which is so paradoxically imbued today with Whig
and Liberal traditions' and which was opposed to increased government
supervision of the economy.[2] From a different political quarter but at the

1 R. Boothby *et al.*, *Industry & the State: a Conservative View* (London, 1927),
  pp.175–6.
2 ibid., p.213. On the influence of Liberal ideas, see also F. J. C. Hearnshaw,
  Conservatism in England: an Analytical, Historical, and Political Survey (London,
  1933), p.4; and P. Smith, *Disraelian Conservatism and Social Reform* (London, 1967),
  p.321.

same period, the Liberal Yellow Book referred to opposition to state intervention as being characteristic of extremists on the right wing of politics.[3] And much more recently a CPC pamphlet, while not itself urging this view, likewise noted the number of Conservatives who still 'embrace the doctrines of Manchester School Liberalism'.[4] In fact the historical perspective implied in these judgements is somewhat misleading in so far as an emphasis hostile to government intervention was firmly established in Tory circles well before the influx of Liberal Unionists and others in the late nineteenth century. But it is certainly true that the anti-statist point of view emerges much more strongly among Conservatives once the apparently inexorable pressures of collectivism had firmly declared themselves in particular through the consequences of the extension of the franchise, the manifest tendency of Liberal legislation after 1905, and the rise of the Labour Party.

The ideological influence most important in the development of the libertarian theme was undoubtedly that of Herbert Spencer. He had himself acknowledged the political transformation under way. As early as 1884 he commented, apropos the reception of his articles on 'The New Toryism', that 'oddly enough' he was 'patted on the back by the conservatives' which was 'a new experience' for him. And he wondered, too, in *The Man Versus the State* whether it might not be the Tories who would become the 'defenders of liberties which the Liberals, in pursuit of what they think popular welfare, trample under foot.'[5] And at least one Liberal publicist also recognized the same drift of events when he observed just before the Great War that Spencer's individualism 'might fairly be credited with generating . . . a very large amount of the more rational Conservatism of our time.'[6]

But while the form and tone of Spencer's ideas were predominant in the formation of this Conservative libertarianism they were not exclusive. Overall a notable range of argument was involved based on rather varied premisses. These are sometimes social and economic, sometimes religious and philosophical, depending, of course, on the interests and disposition of the exponent. But broadly disciples of the doctrine fall into two groups. First there are the extremer adherents of a more or less orthodox *laissez faire* and free-trade position. Then there are the supporters of a more moderate view which accepts the need for a greater

3 Liberal Industrial Inquiry, *Britain's Industrial Future* (London, 1928), p.453.
4 N. Lawson, 'The Need for a National Policy', R. Blake *et al.*, *Conservatism Today* (CPC no. 350; London, 1966), p.49ff.
5 H. Spencer to E. L. Youmans (15 February 1884), in D. Duncan, *The Life and Letters of Herbert Spencer* (London, 1908), p.239; H. Spencer, *The Man Versus the State* (1884; Penguin, 1969), p.81 n.
6 J. M. Robertson, *The Meaning of Liberalism* (1912; 2nd edn, London, 1925), p.170 (p.198 in 1st edn).

degree of state activity in some fields while wishing to limit the range or type of intervention allowed elsewhere. And this might be done, for instance, by drawing a distinction between social and economic regulation, the former being regarded as permissible and the latter generally not. In this chapter and the next something will be said of the pedigree and development of these libertarian ideas as they have been deployed over the years by Conservative politicians and propagandists. It is a style of thought which has indeed lately assumed some prominence in the party counsels and is, therefore, of more than merely quondam significance. Nor can denial that these views have anything to do with Conservatism be historically accurate.[7]

SOME NINETEENTH-CENTURY INSTANCES

> . . . it is out of the power of an Act of Parliament . . . to cure our social
> evils. . . . no Government can insure to willing labour 'a fair day's wages
> for a fair day's work'. . . .
> LORD ELCHO, 77 Parl. Deb. 3s., 4 February 1845, col. 49

Fear of centralized power and the danger of its growth was one of the major themes of British politics from at least the seventeenth century onward; and Conservatives like others were much concerned with the issues this matter raised. In particular, of course, the question took the form of delimiting the proper sphere and functions of government. Burke, always a major influence on Conservative thinking, had laid down certain guide-lines in his posthumously published *Thoughts on Scarcity* (1795), a tract the general tenor of which is revealed by the fact that it was later praised by Richard Cobden in the highest terms.[8] It is, Burke wrote, 'one of the finest problems in legislation' what the state ought to undertake and what it ought to leave 'with as little interference as possible' to individual discretion. Certainly there is no absolute or hard and fast rule that can be determined but he thought the 'clearest line of distinction' was that

> the state ought to confine itself to . . . the exterior establishment of its
> religion; its magistracy; its revenue; its military force by sea and land;
> the corporations that owe their existence to its fiat; in a word, to
> everything that is *truly and properly* public, to the public peace, to the
> public safety, to the public order, to the public prosperity.

Whatever remains, he adds, 'will, in a manner, provide for itself'; and it is a mistake for statesmen to move beyond their proper sphere. 'They ought to know the different departments of things; what belongs to laws, and

7 e.g. R. Scruton, *The Meaning of Conservatism* (Penguin, 1980), pp. 15–16, 33.
8 J. Morley, *The Life of Richard Cobden* (London, 1881), i. 167. Cf. the brief discussion in H. J. Laski, *The Rise of European Liberalism* (1936; Unwin Books, 1962), pp. 130–2.

what manners alone can regulate.' These are generalities, of course, and capable of a wide variety of interpretation; but it was not Burke's intention to leave the matter thus unclear. He specifically excludes local and domestic affairs from centralized interference and condemns in this context, however well-intentioned, 'a restless desire of governing too much.' 'My opinion', he concluded, 'is against an over-doing of any sort of administration, and more especially against this most momentous of all meddling on the part of authority; the meddling with the subsistence of the people.'9 The state is thus authoritatively and explicitly warned to leave economic life well alone.

This was the orthodox belief that continued throughout the following century, supported (it was supposed) by the authority of the classical economists. And here at least one connexion was explicit, for Burke was full of praise for *The Wealth of Nations* and, in turn, Adam Smith said that Burke was the only man who, unprompted, thought on economic matters exactly as he did himself.[10] The combined influences of the great Whig politician and theorist together with what was taken to be the dominant economic orthodoxy of the day are more than adequate to account for the opposition of many Conservatives to state interference: the creed meant non-intervention at home and free trade abroad. Various considerations were urged to sustain this point of view.

Thus there was a basic point of a metaphysical kind that a great many of the ills of existence were quite beyond human control. They were part of the nature of things, divinely ordained almost, so that it was to no purpose to pass legislation in the attempt to ameliorate them: apparently unsatisfactory conditions had rather patiently to be suffered by the poor and distressed until relieved by God's grace.[11] Moreover any interference would be likely to disturb organic growth and progress and have an untoward rather than a beneficial effect. Something of this theme is revealed in the following report of a speech made by Lord Liverpool, then Prime Minister, in 1819:

> Personally he sympathised deeply with the distress. Every man must look with an anxious desire towards any measure which was calculated to afford relief to the lower classes of people in this country, and more especially to the manufacturing population. But the Legislature must proceed with great caution. Measures of that kind

9 Burke, *Works* (World's Classics, London, 1906–7), vi. 30–1, 32, italics in original. Burke's attachment to free trade is also evident in his *Two Letters to Gentlemen in the City of Bristol* (1778), ibid., ii. 290, 293, 301; also in his *Letter to Thomas Burgh, Esq.* (1780), *Works*, ed. Bohn (London, 1855), v. 497.
10 Burke, in *The Annual Register*, xix (1776), p. 241 (second pagination); J. Prior, *Life of . . . Edmund Burke*, 5th edn (London, 1854), p. 61.
11 Cf. J. Hart, 'Nineteenth Century Social Reform: a Tory Interpretation of History', *Past and Present* (no. 31, July 1965), p. 56.

could not be viewed as matters of indifference. If they did not effect good, it was possible that they might do much harm, and he believed that for one instance in which benefit was produced by Legislative interference in matters of trade and commerce, ten cases might be pointed out in which injury had been the consequence. This was a doctrine which could not be too often or too strongly impressed on the people of this country. They ought to be taught that evils inseparable from the state of things should not be charged on any government; and, on enquiry, it would be found that by far the greater part of the miseries of which human nature complained were in all times and in all countries beyond the control of human legislation.

> 'How small, of all the ills that men endure,
> The part which Kings or States can cause or cure!'

He was here arguing in a statesman-like but peculiarly English spirit. The Legislature of no other country whatever has shown so vigilant and constant a solicitude for the welfare of the poorer classes; no other has so generally abstained from interference with the details and operations of trade; and it is almost equally demonstrable that the pre-eminent prosperity of our trading classes of every kind has been caused, or at least very greatly aided and promoted, by that judicious abstinence.[12]

Clearly it was not difficult to attach to this kind of 'administrative laissez-faire' (to use Professor Roberts's phrase) the increasingly fashionable doctrine of evolution and natural selection, legislative intervention being seen as something that would inhibit rather than aid the process of economic and social advance. Equally such interference could be criticized as a hopeless attempt to forestall or control the natural laws of political economy. It would, too, adversely affect the foundations of national prosperity.[13]

Associated with this belief was the corollary that the condition of the people would be more effectively improved through self-help and voluntary action which had, too, the added advantage of being more conducive to moral improvement. State aid was only appropriate in special circumstances and even then only as a supplement to, not as a replacement for, the efforts of individuals themselves. This sort of

12 Speech in House of Lords, 23 [sic] November 1819, cited in R. J. White (ed.), *The Conservative Tradition* (1950; 2nd edn, London, 1964), pp.218–19. This speech was in fact made on 30 November 1819; the reports in Parl. Deb. and *The Times* are somewhat shorter than that cited here but of the same general tenor.

13 Cf. D. Roberts, 'Tory Paternalism and Social Reform in Early Victorian England', *American Historical Review*, lxiii (1957–8), p.334; P. Smith, *Disraelian Conservatism and Social Reform* (London, 1967), p.33.

argument was used to reject the notion, increasingly prevalent among the unenfranchised classes, that once they got the vote they would be able to force Parliament to remedy the evils of their condition, a belief both mistaken and unnecessary. The real truth was that the disadvantages endured by the labouring classes were, if remediable at all, only to be dealt with by themselves and in their individual rather than in their collective capacity, by their own thrift and self-denial, not by pressing government to do that for them which they are able, if they will, to do without it. It was also morally ludicrous for working men to want the legislature to compel them to educate their children or force them in Lowe's phrase (if a Liberal view may be permitted here) 'to practise an involuntary abstinence from intoxicating liquors'![14] As Lord Derby said equally bluntly a little while afterwards to the Liverpool Working Men's Conservative Association, 'for those social improvements which we all desire, and which are in everybody's mouth, we must look to the community acting for itself in the first instance, and to Governments and legislators only in rare and exceptional cases.'[15] Northcote, in a letter written in 1875 to the Co-operative leader G. J. Holyoake, likewise stressed self-help rather than state action as the right and effective way to raise the people's condition. The working classes, he said, must be got 'to work out their own improvement for themselves.'[16] Northcote was, of course, a life-long free-trader who supported repeal of the Corn Laws even before Peel's conversion and, as President of the Board of Trade in the 1860s, had (during a Commons' discussion of regulation of the conditions of service of merchant seamen) pointed to the limits of state intervention in this and cognate respects and to the need for the men to act in their own behalf. At the same time, as a practical man of affairs, he was prepared to compromise if the claims concerned were absolutely pressing as with those of women and children who were often unable to protect their interests. But, he believed, the conditions of economic life in general were largely beyond control and he was, in consequence, sceptical about attempts at state regulation.[17] A good many Conservatives were only prepared to accept public action with reluctance, therefore, and only after the most careful scrutiny of the policy proposed. This was the case, for instance, with one of the most important of the statutes they sponsored during the Disraelian hey-day, the

14 R. Lowe, *Speeches and Letters on Reform* 2nd edn (London, 1867), p.8.
15 Reported in *The Times* (10 January 1872), p.10.
16 Cited in Smith, op. cit., p.205.
17 ibid., pp.53–4, 238–9. This diffident attitude was obviously one factor in the antipathy which existed between Northcote and Randolph Churchill. On Northcote's views see also E. J. Feuchtwanger, *Disraeli, Democracy and the Tory Party* (Oxford, 1968), pp.32–3.

Artizans' Dwellings Act of 1875.[18] Sir Henry Maine related this theme to his study of popular government which, he feared, might establish a new 'fiscal tyranny' by promising the population a living of idleness at the expense of those who 'willingly labour' and are thrifty. But this would adversely affect the motives, not only of the recipients of the dole but, much more importantly, of those on whose industrious shoulders the production of wealth depends. Maine specifically invokes Spencer's *The Man Versus the State* and the tone of the passage and its inspiration is clear from the references to 'the strenuous and never-ending struggle for existence' reflected in that 'beneficent private war which makes one man strive to climb on the shoulders of another and remain there through the law of the survival of the fittest.'[19] The general attitude was epitomized in that of one Tory radical MP, Albert Pell, who was convinced that indiscriminate aid encouraged only improvidence. He wrote his own epitaph (in Spencerian mood) as follows: 'Of long experience as a guardian of the poor in London and in the country, he condemned Poor Law Relief as inconsistent with real beneficence and adverse to the best interests of the poor'.[20]

There was also advanced an argument to the effect that the extension of state intervention could only be made at a heavy sacrifice of individual liberty. There were two main aspects to this constitutional case. One was based on the traditional fear that the growth of central administration entailed would threaten that local autonomy which was the key to our free institutions. The virtues of the citizen and the basis of civil freedom alike were to be found in independence, respect for property, local self-government, and the particularism of special groups and interests. Coleridge had always expressed a deep suspicion of Whitehall and Westminster and believed that Christian society should be promoted by the squire, magistracy, and local clergy. Of course, this was also one of Disraeli's early themes. And, for instance, in 1848 the Tory journal *John Bull*, reflecting the views of the squirearchy, argued against the Public Health Act of that year and against the idea of central boards or bureaux in favour of locally based corporations.[21] Similarly in the 1840s and 1850s the Tory publicist and barrister J. Toulmin Smith conducted a campaign against the growth of central government which he attributed to a mistaken humanitarianism on the part of the Whigs. Something will be said in more detail in a later volume about his championing the concept

18 See the passages cited in Smith, op. cit., pp.220–1.
19 Sir H. Maine, *Popular Government* (1885; 2nd edn, London, 1886), pp.49–50.
20 Smith, op. cit., p.141 and n.1. For Pell, see *DNB* ii.2831. His posthumous *Reminiscences* (London, 1908) were edited by the extreme libertarian Thomas Mackay who also supervised the anti-Fabian *A Plea for Liberty* (London, 1891).
21 *John Bull* (13 May 1848), cited in Roberts, art. cit., p.333.

of local self-government and his attack on what he called 'presumptuous *empiricism*', that is, the piecemeal but cumulative collectivist tendency which he saw as undermining the principles of English liberty.[22] But the gist of his view, which was typical, that state action was anathema is revealed in the following characteristic passage in which he rejects the centralization involved in such action because it would

> take away the free action of every man over his own property [and] stay the free use by every or any man of his own resources and his own ingenuity. Universal obedience to the schemes and crotchets of one or two closet-theorists is proclaimed to be more conducive to human progress than the ceaseless and multitudinous energy and enterprise of millions of active, intelligent and practical men, daily meeting face to face the difficulties to be overcome, and directly interested in attaining the best results and making the furthest advances. *This is what Centralization really is*, stripped of the specious disguises under which its advocates seek to cover its natural repulsiveness. The crotchets of individuals, having no special gift and no possible special ubiquity or omniscience . . . are to be enforced as *Law* upon the whole land. Every man is to be permitted to do *that only* with his own which these individuals may be pleased to let him.[23]

Nor was this view later lost to sight. Speaking in 1879 on the question of educational provision, Auberon Herbert made very clear his hostility to a centrally imposed scheme:

> I dread the uniformity of system, the monotony and the routine that Government is inflicting upon us. I am exceedingly jealous of this power exercised by the centre. I want to give the parts more room and a fuller sphere of action. I want to throw more responsibility upon them, and I want to leave them freer each to chose a plan which seems best suited to their own needs and wishes.[24]

There was, too, a like fear that Parliament, dominated by the representatives of a popular majority mandated to carry out its will, would constitute the basis of a new tyranny more effective and extensive even than royalist absolutism. In the terms later popularized by Spencer, the divine right of kings would be replaced by the divine right of Parliament as the great superstition of the day.[25] For example, in 1874,

---

22　See vol.iii, *A Much-Governed Nation*, ch.2. The phrase cited is from Smith's *Government by Commissions Illegal and Pernicious* (London, 1849), p.367, italics in original.

23　J. Toulmin Smith, *Centralization or Representation?* (London, 1848), p.x note*, italics in original.

24　Cited in S. H. Harris, *Auberon Herbert: Crusader for Liberty* (London, 1943), p.283.

25　Spencer, *The Man Versus the State* (1884; Penguin, 1969), pp.151, 254.

Lord Salisbury, speaking on the issue of temperance and licensing, warned against entering 'the regions of paternal Government' for, given 'a political system where power resided with the greatest numbers', authority under such a régime might in time be used in undesirable ways.[26] Hence the famous opinion of W. C. Magee, the Tory Bishop of Peterborough (and later Archbishop of York), that he would rather see England free than compulsorily sober. There was, he said (in 1876), 'too great a tendency on the part of those who were gaining political power in the State to believe that legislation could do everything for them, and that as little as possible was to be done by themselves.' Working men 'were too willing to give up their own freedom . . . by bringing about some larger and sweeping action on the part of the State.'[27] It was, perhaps, one thing to use the power of government for purposes of social amelioration at the initiative or in the interest of the propertied classes; it was quite another to acquiesce in reform carried out more and more at the behest of a mass electorate, for this could only end in redistributive taxation, the insecurity of property, a threat to liberty, and thus to the social order itself. One Conservative MP, discussing a Scottish Education Bill, deplored the tendency to subject 'all mankind' to such 'penal legislation'. 'If anybody were called on to portray the advancing civilization of England, it might be fitly conveyed by the representation of a large prison.'[28]

Many Conservatives, then, commonly believed in the minimal or limited state, holding to the view that the 'province of legislation was simply to maintain law and order' and not to interfere with the morals and activities of the people.[29] This is, of course, simply the Burkeian point with which this section began. Professor Smith's summary of the position as it was in the middle decades of the century is that the Conservative Party 'was, in fact, predisposed against rather than towards the extension of governmental intervention in social questions.'[30] It was not at all inappropriate, therefore, for one MP to observe, in a debate at this time, that all the free-trade arguments were coming from the Conservative benches.[31]

Many examples of this libertarian Conservatism might be indicated of which the following must stand as representative.

One leading, if somewhat eccentric, expositor of these sentiments was

26 220 Parl. Deb. 3s., 7 July 1874, col. 1190. Disraeli had earlier expressed similar views e.g. W. Hutcheon (ed.), *Whigs and Whiggism: Political Writings by Benjamin Disraeli* (London, 1913), pp.148–9, 158, 185, 354.
27 230 Parl. Deb. 3s., 30 June 1876, cols 724–5.
28 211 Parl. Deb. 3s., 20 June 1872, col.2013 (J. H. Scourfield).
29 229 Parl. Deb. 3s., 14 June 1876, col.1839 (A. Mills).
30 Smith, op. cit., p.34.
31 229 Parl. Deb. 3s., 14 June 1876, col.1862 (G. Storer).

Francis Charteris, who from 1853 was known as Lord Elcho until he succeeded thirty years later to the title of 10th Earl of Wemyss and March.[32] A landed aristocrat with some industrial interests, he had early in life been a Young England Tory but in 1846 became a Peelite and never subsequently wavered in his devotion to free trade. He ultimately came to rest in the Conservative ranks. Elcho was concerned to defend both the political and social position of his order and the basic truth of the laws of political economy. He was thus prepared to oppose the challenge of middle- and working-class power and to resist the attempt to impose any great degree of state regulation on the free market. This meant that there were fairly severe limits to the degree of legislative action or supervision he would condone. He was prepared for the state to help protect innocents who might otherwise be harshly dealt with by the 'invisible hand', say, women and children in bad factory conditions; but he would not go much further. Political reform he rejected as leading to the dominance of the lower classes and likely, therefore, to stimulate further demand for state intervention.[33] He had indeed been a leading 'Adullamite' opposed to the enlargement of the franchise in 1867. A later foe, especially after 1880, was the collectivism to which the extension of the vote to the urban householder inevitably led.[34] It is not surprising, therefore, that he was a founding member and major financial supporter of the Liberty and Property Defence League.

This body was set up in July 1882 to resist overlegislation, maintain freedom of contract, advocate individualism, and combat attempts at government control of economic and social life.[35] It was a most active

32 On Earl Wemyss (1818–1914), see *DNB*, and two papers in K. D. Brown (ed.), *Essays in Anti-Labour History: Responses to the Rise of Labour in Britain* (London, 1974): one is by C. J. Kauffman, 'Lord Elcho, Trade Unionism and Democracy', a useful account of Elcho's ambivalent attitude towards the growing power of trade unionism; the other is by N. Soldon, 'Laissez-Faire as Dogma: the Liberty and Property Defence League, 1882–1914'. In addition two so far unpublished PhD theses are full of information on Elcho and related matters: N. Soldon, *Laissez-Faire on the Defensive: the Story of the Liberty and Property Defence League, 1882–1914* (University of Delaware, 1969), esp. ch. II; and E. J. Bristow, *The Defence of Liberty and Property in Britain, 1880–1914* (Yale University, 1970). Part of the material in Dr Bristow's thesis as well as some new matter is contained in his 'The Liberty and Property Defence League and Individualism', *Historical Journal*, xviii (1975), pp. 761–89.

33 Kauffman, in Brown, op. cit., p. 201.

34 An interesting comment is provided by a letter Wemyss wrote on 5 May 1899 to Lord Salisbury (who had helped him oppose, though unsuccessfully, a bill to enforce the compulsory provision of seats for shop assistants): 'Thanks for last night. Let us hope that the House of Commons, having taken shop girls seats in hand, has thus touched bottom in Social Legislation', Salisbury Papers, cited in Bristow, *The Defence of Liberty and Property in Britain*, p. 96.

35 There is very full description of the League and its work as well as that of the many like associations of the time in the volumes cited in n. 32 above.

pressure group in this cause and often cited by Socialists as representative of the libertarian point of view.[36] Though ostensibly not partisan, its membership consisted largely of Whigs and Conservatives with the latter predominating as time went on.[37] These people were of various sorts: landowners and landlords worried by contemporary legislative tendencies; members of the 'trade' (quite a lot of these); employers who felt threatened by union activity or statutory control; and ideologues who sustained an uncompromising individualism. The main doctrinal inspiration was, of course, Herbert Spencer; and two of his disciples Wordsworth Donisthorpe and W. C. Crofts were especially involved in the foundation and activities of the League.[38] In fact, they were also closely involved in the Personal Rights Association founded in 1871 (and still in existence) to campaign against (among other things) the state regulation of prostitution, compulsory vaccination, and vivisection. Its journal was called the *Individualist*, a title which indicates the political stance clearly enough. A couple of years later they had set up another individualist group, the name of which – the Political Evolution Society – suggests its Spencerian style and whose purpose was to warn of the 'dangerous principle' which lay behind 'measures of a repressive or paternal character'.[39] The weekly journal associated with this society was (equally indicatively) entitled *Let Be*. In 1880 they changed the name of the latter group to the State Resistance Union and in due course became associated with Lord Elcho in the attempt to found a non-party organization to resist collectivist legislation and to sustain freedom of contract. The result was the foundation of the LPDL.[40] It became linked with various trade associations and other bodies with interests similar to its own such as the London Ratepayers Defence League, the various Free Labour Associations, and the Middle Class Defence League. It conducted propaganda activities at both national and local levels; published a

---

36 e.g. S. Webb, *The Difficulties of Individualism* (Fabian tract no. 69; London, 1896), p. 18; *idem*, *English Progress Towards Social Democracy* (Fabian tract no. 15; 1892; London, 1906), p. 3; G. B. Shaw *et al.*, *Fabian Essays* (1889; Jubilee edn, London, 1950), p. 49; S. Ball, *The Moral Aspects of Socialism* (Fabian tract no. 72; 1896; London, 1906), p. 12; W. Clarke, 'The Fabian Society and its Work', *Socialism: the Fabian Essays* (US edn, Boston, 1894), pp. xxx–xxxi.

37 H. Spencer, *The Man Versus the State*, p. 81 n. Cf. Spencer's letter to the Earl of Wemyss (1 March 1884), in D. Duncan, *The Life and Letters of Herbert Spencer* (London, 1908), p. 242. Sidney Webb recognized its political inclination when he argued that its propaganda was ineffective 'even' with Conservative Parliaments, Shaw *et al.*, *Fabian Essays*, p. 49. Cf. Bristow, op. cit., ch. 1, esp. pp. 7–9.

38 For a specific acknowledgement of Spencer's influence, see e.g. Lord Bramwell, *Laissez-Faire* (London, 1884), p. 5.

39 Cited by Soldon, in Brown, op. cit., p. 210.

40 Soldon in Brown, op. cit., pp. 210–12; Soldon, *Laissez-Faire on the Defensive*, pp. 108, 110 ff. See also *Self-Help v. State-Help. The Liberty and Property Defence League: its Origins, Objects and Inaugural. 1882* (London, 1883).

journal called, at first, *Jus* or the *Liberty Annual* and then the *Liberty Review* (whose editor was Frederick Millar, an admirer of the individualist Auberon Herbert); tried to influence the course of Parliamentary proceedings; and so on. Under its aegis a series of pamphlets was issued to help sustain its case, much of this propaganda being in the style of Toulmin Smith and his *Parliamentary Remembrancer* a generation before.[41] The slightest extension of government control at either central or local level was attacked as incompatible with a genuine individuality. For instance, a Bill to pay from the rates the expenses of the metropolitan fire brigade was regarded as 'a confiscatory measure of the worst order' and as reflecting 'one of the best illustrations of the rapid advance and mischievous effects of state-socialism.'[42] Centralization, a major target, was held only to educate a nation 'to political incapacity'.[43] And, of course, the general anti-collectivist theme was much explored. For instance, one speaker addressing the League in 1884 said that the main political problem in the democratic age now in prospect was to limit the power of the many and to protect the individual against state intervention and growing public expenditure (financed out of increased taxation) in respect of services provided for the masses. All such interference involved infringement of personal liberty and was, therefore, wrong.

> Freedom is the true solution for many of our troubles – the utmost freedom that can be given to industry – the utmost freedom for a man to contract, or to bestow his labour upon any subject he chooses, without State interference, while the only protection which the Government has a right and duty to extend over its subjects is the protection of life, liberty, limb, and property, from injury by others. . . .[44]

Lord Bramwell, a famous judge and supporter of the League, wrote a paean of praise for the laws of political economy which, he claimed, taught *laissez faire* and free trade:

> Leave every one to seek his own happiness in his own way, provided he

41 e.g. *Overlegislation in 1884. Review of the Bills of the Session . . .* (London, 1884); the Earl of Wemyss, *Socialism at St. Stephens in 1883* (London, 1884); W. Donisthorpe, *Liberty or Law?* (London, 1884); and perhaps the most comprehensive, T. Mackay (ed.), *A Plea for Liberty* (London, 1891) written as a riposte to the *Fabian Essays* of 1889. On Mackay, see J. W. Mason, 'Thomas Mackay: the Anti-Socialist Philosophy of the Charity Organisation Society', in Brown, op. cit., ch. 12.

42 *Overlegislation in 1884*, p. 8.

43 M. J. Lyons, *Radicalism and Ransome* (London, n.d. [1888?]), pp. 8–9.

44 E. Pleydell-Bouverie, *The Province of Government: an Address Delivered Before the Liberty & Property Defence League* (London, 1884), *passim*, the passage cited being at p. 15, Bouverie had been a prominent Liberal of the old Whig school but in 1873 he broke with Gladstone and retired from active politics four years later; he was a close friend of Wemyss's.

does not injure others. Govern as little as possible. Meddle not, interfere not, any more than you can help. Trust to each man knowing his own interest better, and pursuing it more earnestly than the law can do it for him.[45]

The League was aware that Liberal radicals and Tory Democrats alike were disposed to advance collectivist schemes and indeed to rival one another in so doing; but it was hoped that true Conservatives would soon disengage themselves from 'this disastrous contest.'[46] They should recognize that many evils – like the drink problem – simply cannot be tackled by law.[47] The League in fact lingered on until the 1930s continuing its opposition to collectivist development; it seems its last manifestation was a letter in *The Times* in 1929 from its then secretary, Frederick Millar, protesting about the dangers of extending municipal trading. But, of course, by then, in an age of large organization and after a century of state intervention, its individualist stress seemed to many anachronistic.[48] Though it was not so to all as will be seen.

It is certainly clear, however, that at the end of the nineteenth century the libertarian wing of Conservatism was most active and of some significance. It had leaders of note and could draw on considerable electoral and other support.[49] Some of the Unionists who split from the Liberals over Home Rule were free-traders and (like Chamberlain on the other side of the doctrinal fence) carried their ideas with them into the Conservative ranks thus reinforcing the libertarian ideas already strongly present there. Nor, when the issue arose, was opposition confined to the protection of home industry alone; it was recognized there was logically a duty to reject proposals to extend public control in other ways. Lord Cromer who, after a long military and diplomatic career, entered politics as a Unionist free-trader wrote in a letter in 1910: 'I have never accepted the view that a Free Trade policy means merely an absence of taxes imposed for protective purposes. . . . It means the support of individualism against collectivism'.[50]

Goschen is a particularly good example here. Although he spent most of his political life supporting the Liberal cause Goschen finally joined the Conservative Party in 1893 having, of course, been formally aligned with it since he accepted Cabinet office under Salisbury in 1886 after Randolph Churchill's resignation. He was a lifelong libertarian. In 1861

---

45 Lord Bramwell, *Economics v. Socialism* (London, 1888), p.10. Cf. his *Laissez-Faire* which he concludes with the call, '*Vive Laissez faire!*', ibid., p.22.
46 Liberty and Property Defence League, *Annual Report* (1893–4), pp.6–7.
47 Lord Bramwell, *Drink* (London, 1885).
48 Soldon in Brown, op. cit., pp.231–3. Millar died in 1933.
49 Cf. R. B. McDowell, *British Conservatism, 1832–1914* (London, 1959), p.168.
50 Cromer to B. Mallet (23 February 1910), in Marquess of Zetland, *Lord Cromer* (London, 1932), p.323.

he had brought out a well-known book on the theory of foreign exchanges in which the orthodox economic position about self-regulating markets and the like is taken up. Early in his Parliamentary career – he entered the House of Commons in 1863 – his speeches (as he later said) 'struck the note of that objection to the encroachments of Government interference on the freedom of individual action which . . . has coloured to a certain extent my political opinions throughout my career.'[51] And although he had supported electoral reform in 1867 he was always concerned about the possible collectivist impact of the change and in fact opposed further legislation of the kind mainly for this reason.[52] He was a fervent opponent of compulsory equality because the attempt to achieve it would annihilate freedom.[53] Opposition to Home Rule finally drove him out of the Liberal fold – as it did Joseph Chamberlain. But otherwise they were poles apart. Although they served together in the Unionist Cabinet from 1895 to 1900 (when Goschen retired) Chamberlain's tariff reform campaign brought Goschen back into politics to defend free trade on the ground that tariffs would increase government power and further pave the way to state Socialism.[54]

Other members of this Conservative and Liberal Unionist free-trade group were Hicks-Beach, C. T. Ritchie, Lord Hugh Cecil and his brother Robert, Elliot (Goschen's biographer and editor of the *Edinburgh Review*), and John St Loe Strachey of *The Spectator*.[55] Strachey for another reflects a syndrome of actions and attitudes similar to those of Goschen. He ceased supporting the Liberals over Home Rule yet differed with many Conservatives about tariff reform. Under his sway *The Spectator*, though strongly Unionist and imperialist, favoured non-intervention in domestic affairs and was firmly even vituperatively opposed to the kind of social policies espoused by Chamberlain and George.[56] This sort of sentiment was of some importance at that time. Hostility to the interventionist and welfare policies of the new Liberalism drove some previously Liberal supporters into the Tory ranks despite the tariff reform campaign. Many of the Manchester cotton industrialists

51 A. R. D. Elliot, *The Life of George Joachim Goschen, First Viscount Goschen, 1831–1907* (London, 1911), i.60. See e.g. the following speeches: 172 Parl. Deb. 3s., 8 July 1863, col. 407; 174 ibid., 3 May 1864, col.2126; 177 ibid., 23 February 1865, cols 630–1.
52 See vol.1, *The Rise of Collectivism*, pp.214–15.
53 Goschen's *Addresses* (Edinburgh, 1885), p.12 and other references cited by T. J. Spinner, Jr, 'George Joachim Goschen: the Man Lord Randolph Churchill "Forgot"', *Journal of Modern History*, xxxix (1967), pp.415–16.
54 ibid., p.424.
55 McDowell, op. cit., p.168.
56 ibid., pp.169–70. Cf. Strachey's *The Adventures of Living: a Subjective Autobiography* (London, 1922), chs xxvi, xxvii. In 1908 Strachey published a work on *The Problems and Perils of Socialism*.

reacted in this way believing that free trade (to which a good number of them had not been wholly committed in any case) was, in the face of a Socialist threat, an expendable part of *laissez faire*.[57] Strachey wrote in 1909 that 'Old Age Pensions is going to turn out the grave of Free Trade', and he was disinclined to recognize as true free-traders those 'who confine their observation of free-trade principles to exports and imports and violate those principles in the most cynical way in all the other departments of public activity'.[58]

The opposition to Tory democracy, or indeed any extensive form of collectivism, was expressed in the anonymous Spencerian pages of a tract published in 1892 the author of which thought the Conservatives were giving way too much under the democratic pressures of the day.[59] It was conceded that a limited state intervention was legitimate to deal with manifest evils; but government should never attempt to do for people what they could reasonably be expected to do for themselves. The purpose of the state was prevention or warning not promotion by compulsion.[60] With the current tendency to interfere, which Conservatives were themselves misguidedly encouraging, it would not be long before there was created a 'sort of vast foundling hospital' looking after people from the cradle to the grave.[61] Under this form of social democracy the state will become 'the universal regulator of morals and manners, the sole director of education, the employer, the paymaster, and the landlord of the nation, the irresponsible dictator of society.' It will thus 'pervade and dominate all departments of human life'.[62] And if in the stern arena of international competition the British Empire shall ever falter and fail it will be because the energies of its people will thus have been sapped from within, 'dying from sheer poorness of blood, from the State-aided survival of the unfittest.'[63]

Two of the most extreme and well-known libertarian publicists with Conservative affiliations were Auberon Herbert and Wordsworth Donisthorpe. Herbert (1838–1906) was in the true line of aristocratic eccentrics, interested in a whole range of things from war to bicycling, from psychic research to prehistoric artefacts. Beatrice Webb, referring to his continual (and, as she believed, ineffectual) battle with the growing strength of the collectivist foe, called him 'the Don Quixote of the

57 P. F. Clarke, 'The End of Laissez Faire and the Politics of Cotton', *Historical Journal*, xv (1972), pp.493–512.
58 Cited ibid., pp.507–8.
59 'A Plain Tory', *Tory Democracy and Conservative Policy* (London, 1892), pp.4–5, 10.
60 ibid., pp.149–50, 152–3.
61 ibid., p.152.
62 ibid., p.194.
63 ibid., p.152.

nineteenth century'.[64] He was a staunch Conservative in his younger days and for long had close links with the party.[65] However he then began to incline more towards Liberalism and in 1870 was elected to Parliament in that interest.[66] Nevertheless (to complete this aspect of his story) he gradually returned to the Tory allegiance which both his training and temperament made more natural.[67] This was specifically because he found (with Spencer and many others) that the individualism, which he saw as increasingly important and congenial, was more sympathetically reflected in Conservative circles. Crucial to this transformation of affiliation and doctrine was Herbert's meeting and 'memorable' talk with Spencer at the Athenaeum in the early 1870s, the significance of which he later described as follows:

> I have often laughed and said that, as far as I myself was concerned, [Herbert Spencer] spoilt my political life. I went into the House of Commons, as a young man, believing that we might do much for the people by a bolder and more unsparing use of the powers that belonged to the great law-making machine; and great, as it then seemed to me, were those still unexhausted resources of united national action on behalf of the common welfare. It was at that moment that I had the privilege of meeting Mr. Spencer, and the talk which we had – a talk that will always remain very memorable to me – set me busily to work to study his writings. As I read and thought over what he taught, a new window was opened in my mind. I lost my faith in the great machine; I saw that thinking and acting for others had always hindered not helped the real progress; that all forms of compulsion deadened the living forces in a nation; . . . . I no longer believed that the handful of us – however well-intentioned we might be – spending our nights in the House, could manufacture the life of a nation, could endow it out of hand with happiness, wisdom and prosperity, and clothe it in all the virtues.[68]

The basic lesson Herbert learned from this study was that the end of all legislation should be the care, preservation, and extension of individual liberty. It followed, as stated in the principles of the Personal Rights and Self-Help Association (which Herbert helped to launch), that it was necessary to oppose the multiplication of laws tending to control and

64 B. Webb, *Our Partnership* (London, 1948), p. 32.
65 S. H. Harris, *Auberon Herbert: Crusader for Liberty*, pp. 38, 54, 71 ff. On Herbert, see also N. Soldon's thesis, *Laissez-Faire on the Defensive*, esp. pp. 258–61.
66 Harris, op. cit., pp. 75, 82 n., 85, 98.
67 ibid., pp. 210, 320.
68 A. Herbert, 'Mr. Spencer and the Great Machine', *The Voluntaryist Creed* (London, 1908), pp. 5–6. Cf. the passage about this meeting from Herbert's Journal, cited in Harris, op. cit., pp. 155–6; also ibid., p. 266.

direct the affairs of the people.[69] No one, Herbert thus believed, will do any good in politics unless he acts on Spencer's 'great truth', that 'man must be free if he is to possess happiness'.[70] In glossing this principle Herbert went indeed farther in the individualist direction than the Master himself asserting in a more extreme way the principle that any service the people requires 'must be done by themselves' acting where necessary 'by means of voluntary association.'[71] So in addition to the usual sort of policies that there must be no state ownership of land or other property, no legislative protection of labour or educational provision, there was also the startling and extraordinary proposal that all taxation must be voluntary for otherwise coercion is involved which is always unjust.[72] Government, politics itself, with all the wastes and frustrations entailed, must be reduced to the uttermost minimum for in no other way will human energy be fully released and faculties satisfied.[73] For Herbert, even national defence should so far as possible be conducted on voluntaryist and local lines.[74] He never wavered from the belief that 'it is not laissez-faire that has failed' but rather the courage to see and expound the essential truth it contains, 'to point towards the true remedies' and away from the sham panaceas of collectivism.[75] It is really hardly any wonder that T. H. Huxley could discern no 'logical boundary between Mr. Herbert's position and that of Bakounine', the anarchist.[76]

While often assuming a similar stance on most questions of practical politics, Wordsworth Donisthorpe, a Tory barrister, did not adopt quite so extreme a theoretical position as Herbert. He believed most fervently in what he called the principle of 'Let Be' and that in the long run events must tend in the direction of a diminishing role for government. At the same time he was prepared to accept that the existing state of affairs regrettably required some degree of collective action: so the key contemporary issue was what limits to liberty were appropriate for the

69 See the passages cited in Harris, op. cit., pp.189, 206–7.
70 A. Herbert, *A Politician in Trouble about his Soul* (London, 1884), p.222. Cf. esp. the papers published as *The Right and Wrong of Compulsion by the State* (London, 1885).
71 Herbert, *A Politician in Trouble about his Soul*, p.255. But not any form of association is proper and just: see e.g. Herbert's attack on the coercive and restrictive aspects of the 'New Unionism' in 'The True Line of Deliverance', T. Mackay (ed.), *A Plea for Liberty: an Argument against Socialism and Socialistic Legislation* (1891; 2nd edn, London, 1891), ch.XII.
72 Herbert, *A Politician in Trouble about his Soul*, pp.268ff.
73 ibid., pp.283–6. Cf. Harris, op. cit., p.302.
74 R. Barker, *Political Ideas in Modern Britain* (London, 1978), p.56.
75 Herbert, *A Politician in Trouble about his Soul*, p.223.
76 T. H. Huxley, 'Government: Anarchy or Regimentation', *The Nineteenth Century*, xxvii (1890), p.860. Though see also a response from Herbert, 'What is Anarchy?' in the letter column of *The Westminster Gazette* (7 August 1894), p.2. The vendetta continued: see ibid. (11 August 1894), p.2; and 'The Anarchist Peril', ibid. (20 August 1894), p.3; etc.

moment.[77] Donisthorpe did not think any abstract, general answer was possible; but he forcefully observed in Spencerian fashion that much the state has tried to do in the past has not at all diminished the evils aimed at and often had untoward consequences in itself. So in this respect the lesson and tendency of history were clear.[78] He was a close associate of Spencer's and, for instance, involved with him in an abortive scheme to tabulate Acts of Parliament with a view to contrasting their intended purpose with the undesirable effects that actually followed.[79]

Notions of this kind were in fact widespread throughout the libertarian wing of Conservatism. Referring to one of the leading members of the LPDL, Lord Bramwell, Sidney Webb wrote that he 'will give cogent reasons for the belief that absolute freedom of contract, subject to the trifling exception of a drastic criminal law, will ensure a perfect State.'[80] Not insignificantly – perhaps indeed, most important of all – Lord Salisbury himself (who was Prime Minister for more than a decade in all at the end of the century) was strongly opposed to collectivist legislation as deleterious in its effect on a sense of personal responsibility and obligation.[81]

In a Fabian tract first published in 1893 G. B. Shaw summed up what all these people stood for, drawing attention also to their diverse party origins:

> The old Whigs and new Tories of the school of Cobden and Bright, the 'Philosophic Radicals,' the economists of whom Bastiat is the type, Lord Wemyss and Lord Bramwell, Mr. Herbert Spencer and Mr. Auberon Herbert, Mr. Gladstone, Mr. Arthur Balfour, Mr. John Morley, Mr. Leonard Courtney: any of these is, in England, a more typical Anarchist than Bakounin. They distrust State action, and are jealous advocates of the prerogative of the individual, proposing to restrict the one and to extend the other as far as is humanly possible, in opposition to the Social-Democrat, who proposes to democratize the State and throw upon it the whole work of organizing the national industry, thereby making it the most vital organ in the social body.[82]

Many of these strands of anti-statist sentiment were brought together

77 W. Donisthorpe, 'The Limits of Liberty' in Mackay, op. cit., pp.65, 68–70, 78.
78 ibid., pp.87, 99–100, 106.
79 D. Duncan, *The Life and Letters of Herbert Spencer* (London, 1908), pp.316–17. On Donisthorpe, see also Soldon, *Laissez-Faire on the Defensive*, pp.252–7.
80 In Shaw *et al.*, *Fabian Essays*, p.30.
81 See A. Jones and M. Bentley, 'Salisbury and Baldwin' in M. Cowling (ed.), *Conservative Essays* (London, 1978), pp.27–8. At the same time Salisbury was not prepared to rule out some social responsibility for government where special circumstances might warrant it: see above pp.228–9.
82 G. B. Shaw, *The Impossibilities of Anarchism* (Fabian tract no.45; n.d. [1893]; London, 1895), pp.4–5.

after 1905 in the British Constitution Association, an interesting if not very long-lived body which has, until quite recently, received little attention. But because of its very representativeness it demands some notice here.

'THE NEW CANUTE'

... as the waters approached, he commanded them to retire ... but ...
the sea still advanced towards him. ...
D. HUME, *The History of England*, ed., 1773, i.152

One commentator, writing in 1908 about the development of imperialist policies, observed that to the new generation of Tories an extended use of state machinery was not at all unthinkable. 'Gone, indeed', he said, 'is the pure individualism of Lord Morley and Lord Hugh Cecil, with its profound distrust of all State action, and its indifference to the use or waste of the national man-power.' But, he added, a 'devoted few under the aegis of Lord Hugh and Mr. Strachey' have raised the 'last sanctuary' of this libertarian doctrine 'in the British Constitutional Association'. And he correctly noted, too, the relevance in these debates of 'the great corollaries of evolution.'[83]

The Association was founded in 1905 with an ostensibly all-party appeal but it had in fact a largely Conservative membership. Its main contemporary role was to provide a focus and rationale for resistance not only to the programme of the new Liberal government but also to the pressure in the Conservative Party itself to rethink its attitude to social change so that it might be in a more competitive electoral position. In terms of intra-party tendencies the Association was opposed to everything that Joseph Chamberlain stood for in respect of economic and social reform generally and, very specifically, in respect of his repudiation of Spencer's doctrines. The Association's first President was Lord Hugh Cecil who was succeeded by Lord Balfour of Burleigh, the Scottish Conservative peer. Its leading members included such well-known Conservatives and Unionists as Lord Avebury, A. V. Dicey, Lord Courtney, and John St Loe Strachey, as well as some non-political public figures such as Professor Flinders Petrie. Others connected with the Association included Mrs T. H. Green, J. A. R. Marriott, F. A. Sibly, A. L. Smith, and Percy Wyndham.[84] This membership has recently been described, somewhat pejoratively, as 'a curious mixture of unionist free traders, orthodox poor law administrators, and followers of Herbert Spencer.'[85] The Association did not have a long effective life though it

83 Norman Chamberlain, 'The New Imperialism and the Old Parties', *The National Review*, li (1908), p.646.
84 BCA, *Constitution Papers* (no.3, August 1906), p.5.
85 K. D. Brown, 'The Anti-Socialist Union, 1908–49' in K. D. Brown (ed.), *Essays in*

lingered on till 1918. But its existence even for this short space of time provides evidence of Conservative fears about the positive state then being zealously constructed. A contemporary newspaper entitled an article about one of the BCA conferences, 'The New Canute', because the Association was trying to 'check the further advance of the Collectivist tide.'[86]

In a symposium published in 1908 to expound 'British Constitutionism', it was stated that the central purpose was 'to uphold the fundamental principles of . . . personal liberty and responsibility – and to limit the functions of governing bodies accordingly.'[87] The strength of a nation, it was argued, depended on the quality of its citizens and on the greatest possible elevation of their character through self-help. This could only be achieved by ensuring that people assumed all their personal responsibilities and by encouraging them to do things for themselves either as individuals or through voluntary co-operation. Interference in this would bring the capable down to the level of the inefficient and so promote social weakness.[88] It seemed to follow that the 'spread of Collectivist ideas', being of a contrary tendency, would threaten

to destroy the moral fibre of the British people by encouraging all classes to rely for their well-being upon Parliament or Municipalities rather than upon their own efforts. No legislation will make a people religious, or moral, or temperate, or industrious, and the Association has set itself to the work of bringing home to the public conscience the truth that the source of well-being is individual effort. . . .[89]

The Association held, therefore, that the trammels of bureaucracy were to be deplored wherever they appeared and that the state should so far as possible be restricted to its 'primary functions' of protecting the country from invasion and securing the administration of justice. Its encroachments elsewhere must be challenged and hampered; and it was fortunate that with the 'advance of civilisation' it would be more and more feasible to reach in this respect the 'irreducible minimum'.[90]

Anti-Labour History: Responses to the Rise of Labour in Britain (London, 1974), p.239. Cf. ibid., p.284; also E. J. Bristow, *The Defence of Liberty and Property in Britain, 1880–1914* (unpublished PhD thesis, Yale University, 1970), pp.29, 308–9.

86 *Oxford Chronicle* (19 July 1907), cited in M. H. Judge (ed.), *Political Socialism: a Remonstrance. A Collection of Papers by Members of the British Constitution Association. . . .* (Westminster, 1908), pp.151–2.

87 ibid., p.179.

88 ibid., pp.1, 3–4, 92–3, 179.

89 ibid., pp.179–80. Cf. C. W. Saleeby, *Individualism and Collectivism: Four Lectures* (London, 1906), ch.III, esp. pp.92, 101. It should perhaps be noted that Dr Saleeby later so far changed his allegiance as to join the Fabian Society; see B. Webb, *Our Partnership* (London, 1948), pp.460, 523.

90 Judge, op. cit., pp.180–1.

The implications of this attitude for social and economic life were accepted and clearly spelled out. Because, as Dicey said, 'State help kills self-help', opposition was expressed to a universal state scheme of old age pensions, unemployment relief, limitation of the working-day (as in the Eight Hours Bill proposed for the coal-mines in 1908), municipal trading, and the like.[91] Particular objection was taken to increased expenditure on a system of compulsory education on the ground *inter alia* that responsibility for seeing children were educated lay with the parents.[92] In the context of this question, Dicey again bluntly expressed the Spencerian view of the Association by querying the proposal to provide meals for schoolchildren either from the rates or general taxation. Why, he wrote, should a man 'who first neglects his duty as a father' (by not feeding his children properly) and who 'then defrauds the State' (by accepting meals paid out of public funds) 'retain his full political rights'?[93] Opposition was also expressed to proposals to tax land values and to relieve the stringency of Poor Law relief.[94] So far as economic affairs were concerned, government was warned to refrain from interfering where work could be done more economically and efficiently by private enterprise. Similarly redistributive taxation was held to be unacceptable in its effects.[95]

The doctrine was summarized by Lord Balfour of Burleigh in an address on the dangers of 'political Socialism':

> The essential condition for the progress of a community is that the incentive to efficiency on the part of its individuals shall be of the strongest possible kind. This required incentive can only be supplied by a strict application of the principle that the earnings of each individual shall be securely preserved to him. The development of our system of justice has been governed by this principle, and its chief aim has been to prevent individuals from plundering one another, and to maintain intact for each whatever he has earned. But it is forgotten that the evil to the community is as great whether the plunderer be merely an individual member of society or society itself. In either case the citizen is deprived of the fruits of his labours, and the result to him is the same. Year by year more legislation is proposed of which the effect is to draw upon the earnings of the efficient for the benefit of the inefficient. Year by year Parliament makes life harder for those whose

91 A. V. Dicey, *Lectures on the Relation Between Law & Public Opinion in England During the Nineteenth Century* (1905; 2nd edn, London, 1920), pp. 257–8.
92 See e.g. the BCA leaflet *The Education Act of 1906*; Saleeby, op. cit., p. 16; *Constitution Papers* (no. 3, August 1906) pp. 9–10.
93 Dicey, op. cit., intro. to 2nd edn, p. 1. Cf. the similar criticism of the old age pension scheme, ibid., pp. xxxiv–xxxv.
94 *Constitution Papers* (1909), *passim*.
95 Judge, op. cit., p. 182.

labour benefits the State, and easier for those who are a drag upon it.

In the supposed interests of the 'majority,' now one now another section is victimised, and the 'liberty of the individual' through constant infringement becomes little more than a phrase.[96]

It should always be remembered, indeed, that government expenditure is itself unproductive and that the state can give nothing to one section of the people 'which is not taken from another'. 'Political socialism' was, in fact, defined as legislation in the interests of a special class, namely, those who are the least efficient, and it was to be deplored whether it came from Liberal or Unionist quarters.[97] Dicey was quite specific. Speaking to the Association's conference in 1908 on the subject of guarantees against oppression, he said, 'We dread the passing of laws, and still more the administration of the law, in accordance, not with the deliberate and real will of the majority of the nation, but with the immediate wishes of a class, namely, the class . . . of wage earners. *We fear class legislation*'. He then indicated what he had in mind by referring to the Trade Disputes Act, which gave special legal privileges to this class, and the Old Age Pension Act which, in his view, introduced 'a calamitous revolution of our whole social system'. 'Look wherever we will', he went on, 'we see Statutes which limit the freedom of men or of women to enter into otherwise lawful contracts and to sell their own labour on such terms as they themselves see fit to accept.' The motive is benevolence and electoral popularity; but the interference with personal freedom and responsibility which is involved can only lead to disaster.[98] As Dicey was aware, if the mass of electors was determined to have this kind of policy then nothing could stop it. But in this situation he and others looked to various institutional devices – such as the maintenance of the House of Lords' suspensory veto, the use of the referendum, and the introduction of proportional representation – to delay the pursuit of such legislative folly.[99]

In elaborating these themes members of the Association acknowledged, of course, the libertarian aspects of the writings of J. S. Mill and the 'older economists'.[100] But from the surviving documents it is quite clear that Herbert Spencer's was the main intellectual influence at work. His

96 ibid., pp.174–5.
97 ibid., pp.5, 182; *Constitution Papers* (no.4, 15 November 1907), p.17. Not surprisingly W. H. Mallock's *A Critical Examination of Socialism* (1908) was favourably received, ibid. (no.9, 15 April 1908), pp.62–3.
98 *Constitution Papers* (no.14, 15 September 1908), pp.117–18, italics in original. This is the general burden, too, of Dicey's *Law & Public Opinion*: see especially the intro. to 2nd edn (1914).
99 *Constitution Papers* (no.3, August 1906), pp.10–11, 12; ibid. (no.9, 15 April 1908), p.59; ibid. (no.14, 15 September 1908), pp.118–19.
100 e.g. Judge, op. cit., pp.157–9.

authority is very frequently invoked and there is a great deal of quotation from his writings.[101] As a result the collectivist evolutionary ideas associated with Benjamin Kidd were correspondingly ill-received.[102] On this basis the Association's doctrine (as just described) was regarded as having scientific warrant and collectivism seen as contrary to the laws of nature, specifically to the process of evolution. 'Progress is difference' in the words of Spencer's maxim. All 'valid' advance rests (in the biological idiom) on the due production of variations and the selection of the fittest among them.[103] Each individual, therefore, needs to be exposed to the environment in which his faculties can develop to the full and any special potentialities flourish. This can only occur where he is as free as possible to act as he will and to bear the consequences of what he does. Public interference can only inhibit this process for its administration will tend to pursue equality of condition, rest on uniformity of treatment, and involve the suppression of differences.[104] Spencer's law of equal freedom must rule, therefore: 'The function of the State' is 'to maintain the freedom of the individual, limited only by the like freedom of other individuals'.[105]

Nor was the British Constitution Association the only body created at this time to urge the libertarian case. There was also, for instance, the Anti-Socialist Union founded in 1907–8 as a means of extending and co-ordinating in a more effective way and on a national scale the drive against contemporary collectivism in whatever quarter this appeared. It had in view protectionist ideas in the Conservative Party as much as the policy of the Liberal government and the rise of Labour.[106] Again its supporters were largely of Conservative persuasion. A prime mover was R. D. Blumenfeld, editor of the *Daily Express*; its first President was the Duke of Devonshire; a number of Unionist MPs were members including Walter Long, one of the party's leaders; there were also representatives of commerce and industry; and W. H. Mallock was on the committee.[107] Links were established with cognate organizations such as the Industrial Freedom League (which had been formed in 1902 to sustain the interests

101 e.g. ibid., pp. 87ff., esp. p. 91 on 'the value and truth of Herbert Spencer's teaching'; see also the paper 'Man *versus* State', ibid., pp.161–8; and Saleeby, op. cit., *passim*.
102 See e.g. *Constitution Papers* (no.10, 15 May 1908), pp.70–1. For Kidd, see vol.i, *The Rise of Collectivism*, pp. 263–5.
103 Judge, op. cit., p.90; Saleeby, op. cit., pp.9–10, 104–5.
104 Cf. the specific invocation of Spencer's *First Principles*, in Judge, op. cit., p.87; see also Saleeby, op. cit., pp.8–10.
105 Judge, op. cit., p.181. Cf. ibid., p.1.
106 K. D. Brown, 'The Anti-Socialist Union, 1908–49', Brown (ed.), *Essays in Anti-Labour History*, pp.239–40; Bristow, *The Defence of Liberty and Property in Britain, 1880–1914*, pp.325ff.
107 Brown, op. cit., pp.240–1, 248–51. Later members included Cdr Locker-Lampson and Sir Samuel Hoare: see the list ibid., pp.260–1.

of private traders against municipal Socialism); conferences were held; trained lecturers toured the country; pamphlets, newspapers, and similar literature were produced. In order to stress the importance of individuality and responsibility, the Union opposed municipal commercial enterprise, nearly all the paternalist welfare schemes then being proposed, and stressed the doctrine of self-help rather in the style of Samuel Smiles. At the same time the ASU emphasized the importance of profit-sharing and charitable work of a social kind as a means of trying to palliate unrest that would otherwise turn the attention of the masses to collectivist change.[108]

The ASU continued its activities during the 1920s and 1930s (for the first few years under the name of the Reconstruction Society) though it tended to be rather negative in its approach and it was overall less effective than before the Great War.[109] A typical publication was the pamphlet on the value of individuality by G. K. Peto which harped on the evils of state trading and the bad record of public agencies as employer. Another such tract was that by Herbert Williams attributing the current level of unemployment to high taxation; while elsewhere Duff Cooper and Sir Duncan Grey queried the practicability and desirability of various Socialistic proposals particularly in respect of the pursuit of equality.[110] Winston Churchill also addressed the ASU on a number of occasions.[111] One of its chairmen during the 1930s was Lord Mount Temple who brought out an attack on the tyranny and cost of bureaucracy.[112] This group survived until 1949 when it was wound up and its assets transferred to the Economic League which had itself been founded in 1919.

Of course the impact of these bodies and others such as the Middle Class Defence League and the Anti-Waste League (founded in 1921 to press for reductions in public expenditure) was minimal in the sense that, for all their effort and expenditure (which was on a by no means insubstantial scale), the collectivist tide of legislation continued to

---

108 ibid., pp.244–7.
109 ibid., pp.252–7.
110 G. K. Peto, *The Value of Individuality* (ASU no.100; London, n.d. [1926]); H. G. Williams, *The National Income* (ASU no.103; London, n.d. [1926]); A. Duff Cooper, *The Impossibility of Socialism* (ASU no.106; London, n.d. [1927]); Sir D. Grey, *The Follies and Fallacies of Socialism* (ASU no.107; London, n.d. [1927]). See also H. G. Williams, *Why I am Not a Socialist* (London, 1930) in which the virtues and advantages of individualist capitalism are reviewed; as well as his *What is Socialism?* (NUA no.2012; London, 1921; 2nd enlarged edn, 1924); and *idem, Elementary Principles of Political Economy* (NUA no.2027; London, 1921).
111 See e.g. his *The Coming Struggle* (ASU no.95; London, n.d. [1926]).
112 Lord Mount Temple, *Tyranny of Bureaucracy* (Anti-Socialist Union; London, 1937), a reprint of his speech in 101 H.L. Deb. 5s., 15 July 1936, cols797–812.

flow.[113] And, of course, industry and commerce (from which nearly all the funds came) was often not loath to accept the helping-hand proffered by the state and indeed often urgently sought it. But organizations like the BCA and the ASU reflected a type of Conservative activity and interest that continued and showed later manifestations as in Ernest Benn's Individualist Movement and such bodies as Aims of Industry and the Institute of Economic Affairs.

In the first part of this century, then, Conservatism contained a vociferous anti-statist element, one which was all the more assertive because its ideas were under attack by those who, for one reason or another, took a more positive view of government intervention and who for the time seemed triumphant. Beatrice Webb observed this situation when she wrote in her diary in 1906: 'Meanwhile, Balfour has succumbed to Chamberlain, and the Conservative Party has become definitely protectionist – for the time – so long as Chamberlain lives. In so far as it commits the most *laisser-faire* party to the policy of state control and increase of taxation, we rejoice in it.'[114] It was not, of course, that the entire party leadership succumbed whole-heartedly to the current pressures making in a collectivist direction. Bonar Law, for instance, was one of those who were much concerned about the increasing welfare provision which was part of the pre-war Liberal programme. He believed it was undesirable for Conservatives to be openly and closely associated with such a social reform policy and on this basis led the opposition to the 1911 National Health Bill.[115] And another leading Conservative politician who fought a staunch rearguard action in defence of libertarian principles was Lord Hugh Cecil.

THE RELIGIOUS BASIS: LORD HUGH CECIL

'But, they say, there are no politics in the New Testament –'
'Well, they're right enough there, ...'
G. ELIOT, *Felix Holt*, 1866; Everyman, 1934, p.60

Lord Hugh Cecil was the first President of the British Constitution Association and, in the interesting and quite extensive corpus of his writings and speeches, developed at some length a rationale for the view

113 At one stage an attempt was made without success to unite these separate but cognate groups into one 'Citizens' Union', Bristow in Brown, op. cit., p.284. On the Anti-Waste League which operated largely through the Unionist Party, see C. Cook, *Sources in British Political History 1900–1951* (London, 1975–7), i.11.
114 B. Webb, *Our Partnership*, p.332. Cf. ibid., p.335.
115 R. Blake, *The Unknown Prime Minister: the Life and Times of Andrew Bonar Law, 1858–1923* (London, 1955), p.140; J. S. Saloma, *British Conservatism and the Welfare State: an Analysis of the Policy-Process within the British Conservative Party* (PhD, Harvard University, 1961), pp.330–42.

of Conservatism involved and one notably different from that usually urged. And if Cecil's political manner could be uncompromising – his animosity and that of his friends during the constitutional crisis of 1911 earned them the title of 'Hughligans' – his intellectual style was very different, too, from the kind of secular Toryism presented by Lord R. Churchill or J. Chamberlain. He once referred to Chamberlain and his like as alien immigrants in the Conservative Party.[116] For not only was Cecil a fervent believer in the limited state, an extreme individualist who (as Chesterton said) would have been quite at home in the Manchester School, his theoretical defence of this position is subtle and rooted in a biblicizing form of Anglicanism. Mrs Webb recorded in her diary in November 1903: 'Dined at the Asquith's. Lord Hugh Cecil . . . disappointing – a bigot even on fiscal questions, dominated entirely by a sort of deductive philosophy from *laisser-faire* principles held as theological dogma. . . .'[117] Or, as Sir Oswald Mosley commented many decades later, Cecil's 'religious convictions traversed and permeated his whole political being' and he could hardly write a letter to *The Times* about free trade without dragging them in.[118]

Cecil saw Conservatism as a creed brought into existence by the forces unleashed during the French Revolution: hence the importance he attributed to Burke's great insights.[119] And in Cecil's eyes the clear duty of supporters of this doctrine was to resist Jacobinism in all its forms. This did not mean a wholly unyielding attitude to all change but it did entail approaching each proposal for reform with a firm scepticism and an appropriate prudence. Consequently the major question Cecil faced was how to establish a standard of judgement in these matters by reference to which a consistent attitude might be adopted to the march of events and a mere opportunism avoided.[120] The basis on which he rested his case was, as already intimated, a particular view of the Christian ethic – Harold Laski's suggestion that Cecil's defence of the existing system of private property abandons any attempt at moral justification is simply a most careless, and utterly absurd, misreading of the texts.[121] Yet it is true that Cecil's statement was not wholly unaffected by the popular version of Spencer's evolutionism then current; this was after all central to the ethos of the BCA with which he was so closely associated. His analysis has to be seen, too, in the specific political context which was the immediate occasion of its initial exposition.

116 J. L. Garvin and J. Amery, *The Life of Joseph Chamberlain* (London, 1932–69), vi. 815.
117 B. Webb, *Our Partnership* (London, 1948), p.274. For Chesterton's remark, see his *Autobiography* (1936; London, 1937), p.264.
118 Sir O. Mosley, *My Life* (1968; London, 1970), p.148.
119 Lord Hugh Cecil, *Conservatism* (1912; London, 1928), pp.47–8.
120 ibid., part I.
121 H. Laski, *A Grammar of Politics* (1925; 5th edn, London, 1948), p.178.

By the first decade of this century not only had the policies of the Liberal Party become increasingly collectivist in many ways – as reflected in the programme for social and economic reform put forward by Campbell-Bannerman's and Asquith's governments – but, as well, the new Labour Party and the trade unionism it represented had begun to emerge as major political forces. Moreover, as already remarked in the previous chapter, there were notable interventionist tendencies at work in the Conservative Party itself and these were strengthened both by the tariff reform ideas then being increasingly canvassed and by the feeling that if the party was to regain the ground disastrously lost in the 1906 general election it would have to refurbish its appeal to the voters in particular on the matter of social change. The British Constitution Association had, of course, been established to resist these collectivist tendencies in political life generally and in the Conservative Party in particular. In his presidential address to the Association's annual conference in 1907, Cecil deployed the usual case against 'constructionism' or 'political socialism'.[122] This tendency is attacked because of its untoward effect on individual enterprise and initiative which are the main determinants of the level of economic activity. There are also the usual Spencerian overtones about the enervating results of growing dependence on the state and the deleterious consequences for the national character.[123] And although the naturalistic themes never bulked large in Cecil's description of Conservative doctrine, there are continual reminders of Spencer's influence in, for example, the suggestion about the inefficacy and failure of legislative control and also perhaps in the frequent stress on the importance of allowing human instincts and capacities as much free play as possible.[124] But the greatest weight of Cecil's argument about the nature and purpose of government is thrown on his interpretation of Christianity and the ethical tenets he takes to be implied in it. These provide the normative standard by which in his view political policy is to be judged.[125] As he put it in a post-war pamphlet, 'The authority of the State may be at every point challenged and required to justify itself according to the law of God.'[126]

The point of departure, then, is that 'Conservatism must not shrink from the appeal to Christian morality. Its characteristic as a party ought

---

122 The address is reprinted in full in M. H. Judge (ed.), *Political Socialism: a Remonstrance. A Collection of Papers by Members of the British Constitution Association.* . . . (Westminster, 1908), pp. 33–50.
123 ibid., esp. pp. 48–9.
124 e.g. Cecil, *Conservatism*, pp. 190–2; *Natural Instinct: the Basis of Social Institutions* (London, 1926), esp. pp. 7–8; *Conservative Ideals* (NUA no. 2184; London, 1924), pp. 7–8.
125 Cecil, *Conservatism*, pp. 116–17.
126 Cecil, *Nationalism and Catholicism* (London, 1919), p. 18. Cf. ibid., p. 59.

to be . . . the readiness to apply a religious standard to politics.'[127] While, of course, this has been a common Conservative theme, it has (as Cecil admits) also been at least as frequently urged by those of different political persuasion.[128] What is important, therefore, is not this kind of pious generality as such but the particular religious doctrine or text invoked and the specific points of policy and programme elicited from it (or simply associated with it). And here Cecil is honestly blunt: 'there is immense difficulty in applying the teaching of revealed religion directly to the problems of social and political reorganization.'[129] Thus the source of principle he has in mind is that of 'Christian morals as revealed in the New Testament'. But there is the major problem that the 'direct teaching' of this guiding document on matters of state is 'slight and even meagre.'[130] However, it is precisely this absence of specific instruction that Cecil turns to polemical advantage. For he points out that all the New Testament positively affirms about politics is that 'obedience is due to the authority of the State within its own sphere' (and as well that this sphere 'does not extend to purely spiritual matters.')[131] And the one thing, he suggests, that this 'meagre' reference cannot be held to justify is state Socialism.[132] First this is because so far as the role of government is implied at all it seems to be limited to 'the elementary duty of maintaining order and repressing crime.' But further, and much more importantly, political matters are put firmly in second place, the main didactic emphasis being given to questions concerning on the one hand, the individual character and conscience and, on the other, spiritual society.[133]

For example, while there are in the New Testament plenty of warnings addressed to the rich or references to the blessings of the poor, nothing is said or implied about its being the duty of the state to relieve poverty and distress or about the need for a general readjustment of social conditions: the whole emphasis of the text is rather on how wealth may affect the spiritual well-being of the individual and the possibility of his entry into the kingdom of heaven.[134] Christ was not a social reformer, even though the Christian may be driven to become one and to do what he can within his own circle of influence.[135] Cecil does agree that the 'competitive system' and 'the existing organisation of commerce and industry', being

127 Cecil, *Conservatism*, , p.210.
128 ibid., p.74.
129 Cecil, *Natural Instinct*, p.6.
130 Cecil, *Conservatism*, pp.73–5.
131 ibid., p.75. He refers, of course, to the dictum that the Christian should 'render unto Caesar' etc.
132 ibid., pp.75–82, 95–6.
133 ibid., pp.81–2.
134 ibid., pp.83–5.
135 ibid., pp.86–7.

based on self-interest, have a lower moral status than arrangements based on the ethic of love.[136] But again he refuses to believe that this premiss necessarily leads to a commitment to radical reform of social and economic institutions. If by political action private enterprise is replaced by state regulation of economic life this will simply transform the mode of competition; it will not eliminate it. To do this requires the regeneration of individual character, an object that will not be effected by a mere change of political and social machinery.[137] 'Character', he writes, 'will transform the social system, but it takes something more vivifying than a social system to transform character.'[138]

Of course, this view about the moral limitations of institutional and cognate reform was one shared by many devout people of different political persuasions: R. H. Tawney is a case in point.[139] It is an attitude that was also shared by other Conservatives. There is, for instance, an interesting reflection of it in some correspondence in 1907 between the Marquess of Salisbury and the Earl of Selborne. The former objected 'to public almsgiving in any form to the working classes' but happily accepted the use of the machinery of the state to enable them to help themselves. In a later letter he put this view in a moral context stressing the importance of personal regeneration:

> the investment of public money for the advantage of members of the public must be judged in each case on its merits. One criterion for this judgement is the answer to the question whether a measure panders to the covetousness or laziness of individuals or classes. If so this would be a moral bar. But the protection and care of the weak are not barred.

The basic social malady 'is not economical or political but moral. The vice of the poor, the selfishness of the rich, the hardness of the middle classes are moral evils and must be controlled by moral weapons. You will anticipate the conclusion. The solution is beyond the sphere of the politician. . . .'[140]

Cecil argues, then, that the kind of political change demanded by the radical reformer cannot achieve the purpose in view or be justified by reference to the ethical principles laid down. Moreover he goes on to assert that the methods envisaged are themselves incompatible with Christian moral standards. There are severe warnings in the Gospels about the selfish enjoyment of riches and the like. But it does not follow

136 ibid., pp. 89–90. Cf. R. B. McDowell, *British Conservatism, 1832–1914* (London, 1959), p. 150, and the references to Cecil's speeches in Parliament there cited.
137 Cecil, *Conservatism*, pp. 90–6.
138 ibid., p. 91.
139 See below pp. 443–6.
140 Salisbury to Selborne (20 September 1907); same to same (3 October 1907). I owe these texts to Dr D. G. Boyce.

that it is a Christian act 'to deprive selfish people of the wealth they misuse and to transfer it to those who are poor.' The very idea is a fundamental error for it misses the main point of the teaching which is that acts of self-denial lose their Christian character if they are done under duress: 'Compulsory unselfishness is an absurdity, a contradiction in terms.' Virtue consists not merely in doing right but, through self-discipline, in choosing so to act. The Good Samaritan aided the distressed man at his own cost; he did not run after the Priest and the Levite and force them to minister to the poor man's sufferings; and *a fortiori* the Gospel story does not justify the case of the wounded traveller himself compelling those who would pass him by to give him relief for if he did he would be little better than the footpads who had despoiled him. Yet this is, thinks Cecil, 'a fair parallel for a majority of voters' who exert their political power to confiscate wealth by law and distribute it among themselves. From the moral point of view the mere transfer of material wealth from one pocket to another is indifferent if done by just means and dishonest if otherwise achieved.[141]

How, then, does Cecil view the specific role and duty of the state? As already intimated his concern is with the moral framework of political action and he puts this in terms of a discussion of 'Justice'. By their very nature acts of government are likely to have a greater effect than those of any other group or individual. It is all the more important, therefore, that the state should act justly even when it is acting on behalf of the public as a whole. This means it must not inflict undeserved injury or withhold a benefit rightly belonging to someone (except as punishment for a crime).[142] What is particularly involved in this view of justice is indicated by Cecil's discussion of property and of legitimate state functions.

The basis of the argument about private property is developed with some skill and sophistication. It is that where the right to property exists – and Cecil regards it as an instinctive part of 'the Divine equipment of man' and therefore 'a sacred thing'[143] – the principle that it is unjust to inflict an injury or pain on any person is adequate to sustain that right; for an individual would certainly be maltreated if he were deprived of what he owns without sufficient reason. This is part simply of the elementary Christian duty that no man should harm his neighbour.[144]

---

141 Cecil, *Conservatism*, pp. 96–9; *Liberty and Authority* (London, 1910), pp. 16–18, 24. Cf. Enoch Powell's remarks about the concept of 'compassion' in his *Still to Decide* (Paperfront, 1972), pp. 22–3; and for an interesting contemporary comment (on Cecilian lines) about the Samaritan and similar themes, see J. R. Vincent, 'A Manifesto for Marginals', *TLS* (11 September 1981), p. 1023.

142 Cecil, *Conservatism*, pp. 165–8.

143 Cecil, *Conservative Ideals*, pp. 5–8; *Natural Instinct*, pp. 6–7, 8–10, 12–14; *Conservatism*, p. 118.

144 Cecil, *Conservatism*, pp. 120–1.

The way in which the property was acquired (for example, whether it was earned or not) or the use to which it is put are irrelevant to this consideration. Nor is any 'element of desert' involved, that is, whether the owner ought to have what he possesses.[145] This is because the economic process depends not on any conception of merit, which is irrelevant to it, but on the technical pressures of the market: the 'forces that make wealth are never ethical' and a title to property does not rest on its owner's virtues.[146] Nor can 'a nobler standard' of conduct and reward be enforced through state action, through, say, a policy of redistributive or confiscatory taxation. For one thing the state as such has no means of establishing proper categories of merit. Could it possibly examine the origin and ownership of all property in the country? If it should attempt to do so the result is only too likely to be dishonesty and hypocrisy on the part of those affected.[147] Then further – and here the basic principle of morality as Cecil conceives it is again invoked – to tax a particular class especially is to punish its members. And 'to punish except for crime is unjust; and to commit injustice in order to profit by it is dishonest.'[148] Of course, public authorities have to levy taxes on property to meet expenses necessary in the service of the whole community; but this is a different matter from relieving the wants of particular classes. If this latter end is the purpose of an impost forced on everyone then it is no more than theft disguised as philanthropy. Taxation legitimately imposed for general purposes and interests must be distinguished from confiscation intended to benefit a specific group.[149] Property owners must thus be guarded against undeserved injury and this necessarily imposes limits on the general revenue and so on state activity.

Cecil believes, then, that the duty of public authority is limited to the provision of services required for the welfare of the entire society. And while his view is in some respects similar to Spencer's, on the whole his attitude to this matter is less limited and he is prepared to concede that legitimate state activity covers not simply the vital functions of maintaining the security of life and property but also such matters as public health, transport, lighting, and similar amenities of universal benefit.[150] Yet, because of the restrictions on the state that Cecil persists in envisaging, his view may still be regarded as clearly libertarian in nature.

For, first of all, Cecil asserts the necessity of sustaining a large sphere

145 ibid., pp.121, 123–4; Liberty and Authority, pp.25–6.
146 Cecil, Conservatism, pp.124–7, 141. On land ownership in particular, see ibid., pp.127–41.
147 ibid., pp.143–5.
148 ibid., p.150; Conservative Ideals, pp.8–9.
149 Cecil, Conservatism, pp.152–8.
150 ibid., pp.139–40.

of individuality on which the community may not entrench because the widest possible opportunity of choice is essential for the development of the individual and of the race. Only the most exceptional circumstances could warrant putting aside this principle in favour of the 'costly palliative' and 'enervating hand' of government interference.[151] Cecil is very critical of Matthew Arnold and those like him who speak of the development of the 'best self' under the tutorial guidance of the state. He naturally rejects, too, the authoritarian pursuit of equality as both unreal and incompatible with essential liberty.[152] He looks forward instead (in terms of what might be called a Christianized Spencerism) to a gradual evolution towards a sort of libertarian anarchy in which men live together without coercion in a 'spontaneous cohesion of virtuous wills.'[153]

Further, Cecil holds that the role of the state in economic life is of the second order. It cannot itself directly create value and can do no more than clear the way for the optimum operation of primary economic forces. Government, he says, ministers to the productive process only by 'facilitating the working of the energies and desires of its citizens.'[154] He is perturbed, therefore, by the statist implications of tariff reform in respect of the regulation of trade and industry.[155] And he believes, pursuant to his stress on the superiority of voluntary action, that workers should not look to legislation to sustain them in respect of any inequality in bargaining but should to this end combine themselves in trade unions.[156] Similarly Cecil is loath to accept any public responsibility for the relief of suffering or for a programme designed to eliminate inequalities of wealth. This could only be achieved by an attack on property: and no one may rob to give alms.[157] His attitude is also reflected in his views about education. He thinks there might be a case for using powers of compulsion to see children are suitably educated. But as a permanent solution there are major dangers in this both to personal liberty and to the sense of parental responsibility.[158]

Cecil is concerned, therefore, to show that (as he sees it) Christianity does not imply extensive social reform and economic control by the state. Increments of either may be necessary but they are to be kept to a severe minimum because they involve compulsion and perhaps injustice. The stress is rather upon individual or group action and the moral

151 Cecil, *Liberty and Authority*, pp.16–18, 24, 36–7, 46, 67.
152 ibid., pp.26ff., 51–62.
153 ibid., pp.68–9.
154 Cecil, *Conservatism*, p.140.
155 ibid., pp.192–5.
156 ibid., pp.187–90.
157 ibid., pp.172–87, 197.
158 Cecil, *Liberty and Authority*, pp.37–45.

regeneration of character through this voluntary process. Of course, not all Conservatives accepted the attempt to base their creed on this kind of moralizing Christianity. Party propaganda was likely to adopt a more simple and robust view anticipating (if the anachronism may pass) visions of 1984 and exhorting a hostility to state ownership and Socialism generally by, for instance, suggesting they would make every one a puppet and compel people to live in gigantic barracks. Or Socialism is simply equated with 'slavery, tyranny, famine and rule by force' as in Russia, with the regulation of 'everybody at all times.'[159] Some Conservatives feared that to press Cecil's type of argument might possibly open the door to all sorts of undesirable doctrines, Christian Socialism for instance. I fancy it was with obvious reference to Cecil that K. Feiling wrote there was 'no justification for importing the New Testament into politics' at all.[160] Of course, this was (in a way at least) precisely Cecil's point in criticism of Socialists who used Christianity to bolster their demands for radical reform; and it is a point that has not gone unrecognized since his day. As one recent commentator remarked, 'the religious dispensation of Christ did not include a blue-print for the social or political order.'[161] It is not surprising, therefore, that a libertarian Conservatism has often been established not on some theological basis but on other, secular, grounds, as the representative writings of Ernest Benn will illustrate.

PRIVATE ENTERPRISE AND SELF-HELP: THE INDIVIDUALISM OF SIR ERNEST BENN

> Let's stop somebody from doing something!
> Everybody does too much.
> People seem to think they've a right to eat and drink,
> Talk and walk and respirate and rink,
> Bicycle and bathe and such.
> So let's have lots of little regulations,
> Let's make laws and jobs for our relations,
> There's too much kissing at the railway stations –
> Let's find out what everyone is doing,
> And then stop everyone from doing it.
> A. P. HERBERT, cited in E. J. P. BENN, *Account Rendered*, 1930,
> repr. 1931, p. [vi]

Benn's point of view – basically an attack on 'this thing called the State' – is, in fact, mannered in presentation, never systematic, and (in this sense)

---

159 NUA, *What Socialism Really Means* (no. 1087; London, 1914). Cf. *Why You Should Be Unionist* (no. 2059; London, 1922).
160 K. Feiling, *What Is Conservatism?* (London, 1930), p.10.
161 E. Norman, 'Christianity and Politics', M. Cowling (ed.), *Conservative Essays* (London, 1978), p.73.

peculiarly his own.[162] It is nevertheless broadly representative of a
notable range of Conservative opinion in the decades after the end of the
Great War and indeed of recent years. Writing in 1927 Keynes said that
the 'very extreme Conservatives, led by Sir Ernest Benn and his friends
. . . would like to undo all the hardly-won little which we have in the way
of conscious and deliberate control of economic forces for the public
good'; and added sarcastically that the course they favoured was nothing
more than 'a return to chaos.'[163] Less pejoratively Harold Macmillan
(looking back a little while ago to the 1930s) said there were many in the
Conservative Party

> who believed that private enterprise, left alone and allowed to operate
> untrammelled, would in the long run produce wealth on a greater scale
> than any other system. It is true that the supporters of the *laisser-faire*
> view had been recently divided by the question of protective duties,
> and correspondingly weakened by the final triumph . . . of protection-
> ist policies. Moreover, all the interference with the free market that
> had grown up with the trade union system had largely destroyed the
> old classical position. Nevertheless, most Conservatives, having
> carried tariff reform, had not faced the logical consequences of their
> success. In any case, since many of them were originally Whigs or
> Liberals, they cherished their opinions like heirlooms. Their general
> view was 'the less interference the better; let private enterprise get on
> with it'.[164]

One instance of this attitude (though, surprisingly in an academic
polemic, one that hardly expounds adequately the basis of the point of
view) is Professor Hearnshaw's *Conservatism in England* (1933) which
manifests a ferocious hostility to the development of collectivist
government and attacks 'the swelling extravagance of the state' as the
main feature in the collapse of British finance.[165] Looking ahead to the
later 1930s and after, Hearnshaw urges Conservatives not to attempt to
outbid Liberals in promises of democratic change and Socialists in
promises of welfare assistance. Nor should they follow the fashionable
lead in giving so much emphasis to 'economic concerns' at all.[166] The
positive solution proposed is curious and contains what, to latter-day
eyes, may seem unfortunate references to sterilization of the unfit and the
eugenic purification of the race. But the stress that is relevant here is that

162 The phrase cited is from E. J. P. Benn, *The Confessions of a Capitalist* (1925; 12th
     edn, London, 1932), p.211.
163 J. M. Keynes, 'Liberalism and Industry', *The Collected Writings* (London, 1971 ff.),
     vol. xix, part II, p.640.
164 H. Macmillan, *Winds of Change, 1914–1939* (London, 1966), p.501; cf. ibid., p.510.
165 F. J. C. Hearnshaw, *Conservatism in England: an Analytical, Historical, and
     Political Survey* (London, 1933), pp.285–6.
166 ibid., pp.291–2, 294–5.

while 'the true conservative is profoundly concerned for the condition of the people' he is convinced that

> no permanent improvement of this condition can come by means of indiscriminate charity, or promiscuous doles, or any other device that debilitates, demoralises, and degrades. He sees the way of improvement to lie . . . along the line of intelligent self-help, cultivated ability, enhanced skill, increased specialisation, bettered physique, elevated character, enlarged faith. . . . His ideal is not that of a pauper proletariat dependent on the state (i.e. on other people's confiscated possessions), but of a property-owning democracy.[167]

And the establishment of this ideal involved the maintenance of the capitalist system as the condition of economic freedom and individual development. At the same time it was recognized that restoration of economic prosperity might well involve a circumvallation of protection and financial control. But apart from this Hearnshaw was convinced that Conservatism was the only defence of liberty against the collectivist menace.[168]

Nor was this an uncommon theme in the Conservative literature of the 1920s and 1930s. A few other instances among many may be given as illustration. First a propaganda leaflet issued in 1925 urged the voter to support the Conservative Party because it opposed 'excessive State Control and bureaucratic interference with individual freedom' and opportunity. The state 'cannot successfully direct industrial operations . . . and take the risks which individuals do': economic progress depends on 'individual enterprise'.[169] Secondly Dorothy Crisp in *The Rebirth of Conservatism* asserted the primary rights of family, property, and liberty and on this basis attacked theft by taxation and the 'meaningless half-Socialism' which had latterly come to corrupt Conservative policies and principles.[170] The libertarian theme is summed up in the sentence: 'Conservatism considers it the duty of a government to interfere as little as possible, and not as much as possible, in national life.' And it should eschew the policies involved in pursuing 'that evil absurdity, the doctrine of equality.'[171] Thirdly Sir Bolton Eyres Monsell (later 1st Viscount Monsell), then Conservative chief whip, suggested in 1931 to the Commons Select Committee on Procedure in the Public Business that there was too much legislation. He was rebutting the view expressed to the committee by his Labour counterpart Thomas Kennedy, who had

167 ibid., pp. 303–4.
168 ibid., pp. 304, 306–7. Cf. his later booklet on *The Socialists' 'New Order'* (1941; 2nd edn, London, 1943), a repudiation of collectivism of whatever provenance.
169 *Why You Should be Conservative & Unionist* (NUCUA no. 2078; London, 1925).
170 D. Crisp, *The Rebirth of Conservatism* (London, 1931), pp. 8, 28.
171 ibid., pp. 39, 84.

urged persistently that legislative output in the interest of the majority must be increased and procedure reformed accordingly, a typically collectivist viewpoint brusquely and starkly put.[172] Sir Bolton rather deplored the tendency to increase government's power and the corresponding view that

> it should be made easier for the House of Commons to turn out legislation. There seems to me a great impatience among certain people of any criticism at all of legislation in these days. I suppose the idea underlying this is that the country wants legislation. I myself believe that to be a complete fallacy. I think we have suffered a good deal from too much legislation. I believe it is very hard to frame any Act nowadays which will get the consent of a majority in the country. I should put the legislative function of the House of Commons last.[173]

But he admitted that in terms of recent experience the Conservative government of 1924–9 was in this respect 'almost the worst offender that I know of', the pressure coming largely from the departments.[174] Winston Churchill likewise expressed to the committee a similar view that legislation was overdone and indicated his disquiet about the enormous number of bills being passed.[175] Another rather quaint and fascinating exposition of the Tory creed, while fully acknowledging in Disraelian terms the authority and duty of the state, was primarily concerned to repudiate the idea of government as the universal provider and to sustain belief in the liberty, initiative, and responsibility of the individual. Thus Toryism (it was urged) 'must see that State Interference is reduced to the minimum compatible with the spiritual and physical welfare of all the citizens.'[176] Finally that staunch Tory Rudyard Kipling expressed his social philosophy in the address he gave at St Andrew's University in 1923 on the occasion of his election as Lord Rector. He spoke of the crucial importance of a man owning himself especially amid the press of the modern world:

> Partly through a recent necessity for thinking and acting in large masses, partly through the instinct of mankind to draw together and cry out when calamity hits them, and very largely through the quickening of communications . . . the power of the Tribe over the individual has become more extended, particular, pontifical, and,

172 Procedure on Public Business. Sel. Cttee. Spec. Rep., 1930–1 (vol. viii), H.C. Paper 161, qq. 574–82, 596, 605, 609, 674–84, 875–92.
173 ibid., q. 1282. Cf. ibid., qq. 1403–4, 1449–51.
174 ibid., q. 1348.
175 ibid., q. 1521.
176 P. Loftus, *The Creed of a Tory* (London, 1926), pp. 37, 139. The book combines, fascinatingly in this day and age, the old ideas of Order, a Great Chain of Being, the plurality of worlds, Gothicism, and other such venerable themes.

using the word in both its senses, impertinent, ... Some men accept this omnipresence of crowds; some may resent it. To the latter I am speaking.

'Nowadays', he added, 'to own oneself in any decent measure, one has to run counter to a gospel, and to fight against its atmosphere'.[177]

But perhaps one of the most sustained defences of the libertarian position by a Conservative publicist during the period between the wars was that of Sir Ernest Benn. In terms of the case he put, he was (so to say) the Samuel Smiles of his day; or alternatively he might be seen as a perhaps rather superficial disciple of Herbert Spencer, one who followed the latter's political line but without any methodical statement of the evolutionary metaphysic by which it was originally underpinned. Certainly Benn was, as his friend Sir Carleton Allen wrote, an adherent of 'the principles of undiluted *laissez-faire*'.[178]

Benn's family was active in Liberal and Progressive Party politics and in his young days he was himself involved in these affairs being not surprisingly affected by the twin forces of evangelicalism and utilitarianism that had moulded this domestic background.[179] Then, as a result of his experience as a temporary civil servant at the Ministries of Munitions and Reconstruction during the Great War, he was much impressed by the possibilities of state action. At this period he believed it was necessary to ensure close collaboration between government and industry through a supervising Minister of Commerce. Such an expedient, he thought, was vital if the trade war was to be won and other likely economic problems of the post-war period effectively tackled. This attitude was expressed in his first three books.[180] He was also connected with the establishment of the Whitley Council system in the public service. Later, however, he referred to these ideas and activities as 'my economic wild oats' and came to wish that the publications which had resulted could be forgotten.[181] For he had quite quickly changed his mind, repudiating this 'mild collectivism' and becoming instead an 'unbending individualist'. Perhaps it was the leaven of his commercial experience that was at work in this change. He had early joined his father's publishing firm in a junior capacity and was subsequently, with very considerable commercial success, to be its director. Perhaps it was, too, the result of a visit he made in 1921 to the USA during which he was greatly impressed with the

177 Cited in C. Carrington, *Rudyard Kipling: His Life and Work* (1955; Penguin, 1970), pp. 535–6.
178 Cited in D. Abel, *Ernest Benn: Counsel for Liberty* (London, 1960), p. 11.
179 See A. G. Gardiner, *John Benn and the Progressive Movement* (London, 1925), e.g. pp. 465–9.
180 *Trade as a Science* (London, n.d. [1916]), *The Trade of Tomorrow* (London, 1917), *Trade Parliaments and their Work* (London, 1918).
181 E. Benn, *Happier Days: Recollections and Reflections* (London, 1949), ch. VII.

energy, efficiency, and freedom of economic life there.[182] Also there was the undoubted effect at this time of his acquaintance with Sir Hugh Bell the Yorkshire steel-master and ardent free-trader. The flavour of the opinions Benn had come to hold and which he subsequently asserted with never-diminishing fervour is reflected in the titles of three of his books: *The Return to Laisser-Faire* (1928), *Modern Government 'as a busybody in other men's matters'* (1936), and *The State the Enemy* (1953).

From the mid-1920s, then, when Benn's opinions underwent this rather dramatic reversal, individualism became 'the very kernel' of his political creed. The state was now the 'acme of immorality'; the individual was good and the collective evil.[183] With Sir Hugh Bell he launched in 1926 the Individualist Movement, almost it might seem as a belated ideological counterblast to the Progressive Movement his father had founded. It began with a bookshop, and meetings and talks soon followed. He broke formally with the Liberal Party in 1929 because he objected to the 'socialistic liberalism' of George and the Yellow Book. He then gave his support to the Conservatives or rather to their libertarian wing. He described his later attitude as 'a full-blooded, die-hard Tory point of view.'[184] At the same time he recognized that amongst an individualist's more important work was the task of rooting 'socialism' out of the Conservative Party itself; and he was in some respects averse to being seen solely and simply as one of its supporters because of the party's ambivalence on the matter of collectivism.[185] In 1931 he was connected with a group called 'The Friends of Economy' concerned to attack swollen state expenditure. Two years later Benn founded a short-lived weekly paper *The Independent* to expound his libertarian views. Just after the outbreak of the Second World War there began his most important campaign to defend 'personal and civil liberty, the rule of law and the free market' and to resist 'bureaucratic controls' and 'every project for a state-planned economy.'[186] In 1942 he issued a 'Manifesto of British Liberty' doing this together with a number of other sympathizers including C. K. Allan, F. J. C. Hearnshaw, Lord Leverhulme, and F. W. Hirst. Shortly afterwards Benn helped to found the Society of Individualists (later the Society for Individual Freedom) of which he became President. This association had a quite numerous following drawn from all parties including a number of Tory MPs who had themselves been active in the establishment of a National League of

182 Benn, *The Confessions of a Capitalist*, ch. x; *Happier Days*, p.188; Abel, op. cit., pp.27–31.
183 D. Abel, 'Sir Ernest Benn', *DNB*, ii.2511.
184 Benn, *Happier Days*, pp.160–1.
185 Abel, *Ernest Benn*, pp.131, 136.
186 Abel, 'Sir Ernest Benn', *DNB*, ibid.

Freedom against bureaucracy and state control.[187] Among the Conservative back-benchers thus involved were Douglas Hacking, Patrick Hannon, Waldron Smithers, Leonard Lyle, and A. M. Lyons; and something of what they stood for is indicated in the declaration of the League's manifesto that its aim was to 'fight the strong movement now on foot to continue unnecessary official control of trade, industry, business and private lives after the war.'[188] Subsequently a news-letter or magazine called *Freedom First* was issued which at one stage reached a circulation of some 20,000 copies.

Despite this array of activity Benn found time to become one of the most prolific publicists of his day in the cause of Tory individualism: as he said himself, he was 'an incorrigible controversialist'.[189] He contributed many articles to the newspaper and periodical press and, in the three decades or so before his death in 1954, he wrote over twenty books and as many tracts and pamphlets to expound his opinions. None of these is anything like a systematic treatise though constantly reiterated and consistent themes can be discerned in the sometimes rambling discussion. There are, in fact, two basic aspects to his varied excursions into these matters – a traditional constitutional libertarianism; and a belief in the superior moral virtue and economic efficiency of free enterprise and profit-seeking – though the latter is by far the more extensively developed of the two ideas. Overall, government intervention was always the foe to be attacked.

Liberty in the classical, negative sense is for Benn the supreme value as only through free choice can the moral qualities of the individual develop. Progress is always 'in direct ratio to the free play upon man' of external forces.[190] The antithesis of freedom is, therefore, the growth of government action, of the continual and growing need for permission to do things.[191] The state itself lacks the moral elements inherent in the individual; but it can all too easily inhibit their growth in him by the entanglements and controls it creates.[192] 'Our habit', he wrote, 'is to think of government as something that is good, that is great, that is desirable, whereas we ought to think of government as, at its best, a necessary evil.'[193] Consequently state interference with the freedom of the subject must be reduced to a minimum; the executive must be once

187 Abel, *Ernest Benn*, chs VII–VIII.
188 *Daily Herald* (17 April 1943), cited in P. Addison, *The Road to 1945: British Politics and the Second World War* (London, 1975), pp.231–2.
189 Benn, *Happier Days*, p.80.
190 E. Benn, *Account Rendered, 1900–1930: Being an Attempt to Estimate the Moral and Material Cost of the New Ideas Expressed in the Political Activities of Great Britain During This Period* (1930; London, 1931), pp.159, 165, 173.
191 Benn, *Happier Days*, ch.xviii.
192 Benn, *The State the Enemy* (London, 1953), pp.120–3.
193 ibid., p.140.

again subordinated to the legislature and judiciary; the rule of law must
be fully asserted; administrative decentralization should be encouraged;
the tendency of people to depend less on self-help and more on a
paternalistic government is to be deplored. His message was blunt: 'Our
future depends upon how far we have realised and understood the folly
of our recent ways.'[194]

The main concern was with the tendency for the state to assert itself
more and more in the economic field. This was an area from which in
Benn's view it should as much as possible keep clear, leaving things to
private enterprise and intervening only to eliminate restrictions on trade.
The most extensive defence of the free-market economy which he wrote,
and which is probably his most well-known book, is *The Confessions of
a Capitalist* first published in 1925 and which was, interestingly enough,
still in print in the late 1940s after selling some quarter of a million copies.
The basic economic idea, which involves a repudiation of the labour
theory of value, is that wealth is a by-product of exchange and the
specialization of function this presupposes.[195] Nothing, Benn said, 'can
ever alter the fact that if we wish to be civilised we can only live by the
will of others, who are willing to give us those things which we require in
exchange for something which we have to offer.'[196] An extremely
complex organization of production and distribution has grown up to
satisfy individual wants and in this intricate mechanism the businessman
is an essential agent who takes the risk of loss.[197] Profit is simply a saving
or advantage derived from this process of exchange, a premium on
economy and efficiency in meeting demand as expressed through the
market. It is thus not at all illegitimate but rather both necessary and
desirable, especially when it is seen as the major source of increased
saving and capital on which future progress depends.[198] The price
mechanism is (or would be if it were allowed to work freely) no more
than the index through which the needs and offerings of people are
registered.[199] Benn is 'an unrepentant believer' in this system because he
thinks it is the most effective means available of producing a growing
range of material goods and services and of satisfying the wish for a
higher standard of living. To restrain or abolish it is to destroy the
possibility of improved human comfort.[200] Moreover it provides a

194 ibid., pp. 57–8.
195 Benn, *The Confessions of a Capitalist*, pp. 53–4.
196 ibid., p. 54.
197 ibid., pp. 56–7, 59, 60–1, 72 and ch. vii *passim*.
198 ibid., esp. p. 68 and ch. vi; on 'excessive profits' see ibid., pp. 110–12, and on profit-
     sharing, ibid., pp. 112–14, 173–6. Also Benn's pamphlet *The Profit Motive* (1941) in
     Abel, *Ernest Benn*, app. ii; and in *The State the Enemy*, pp. 127–35.
199 Benn, *Happier Days*, pp. 61–2.
200 Benn, *The Confessions of a Capitalist*, pp. 19, 33, 85.

uniquely satisfactory array of incentives to work and of outlets for the characteristic acquisitive instincts of human kind.[201] Nor is the situation, simply because it is competitive, necessarily to be regarded as a matter of cut-throat rivalry: on the basis of his own early struggles and experience in commerce, Benn believed that 'there was more of the real spirit of Christianity to be found in business circles than in many churches'.[202] Moreover these arrangements of the market were the only circumstances in which the power of consumer demand was sovereign, which ensured that the buyer gets the article he wants instead of what someone else thinks he ought to have. The free-market economy is indeed the analogue of political democracy: each is the most effective means of registering and securing popular wishes.[203]

These arrangements are hindered by interference with the process of free choice whatever the quarter from which the restraint comes. Usually its object is to avoid the burden of risk and may take the form of restriction by a trade union or association, the development of monopoly or a ring to maintain a market price, or, above all, direct intervention by the state.[204]

A book he wrote in 1930 called *Account Rendered* was an examination of 'the new politics' and an attempt to estimate the moral and material costs of growing collectivism and the burden they represent for future generations.[205] Action by government was always likely to be disastrous. Interference with the price mechanism and the introduction of what Benn called 'political money' (as with managed currencies, a vast public debt, and manipulated exchange rates) were responsible 'for a very large share of the troubles from which the world is suffering' in particular the terrific rise in prices in the period since the latter part of the nineteenth century.[206] Naturally, too, he opposed high levels of taxation and public expenditure. This was partly because of 'the frightful discouragement' it offered to new enterprises. But it was also because, though mainly spent, it is true, on worthy subjects, the ends in view were not in fact to be attained in this way. Moreover their pursuit through this means led to the toils and extravagances of bureaucracy. 'Red tape' was the inevitable and indeed quite proper concomitant of public action; but this was all the

201 ibid., p.134.
202 ibid., p. 81.
203 ibid., pp.108–9, 161; *The State the Enemy*, pp.138–9.
204 On the deleterious effects of trade union practices, see e.g. Benn, *The Confessions of a Capitalist*, pp.67–8, 190–5. He believed, too, it was a most untoward idea that a worker or producer can justify his price, not by value given, but by his needs or commitments; the cost of living, for instance, is a reason for wanting a wage but has nothing to do with the way it might be obtained: see *Account Rendered*, chsiii–iv.
205 *Account Rendered*, esp. chsv–vi, viii.
206 Benn, *The Confessions of a Capitalist*, pp.66–7; *Happier Days*, ch. v and pp.73–7.

more reason why such activity and organization should be minimized.[207] Every new department of government, he wrote, in summary of these themes, 'stands in the way of individual action and personal initiative, and every one of them constitutes at innumerable points a discouragement to those who would be glad to get along with the work of reconstructing the world and supplying the needs of mankind.' He went on to compare directly public and private enterprise:

> Public expenditure must, from its nature, be wasteful. It is as well that we should recognise that inherent weakness in it. State work tends to be done at an uneconomic price. . . . This difficulty does not arise from greed or avarice or chicanery on the part of public servants. The trouble is deeper seated. It arises from the fact that in public work, as distinguished from private work, there is no real test of service. If private work is bad, private persons decline to have it. The test of competition, the freedom of choice, the checks on extravagance, and the incentives to betterment, which are essential elements of private business, are absent in dealings with a public body. A bad piece of work sold to a private person brings discredit on a private trader and robs him of future business. A bad, useless, or extravagant piece of work sold to the public is invariably blamed upon the politicians.[208]

Again he pointed out elsewhere that the civil servant and the businessman exist in quite separate worlds. The former ultimately works by legal compulsion while the latter has to win the favour of the public or he goes bankrupt.[209]

So the conclusion is clear: the main cause of our economic and political difficulties is 'the modern mania for invoking public action', for 'organising everything', for taking money out of private hands where it could be productive and placing it instead in 'the dead hands of the State machine' where it is sterile. This tendency to rely on government made people 'lean' on the support proffered instead of cultivating energetic qualities and so it created a 'safety first' state of mind.

> This generation turns to government as its grandfathers turned to God, and looks upon it as an ever present help in trouble. Some of us believe in the efficacy of prayer, but a great many more believe in the power of government to fix a wage, find us work, or to save us from our own incapacities.[210]

207 Benn, *The Confessions of a Capitalist*, pp. 200–5, 217; *Account Rendered*, p. 33.
208 Benn, *The Confessions of a Capitalist*, pp. 204–5; cf. *Account Rendered*, pp. 88–90, 92.
209 Benn, *Happier Days*, pp. 96–7.
210 Benn, *The Confessions of a Capitalist*, pp. 184, 224; *Account Rendered*, pp. 32, 107 and ch. xiii *passim*.

In one book, Benn formulated this doctrine in three basic points: '(1) . . . strict economy in public affairs is the first essential to prosperity. (2) . . . self-help is the only sure and certain remedy for industrial and commercial ills. (3) . . . political action in business matters generally accentuates the evil that it is designed to cure.'[211] Nor, I think, was he ever impressed by Keynesianism: it was because of excessive taxation and public expenditure already existing that problems about saving and investment arose at all. On this basis, then, Benn opposed general attempts by government to manage the economy and as well specific items of state supervision and aid such as nationalization, public trading, the provision of working-class housing, subsidies to industry, licensing systems, customs inspections, passports, consumer protection, compulsory marketing boards, and so on and so forth.[212]

And one especial social policy that he criticized as particularly foolish and dangerous was the attempt to achieve and enforce egalitarianism. Though Benn did not at all favour a rigid social structure based on heredity or unchanging class barriers, he thought some inequality was inevitable. Pride in superior quality or status was, he believed, 'a proper value' and necessary to progress. In this context he invokes Pareto's 'law' of income distribution to show that there must always be degrees of wealth which rise or fall together.[213] And given that society must be a hierarchy, it is best that the grading process is based on the money test of the competitive system for this means that each person is subjected to the opinion of his fellows: 'Under Capitalism every act performed by anyone of us is tested and found good or bad by the judgement of those whom it affects.' And this is certainly a better way, in Benn's opinion, of selecting the higher grades of society than any alternative.[214]

Hence all Benn's criticisms of high state expenditure, its waste and lack of economy, the inflation of prices and creation of money to which it can lead, the obstacles state control can place in the way of development and increased production, the uniformity of treatment involved, the absence of effective and proper standards of state conduct, the weakening of the individual (as also of family ties and the sense of parental responsibility), the growth of bureaucracy, the decline of freedom both personal and commercial, and the suppression of the voluntary principle: all of which adds up (in his view) to the demoralization of the country and the impoverishment of the citizen. And if these views were not worked out as a coherent ideology – he was a pamphleteer not a political

211 Benn, *The Letters of an Individualist to 'The Times', 1921–1926* (London, 1927), p.84.
212 ibid., *passim*; *Happier Days*, pp.44–5, 49, 86–90; *Account Rendered*, ch.x; *The Confessions of a Capitalist*, pp.60–3.
213 Benn, *The Confessions of a Capitalist*, ch.ix, pp.180–4; *Happier Days*, p.85.
214 Benn, *The Confessions of a Capitalist*, p.161.

theorist – their provenance is nevertheless clear. Benn was very well read in the literature expounding and defending the capitalist economic system.[215] And something of the intellectual ancestry he acknowledged may be gleaned from the following remark: 'In the ideal state of affairs, no one would record a vote in an election until he or she had read the eleven volumes of Jeremy Bentham and the whole of the works of John Stuart Mill, Herbert Spencer and Bastiat as well as Morley's "Life of Cobden."'[216] Nor does he fail to invoke Samuel Smiles and the virtues of self-help.[217] Probably he derived most guidance from Spencer to whom he refers indirectly or specifically in many passages.[218]

Benn's case is not argued then, in the manner of an intendedly exhaustive and consistent academic study. It is an assertive *ex parte* plea put selectively (and acknowledged as such), a restatement of a few simple principles dear to the heart of an honest and successful businessman who believed fervently in the virtues of self-help and private enterprise and who looked back in anguish to the decline in his lifetime from the standards and achievements of the Victorian era. He had no real historical sense and did not, for instance, understand how the development of collectivism could be discerned, growing quite strongly, in the very period of freedom which he adulated. He must (like Spencer before him) have been disappointed and saddened by the way in which few seemed to listen to his preaching, and how events seemed always to go ever more strongly in the direction he deplored. Yet he was never without support: a good many persons as old-fashioned as himself (including the clerical publicist Dean Inge) agreed with him as did many rank and file members of the Conservative Party. There were those in Parliament who held to a similar point of view, back-bench Tory MPs like Sir Waldron Smithers and Sir Herbert Williams, for instance, who while they never held major office were not without influence in the party. One semi-official Conservative reflection of libertarian doctrine was a pamphlet *Why I am a Conservative* published in 1943 at the height of the wartime system of controls. It recognizes that there are certain public services it is proper for the state to perform and that it may be necessary from time to time to add to these. But the general emphasis is clear: the Conservative (it is said) 'believes that the less the State interferes with the life and liberty of the individual the better, and that restrictive action by the State should be limited to protecting the community against any abuse of individual liberty.' It follows that the author asserts the superiority of

215 See e.g. Benn, *The Letters of an Individualist*, ch. xi.
216 ibid., p.13.
217 Benn, *Happier Days*, pp.92–3.
218 See e.g. Benn, *The Confessions of a Capitalist*, pp.202–4; *Happier Days*, pp.92–3; and the extensive excerpts from Spencer's 'The Coming Slavery', cited in *The State the Enemy*, pp.155–75; also ibid., pp.8–9, 19.

private enterprise and rejects the more inefficient form of state activity and bureaucracy.[219] In 1943 the Progress Trust was set up to sustain this point of view and to counter the influence of the Tory Reform Committee. Sir Spencer Summers, one of the Trust's founder members, has stated that it was motivated by fear that the 'Beveridge Society' would be carried too far and that the belief that the state should care for everyone would undermine the principles of individual self-help and responsibility and be inimical to the private enterprise system.[220]

Benn's own organizational influence was largely exerted through the Society for Individual Freedom which (as mentioned above) he helped to found. While formerly open to members of any political persuasion this association tended to have Conservative affiliations though of a kind that were, on the whole, remote from the party leadership.[221] For instance, the President of the Society for a long period until 1970 was Anthony Lambton, Conservative MP for Berwick-upon-Tweed, who for a time held office in the Heath administration; other Tory MPs who were members included Ronald Bell and Donald McI. Johnson. The Society deals with a certain amount of work on behalf of members who are in dispute with public bodies. But arguably its most effective effort in recent years was its role in the campaign to establish an Ombudsman in Britain. For instance, it commissioned T. E. Utley's study of the subject which appeared in 1961 and which was one of the factors helping to create a body of informed opinion on this issue (the Society sent a copy of this study to every MP).[222] Moreover, when a legislative proposal was finally put forward, the Society's views were among those consulted by the leaders of the Conservative opposition; though one reason perhaps why they were lukewarm towards the proposal was that, in contrast to the Society's libertarian view, that leadership was largely dominated by paternalistic and statist ideas of Conservatism.[223]

Of course, lawyers have often tended to be individualists of this kind: as with Lord Hewart's attack on the 'new despotism' and G. W. Keeton's questioning whether Parliament can survive in view of the growth of the executive. And Sir Ernest Benn's long-time friend and colleague in the Individualist movement, the constitutional lawyer Sir Carleton Allen is well-known for his libertarian reflections on the harmful effects of

219 David Stelling, *Why I am a Conservative* (London, 1943), pp.25–6. For other reflections of 'neo-liberal' Conservatism during the war, see H. Kopsch, *The Approach of the Conservative Party to Social Policy during World War II* (PhD, London University, 1970), pp.63–72.
220 In an interview with H. Kopsch, cited in the latter's thesis, loc. cit., pp.71–2.
221 For this paragraph I have drawn on details in F. A. Stacey, *The British Ombudsman*, (Oxford, 1972), pp.28–32, 37, 67–8, 340.
222 Cf. ibid., pp.30–2.
223 ibid., pp.35–6.

growing state intervention and, in particular, of the increase in executive power which in his view amounts to an unfortunate shift in the constitutional centre of gravity. He has in this regard commented especially on the growth of administrative justice and delegated legislation.[224] Likewise some other publicists in this field have, in terms very like Benn's, opposed the development of a welfare-oriented society and the undermining of free enterprise. For instance, G. L. Schwartz in a Conservative sponsored booklet published in 1944 analysed and rejected the idea of national planning in favour of the order and co-ordination brought by the free-enterprise economy which as well allows maximum personal choice. And he concludes that 'In a free democracy the task of the State is not to plan enterprise, but to establish and maintain such conditions that free enterprise is synonymous with planning to meet the freely expressed demands of the community.'[225] Similarly in a book published in 1950 (by E. Benn Ltd) Thomas Hewes condemned the slavish following of 'the common pattern of collectivism' as incapable, whatever people think, of leading to the good life or economic security. The need is to revitalize 'the tested principles of individual liberty and equality of economic opportunity by aggressive decentralization on many fronts'.[226]

Manifestly this kind of Conservative libertarianism was hardly a dominant emphasis in the counsels of the party during the flush collectivist period of the war and after. Yet it is a point of view that has not lacked notable exponents; and it has, in very recent years, experienced a notable stimulus or revival. These latter developments are briefly reviewed in the next chapter.

224 C. K. Allen, *Law and Orders: an Inquiry into the Nature and Scope of Delegated Legislation and Executive Powers in England*, 1st edn (London, 1945) esp. ch. 11. In the latest edition (1965) the general point of view is unchanged though the diatribe is somewhat mellowed and some critical passages eliminated. See also Allen's earlier *Bureaucracy Triumphant* (London, 1931) and other tracts with a similar theme e.g. *What Price the British Constitution?* (London, 1941), and *Democracy and the Individual* (London, 1943). These matters (including the establishment of the Ombudsman) are examined in vol. iii, *A Much-Governed Nation*, chs 9, 10.
225 G. L. Schwartz, *Why Planning?* (London, 1944), p. 40.
226 T. Hewes, *Decentralize for Liberty* (London, 1950), p. 7.

9

DECLINE AND RENEWAL

May freedom's oak for ever live
With stronger life from day to day;
That man's the true Conservative
Who lops the moulder'd branch away.
TENNYSON, 'Hands All Round', 1852, in *The Works*, 1894, p. 575

AFTER 1945: UNDERTOW

The battle within the party is fought between the Tory individualists who follow ironically enough, the creed of nineteenth-century Liberalism and the Tory Reformers who raise the banner, or rather wave the pocket handkerchief, of Disraeli's Young England. Their ideas may be described as Socialism without Socialists. . . . I prefer the old Pretenders to the new. But that does not mean I believe the Old Guard of Tory Janissaries massed round the glorious but tattered banner of Free Enterprise are more likely to win a victory within the party or with the electorate.
LORD BEAVERBROOK to E. J. FLYNN, 11 October 1945, cited in A. J. P. Taylor, *Beaverbrook*, 1972; Penguin 1974, pp. 728–9

AS LORD BEAVERBROOK'S opinion indicates, the Conservative Party entered the post-war period in a state of some ideological disarray. The Coalition government had formulated an extensive programme of social and economic reform and the party was, therefore, formally associated with, even committed to, these policies. Yet there was in some circles a definite reluctance to accept them and even a sense of positive alienation from the principles involved largely because of the degree of state intervention and the level of taxation entailed. If the party had thrown up the Tory Reform group, committed to the government's reconstruction programme, there was also (as already mentioned in the previous chapter) the Progress Trust with its libertarian concern over these tendencies. Beaverbrook himself who had long believed in individual enterprise free of government supervision objected (on the whole) to controls and plans.[1]

1 A. J. P. Taylor, *Beaverbrook* (1972; Penguin edn, 1974), pp. 222–4, 522.

One preliminary skirmish that occurred in 1944 intimated the nature of the controversy that loomed.[2] The topic concerned was the continuance into the peace of wartime controls, the issue arising because the Ministry of Reconstruction was thinking ahead about such questions as the reallocation of manpower.[3] In August of that year a number of people including several Conservative MPs, such as D. L. Savory, W. Smithers, J. G. Braithwaite, and Sir R. Tasker, had signed a letter, a copy being sent to the Prime Minister, supporting the creation of 'a fighting fund for freedom' so that propaganda against state control could be issued and appropriate candidates helped with their election expenses. Among other things the letter said:

> We are fighting this war for eternal values, for Christian principles, for Liberty and Freedom and for the soul of man; for freedom to lead our own lives, for freedom from State interference, for freedom from filling up endless forms and from dictation and direction by Government officials, and for freedom from the continuance of State control after the war. We have *lent* our personal Freedom to the Government for the duration – it is vital that the loan be repaid after the war is over. . . . Today the trend of post-war legislation is in the opposite direction. Bill after bill is being introduced, or envisaged, which involves compulsion and loss of personal Freedom.[4]

Then, with an approving reference to Hayek's 'epoch-making' *Road to Serfdom*, a plea is made to halt this 'race down the road to the Totalitarian State' because the farther we go along it the more difficult it will be to turn back. 'Have we fought this war to preserve our Freedom from foreign tyranny in order to lose our Liberties to the Bureaucrats at Home?' The final and perhaps despairing shaft is that 'if a People will not save themselves, no Government can save them'.[5] In a later letter to the Premier, Waldron Smithers urged the crucial need to give full scope to the people's initiative in dealing with the economic problems of the peace and to avoid the continuance of controls.[6] Nor was this a unique flurry of controversy. There were also substantial and basic differences of opinion in Conservative ranks about such matters as the Catering Wages Bill and the Beveridge Report, educational policy and town planning.[7]

2 The papers referred to in this paragraph are at the PRO in PREM 4 88/2.
3 e.g. ibid., pp. 371 ff., memorandum of 10 October 1944, WP (44) 563.
4 ibid., p. 367, italics in original. I imagine this letter may subsequently have been published but I have only seen it in the form and place cited.
5 ibid., pp. 367–8.
6 Smithers to Churchill (16 November 1944), ibid., pp. 364–5. In this file there are also papers revealing an interesting difference of opinion on these matters between the secretaries in the Prime Minister's Private Office, ibid., pp. 356–64.
7 These intra-party debates are reviewed in detail in H. Kopsch, *The Approach of the*

After the traumatic electoral defeat in the summer of 1945, attempts to rethink the party's position and restore its popular image, basically on the lines of the coalition programme, brought sustained resistance. Thus the policy founded on the Industrial Charter of 1947 – the major document of Conservative rethinking in the immediate post-war period – was not worked out and presented without arousing notable expressions of concern and even opposition. For instance, Heathcoat Amory, who was a member of the industrial policy committee of the Conservative Shadow Cabinet, had doubts about the practicability at least of some of the proposals being himself rather more close to traditional free enterprise ideas than the rest of his colleagues. Official party publications, too, frequently stressed that 'free enterprise must not be trammelled by State control or superseded by monopolistic State ownership' and that party policy placed the 'freedom of the individual' from public restraint at the forefront of its programme.[8] Similarly Lord Woolton in a broadcast talk stressed that, while concerned with social reform, Conservatives equally rejected a state-controlled society and believed fundamentally in the power of individuals not of government.[9] Given the context of the day and this sort of encouragement it was not surprising that the anti-state Conservatives were in full voice. It was even necessary for Maxwell Fyfe to be given the special task of placating those Tories who thought the Charter was 'pink'.[10] Sir Waldron Smithers was foremost among this group in the House of Commons which also included such well-known back-benchers as Sir Herbert Williams. At the party conference in October 1947 Smithers called for the rejection of the Charter as no better than 'milk and water Socialism'.[11] Two years later he unsuccessfully tried to refer back the policy statement *The Right Road For Britain* on the ground that it was 'fatal' for Conservatives 'to compete with the Socialists in promising a Welfare State.'[12] Lord Beaverbrook's hostility was expressed through the columns of his newspapers. Likewise the editors of the weekly journal *Truth* represented Conservative concern at Socialistic developments in the party's policy, writing thus in 1949:

> Does official Conservatism wish to conserve the great tradition that the individual citizen and his family are the sound unit of society, or

    Conservative Party to Social Policy during World War II (PhD, London University, 1970), sections II–IV; cf. the summary in section V.
8 NUCUA, *Notes on Conservative Policy* (no. 3835; London, 1946), p8; *10 Points of Conservative Policy* (no. 3849; London, 1946); *We Shall Win Through* (London, 1952), pp. 8–10, 20, 32.
9 Lord Woolton, *The Modern Conservative* (CPC no. 3894; London, 1948), pp. 3–5.
10 Lord Butler, *The Art of the Possible* (London, 1971), pp. 143–4.
11 *KCA* (1946–8), p. 8945.
12 ibid., (1948–50), p. 10285A (10286).

does it wish to agree that the State is the sole unit to which the citizen and his family must be serflike in their subservience? Does Toryism teach that it is right and just that a man or woman should have special rewards for special services, or does it believe in a sentimental egalitarianism whatever its effect on productivity and the human character?[13]

The party's current obsession with planning was denounced as Fabian.[14] Referring to these views Harold Macmillan, a leading protagonist, of course, of the other brand of Conservatism, wrote later in his memoirs:

> In the House of Commons a number of Conservative Members were critical and alarmed. . . . Sir Waldron Smithers . . . fondly believed himself to be a good Tory, but in fact held opinions on economic and social matters indistinguishable from those of the Manchester *laissez-faire* school in the middle of the nineteenth century.

He added that, despite such opposition, those whom he himself called the 'true Tories' accepted 'with growing enthusiasm' a Conservatism oriented towards planning and the welfare state.[15] And it is the case that libertarian criticism of the so-called 'new Conservatism' of the post-war period, while often very vocal, attracted relatively little support at the time especially in the higher reaches of the Parliamentary leadership. Those elements in Conservative doctrine compatible with the positive state received most emphasis. Nevertheless as time wore on the other strand was reinforced by the natural and tactically desirable tendency to repudiate state Socialism and all its works. Slogans such as 'Set the people free' tended to predominate; and by 1955 the election cry was 'Conservative freedom works'. In 1950 one party publication (citing a speech by Churchill) put the issue in this way:

> The choice is between two ways of life; between individual liberty and State domination; between concentration of ownership in the hands of the State and the extension of ownership over the widest number of individuals; between the dead hand of monopoly and the stimulus of competition; between a policy of increasing restraint and a policy of liberating energy and ingenuity; between a policy of levelling down and a policy of opportunity for all to rise upwards from a basic standard.[16]

13 *Truth* (21 January 1949), p.61, cited in A. Gamble, *The Conservative Nation* (London, 1974), p.44.
14 *Truth* (27 June 1949), p.119, cited ibid., p.45.
15 H. Macmillan, *Tides of Fortune, 1945–1955* (London, 1969), pp.303–4.
16 *Conservatism 1945–50* (CPC no.90; London, 1950), pp.106–7. Cf. the emphasis in D. Spearman, 'The Freedom of the Individual', *Swinton Journal*, iv (no.2, September 1957), pp.41–4.

This antagonism was presented, of course, as one between the parties. But it might equally properly be seen as one between the different types of Conservatism itself.

Most expressions of the ideology reflected the attempt to achieve some kind of balance between the antithetical tendencies. This feeling is indicated in a book published by one MP in 1949. Its author Christopher Hollis is most concerned with constitutional problems and the need for institutional change but does place his analysis in a wide context, that of 'Freedom in an Industrial Age'.[17] He was clear Conservatism could not be simply a hankering after *laissez faire* because it had somehow to grapple with the new problems that had emerged from traditional capitalism, the irreligious ethos of the day, and the anomie created by vast social and industrial organizations in which man felt lost and 'disintegrated', not at home, bereft of all meaningful organic relationship. Yet it is not enough to invoke the state as a solution, for this may simply aggravate 'the disease of our age'. The crucial problem is, therefore, 'the discovery of a method of giving to the ordinary man a real membership in the large units in which modern conditions compel him to work.'[18] And the answer (Hollis here follows the analysis of Peter Drucker) is '"to prevent centralized bureaucratic despotism by building a genuine local self-government in the industrial sphere".'[19] Hollis writes about the general tendency towards collectivism which has been going on a long time: Conservatives, Liberals, and Socialists alike 'all were going, willy-nilly, in the same direction. But whether it was a right direction is a wholly different question.'[20] And in the kind of emphasis and solution he envisaged Hollis latches, of course, on to a decentralizing and property-diffusing tendency that had long been characteristic of certain kinds of Conservative thinking (as well as of Distributism with which, as a Catholic, Hollis was almost certainly familiar).[21]

Signs of a similar concern to Hollis's are also visible in aspects of the publications and speeches of the so-called 'One Nation Group' of Conservative MPs who were all elected to the House for the first time in 1950. The group initially consisted of C. J. M. Alport, R. Carr, R. Fort, E. Heath, G. Longden, I. Macleod, A. Maude, J. E. Powell, and J. Rodgers.

17 C. Hollis, *Can Parliament Survive?* (London, 1949), ch. 1.
18 ibid., p.12.
19 ibid., p.13, citing P. Drucker, *The Future of Industrial Man*.
20 ibid., p.45.
21 On the long-standing Conservative emphasis on the diffusion of land-ownership, profit-sharing, co-partnership schemes, and the like, see E. J. Bristow, *The Defence of Liberty and Property in Britain, 1880–1914* (unpublished PhD thesis, Yale University, 1970), pp.263–7, 269ff., 302ff. One particularly well-known and influential early statement in this context is W. H. Mallock's 'Conservatism and the Diffusion of Property', *National Review*, xi (1888), pp.383–404. For Distributism, see ch.3, pp.88–95 above.

In the early, eponymous pamphlet, the title of which clearly indicated the Disraelian heritage, a certain stress was nevertheless put on the need for a discriminatory attitude to welfare, for a departure from universal schemes so as to deal more effectively with real cases of want.[22] In truth there were more strands than one in the ideas of this group. Nevertheless in a later booklet *Change is our Ally* (which is subtitled 'A Tory Approach to Industrial Problems') the libertarian attitude is indicated by the title of that part of the work which discusses Conservative policy in the period since 1951, 'The Return to a Free Economy'. After a review of the years between the wars to show how public intervention in industry had increased, the contemporary point is introduced as follows:

> The formation of a Conservative government in October, 1951, marked a reaction in opinion against the trend not merely of the years of Socialism since 1945 but in many respects of the whole period since the first World War.
>
> A change of direction was at once initiated. Physical controls and State trading were progressively eliminated. Bank rate was immediately used to help in restoring supply and demand for capital to equilibrium, thus combatting [*sic*] inflation by purely economic means. The reduction of consumer subsidies in the first Conservative Budget began to bring prices into line with real costs.
>
> The new attitude was most strikingly expressed in three measures, all introduced in 1952, to denationalise road haulage, the iron and steel industry, and development rights in land.

But this, it was hoped, was only a beginning.[23]

The ethos represented by this group was sufficiently clear at least to John Strachey who in the *New Statesman* said that the pamphlet on industrial policy (which was, in fact, much influenced by Enoch Powell's ideas about the free-market economy) should have been called 'Back to Laissez Faire': 'Here', Strachey wrote, 'are a group of young Tories preaching the pure milk of the gospel of classical liberalism. . . .'[24] Certainly *Change is our Ally* expressed sentiments like the following:

> In the second half of the twentieth century the creation of new wealth has become our most urgent need. If this is to be achieved, we believe that the pendulum must swing back towards a more competit-

22 I. Macleod and A. Maude (eds), *One Nation: a Tory Approach to Social Problems* (CPC no.86; London, 1950), p.9.

23 E. Powell and A. Maude (eds), *Change is our Ally* (CPC no.133; London, 1954), p.47.

24 Cited in A. Roth, *Enoch Powell: Tory Tribune* (London, 1970), p.111. R. A. Butler's reference to the group as 'Tory "neo-Fabians"' is most misleading: see his 'A Disraelian Approach to Modern Politics', R. A. Butler *et al.*, *Tradition and Change* (CPC no.138; London, 1954), p.10.

ive system. We recognise that social and political considerations should often override economic ones, and that it may therefore be necessary to mitigate the effects of economic change. But as a general rule we reject the distortion of the natural forces of supply and demand for avowedly economic purposes. At best it is usually ineffective; at worst it can be positively harmful. [Any] exceptions . . . do not invalidate the general principle that freely-operating competition is the most effective means of promoting economic advantage.[25]

On this basis two main themes were developed. The first is that 'efficient co-ordination depends not on centralised planning but on the exercise of consumer choice based on economic costs competitively determined.' The creative force in industry is consumer demand which is also 'the most effective co-ordinating force' provided consumers are able to 'choose between different goods and services offered at true economic cost.' Yet this is not an argument for complete *laissez faire* for it may be beneficial to control generally the 'economic temperature', say to mitigate the effects of economic change for social purposes or to protect the economy from world conditions.[26] The second, and more important, theme is the need for economic change itself and for a structure of industry that will encourage it. The attempt to maintain the *status quo* through 'rationalisation' – the received doctrine of the 1920s and 1930s – is not enough. Redeployment and flexibility are now required and are to be achieved not through central direction but through various forms of incentive to capital, management, and labour.

A further One Nation Group pamphlet which came out at the end of the 1950s concerned itself with a cognate theme, 'the process of restoring balance between the power of the State and the rights of the individual.'

> In 1951 we inherited a society in whose life the State was playing a heavy and expanding role. . . . We found . . . that in social and industrial affairs more and more power was being taken and wielded by the executive; scope for the individual was, correspondingly, diminished. During the next eight years, particularly since 1955, . . . the Conservative Government has gone some way towards halting and reversing this trend towards State domination [and] this has been a most beneficial result of Tory rule. . . . Reviewed in this light much of the work and policy of the Conservative Government assumes a coherence and purpose which is not widely perceived or appreciated.[27]

The object was to show how this trend might be developed in the future and how the Tory middle ground between extreme individualism and

25 Powell and Maude (eds), *Change is Our Ally*, p.96.
26 ibid., pp.96–7.
27 Lord Balniel *et al.*, *The Responsible Society* (CPC no.200; London, 1959), pp.5–6.

excessive 'State parentalism' might be defended.[28] Given that this was the period of Crichel Down when concern for the individual's rights in relation to public agencies had been intensified and when, the bonfire of controls phase having passed, Macmillanite collectivism was in the ascendant, it may be these opinions are somewhat jejune. Yet they indicate a psychology of interest and would certainly have appealed to anti-statist elements in the party, perhaps helping to allay their fears while the leadership went about doing something quite different.

These expressions of opinion owed a good deal to the influence in the group of Enoch Powell. In fact, possibly the most extensive and coherent statement of Conservative libertarianism by a politician in the past two or three decades is embodied in his speeches and writings.

ENOCH POWELL AND THE FREE SOCIETY

Mr. Powell is an economic Whig but a political Tory. . . .
J. CRITCHLEY, *The Times*, 15 February 1969, p.8

Enoch Powell is a polymath of astonishing intellectual range and industry. He must surely be unique among today's politicians at Westminster in the breadth let alone the testing depth of his interests. From the past, but still no dry relic, there is the poetry and classical scholarship, the fascination with German philosophy and literature, and the astonishing linguistic competence. There is the current immersion in and the grasp of technical problems in so many disparate fields from theology and economics to medieval history. And this altogether apart from everyday preoccupations. It is hardly surprising that his numerous political utterances bear the mark of a profound and rigorous mind consciously dedicated to a consistent statement of public issues which, if not embodied in a single systematic treatise, is none the less indicated by the thematic arrangement of ideas implicit in his published volumes of political addresses.[29] Something he himself said about Aneurin Bevan (whom he much admired) is an apt comment: 'He had a characteristic not common among politicians . . . : he was never satisfied with a debating argument or a particular train of reasoning unless he could relate it to some general principle and inform his contentions with the light which that general principle shed.'[30] One interesting review of Powell's *Freedom and Reality* observed that its character was of a 'collection of political speeches . . . made to figure as a philosophical construction with

28 ibid., pp.6, 7–8, 11.
29 e.g. J. Wood (ed.), *A Nation Not Afraid: the Thinking of Enoch Powell* (London, 1965); J. E. Powell, *Freedom and Reality* (Paperfront, 1969); J. E. Powell, *Still to Decide* (Paperfront, 1972); J. E. Powell, *The Common Market – the Case Against* (Paperfront, 1971).
30 Cited in Andrew Roth, *Enoch Powell: Tory Tribune* (London, 1970), p.132.

a proudly philosophical title. . . . [What] other politician of the age would offer us the pretension – let alone the substance ?'[31]

This aspect of Powell's ideas has latterly tended to be forgotten in the furore created by his views on the EEC and even more on immigration policy as well as by his subsequent departure from the Conservative Party. But in the present context it is proper to direct attention to the more general range and pattern of his opinions concerning the role and function of government which he has himself discerned as among the central issues of our time.[32] And here there is a basic consistency of view whatever *bouleversements* may have occurred in respect to other fields of policy in which concepts once firmly held have been ruthlessly cast aside on being revealed as illusions incompatible with reality. The most obvious instances of such a transformation of political values have occurred in the area of foreign and empire policy. For example, from originally being preoccupied with sustaining Britain's imperial role, Powell came to realize in the mid-1950s that the commonwealth co-operation of which he had dreamed was quite impossible; and so he was led instead to advocate a policy of withdrawal from distant overseas commitments and a concentration on Britain's own concerns in Europe and its defence.[33] Likewise Powell has altered his view on the Common Market.[34] In each such case, no doubt genuine changes of sentiment become indistinguishably mingled with questions of political tactics.[35] But the concern here is primarily with the collectivist issue, specifically the domestic task and duty of government, and on this it is clear – despite suggestions to the contrary – that Powell has not changed much at all since he entered politics after the last war though he may have become more uncompromising.[36] His position, a firm defence of the free-market economy, is based first and foremost on acceptance of the classical economic tradition, the belief that the real world is here governed by ineluctable laws. Illusion is the supposition that these hard principles can be avoided or their consequences mitigated by political sleight of hand.

31 R. Jackson, 'Enoch Powell: Paradox of Politics and Poets', *The Times* (24 April 1969), p.11.

32 Powell, *Freedom and Reality*, p.187.

33 ibid., chs 11 and 12, and pp.321ff., 337; Powell's essay on 'The Empire of England', in R. A. Butler *et al.*, *Tradition and Change* (CPC no.138; London, 1954), pp.41–53. See also Roth, op. cit., *passim*, but esp. pp.115–16; and T. E. Utley, *Enoch Powell: the Man and his Thinking* (London, 1968), pp.61–6, 69–70.

34 Powell, *The Common Market – the Case Against*, pp.9–11, 19, 60, 71–2.

35 For a detailed analysis of Powell's 'nationalism' and his views on these recent issues, see K. Phillips, 'The Nature of Powellism', N. Nugent and R. King (eds), *The British Right: Conservative and Right Wing Politics in Britain* (Farnborough, Hants, 1977), ch. 5, esp. pp.110ff.

36 See e.g. Utley, op. cit., pp.58–60, 74–5. Cf. the ironical comment of Aneurin Bevan in 1956, cited in Roth, op. cit., p.133; also ibid., pp.221, 223.

In addition there is his strong sense of the continuity of British history, and so of the national conventions and institutions which are conceived in compatible libertarian mould. Such are the political realities in which freedom is enmeshed and on the principles of which policy must be based. This position, not surprisingly, issues in a fervent hostility to the *dirigiste* tendencies which have (he believes) become so predominant and uncongenial a feature of our political life and which have affected so strongly, too, the Conservative Party itself.[37]

Yet Powell's point of view is not at all (as many critics suppose) a straightforward, across-the-board *laissez faire* attitude like that of Spencer or Sir E. Benn. He has specifically denied holding such a view and, far from accepting the notion of 'the neutral state', accepts that government must take some important decisions on behalf of the community as a whole.[38] Suggestions that Powell possibly wishes even to abolish the police, the fire service, and the armed forces, and to hand them over to private companies to run at a profit are absurd.[39] He is not and never has been an extreme 'voluntaryist' like Auberon Herbert. In 1970, when it was widely expected that state intervention would be notably diminished by the Heath administration, Powell clearly recorded his own view:

> 'Less government' does not mean less government everywhere. It is not only consistent with there being more government in some spheres and directions, but it positively demands it. If *laissez-faire* means that government withdraws from those functions in society which the citizens must not or cannot try to perform for themselves, then the Tory Party is not, never has been, and never can be, the party of *laissez-faire*.[40]

In fact, his position rests on a distinction between three areas of policy the role of government being different in each.[41]

The first field is both basic and fairly clear. It is the duty of government to ensure for the community a secure framework of living and this means

---

37 Powell, *Freedom and Reality*, pp.7–8; Wood, *A Nation Not Afraid*, pp.ix–x, 31; Roth, op. cit., pp.311, 316, 317; P. H. Douglas and J. E. Powell, *How Big Should Government Be?* (Washington, DC, 1968), pp.46–8; 'Conservatism and Social Problems', *Swinton Journal*, xiv (no.3, Autumn 1968), pp.8–16.

38 Powell, *Freedom and Reality*, p.23; Douglas and Powell, op. cit., p.166; speech (1964), cited in Roth, op. cit., p.305 (in which he attacks, too, the 'wishy-washy' compromise with Socialism which had characterized the recent policies of Conservative governments).

39 B. Levin, *The Pendulum Years* (1970; Pan, 1972), pp.168–9.

40 Powell, *Still To Decide*, p.11.

41 This kind of analysis with its corollary of limited government action has been specifically criticized by D. Howell in his paper 'Towards Stability', R. Blake *et al.*, *Conservatism Today* (CPC no.350; London, 1966), pp.35, 43.

the provision of adequate defence against external attack and the domestic maintenance of law and the prevention of crime: the most elementary function of the state is 'the protection of the physical safety of its members'. This attention to national security in the widest sense is 'the outer frame or condition precedent of the nation's life.'[42] But secondly this security must also be the framework of a civilized way of living. And in Powell's view the provision of the necessary common services to this end may or may not involve the state. He thinks that what is done in this respect in any given country will hinge on its history and circumstances. A motorway, for example, might be built and run as a public highway or as a privately-constructed toll road; and a hospital could be the responsibility of central government, or a municipality, or some voluntary body. It depends. And so far as Britain is concerned Powell thinks that, while it might have been otherwise, we have in these respects become used to a good deal of public control and operation and to rely extensively on state initiative. And all this he is prepared – perhaps with a certain reluctance in some respects – to accept. He comments, too, on the high standards which have been achieved in this way in fields such as education, roads and traffic, the great urban services such as town planning, public health, welfare, and social security.[43] He is especially a defender of the range of services for which he was personally responsible as Minister of Health and does not anticipate or advocate any scheme radically different from the present nationally organized and financed arrangements though he is quite aware of the problems and defects involved. In this latter respect in particular he is concerned that while public services may lay down minimum provision they should not necessarily become all-embracing and exclusive.[44] But, in such contexts as these, Powell generally thinks in terms of 'the limits of laissez-faire' and of the irrelevance of economic criteria: of course, such provision has a cost but in regard to these matters this may be a secondary consideration.[45] Naturally if voluntary or private activity, perhaps in the pursuit of profit, will effectively get something done in this 'mixed' area then there is no need for state action. But when 'non-profit' or apathy prevails then government is 'necessarily and functionally concerned.' There are dangers in this resort, to spontaneous development and change, but the alternative may be, too, a pitiful narrowing of human possibilities.[46]

42 Wood, *A Nation Not Afraid*, p.32; Powell, *Still to Decide*, pp.11–12, 18; Douglas and Powell, op. cit., p.49.
43 Wood, *A Nation Not Afraid*, pp.32–3; Powell, *Freedom and Reality*, p.36.
44 Wood, *A Nation Not Afraid*, pp.28, 44; Powell, *A New Look at Medicine and Politics* (London, 1966); Douglas and Powell, op. cit., pp.190–2.
45 Powell, *Freedom and Reality* p.94; 'The Limits of Laissez-Faire', *Crossbow*, iii (no.11, Spring 1960), pp.25–8; Douglas and Powell, op. cit., pp.173–4.
46 Wood, *A Nation Not Afraid*, pp.29, 42–3, 49–51; Powell, *Freedom and Reality*,

Yet thirdly, in the economic sphere itself, things are quite otherwise. For Powell is an unrepentant critic of the 'superstition' that government can and should try to control the economy.[47] He is rather an ardent believer in capitalist free enterprise as indicated by the remark he was once reported to have made that when kneeling in church he often thought how much God should be thanked for the gift of capitalism.[48] His preferred definition of 'Powellism' is 'an almost unlimited faith in the ability of people to get what they want through peace, capital, profit and a competitive market.'[49] This commitment to the free-market economy arises because it is seen as 'the unique key, to unlock imprisoned energies.'[50] In order to ensure optimum economic growth there must be no obstacles to change and the free play of initiative. Normally consumer demand must not be frustrated or the working of the profit motive prevented. Ingenuity, effort, and judgement must be allowed to reap the rewards of their success for they multiply wealth. And, in fact, unless the capitalist system is largely allowed its head there will not be available that surplus of resources needed to sustain improved standards of security and common service.[51] The essential role of government in this respect is 'to abolish and remove man-made obstacles' to the economic process and to see it goes on as undisturbed as possible.[52] But the task of public authority is not, therefore, uniform. Sometimes its duty is 'to do nothing and let things happen'; and this may not infrequently require a great deal of political courage.[53] Sometimes positive action is necessary to remove obstacles or stop interference with the free flow of economic forces as with the abolition of rationing or state purchase, the removal of subsidies, dismantling economic controls, and the like.[54] Further it may be appropriate for government to adjust to this same end the 'framework of law' within which industry and commerce operate as by the prevention of restrictive practices, the revision of trade union law, or the treatment of monopoly.[55] Also (as already noted) it may be necessary in

---

pp.13, 32, and *Still to Decide*, pp.12–13. There is a detailed analysis of Powell's views about welfare provision in K. Phillips, 'The Nature of Powellism', loc. cit., esp. pp.99–106.

47 Lecture given in 1961, cited in Roth, op. cit., p.260.
48 Cited ibid., p.306.
49 Powell, 'Conservatism and Social Problems', *Swinton Journal*, loc. cit., p.15.
50 Powell, *Freedom and Reality*, p.27.
51 Wood, *A Nation Not Afraid*, pp.7, 32, 34, 82; Powell, *Freedom and Reality*, pp.7, 28, 32–3, 144–5, 160–3.
52 Wood, *A Nation Not Afraid*, p.32; Douglas and Powell, op. cit., pp.66–7.
53 Wood, *A Nation Not Afraid*, p.33.
54 ibid., pp.4, 33–4.
55 ibid., pp.14, 119ff.; Powell, *Freedom and Reality*, pp.193–214; Utley, op. cit., pp.127–8.

connexion with the provision of security or desirable common services for the profit motive to be superseded altogether, though even here Powell does not give government *carte blanche* in its mode of action, distinguishing between general regulation of a spontaneous or automatic system of decision (which is acceptable) and specific intervention (which is not).[56] But basically in the field of business, commerce, and industry, 'where the economic motive reigns', it is necessary, he believes, to be 'whole-hoggers' and 'to put the state in all its guises under "notice to quit".'[57]

Given these views it is not surprising, therefore, that Powell is extremely critical of government intervention beyond the limits envisaged. Nationalization or other forms of public ownership are unacceptable and the existing sector of the economy falling under this description should be reduced as quickly as possible so that the enterprises concerned may 'resume their proper integrated place in a free economy.'[58] National planning or anything like it is, of course, completely anathema. It is an illusion and will not work. The complexities involved are too great; the information available for decision-making on this scale is all too likely to be woefully inadequate both in quantity and 'promptitude'; and too much weight rests on the calibre and in the hands of a small body of public servants.[59] Moreover given the national scope of the exercise any mistake made will be enormous in its consequences.[60] A national plan will also be rigid, too slow to adapt to changing circumstances and this not least because of the political factors involved which are likely to make it difficult to admit anything is wrong 'until disaster has occurred'. In this way, again, a plan will inhibit the flexibility and possibility of development so desirable in the economy: it will, for instance, freeze a certain distribution of labour and other resources, prevent the satisfaction of varying demand, and inhibit the achievement of technological advance.[61]

In this changing world poor Leviathan is left lumbering behind; for the great machine is bound to be working on a conception of the nation as it no longer is, perhaps as it has long since ceased to be. There is always

56 See the speech reported in Utley, op. cit., pp.119–23; Douglas and Powell, op. cit., pp.48ff.
57 Powell, *Still to Decide*, p.13.
58 Wood, *A Nation Not Afraid*, p.81; Powell, *Freedom and Reality*, pp.73–6; Douglas and Powell, op. cit., pp.65–6.
59 Powell, *Freedom and Reality*, pp.22, 38, 41–6, 48, 58, 91–2; Utley, op. cit., p.125; E. Powell and A. Maude (eds), *Change is our Ally* (CPC no.133; London, 1954), pp.26–27, 31–2, 38; Douglas and Powell, op. cit., pp.59–60.
60 Powell, *Freedom and Reality*, p.23.
61 ibid., pp.22–3, 38–9, 49, 55–6, 264–80; Wood, *A Nation Not Afraid*, pp.66–8, 71–3, 74–5, 88–9; Powell and Maude, *Change is Our Ally*, p.38.

a time-lag before Parliaments, Ministers, bureaucrats, and politicians set off again in pursuit of the world which has moved on.[62]

Specifically the kind of control involved in planning can cause hardship and scarcity. Powell believes, for instance, that the shortage of housing and the unhappiness it causes are the direct result of government attempts to peg rents, subsidize building, and ration or allocate output.[63] Equally planning inhibits energy and enterprise and thus helps to reduce the reservoir of wealth on which the adequate provision of common services depends.

But above all a national plan is the enemy of free choice. It brings in its train a kind of society which in the end must reflect the antithesis of freedom: where consumer choice exercised through price and profit does not decide, 'there the state must and will.' Planning means control.[64]

> I happen to believe that when a society's economic life ceases to be shaped by the interaction of the free decisions of individuals, freedom is in a fair way to disappear from other sides of its existence as well. The terms 'free economy' and 'free society' are to me interchangeable.[65]

In a paean of praise reminiscent, for instance, of Ernest Benn or, to take a later example, of Milton Friedman, Powell says:

> The free enterprise economy is the true counterpart of democracy: it is the only system which gives everyone a say. Everyone who goes into a shop and chooses one article instead of another is casting a vote in the economic ballot box: with thousands or millions of others that choice is signalled through to production and investment and helps to mould the world just a tiny fraction nearer to people's desire. In this great and continuous general election of the free economy . . . we are all voting all the time.

Or, again:

> The collective wisdom and the collective will of the nation resides not in any little Whitehall clique but in the whole mass of the people – in the producers, listening to the voice of the customer at home and abroad; in the savers and investors, using their eyes and their brains to lay out their resources to the best advantage; in the consumers themselves expressing through all the complex nervous system of the market their wishes, their needs, their expectations. In short, the true

62 Wood, *A Nation Not Afraid*, p.43.
63 Powell, *Freedom and Reality*, pp.92–3, 95, and *Still to Decide*, pp.19–25; Wood, *A Nation Not Afraid*, pp.7, 60–1, 90; Douglas and Powell, op. cit., p.176.
64 Powell, *Freedom and Reality*, pp.34–6, 41–5, 49–51, 102; Powell and Maude, *Change is our Ally*, pp.37–8.
65 J. E. Powell, *Saving in a Free Society* (1960; 2nd edn, London, 1966), p.8.

national economic plan is being made all the time by the very people and institutions which the intellectual arrogance of the Socialist affects to despise.[66]

He also believes that the evils of inflation – surely the major economic issue of the day? – are a direct consequence of the excessive government expenditure entailed by so much intervention and the way this is financed; just as the recurrent balance of payments crises are attributed to control of exchange rates.[67] He finds particularly objectionable and insidious the collectivism by stealth involved in the procedure (which has latterly been more and more extensively employed) of 'government by request' or by intimidation, that is, so-called voluntary co-operation not required by law with state intervention or supervision of economic life. Examples are voluntary price or wage restraint or their counterparts in investment and industrial policy. Such decisions are based on government persuasion, advice, bullying, or exhortation and really reflect a covert use of compulsion. All this should be opposed: first because government in order to apply this kind of pressure needs a single body to deal with and, as this organization has to be representative, it must involve a closed shop and a harsh way with recalcitrants; and secondly because it is 'an arbitrary and lawless use of power'. There is a profound distinction which must not be blurred between this 'Rule of the Threat of Law' and the rule of law itself, between what government wants and what the law requires.[68]

Reality for Powell is simply another name for freedom and the natural necessity of things. And it will always in the end force itself through illusions about the controlled economy though not perhaps before these dreams or fallacies have wrought all sorts of untoward consequences. 'How much better to face [the facts] steadily and continuously, by letting price – genuine, competitive, market price – tell us the truth.'[69]

Given all this, Powell naturally holds that the Conservative Party should stand clearly for capitalist free enterprise and against all forms of economic *dirigisme*. He recognizes, too, that this will require the repudiation of certain paternalistic or collectivist tendencies in the party's own tradition and record.[70]

66 Powell, *Freedom and Reality*, pp.11, 33. Cf. ibid., p.22; Douglas and Powell, op. cit., pp.61, 68. On Friedman, see vol.i, *The Rise of Collectivism*, ch.3, pp.154–61.
67 Powell, *Freedom and Reality*, pp.98ff., 123–4, 143, 149–52, 168–71, 177, 180, 183, 192; Wood, *A Nation Not Afraid*, pp.19, 22–3.
68 Powell, *Freedom and Reality*, pp.46, 64–73, 79–82, 115ff., 127ff., 164, 166–7, 198, 209; Powell, *Still to Decide*, ch.3, esp., pp.67ff.; Utley, op. cit., p.116. Cf. the similar attack on the 'Appeal Response' by David Howell, M. Wolff et al., *The Conservative Opportunity* (London, 1965), pp.97–8.
69 Powell, *Freedom and Reality*, p.114.
70 ibid., pp.23–5.

One of the historic duties of the Conservative Party is to moderate the mania for seeing and seeking the hand of government in everything and to oppose the superstition that government action is the panacea for mankind's ills.

Whatever else the Conservative Party stands for, unless it is the party of free choice, free competition and free enterprise, unless – I am not afraid of the word – it is the party of capitalism, then it has no function in the contemporary world, then it has nothing to say to modern Britain.

. . . we are a capitalist party. We believe in capitalism. When we look at the astonishing material achievements of the West, at our own high and rising physical standard of living, we see these things as the result, not of compulsion or government action or the superior wisdom of a few, but of that system of competition and free enterprise, rewarding success and penalising failure, which enables every individual to participate by his private decisions in shaping the future of his society. Because we believe this we honour profit competitively earned; we respect the ownership of property great or small; we accept the differences of wealth and income without which competition and free enterprise are impossible.[71]

Powell has often felt, however, that his party had become so imbued with the collectivist illusion (it was, for instance, a Conservative government which had initiated attempts to control incomes and set up NEDC and the 'little Neddies') that it was necessary to urge a total redefinition of doctrine and policy so that support would no longer be given to state ownership, pretentious attempts at planning, subsidizing or otherwise bolstering uncompetitive industries or regions, and the like.[72] And before his dismissal from the Shadow Cabinet in 1968 Powell did have some definite influence to this end in the policy study groups which the party had set up.[73] In 1967 he made one of his most pointed attacks on the tendency towards collectivism and stressed the part Conservatives must play in reversing it:

Today an enormous and steadily increasing dead weight of organization and constraint pins the nation down. It is an incubus which has grown so steadily and with such acceptance that most people are scarcely conscious of its deadening presence. There is the whole range of the nationalized industries. There is the whole gamut of government intervention in non-nationalized industry. There is the

71 ibid., p.18; Wood, *A Nation Not Afraid*, pp.18, 25. Cf. ibid., pp.87, 88, 91.
72 Powell, *Freedom and Reality*, pp.23–34; Wood, *A Nation Not Afraid*, pp.68, 76, 96–8; Roth, op. cit., pp.318–20; Utley, op. cit., p.35.
73 Roth, op. cit., pp.325–6.

great and growing host of organizations advising, exhorting, cajoling, planning, interfering with our industry and commerce. There is the system of a welfare state designed to promote uniformity and eliminate all scope for choice and initiative. There is the range of policies, from incomes and prices to industrial location, which aim at averaging everything and everybody.

No wonder so many people say: 'This is the way of the world; there is no escaping, no reversing it, so let us acquiesce. . . .' But it is not the way of the world. The world swirls by, leaving us behind, with an adventurous, achieving spirit, that contrasts with the atmosphere of Britain.[74]

Between the 'two inherently different systems' the Conservative Party must choose. If it chooses to 'go on adding more elements of state control to the large accumulated load the nation already carries, . . . there will soon be no longer a real role in this country for the Tory Party.' But if it resolves really 'to set the people free' there nevertheless lies ahead of it 'a task of heroic dimensions', a 'return to freedom' that will mean 'nothing less than a revolution in the whole form and organization of our life and economy in Britain.'[75]

And such a change is vital. The free economy of capitalism must be sustained by Conservatives though not merely, perhaps not even mainly, for material reasons:

We believe that a society where men are free to take economic decisions for themselves – to decide how they will apply their incomes, their savings, their efforts – is the only kind of society where men will remain free in other respects, free in speech, thought and action. It is no accident that wherever the state has taken economic decision away from the citizen, it has deprived him of his other liberties as well. . . .

We uphold the capitalist free economy, then, as much more than a mechanism for ensuring that the nation gets the best material return for its energies and resources: we uphold it as a way of life, as the counterpart of the free society, which guarantees, as no other can, that men shall be free to make their own choices, right or wrong, wise or foolish, to obey their own consciences, to follow their own initiatives.[76]

It is clear, then, that Powell is not a classical Liberal *tout court*. He is prepared to have government play a significant role in the affairs of the

74 Powell, *Freedom and Reality*, p.77.
75 ibid., p.79. Contrast the view that Powell's economic ideas are incompatible with the 'central tradition of English conservatism', Utley, op. cit., pp.136–7.
76 Wood, *A Nation Not Afraid*, pp.25–6. Cf. J. Wood (ed.), *Powell and the 1970 Election* (Paperfront, 1970), pp.122–4; Utley, op. cit., p.117.

community in respect of public order and in matters which concern the quality of the common life. But he is undoubtedly very dubious indeed about the contemporary tendency to extend state control over the details of economic activity whether this be reflected in the conscious pursuit of state Socialism or in the perhaps less committed but nevertheless ominous march toward the mixed economy or the middle way which has found substantial support in the leadership and body of all major parties at least for the last forty or fifty years. To this degree Powell certainly wants to turn the clock back; or leap forward: it depends how you see it. For Powell, therefore, the Conservative Party must be a libertarian party free of a universal statist tendency; or it is nothing. His fear is that people will, from apathy, ignorance, or a false conception of their real interest welcome the embrace of collectivism.[77] And the politician's task is precisely to prevent such images, myths, and illusions about the world from being thus in conflict with its reality.

LIBERTARIAN OPPORTUNITY?

The essence of an English Conservative is that he believes in the spontaneous forces of society and is sceptical of the wisdom and efficacy of government.
T. E. UTLEY, in 'Intellectuals and Conservatives: a Symposium', *Swinton Journal*, xiv, no.2, Summer 1968, p.31

During the 1950s and early 1960s Powell seemed often to be a lone Conservative voice urging the claims of the limited state. Of course, he was not in fact unique in holding such views. But this was the Butler-Macmillan era in which the dominant note sounded was that of the middle way and successive Tory governments were busy demonstrating that they were not afraid of using the power of the state to tackle economic and social problems. However, following the departure of the major figures who had presided over this Conservative version of 'consensus' politics, a reaction set in. This was subsequently reflected in a short-lived journal that appeared in the late 1960s. Its director, Sir Anthony Meyer, explained his policy in the first editorial to appear. Public and party opinion alike, he suggested, were moving to the right, a tendency which 'is largely the result of the conspicuous failure in action of the ideas – economic planning, universal state welfare – which during most of this century have activated not only the Labour Party but' – the admission is significant – 'much of the Conservative Party too.'[78] One commentator of the time more specifically still accused the Macmillan administration of having been 'a good deal too collectivist'; another (in a

77 Wood, *A Nation Not Afraid*, p.31. Cf. ibid., p.2; Powell, *Freedom and Reality*, pp.13, 60–2.
78 *Solon: a Right Wing Journal*, i (no.1, October 1969), p.4.

curious misreading of the party's ideological tradition) even asked whether 'Conservative welfarism' was not a contradiction in terms.[79] And these libertarian stirrings became, of course, much more apparent after the party's defeat in the 1964 general election. An almost automatic response to this political failure was to set in train a process of examining party principles and policy as a means of stimulating a Tory revival. What has happened, in effect, from that day to this is that more and more Conservative opinion has become aware of that strand in its ideological tradition which justifies a dubiety about or even hostility to a substantial and increasing role for the state in the regulation of society's affairs. A long experience of the growth of government had, it seems, at last bred a notable scepticism about its augmented role and led to a feeling in the party that too many people had been too ready to accept state intervention and had ignored their 'liberal economic heritage'.[80] A new emphasis was, therefore, sought in doctrine and programme, and Conservatives were increasingly urged to forsake the collectivist path which they had latterly taken and to defend instead the capitalist free economy and generally what one of them called 'classical liberalism'.[81] In what is arguably one of the most cultured and wide-ranging reviews of these matters undertaken by an active politician, Angus Maude wrote in 1969 that if Conservatives opposed the policy of limiting state action for perfectly sound reasons when that view was dominant then now, when collectivist programmes were in the ascendant, 'they are inclined to be attracted by the intellectual arguments for laissez-faire.'[82] This point of view and the case made in its behalf is clearly important not least because in purely practical terms it has been a factor crucial to the creation of that background of opinion from which the policies of the Thatcher government have emerged, policies which deliberately set out to challenge the dominant collectivist tendencies of the age. What, briefly, is the nature of the arguments offered as 'an intellectually based and firmly stated alternative'?[83]

Publicists being what they are, the identity of the guides and mentors

79 R. Lewis in 'Intellectuals and Conservatism: a Symposium', *Swinton Journal*, xiv (no.2, Summer 1968), p.17; E. Kedourie, 'Conservatism and the Conservative Party', *Solon* (no.4, October 1970), p.48.
80 T. Raison in 'Intellectuals and Conservatism: a Symposium', loc. cit., p.21.
81 This phrase occurs in N. Lawson, 'The Economic Setting: the Need for a National Policy', R. Blake *et al.*, *Conservatism Today* (CPC no.350; London, 1966), p.57. Cf. P. Worsthorne, 'The Ideological Setting: Priorities for Capitalism', ibid., pp.18–24, 26, 28–30; also T. Szamuely, *Unique Conservative* (CPC no.531; London, 1973), pp.25–6, and the broadly anti-collectivist emphasis of a number of those responding to one of Szamuely's articles, J. Biffen *et al.*, 'Intellectuals and Conservatism: a Symposium', loc. cit., pp.9–35.
82 A. Maude, *The Common Problem* (London, 1969), p.287.
83 The phrase cited is from T. Szamuely, 'Intellectuals and Conservatism', *Swinton Journal*, xiv (no.1, Spring 1968), p.13.

328 The Ideological Heritage

whose influence is at work in their articles and pamphlets has invariably
to be guessed at. There is more than a touch of Samuel Smiles or Spencer
in what they say but it is to be doubted whether they have spent many
hours poring over the pages of the Synthetic Philosophy or even of the
perhaps more familiar volumes of the classical economists and J. S. Mill.
Brooding omnipresently as well over the appearance of these libertarian
ephemera is the spirit of such profound contemporary writers as M.
Oakeshott and F. A. Hayek who have in recent years produced, in their
different ways, a telling criticism of 'teleocratic' government and a most
sophisticated defence of 'the political economy of freedom', of a society
infused with a sense of individuality and the rule of law. Yet, some
academic adherents of the libertarian cause apart, few will follow them
in their arcane reference of these matters to certain implications of
Idealist philosophy or the history of scientific rationalism. In any case,
for his part Hayek has denied he is a Conservative (though it is
presumably only the collectivist brand of the doctrine he finds unacceptable); Oakeshott's allegiance in this respect is, however, clear.[84] A
more obvious and immediate affinity is to the libertarian case stated on
many platforms by E. Powell though, in a notable example of political
ingratitude, it has been rare since he left the Conservative Party for this
similarity or indebtedness to be properly acknowledged.[85] Another most
immediate influence is, of course, that of Professor M. Friedman, a brief
account of whose monetarist doctrine and its implications was given in
the previous volume.[86]

The kind of Conservatism expounded by its libertarian supporters
does not on the whole sustain a merely 'blind rush in the direction of less
and less government'. It is recognized that there has to be some
regulation of the market for social or environmental reasons. But it is
highly desirable all the same to take a hard look at, for instance, the
preoccupation with 'growth' at any price, at the pursuit of egalitarian
goals, and at the array of welfare and educational policies created in

84 See M. Oakeshott, *Rationalism in Politics and Other Essays* (London, 1962), and *On
    Human Conduct* (Oxford, 1975). See also my *Oakeshott's Philosophical Politics*
    (London, 1966), and 'Idealism, Modern Philosophy and Politics', P. King and B. C.
    Parekh (eds), *Politics and Experience*. . . . (Cambridge, 1968), which also contains a
    bibliography of Oakeshott's writings to that date. For Hayek, see esp. his recent *Law,
    Legislation and Liberty* (London, 1973–9), and his *Road to Serfdom* (London, 1944),
    The Counter-Revolution of Science: Studies on the Abuse of Reason (New York,
    1955), *The Constitution of Liberty* (London, 1960). For comment, see E. Streissler *et
    al.*, *Roads to Freedom* . . . (London, 1969).
85 In 1968 a foreign observer, Senator Paul Douglas, even told Powell he did not really
    belong in the Conservative Party: P. H. Douglas and J. E. Powell, *How Big Should
    Government Be?* (Washington, DC, 1968), p.99. And for a domestic instance of
    agreement with this view, see F. Mount, 'Facing Mr. Powell', *Solon*, i (no. 3, April
    1970), pp.7–14.
86 See vol.i, *The Rise of Collectivism*, ch.3, pp.154–61.

recent years by the interventionist 'consensus'.[87] The basic principle is one that was stated epigrammatically many years ago by Walter Lippmann: 'in a free society the state does not administer the affairs of men. It administers justice among men who conduct their own affairs.'[88] There must thus be a reasonably clear understanding of the limits of the public sphere in these terms. One Conservative journal said in the mid-1960s that the purpose of the state was 'to provide the conditions in which the private sector can flourish. . . . Society is composed of individuals who are best served by being made free to make choices of their own. The job of Government is to make possible this freedom by ensuring competition, education and security.'[89] Later discussion in the same place equally stressed the importance of affirming the role of government to be the restoration and then the sustainment of the free market and price mechanism and of recognizing that this will involve facing up to a notable reduction in the existing level of public agency.[90] A CPC 'masterbrief' put out in 1969 took a look at this problem of reducing the scope of government. It reviewed the various indices of growing state control, the forms it takes, and various policies to deal with this growth that a libertarian Conservative administration might follow.[91] So a common theme at this time, uniting the members of the Monday Club and the Bow Group alike, was the need to eliminate unnecessary restrictions and to ensure more effective competition. It was vital to rebel against the 'surfeit of bad laws designed to control and regulate' the way people act and to improve the quality of life by restoring the dominance of free enterprise and halting the expansion of bureaucracy.[92] Another Monday Club pamphlet, urging that the freedom of the individual was a fundamental principle of Conservatism, complained it was astonishing that the party had failed to take effective action in defence of individual liberties in a period when these have been progressively diminished. In a rash of bold type it was asserted that Socialism was to be completely rejected along with the centralization of decision-making in the hands of government, 'even a Conservative one'. 'We believe in Free Enterprise, in risk-taking, in the prospect of success.'[93] Another Tory MP, writing

---

87 Maude, *The Common Problem*, pp.127–8, 290–4.
88 W. Lippmann, *An Inquiry into the Principles of a Good Society* (Boston, 1937), p.267.
89 'Themes for a Tory Revival', *Swinton Journal*, xi (no.1, Summer 1965), p.6. For Powell's view, see his 'The Consequences of the General Election', ibid., pp.12–13.
90 e.g. editorial on 'Rethinking the Role of Government', ibid., xiv (no.1, Spring 1968), pp.2–4; D. Alexander, 'Facing the Facts about the Public Sector', ibid. (no.4, Winter 1968–9), pp.37–41. Cf. N. Lawson, 'The Economic Setting: the Need for a National Policy', R. Blake *et al.*, *Conservatism Today*, pp.55–7, 59–60.
91 'Scaling Down Government' (CPC no.436; London, 1969).
92 J. Gouldburn, *We Must Revolt* (Monday Club; London, n.d. [1969]), pp.2–3, 5, 7.
93 T. Stacey, *The Vanishing Individual* (Monday paper no.4; London, 1966), pp.3, 8.

under the same aegis, urged his party to adopt a programme of reform involving a reduction in public expenditure and, therefore, in taxation, a transfer from direct to indirect methods of raising revenue, and an overhaul of the social services so that only those persons really in need received state help. He added that the

> effect of a return to self-providence on the individual could be remarkable. It would markedly reduce the present tendency to lean on the State; it would automatically inculcate a greater sense of responsibility; the individual would once more have to decide his own priorities in providing for the needs of his family.[94]

Equally a series of Bow Group essays explored similar themes. There was a demand for greater choice and freedom in the social services and more decentralization of control generally. One particular paper on managing the economy argued the need to develop in economic life 'a sharp and tough competitive climate', a goal that would entail substantial change in the practice of both sides of industry. Similarly Sir Edward Boyle (as he then was), while accepting as proper a substantial range of government activity, nevertheless urged the need for decentralization and some reduction in the existing power of the state. P. Goldman (then Director of the Conservative Political Centre) had likewise stressed, a few years before, that Conservatism, while recognizing the social nature of man, rested on an understanding of the importance of a diversified society. It was thus the traditional enemy of centralization and the champion of the diffusion of power and property.[95] An official discussion booklet similarly emphasized the little platoon, the role of families, groups, and associations; and, while acknowledging the need sometimes to use the public power in favour of hard-pressed individuals, asserted that nevertheless Conservatives believed in principle in less rather than more government intervention.[96] Likewise T. Raison expressed similar views, recognizing the essentially secondary nature of government's true role and stressing the need for constructive tension and a real diversity of opportunity. That great fetish

---

94 V. Goodhew, *Self-Help Reborn* (Monday Club; London, n.d. [1969]), pp.1, 9–10. Cf. the recanting comments of V. Montagu, *The Conservative Dilemma* (Monday Club; London, 1970), pp.14–23. Montagu had been a founder of the Tory Reform Committee (see pp.255–6 above) but by the late 1960s had come to believe that government had become too large and intrusive and needed to be radically cut back.

95 M. Wolff *et al.*, *The Conservative Opportunity*, pp.99–104; E. Boyle, 'Government and Society', *Swinton Journal*, xv (no.1, Spring 1969), pp.8–15; P. Goldman, *Some Principles of Conservatism* (CPC no.161; 1956; London, 1961), p.10.

96 [G. D. M. Block], *Society and the Individual* (Young Conservative and Unionist Organisation; London, 1962), pp.1–3. Cf. D. Howell on controlling government growth, *The Times* (14 March 1967), p.13, and ibid., (28 May 1968), p.11.

of the day, an incomes policy, is repudiated as 'a logical nonsense' incompatible with this 'framework of greater competition'; and it is urged that a buoyant economy, free because untrammelled by excessive state regulation, is alone the basis for effective social justice.[97] In this context one particular theme that became increasingly popular was the need to move away from compulsory universalism in social provision to more discriminating arrangements that would, through a reduction in abortive social expenditure, allow more generous treatment of the most needy and a greater degree of choice. Arthur Seldon of the Institute of Economic Affairs is one of those who has in particular explored the possibilities of the various policies and devices involved.[98] I confess I refer to Seldon here with a certain diffidence because he has said he normally votes Liberal – yet in the same breath he describes his social philosophy as one of radical Conservatism. What is clear is his personal commitment to the primacy of the individual and to liberty and his recognition that government must be limited in scope and decentralized in administration.[99]

The Institute of Economic Affairs is itself relevant in the present context. It is one of those bodies which may feasibly be seen as a latter-day equivalent of the Liberty and Property Defence League, the British Constitution Association, or the Anti-Socialist Union. The last of these earlier pressure groups, the ASU, was wound up in 1949 and its assets transferred to the Economic League which had been founded after the Great War to help preserve 'personal freedom and enterprise' and to oppose 'all subversive forces' seeking 'to undermine the security of Britain in general and of British industry in particular'.[100] It is true that the IEA, like other bodies of the same sort, is not associated in any formal way with a political party or dependent on one either ideologically or financially. But there is an undoubted affinity in most respects with libertarian Conservatism and views congenial to this doctrine were thus sustained by the activity of these organizations. The Institute was founded in 1947 as a 'research and educational trust' to study markets and pricing systems as technical devices for apportioning resources and registering

97 T. Raison, *Conflict and Conservatism* (CPC no. 313; London, 1965), pp. 9, 11–15. Cf. an article in *The Times* by 'A Leading Conservative' (8 October 1970), p. 10.

98 On the general criticism of universalism, see e.g. R. Harris, *Choice in Welfare* (London, 1963); also A. Seldon, 'The Humane Society: Some Thoughts on the Social Services in the Second Half of the Twentieth Century', *Swinton Journal*, vii (no. 1, March 1961), pp. 7–15, and his 'Thaw in the Welfare State', *Lloyds Bank Review*, (July 1972), pp. 18–33.

99 See his contribution to the symposium on intellectuals and Conservatism, *Swinton Journal*, xiv (no. 2, Summer 1968), esp. pp. 21, 24, 25.

100 K. D. Brown, 'The Anti-Socialist Union, 1908–49', K. D. Brown (ed.), *Essays in Anti-Labour History: Responses to the Rise of Labour in Britain* (London, 1974), pp. 257, 384–5 n. 94.

preferences. A number of prominent academic economists has figured among those comprising the Institute's trustees and advisory council including Sir Sydney Caine, Colin Clark, John Jewkes, A. T. Peacock, G. Schwartz, and J. Wiseman. As well, by no means all its publications are ideologically oriented but there is no doubt about the general libertarian propensity at work albeit in an undoubtedly scholarly context. This is well reflected, for example, in Professor H. B. Acton's *The Morals of Markets* (1971), a study by a professional philosopher of the deficiencies of the collectivist case and of the superior ethical status of the arguments in favour of a free economy.[101]

A cognate body, but one which is much more directly concerned to forward the interests of industry and commerce, is Aims for Freedom and Enterprise (formerly Aims of Industry). It was established by leading industrialists in 1942 to work for the defence of private enterprise and to promote the market economy and the efficiency of capitalism. In origin it may thus be seen as a reaction to the extreme degree of direction of economic life which occurred during the war and which many feared would be continued afterwards. One vital political theme that is always urged is that there is a direct relationship between the free economy and the general liberty of the individual and, conversely, that state ownership of the means of production and distribution leads inevitably to the general suppression of opposition, free speech, and so forth.[102] The ethos involved is nicely caught in the following passage from one of the many pamphlets issued by Aims, one written in this case by an academic sympathizer:

> The liberal democrat knows that there never has been and can never be a purely laissez-faire system. The crucial problem he faces is how much State intervention there should be and the forms which it should take. Even if the answers were clear and simple, it would be a frightening task to explain them. . . . What he can assert with the utmost confidence is that every experience of a centrally-controlled economy has led to an increasing centralization of political power and an ever-diminishing degree of political and personal freedom for the overwhelming majority of citizens.[103]

Among specific campaigns that have been mounted by this organization are those attacking further nationalization, 'Government intervention-ism', the size of the civil service, excessive public spending and borrowing, high taxation, and direct labour schemes. The invention of

---

101 H. B. Acton, *The Morals of Markets: an Ethical Explanation* (London, 1971).

102 See e.g. T. Szamuely, *Socialism and Liberty* (1971; London, 1977); R. Lewis, *Neither Freedom Nor Enterprise* (London, n.d. [1975]); R. Harris, *Freedom of Choice: Consumers or Conscripts?* (London, n.d. [1976]).

103 K. W. Watkins, *Influencing the Political Future* (London, n.d. [1973]), p.5.

2

'Mr. Cube', the symbol of private enterprise sugar, was one of Aims's greatest successes.[104] In a public message issued in 1971 the then Chairman of the organization stated that

> The battle of ideas between those who believe in a State society and those who believe in a free economy is by no means over. . . . We are concerned with the interests of free enterprise commerce and industry. . . . We will watch, especially, for trends towards expansion of intervention by government – central or local – and continue to urge a reduction in its scope. . . . Free enterprise and therefore the freedom of everyone in this country have been eroded in recent years. Only determination can halt the trend. . . .[105]

And Aims's publications often explicitly accept that, so far as the advance of collectivism is concerned, it is difficult to say whether the Labour Party or the Conservative Party is more to blame.[106] What is clear is the need to re-establish a more competitive state of affairs in many key industries and to restore the power of decision-making where it properly belongs, to industry's professional managers. This means opposing further state intervention, whether overt or covert, as in the use of planning agreements or through the 'creeping State ownership' represented by the operations of the National Enterprise Board.[107] Some of the harsher implications of reducing state involvement are bluntly faced including cutting down a whole range of present activities and services in such areas as coal mining, gas production, telephones, transport, hospitals, and schools.[108] The academic contribution is often the most fervent. Recently Professor Ferns commented that there 'no longer exists in British society an effective agency or force capable of defining and limiting the role of government in the community' especially in the aftermath of the disastrous taxation policies followed in recent years. The prime necessity, he urged, was to create a movement capable of actually 'setting limits to public expenditure'; and a refusal to pay taxes *à la* Hampden was envisaged – an extreme tactic the recommendation of which is not at all characteristic of the group's general manner.[109]

104 A. Sampson, *Anatomy of Britain Today* (1965; Harper Colophon, 1966), p.655.
105 Advertisement entitled 'Free Enterprise – the new battle of ideas', *Spectator*, (23 October 1971), p.581.
106 e.g. N. Ridley, *A Nation of Monopolists?* (London, n.d. [1975]), pp.1, 20.
107 D. F. Channon, *Strategy and Structure of Management in Private and State Industry* (London, n.d. [1974?]), p.1 Cf. *idem, The Strategy and Structure of British Enterprise* (1973; London, 1974), pp.232–4, 243–5.
108 R. E. Dunstan, *Government. . . . : Wise Parent or Tycoon* (London, 1974), pp.14–16.
109 H. S. Ferns, *The Radicalism the Case Requires* (London, 1976), pp.2–4, 8–9. More typical of Aims's concerns are such surveys as F. Knox, *The Growth of Central Government Manpower* (London, 1969); J. L. Marshall, *The Role of Government in the Economy* (London, 1970); *Reducing the Growth of Civil Servants* (London, 1971); and their like.

Then – a final example of this sort of libertarian pressure group – there is the more recent National Association for Freedom publicly launched in 1975 as a memorial to Ross McWhirter after his murder by the IRA. Four years later it was renamed the Freedom Association. It has indulged in the usual attack on the enveloping meshes of an increasing machinery of government but what is stressed is rather the importance of extending personal liberty by securing a more effective protection of basic rights for the citizen in an age of extending and intrusive public agency. The main constitutional devices recommended to this end are the promulgation of a Bill of Rights and the establishment of a Supreme Court with power to veto unconstitutional legislation.[110] At the same time sight is not lost of the importance of private ownership and enterprise or of the opportunity to choose services other than those provided by the state.[111] Its practical concerns have to a great degree centred on the need to protect individual freedom *vis à vis* trade union power. It was actively involved in the Grunwick affair, for instance. Similarly it assisted the Tameside Council in its legal fight against the imposition of the comprehensive principle in its secondary schools.[112]

A useful summary of all such libertarian views expressed in so many different quarters is, as it happens, provided by one particular CPC pamphlet which appeared in 1969. It was written by Geoffrey Rippon and had the title *Right Angle: a Philosophy for Conservatives*. The main assertion is that there 'is neither health nor joy in the collectivist society' on the premiss that individual choice, freedom, and responsibility (that alone can secure those ends) depend on 'limiting the sphere of government'. The 'proper functions' to which it should be restricted are defence, foreign policy, and 'the provision of those essential services that can only be provided by and on behalf of the community as a whole.'[113] In this context the 'four major objectives' of Conservative radicalism are said to be an effective degree of restriction on the power of the modern state; stronger safeguards for individual rights; protection for private property and the encouragement of personal capital creation; and the defence of freedom in all its aspects.[114] And this is all epitomized in an attack on centralization and over-government together with a stress on

110 On such matters, see vol.iii, *A Much-Governed Nation*, ch.10.

111 e.g. NAF, *The Campaign for Freedom* (London, n.d.); *Constitutional Notes on Rights and Liberties* (London, n.d.); and the speech of Lord de l'Isle in a press release (2 December 1975), pp.3–5.

112 There is a curiously jaundiced account in R. Clutterbuck, *Britain in Agony: the Growth of Political Violence* (1978; Penguin, 1980), pp.255–7 (and see index for other detailed references).

113 G. Rippon, *Right Angle: a Philosophy for Conservatives* (CPC no.427; London, 1969), pp.6–7.

114 ibid., p.9.

local autonomy that would have gladdened the heart of Toulmin Smith (though it is the authority of Maitland, no less, which is invoked). There is also assertion of the further need to return major public industries to private ownership and to refuse to embark on experiments in 'paternalistic bureaucracy' such as the control of prices and incomes.[115] We need, too, new devices such as a Bill of Rights to protect the individual, a more equitable attitude to taxation, more opportunity, and less stress on artificial levelling.[116]

By the late 1960s, then, a substantial, or at least a very vocal, body of opinion in the Conservative Party (or that existed in ideological affinity to it) was moving in a libertarian direction, was in the pursuit of more individual freedom from state control than had been enjoyed for many years. The task in view was surely immense: nothing less than to halt and then reverse the process of collectivist growth which had been gathering momentum for so long. But it was not seen as practically impossible. One academic contributor to the discussion urged, for instance, that while there might be irreversible processes in the realm of nature, 'political science knows of none such.' Consequently 'talk of the impossibility of turning the clock back . . . is only misleading metaphor.' If collectivism is inevitable, how did we ever escape from the previous state of affairs?[117] All these people were, therefore, increasingly optimistic about the prospects ahead.

But, of course, none of this party or other propaganda could do more than influence opinion. In the last resort any major political significance could only accrue if all this publicist activity were preparation for a fundamental switch of policy to be introduced by a Conservative Cabinet committed to halting the growth of government. And it was indeed the declared initial strategy of E. Heath and his colleagues when they took office in 1970 to do precisely this, to change the collectivist direction of affairs and to initiate instead an individualist tendency. Discussion of their proposed policy had brought out its intention of being 'something of a revolution' in the way it would foster private enterprise, cut government expenditure, and the like.[118] Heath himself said, 'We want to clear away the debris of half a century'.[119] As Leader of the Opposition he had told the party conference in 1969: 'We will remove the shackles of government from industry. We will banish the regulation and control of business activities. We will withdraw the Government from holdings in

115 ibid., pp. 9–11.
116 ibid., pp. 11–14.
117 P. Day, 'Conservatism and Liberty', Solon, i (no. 3, April 1970), p. 38.
118 See e.g. A. Fergusson, 'The Tory Alternative', The Times (12–16 May 1969).
119 Cited in A. Roth, Heath and the Heathmen (London, 1972), p. 198. Cf. P. Cosgrave, 'Edward Heath's Strategy', Spectator (16 October 1971), pp. 546–7.

private firms. We will begin to reintroduce private ownership into nationalized industries.'[120] Of course, this was the sort of thing conference wanted to hear; and the same kind of sentiment was presented the following year as well (by which time Heath was Prime Minister) when (wreathed in Smiles, as it were) he told the delegates their purpose was to make fellow citizens 'recognize that they must be responsible for the consequences of their own actions' and 'learn that no one will stand between them and the results of their own free choice.'[121] Certainly Heath had been the minister largely responsible for the abolition of resale price maintenance and he had long given the impression of being committed to such policies as letting industrial lame ducks go to the wall, eliminating regional subsidies, and generally disengaging government from economic intervention as reflected, for instance, in the search for an incomes policy. Moreover, entry to the Common Market was in many ways seen as providing a stimulating degree of competition.[122] Again 'less government' was the goal in respect to which a specific commitment was made in the 1970 White Paper on *The Reorganisation of Central Government*.[123] And, to take one further instance among many possible examples, the then Chancellor of the Exchequer, in a speech delivered late in 1970, pledged the administration to 'the cutting of public expenditure' and 'the reining back of state intervention and control in industry'.[124] There is no room for doubt that, though Heath never adopted an extremist view of these matters, the general tone of his policy statements was (as one academic observer put it) 'anti-interventionist, and in favour of competitive market solutions to problems.'[125] Similarly the then ambassador to the United States, Lord Cromer, publicly expressed his belief that there was in train, through the Heath government, a reaction against Conservative collectivism.[126] None the less a wary scepticism about these possibilities was expressed in some quarters.[127] And, of course, with the change of attitude on incomes policy, lame ducks, and so forth, there was clearly intimated a 'reversion to paternalism' (as Professor Peston called it).[128] It is not for me to defend

120 Cited in Fergusson, loc. cit. (12 May 1969), p.11.
121 Cited in Roth, op. cit., p.210.
122 ibid., pp.xv, 5, 65–6, 177, 181, 189–90, 211–12, 216–18.
123 Parliamentary Papers, 1970–1 (vol.xx), Cmnd.4506, p.4 §5.
124 Reported in *The Times* (16 October 1970), p. 23.
125 M. Peston, 'Conservative Economic Policy and Philosophy', *Political Quarterly*, xliv (1973), p.411.
126 See the speech, 'Lord Cromer on "New Freedom" in Britain', reported in *The Times* (20 February 1971), p.4.
127 e.g. Aims of Industry, *Annual Report, 1970–1971* (London, 1971), p.4.
128 Peston, art. cit., p.416. Cf. the discussion of J. Davies's turnabout on the lame duck policy, D. Wood, 'BennTech Rises Like the Phoenix', *The Times* (15 May 1972), p.15.

the Heath government's switch of emphasis to a Conservative style rather different from that clearly expressed in its early intentions.[129]

After the impact, even shock, of this reversion, and given the disasters of 1973–4, it is hardly surprising that there was a further and growing reassertion of libertarian attitudes by those disappointed with the Heath record. It constitutes a more urgent assertion still of the themes which, as has been seen, have been growing in importance within Conservatism since the mid-1960s. One early instance of this is a paper that appeared in 1975 in the *Political Quarterly* written by a young Tory of anti-collectivist persuasion. It discerned the 'enlargement of the role of Government' and its increasing incapacity as the main factor in British economic decline and in this context spoke bitterly of the 'failure of nerve, lack of imagination and intellectual confusion' of the Heath government.[130] A return to first principles is urged based on reference to an 'alternative vision of society', one that is (because based on freedom of choice) 'morally richer and spiritually more satisfying' than the collectivist condition to which we have been led by all parties alike. The two main targets of attack are the 'universalist' welfare state and nationalization.[131] The libertarian point of view is also clear in a symposium on the 'Conservative Opportunity' which appeared in 1976. In a foreword Lord Hailsham urged that the main contemporary enemy is uniformity which is being imposed to an extent incompatible with freedom. We are faced, he says, 'with a constitutional crisis largely brought on by the process of over-centralisation, over-government, and excessive taxation.' The peril in which we find ourselves, he adds, 'is largely produced by Socialist collectivism.'[132] This is, of course, a misleading attribution for, as has often been stressed in this survey, the collectivist tendency has been not a little aided by Conservative efforts. And recognition of this is indeed the specific starting-point of the various contributions to this volume: that the Conservative Party is going through 'a period of major rethinking' which reflects 'an intellectual revolt against the orthodoxies which have ruled public life since the early 1940s', misgivings about prevailing economic and welfare policies, 'a surge of feeling against "bureaucracy"', and so forth.[133] In many places the tone is positively Spencerian. And one of the editors, Lord Blake, explicitly acknowledges the dual inheritance of the party and its ideology:

129 The change of direction is discussed by e.g. J. Bruce-Gardyne, *Whatever Happened to the Quiet Revolution? The Story of a Brave Experiment in Government* (London, 1974), ch.1 of which analyses the nature of the libertarian intention.

130 P. V. Elst, 'Radical Toryism – the Libertarian Alternative', *Political Quarterly*, xlvi (1975), pp.66, 67–8.

131 ibid., pp.69, 71–2.

132 Lord Blake and J. Patten (eds), *The Conservative Opportunity* (London, 1976), pp. vii–viii.

133 ibid., pp.1, 4–5.

There have been in the past two sometimes conflicting and contradictory traditions in the party's attitude – paternalism and libertarianism. There has been a case in the past for paternalistic interventionism to soften the rigours of doctrinaire *laissez-faire* capitalism. All this belongs to the days when the Liberal Party of Cobden and Bright was the enemy. It is largely irrelevant now. The common feature of all the essays in this book which deal with home affairs is libertarianism – less government, less public expenditure, fewer public servants, lower taxation, greater freedom. The enemy is not *laissez-faire*, but *étatisme*. Paternalism is out, along with the welfare consensus.

We have reached a parting of the ways in terms of attitudes to society and economic management.[134]

Thus there is, it is hoped, 'more of a desire to get government off our backs' than at any time since 1950.[135] 'Nothing less will suffice than a major reversal of the trends which ever since 1945 Labour has promoted and Conservatives have accepted.'[136] The volume consists, in fact, of a series of essays by Oxford academics which explores various aspects of this theme: the importance of pluralism (an interesting revival this, showing that the notion has appeal not only on the contemporary left); the need to consider afresh the proper level of government intervention in economic life; should central power be broken up by devolution? could there be advantages in a Bill of Rights? electoral reform? relaxation of the secrecy laws and more open government? Overall, especially in connexion with economic questions about government action to achieve 'the public good' and to manage the economy, the general spirit is very like that of Enoch Powell, though (as usual in recent Conservative literature) his name is, churlishly, largely unmentioned in these pages. The position adopted is thus that it is impossible to have a completely free-market economy in everything: not all welfare matters can be looked at in that context, for instance, though existing schemes are hardly effective or economical. At the same time there are crucial areas where the case for state intervention is very weak and attempts to impose it will produce disastrous distortions and difficulties. The book as a whole is an excellent, systematic analysis of the alternative view presented by Conservative libertarianism. Generally, too, its tone is considered and moderate though this tenor is not always reflected in the cognate party literature. Symptomatic of this is an outspoken attack by Eldon Griffiths on the 'collective mystique' and what it entails as a challenge to progressive capitalism and individual liberties. Writing in 1977 he

134 ibid., p.8.
135 ibid., p.10.
136 ibid., p.12.

believed the time had come for the Conservative Party to 'shift over to the offensive' and proclaim loudly the superiority of libertarian values and practices.[137]

Views of this kind were shared, of course, by a number of the party leaders. M. Thatcher had herself gone on record as supporting policies designed to diminish the role of the state as, for example, in a pamphlet she produced for the CPC in 1968. She argued that while it was no doubt necessary for government to continue with a substantial role during the period of post-war reconstruction this had continued too long, sustained during the 1960s by the contemporary emphasis on growth. It had led, she said, to 'the totally unacceptable notion' that government should even fix the increase of wages and salaries.[138] Government had, at the same time, become more distant:

> We started off with a wish on the part of the people for more government intervention in certain spheres. This was met. But there came a time when the amount of intervention got so great that it could no longer be exercised in practice [save] by more and more officials or bureaucrats. Now it is difficult if not impossible for people to get at the official making the decision and so paradoxically although the degree of intervention is greater, the government has become more and more *remote* from the people. The present result of the democratic process has therefore been an increasing authoritarianism.

And inevitably 'Once everything is provided and controlled by the State, the voice of the individual is silenced, the ability to choose eliminated.'[139] She believed the solution is clear:

> *the way to get personal involvement and participation is not for people to take part in more and more government decisions but to make the government reduce the area of decision over which it presides and consequently leave the private citizen to 'participate' . . . by making more of his own decisions.* What we need now is a far greater degree of personal responsibility and decision, far more independence from the government, and a comparative reduction in the role of government.[140]

The policy implications of this stance must, Thatcher urged, be followed through in terms of tax reductions and the like in particular to permit competition to flourish and the individual to play a greater part in

---

137 E. Griffiths, *Fighting for the Life of Freedom* (CPC no.601; London, 1977), p.22.
138 M. Thatcher, *What's Wrong with Politics?* (CPC no.419; London, 1968), p.8.
139 ibid., pp.8–9, italics in original; *idem*, foreword to C. E. Bellairs, *Conservative Social and Industrial Reform: a Record of Conservative Legislation between 1800 and 1974* (CPC no.600; rev. edn, London, 1977), pp.7–8.
140 Thatcher, *What's Wrong with Politics?*, p.9, italics in original.

looking after his own future. The state would continue to sustain basic standards and concentrate on providing things that citizens cannot. But beyond this the 'atmosphere of restriction' must be cleared to make it possible for increasing responsibility to accrue to the citizen and his family pursuing their own good in their own way.[141]

Similarly D. Howell (subsequently a member of Thatcher's Cabinet) continued to call for a new Conservative approach to the problems of the 1970s and 1980s. He had, of course, been an early exponent of the libertarian possibilities though (as has already been seen) these seemed to disappear under the pressure of events to which the Heath administration was exposed.[142] Notwithstanding this experience a later pamphlet from Howell's pen once more demanded a complete rethinking of the Conservative attitude to 'a disgracefully inefficient and over-centralised public sector', to the failure (or rather increasingly manifest irrelevance) of Keynesian economic policy, and to the excessive public spending which has necessarily been entailed.[143] It is a partisan review, of course: the failure of post-war politics is attributed a little too much to Socialist deficiencies and the part which has been played by Conservative administrations and ideas is admitted not at all, at least explicitly. Yet the call is clear: it is for a move away from bureaucratic centralization and collectivist paternalism, a plea (for instance) that policy proposals must in future 'involve a minimum of legislation' and look, too, to 'a far tauter, less costly, central administration', and to 'a thriving free enterprise sector, burdened by fewer government overheads.'[144] Of course, this means limiting the ambitions of central government, achieving stable money, and the like. But, most interestingly, one element of the new policy that is picked out for emphasis is the need for more popular involvement in both political and especially economic affairs, specifically more worker participation in industry and more sharing of the profits of its operation. A 'more genuine industrial democracy', 'worker capitalism', or 'worker co-operatism' seem to be the new – or rather the revived – slogans.[145] Certainly it is the genuine tradition of libertarian Conservatism that is reflected in the sentiment with which Howell concludes his brochure: 'The future in Britain . . . lies not in idolising the State and condemning private property and profit,

141 ibid., pp.10–12.
142 See Howell's pamphlets *Whose Government Works?* (CPC no.407; London, 1968), *A New Style of Government* (CPC no.463; London, 1970), and *A New Style Emerges* (CPC no.494; London, 1971).
143 D. Howell, *Time to Move On: an Opening to the Future for British Politics* (CPC no.581; London, 1976), pp.7–11.
144 ibid., pp.6, 15, 16.
145 ibid., pp.17–22. Cf. the earlier B. Cassidy, *Workers on the Board: a Study in Employee Participation* (CPC no.522; London, 1973).

but in the making and sharing of profit and in the recognition that as yet too many people have not enough private property and not enough private choice.'[146]

Other leading members of the party also went on record to attack the excessive amount of regulation from which the country was suffering and which inhibited economic growth, as with Sir Geoffrey Howe's discussion of what he called 'legislative pollution'.[147] But perhaps the most considered review of the libertarian prospect that has recently been undertaken by a leading Conservative politician is that of Sir Keith Joseph. This is hardly surprising for not only does he seem to approach these matters in a rather academic frame of mind but also he was in 1975, as a member of the Shadow Cabinet, given overall responsibility for the supervision of party policy and research.[148] His appointment to this task was presumably an indication that Thatcher intended there should be a basic review of Conservative policies and principles in the sense of moving away from the so-called post-war consensus with its emphasis on state-provided welfare and Keynesian-inspired economic regulation. Many of the results of this programme of self-analysis have been issued under the auspices not of the Conservative Political Centre but of the Centre for Policy Studies, a body set up by Thatcher and Joseph in 1974 to explore the implications in particular of the social-market economy and to urge that this kind of economic arrangement alone provides the basis for an improved standard and quality of life as well as for effective freedom of choice.[149]

There is the belief that Conservatives themselves have too often revelled in 'the new power' of government; equally there is a specific repudiation of the doctrine of the 'Middle Way' which has proved in many respects a 'costly obsession', the slippery slope to collectivism.[150] As well, Keynesian policies of demand-management and high taxation have been a major cause of the economic difficulties we now face. It is not that the goal of a high and stable level of employment is repudiated but rather the by now conventional wisdom about how this aim might be attained. Indeed it is the means adopted by successive governments in the

146 Howell, op. cit., p.23.
147 Sir G. Howe, *Too Much Law? The Effects of Legislation on Economic Growth* (CPC no.610; London, 1977).
148 *KCA* (1975), p.26989A (26991). Crossman described him in 1970 as an 'intelligent', 'civilized, cultivated man': see *The Diaries of a Cabinet Minister* (London, 1975–7), iii.952.
149 Cf. Centre for Policy Studies, *Why Britain Needs a Social Market Economy* (London, 1975).
150 Sir K. Joseph, *Freedom under the Law* (CPC no.569; London, 1975), p.17; *Stranded on the Middle Ground? Reflections on Circumstances and Policies* (London, 1976), pp.19ff. And for what follows, ibid., *passim*.

post-war era to try to achieve full employment and the creation of the welfare society that have, through the overspending to which these programmes have led, been the main and continuing cause of inflation and so of the attempted assertion of tighter control over wages and prices to try to make the plan work. The present problem of inflation plus unemployment is the inevitable outcome of the policies pursued. Government deficit-financing to expand domestic demand is by definition inflationary. It may seem to work for a while but then shortages emerge in materials, in skilled and other labour, and in finished goods; so prices and imports begin to rise. At the same time welfare and similar spending was continued or increased on the assumption that production would grow to match it; and yet when this did not happen the level of spending was maintained thus increasing the inflationary pressure still more. Further, taxation is raised to penal levels with disastrous effects on industrial and commercial enterprise the buoyancy and success of which can alone be the foundation for social service or other non-productive public expenditure. Nor is the matter helped by the subsidizing of high-cost and over-manned 'lame ducks', a policy which rigidifies pockets of the economy, prevents the appropriate movement of resources to more profitable outlets, and makes the task of the unsubsidized sector all the more difficult, helps indeed to create further unemployment there.[151]

Following this diagnosis the basic proposal is that government expenditure must be reduced for unless the money supply is properly adjusted nothing else will come right. But though vital this is only the beginning: in itself monetarism is not enough. There must also be a reduction of the public sector and more essential encouragement of private enterprise.[152] And all the detailed structural questions remain to be tackled: those relating, for instance, to wage-levels, productivity, mobility of labour both geographical and in terms of willingness to take jobs available, retraining, housing policy, profitability, business efficiency, and so on.[153] And Joseph believes that a solution will only be achieved within the framework of a social-market economy. This stands in contrast to the kind of 'command' or 'permanent war' economy which we have been building for ourselves over recent decades and with such disastrous results. The free economy alone promotes economic efficiency and sustains political liberty and so the pursuit of the cultural and moral ends which these achievements make possible. Joseph clearly rests this point of view on a fundamental belief in the rule of law and the rights of individuals (especially in respect of property).[154] But he specifically

151 e.g. Joseph, *Monetarism Is Not Enough* (London, n.d. [1976]), pp.13–14.
152 Joseph, *Stranded on the Middle Ground?*, p.11; *Monetarism Is Not Enough*, p.19.
153 Joseph, *Stranded on the Middle Ground?*, p.10.
154 Joseph, *Freedom under the Law*, pp.5–8.

repudiates the idea of an extreme *laissez faire* and recognizes, too, that 'market principles' cannot be slavishly adhered to in all things.[155] There must, for instance, be intensive government action to restore the circumstances in which real competition can flourish.[156] And while such goals as income egalitarianism will be severely eschewed it will nevertheless be proper to attend to the care of those who cannot look after themselves by, for instance, a negative income tax or other suitable means.[157] But basically Joseph makes a firm distinction of principle in respect of the role and office of government in this regard: it should create a framework of laws, taxes, and services within and by which people are encouraged to run their own lives in such a way that the public interest is also achieved. It is not the function of government to control this activity substantively, at first-order level, but simply to regulate and place limits on it. Government cannot as a kind of pseudo-entrepreneur manage economic life profitably and efficiently; though it can and must help create the conditions in which others can do so.[158] 'We oppose socialism', he says in one place, 'because it means a government that runs men rather than makes rules for men who run themselves.'[159] Of course, to reduce public spending to the extent required, 'cutting subsidies to housing, food, make-work, lame ducks' and more, so to reduce taxation and borrowing, 'will need strong nerves'.[160] And the likelihood of its success will rest, too, on the support of public opinion in the pursuit of these ideas which have been allowed over the decades to become all too unfamiliar. However, Joseph believed that the task was by no means impossible because, he claimed, the country increasingly realized that it had somehow gone astray since the proud, confident morning of 1945.[161] At least one great virtue of the sort of inquiry he embarked on is that (as against the conventional Tory diffidence) it rests on the assumption that politics is fundamentally about ideas which form the climate of opinion within which decisions are taken and institutions set to work.[162] Thatcher herself has similarly been associated with 'conviction' rather than 'consensus' politics.[163] Certainly if, after decades of collectivist development, a libertarian revival is to be at all feasible, an intellectual

---

155 *Stranded on the Middle Ground?*, pp.59, 62, 70. Cf. Joseph, 'The Economics of Freedom', K. Joseph *et al.*, *Freedom and Order* (CPC no.576; London, 1975).
156 Joseph, *Stranded on the Middle Ground?*, p.60.
157 See the article on 'Equality: an Argument Against' (1976), ibid., pp.75–9. Cf. CPS, *Why Britain Needs a Social Market Economy*, p.9.
158 e.g. Joseph, *Stranded on the Middle Ground?*, pp.28, 62.
159 ibid., p.70.
160 ibid., pp.16, 46.
161 ibid., p.34.
162 ibid., p.49.
163 See e.g. the interview recorded in *Time* magazine (14 May 1979), p.14.

and psychological transformation is necessary. This in part is the significance of recent academic interest in these matters.

The truth is that the Tory Party tends to be (or likes to think it is) apprehensive about, even distrustful of, abstract thinkers and prefers to believe its principles derive from the experience of men of action.[164] But latterly this has not been true at least of the libertarian wing of the party which has sought intellectual respectability by invocation of the ideas of such mentors as Hayek, Oakeshott, and Friedman. And there has been other recent academic support though not always of a helpful kind. In a short but often bewildering investigation, Professor H. S. Ferns asserted that 'government is not the doctor, but the disease' and urged the case for a marked reduction in the role of the state and the re-creation of the free-exchange economy.[165] Reference has already been made to the Oxford symposium on the Conservative opportunity. There is also the series of essays, sponsored by the 'Salisbury Group', which appeared in 1978 under the editorship of Maurice Cowling. In a review of this volume, Michael Oakeshott – whose spirit seems to brood omnipresently over its pages – suggested it was the latest of several attempts made in recent years to retrieve from decline the concept of government as an institution concerned, not with the substantive management of our affairs but rather with the framework of rules and conditions within which free citizens go about their own diverse business. This view, he says, if it has a home anywhere in our politics must surely find it in a Conservative Party.[166]

The dustcover of this last-named book of essays claims that in its pages 'the new Conservatism of the past fifteen years finds its authoritative completion'. This asserts both much too little and too much. The volume itself and its authorship are important straws in the wind: of this there is no doubt. But none of it is really new; and no service is done to the Conservative cause by suggesting it is, as if there were no long tradition of libertarian attitudes to be discerned in the history of the Conservative Party in modern times and no growing discussion of these matters over the last two decades. The quality of the papers themselves is somewhat varied: some are thin and bear the marks of an opacity that indicate both hurry and confusion. And while indeed there is some general measure of agreement that the 'liberal Conservatism' of Butler's and Macmillan's day has to be repudiated, there are, in fact, two apparently similar but rather different views about the nature of the 'new Conservatism' that should replace it. There is first of all the blunt and direct call to 'roll back the frontiers of the state', a phrase (or something like it) which is often

164 e.g. P. Dean, 'Tory Principles Today', P. Dean et al., Conservative Points of View (CPC no. 306; London, 1964), p.6.
165 H. S. Ferns, The Disease of Government (London, 1978), pp. 5, 130, 138.
166 M. Oakeshott, 'Conservatism: Foundations and Fallacies', Daily Telegraph (29 June 1978), p.18. I owe this reference to Mr P. P. Nicholson of the University of York.

repeated.[167] But there is secondly a more subtle position explored which suggests that such simple libertarianism is likely to be both electorally disastrous and irrelevant to the major issues of the day. This latter case might be put baldly in the following terms. Certainly the state has tended to meddle much too much in what does not concern it; it has improperly attempted to manage all the details of economic life, and so on. But to acknowledge this is not to imply that its functions should be reduced as near as possible to zero. On the contrary the state needs to be strong to attend to its proper business of sustaining the rules or framework within which people may see to their affairs. In particular its major task in present and foreseeable circumstances will be to restore public order and social discipline, authority and the rule of law. If this is true – and especially if this is recognized by the public to be the case – mere economic libertarianism sadly misses the boat. In different ways this is, I believe, the theme of the two best essays in the book: that by Peregrine Worsthorne on 'Too Much Freedom' and that by S. R. Letwin who provides a subtle and superbly articulated account of 'civil association' on Oakeshottian lines.[168]

Recently there has been, then, ample discussion and assertion of a libertarian kind. And emerging from this ideological flurry the dominant aims of contemporary Conservatism are clear. An official statement of policy issued in 1976 concedes that the state must have a notable role 'as the trustee of the whole community', for instance, by 'holding the balance between different interests.'[169] But in present circumstances it is made quite clear also that the public realm must be controlled and pruned and self-help encouraged, particular stress being laid on 'the individual and his freedom'.[170] In sum:

> Our policies are designed to restore and defend individual freedom and responsibility. We mean to protect the individual from excessive interference by the State or by organisations licensed by the State, to stop the drift of power away from the people and their democratic institutions, and to give them more power as citizens, as owners and as

167 M. Cowling (ed.), *Conservative Essays* (London, 1978), e.g. pp. 14, 39, 192–3. For an earlier use of this phrase, see J. E. Powell's speech of February 1970, cited in *Still to Decide* (Paper front, 1972), p. 26; and for some other occasions, see R. Boyson, 'Roll Back the State', *Swinton Journal*, xvii (no. 4, Winter, 1971–2), pp. 23–31; T. Renton, in the *Daily Telegraph* (24 February 1978), p. 16; and 969 H.C. Deb. 5s., 25 June 1979, col. 71 (C. Morrison).

168 P. Worsthorne, 'Too Much Freedom', Cowling (ed.), *Conservative Essays*, esp. pp. 148–9; S. R. Letwin, 'On Conservative Individualism', ibid., pp. 52–68. Cf. T. E. Utley's comments, ibid., p. 51; also Thatcher's interview with B. Connell, reported in *The Times* (5 May 1980), p. 6.

169 Conservative Central Office, *The Right Approach: a Statement of Conservative Aims* (London, 1976), p. 18.

170 ibid., pp. 7–8, 17, 24, 27.

consumers. We shall do this by better financial management, by reducing the proportion of the nation's wealth consumed by the State. . . .[171]

This same stress was most apparent, too, in the campaign the Conservatives fought in the general election of May 1979. A few weeks only before the poll was announced a *Daily Telegraph* editorial put the central issue clearly enough: 'Either the tide of collectivism must be turned back' (as the Tory leadership proposes) or (as Labour suggests) 'the State's authority must be extended still further'.[172] A major theme of the party manifesto was the importance of redressing the balance of affairs in favour of the citizen and against the state.[173] This priority was also reflected in the specific proposals of the subsequent Queen's Speech: the promises to restrict 'the claims of the public sector on the nation's resources', to establish 'more effective competition', to restrict the activities of the National Enterprise Board, to cut down the nationalized industries, to limit trade union power, and so forth.[174] The provisions of the first budget, the corollary reductions in public expenditure, the decision to begin selling off certain nationalized assets, and the like are an undoubtedly appropriate part of the required pattern. But it is perhaps salutary to recall that we were here before just over a decade ago with Mr Heath. Perhaps the will of Thatcher and her colleagues will prove stronger: or their fortune greater. On the libertarian assumption that a great deal of our machinery of control is defunct and inhibiting, restrictive of individual liberty of choice and of economic expansion alike, the motto should be in tune with the spirit of Tennyson's verse which serves as general epigraph to this chapter. There is indeed much to lop away. It will be a hard and revolutionary task to remodel the vast mass of collectivist legislation, institutions, practices, and attitudes which has for so long been in the making. As Powell warned over ten years ago, when the prospect was but a dream, Conservatives 'should be aware that the undertaking is an immense one.'[175] We are currently (1982) witnessing the first difficult and faltering steps on the road to its success; or the beginning of its failure. Time alone will tell.

171 ibid., p.71.
172 'Enough Is Enough', *Daily Telegraph* (26 March 1979), p.20.
173 *KCA* (1979), pp. 29633–8. Cf. Thatcher's stress on limiting state control and giving the individual greater freedom of choice, *Time* (14 May 1979), p.11, 13, 15.
174 *KCA* (1979), pp.29705–6.
175 J. E. Powell, 'Conservatism and Social Problems', *Swinton Journal*, xiv (no.3, Autumn 1968), p.13. For a series of critical contemporary comments on the government's performance, see P. Jackson *et al.*, *Government Policy Initiatives 1979–80: Some Case Studies in Public Administration* (London, 1981).

PART FOUR
THE DUALITY OF SOCIALISM

... modern socialism is a doctrine with a double aspect. . . . It is a
doctrine of emancipation ... and it is a doctrine of organization. . . .
E. HALÉVY, *The Era of Tyrannies*, 1938, trans. edn, 1967, p.80

10

SOCIALISM: CHARACTER
AND SOURCES

Socialism is an intellectual Proteus. . . .
H. G. WELLS, *The New Machiavelli*, 1911, Penguin, 1946, p. 91

THERE is no doubt about the variety of shape or emphasis which Socialist doctrine can assume. It is pretty obvious and the fact has frequently been observed. Professor Tawney spoke glowingly of 'the radiant ambiguity of the word Socialism'; while the great French historian Elie Halévy commented on its 'inner contradiction'.[1] In pejorative vein Lord Milner urged at the beginning of the century that it was the 'most vague and misleading of all the catchwords of current controversy'; and in a paper published just after the last war, Professor R. A. Dahl described how, as he saw it, there was inherent in Socialist thought a conflict of ideas and emphasis.[2] And – a final example – Dr Robert Berki has in a recent monograph described a number of rather different, not to say contrasting, 'basic tendencies' which he detects within the Socialist movement.[3] Nor, as detailed exegesis makes clear, is this dichotomy or array peculiar to British Socialism alone, for it is also profusely reflected in exotic varieties of the belief.[4] It is indeed a volatile creed which embraces the ideas and nostrums of prophets so dissimilar as Marx and Ruskin, Keir Hardie and Chairman Mao, Stalin and

1 R. H. Tawney, *The Attack and Other Papers* (London, 1953), p. 60; E. Halévy, *The Era of Tyrannies: Essays on Socialism and War* (1938; trans. edn, London, 1967), pp. 80–1, 198–200; cf. ibid., pp. 204, 212, 238.
2 A. Milner, 'Reminiscence', A. Toynbee, *Lectures on the Industrial Revolution of the Eighteenth Century in England . . .* (1884; rev. edn, London, 1908), p. xxvi; R. A. Dahl, 'Workers' Control of Industry and the British Labor Party', *American Political Science Review*, xli (1947), pp. 875, 876. Among similar observations of the different strains of thought in the British Labour movement, see B. Crick, *The Reform of Parliament* (1964; 2nd edn, London, 1968), p. 211; M. Shanks, 'Labour Philosophy and the Current Position', *Political Quarterly*, xxxi (1960), pp. 242–3.
3 R. N. Berki, *Socialism* (London, 1975), an admirable synoptic study.
4 Cf. K. L. Shell, 'Industrial Democracy and the British Labor Movement', *Political Science Quarterly*, lxxii (1957), pp. 515–16.

G. Orwell, and which, on the domestic scene, in some fashion places J. Callaghan or D. Healey alongside the most ardent and *avant-garde* apostle of, say, the Militant Tendency or the Workers' Revolutionary Party, or a fire-eating catastrophist beside an old-fashioned exponent of Mill such as A. W. Benn. Of course, any actual relationship within this multiformity may be non-existent or merely limited to an exchange of insults. But always the claim is there, advanced from these so very different quarters, to represent the genuine core of Socialist faith.

In the face of this somewhat bewildering array it is difficult to see that Socialists, thus broadly denominated, share any essential ideas in common.[5] Of course, it is possible to adopt what might be called a technical meaning for the term, to establish its theoretical context or implications, and rigidly to exclude from the ideological fold all those whose ideas and policies do not conform to this ostensive standard. Yet this procedure is abstract and artificial and is likely in any case to overlook or underestimate the differences that will still remain, especially over a period of time, either between those that are not sequestered by the shibboleth or within an individual. So, even with a particular doctrine, like that which has appeared in this country over the past 150 years or so, a more complex and diffuse process of designation is required. It is necessary to recognize a range of Socialisms associated through a series of interlocking connexions; a diversity yet not one that is boundless. For the heterogeneity does have certain limits set by the reaction to the problems of urban industrialization and the like. What, then, is the nature of the variety to be observed in the British form of the ideology?

In fact, the demarcation of the native brand of the doctrine seems to be set by the two rather distinct, and ultimately contrasting, motives or goals that have been at work in this Socialism over the past century and a half. These poles of endeavour, potentially so antithetical, are (on the one hand) organization and efficiency, and (on the other) liberty, fulfilment, and moral regeneration. Of course, these ends may be intertwined or pursued in tandem, regarded simply as different aspects of the same purpose. But equally they may involve distinct emphases that emerge in a more than notional separation. This is especially the case so far as the central aspect of modern political thought is concerned: that is, the attitude to be adopted to the state and its proper form and office. For if the object is to organize society properly, indeed scientifically, to eliminate all the wastes and defects that have hitherto disfigured the conduct of our industrial and technological affairs, our economic and social life generally, then the achievement of this purpose will involve supervision and control. It will necessarily mean a growth in governmental or some surrogate power and this may not be easily compatible with the

5 Cf. the discussion of the analysis offered by Dr B. C. Parekh, pp.12–14 above.

continuation of extensive freedom of personal choice and action. Yet the alternative aim of realizing an ethical ideal, it may be of making it possible for the individual to develop his abilities and achieve his potential, must in the end have a different kind of motivation or order of priorities. The protest here is not primarily about the inefficiency of the existing arrangements but rather about their pitiless inequity, their immorality, and godless nature even. And while in the reform of this state of affairs the role of public authority may not be unimportant it can (from this second point of view) never be more than a means of transient significance. Indeed – and this is the crucial point of difference – because of the control this governance involves, it may be seen as a positive hindrance to the fulfilment of the moral purpose, and so the restriction or even elimination of the state may be a condition of the achievement of the Socialist ideal interpreted in this way.

This abstract generalization about the twin and antithetical versions of Socialist ideology remains to be illustrated in the concrete and this will be done at large in the following chapters. But in the rest of this brief introduction it will simply be noted that the origins of the British Socialist tradition of thought are many and varied like those of Liberalism with the genesis of which indeed Socialism has often much in common.

It is possible, and sometimes profitable, to trace the matter back to medieval, early Church, and even classical times, noting affinities between certain aspects of modern Socialist thought and, say, the communism of the philosophers in Plato's *Republic* or the belief of some Christians that private property is sinful (being one of the results of the Fall) and that privilege is incompatible with the equal humility of all before God.[6] Certainly the whole natural law tradition has often stressed an original state of joint possession and universal liberty. There was, too, the old social radicalism associated with the, no doubt vague, opinions of John Ball, the Friars, and their like.[7] Similar tendencies of thought were at work in the early modern period, for example in the social criticism of More's *Utopia* and the ideas of the Levellers and Diggers during the civil wars. Here can be found the notions of common ownership and of labour as the source of wealth and standard of value. Though hardly Socialistic ideas in the modern sense, there is a strong family resemblance in certain respects and they do reappear in more influential guise in the writings of people such as Locke and Smith. And, of course, a general radicalism abounded. It is Oliver Goldsmith who, in a prospect of contemporary

6 For a recent instance, see A. W. Benn, *Arguments for Socialism* (1979; Penguin, 1980), pp.23–9, 146.
7 For a sympathetic and brief résumé of the various early tendencies, see B. Jarrett, *Medieval Socialism* (London, n.d. [1913]).

society, observed that 'Laws grind the poor, and rich men rule the law'.[8] But on the whole it is probably more fruitful to look for the birth of modern Socialist doctrines in the period of great political and social upheaval at the end of the eighteenth and the beginning of the nineteenth centuries. It was then, indeed, that the term Socialism seems first to have been used in print in this country. In 1827 the editor of *The Co-operative Magazine* argued that the value of a commodity consisted of both present and past labour and urged that the main question arising was whether this value should be owned individually or not. Those who held it should be so owned were the political economists while those who thought it should be held in common were the 'Communionists and Socialists'.[9] Of course, it may often be helpful for all sorts of reasons to look back beyond this major period of inception to discern strands of what might be called 'proto-Socialism'; but it is from the modern era that the major formative factors in the development of Socialist thought are likely to be derived or, at least, to coalesce in a relevant way.

One of the main driving forces was religion, a factor assuming many forms in this regard. There was the critical humanitarianism of the Evangelicals important, for instance, in the development of factory reform. There was the Christian Socialism of the Anglican establishment, specifically of people such as Kingsley and Maurice. The latter said in 1849 he seriously believed that Christianity was 'the only foundation of Socialism' and that 'a true Socialism' was 'the necessary result of a sound Christianity.'[10] In this style there was, too, the general social concern of ecclesiastics of varied persuasion such as Booth, Manning, Gore, and Temple. Christ was often seen as having come to earth as a working man; he exalted the cause of the poor and lowly; and urged a person's duty to his neighbour. The great enemy of true religion is riches. Individualism, competition, and self-help were to be eschewed as ideals and replaced by co-operation to achieve the end of human brotherhood. And only a Socialism that was fully Christian could genuinely achieve that conversion of the heart of man to a moral ideal which is the real need of modern society.

Of course, Nonconformity was of especial importance in the history of the Labour movement. It was often the faith of the underprivileged, a

8 O. Goldsmith, 'The Traveller, or a Prospect of Society' (1764), *Poems and Essays*, ed. A. Ridgway (London, n.d. [1925]), p.25.
9 M. Beer, *A History of British Socialism* (1919; London, 1953), i.187. These and similar terms were in fact largely continental in propagation: see A. J. Bestor Jr, 'The Evolution of the Socialist Vocabulary', *Journal of the History of Ideas*, ix (1948), pp.259–302.
10 Cited in P. Dearmer, *Socialism and Christianity* (Fabian tract no.133; 1907, new edn, London, 1907), p.3. Cf. the conclusions of the Pan-Anglican Conference of Bishops (1888), cited ibid.

belief which stressed the sanctity of the individual soul as such, thus providing a spiritual basis for objection to a merely established Church and to the authority of the classes associated with it. Many of the old-style Labour leaders were personally devout, notable in chapel as preachers, trained (as one historian put it) 'in the administrative habits of Methodism, equally accustomed to declamation and conference'.[11] Beatrice Webb remarked on the intimate and complete way in which the working society she encountered while living at Bacup was formed, in both thought and action, by the chapel and its tenets. These people were thus being prepared, she mused, for democracy and self-government.[12] Nor was the historical veneration, like that of Coleridge or the Tractarians, for the ideal Church of the past without a popular impact.[13] Among other things it directed men's minds back to the period before individualism had been dominant, when society was seen to consist of corporate groups in which each person had a fixed status and role and which in turn had a sense of responsibility for its members and their welfare. In this fashion it necessarily impressed men with the social and ethical rules of the medieval Church and its doctrine. Generally, as well, by its stress on historical, organic change, this Coleridgean viewpoint made familiar the notion that class relations and concepts of property and social duty could alter and improve: the principles and implications of political economy were not, therefore, completely immutable.[14] Finally it must be noted, as part of this religious impact on politics, that in the development of the radical ferment of the late nineteenth century an important impetus was provided by a sense of guilt about the condition of the less fortunate that seems to have arisen among many of the socially privileged. Mrs Webb, again, commented on this 'new consciousness of sin among men of intellect and men of property' alike. 'When I say the consciousness of sin', she wrote, 'I do not mean the consciousness of personal sin'. J. S. Mill, like the Webbs themselves,

> did not alter his modest but comfortable way of life when he became a Socialist. . . . The consciousness of sin was a collective or class consciousness; a growing uneasiness, amounting to conviction, that the industrial organisation, which had yielded rent, interest and profits on a stupendous scale, had failed to provide a decent livelihood and tolerable conditions for a majority of the inhabitants of Great Britain. . . . This class-consciousness of sin was usually accompanied by devoted personal service, sometimes by open confession and a

11 G. M. Young, *Victorian England: Portrait of an Age* (1936; 2nd edn, London, 1966), p.170.
12 B. Webb, *My Apprenticeship* (1926; Penguin, 1938), i.185–6, 190–2.
13 Young, op. cit., p.170.
14 Beer, op. cit., i.273.

deliberate dedication of means and strength to the reorganisation of society on a more equalitarian basis.[15]

Of course, not all Socialists were of this spiritual sensibility and naturally there was an element of expediency about this concern, an awareness of the possible consequences of economic depression and electoral reform if nothing was done to ameliorate conditions for the poorer classes. But the significance of the strongly felt sense of wrong referred to is undoubted and contributed not only to an extension of personal charity but also to the creation of that social ethos from which all sorts of Christian Socialism and Fabianism itself emerged.

Nor must the cognate aesthetic dimension be overlooked. It was, for instance, certainly a major influence in some forms of Guild Socialism – especially that of A. J. Penty – and may be best exemplified by reference to such writers as Morris, Ruskin, and Carpenter. Following Carlyle they realized that the growth of wealth is not the same as prosperity for the people. Thus Morris basically saw man as a creative animal and resorted to politics (becoming himself a revolutionary Socialist) because he believed that bourgeois society restrained and warped the creative instincts of humankind. Capitalism had destroyed art and polluted the very physical environment. He envisaged instead a simple society of equals in which all could find joy and satisfaction in creative work, an ideal at once aesthetically and emotionally pleasing.[16]

The tradition of radical ideas which emerged from the English and French Revolutions of the seventeenth and eighteenth centuries was also important. The theories of the Levellers and of the eighteenth-century 'commonwealthmen' in this country and the concept of equality thrown up after 1789 in France helped to establish a mode of attack on the existing distribution of private property, even on the institution itself. Rousseau, for instance, saw distinctions founded on inequality of wealth as the great source of social and political unrest and of moral evil. And he was followed in this by a number of the writers of the revolutionary period such as Mably, Morelly, and Babeuf all of whom affirmed that men's natural destiny was to be equal and that private property was the cause of all human misfortune. It made men grasping and idle, it led to

15 B. Webb, op. cit., i.204, 206–8. Cf. Hubert Bland's comments on the 'deep discontent' generated in 'the educated classes' by the presence of 'a vast mass of human misery', in his 'The Transition to Social Democracy: the Outlook', *Fabian Essays* (1889; Jubilee edn, London, 1950), p.204.

16 For an excellent brief review, see S. Ingle, 'Socialist Man: William Morris and Bernard Shaw' in B. C. Parekh (ed.), *The Concept of Socialism* (London, 1975), pp.73–82. This whole paper, ibid., pp.72–94, is particularly interesting, too, because it presents the antithesis between two opposing forms of Socialism, the almost anarchic egalitarianism of Morris and the meritocratic leadership envisaged by Shaw.

exploitation, and it was the source of social unrest and conflict. If this institution were abolished, along with others that have grown up around it, the fundamental goodness of human nature would, no longer being corrupted by its surroundings, be able to emerge. This egalitarian attack on private property was perpetuated by other continental writers such as Fourier, Proudhon, Louis Blanc, and Marx, who had influence in this country. For instance, Hyndman's Socialism, and that of the Social Democratic Federation which he founded and led, was Marxist in inspiration. Similarly Marx had an impact on some of the Fabians. At the same time it is manifest that this particular exotic influence was hardly so great as some commentators have suggested.[17] Clearly, however, it was not of no account and in certain quarters was considerable especially in the decades after the Great War. If one looks, for instance, at the collection of some 5000 pamphlets in the South Wales Miners' Library at Swansea then, while earlier examples tend to show a substantial Syndicalist influence especially that of the Americans E. Debs and D. de Leon, material from the 1930s and after is undoubtedly very often Marxist or rather Communist in nature. A straw in the wind in this regard is a publication called *Socialism as a Science* which more or less defines 'science' as the Marxist idea of historical development, of progress based on the material conditions of life.[18] In truth, however, it was not really necessary to invoke in this regard any exotic notions because (as already intimated) a very radical, even a revolutionary, tradition of ideas of domestic provenance and substantial lineage was well established. It is only necessary to refer to the work of Godwin, Paine, Cartwright, Thelwall and his associates in the London Corresponding Society, the various writers collectively called the early English or Ricardian Socialists, and the Chartist agitation to indicate what is in mind. Paine's *Rights of Man* alone contains a remarkable assemblage of progressive political programmes together with the view that government, if properly reformed and controlled so as to be the instrument of social conscience, is the means whereby these reforms may be introduced.[19] Godwin familiarized the notion that man has no innate character or defect but may be perfected by the rational transformation of his conditions of life. Owen, in particular, had a great deal of influence not only in expounding this Godwinian notion but also in his belief that

17 See the very full assessment in S. Pierson, *Marxism and the Origins of British Socialism: the Struggle for a New Consciousness* (Ithaca, New York, 1973). Dr Berki is quite firm, and rightly so: in Britain, Marx's direct influence at that time was almost negligible, op. cit., p.71; cf. G. Watson, *The English Ideology* (London, 1973), pp.223–4.
18 M. P. Price, *Socialism as a Science* (Gloucester, 1923), *passim*.
19 Cf. D. C. Somervell, *English Thought in the Nineteenth Century* (1929; London, 1964), p.31.

the change in humankind was to be paternalistically achieved by 'the directors of the system'.[20] Thus any community might be so organized as to make individuals happy.[21] The revolutionary theory of the 'Norman Yoke' with its rejection of the established political and social system as the imposition of an alien ruling caste was still strong; it appeared, for instance, in the writings of Bronterre O'Brien and others and was still in use as late as the early years of the present century.[22] Chartism, of course, with its long career over three decades reflected no nicely systematic or coherent body of thought; nor did it embody a single set of policies. Yet among its various strands may be found: a stress on common ownership; an Owenite desire for social reform; the development of trades unionism and the political and other education of the masses; and, based on a sort of natural rights doctrine, a claim that the worker should receive the full product of his labour. The political gist of the Chartist programme was, of course, embodied in the six demands of the People's Charter of 1838: universal manhood suffrage, equal electoral districts, secret ballot, annual Parliaments, no property qualifications for and payment of MPs. The specific domestic attack on the unequal distribution of property was without doubt of long standing. In addition to the themes and causes already mentioned, the Agrarian Socialists, such as Thomas Spence and William Ogilvie, established in the late eighteenth century (and at a time when enclosures were causing some distress) the doctrine of land-ownership as theft and demanded in this respect the equal right of all. Other Early English Socialists such as Charles Hall, William Thompson, John Gray, and Thomas Hodgskin developed, in the context of their egalitarian attack on private property, a theory of surplus value and class exploitation based on the idea that labour is the sole foundation of wealth. Nor were these notions unfamiliar to the classical economists: Ricardo's theory of the exploitation of the farmer by the landlord is of obvious reference here. And, in its collectivist aspect (to which reference has already been made in another context), Benthamism was not without significance though it made for constitutional rather than revolutionary change.[23] The co-operative movement and the reformist aspects of philosophical idealism also had their part to play. Nor, of course, can the

20 R. Owen, *A New View of Society and Other Writings* (Everyman, 1949), p. 36.
21 ibid., p. 110.
22 See C. Hill, *Puritanism and Revolution: Studies in Interpretation of the English Revolution of the 17th Century* (London, 1958), ch. 3, esp. pp. 116–22.
23 Cf. Keynes's interesting remark that Marxism was *the reductio ad absurdum* of Benthamism, *Two Memoirs* (London, 1949), p. 97. I take it the reference is to (i) the generalization of Ricardo's and James Mill's theory of exploitation and the development of the Ricardian theory of 'rent' into one of 'surplus value'; (ii) the elaboration of the concept of social and economic struggle implicit therein; and (iii) the common trait of scientism. Though, of course, as with all epigrams, so much is excluded.

vital role of the trades unions be overlooked: as S. Haseler suggested recently, 'Ernest Bevin, not Methodism or Marxism, is Labour's heritage.'[24] This may not be true of many Socialists but it definitely makes a valid, if limited, point.

Something of the innumerable and perhaps even rather odd or eccentric strands that went to make up the Socialist ethos in Britain at the beginning of this century is manifested in the remarks of Alfred Orage about his own brand of the doctrine:

It was . . . a cult, with affiliations in directions now quite disowned – with theosophy, arts and crafts, vegetarianism, the 'simple life,' and almost, one might say, with the musical glasses. Morris had shed a medieval glamour over it with his stained-glass *News from Nowhere*. Edward Carpenter had put it into sandals, Cunninghame Graham had mounted it upon an Arab steed to which he was always saying a romantic farewell. Keir Hardie had clothed it in a cloth cap and a red tie. And Bernard Shaw, on behalf of the Fabian Society, had hung it with innumerable jingling epigrammatic bells – and cap. My brand of socialism was, therefore, a blend or, let us say, an anthology of all these, to which from my personal predilections and experience I added a good practical knowledge of the working classes, a professional interest in economics which led me to master Marx's *Das Kapital* and an idealism fed at the source – namely Plato.[25]

In his studies of the radical tradition, R. H. Tawney, noting again that Socialism is obviously a word of more than one meaning, its character varying substantially with political realities and the specific environment in which it develops, deduced from this that it was unprofitable to discuss the doctrine in general terms without defining the particular type of it under consideration.[26] There is obviously very sound sense in this suggestion. And it means that the task now to be faced is that of illustrating concretely something of the varieties of British Socialism which have been manifested in modern times and thus of indicating the doctrine's necessarily ambivalent and contradictory character. And we are not without authoritative guidance in this regard. For, at a relatively early stage in the development of the creed, J. S. Mill pointed most perceptively to the sort of antinomy involved. There are, he said, two kinds of persons who call themselves Socialists: those whose plans for a new order of society rest on the vision of a free association of small, self-governing units; and another class who propose a bolder scheme to manage the entire productive resources of the country through the

24 S. Haseler, *The Gaitskellites: Revisionism in the British Labour Party, 1951–64* (London, 1969), p.1.
25 Cited in P. Mairet, *A. R. Orage: a Memoir* (London, 1936), p.40.
26 R. H. Tawney, *The Radical Tradition* (1964; Penguin, 1966), p.146.

concentrated agency of central government. He himself favoured the first
of these two possibilities and believed the latter to be characteristic in his
time of continental rather than British views.[27] In this he was to prove
wrong. But he had undoubtedly correctly sketched the two limiting and
contrasting styles which Socialist thought in Britain would freely
exemplify over the ensuing century.

27 J. S. Mill, 'Chapters on Socialism' (1879), *Collected Works*, ed. J. M. Robson *et al.*
(London, 1963ff.), v.737.

11

THE FABIAN MODEL

The creed of scientific preparation and organization was sweeping
before it the philosophy of instinct, improvization, and liberty.
E. HALÉVY, *A History of the English People in the Nineteenth Century*,
1913–46; trans. edn, 1961, vi.174

A CAMERALIST TRADITION

. . . collectivism . . . demands expert government . . . 'the aristocracy of
talent' of which Carlyle wrote. The control of a State with powers so vast
will obviously need an exceptional and exceptionally large aristocracy.
E. BARKER, *Political Thought in England 1848–1914*, 1915, 2nd edn
rev., 1947, pp.192–3

OPPONENTS, even when they recognize the variety of doctrine
involved, invariably go on to insist that Socialism necessarily means
increasing state control especially of the means of production.[1] It is
perhaps a contradictory view; but it does undoubtedly point to a major,
even the dominant, stream of ideas in the British Socialist tradition. And
what the statist aspect of Socialism may entail is suitably represented by
the Fabians who believed that the key to the transformation of society
was not so much the cultivation and recognition of democracy or
individuality but rather wise and authoritative direction from above.
Sidney Webb was as honestly blunt about this in public as his wife was in
the privacy of her diary. He was certain the best government was no
longer that which governed least but that which could 'safely and
advantageously administer most.' It was foolish, he wrote, to suppose
that the affairs of 'a complicated industrial state' could be run 'without
strict subordination and discipline, without obedience to orders'; it was
'to dream, not of Socialism but of Anarchism.' In any such community,
however formally democratic it might be, affairs would perforce become
'more and more the business of elaborately trained experts, and less and

1 For an old but typical instance, see the NUCCA handbook *The Case Against
Radicalism 1909: a Fighting Brief for Unionist Candidates, Agents and Speakers*
(London, n.d. [1910]), pp.31, 45.

less the immediate outcome of popular feeling.'² As well the order of priorities was undoubted: 'the perfect and fitting development of each individual is not necessarily the utmost and highest cultivation of his own personality, but the filling, in the best possible way, of his humble function in the great social machine'.³ It was not that the individual's best interest would not be served; but efficiency in production and the achievement of the national minimum or other forms of betterment demanded a society deliberately organized on 'scientific' principles by an administrative élite of superior knowledge and experience. Mrs Webb recorded a like sentiment and purpose in this way: 'we have little faith in the "average sensual man", we do not believe that he can do much more than describe his grievances, we do not think that he can prescribe the remedies. . . . We wish to introduce into politics the professional expert' and through him 'to extend the sphere of government'.⁴ H. G. Wells (who had rather similar beliefs, of course) accurately hit the mark so far as the Webbs were concerned when, having presented them with a copy of his book *A Modern Utopia*, he said that the idea of a ruling class of 'samurai' (which he had expounded in that work) would pander to all their worst instincts.⁵ Shaw, too, accepted that, always and everywhere, 'the few will . . . organize the many.'⁶

But these were hardly surprising views for the Fabians to have. Most of them were bourgeois with a healthy and proper disrespect for the lower orders though with a sense – arising perhaps out of interest, maybe out of conscience, or even a feeling of sin – that something must be done to improve their lot and that this required radical social change. Many of them were civil servants not a little impressed with their own abilities and imbued with the idea of a mandarin responsibility: theirs was the notion writ large of the 'intellectual' official described in the Northcote-Trevelyan report as the key to bureaucratic efficiency. They also reflected in this regard the impact during the nineteenth century of the development of a professional class with its own ethic implying the concept of a society functionally based on expertise and selection by merit.⁷

2 S. Webb, *The Basis & Policy of Socialism* (Fabian Socialist Series no. 4; London, 1908), pp. 57, 71; *The Necessary Basis of Society* (London, 1908), p. 6. Cf. *The Difficulties of Individualism* (Fabian tract no. 69; London, 1896), pp. 5–6.
3 S. Webb, 'The Basis of Socialism: Historic', G. B. Shaw *et al.*, *Fabian Essays* (1889; Jubilee edn, London, 1950), p. 54.
4 Diary entry (29 December 1894), in B. Webb, *Our Partnership* (London, 1948), p. 120. Cf. ibid., p. 97.
5 ibid., p. 305.
6 G. B. Shaw, *Socialism and Superior Brains: a Reply to Mr. Mallock* (Fabian Socialist Series no. 8; 1909, 2nd edn, London, 1910), p. 51.
7 Shaw commented on the contrast in class background between the middle-class Fabians and the proletarian rank and file of the Socialist League and the SDF in his *The*

They were, too, in touch with a tradition of ideas of very notable lineage indeed. Of course, the concept of a ruling intellectual élite is hardly new. Its origin might be sought in Plato's philosopher kings or in the actual role of the medieval clerisy. Since then many reformers, especially those of a utopian frame of mind, had looked to such a group for a solution to the besetting social ills and political turmoil of their day. The achievements of modern science added impetus to the dream. The early academies such as the Royal Society were founded to act as centres of learning, as repositories of natural knowledge in particular, through which the condition of the world might be transformed. This stream of ideas was crucially embodied in Francis Bacon's vision of a science of man and nature that would enable the human race to make the world its servant, an instauration symbolized in the Solomon's House of his *New Atlantis*. And as his influence was second to none in forming the minds of so many people in the educated classes during the two centuries after his own time – the 'Bacon-fac'd generation' – his character as a writer who established an early paradigm of the managerial state is central.[8] This sort of attitudes was nourished, too, and in a most important way by the various policies associated with the so-called mercantile system which looked with favour on state action as a means of furthering the economic ends in view, in particular the achievement of a favourable balance of trade. In these terms one of the main functions of government was the development of industry and the regulation of commerce either by direct state intervention (as by the fixing of prices and wages or the stimulation of exports through bounties and duties) or through the agency of quasi-public trading companies and monopolies. In an important sense, therefore, mercantilism was concerned with making the state powerful in its economic aspect. Sir Alexander Gray summarized the matter in these words:

> . . . in all their schemes the mercantilists looked to a benevolently paternal government, assumed wise enough to interfere everywhere. Mercantilism was a policy of ubiquitous and perpetual government

Fabian Society: What It has Done & How It has Done It (Fabian tract no.41; London, 1892), p.4. On the development of the professional classes, see H. Perkin, *The Origins of Modern English Society, 1780–1880* (1969; London, 1972), pp.252ff.; and for the Fabian reflection of their ideal, ibid., pp.261–2, 265; also R. Dahl, 'Workers' Control of Industry and the British Labor Party', *American Political Science Review*, xli (1947), p.878.

8   Cf. M. Oakeshott, *On Human Conduct* (Oxford, 1975), pp.287–91. On the impact of Baconian ideas, see e.g. S. B. L. Penrose Jr, *The Reputation and Influence of Francis Bacon in the Seventeenth Century* (New York, 1934); R. F. Jones, *Ancients and Moderns: a Study of the Background of the 'Battle of the Books'* (1936; 2nd edn, St Louis, Mo., 1961).

activity. There was nothing the Government might not do, if thereby its activity was calculated to promote the general well-being.

There is, he adds (after a review of the typical policies involved), 'an obvious kinship between Mercantilism and State Socialism'.[9] Sir Alexander was not perhaps a wholly neutral observer of these matters but with some qualification this general judgement about the mercantilist sense of the need to strengthen the power of the realm is elsewhere confirmed: there was to be, as James Bonar said, 'an interference at every point'.[10]

And if in Britain certain aspects of these themes were subsequently impugned by the doctrines of Adam Smith and his followers, they were nevertheless sustained elsewhere by the important cameralist school of thinkers which flourished in Germany and Austria during the eighteenth century and which was much concerned with the problems of administration and control arising in the pursuit of 'enlightened government'.[11] The cameralists were rationalists in the sense that they believed in the possibility of discovering rules, independent of the activity of politics, to give that activity purpose and direction and as well means to achieve the goals indicated. Political discussion is thus an analysis of techniques and of solutions to social and economic problems achieved by their application. A sort of particularized utilitarianism is at work also. The aim is happiness and this may be achieved through the creation in the state concerned of specific conditions necessary to this general consummation: adequate security, a growing population, the development of economic resources, the establishment of welfare services. Government is thus seen as a eudemonic machine capable of producing comfort and content. Its power is to be used and used systematically to this end. Indeed, one of the numerous German academics who expounded these views urged that the first essential of any wise government was a well-conceived plan.[12] And the ideal of paternalist and absolute monarchy

9 Sir Alexander Gray, *The Development of Economic Doctrine: an Introductory Survey* (1931; London, 1963), ch.III, citations at pp.64–5.
10 J. Bonar, *Philosophy and Political Economy in Some of their Historical Relations* (1893; 3rd edn, London, 1967), p.133. See also e.g. Sir E. Roll, *A History of Economic Thought* (1937; new edn, London, 1957), pp.61–85, esp. pp.61–4; W. Stark, *The History of Economics in its Relation to Social Development* (London, 1944), pp.8–14; E. Lipson, *A Planned Economy or Free Enterprise: the Lessons of History* (London, 1944), ch.2 'England's First Planned Economy'.
11 The literature in English on this school is not considerable but see e.g. A. W. Small, *The Cameralists: the Pioneers of German Social Polity* (Chicago, 1909); L. Sommer, 'Cameralism', *Encyclopaedia of the Social Sciences* (New York, 1950), iii.158–60; G. Parry, 'Enlightened Government and its Critics in Eighteenth-Century Germany', *Historical Journal*, vi (1963), esp. pp.180–5; and the luminous summary in Oakeshott, op. cit., pp.299ff.
12 Parry, art. cit., p.184 referring to J. H. G. von Justi, *Gesammelte Politische- und Finanzschriften* (Copenhagen and Leipzig, 1761), iii.75–6.

involved seemed to entail three concepts relevant here. One is the concentration of authority in the hands of the prince and the elimination of any intermediate stratum of autonomous associations such as the guilds or corporations which had hitherto stood between subject and ruler. The second is a notion of efficient and economical, indeed scientific, administration conducted centrally by a body of professional officials. The other is a view of civil society as a kind of estate to be managed in the most rational and beneficent way, its workers or retainers being kept busy producing the wealth necessary for their own maintenance as well as for that needed to support the functionaries and for the pursuit of public purposes. This was lordship of an effective and extensive kind involving the constant improvement, and so the enlargement, of official interference. The cameralists thus centred their attention on 'the problem of the rising state'.[13] von Justi wrote that a 'properly constituted state must be exactly analogous to a machine, in which all the wheels and gears are precisely adjusted to one another; and the ruler must be the foreman, the mainspring, or the soul . . . which sets everything in motion.'[14]

There is manifestly a strong family resemblance between this sort of theory and similar notions that were perhaps more widely deployed. There was, for instance, St-Simon's concept of a Council of Newton and the cognate ideas of his disciple, Auguste Comte, of a society rationally administered by a caste of expert and professional *polytechniciens*.[15] During the nineteenth century such meritocratic beliefs became almost a commonplace: witness Coleridge's emphasis on the vital reformative role of a new 'clerisy'; Carlyle's on the 'grand problem', the need for government to be by a real 'Aristocracy of Talent', 'Hero-Kings', rather than the ballot box, and his recognition that a just despotism is essential; J. S. Mill's on the cultural and political influence of a superior few whose position in a mass age had to be safeguarded by appropriate institutional devices; and the general Benthamite stress on the achievement of a social harmony of interests through the tutorial activity of command.[16] To all this has to be added the force of the considerable scientism of the day, for

13 Sommer, loc. cit., iii.160.

14 von Justi, op. cit., iii.86–7, cited and translated in Parry, art. cit., p.182. Cf. de Tocqueville's comments in *Democracy in America* (1835–40; Fontana, 1968), ii.869–70 as in the passages cited in vol.i, *The Rise of Collectivism*, pp.22–3.

15 Cf. F. A. Hayek, *The Counter-revolution of Science: Studies on the Abuse of Reason* (1955; Glencoe Free Press, 1964), partII; E. Halévy, *The Era of Tyrannies: Essays on Socialism and War* (1938; trans. edn, London, 1967), pp.17ff. For a pejorative (and French) view of the *polytechnicien*, see A. Maurois, *The Silence of Colonel Bramble* (trans. edn, 1919; London, 1930), p.148.

16 In one place at least Sidney Webb specifically claimed for Socialists the mantle of Benthamism: *The Basis & Policy of Socialism*, p.55. Cf. B. Webb, *Our Partnership*, p.210; and A. M. McBriar, *Fabian Socialism and English Politics, 1884–1918* (1962; Cambridge, 1966), pp.149–55.

instance the hyper-Darwinist belief of people like Huxley and Kidd that, as the evolutionary process went on, the more complex organisms produced demanded mechanisms of greater control.[17] There were also the contemporary ideas (developed from the 1880s on) of 'scientific management', techniques of improvement in industrial production worked out by a new class of specially trained experts. These themes were associated in particular with the writings of F. W. Taylor and involved 'a fully fledged technocratic ideology for a new society'.[18] It is easy to see why many Socialists – and not only them, of course – should find all such notions congenial. They were akin to, say, Robert Owen's paternalist schemes for the proper direction of production and for the creation, in behalf of the dependent workforce, of the proper environment in which alone their lives and characters could be educated and moulded for happiness. It was in similar vein, too, that John Ruskin had urged that the economic and social evils of the day could only be dispersed by a trusteeship of power in Platonic fashion by what he called a new chivalry.

In this broad context of ideas, then, the Fabians easily slip into place as exponents of a directorial Socialism: as Michael Oakeshott recently noted, 'the connection between Fabianism and Cameralism is unmistakable'.[19]

THE FABIAN SOCIETY

For just experience tells, in every soil,
That those who think must govern those that toil. . . .
O. GOLDSMITH, 'The Traveller, or a Prospect of Society', 1764,
ll. 372–3

In H. G. Wells's novel *Ann Veronica*, the following passage occurs:

'I have heard of the Fabians,' said Ann Veronica.
'It's *the* society!' said Miss Miniver. 'It's the centre of the intellectuals. Some of the meetings are wonderful! Such earnest, beautiful women! Such deep-browed men! . . . And to think that there they are making history! There they are putting together the plans of a new world. Almost light-heartedly. There is Shaw, and Webb . . . – the most wonderful people! There you see them discussing, deciding, planning! Just think – *they are making a new world!*'
'But *are* these people going to alter anything?' said Ann Veronica.
'What else can happen?' asked Miss Miniver, with a little weak

17 For hyper-Darwinism, see vol.i, *The Rise of Collectivism*, pp.261–7.
18 The phrase comes from K. Minogue's review of J. A. Merkle, *Management and Ideology*, TLS (29 May 1981), p.591.
19 Oakeshott, *On Human Conduct*, p.311.

gesture. . . . 'What else can possibly happen – as things are going now?'[20]

Of course, when Wells wrote this passage he was, for all sorts of personal and other reasons, disenchanted with the Fabian; so he continues by having his emancipated young woman, Ann Veronica, query whether her interlocutor's optimism is justified and whether the Society is really going to alter anything. But his irony does not at all misrepresent what the group had come to stand for: pointing the way to a more efficiently organized and, therefore, more humane state of things. If its origins reveal somewhat diverse motives and divided objectives, a crisp down-to-earth reformism began quite quickly to dominate its activities.

The Fabian Society proper was founded in 1884 but it grew out of other groups which had been established a little earlier, in particular the Fellowship of the New Life which had been started by a civil servant, Percival Chubb, and an itinerant mystic named Thomas Davidson whom Havelock Ellis once described as 'one of the most remarkable men I have ever known.'[21] The Fellowship was dedicated to personal regeneration (described as 'the cultivation of a perfect character in each and all'), to what used to be described as 'higher thought', to the simple existence of a self-contained, co-operative commune, and to humanitarianism of a kind influenced by Christian Socialism and the doctrines of 'eternal justice' expounded by the Catholic moralist Antonio Rosmini-Serbati: an eclectic and heady mixture.[22] But then a schismatic transformation occurred that is described in a letter Bernard Shaw wrote many years later to Kingsley Martin about the impact of Sidney Webb and himself on this band of high-minded do-gooders. The terms, if a little over-simplified, are graphic:

> Webb was not the founder of the Fabian Society. It was founded by a Rosminian philosopher named Davidson and was excessively un-

20 H. G. Wells, *Ann Veronica* (1909; Penguin, 1968), p.113, italics in original.
21 In W. H. Auden *et al.*, *I Believe: the Personal Philosophies of Twenty-Three Eminent Men and Women of our Time* (London, 1940), p.83. See also N. MacKenzie, 'Percival Chubb and the Founding of the Fabian Society', *Victorian Studies*, xxiii (1979–80), pp.29–55.
22 A. Fremantle, *This Little Band of Prophets: the British Fabians* (1959; Mentor Books, 1960), pp.26–7. On the utopian and morally regenerative ethos of the Fellowship and its origins, see N. and J. MacKenzie, *The First Fabians* (London, 1977), ch.1. On Rosmini (1797–1855), ibid., p.302; and W. Wolfe, *From Radicalism to Socialism: Men and Ideas in the Formation of Fabian Socialist Doctrines, 1881–1889* (New Haven, Conn., 1975), p.154, and the references there given. Davidson had edited and translated Rosmini's works and had in view, too, a new edition of those of St Thomas. Given this sort of interest one wonders about the influence the late nineteenth-century papal encyclicals might thus have exerted, albeit indirectly, on Fabian ideas.

fabian, dreaming of colonies of Perfect Lifers in Brazil, and discussing the abolition of money and the substitution of pass-books, and constitutional anarchism and all sorts of nonsense. . . . It split into a political section led by Hubert Bland, calling itself the Fabian Society, and a Fellowship of the New Life, with perfectionist views. The Fabian section had one working man member named Phillips; and it managed to get out a tract entitled *Why are the Many Poor?* This tract came my way. I, being a newly converted Marxist looking for a political shop, saw that the title Fabian, obviously educated, was an inspiration. I joined it and found it a handful of hopeless amateurs needing above all things Webb, whom I had picked out as a political genius. . . . I roped him into the Fabian; and his knowledge, ability, and administrative experience as an upper division civil servant at once swept all the nonsense and Bohemian anarchism out of it, and made it what it finally became.[23]

Of course, despite the change of emphasis, some element of ethical appeal or a sense of humanitarian values were never subsequently absent. It was this aspect of the Fabian that Annie Besant originally found congenial.[24] For some Fabians indeed this attempt to reconstruct society in accordance with the highest moral possibilities continued to be the strongest strand of motivation as, among early members, for Sydney Olivier and Sidney Ball. But concentration on or the exposition of this side of things was never a Fabian *forte* at least during the years of the Society's maturity. Olivier's paper in the *Fabian Essays* on the moral basis of Socialism is hardly a distinguished contribution to the subject; and Ball's analysis elsewhere of the same topic is a rather shapeless ethical *mélange*: some of the obscurer aspects of philosophical idealism garnished with a dash of Ruskin and expressed in the language of natural selection.[25] This was really the kind of thing the Fabians ultimately decided they wanted to get rid of after they had 'seceded from the Regenerators' and put thoughts of the New Jerusalem aside in favour of a thorough understanding of the theory of rent and a practical grasp of the sanitary regulations of a London borough.[26] And instead of the existing 'scramble for private gain', what they sought was 'the introduction of design, contrivance, and co-ordination' in the conscious pursuit of 'collective welfare'. These are Shaw's words commending the original programme;

23 G. B. Shaw to K. Martin (14 October 1947), cited in C. H. Rolph, *Kingsley: The Life, Letters and Diaries of Kingsley Martin* (London, 1973), p.131.
24 N. and J. MacKenzie, op. cit., p.54.
25 S. Ball, *The Moral Aspects of Socialism* (Fabian tract no. 72; London, 1896). Cf. his 'The Socialist Ideal', *Economic Review*, ix (1899), pp.425–49.
26 The phrase cited is from G. B. Shaw, *The Fabian Society: What It has Done & How It has Done It* (Fabian tract no. 41; London, 1892), p.4. Cf. Shaw's 'Sixty Years of Fabianism' (1947), Shaw *et al., Fabian Essays* (1889; Jubilee edn, London, 1950), p.229.

but their spirit is echoed by Webb when, in a later exposition, he says that what the Fabians wanted was an improvement in real conditions to be achieved by more efficient economic arrangements than those obtaining under capitalism.[27] Shaw, again, summed up the transformation in the group's ethos: 'Certain members of that circle, modestly feeling that the revolution would have to wait an unreasonably long time if postponed until they personally had attained perfection, set up the banner of Socialism militant'.[28] And if recent commentary has properly indicated the ethical basis or undercurrent of early Fabian thought, it is nevertheless true that, by 1894, the Webbs were quite baldly stating that from the late 1880s onward the chief effort of the 'English Socialist Movement' as a whole and of the Fabian in particular was to bring about a society infused with collectivist principles and techniques.[29]

What was particularly involved in this campaign naturally depended on the membership. This was never very large but, in the early days, included such people as Shaw, the Webbs, Olivier, Annie Besant, Wells, and Graham Wallas. Later, and similarly sometimes transient, adherents were A. J. Penty, R. H. Tawney, G. D. H. Cole, H. Laski, and B. Russell. A group composed of such headstrong individualists naturally produced an array of often contrasting opinions about what the pursuit of Socialism entailed. But among the plethora of ideas, held with a varying strength of conviction as circumstances and the dominant personalities changed, certain leading themes frequently emerged. Of course, there was (as will be seen) an extensive array of particular programmes and policies ranging from the provision of public baths to the socialization of communications.[30] But what is most important is the manner or style in which these proposals were made and their implementation envisaged.

The nature of the people involved, the kind of group they constituted, and as well the sort of persons on whom they sought to bring their influence to bear, led easily to a belief in wise and authoritative direction from above, a view the cameralist background of which has already been

27 Shaw, 'Preface to the 1908 Reprint', *Fabian Essays*, p.xxx; S. Webb, 'The Spirit of the Fabian Society', *The Green Leaf* (no. 3, February 1927), p.13. This periodical is not, as the innocent reader might assume, the house journal of the author's family but a bilingual review devoted to the radical reconstruction of society which was published by a group of Labour supporters in Paris in the 1920s. The title (otherwise *La Revue Verte*) is obscure (to me) in both origin and symbolic intent (unless it refers to the cockade snatched by Desmoulins in 1789). Yet I cannot say the advice with which the magazine's contents page was often headed is not sound, to wit, that 'The Green Leaf Should Be Read By All Those For Whom The Reconstruction Of Society Is Of Deep Interest'.

28 G. B. Shaw, *The Fabian Society* . . . , p.3.

29 S. and B. Webb, *The History of Trade Unionism* (1894; new edn, London, 1907), p.400 and n.1.

30 For a good, very brief, summary, see H. G. Wells, *New Worlds for Old* (London, 1908), ch.XII, esp. pp.265–6.

described. It was shared by such native preceptors as Owen, Carlyle, and Ruskin none of whom ever cared much for political democracy or who, like J. S. Mill, were acutely aware of its deficiencies. Such attitudes are crucially reflected by the Webbs (whose ideas are looked at in more detail below) and by Wells. Here another illustration of this posture of superiority may be taken from the pages of Leonard Woolf's auto-biography. If trivial the example is nevertheless characteristic of Fabian hauteur. For long the Society's leading expert on international and imperial affairs, Woolf was in his younger days a colonial administrator in Ceylon. He writes rather snobbishly of a colleague there, a police magistrate, commenting on his lower middle-class origin and the scrappy superficiality of the self-education in which he had indulged. There is no sense in the portrait of sympathy for someone struggling to better himself, only the expression of class disdain. Again Woolf remarks of a servant he once had that 'she was one of those persons for whom I feel the same kind of affection as I do for cats and dogs.' More generally, while deploring any illegality or use of excessive force, he was a strict, even stern, authoritarian when it came to the maintenance of law and order in his Ceylonese domain.[31] The self-description reveals, albeit unconsciously, that paternalistic, upper-class 'habit of authority' which A. P. Thornton has so convincingly analysed, an attitude reflected in the general Fabian view of the cultural and intellectual superiority of their class at home and of the white race abroad.[32] When in any situation occasioning concern or trepidation, Beatrice Webb used to repeat to herself (as a means of acquiring courage) that she was the cleverest member of the cleverest class of the richest country in the world. It was easy and natural for such people to assume the need for both domestic and colonial tutelage. In his usual deliberately outrageous way, Shaw likewise indicated the Fabian contempt for the masses. Of course, there was a quite sincere support for an improvement in their conditions and firm acknowledgement of the need for a formal equality of rights and opportunities. But to reach these very goals exceptional ability had to be detected and the emergence of a 'Democratic Aristocracy' of talent encouraged. In many ways the sentiment is simply repetition of the concern expressed so many years before by J. S. Mill and others, the keen recognition that 'mobocracy' or 'Government by the Unfittest' may well be the main obstacle to the desired reorganization of society. The extreme and provocative tone of the Shavian formulation emerges most

31 L. Woolf, *Growing: an Autobiography of the Years, 1904–11*, (London, 1961), pp.63–5, 79, 169; *Beginning Again: an Autobiography of the Years, 1911–18* (London, 1964), p.173.

32 A. P. Thornton, *The Habit of Authority: Paternalism in British History* (London, 1966), e.g. pp.16–17, 321–2; A. M. McBriar, *Fabian Socialism and English Politics, 1884–1918* (1962; Cambridge, 1966), pp.126ff.

clearly, however, in the view that the necessary élite should be selected not by popular vote but by a panel of experts, that under Socialism social misfits should be 'painlessly liquidated', and that those who are not able 'to prove their social solvency' should be made to do useful work or be put to death![33] One never really knows with Shaw whether he means exactly what he says or is simply trailing his coat. Certainly this particular expression of opinion is the *reductio ad absurdum* of that alliance between eugenic selection and benevolent despotism that Shaw always favoured.[34] And if it was, admittedly, formulated long after the Fabian hey-day, earlier (if more modest) expressions of its political implications are not hard to find. In 1896, for instance, Shaw carefully explained to the trade union movement, on behalf of the Fabian Society as a whole, that the extreme devices of democracy were undesirable. Legislative and administrative power should always remain in skilled hands: the 'organized, intelligent and class-conscious Socialist minority', he said, must not be placed at the mercy of the unorganized and apathetic rabble of electors or routine toilers.[35] Fabians thus invariably accepted the need for discipline and guidance expressed through an intensification of collective regulation. Modern society was so large and complex it required efficient bureaucratic control, the scientific and benevolent rule of 'official archangels'.[36] And if Fabians did not create this necessity for control their interest was undoubtedly to see that the essential element of supervision was of 'high quality' so that the 'deliberate and instructed will' of the community might prevail with the minimum of friction.[37] Inevitably there was often associated with this opinion a rather cavalier attitude towards existing political arrangements, a disenchantment that Shaw stated epigrammatically when he said that 'the ocean of Socialism cannot be poured into the pint pot of a nineteenth century parliament'.[38] These are the sort of sentiments that ought always to be remembered and placed alongside any protestations of democratic faith and enthusiasm for local self-government.

The implications were obvious and libertarian critics were never slow to condemn those impatient of traditional institutions and the rule of

33 For these views and phrases, see Shaw, 'Sixty Years of Fabianism', *Fabian Essays*, pp.217–28.
34 Cf. Mrs Webb's consideration of 'the subject of human breeding' as 'the most important of all questions', diary entry (16 January 1903), cited in *Our Partnership* (London, 1948), pp.256–7. On the role of eugenics in the development of statist society, see vol.i, *The Rise of Collectivism*, ch.5, pp.269–72.
35 Shaw, *Report on Fabian Policy* . . . (Fabian tract no.70; London, 1896), pp.13–14.
36 The phrase cited is from H. G. Wells, *The Bulpington of Blup*. . . . (London, n.d. [1932]), p.107.
37 See R. Fraser, *A Social Philosophy for Fabians* (Fabian tract no.234; London, 1930), pp.7–8, 10.
38 Shaw, 'Preface to the 1931 Reprint', *Fabian Essays*, p.xiv.

law; and in so doing they revealed the thrust of the Fabian position. One typical and perceptive statement is from the pen of Ramiro de Maeztu, the Spanish diplomat and politician who, as a journalist, had in his younger days lived in England for a number of years and become closely associated with Fabian and other radical circles. Many members of the Society, he noted, 'looked upon officialism as the instrument of Divine Providence for the solution of social problems.'[39] As Socialists they were certainly enemies of a confined opulence but the means of dispersal they envisaged did not involve subjecting 'the power of the powerful' to popular control.

> . . . State Socialism will entirely abolish the wealth of the rich when it establishes the ownership in common of the means of production, distribution, and exchange. But the State which does such a thing will not be, as the idealogues [sic] appear to think, a pure entity of reason, but a government, an executive power, a bureaucracy; and the men who will assume the power under it now possessed by the capitalists will consequently be men of flesh and bone, constituted as a governing class. It is quite possible that, under such a régime, the workers might attain a position of greater security than they now enjoy. But, at bottom, they will have done no more than change their masters and their form of government. The bureaucrats will replace the capitalists; political power economic power; the present State will be replaced by the Servile State, . . . and the life of the masses, as at present, would lie at the mercy of a few men.[40]

Nor has similar assessment of the functionary state envisaged by the Fabians been wanting either at that time or since.[41] Roy Campbell's poetic comment at least must be cited:

> . . . whose collective dictatorial rule
> Would wake the devil in the tamest mule –
> For they're all members of the self-same school,
> And drilled, like Fascists, to enforce on all
> The standards of the middling and the small: . . . .[42]

This wise and authoritative direction was to be expert and calculated,

---

39 R. de Maeztu, *Authority, Liberty and Function in the Light of the War* . . . (London, 1916), p.92.
40 ibid., pp.199–200. For Belloc's concept of the 'Servile State', see above pp.91–3.
41 For random instances that lie to hand, see H. G. Wells, *New Worlds for Old*, pp.276–7; H. Belloc, *The Servile State* (1912, 3rd edn, London, 1927), pp.127–30; L. T. Hobhouse, *Liberalism* (1911; Galaxy, 1966), pp.89–90; Lord Hewart, *The New Despotism* (London, 1929), pp.14–16; and M. Oakeshott, *On Human Conduct* (Oxford, 1975), pp.300–1.
42 R. Campbell, 'The Georgiad' (1933), *The Collected Poems* (1949; London, 1955), p.240.

a paternalism rationally organized and efficiently sustained. The epithet 'scientific' was continually used by the Fabians to describe this manner of governance. It was clearly a term that through constant repetition was intended to inspire confidence in the flow of analysis and recommendation in which it was embedded. It was often associated, too, with the equally common and fashionable references to evolution and the growth of the social organism on biological lines. Shaw, for one, saw the case for enforcing an equality of incomes in biological terms. A stable civilization needs adequate leadership and this will only appear if human development through the widest possible sexual selection is uninhibited by the class distinctions that now prevent intermarriage. Equally Sidney Webb sometimes used biological language to hyper-Darwinist purpose.[43] However, the usual Fabian use of the term 'scientific' did not necessarily refer to this specific context or entail application of the strict mathematical and testing experimental techniques of the laboratory. Rather it meant simply that, given any object or policy in view, it should be rationally conceived, its implications patiently and thoroughly explored, relevant data methodically collected and presented, all with a view to practical implementation given the realities of human nature and the social situation.[44] At least, Fabians believed, this investigative procedure stood in favourable contrast with the merely visionary proposals for change which had been so common among reformers hitherto. They rejected such utopian schemes with contempt.[45] Perhaps the one feature of Marxism that Fabians as a whole found acceptable was its attempt (as they perceived it) scientifically to establish carefully verified facts about modern capitalism.[46] Not that everyone was impressed with this Fabian manner even if in principle the power of

43 Shaw, 'Sixty Years of Fabianism', *Fabian Essays*, pp.217ff.; Webb, 'The Basis of Socialism: Historic', ibid., pp.53–4.
44 For some examples of the use of 'scientific' and cognate terms in this broad sense, see e.g. *Fabian Essays*, pp.26–7, 41, 46, 53, 54, 106, 165, 229; Shaw, *The Fabian Society*, pp.15, 16, 25, 27; J. Burns, *The Unemployed* (Fabian tract no.47; London, 1893), pp.4, 7, 13, 16; Shaw, *Report on Fabian Policy*, p.9; S. Ball, *The Moral Aspects of Socialism* (Fabian tract no.72; London, 1896), pp.3, 4, 7, 10, 11; W. P. Reeves, *The State and its Functions in New Zealand* (Fabian tract no.74; London, 1896), p.4; W. S. Sanders, *The Case for a Legal Minimum Wage* (Fabian tract no.128; London, 1906), p.3; Mrs E. C. Townshend, *The Case against the Charity Organisation Society* (Fabian tract no.158; London, 1911), p.3; S. Webb, *The Necessary Basis of Society* (London, 1908), p.7; B. Webb, *Our Partnership*, p.300; and H. G. Wells, *New Worlds for Old*, pp.265, 268, 273. There are some interesting suggestions about the possibly deleterious effect of positivism on Socialist thought in A. Arblaster, 'Socialism and the Idea of Science', B. C. Parekh (ed.), *The Concept of Socialism* (London, 1975), ch.7, esp. pp.148–9 on the Fabians.
45 e.g. *Fabian Essays*, pp.29, 32; S. Webb, *The Difficulties of Individualism* (Fabian tract no.69; London, 1896), p.3.
46 Shaw, *Report on Fabian Policy*, p.7, significantly in a section on 'Fabian Natural Philosophy'. See also *Fabian Essays*, p.166.

science seemed considerable. One of H. G. Wells's heroes (if that is the right word), Theodore Bulpington, is used to express doubts felt about its real status:

> He imposed upon all that slow earthbound Fabian stuff, that collection of doubtful statistics, that meticulous open-minded assembling and sorting of facts, that sedulous imitation, in an uncongenial field, of the methods of physical science, the word '*bourgeois*'; and at a stroke the convergence of obligation it implied was foiled.[47]

Of course this is negative – at that point of the story Bulpington was in the throes of a conversion to Communism – but it does reliably characterize the Fabian style in the respect now in question: 'the grip of science closing in upon social and political problems in the most effective fashion . . . to make a "planned world" . . . on a larger scale than ever. . . .'[48] 'Science' is undoubtedly one of the grandest and most persuasive words in the world and the Fabians used it to good effect and surely in all sincerity. What they really never allowed for was the difficulty that it meant getting outside man and trying to see him (as Chesterton's Father Brown once said) as if he were a gigantic insect: whereas the real secret was to 'get inside' him.[49]

Apart from the concrete and careful method of inquiry and prescription the Fabians claimed to adopt, a scientific dimension was, they believed, also given to their point of view by the sort of economic arguments they deployed. It was, Webb wrote in 1920, the part of their case that had been most sustained by subsequent experience.[50] And, of course, then as now economics was regarded as the most exact of the various social studies. The Fabian case rested on a rejection of some of the principles of classical political economy, the notions of the benevolent guiding-hand and of competitive *laissez faire*, for instance.[51] Yet though the discussion might sometimes seem to have a Marxist ring about it – and certainly many of the Fabians knew their Marx well – there is little evidence to sustain any suspicion of real intellectual affinity in this respect. In particular the Fabians firmly dissociated themselves from the usual Marxist paraphernalia about the increasing degradation of the workers, the inevitability of a growing class struggle, and so forth and

---

47 Wells, *The Bulpington of Blup*, p.113, italics in original.
48 ibid., pp.352–3. Cf. Wells's stress elsewhere that the 'essential Socialist idea' rests on 'a sufficiency of CONSTRUCTIVE DESIGN', *New Worlds for Old*, p.26 and ch.II *passim*, capitalization in original.
49 G. K. Chesterton, *The Secret of Father Brown* (1927; Penguin, 1974), pp.12–13. For a perhaps more acceptable (but not necessarily more authoritative) statement of the same point, see R. H. Tawney, *The Webbs in Perspective* (London, 1953), pp.11–12.
50 S. Webb, 'Introduction to the 1920 Reprint', *Fabian Essays*, p.xviii.
51 Shaw, 'The Basis of Socialism: Economic', ibid., p.26.

asserted instead the prospect of a gradual and constitutionally achieved improvement. This would alone have been enough to create a genuine and major contrast. In fact the main Fabian inspiration seems to have come from the writings of Mill and Jevons and thus some of the more acceptable parts of the classical doctrine itself.[52] Its centre was a theory of rent (originally derived from the Ricardian analysis) to the effect that the landlord exploits his tenants, those who actually work the land, by pocketing the economic 'rent', that is, the surplus value produced by any given land over marginal land (which is only just worth cultivating because it provides no more than a subsistence for the farmer).[53] This doctrine was extended to apply to more general economic circumstances, to movable capital as well as real estate. Wages were seen as being pressed to subsistence level, and the surplus of the value produced by labour ('rent') as accruing to the employer and owner of the instruments of production.[54] 'The modern form of private property is simply a legal claim to take a share of the produce of the national industry year by year without working for it.'[55]

Given this, the conclusion drawn was the need to appropriate 'all forms of economic rent of land and capital' on behalf of the nation as a whole.[56] Of course, reform of this kind as applied to the land was a long-standing theme, a key manifestation of hostility to the established classes. It was shared by people so different as H. Spencer, P. E. Dove, T. H. Green, Henry George, and A. R. Wallace. In 1870 J. S. Mill had helped to found a Land Tenure Reform Association with the object of urging ultimate state ownership and control of the soil; and other similar organizations also existed.[57] In this respect, then, so far as the taxation of land values, the nationalization of rent and even of land itself, were concerned, the Fabians were simply swimming with a long-set radical tide. What was advocated was either heavily progressive levies of various

---

52 On these matters, see e.g. H. J. Laski, *Communism* (London, 1927), p.91, and his introduction to R. Fraser, *A Social Philosophy for Fabians*, p.2; M. Beer, *A History of British Socialism* (1919; London, 1953), ii.238–9; S. Webb, *English Progress Towards Social Democracy* (Fabian tract no.15; 1892, London, 1893), p.11, and his *Towards Social Democracy: a Study of Social Evolution During the Past Three-quarters of a Century* (London, n.d. [1916]), pp.37–8. For scepticism about or repudiation of Marxist economic doctrine, see G. Wallas, cited in Fremantle, *This Little Band of Prophets*, p.49.

53 Shaw, 'The Basis of Socialism: Economic', *Fabian Essays*, pp.5–8, 10.

54 ibid., pp.18–19, 25.

55 ibid., p.24.

56 Shaw, *Report on Fabian Policy*, p.5.

57 See the review of these doctrines and groups in Beer, *A History of British Socialism*, ii.238–45; also E. E. Barry, *Nationalisation in British Politics: the Historical Background* (London, 1965), chs1–11; W. Wolfe, *From Radicalism to Socialism*, pp.79ff.

sorts or the actual take-over and operation of the assets concerned by appropriate public authorities. It will be found, in dealing with the landlord, Webb wrote, that

> the resources of civilization are not exhausted. An increase in the death duties, the steady rise of local rates, the special taxation of urban ground values, the graduation and differentiation of the income-tax, the simple appropriation of the unearned increment, and the gradual acquirement of land and other monopolies by public authorities, will in due course suffice to 'collectivize' the bulk of the tribute of rent and interest in a way which the democracy will regard as sufficiently equitable even if it does not satisfy the conscience of the proprietary class itself. This growth of collective ownership it is, and not any vain sharing out of property, which is to achieve the practical equality of opportunity at which democracy aims.[58]

Arguing in a similar fashion, the Fabians supported public regulation or ownership of the main resources and services (including, in addition to land, the railways and coal-mines) as well as considerable extension of governmental powers over conditions of work and living. This control was to be assumed 'scientifically' so as to ensure social efficiency and at least 'the national minimum' for all.[59] Specifically the object was 'vesting the organization of industry and the material of production' in the state.[60] George Bernard Shaw stressed that the Fabians advocated exclusively 'State Socialism'; and Sydney Olivier explained this meant basically 'collective property . . . in the instruments of production'.[61] Describing the Fabian policies of the 1890s, Mrs Webb (who claimed she then had the status of observer rather than participant) wrote that they comprised 'essentially collective ownership wherever practicable; collective regulation everywhere else; collective provision according to need for all the impotent and sufferers; and collective taxation in proportion to wealth, especially surplus wealth.'[62] Sometimes the Fabians envisaged that movement in this direction would proceed a quite long way to deal intensively with matters of even personal amenity and interest. For instance, Graham Wallas, writing of property under Socialism, looked forward, apparently with eagerness, to a future in which the family and all such selfish concerns and institutions were replaced by 'the public kitchen', 'the public store', the public teacher, and the like. 'Then at last

58 S. Webb, *The Difficulties of Individualism*, pp.10–11. Cf. *Fabian Essays*, pp.25, 167–9, 171, and Webb's *The Basis & Policy of Socialism* (Fabian Socialist Series no.4, London, 1908), pp.27, 30.
59 S. Webb, *The Basis & Policy of Socialism*, pp.82–95. The slogan 'national efficiency' was coined by the Webbs in their *Industrial Democracy* (1897).
60 'Preface' (1889), *Fabian Essays*, pp.xxxix–xl.
61 G. B. Shaw, *Report on Fabian Policy*, p.5; Olivier, 'The Basis of Socialism: Moral', *Fabian Essays*, p.96.
62 B. Webb, *Our Partnership*, p.107.

such a life will be possible for all as not even the richest and most powerful can live today.' Similarly Mrs Besant had a policy for the 'County Farm' with its 'public meal-room' and similar communal facilities to support which institutions the necessary labour would be compulsorily sent.[63]

Yet this latter and rather ludicrous element of Platonic communism – a relic presumably of New Life utopianism – was not really characteristic of the Fabian viewpoint as a whole. What is undoubtedly true is that the Society urged, in rather Benthamite fashion, that once government and its machinery was reformed so that it was both representative and administratively efficient, the transfer to it of economic resources was both feasible and desirable. The state, said Shaw, may thus be 'trusted with the rent of the country, and finally with the land, the capital, and the organization of the national industry – with all the sources of production in short'.[64] This is obviously a prescription for a most notable extension of government interference in economic life; and the impression is sustained by the considerable array of social reforms the Fabians supported from time to time in addition to proposals for the nationalization of land, mines, transport, and other general services. The programme embraced the extension of state powers of supervision and protection in respect of factories, housing, and health including such matters as water and milk supply; provision for the unemployed; the establishment of compulsory education; and much else. The proposals made in the Society's numerous tracts and pamphlets to sustain the goal of the national minimum in fact indicated a very substantial collectivist prospectus indeed.

As a result even the Fabians were troubled, or some of them were some of the time, about the prospect of a society increasingly dominated by a centralized state bureaucracy, though it is not always clear how deep this concern really went. To a group many of whom had little faith in the average man and who were, too, so imbued with the bureaucratic ideal, a problem about, for instance, whether a public service should be administered on a central or a local basis was more likely to be a technical question of administrative appropriateness than a matter of popular responsibility in any but a formal sense.[65] This is perhaps shown by the way in which some Fabians tended to be rather scornful about the fashionable idea of co-operative organization.[66] However it is un-

---

63 G. Wallas, 'Property under Socialism', *Fabian Essays*, pp.138–9; A. Besant, 'Industry under Socialism', ibid., pp.143–4. Nor have horrors of this kind lost their appeal: cf. references to the neighbourhood laundry, baker, and hairdresser in E. Luard, *Socialism Without the State* (London, 1979), p.152.

64 Shaw, 'The Transition to Social Democracy', *Fabian Essays*, p.169.

65 Cf. S. Webb, *The Basis & Policy of Socialism*, pp.58–9.

66 e.g., ibid., pp.17–18; cf. ibid., pp.71–3 on the 'Peasant Proprietorship fallacy'; and *The Difficulties of Individualism*, p.13.

doubtedly true that they were particularly associated with the concept of 'Municipal Socialism', the idea that much of this collectivized respons-ibility should accrue to democratically elected and autonomous local authorities.[67] In an early tract written by Sidney Webb and called *The Workers' Political Programme*, the aim was put like this:

> We want the Town and County Councils, elected by adult suffrage, and backed with the capital derived from the taxation of unearned incomes, and with compulsory powers of acquiring the necessary land upon payment of a reasonable consideration to the present holders, to be empowered to engage in all branches of industry in the fullest competition with private industrial enterprise. . . . Local Self Government can be but a mockery to the poorer workers until it means the democratic control and administration not merely of a park or a sewer, but of the shops and factories in which the worker has to earn his living.[68]

Despite the apparent idealism, there was also in this line of Fabian thought an element of hard calculation and even self-interest involved. They were all very much aware that in the gradual and 'unconscious' development of collectivism that had been taking place since the beginning of the nineteenth century, the municipalities had played a crucial role.[69] But in fact London, where many of the leading Fabians lived, had been lagging behind the achievements of the most progressive provincial authorities. Of course, there was no general London govern-ment until the foundation of the LCC in 1888. When this body was established, the Fabian (in contrast to the Conservatives and their allies who wanted to break up the County Council and create a number of independent municipalities) saw the opportunity to use it and to bring to the metropolis the benefits of all the advances obtained elsewhere. Sidney Webb wrote of the need 'to lift London to the level of Lancashire'; and W. T. Stead, then editor of the *Pall Mall Gazette*, said in 1892 he believed that Webb wanted to emulate the leader of radicalism in Birmingham

---

67 See e.g. S. Webb's 'Introduction to the 1920 Reprint', *Fabian Essays*, p. xx. Also his remarks in *Socialism in England* (London, 1890), pp. 109–10; and, on the need to avoid an undue concentration of political authority, *Towards Social Democracy*, p. 5. This idea of a local ownership of property and other wealth may be linked to a much earlier radicalism, see C. Hill, *Puritanism and Revolution: Studies in the Interpre-tation of the English Revolution of the 17th Century* (London, 1958), pp. 106–7. Likewise the municipal ideal continues long after the Fabian hey-day: see e.g. W. A. Robson, 'The Outlook', H. J. Laski *et al.*, *A Century of Municipal Progress, 1835–1935* (London, 1935), pp. 460–1.

68 S. Webb, *The Workers' Political Programme* (Fabian tract no. 11; London, 1890), pp. 8–9.

69 S. Webb, 'The Basis of Socialism: Historic', *Fabian Essays*, p. 47; S. Webb, *Socialism in England*, pp. 116–17. And cf. vol. iii, *A Much-Governed Nation*, ch. 2.

and become the Joseph Chamberlain of London.[70] Lord Rosebery even described the Fabian proposals as 'not Socialism at all' but simply 'a vital necessity for a great city.'[71] Be that as it may, it was clear that the municipalities had indeed played a great part in the development of the public intervention that had so far occurred; and, as well, that the Fabians saw the LCC as (at that stage) 'a better platform from which to bring about collectivism than the House of Commons.'[72] For both sorts of reason, therefore, it was argued that the wide achievement of democratic local self-government would create the machinery for and basis of Socialism.[73] In this way, too, it would be possible to avoid the tyranny of a single national employer and the cramping uniformity and red-tape, and so inefficiency, to which it might give rise. Given this Webb could indignantly repudiate the accusation that the Fabian policies would lead to the 'Servile State' and 'one employer'.[74] It was urged, as a counter to this charge, that genuine municipal experiment and variation would be possible on the basis of local differences of need and circumstance: almost as though (Webb said) someone who lived in Hampstead and did not like the local arrangements could move to Highgate and there enjoy a different dispensation.[75] Much, in particular, was hoped in this regard from the proliferation of municipal trading.[76] Looking back in 1920, Sidney Webb summarized the Fabian view as follows: 'We accordingly saw our way to a vast increase in the consciousness of personal freedom, a vista of endless diversity, the practical opportunity for an indefinitely varied development of human personality, under the complete and most all-embracing Collectivism.'[77]

Nevertheless this concept of municipal Socialism gradually sank into the background in particular because of the technical demands of the new public services (such as the production and supply of electricity) and the need to compromise with the *ad hoc* bodies set up to manage them.[78] But it can reasonably be urged that what the Fabians did was to seize on

70 S. Webb, *Labor in the Longest Reign (1837–1897)* (Fabian tract no. 75; 1897, 2nd edn, London, 1899), p.19; B. Webb, *Our Partnership*, pp. 57–8. Cf. ibid., pp. 62–4, 83, 121; E. Halévy, *A History of the English People in the Nineteenth Century* (1913–46; trans. edn, London, 1961), v.240–2 and p.240 n.1.
71 Cited in McBriar, op. cit., p.195.
72 Diary entry (20 January 1895), in B. Webb, *Our Partnership*, p.121.
73 Shaw, 'The Transition to Social Democracy', *Fabian Essays*, pp.174–5.
74 *Crusade* (August 1912), suppl., p.152, cited in McBriar, op. cit., p.109.
75 S. Webb, 'Introduction to the 1920 Reprint', *Fabian Essays*, p.xx. A fascinating literary expression of this contemporary pluralism is G. K. Chesterton's *The Napoleon of Notting Hill* (1904).
76 See e.g. the case argued in A. Maude, *Municipal Trading* (Fabian tract no. 138; London, 1908).
77 *Fabian Essays*, p.xx.
78 McBriar, op. cit., pp.222–33.

existing municipal developments and fashion their implications into a general theory of political and economic evolution.[79] Libertarian opponents were hardly deceived in any case. On the contrary they recognized that municipal Socialism was 'one of the gravest and most insidious maladies' to threaten 'modern civilization.'[80]

It will be readily apparent from all this that the Fabians believed in constitutional change rather than revolution as a means of achieving the reforms they advocated. Like their Shakespearian namesake, they urged 'No way but gentleness'.[81] Their case is indeed rather reminiscent of the old radical-Chartist claims. But there is again the sense that this advocacy of the peaceful road to change is a considered expediency rather than a matter of principle. So much had already been achieved in this way; so much would be lost by a period of political disorder. But, whatever the motive at work, this attitude is clearly yet another indication that the Fabian view involves repudiation of the Marxist concept of politics. The latter characteristically regards the capitalist state as an instrument of oppression. But to the Fabians it was potentially the key instrument of radical reform, the sole means indeed through which the good society might be established and sustained. Preference for the constitutional tactic was in that sense deliberate and described in typical Shavian style as follows:

> The Fabian knows that property does not hesitate to shoot, and that now, as always, the unsuccessful revolutionist may expect calumny, perjury, cruelty, judicial and military massacre without mercy. And the Fabian does not intend to get thus handled if he can help it. If there is to be any shooting, he intends to be at the State end of the gun. And he knows that it will take him a good many years to get there. Still, he thinks he sees his way – or rather the rest of the way; for he is already well on the road.
>
> It was in 1885 that the Fabian Society, amid the jeers of the catastrophists, turned its back on the barricades and made up its mind to turn heroic defeat into prosaic success. We set ourselves two definite tasks: first, to provide a parliamentary program for a Prime Minister converted to Socialism as Peel was converted to Free Trade; and second, to make it easy and matter-of-course for the ordinary respectable Englishman to be a Socialist as to be a Liberal or a Conservative.
>
> These tasks we have accomplished, to the great disgust of our more

---

79 Cf. R. C. K. Ensor, *England 1870–1914* (1936; Oxford, 1968), pp. 128–9.
80 P. Leroy-Beaulieu, *Collectivism: a Study of Some of the Leading Social Questions of the Day* (trans. and abr. edn, London, 1908), p. 303.
81 *Twelfth Night*, III.iv.112.

romantic comrades. Nobody now conceives Socialism as a destructive insurrection ending, if successful, in millenial absurdities.[82]

After the very early days, then – when the Fabians were in truth as 'catastrophist' as many other Socialist groups – there was always in their doctrine an emphasis on legislative reform, on a 'resolute constitutionalism'.[83] Sidney Webb was insistent that the fundamental changes it was intended to bring about should be 'democratic' (in the sense of having become acceptable to the majority of the people and not regarded as wrong or excessive), 'gradual' (not causing dislocation), and 'constitutional' (achieved by the usual process of peaceful change).[84] The development of a Socialist society was regarded as assured and inevitable through, for instance, the extension of the franchise. The industrial revolution may have left the labourer 'a landless stranger in his own country' but the 'political evolution is rapidly making him its ruler.' For, once all men have the vote, the legislature will be bound to act in the interests of the most numerous, that is, the working class.[85] More than this: the change was already going on in the growing government interference of the time and was being thus assisted even by those who were in principle fervently anti-Socialist. This tendency was so strong that there was little or no prospect of its pace slackening; quite the contrary in fact.[86] The Fabian view was that what was needed was simply 'the well-devised extension' of the process.[87] It would be simply foolish, or criminal, to interrupt this *de facto* progress in the name of some romantic theory. Mrs Webb wrote in her diary: 'we don't want to pull down the existing structure – all we want is slowly and quietly to transform and add to it.'[88] The specific and basic nature of this 'silent'

82 Shaw, 'Preface to the 1908 Reprint', *Fabian Essays*, p.xxxiii. For similar rejection of 'catastrophism', see Shaw, 'The Transition to Social Democracy', ibid., pp.170–1; H. Bland, 'The Outlook', ibid., pp.188–9; and S. Webb, *The Basis & Policy of Socialism*, p.51.

83 Shaw, 'Preface to the 1931 Reprint', *Fabian Essays*, p.viii. Cf. his reference to 'Fabian Constitutionalism', *Report on Fabian Policy*, p.4. And for the early insurrectionist spirit, see Shaw, *The Fabian Society*, pp.3–4.

84 Webb, 'The Basis of Socialism: Historic', *Fabian Essays*, p.32. Cf. his *Socialism in England*, p.9, and *English Progress Towards Social Democracy*, pp.12–13, 15.

85 Webb, *Fabian Essays*, p.37; Shaw, *What Socialism Is* (Fabian tract no.13; London, n.d. [1890]), p.[3].

86 e.g. the references to 'our unconscious Socialism' and the like, *Fabian Essays*, pp.43–9; Shaw, ibid., pp.171–3; Webb, *The Basis & Policy of Socialism*, pp.47–9; *English Progress Towards Social Democracy*, *passim*. And cf. (from a contrasting viewpoint, of course) Spencer's remarks in *The Man Versus the State* (1884; Penguin, 1969), pp.98–106.

87 e.g. Webb, *Labor in the Longest Reign*, *passim*, but esp. p.19; Wells, *New Worlds for Old*, p.263.

88 Diary entry (6 December 1903), cited in B. Webb, *Our Partnership*, p.277. Cf. M. Cole (ed.), *Beatrice Webb's Diaries, 1924–1932* (London, 1956), p.70.

revolution, the technical, economic, and social changes at work, is outlined most clearly and succinctly from the Fabian point of view in William Clarke's contribution to the original series of *Fabian Essays*. Further, in explaining Fabian doctrine to an American audience, Clarke made clear that the Society rejected both revolutionary policies (like those of the Social Democratic Federation) and the emphasis on spiritual regeneration alone (as with the Fellowship of the New Life).[89]

The basic tenet of action so far as the Fabian was concerned was (in Webb's famous phrase) the 'inevitability of gradualness'. The term is apt, though invented later.[90] At the time the process was usually called 'meliorism', that is, social improvement none the less radical for being achieved by perhaps slow and piecemeal reform on the basis of a prior and intensive preparation, including careful investigation of the facts and possibilities, and appropriate publicity and propaganda. The Fabian object was to stimulate this process by the tactics of 'permeation', 'the inculcation of Socialist thought and Socialist projects into the minds not merely of complete converts, but of those whom we found in disagreement with us'. Mrs Webb's version of the tactic was, 'The truth is that *we want the things done* and we don't much care what persons or which party gets the credit'. Or, as Shaw put it over half a century later: 'The Fabian policy was to support and take advantage of every legislative step towards Collectivism no matter what quarter it came from, nor how little its promoters dreamt that they were advocating an instalment of Socialism.'[91] Halévy, in his *History*, nicely referred to the 'disinterested Machiavellianism which was the essence of the Fabian method.'[92]

Thus the Fabians made themselves a sort of 'institute for social engineering' and, so far as opportunities allowed, plied people of influence in all quarters and of all opinions with ideas and projects thought to tend in the desired direction.[93] It was this purpose that helped stimulate the large numbers of Fabian tracts published on many of the specific questions of the day: factory conditions, sanitary reform, public health generally, the organization of agriculture, land nationalization, death duties, taxation, and much else. Each was a close analysis of the

89 W. Clarke, 'The Basis of Socialism: Industrial', *Fabian Essays*, pp. 58–95; 'The Fabian Society and its Work', in *Socialism: the Fabian Essays* (Boston, 1894), pp. xxii–xxiii.
90 It seems to have been used first in the Chairman's address to the Labour Party annual conference in 1923, C. L. Mowat, *Britain Between the Wars 1918–1940* (1955; London, 1968), p.153. In this original use the phrase referred to the growth of the Labour vote.
91 S. Webb, 'Introduction to the 1920 Reprint', *Fabian Essays*, p.xxvi; B. Webb, *Our Partnership*, pp.67–8, italics in original; Shaw, 'Sixty Years of Fabianism', *Fabian Essays*, p.211. Cf. S. Webb, *Socialism in England*, pp. 3, 8, 24–5, and B. Webb, op. cit., pp.7, 122.
92 Halévy, *A History of the English People in the Nineteenth Century*, v.207.
93 Beer, op. cit., ii.287.

facts of the case, thought through, and with proposals for change worked out in some detail. The flavour of the enterprise may be savoured through some examples of the titles issued: 'The Truth about Leasehold Enfranchisement', 'The Case for an Eight Hours Bill', 'The Municipalization of the Gas Supply', 'Allotments and How to Get Them', 'Municipal Slaughter Houses', 'The London Education Act, 1903: How to Make the Best of It', and so on.[94] Clearly if this was Socialism it had moved on a long way from the utopianism of the continental theorists and anarchists and also the sentimental romanticism of some English reformers. As Sir Alexander Gray said, 'the transition from the Rights of Man to the Tenant's Sanitary Catechism is, in its way, symbolical of what Fabianism achieved.'[95] Though at the same time due tribute must be paid, in considering this practical, down-to-earth emphasis, to the detailed schemes previously produced by a wide range of reformers from Bentham to Toulmin Smith.

Through such ideas, then, Fabianism did much to spread and make respectable the collectivist point of view. It may be the actual influence of the Society has in some respects been exaggerated: not least it should be remembered that in the 1880s and 1890s its members were all quite young and that it constituted a mere intellectual coterie on, if not quite beyond, the fringes of power. But there is no doubt – and it is a surprising and astonishing achievement – that at certain times and in particular areas of policy it had an important effect. For instance, if the Fabian influence on the Labour movement before 1914 was weak, there is clear evidence that it crucially affected the development of the Labour Party during and after the Great War, for the demands that conflict made on society created circumstances in which Fabian doctrine could flourish.[96]

It should be clear now what the Society as a whole stood for. Something of the starker aspects of its statist doctrine emerged in the writings of the Webbs.

THE WEBBS

English socialism was Fabian socialism. Fabian socialism was Webbian socialism. And much of the language in which it was discussed was Webbian language.

ANON., 'A Partnership of Ideals', Times Literary Supplement, 5 July 1963, p.485

Sidney and Beatrice Webb made a major contribution to British

94 See the list of tracts and other publications from 1884 to 1958 in Fremantle, This Little Band of Prophets, pp.269–85.
95 Sir Alexander Gray, The Socialist Tradition Moses to Lenin (1946; corr. edn, London, 1947), p.388.
96 Cf. McBriar, op. cit., pp.343, 348–9; J. M. Winter, Socialism and the Challenge of War: Ideas and Politics in Britain, 1912–18 (London, 1974), p.6.

Socialism. Tawney said (correctly one would guess) that they were widely regarded as the movement's ideological leaders; while Bertrand Russell believed they 'did a great work' in giving the doctrine its 'intellectual backbone'.[97] But this crucial contribution was indirect in the sense that it did not take the form of writing extensive and systematic treatises about Socialism as such. This was, Tawney continued in the lecture already cited, because they saw the creed not as a series of principles to be imposed on politics from outside but 'as an organic growth from already vigorous roots.' The task was not

> to draw designs for imposing new palaces on non-existing vacant sites. It was to reveal the significant features of the transformation under way about them; to elicit conclusions of general application from the mass of raw experience provided by it; and thus to make possible a progress no longer haphazard and halting, but deliberate and sustained.

Consequently their views about Socialism are rarely 'cast in a doctrinal mould. They emerge as a synthesis of generalizations suggested by the institutions explored in their descriptive and historical works.'[98] For instance, their voluminous study of the agencies of local administration while not (except in the case of the Poor Law) going beyond the 1830s was conceived, not merely as history, but as an indication of the way in which such institutions might become a major instrument of collective welfare and control.

Something of their ideas will already have been gleaned from the preceding pages on the Fabian Society. But, given their intrinsic importance to the history of Socialist development in this country, it is necessary and proper to look a little more closely at their particular contribution, to establish the nature and basis of their belief in the necessity and propriety of collectivist development and the use of the power of the state to achieve this end.

Their partnership

In a valedictory tribute it was said it is always necessary to consider the Webbs together, 'for one cannot think of them apart.'[99] Certainly in their lives and ideas each of them embodied many of the attributes of class and intellectual superiority. 'Neither was by temper, instinct or training, democratic. Sidney was a born bureaucrat; Beatrice a born aristocrat. In each case, the impulse was benevolent and entirely disinterested; in neither equalitarian.'[100]

97 R. H. Tawney, *The Attack and other Papers* (London, 1953), p.115; B. Russell, *Autobiography* (London, 1967–8), i.79.
98 R. H. Tawney, *The Webbs in Perspective* (London, 1953), pp.9–10.
99 R. H. Tawney, 'In Memory of Sidney Webb', *Economica*, n.s., xiv (1947), p.245.
100 M. A. Hamilton, *Remembering My Good Friends* (London, 1944), p.260.

A more blunt comment is that they were both snobs.[101]

Beatrice Potter was, as John Strachey said, 'born into the highest ranks of the new class of captains of industry'.[102] Her father, who was extremely rich, had substantial railway and other interests both in Britain and abroad. Though he recognized the need to compromise with emerging popular forces, he was no democrat and held firmly to the conviction that a country's rulers ought to be drawn from a leisured class, all the better if its position was based on inherited property.[103] Something of this élitism and paternalism always remained in his daughter's attitude: she was always (she wrote) conscious of her family's 'superior power' and that she 'belonged to a class of persons who habitually gave orders, but who seldom, if ever, executed the orders of other people.' And she described herself as being 'anti-democratic through social environment'.[104] Another and quite different side of her character reflected that of her mother, a woman of unusual ability and also from a wealthy background. She was very religious and spent a lot of time studying (amid much else) the Church Fathers and the Greek Testament: 'Her soul longed for the mystical consolations and moral discipline of religious orthodoxy.'[105] Something of this intense religiosity and mystical craving was inherited by her daughter who, after a crisis of faith, emerged with her beliefs still firm if no longer wholly orthodox.[106] She was she wrote later always full of 'a yearning for the mental security of a spiritual home' and discovered that her 'incipient religious temperament' found an outlet in prayer. It was by this worship that her 'emotional Will to Believe' tried 'to attain the consciousness of communion' with an 'all-pervading spiritual force' and through which, she intuitively felt, 'the soul of man discovers the purpose or goal of human endeavour'.[107] Nor was this religiosity hidden: the young Harold Laski commented in his correspondence with Mr Justice Holmes on Mrs Webb's 'love of religious mysticism', her belief in 'the universal efficacy of prayer', and on the satisfaction she seemed to derive from 'genu-

101 See M. Foot, *Aneurin Bevan: a Biography* (London, 1962–73), i.121; also M. Muggeridge, *Chronicles of Wasted Time* (London, 1972–3), i.141, 143. Muggeridge is Mrs Webb's nephew by marriage and knew her and her husband well.
102 J. Strachey, 'Sidney and Beatrice Webb', *The Listener*, vol.lxiv (13 October 1960), p.617.
103 B. Webb, *My Apprenticeship* (1926; Penguin, 1938), i.25–6.
104 See the vivid, social and self-analysis, ibid., i.61ff. Cf. M. Cole (ed.), *Beatrice Webb's Diaries, 1924–1932* (London, 1956), p.27.
105 B. Webb, *My Apprenticeship*, i.31.
106 ibid., i. 95ff.; see also the contribution to W. H. Auden *et al.*, *I Believe: the Personal Philosophies of Twenty-Three Eminent Men and Women of our Time* (London, 1940), pp.334–5.
107 Auden *et al.*, op. cit., pp.332–3; M. Cole (ed.), *Beatrice Webb's Diaries, 1912–1924* (London, 1952), pp.48–9; B. Webb, *Our Partnership* (London, 1948), pp.429, 448–9.

flexion'.[108] She was aware of the strength of other views and held that
human existence constituted a kind of continuous dialectic between 'the
Ego that affirms and the Ego that denies' the validity of religious
experience.[109] As for science itself, that great annihilator of religious and
other mysteries, this was also another shrine at which she worshipped.
And a satisfactory fusion of the claims of each was achieved in the belief
that if 'scientific method' was properly applied to understand and control
'the process of life', then the purpose of existence itself was to be directed
by prayer and derived from spiritual insight.[110]

As was perhaps to be expected, given her home background, Beatrice
Potter's first ideas reflected a hostility to collectivism. She refers to having
been brought up 'in a stronghold of capitalism, under the tutelage of the
great apostle of *laissez-faire*, Herbert Spencer'.[111] He was in fact a great
friend of the family and a frequent visitor to their home. Late in life, in a
broadcast talk, she still recalled his early impact on her as 'guide,
philosopher, and friend'.[112] A comment which she penned in 1884 clearly
brought out the bias of her mind in those young days:

> . . . as a citizen looking to the material and spiritual welfare of my
> descendants, I object to these gigantic experiments, state-education
> and state-intervention in other matters, which are now being in-
> augurated and which savour of inadequately thought-out theories –
> the most dangerous of all social poisons. Neither do they seem to me to
> be the result of spontaneously expressed desires of the people; but
> rather the crude prescriptions of social quacks seeking to relieve vague
> feelings of pain and discomfort experienced by the masses.[113]

But soon, quite firmly and quickly, her viewpoint began to change.[114]
She became disenchanted and dissatisfied with the upper-class round of
London society, trying to break out of its grasp into more intellectually
satisfying and politically significant realms. She read widely and, for
instance, used to spend long hours listening to debates in the House of
Commons. She became interested in the world of labour and decided the
best form of social service she could offer was to be an independent

108 Laski to Holmes (11 January 1927, 20 August 1929), in M. de W. Howe (ed.), *Holmes-Laski Letters: the Correspondence of Mr. Justice Holmes and Harold J. Laski, 1916–1935* (London, 1953), ii.912, 1176.
109 B. Webb, *My Apprenticeship*, i.126.
110 B. Webb, *Our Partnership*, p.429; *My Apprenticeship*, ii.391–2.
111 B. Webb, *Our Partnership*, p.19. Cf. ibid., p.197; *My Apprenticeship*, i.47, 157.
112 B. Webb, 'The Nature and Classification of Social Institutions', M. Adams (ed.), *The Modern State* (London, 1933), p.172.
113 B. Webb, *My Apprenticeship*, i.219. Cf. the obvious marks of Spencerian individualism in her letter to J. Chamberlain (4 March 1886), cited in K. Muggeridge and R. Adam, *Beatrice Webb: a Life, 1858–1943* (London, 1967), pp.96–7.
114 S. and B. Webb, *Methods of Social Study* (1932; new edn, London, 1975), pp.36ff.

investigator.[115] To acquire experience and knowledge she visited Soho slums on behalf of a Charity Organization Committee, collected rents in the East End, and worked in a sweat-shop. In 1883 she went further afield, to Bacup in Lancashire, to stay with some lower-class relatives and studied the weavers there, commenting (as previously noted) on their simple piety. She took an active part in the work involved in her cousin, Charles Booth's, inquiry into the *Life and Labour of the People of London*. She began to publish the results of her studies and was coming to believe in the need for a radical reform of the existing system to remedy its manifest evils.[116] She later described the mixture of motives involved:

> What happened was that the time-spirit had, at last, seized me and compelled me to concentrate all my free energy in getting the training and the raw material for applied sociology; that is, for research into the constitution and working of social organisation, with a view to bettering the life and labour of the people. . . . There was the current belief in the scientific method, in that intellectual synthesis of observation and experiment, hypothesis and verification, by means of which alone all mundane problems were to be solved. And added to this belief in science was the consciousness of a new motive; the transference of the emotion of self-sacrificing service from God to man.[117]

Perhaps predominant among the strands of motive was, not surprisingly, a religious sense of sin.[118]

In any event, Miss Potter became convinced that individualism and *laissez faire* were no longer tenable principles and that it was necessary to replace the private ownership of the main instruments of production and the profit motive as the basic economic features of industrial society.[119] Her studies in the East End of London revealed to her the physical misery and moral debasement of the swarming urban centres. There was also the problem of preventing or mitigating the recurrent periods of prosperity and depression and their effects on the level of employment, for instance. It was equally necessary to meet the needs of the aged and infirm and to ensure the provision of adequate services of various kinds from education to parks. Something to achieve these ends would result from trade union pressure and legislation. But, at this stage, spurning the nostrums of the SDF as unreal and utopian, she found most to hope for in

---

115 B. Webb, *My Apprenticeship*, i.174–5, 197.
116 ibid., i.175ff.; ii.263ff., 306ff.
117 ibid., i.152–3.
118 See the passages cited pp. 353–4 above.
119 For what follows in this paragraph, see B. Webb, *My Apprenticeship*, ch. vii, 'Why I Became a Socialist', esp. ii. 395–6, 422–42.

the co-operative principle as applied to the organization of both production and consumption.

It was at this point that she came into contact with the Fabian Society and, through its influence, to appreciate the crucial importance of extensive and continuous state action, whether central or local, in order to overcome the evils of a class-divided nation and attain that national minimum of provision necessary to secure a 'Civilised Life' for all.[120] In her diary in February 1890 Beatrice Potter listed all the contemporary issues and trends she thought significant and commented:

> . . . the whole seems a whirl of contending actions, aspirations and aims, out of which I dimly see the tendency towards a socialist community, in which there will be individual freedom and public property, instead of class slavery and private possession of the means of subsistence of the whole people. At last I am a socialist![121]

On joining the Fabian she met Sidney Webb who impressed her with his intelligence and remarkable knowledge. He helped her with her work on the co-operative movement and trade unionism in Britain; and her commitment to Socialism seemed to grow under his influence. From this association, though not without much uncertainty on her part (he on the contrary seems to have welcomed being thus ensnared by the life-force), sprang their marriage in 1892.

Sidney Webb was born in 1859 into a lower middle-class family in London. His circumstances were not poor but there was a world of difference between his background and that of Beatrice Potter. He went to work at 16 as a clerk in the City, later took the civil service examination, and ultimately entered the Colonial Office in the upper division. He was thus one of the 'picked clever young men' who benefited from the Northcote-Trevelyan proposals of mid-century and the reforms later introduced to improve administrative recruitment. Shaw called him 'the ablest man in England'.[122] He joined the Fabian Society, became one of its leading members, and was the author of many of its tracts. Wells said he was the Society's 'idea factory'. Like his father, a disciple of Mill, his political and cognate views were largely formed by this influence though he seems to have become specifically committed to Socialism (which he did not at first find attractive) by reacting against the views of a lecturer at Birkbeck College who was opposed to public ownership. He believed William Morris to be the greatest exponent of the creed.[123] In

120 ibid., ii.386, 442–3, 450ff.
121 ibid., ii.456.
122 G. B. Shaw, *Sixteen Self-Sketches* (London, 1949), p.65.
123 R. H. Tawney, 'In Memory of Sidney Webb', loc. cit., p.247, 253; Muggeridge and Allen, *Beatrice Webb: a Life*, p.121; M. Cole (ed.), *The Webbs and Their Work* (London, 1949), p.6. For a Shavian comment on the slight influence Marx had, see

1892 he became a London County Councillor, one of six Fabians then elected in the Progressive interest.

Some observers have detected in him (beneath the bureaucratic habits, the statistics, and blue books), the humanitarian spirit of a poet and idealist even to a Quixotic degree. His wife sometimes wrote (though not very persuasively) as though he basically shared her own religious beliefs, albeit expressed in a less demonstrative way. And certainly it was true that his earliest views suggested the importance of 'moralisation' rather than merely practical reform and that the Comteian religious feeling was important to him.[124] But more generally he had the public image at least of an intellectual machine capable very swiftly of absorbing and categorizing a vast array of data: a superb organizer and 'social engineer' (again his wife's phrase). Halévy – certainly no friend to what Webb stood for – was reported to have held he had all the qualities essential to the 'Prussian methods of organized bureaucracy.' And the early Comteian influence surely encouraged belief in a well-ordered society regulated by a professional élite.[125] Similarly E. R. Pease (for long secretary of the Society) who knew him well often said, with reference to these administrative skills, that if Webb were a member of a committee it could be assumed that, unless there were evidence to the contrary, any report or resolution adopted had been drafted by him.[126] Arthur Penty recorded that Webb was the only man he had ever met who understood collectivism and wholeheartedly believed in it and all its implications.[127]

Beatrice Potter had a private income (of some £1000 p.a., a substantial sum in those days) which enabled Sidney Webb to resign his civil service post so that together they could work on their schemes of social inquiry. Typically they plunged into work even during their honeymoon, investigating the origins of workers' associations in Ireland and delving into Glaswegian 'municipal cellars for sociological facts, starting out straight away, like Maeterlinck's Mytil and Tytil, with their scientific sociological cage, to capture the bluebird of collective happiness.'[128]

'The Webbs and Social Evolution', *New York Times Magazine* (18 November 1945), pp.19–20. Wells's remark is in *New Worlds for Old* (London, 1908), p.263.

124 See e.g. B. Webb, *Our Partnership*, p.449; Tawney, art. cit., p.253; V. Marrero, *Maeztu* (Madrid, 1955), p.325; and, most importantly, W. Wolfe, *From Radicalism to Socialism: Men and Ideas in the Formation of Fabian Socialist Doctrines, 1881–1889* (New Haven, Conn., 1975), ch.6; N. MacKenzie (ed.), *Letters of Sidney and Beatrice Webb* (London, 1978), i.73, 75.

125 C. Bouglé, 'Preface to the Original Edition', E. Halévy, *The Era of Tyrannies: Essays on Socialism and War* (1938; trans. edn, London, 1967), p.xxi; B. Webb, *Our Partnership*, p.6.

126 See e.g. M. Cole (ed.), *The Webbs and Their Work*, p.23. McBriar discusses Webb's administrative impact, ibid., pp.78–97.

127 A. J. Penty, *A Guildsman's Interpretation of History* (London, 1920), p.300.

128 B. Webb, *Our Partnership*, p.31. The citation in the text is from Muggeridge and Allen, op. cit., p.129.

Their concerns were in one respect limited: they had little interest in abstract concepts or ideals. Likewise certain areas of public policy, imperial and foreign affairs in particular, aroused hardly any curiosity. But their concentration of attention made their gaze more intense. What they specifically had in mind was a series of investigations into the history, structure, and functions of the new forms of social organization created by the problems of the industrial age whether, as with the co-operative movement and the trades unions, they were developed by like-minded citizens as means of self-expression and protection, or, as with local government and the Poor Law, involved as well increasingly substantial elements of public agency. This was the '"Webb speciality"'.[129] They also extended this interest, in due course, into a more futuristic field considering the political arrangements that would be appropriate to a Socialist Britain, the meaning of Soviet Communism, and much more. And from all the data and other considerations acquired, they were concerned not simply to categorize the many varieties of institution studied and to establish if possible their 'recurrent uniformities' in constitution and activity but also, in some dynamic fashion, to show 'the main lines of development'.[130] Basically it was institutions of social control with which they were concerned; and their work on these topics, however scholarly, was definitely intended to have a practical effect and value. As Leonard Woolf put it, in his perceptive, brief study of their thought:

> It was . . . not unnatural that the Webbs, when they decided that society or sociology was the right object of scientific study, should have immediately been attracted by [a] new and gigantic phenomenon, this pullulation of organisations and institutions, continually increasing in size or extending the tentacles of their control over new spheres of life. [But] they were not merely scientific researchers into the morphology and pathology of society and its institutions, they were also, at the same time and all the time, intensely interested in clinical treatment, in the practical problems of how to make the institutions work efficiently. . . .[131]

In addition there was their more direct activity in the political field itself. Mrs Webb was a crucial member of the important Poor Law inquiry and in the famous Minority Report laid down a scheme for an all-embracing system of social security through which the state would regard it as a major duty to sustain those members of society who were inadequately provided for. For his part Sidney Webb became a major figure in London

129 S. and B. Webb, *Methods of Social Study*, p.89.
130 B. Webb, *My Apprenticeship*, ii.476.
131 L. Woolf, 'Political Thought and the Webbs', M. Cole (ed.), *The Webbs and Their Work*, p.256.

government and a member of the two Labour Cabinets of the 1920s. Together they were largely instrumental in founding the London School of Economics and the journal *The New Statesman*. Undoubtedly their behind-the-scenes influence could be substantial: for instance, Sidney affected the form of the 1902 Education Act.[132]

The Webbs' attitude to the Labour movement and its leaders was for long unfavourable. They did not believe it would come to anything and preferred to work through the existing political establishment.[133] But in time they came to think that reform thus achieved was not moving fast enough, that there was indeed active hostility and opposition to their work on both wings of the Liberal Party; and Campbell-Bannerman, for instance, had a low opinion of Sidney Webb.[134] Further, some Fabians – such as Henry Slesser, Clifford Allen, and Clifford Sharp, who formed the so-called Fabian Reform Movement – had always had doubts about the effectiveness of a permeation policy and urged the need to establish a separate Socialist party.[135] The Labour movement itself was not then Socialist, of course, but the Webbs thought they might be able to mould it by providing the intellectual leadership it so obviously lacked. Consequently as they lost touch with or faith in the Liberal and Conservative leaders, they moved into a phase of open campaigning and propaganda above all in respect of Poor Law reform, and from thence to a position inside the new Labour Party itself with a view to giving it a definite and fully worked-out collectivist programme.[136] Their real impact began after 1914 when Sidney Webb became a member of the Labour Party's War Emergency Workers' National Committee, 'the only independent voice of the United British Labour Movement' and apart from which the party hardly existed as a national organization during the Great War.[137] He also became a member of the Labour Party Executive. He was quite clear himself that he could, from this vantage-point, help

132 E. Halévy, *A History of the English People in the Nineteenth Century* (1913–46; trans. edn, London, 1961), v.207; B. Webb, *Our Partnership*, p.233 on 'Webb's bill'.

133 See e.g. the diary entries for 8, 10 July 1895, cited in B. Webb, *Our Partnership*, pp.125, 126. Cf. R. C. K. Ensor, in M. Cole (ed.), *The Webbs and their Work*, pp.67–8.

134 Diary entry (19 March 1902), cited in B. Webb, *Our Partnership*, p.232; J. Wilson, *CB: a Life of Sir Henry Campbell-Bannerman* (London, 1973), pp.360, 371.

135 H. Bland, in *Fabian Essays* (1889; Jubilee edn, London, 1950), p.201–3. Shaw says that a good number of Fabians realized as early as 1896 that the permeation game was played out, *The Fabian Society: its Early History* (Fabian tract no.41; 1892; London, 1906), pp.20–1, 28.

136 B. Webb, *Our Partnership*, pp.423, 460–2, 469, 471.

137 J. M. Winter, *Socialism and the Challenge of War: Ideas and Politics in Britain, 1912–18* (London, 1974), pp.184, 189. Ch.7, ibid., gives a full account of this Committee and Webb's role in its deliberations; also J. S. Middleton, in M. Cole (ed.), *The Webbs and Their Work*, pp.167–71.

transform war experience into a powerful vehicle for progressive social change and to do this in a way congenial to Webbian ideas.[138] And, in fact, his contribution to the formulation of a coherent Labour programme and the establishment of a new party structure was 'second to none'.[139] The party had hitherto adopted a politically unsectarian attitude, refusing to subscribe to any particular creed, programme, or ideology. In the words of the Chairman of the 1917 Conference, it had 'refused to adopt any mechanical formulas or to submit to any regimentation either of ideas or of policy.'[140] But as the war drew on and, as well, after the Russian Revolution, it was increasingly felt – especially by MacDonald and Henderson – that it should more firmly establish its own independent viewpoint. It was in this fluid context that Webb was able to play his substantial and even crucial part in producing a memorandum on war aims and helping to prepare a draft party constitution as a basis for post-war policy.[141] The outcome was the key document called *Labour and the New Social Order* which Webb had composed in addition to the new constitution which widened the basis of the party. In this way, he helped substantially to commit it for the first time to a Socialist ideology. The Webbian influence was thus so notable because, at the time when the party was looking for an intellectual lead, there was ready to hand a complete and relevant body of ideas, well-founded in research, elaborately explored, and fully worked-out in terms of the detailed institutional and policy aspects of the process of social change envisaged. In a word, Webb was able to provide the Labour Party with just the kind of theoretically oriented blueprint it was looking for.[142] Beatrice Webb claimed that by the end of 1917, her husband was 'the intellectual leader of the Labour Party'; and there was much truth in this.[143]

The salient features of this doctrine and its contrast with the ideology of libertarian individualism are indicated in the following passage from one of Sidney Webb's early works:

The Socialist is distinguished from the Individualist, . . . by a complete difference as to the main principles of social organization. The essential contribution of the century to sociology has been the supersession of the Individual by the Community as the starting point of social investigations. Socialism is the product of this development, arising with it from the contemporary industrial evolution. On the

138 Winter, op. cit., pp. 221, 222–3; Middleton, loc. cit., pp. 171 ff., M. Cole, in *Beatrice Webb's Diaries, 1912–1924*, pp. 45–6 n.1.
139 Winter, op. cit., p. 234, and ch. 8 *passim*.
140 *Labour Party Annual Report 1917*, p. 82.
141 Winter, op. cit., p. 259.
142 ibid., pp. 274–5.
143 *Beatrice Webb's Diaries, 1912–24*, p. 99; Winter, op. cit., p. 275.

economic side, Socialism implies the collective administration of rent and interest, leaving to the individual only the wages of his labour, of hand or brain. On the political side, it involves the collective control over, and ultimate administration of, all the main instruments of wealth production. On the ethical side, it expresses the real recognition of fraternity, and universal obligation of personal service, and the subordination of individual ends to the common good.[144]

The collectivist emphasis is evident.

The specific policy objective in view was the establishment of the 'national minimum of civilised life', a set of standards of provision in subsistence, leisure and recreation, sanitation, and education below which no one should be allowed to fall and which was the necessary condition of a healthy social order (though the obligations of those thus assisted were not to be overlooked). Beyond all this 'the illimitable realm of the upward remains'.[145] Beveridge believed that this concept of the national minimum was the principal Webb contribution to social thought.[146] There was to be no truck with Syndicalism or 'such nonsense' as Guild Socialism. What Punch in one place called 'Sidneywebbicalism' was to be quite different from all that: 'To bring about the maximum amount of public control in public administration' was the blunt and explicit objective.[147] And Guildsmen, at least, criticized the new Labour Party policy precisely because of 'the enormous emphasis laid throughout on State action.'[148]

There was a rigid dogmatism, even ruthlessness, about the way the Webbs single-mindedly pursued these goals, a characteristic pointedly noted by many observers. One comment to this effect is Max Beerbohm's well-known cartoon of 'Mr. Sidney Webb on his birthday': he is shown kneeling on the floor playing at 'arranging society' moving manikin people and politicians about like so many toy soldiers. Another is G. K. Chesterton's remark that 'Mrs. Sidney Webb . . . settles things by the simple process of ordering about the citizens of a state, as she might the servants in a kitchen.' According to Lord Beveridge, C. F. G. Masterman was rather horrified by Mrs Webb's zeal for disciplining people and said he always prayed that, if ever unemployed, he never fell into her hands.[149]

144 S. Webb, Socialism in England (London, 1890), pp.9–10.
145 S. Webb, The Necessary Basis of Society (London, 1908), pp.9–11. Cf. B. Webb et al., Socialism and National Minimum (London, 1909), esp. pp.43, 49, 65ff.; S. and B. Webb, Industrial Democracy, (1897; new edn, London, 1920), pp.766–84; B. Webb, Our Partnership, pp.229, 272, 452, 478–9, 481–2; B. Webb, My Apprenticeship, ii.386.
146 See Beatrice Webb's Diaries, 1912–24, p.vii.
147 B. Webb, Our Partnership, p.132, citing the diary for 1896.
148 The Guildsman, February, 1918, pp.3–4.
149 The cartoon has often been reprinted, see e.g. M. Cole (ed.), The Webbs and their

They were sure they were right about crucial matters and so never really open-minded. Sidney at least would, it seems, have been prepared, in Platonic fashion, to ban or censure literature found either uncongenial or mischievous.[150] Using the word in its Oakeshottian sense, they were 'rationalists'. Beatrice Webb said the joint task she and 'The Other One' had in life was to be 'pioneers of social engineering'; and it has, she added, 'been real sport thinking out each separate part and making each part fit the others.'[151] Scientific efficiency in social and political organization was their goal and everything had to be subordinated to its achievement. To quote Leonard Woolf again:

> They knew exactly what they wanted. They were convinced of the desirability and inevitability of what they called socialism. This, they thought, required the scientific planning of social life; the adaptation of the structure of social institutions, both public and private, to the functions which the social plan required; the training of a political élite who would be capable of running the machine efficiently and intelligently; the education of the 'ordinary' individual citizen so that he could be fitted fairly and squarely into an appropriate place in the social, but primarily economic, machine. . . . They were convinced that if the machinery of society was properly constructed and controlled efficiently by intelligent people, if the functions of the various parts of the organisation were scientifically determined and the structure scientifically adapted to the functions . . . then we should get an adequately civilised society. . . .[152]

It was indeed a new kind of utopianism.

Something more must now be said in review of two key aspects of this powerful and influential syndrome of ideas: their concept of social science; and their view of the administrative machine.

A science of society

As already noted, the word 'scientific' was a term of approbation in Fabian circles – and not only there.[153] The Webbs reflected or, perhaps better, helped to form this attitude. But they did much more than any

   Work, opp. p.113. For the other comments, see G. K. Chesterton, *The Victorian Age in Literature* (1913; rev. edn, London, 1920), p.91; and W. Beveridge, *Power and Influence* (London, 1953), pp.66–7.

150 See Wells's comment in a letter to B. Webb (19 October 1904), cited in L. Dickson, *H. G. Wells: His Turbulent Life and Times* (1969; Penguin, 1972), p.120n.

151 *Beatrice Webb's Diaries, 1912–1924,* pp.178–9.

152 Woolf, in M. Cole (ed.), *The Webbs and Their Work*, pp.258, 263.

153 See e.g. 'Nunquam' [Robert Blatchford], *Merrie England* (1893; London, 1976), p.44.

other members of the Society to explain the details of the method involved.

Of course, the cult of modern western science was part of the spirit of the age: as Beatrice Webb said, it 'was by far the most potent ferment at work in the mental environment in which I was reared'. She mentions especially the impact of G. H. Lewes's *Biographical History of Philosophy* with its eulogy of science and contemptuous positivist rejection of metaphysics; also of the members of the 'X Club', scientists such as Huxley, Tyndall, and Galton.[154] She was impressed, too, with the 'scientific' style of investigation used by her cousin, Charles Booth, with whom she worked.[155] But the most potent influence in this regard was Herbert Spencer who directly inspired her to devote her life to the scientific investigation of social relations and institutions.[156] In her younger days she had regarded him as a 'Prophet' and, as an 'enthusiastic novice in scientific reasoning', she found his 'ingenious intertwining of elementary observations with abstruse ratiocination was immensely impressive.' And while she came to dissent radically from his political conclusions, his stress on 'the relevance of facts' and much else remained; and she thus continued methodologically in his debt.[157] Her 'old friend' had taught her, she wrote in 1903 (the year in which Spencer died), 'to look on all social institutions exactly as if they were plants or animals – things that could be observed, classified and explained'. If enough was known about them then to some extent their actions might even be foretold and controlled. She described how she read his *First Principles* and then followed his generalizations through the various aspects of the 'Synthetic Philosophy' especially the studies of biology, psychology, and sociology. All this, she confessed, illuminated her mind and (rather ironically) became 'the basis of a good deal of the faith in collective regulation' she afterwards developed. For 'once engaged in the application of the scientific method to the facts of social organisation' she shook herself 'completely free from *laisser-faire* bias'. Spencer's influence even turned her for a time against the possibility of reaching any religious truth; but in due course she began nevertheless 'to listen for voices in the Great Unknown' and to open her 'consciousness to the non-material world'.[158] She had shared, then, in 'the all-questioning state of mind' of the age, torn between the traditional metaphysic of the Christian Church and a scientific agnosticism. In a sense she fused the two sets of pressures by making science her religion and having 'an implicit faith' in its

154 B. Webb, *My Apprenticeship*, i.156–7.
155 ibid., ii.263–84, 292–4, 386; Muggeridge and Allen, *Beatrice Webb: a Life*, pp.110ff.
156 B. Webb, *My Apprenticeship*, i.46–7, 56, 161–2; Muggeridge and Allen, op.cit., pp.38–9, 78–9.
157 B. Webb, *My Apprenticeship*, i.43, 45, 47, 111.
158 ibid., i.56.

possibilities.[159] 'Looking back from the standpoint of today', she wrote in 1926,

> it seems to me that two outstanding tenets, some would say, two idols of the mind, were united in this mid-Victorian trend of thought and feeling. There was the current belief in the scientific method, in that intellectual synthesis of observation and experiment, hypothesis and verification, by means of which alone all mundane problems were to be solved. And added to this belief in science was the consciousness of a new motive: the transference of the emotion of self-sacrificing service from God to man.[160]

The way in which these rather different tendencies were mingled in Mrs Webb's mind was to admit a role for each. The scientific investigator manifestly had a major part to play in the human enterprise; but so had the practical acumen of the man of affairs and the vision of the idealist. She saw her husband and herself as a combination of each, as arch-priests (so to say) of this rather Comteian 'religion of humanity' or perhaps beyond.[161]

> . . . the investigator or scientific man has to discover the process by which a given end can be obtained within a given subject-matter. This means specialisation and all the patient methods of observation, generalisation and verification. The man of affairs has to select the processes, to adapt and adjust them in order to bring about a 'state of affairs'. This entails a knowledge of and a capacity to control men, and perception of general ends, which would be actually obtained by the dovetailing of the processes of the various sciences. But neither the investigator nor the man of affairs could act, unless there was a conception of an end or purpose to be attained. This was given by the idealist. Where did he discover his ideals? Not in science, seeing that science can give processes and processes only. Not in affairs: that meant opportunism. In metaphysics or in religion? In choice of ideals within our own inner consciousness, or perhaps in communion with a higher and nobler life than that of common humanity?[162]

But though the Webbs prided themselves on their use of scientific method to study political and social organization, neither of them was

159 ibid., i.73–4, 104.
160 ibid., i.153.
161 ibid., i.166–8; *Beatrice Webb's Diaries, 1912–1924*, pp.195–6; *Our Partnership*, pp.278–9; 'The Nature of Social Institutions', M. Adams (ed.), *The Modern State* (London, 1933), pp.165–81, esp. pp.180–1.
162 B. Webb, *Our Partnership*, pp.263–4. Cf. *My Apprenticeship*, i.16; W. H. Auden *et al., I Believe*, p.325.

really interested in or knew much about natural science itself. At one time
Sidney Webb had attended some of Huxley's lectures and had, as well,
briefly studied geology; Beatrice Potter tried to teach herself mathematics
and had taken a little instruction in experimental physiology but found it
all rather boring. As Lord Beveridge once said: however much the social
claimed to be emulating the natural sciences the connexion was 'never
more than a name.'[163] As with the Fabians generally, being 'scientific'
meant for the Webbs simply being scholarly, thorough, and objective in
the acquisition of knowledge.[164] They described their investigative craft
in various places: for instance, in analysis of Charles Booth's inquiries; in
the preface to the study of *Industrial Democracy*; and, of course, at
length in *Methods of Social Study*.[165] Really there is little about the
procedures suggested to distinguish them from a great deal of historical
or sociological work untainted by the specious attractions of scientism.
What is stressed is the avoidance of merely abstract consideration and the
importance of close and exhaustive empirical study of social institutions,
the actual behaviour of individuals and classes through personal
observation, participation, interview, examination of all the records, and
so on.[166] So far as there is any systematic logical basis it is merely implicit
and not unlike an elementary form of Baconian induction.[167] The
assumption appears to be that there are 'facts' which can be recorded and
the inductive inspection of which will suggest increasingly valid causal
sequences or categories.[168] At its most naïve, the procedure is little
different from Herbert Spencer sitting in his armchair and sorting all his
notes into different piles around him, hoping they will all fit in. At its best
the practice resembled that of a good historian of institutions studying
the concrete detail of their development.[169] The Webbs were in fact little
interested in matters of scientific logic in any formal sense. Not
surprisingly the larger part of their *Methods of Social Study* is more like a
practitioner's handbook than a theoretical treatise such as Bacon's *New*

163 E. Pease, 'Webb and the Fabian Society', Cole (ed.), *The Webbs and their Work*,
    pp.17–18, 26; B. Webb, *My Apprenticeship*, i.158–60; W. Beveridge, 'The London
    School of Economics and the University of London', in Cole, op. cit., p.47.
164 S. and B. Webb, *Methods of Social Study*, pp.2, 16–17, 41 ff. For the Fabian view, see
    pp.371–2 above.
165 B. Webb, *My Apprenticeship*, ii.263–4, 267–8, 292–4 and apps A–C; *Industrial
    Democracy*, pp.xxiii–xxxii; *Methods of Social Study*, passim.
166 See e.g. S. and B. Webb, *Methods of Social Study*, pp.13–14; B. Webb, *My
    Apprenticeship*, vol.ii, apps A–B; Auden et al., *I Believe*, p.325. Cf. Cole (ed.), *The
    Webbs and Their Work*, pp.267–9, 281.
167 See e.g. the process of classification described in *Methods of Social Study*, pp.58–60.
168 ibid., p.54 and ch.III passim.
169 B. Webb, *My Apprenticeship*, ii.293–4, 337, 482–91. Cf. McBriar, op. cit., p.51, and
    Tawney, art. cit., p.249.

Organon or Mill's analysis of the social sciences: and this difference of emphasis is not at all insignificant as a pointer to the authors' purpose and manner.[170] As usual Sidney Webb seemed to bother little with these theoretical matters. His was the blunt, practical empiricism of the down-to-earth man of affairs. But there is no reason at all to suppose he dissented from his wife's remarks on these methodological issues even if he did not consider their elaboration or analysis particularly important. The joint attitude (if such it may be called) and its political implications were summed up, in somewhat idealized fashion, in *Our Partnership*:

> We were, both of us, scientists and at the same time Socialists. We had a perpetual curiosity to know all that could be known about the nature and working of the universe, animate as well as inanimate, psychical as well as material, in the belief that only by means of such knowledge could mankind achieve an ever-increasing control of the forces amid which it lived. We were, both of us, secularists, in the sense that we failed to find in the universe anything that was supernatural, or incapable of demonstration by the scientific method of observation, hypothetical generalisation and experimental or other form of verification. Like other scientists, we were obsessed by scientific curiosity about the universe and its working. But, unlike the astronomers and the physicists, we turned our curiosity to the phenomena that were being less frequently investigated, namely, those connected with the social institutions characteristic of *homo sapiens*, or what is called sociology. We accordingly devoted ourselves as scientists to the study of social institutions, from trade unions to Cabinets, from family relationships to churches, from economics to literature – a field in itself so extensive that we have never been able to compass more than a few selected fragments of it.[171]

They saw society, therefore, 'as one vast laboratory'.[172] But more than this: their gospel was that the method must be used 'in social service'.[173]

> At the same time, we were active citizens; and, as such, we had to have a practical policy of public life. Our growing knowledge of social institutions led us to a policy of transforming the organisation of wealth production and distribution, from its basis of anarchic individual profit-making to one of regulated social service. That is to say, our action as electors, administrators and propagandists was that of Socialists, instead of that of Liberals or Conservatives. Looking back on half-a-century of scientific investigation and public activity, it

170 Cf. the specific disclaimer, *Methods of Social Study*, p.xliii.
171 B. Webb, *Our Partnership*, p.16.
172 B. Webb, *My Apprenticeship*, ii.391.
173 Cole (ed.), *Beatrice Webb's Diaries, 1912–1924*, p.118.

seems to us in retrospect that every discovery in sociology and, indeed, every increase in our own knowledge of social institutions has strengthened our faith that the further advance of human society is dependent on a considerable further substitution of institutions based on public service for those based on profit-making. We have, accordingly, had the enjoyment of harmony between the two halves of our lives, between our scientific studies and our practical citizenship.[174]

These passages do not tell the whole story: in particular they do not at all bring out the role in Mrs Webb's life of that mystical religious inspiration referred to above; and they do not, of themselves, indicate that the 'scientism' was really only a way of referring to an appropriate form of organized and methodical procedure largely historical in nature. As well, the order of priorities was inverted: as with Spencer, political faith came first and the inquiries simply sustained this goal. But at least, there is here indicated the pair's considered and mature view of their life-work, its method, and its purpose.

For the Webbs, then, a scientific analysis of society was not simply a valuable intellectual exercise in its own right; it was an essential preliminary to the efficient reorganization of society.[175] And it was a token of the mysterious Beyond or at least of a Comteian vision of Humanity.[176]

The administrative machine

Of course, the proposed science of society was so far 'young and very incomplete'; and there was always the major difficulty posed to generalization and prescription by the unpredictability of human behaviour. But, notwithstanding this, the science was capable of 'indefinite extension'.[177] So how could the advantages of a scientifically organized society best be achieved in practice? Basically, the answer given was: through expert control and planned administration. In this respect, 'perfection of the machinery' is the crucial focus of attention and 'efficiency is the sole object' to be achieved by 'technical or scientific' means.[178] The gist of the matter was early revealed: for as Mrs Webb confided to her diary in 1897 'collectivists alone have the faith to grind out a science of politics'.[179] Similarly a few years later, commenting on

174 B. Webb, *Our Partnership*, pp.16–17.
175 Cf. S. and B. Webb, *Methods of Social Study*, pp.28–9 and ch.xii.
176 ibid., pp.258–9.
177 B. Webb, in Auden *et al.*, *I Believe*, pp.328–30.
178 S. and B. Webb, *Methods of Social Study*, p.28.
179 B. Webb, *Our Partnership*, p.137. Cf. ibid., p.168.

the death of Mandell Creighton, Bishop of London, she penned a valedictory encomium that is perhaps more revealing for what it tells of its author than its subject:

> . . . outside the spiritual side of life, Creighton believed implicitly in the scientific method of observation and verification. And he believed in organisation and machinery, in the regulation of conduct by law or public opinion, according to some deliberately conceived idea of social expediency. He had no faith in democracy; though he accepted it as necessary: his contempt for the politician amounted almost to intolerance. Lack of brains was to him the greatest social danger: with brains and good will no change was impracticable. Without intellectual leadership, the average man, however good his conduct, would remain in a state of squalor and mediocrity.[180]

It is clear what the partnership found congenial. And the attitude is generally revealed in a number of contexts.

The first is the Webbs' view of democracy and of the relation between popular and expert opinion. Mrs Webb revealed her basic indifference in the following passage in her diary: 'I have always assumed political democracy as a necessary part of the machinery of government. I have never exerted myself to get it. It has no glamour for me – I have been, for instance, wholly indifferent to my own political disfranchisement.'[181] For his part, her husband often referred to 'a discreetly regulated freedom', the liberty of the masses always being seen in the context of wise guidance from above. Really they were both more interested in administration than politics of a popular kind. A remark of Mrs Webb's, made in 1893, is relevant here. She refers to the LCC and the people who run it: it is (she says with an eye to her husband's role) 'a machine for evolving a committee; the committee is a machine for evolving one man – the chairman. Both alike a machine for dodging the democracy (in a crude sense) by introducing government by a select minority instead of the rule of the majority'. Again, in the following year she wrote:

> . . . we have little faith in the 'average sensual man', we do not believe that he can do more than describe his grievances, we do not think that he can prescribe the remedies. . . . We wish to introduce into politics the professional expert – to extend the sphere of government by adding to its enormous advantages of wholesale and compulsory management, the advantages of the most skilled entrepreneur.[182]

180 ibid., pp.206–7.
181 M. Cole (ed.), *Beatrice Webb's Diaries, 1912–1924*, p.122. The anti-democratic tendency was early manifest: see B. Potter to A. Swanwick (1884), in MacKenzie, *The Letters of Sidney and Beatrice Webb*, i.21–2. Contrast some of her published views in J. M. Winter, *Socialism and the Challenge of War*, pp.52–3.
182 B. Webb, *Our Partnership*, pp.64–5, 120.

It is true that, on the other hand, the Webbs often refer to the basic importance of the ordinary man, the fundamental authority of the mass of the people, the need for a genuinely democratic state, for greater freedom, that is, practical opportunities for exercising one's faculties and fulfilling one's desires.[183] But such remarks are rather formal and to be seen in the context of more frequent and fervent reference to the importance of 'a real aristocracy of character and intellect' and to the popular representative as a mere '"foolometer" for the expert'.[184] Acknowledging the need for safeguards against the evils of bureaucracy, it was nevertheless stressed that it was inevitable society should be governed by officials: the problem was how to combine the maximum of consent with the highest degree of efficiency.[185] In the six lectures on democracy which he gave in 1896, Sidney Webb, while acknowledging that the expert might be responsible, nevertheless gave him a considerable not to say crucial role.[186] Similarly Webb argued in 1908 that the requirements of the coming century would entail in every branch of administration and legislation, a high degree of specialized knowledge and expertise. And these are not matters that can be settled by direct popular vote or formulated by the amateur: they involve 'the highly elaborated technicalities characteristic of the really experienced departmental administrator.'[187] This 'Webb bias in favour of expert administration in all human affairs' was freely acknowledged, as was the fact that this reliance on the 'professional manager' must tend to collectivism. But after all whereas the individualist believed the best government was that which governed least, the Socialist looked to that which could successfully administer most.[188] In 1905 Mrs Webb recorded in her diary H. G. Wells's gift of a copy of his *A Modern Utopia*, a work in which a superior class of controllers called the Samurai is depicted. When Mrs Webb congratulated him on the volume, he 'laughingly remarked' that the chapters on this topic 'will pander to all your worst instincts'.[189] Of course, the Webbian ruler would recognize a duty to his subjects but, as the Squire told Mrs Dale in the Trollope story, '"I do not mean . . . that your duty is to let them act in any way that may best please them for the moment."'[190] In a lecture Sidney Webb gave in 1919 he made clear his

183 e.g. *Beatrice Webb's Diaries, 1912–1924*, p.15; S. Webb, *Towards Social Democracy: a Study of Social Evolution During the Past Three-Quarters of a Century* (London, n.d. [1916]), pp.3–7.
184 B. Webb, *Our Partnership*, pp.138, 231.
185 ibid., pp.293, 300.
186 S. Webb, 'The Machinery of Democracy', *Fabian News* (November 1896–January 1897), in McBriar, *Fabian Socialism and English Politics*, pp.75–7.
187 S. Webb, *The Necessary Basis of Society*, pp.6–7.
188 B. Webb, *Our Partnership*, p.464; *Beatrice Webb's Diaries, 1912–1924*, p.123; S. Webb, *Socialism in England*, pp.26–7.
189 Cited in B. Webb, *Our Partnership*, p.305.
190 A. Trollope, *The Small House at Allington* (1864; Everyman, 1970), p.362.

view of the mass of the people: they were 'apathetic, dense, [and] unreceptive to any unfamiliar ideas'. Of course, they have to be given the vote and their dull characteristics accepted: 'you have got to work your governmental machine in some way that will enable you to get on notwithstanding their denseness.'[191] A flattering view of the workers indeed.

A similar emphasis is observable in the Webbs' specific comments on and proposals for changes in political and administrative machinery. Although on occasion they were prepared to admit that the British Constitution 'has a certain wisdom in it', on the whole they wanted either to reform it more or less drastically on rational lines to make it a less inappropriate system of administration or replace it entirely with something much more efficient.[192] For instance, in 1918 in a tract on the reform of the House of Lords, Sidney Webb proposed not its abolition (the usual Socialist solution) but its reorganization as a 'Committee of Experts'.[193] Similarly Mrs Webb was a member of the Haldane Committee on the Machinery of Government which had to grapple *inter alia* with the problem of relating scientific efficiency in administration to the normal working of the Parliamentary system.[194] The proposals that finally emerged were much more conditioned by considerations of administrative efficiency than by those relating to the party and personal factors so important in practice on the actual political scene.[195] But the high-water mark of the Webbs' comments in this respect was the publication in 1920 of their book on the constitution they had in mind for a Socialist Britain, 'the summing up of our observation and reasoning about political and industrial organisation'.[196] Again, although much attention is paid to the spread of the democratic principle, it is symptomatic of the Webbs' approach that the consideration of party (thought to be an institution of declining importance under Socialism) is restricted to a few pages and a single footnote, albeit a lengthy one.[197] The main concern of the book is really with the structure and working of administrative organizations and with those who will manage them, with the complexities of 'a highly differentiated and systematically co-ordinated social order.'[198] The Webbs believed that the role of the expert

191 S. Webb, 'A Stratified Democracy', *The New Commonwealth* (28 November 1919), suppl., p.5.
192 For the remark about the Constitution (made, be it noted, on the eve of Sidney's elevation to the Cabinet), see *Beatrice Webb's Diaries, 1912–1924*, p.257.
193 S. Webb, *Reform of the House of Lords* (Fabian tract no.183; London, 1918).
194 Cf. the comments in *Beatrice Webb's Diaries, 1912–1924*, p.98.
195 On the Haldane Committee recommendations, see vol.iii, *A Much-Governed Nation*, ch.8.
196 *Beatrice Webb's Diaries, 1912–1924*, p.203.
197 S. and B. Webb, *A Constitution for the Socialist Commonwealth of Great Britain* (London, 1920), pp.82–6, 144–5 n.1.
198 ibid., p.202.

would be crucial but subject to an ever more knowledgeable public opinion so that mere 'government from above' would be avoided.[199] But the analogy with the directors and a shareholders' meeting so acidly drawn by Bertrand Russell is manifestly relevant in this context.[200]

Various aspects of the general political strategy favoured by the Webbs equally revealed the élitism of their attitude. For example, the policy of permeation which they long favoured was one which depended for its success on influencing by all possible means the leadership of the Conservative and Liberal Parties. It was not a policy of popularization; and while there was hope that this technique might be fruitful the Webbs showed little interest in the idea of an independent political party based on the widespread Labour movement.[201] A change of direction occurred, at least in part, when the courtship of the Liberals proved unfruitful.[202] But even then, when the Webbs threw in their lot with the Labour Party, they inevitably saw themselves as a pair of grey eminences directing the new political force towards goals they favoured.[203] They did not in fact think very highly of the leaders of either the Labour Party or the trade unions seeing them rather as material ripe for manipulation.[204] And, as already noted, this was a scheme not without success.[205] Moreover the kind of programme they championed was one calculated to sustain their strategic aims: the crucial concept of public ownership tended in the direction of nationalized monopolies run by technocrats. Their study of *Industrial Democracy* (reissued in 1920) was in effect a 'long panegyric' of state control. As one recent commentator put it, this was 'government for the people but not by them'.[206] The gist of the Webbs' later attitude is revealed in this passage about their relation with Haldane (one which much underplays indeed their quondam faith in a policy of permeation):

> What bound us together as associates was our common faith in a deliberately organised society: our common belief in the application of science to human relations with a view to betterment. Where we differed was in the orientation of political power. Haldane believed more than we did in the existing governing class: in the great personages of Court, Cabinet and City. We staked our hopes on the

199 ibid., pp.196–9.
200 For Russell's comment, see p.410 below.
201 See e.g. M. Cole (ed.), *The Webbs and their Work*, pp.67–8, 147, 167–84; Muggeridge and Allen, *Beatrice Webb, a Life*, pp.148–9; Halévy, *A History of the English People in the Nineteenth Century*, v.229–30.
202 See e.g. B. Webb, *Our Partnership*, pp.232, 423; *Beatrice Webb's Diaries, 1912–1924*, pp.2, 10.
203 B. Webb, *Our Partnership*, pp.116, 125.
204 Cf. Winter, *Socialism and the Challenge of War*, pp.54–6.
205 See above pp.389–90.
206 F. W. Bealey (ed.), *The Social and Political Thought of the British Labour Party* (London, 1970), pp.4–5; Halévy, op. cit., v.142.

organised working-class, served and guided it is true, by an *élite* of unassuming experts who would make no claim to superior social status, but would content themselves with exercising the power inherent in superior knowledge and longer administrative experience.[207]

There is a similar emphasis to be discerned in the Webbs' view that social change of an effective and desirable kind could only come through the action of the state and so of its officials. The paradigm is revealed in effect in the Poor Law Minority Report. The chaos of the existing situation is revealed and a rational alternative proposed in considerable detail, one which does not eschew a notable degree of disciplinary supervision.[208] From the days when she used to do charitable work Mrs Webb rather took a pride in the firm severity with which she could deal with the undeserving poor. And at the very end she was concerned that the universal provision envisaged by the Beveridge Report might produce a race of wastrels and spongers.

Even so specific an enterprise as the foundation of the London School of Economics is indicative of the Webbs' managerial view of things. If the vision was of a Socialist society supervised or run by a class of experts, including those trained in the social sciences, then it was necessary to provide for acquisition of the appropriate technical knowledge. It was in an important way because of this consideration that the Webbs were instrumental in founding the School in 1896. In her diary a couple of years before, Beatrice Webb had stressed the need for such an institution. Reforming society, she wrote, was no light matter; it had to be 'undertaken by experts specially trained for the purpose'.[209] And Halévy, who knew the Webbs quite well at this time, wrote later that they

> pursued methodically and fanatically the end they had proposed to themselves, to transform the old England of individualism and *laissez faire* into an England organized from above. And this School of Economics which they had founded and of which they were the guiding spirits was intended by them to train the bureaucracy of future collectivist England.

Haldane was equally a close contact and in 1906 spoke of the LSE as a sort of training college in the art of administration for both soldiers and civilians.[210] In all this the Fabians were, of course, much influenced by the

207 B. Webb, *Our Partnership*, p.97.
208 Cf. M. Cole (ed.), *The Webbs and their Work*, p.108; Muggeridge and Allen, *Beatrice Webb, a Life*, pp.176–7, 195–6.
209 B. Webb, *Our Partnership*, p.86.
210 Halévy, op. cit., vi.266 and n.2. John Burns wrote to H. G. Wells (16 May 1910) about 'The new helotry in the servile state' being ruled by archivists from the School of Economics: see J. Harris, *Unemployment and Politics: a Study in English Social Policy, 1886–1914* (Oxford, 1972), p.267 n.1.

model of the École Libre des Sciences Politiques founded not long before by Boutmy and Taine with the purpose of reshaping French government after the débâcle of 1870, to be achieved by training an administrative élite in policy-oriented skills. Of course, it was always intended that instruction should be completely scholarly and objective. However it was also felt that such study of the social sciences could not but produce just the right kind of person to run the Socialist state in the efficient way required; and – so they naïvely imagined – would inevitably produce Socialists too.[211]

By comparison with their interest in domestic problems the Webbs, like the Fabians as a whole, at first gave relatively little serious attention to foreign and imperial affairs. So far as there was a wider scope to their interests it was with the social organization of the countries of 'Western Civilization' defined as 'that uncongenial triplet of the Christian Faith, Capitalist Profitmaking and Political Democracy.'[212] Yet this concern, too, always had a didactic aim. If they were fascinated by Bismarckian state Socialism, as they were, it was because they wanted the Prussian model to be copied in Britain; and they urged Joseph Chamberlain to do just this.[213] And, if it served their purpose, they were quite prepared to cast their eyes further afield. For example, they thought very highly of the Japanese and credited them with all the qualities of political and social organization and public spirit which they so much admired.[214] The rise of Japan, they believed, showed what strong central government could do in terms of improving national efficiency. Its success in the war with Russia was greeted excitedly as an instance of idealist and innovating collectivism. When they visited Japan and Korea they saw what they had in mind to see: a country being run in a smooth and orderly way by an enlightened élite, genuine samurai, as it were. It was, they believed, an early example of the future Socialist state and its benevolent bureaucracy.[215] The truth be told they had little love for the play and compromise of multi-party politics and genuinely admired the idea of a one-party system as being more efficient. Dr Winter comments further: 'Authoritarianism, they apparently believed, was a small enough price to pay for efficiency and order in social affairs. This élitist, illiberal aspect of the

---

211 B. Webb, *Our Partnership*, pp.87–9, 195; Cf. Sir William Beveridge's remarks in Cole (ed.), *The Webbs and their Work*, p.44. For a recent analysis of the Webbs' work in respect of education, especially technical and higher education, see E. J. T. Brennan, *Education for National Efficiency: the Contribution of Sidney and Beatrice Webb* (London, 1975), esp. pp.34–9.

212 B. Webb, in W. H. Auden *et al.*, *I Believe*, pp.335–7.

213 Halévy, op. cit., v.141–2.

214 Nor was this favourable opinion confined to the Webbs: see e.g. Sir Oliver Lodge, *Public Service versus Private Expenditure* (Fabian tract no.121; 1905; London, 1907), pp.10–11.

215 Cf. B. Webb, *Our Partnership*, pp.299–300; Winter, op. cit., pp.45–7.

Webbs' thought is expressed . . . in their euphoric appraisal of Japan as it was in their denigration of the rest of the non-white world.'[216] For similar sorts of reasons they were interested in and prepared to praise Turkey.[217]

On returning from their world tour in 1912, full of their new-found admiration for Japan, they realized the case they had hitherto argued for a national minimum under capitalism was going to be very difficult to achieve. They were impressed, for instance, by the great wave of labour unrest that was then sweeping the country constituting, it seemed, a more or less open revolt against the prevailing state of affairs and indicating a greater degree of working-class political awareness than they had thought possible. The cataclysm of the Great War and a disastrous peace settlement followed. In 1923 they published a volume on *The Decay of Capitalist Civilisation* which Mrs Webb described as 'our first indictment of the capitalist system'.[218] Their faith was further disturbed by the great depression which began in the 1920s. During the following decade this economic upheaval continued and the system seemed to be going into still deeper decline. The Webbs had failed to foresee the problem of long-term unemployment and did not understand how it could be tackled in conventional terms. The two Labour governments had been disappointing; had, indeed, failed. Increasingly the Webbs doubted whether the Labour Party would ever be an efficient instrument for the transformation of this country into a scientifically managed collectivist state. Thus the implications were, for them, ominous: in 1931, Mrs Webb expressed doubt about the inevitability of gradualness and the possibility of the peaceful transformation of capitalism; a Communist inspired revolution seemed more likely.[219]

In this context the Webbs' growing interest in and, later, admiration for both Soviet Russia and Marxist theory are not wholly inexplicable.[220] Their example constitutes, indeed, a kind of paradigm case of bourgeois intellectualist radicalism (if the term may be pardoned). They first believe they can influence the establishment of the day by ideas and charm and, so to say, change society from within. Denial of anticipation here dictates a reluctant shift of emphasis to support for a Labour movement the leaders and members of which they rather despise but which they hope to dominate. As this expedient in turn is seen to fail so the questing eye moves further afield to the New Jerusalem arising in the East and to the

216 Winter, op. cit., p.47.
217 J. Parker, 'The Fabian Society and the New Fabian Research Bureau', Cole (ed.), *The Webbs and their Work*, p.244.
218 B. Webb, *Our Partnership*, p.490. But see the Webbs' *A Constitution for the Socialist Commonwealth*, pp.xi–xiii.
219 *Beatrice Webb's Diaries, 1924–1932*, pp.265–6.
220 For one such expression, see *Methods of Social Study*, p.27. The stages of the conversion are described in B. Webb, *Our Partnership*, pp.489–91.

words of its prophet. Where we went hopelessly wrong, Mrs Webb wrote, 'was in ignoring Karl Marx's forecast of the eventual breakdown of the capitalist system as the one and only way of maximising the wealth of nations.'[221] There is an interesting parallel instance in the case of Harold Laski. Both he and the Webbs increasingly adopted the Marxist language of explanation and prescription. But in each case it was a kind of expository mask: in Laski's for his continuing pluralist libertarianism; in the Webbs' for their long-standing belief in bureaucratic collectivism. And this is reflected in their often very different attitudes to the Soviet Union and to Communism. Laski's admiration was linked to a scepticism sometimes little short of abhorrence; the Webbs' was hardly so qualified.[222]

Of course, both the Webbs discerned in Soviet Russia the completely planned Socialist economy they had been advocating steadily for over half a century. And in Mrs Webb's case there was the additional attraction that the USSR seemed to be possessed of and dominated by a 'Spiritual Power': it was a real Church.[223] They believed there had occurred, too, that release of motives and of miracles of co-operative effort that seemed increasingly impossible under capitalism. An alternative principle to making a profit had been found in 'planned production for community consumption', a much stronger force for in it the secular and spiritual coalesce.[224] Moreover the Webbs also found in the ranks of the Soviet administrators their own 'professed faith' in science: 'No vested interests hinder them from basing their decisions and their policy upon the best science they can obtain.' There was, indeed, in the USSR an 'intense preoccupation, and even obsession, with science'.[225]

How could the Webbs, given their long-held interests and ideas, not be impressed by the way an enormous and daunting administrative task was being tackled? And if the normal forms of Parliamentary democracy were not present in the Russian political scene, then there were the new modes of popular self-expression the Webbs detected by which, they believed, large numbers of people participated in the work of government.[226] In many ways the Soviet Union seemed to provide a working exemplification of that 'Socialist Commonwealth of Great Britain' they had themselves described, as indeed the very structure of the work on the

221 B. Webb, *Our Partnership*, p.488.
222 For Laski, see my 'Laski and British Socialism', *History of Political Thought*, ii (1981), pp.586–90.
223 *Beatrice Webb's Diaries, 1924–1932*, p.307. Cf. the passage cited by G. Himmelfarb, 'Process, Purpose and Ego', *TLS* (25 June 1976), p.790.
224 B. Webb, in W. Auden *et al.*, *I Believe*, pp.344–5, 348.
225 S. and B. Webb, *Soviet Communism: a New Civilisation* (1935; 2nd edn, London, 1937), pp.1132–3. Cf. ibid., ch. xi 'Science the Salvation of Mankind'.
226 ibid., e.g. p.viii and ch.xii.

Soviets make clear. It was the case that there was only one party. But they had come genuinely to admire this state of affairs (and not only in Russia); and, the truth be told, they had no great love for the British party system and regarded its leaders as craven incompetents. Moreover in the dedicated élite of the Communist Party of the USSR they saw that 'Vocation of Leadership' which they had always sustained (and which Wells had earlier envisioned in his Order of the Samurai).[227]

Hence their famous, and vast, volume *Soviet Communism: a New Civilisation?* which appeared in 1935 after their trip to the USSR. At the very end of *Our Partnership* (in a passage probably written in the late 1930s or early 1940s) Mrs Webb said in reference to the key issues they had in mind:

> Whether we were right or whether we were wrong in acclaiming Soviet Communism with its multiform democracy, its sex, class and racial equality, its planned production for community consumption, and above all its penalisation of the profit-making motive and insistence on the obligation of all able-bodied persons to earn their livelihood by serving the community, the event will prove. . . .[228]

They themselves were in no doubt at all, which is why they dropped the question mark from the title in the new edition of their book which appeared in 1937: a most famous literary omission. And their feelings of optimism were bolstered by the popular sympathy for Russia that surged forward after the German attack in 1941. In some unpublished papers Lord Samuel has recorded a visit he made to the Webbs in March 1943 shortly before Beatrice's death. They are, he wrote, 'still intensely interested in the fortunes of Soviet Russia, and the conversation usually seemed to curve round to that. Their chief consolation in the infirmities of old age seems to be that their forecasts about the Soviets have turned out to be substantially right.' For her part, Mrs Webb wrote to Samuel of 'the importance of the Soviet Union's living philosophy in reconstructing the world'.[229]

Of course, the Webbs were not alone in thus idealizing the Soviet experiment; and there was always a contrasting view to be found even in radical quarters. R. H. Tawney, for instance, was quite clear that, as he said in 1935, the Russian political system was no more than 'police collectivism'.[230] There has, too, been a lot of scathing comment since about the Webbs' naïvety in this regard. Professor Alasdair McIntyre said they defected from Fabianism to Stalinism simply because they were

227 ibid., p. 1131 and n.2, and ch.v *passim.*
228 B. Webb, *Our Partnership*, p.491.
229 Memorandum on visit to the Webbs (4 March 1943) in HLRO, Samuel Papers A/119(6); Mrs Webb to H. Samuel (11 March 1943), ibid.
230 Cited in R. Terrill, *R. H. Tawney and His Times: Socialism as Fellowship* (Cambridge, Mass., 1973), p.237.

consistent élitists: they always believed in Socialism imposed from above and simply changed their choice of élite. Again Herbert Morrison, who knew the Webbs a little, put the point with characteristic bluntness when he said that these two apostles of gradualism became 'semi-bolsheviks' not so much, he suspected, for ideological reasons 'but because they had lived for a few months in a bureaucrats' paradise and both were bureaucrats to the core.'[231] Two other instances of this sort of comment or explanation must stand for volumes.

The first is the remarks of Malcolm Muggeridge who had direct experience of both the Webbs and the Soviet Union. He had gone there, like the Webbs, convinced it was the country of the future. But, unlike them, he was sadly disillusioned by the experience.[232] He follows a sarcastic reference to 'old Shaw lighting the way to the good Fabian, Stalin' with a general comment on the Webbs' mania for 'scientific method' and its application to Soviet Communism:

> Such masses and masses of documentation! Statistics without end, data of every kind, eye-witness accounts, miles and miles of film, video abounding. Surely out of all this, posterity, if so desiring, will be able to reconstruct us and our lives. But will they? I think of Sidney and Beatrice Webb down at Passfield patiently collecting and collating every scrap of information they could lay hands on about the Soviet regime. Travelling about the USSR to the same end. As experienced investigators, so rigorous and careful. Checking every fact, testing every hypothesis. And the result? – a monumental folly, a volume of fantasy compared with which Casanova's Memoirs, Frank Harris's even, are sober and realistic.[233]

Elsewhere Muggeridge remarks that the Webbs pursued 'truth through facts' and arrived at 'fantasy', sought 'deliverance through power' and arrived at 'servitude'.[234]

The second assessment is that of John Strachey which, coming as it does from an ex-Marxist, is especially interesting. He says that like so many Socialists, including himself, the Webbs

failed to see the extraordinary fact that Keynes's diagnosis and

231 A. McIntyre, *Against the Self-Images of the Age: Essays on Ideology and Philosophy* (London, 1971), p.38; Lord Morrison of Lambeth, *Herbert Morrison: an Autobiography* (London, 1960), pp.113–14. Cf. the similar opinion of G. D. H. Cole in M. Cole (ed.), *The Webbs and their Work*, p.278.
232 M. Muggeridge, *Chronicles of Wasted Time*, vol.i, ch.5. His original account is *Winter in Moscow* (London, 1934). The impressions are cast in the form of a series of fictional sketches; while the preface expresses the intent clearly enough.
233 Muggeridge, *Chronicles of Wasted Time*, i.16, 20.
234 ibid., i.151. This passage ends a vivid, anecdotal account of a visit to Passfield Corner, ibid., i.146–51.

remedy, combined with the obstinate strength, industrial and political, of the wage earners, and combined, too, with the terrific jolt which the second world war was to give to British society, would create a far more favourable opportunity for reformism in the latter part of the twentieth century than had ever existed before.[235]

Strachey goes on to record the impression made on him at the time of its appearance by *Soviet Communism*:

I was then much nearer to the communists than the Webbs ever became; but even I was staggered by the book's utter lack of any critical analysis of Russian society. It was not that the Webbs had seen Stalin's Russia as it was and had come to the conclusion that, nevertheless, since capitalism seemed to be dying, the Soviet system had to be accepted, with all its horrors, as the only remaining way out for human civilization. That was a tenable proposition. But that was not the Webbs' reaction. Their huge . . . work gave the impression of taking Soviet society utterly at its face value. Their extraordinary formalism came out above all in their account of the political side of Soviet society. They described it as if it were in reality what it was on paper. . . . [There] was . . . a fixed determination to see in Soviet Russia the hope of the world. They would not despair; therefore they had to have some repository for their hope. And they found it, not as many of the rest of us did, by concluding that the nightmarish features of Stalin's Russia had to be accepted as the inevitable birth pangs of a new civilization: they found it by firmly shutting their eyes to the existence of any such features. Of course, they were old people by now.[236]

But the Webbs certainly knew about the liquidations, deportations, and the labour camps.[237] It was simply that they were prepared to palliate or even condone them as many left-wing intellectuals did.[238] There was always a certain 'impersonalness' about the Webbs' work, a kind of moral failure to consider the human aspect of what they were studying or recommending.[239]

Tawney, who knew them very well, went out of his way (in discussing their work after they had died) to assert that the 'conventional portrait of the pair as bureaucratic energumens, conspiring to submit every human

235 J. Strachey, 'Sidney and Beatrice Webb', *The Listener*, lxiv (13 October 1960), p.618.
236 ibid., p.619.
237 S. and B. Webb, *Soviet Communism*, ch.VII e.g. pp.566–7, 571–2, 584–5.
238 e.g. ibid., pp.1152–62 on the 'treason trials'. See the interesting discussion 'Did Stalin Dupe the Intellectuals?', in G. Watson, *Politics and Literature in Modern Britain* (London, 1977), ch.3.
239 Cf. A. Toynbee, *Acquaintances* (London, 1967), ch.9, and esp. pp.113–15; R. H. Tawney, *The Webbs in Perspective*, pp.11–12.

activity to the centralized control of an omni-competent State, is a caricature. . . .'[240] No doubt in some sort of ultimate accounting this may be the case. But it is not really the emphasis that emerges from the pages of their work, published or private. It would obviously be wrong to suggest they never showed any awareness of the dangers that lay in the enormous increase and centralization of political authority that was involved in the development of collectivism. They appreciated the need in principle for the control of the collectivist state to avoid its becoming a 'hard tyranny'; and this was why they so often stressed the importance of local authorities in the political scheme of things they envisaged and regarded as desirable the continuation and development of the individual producer and co-operative enterprise in their own spheres outside the publicly controlled economy.[241] They even spoke sometimes of a merely 'limited' application of the collectivist principles.[242] But this was compatible nevertheless with travelling a long way down the road towards the 'housekeeping state': for we 'saw that to the Government alone could be entrusted the provision for future generations'.[243] And Elie Halévy chillingly reported, 'I can still hear Sidney Webb explaining to me that the future lay with the great administrative nations, where governing was done by the bureaucrats and order was maintained by the policemen.'[244] This sort of attitude was not an aberration but an essential part of the Webbian syndrome of ideas, one they handed on to the British Socialists who followed them. As Sidney Webb urged over sixty years ago, in any highly organized community, however formally democratic it may be, government and legislation necessarily become increasingly the business of persons elaborately trained and set apart for the task, and less and less the immediate outcome of popular feeling. This was the characteristically Webbian view.

Their influence was undoubted. Their friend and advocate, R. H. Tawney, wrote as early as the 1920s: 'What made possible the Liberal triumphs after 1832 was the work of Bentham. What has more than anything else made possible that of the Labor movement is the work of the Webbs.'[245] Then later, in the valedictory assessment he offered after they had died, he said:

> They are . . . historical figures . . . whose stature increases as their
> world recedes. They faced great issues, and grappled . . . with them in

240 Tawney, *The Webbs in Perspective*, p.8.
241 See S. Webb's remarks in *Crusade* (August 1912), suppl. p.152, cited in McBriar, *Fabian Socialism and English Politics*, p.109.
242 e.g. B. Webb, *Our Partnership*, pp.117–18.
243 ibid., pp.149–50.
244 E. Halévy, *The Era of Tyrannies*, p.209.
245 R. H. Tawney, 'What British Labor Wants', *New Republic*, xxxvii (1923–4), p.15.

a great way. They changed thought and action. They conquered for knowledge and made habitable by man departments of social life which, before them, had been a trackless jungle. They researched, wrote, agitated, administered, and – since only the last stages of legislation take place in Parliament – were not the less legislators because, save for ten years when both were over sixty, County Hall and the British Museum saw more of them than Westminster. If a man looks back on the successive chapters of English social history from 1880 to 1930, he will find few problems which they failed to illumine, few abuses against which their blows were not the heaviest struck, and few reforms in which they did not play a decisive, if often a deliberately self-effacing, part.[246]

But a more critical assessment of the Webbs and their influence is happily revealed in a vignette from Mrs Webb's own pen of the end of a meeting with the ardent libertarian, Auberon Herbert:

Memory recalls [his] tall figure . . . , wrapped in an old shawl, with vague blue eyes, soft high voice, flowing white beard – the Don Quixote of the nineteenth century, waving one hand at us, while pushing his sailing boat away from the shore; giving us his final blessing: 'You will do a lot of mischief and be very happy in doing it.'[247]

Beatrice Webb died in 1943, her husband four years later. The ashes of both are buried in Westminster Abbey which is surely fitting if the anonymous epigraph cited at the beginning of this section is correct. If it is, it means that the key to Fabianism and of much British Socialism is what Russell called 'the worship of the State.' It was this, he said sharply, which

led both the Webbs and also Shaw into what I thought an undue tolerance of Mussolini and Hitler, and ultimately into a rather absurd adulation of the Soviet Government. . . . Both of them were fundamentally undemocratic, and regarded it as the function of a statesman to bamboozle or terrorize the populace. I realized the origins of Mrs. Webb's conceptions of government when she repeated to me her father's description of shareholders' meetings. It is the recognized function of directors to keep shareholders in their place, and she had similar views about the relation of the Government to the electorate.[248]

*   *   *

246 R. H. Tawney, 'In Memory of Sidney Webb', loc. cit., p.245.
247 B. Webb, Our Partnership, p.32.
248 B. Russell, Autobiography, i.78–9.

Clearly in its extreme form the sort of Socialism represented by the Webbs (and by others such as H. G. Wells) need not be at all democratic. It would be likely to insist on control by the competent class to avoid waste and inefficiency and scientifically to achieve optimum conditions of living and progress. In a phrase, it is a statist or collectivist Socialism. And it is often supposed that this directorial manner is alone characteristic of the creed: it is, in the words of a recent observer, 'doubtful if socialism was ever a libertarian doctrine in any dedicated sense'.[249]

But indeed it often was, or is. There has always been a quite contrary tendency or strand of Socialist thought that has rested its appeal in good part, and sometimes entirely, on a critical concern about the prospect of big government and centralization. From this point of view Socialism could never simply be scientific planning by an administrative élite of civil service mandarins and managers and technocrats however enlightened. Indeed Socialism was not primarily a matter of economic efficiency at all: it was a moral quest rather, a search for individual fulfilment. And no objective of this type was necessarily advanced by a directorial emphasis that would blanket the whole thing in a web (if the term may be excused) of centralized bureaucracy. Harold Laski, whose own work (for all its ambivalence) reflected a preponderant anti-collectivist emphasis, urged (in a Fabian tract, no less) that 'the true Socialism is a libertarian, and not an authoritarian, socialism.'[250] It is to this anti-statist and ethical aspect of the creed that attention must now turn.

249 G. Watson, *The English Ideology: Studies in the Language of Victorian Politics* (London, 1973), p.231.
250 H. J. Laski, *Socialism and Freedom* (Fabian tract no.216; London, 1925), p.12. For discussion of the unity and diversity of Laski's thought, see my 'Laski and British Socialism', loc. cit., pp.573–91.

12

SOCIALISM AND FREEDOM

We should take to socialism because it is ethically right, otherwise we
shall stop short at collectivism.
R. BLATCHFORD, cited in Socialist Union, *Socialism: a New Statement
of Principles*, 1952, p. 3

THE MORALISTIC STRAIN

To understand the Socialist movement, it must be realised that it is
primarily a moral revolt. The movement draws its recruits from among
those who are outraged by the corruption and injustices of our industrial
system, and if we are to see the movement in its proper perspective this
fact must never be forgotten. Its great achievement is to have given to the
world a social conscience.
A. J. PENTY, *Towards a Christian Sociology*, 1923, p. 14

THE APPEAL not to efficiency and scientific administration but to
compassion at the human condition and to the need for the moral
regeneration and fulfilment of the individual, especially in his working
life, goes back to the beginning of modern British Socialism. It is what
lies behind the spirit of co-operation and what is involved in the claims
put forward in behalf of the poor and otherwise underprivileged
members of the community. Of course, the language may be there as
cover merely for the stark and selfish pursuit of class or group interest.
But equally there has always been a substantial element of sincerity and
commitment to an ideal of justice as a fundamental motivating force.
This profoundly ethical strain has revealed itself in the Socialist tradition
in a number of ways not least in the attachment to natural rights and
natural law doctrine as in the manifestoes of the Early English Socialists
and Chartists. Similarly it is closely associated with the simple religiosity
that has so often been a major factor in the development of Socialist
policies and pleas (as it has indeed in those of other ideologies). For
instance, both Robert Blatchford and Keir Hardie founded their opinions
on the Christian concept of the brotherhood of man: the social and
political equality of human beings was simply the reflection of a common

humility before God. Something of the flavour of this point of view is revealed in Blatchford's pamphlet *The New Religion*. He there refuses to attach significance to Marxism and places instead much more emphasis on the inspiration of such writers as Carlyle, Ruskin, Dickens, Thoreau, and Whitman. 'It is from these men', he says, that the industrial population has 'caught the message of love and justice, of liberty and peace, of culture and simplicity, and of holiness and beauty of life.' Socialism is a 'new religion' of 'sweetness and of light' which is 'rousing and revivifying' the masses in matters much greater than mere questions of wages, hours of work, the franchise, scientific government, or economic theory.[1] And if this seems a little oblique, consider another pamphlet of the same period which argues directly that Socialism is implicit in the New Testament, a message that demands for all, and not just a privileged few, the 'right to the spring of God's bounty', 'to drink what is needful of the water of life.'[2] This was a tradition of writing (or rhetoric) that continued to be unashamedly explored as, for instance, in a publication by T. J. Hughes called *State Socialism after the War* which urged the creation of 'a Greater Democracy . . . Founded on the Teachings of Christ'.[3] Tawney, of course, was possibly the most influential exemplar of this latter-day Christian Socialism.[4]

Even where this specifically religious basis was lacking, to many Socialists their creed was a kind of secular ethic: it meant love and service to one's brethren rather than any mere capture of political power or administrative change. There were numerous Socialists of this sort who, like Sidney Ball, argued that the doctrine was a direct deduction from moral principles or it was nothing.[5] The Fellowship of the New Life committed itself to 'the reconstitution of Society in accordance with the highest moral possibilities' rather than attempting to change 'the merely economical aspect' of affairs. The objective was 'the cultivation of the perfect character in each and all' through the principle of subordinating 'material to spiritual things'. The contrast of emphasis was crucial and led, in fact, to a split among the 'Vitanuovans' and so the foundation of the rather differently minded Fabian Society.[6] In a similar mode, Edward

1 R. Blatchford, *The New Religion* (Clarion Pamphlet no.20; London, 1897), pp.2–3.
2. B. J. Harker, *Christianity and the New Social Demands* (London, n.d. [1892]), pp.5, 15.
3 T. J. Hughes, *State Socialism after the War: a Retrospect of Reconstruction after the War, Embracing a Greater Democracy, and Founded on the Teachings of Christ* (1916; 2nd rev. edn, London, 1924).
4 See below pp.439–62.
5 e.g. S. Ball, 'The Socialist Ideal', *Economic Review*, ix (1899), pp.425–49; also his *The Moral Aspects of Socialism* (Fabian tract no. 72; London, 1896).
6 N. MacKenzie, 'Percival Chubb and the Founding of the Fabian Society', *Victorian Studies*, xxiii (1979–80), pp.46–7, 49. And see above pp.365–7.

Carpenter's writings had a substantial effect on Socialists for whom their idealism was a form of religious belief. The South Wales Miners' Library at Swansea contains numerous copies of his works including, of course, the long Whitmanesque poem, *Towards Democracy*; and Fenner Brockway (with, I think, a more than metaphorical intention) described this book as a Bible read regularly on the propaganda outings and rambles of Socialist clubs. E. M. Forster, who knew and admired Carpenter, wrote that he was 'not interested in efficiency or organization, or party discipline, nor in industrialism'. But he undoubtedly wanted to destroy existing abuses such as landlordism and capitalism, and what he offered to replace them with was love and mysticism, a faith in the individual and the beauties of nature.[7] Another particularly good example of this form of Socialist emphasis is the writings and speeches of Bruce Glasier. He was a Socialist of the brand of William Morris and Keir Hardie's successor as editor of the *Labour Leader*. He was also one of the most important early theorists of the ILP. And for him the ideology was in no sense materialistic or just political; rather it was an ethical doctrine, a religion even. It was intended not simply to abolish poverty but rather to save the soul as well.[8] The faith was summed up in some passages from a book on *The Meaning of Socialism* which Glasier brought out in 1919:

> . . . I believe Socialism is inevitable not simply because of the economic and material factors of modern civilisation, but because also of the spiritual factors of social evolution. . . . [It] goes beyond all existing political systems, and ranks in precept with the higher religions. It belongs in ethical affirmation to the common stem from which the social idealism of religion is nourished. It defines man's duty towards man in terms of fellowship and love as well as of citizenship and justice. . . .
>
> Historically, indeed, Socialism is more closely related to religious than to political propagandism. It is from the prophets, apostles, and saints, the religious mystics and heretics, rather than from statesmen, economists and political reformers, that the Socialist movement derives the examples and ideals that inspire its noble enthusiasm and hopes today. . . . [It] means not only the socialisation of wealth, but of our lives, our hearts – ourselves. . . . [It] does not mean mere working class revolt or acquisition. . . .
>
> Socialism, in truth, consists, when finally resolved, not in getting at all, but in giving; not in being served, but in serving; not in selfishness,

7　E. M. Forster, 'Edward Carpenter' (1944), in *Two Cheers for Democracy* (1951; Penguin, 1965), pp.217–18.
8　Cf. J. R. Clynes, 'Mr. & Mrs. Bruce Glasier', H. Tracey (ed.), *The British Labour Party: its History, Growth, Policy and Leaders* (1925; new edn, London, 1948), iii.315.

but in unselfishness; not in the desire to gain a place of bliss in this world for one's self and one's family (that is the individualist and capitalist aim), but in the desire to create an earthly paradise for all. . . .

Thus . . . we see that fundamentally Socialism is a question of right human relationship and is essentially a spiritual principle.

Socialism, therefore, is religion. . . .[9]

Clearly Glasier was no political pragmatist or 'scientific' administrator of the Webbian kind: he was the sort of person to whom the poetry and the idealism were as important as – more important than – politics and economic organization.[10] It is this sort of feeling, fervour even, that has so often kept Socialism in this country alive despite all the odds. Of course, I do not mean anything so naïve and simplistic as that those whom I have so far described broadly as collectivist Socialists were completely unaffected by this kind of ethical or religious spirit. Clearly, for instance, the mystical side of Beatrice Webb's character would have been attuned to this sort of appeal, at least to some degree, even though it would be sternly subordinated in public expression of political analysis and policy. And the continuing concern of the early Fabians (or a good number of them) with ethical questions, especially those concerning the spiritual regeneration of the individual, has recently been made abundantly clear.[11] H. G. Wells, too, had his phases of spiritual mysticism about the crucial role in affairs of the 'redeemer', 'God the Invisible King', and 'the Captain of Mankind'. More than this, there could, between the social engineers and the ethical reformers, often be a notable, if sometimes superficial, affinity on specific issues.

One crucial theme to which the attention of each was frequently directed was the role of the state. The moral concern was invariably focused on the question how personal regeneration could be stimulated if individuals found their lives regimented, increasingly superintended by public authority. Someone like Sidney Webb could equally pay lip-service to this sort of difficulty and, in fact, recognize that his concern was shared by those of otherwise contrasting views. Socialism, he often used to say, does not at all imply 'a rigidly centralized national administration of all the details of life.' To believe it might mean this is 'an entire misapprehension of the Socialist position'. Moreover a society of that sort would be as abhorrent to other Socialists of the type represented by William Morris as to extreme individualists like Auberon Herbert.[12]

9 J. B. Glasier, *The Meaning of Socialism* (Manchester, 1919), pp.222, 224, 225–6, 227, 229.
10 See the study by L. Thompson, *The Enthusiasts: a Biography of John and Katharine Bruce Glasier* (London, 1971).
11 e.g. N. and J. MacKenzie, *The First Fabians* (London, 1977).
12 S. Webb, *Socialism in England* (London, 1890), pp.109–10.

Socialist publications have indeed very frequently stressed the need in pursuing reform to avoid uniformity and the frustration of spontaneity and diversity.[13] Yet, despite the protestations, Webb and those like him have not always avoided advocacy of the degree of centralization and control apparently thus repudiated. However, what is certain is that (as Webb implied in the passage just cited) a good many Socialists, as well as others, have felt a fervent hostility to the collectivist state and its works and on the sort of ground already intimated. A good early instance of this is provided by the ideas of Thomas Hodgskin who, in Halévy's study, appears as a libertarian Socialist with a practical programme heavily marked by a *laissez faire* approach. He was firmly anti-capitalist, asserting the natural right of the worker to the whole product of his labour, but he was strongly opposed to the intervention of law as a means to the end in view: the more limited government was the better.[14] Equally he rejected Owenism because it depended too much on authority; and however desirable the social and moral objectives in view, he would not countenance any educational provision that was state administered.[15]

But while it has not been utterly neglected, this moralistic or anti-statist aspect of British Socialism has not perhaps received its proper share of academic (or other) attention. There has been some comment, of course. A few years ago, for instance, Professor W. B. Gwyn of Tulane University, in a most valuable and all too brief article, did draw attention to the extent that, from the beginning, 'the British Socialist Movement has incorporated the country's libertarian tradition.'[16] He showed (and with a wealth of learned reference) how an insistence on personal freedom and a profound distrust of all organized authority, whether private or governmental, have constituted a vital strand in the Labour Party's history. In the rest of this chapter two major aspects of this often neglected type of British Socialism will be reviewed: first the Guild Socialist protest against the large-scale organization and the centralized bureaucracy and control so often implied by Fabianism; and then the more well-known moral protest against capitalism exemplified in the Christian Socialism of R. H. Tawney. Some of the main issues involved are indicated in a few entries Tawney made in his diary or 'Commonplace Book' shortly after the outbreak of the Great War. In one place he suggested that the question of future social policy might well 'turn very largely on the relation between societies and the state.' In

13   e.g. W. A. Robson, *Socialism and the Standardised Life* (Fabian tract no.219; London, 1926); W. H. Morris Jones, *Socialism and Bureaucracy* (Fabian tract no.277; London, 1949); R. H. S. Crossman, *Socialism and the New Despotism* (Fabian tract no.298; London, 1956).
14   E. Halévy, *Thomas Hodgskin* (1903; trans. edn, London, 1956), pp.45–6, 49, 169.
15   ibid., pp.37–8, 46–7, 86–7, 133–4.
16   W. B. Gwyn, 'The Labour Party and the Threat of Bureaucracy', *Political Studies*, xix (1971), pp.383–402. The citation is at p.385.

particular, in escaping from an extreme individualism (in which, he said, 'no one now believes') it was equally necessary to avoid 'pure collectivism'. Hence, he thought, the importance of some intermediate Socialist possibility like that presented by the Syndicalists or Guildsmen. The most fundamental dimension of the matter, however, concerned not politics at all but the moral question of the motives at work in the pursuit of social reform. A purely utilitarian consideration of the interests of the consumer or the worker was not enough. The English Labour movement, he thought, had made a 'tragic mistake' by aiming 'at *comfort*' instead of 'getting their *rights*, including the right to do their duty.' The result was that the contest was unfortunately 'being fought out on a low plane'.[17]

These, then, are the questions with which the Guildsmen and Tawney were concerned: the search for a proper form of organization that would avoid both anarchy and statism; and the achievement of a correct understanding of the ethical, even spiritual, principles on which an effective Socialism alone can rest.

GUILD SOCIALISM: ITS RISE AND FALL

It rose as a revolt against Fabian socialism; as a protest against collectivism; as a repudiation of the interference of the state . . . in industrial concerns.
F. J. C. HEARNSHAW, *A Survey of Socialism*, 1928, pp. 321–2

If, as often supposed, Socialism is about the abolition or control of the private ownership of the instruments of production, the question of means is obviously crucial. For industry and commerce may (to take extreme possibilities) be conducted either by an authority directly responsible to the government or autonomously by those working in the industry itself. The growth of state intervention in the former manner is one aspect of what is here called collectivism. But a fear of this form of public administration with its dangers of centralization, bureaucracy, and the substitution of one form of 'wage-slavery' for another has been an important element of certain kinds of Socialist thought. The Guild movement reflects an important aspect of this concern and is, therefore, in this sense one of the libertarian forms of Socialism.[18] In 1919 one of its periodicals, *The Guildsman*, cited with approval Chesterton's lines,

17 J. M. Winter and D. M. Joslin (eds), *R. H. Tawney's Commonplace Book* (Cambridge, 1972), pp. 79–80 (entries for 9 August and November 1914), italics in original.
18 Cf. S. T. Glass, *The Responsible Society: the Ideas of the English Guild Socialist* (London, 1966), p.1. For more recent assessments, see A. W. Wright, 'Guild Socialism Revisited', *Journal of Contemporary History*, ix (1974), no.1, pp.165–80; R. S. Barker, 'Guild Socialism Revisited?', *The Political Quarterly*, xvi (1975), pp.246–54.

> The Collectivist State
>   Is a prig and a bandit;
> It may be My Fate,
>   But I'm damned if I'll stand it.[19]

In its opposition to state intervention, as in its stress on industrial rather than political action, Guild Socialism may appear as a sort of Neanderthal offshoot in the development of modern British radicalism. Indeed it did not flourish for many years and seems overall to have had relatively little immediate impact on Labour thought and practice. Yet it may well be that the movement concerned itself with an aspect of industrial and political reform that is, after a long time in limbo, coming once again to the fore in these days of renewed discussion about workers' control and about the predicament of the individual in the face of big government. In any case, its themes were neither unprecedented nor without elaborate sophistication; and they are particularly relevant here in respect of their fundamentally moralistic and anti-statist appeal.

The Guild movement emerged, flourished, and declined during the first quarter of the present century being most active about the time of the Great War. The term 'Guild Socialism' itself appears first to have been used in 1912 in the columns of *The New Age*.[20] While its supporters reflected that moral outrage against the condition of the worker which had always been a strong part of the radical case, their views constituted at the same time a reaction against the then dominant style of British Socialist thinking. For they completely rejected the view that, as it was put by Philip Snowden in 1913, Socialism aimed at 'organising the new society through the State'.[21] They repudiated, that is, the standard belief enshrined in the policies of the Fabians, the Webbs, and the Labour programme of 1918, that it was enough to secure public control of the instruments of production and of the rent, interest, and profit they produce in order to redistribute this wealth, improve conditions of work and life, and otherwise efficiently meet the needs of the people. From the Guildsmen's point of view what was wrong with this programme was that it would undesirably augment the role of the state and as well made no provision for effective self-government in industry or for a role to be played by workers' organizations. Whatever the intention, the situation which would be produced by the standard or official Labour policies would turn out to be a 'servile state' in which the worker would face,

19 *The Guildsman* (February 1919), p.5.
20 *The New Age* (10 October 1912), pp.560–2. For this and other uses of the term, see *OED Supplement* (Oxford, 1972 ff.), i.1317.
21 P. Snowden, *Socialism and Syndicalism* (London, n.d. [1913]), p.132. Cf. A. J. Penty's attack on state collectivism, in *Towards a Christian Sociology* (London, 1923), pp.66–8.

instead of capitalist dominance, a vast collectivist bureaucracy so that he would have no more or even less influence over his working life than he did under private enterprise. He would still be alienated from his work, regarded as a factor of production, merely a 'hand' or 'living tool', rather than (as he should be) a partner.[22] Nor, of course, was this attitude confined only to Guildsmen: Sidney Ball for one had long before argued that the mere substitution of corporate for private administration is the shadow and not the substance.[23] Fundamentally the gravamen of the Guild charge was that Fabian priorities were completely mistaken. The real problem of the day was to free the labouring classes from their slavery to the wage system and the machine and this would not be done by a programme of nationalization which would leave these basic issues untackled. Failing thus to address itself to the really fundamental questions, Socialism (in the hands of the Fabians) 'degenerated into the issue of private and public ownership, and lost its way in a maze of Blue Books, statistics and detailed considerations; gas and water socialism, Poor Law, Housing Reform, etc., on the one hand, and political labourism on the other.'[24] It is a most powerful indictment.

The Guildsmen saw work as the central feature of a man's life. He was primarily a producer and so the just society was one in which he had meaningful control over this vital aspect of his existence, could make it more satisfying, and through it achieve a recognized status and a more active public role. Because a great deal of orthodox Socialist thinking at the time ignored or underestimated this aspect of things, then that thinking was sadly inadequate. Specifically there was need for a different and wider conception of freedom than that which usually prevailed. It was not enough to achieve a degree of formal political liberty, for instance by the occasional exercise of the suffrage; nor was it sufficient even that people were relieved from material cares. As one rather Rousseauistic comment suggested:

> If freedom is to mean anything to the average man it must include industrial freedom. Until men at their work can know themselves members of a self-governing community of workers, they will remain essentially servile, whatever the political system under which they live. . . . Man is everywhere in chains, and his chains will not be broken till he feels that it is degrading to be a bondsman, whether to an individual or to a State.[25]

22 National Guilds League, *National Guilds: an Appeal to Trade Unionists* (NGL pamphlet no.1; London, n.d. [1915]), p.4.
23 S. Ball, *The Moral Aspects of Socialism* (Fabian tract no.72; London, 1896), p.9.
24 A. J. Penty, *Post-Industrialism* (London, 1922), pp.31–2. Cf. ibid., p.34.
25 G. D. H. Cole and W. Mellor, *The Meaning of Industrial Freedom* (London, 1918), pp.3–4. The echoes of Rousseau in this pamphlet are numerous, Cole's edition of the *Social Contract* having been published only four years previously.

Self-government in industry was crucial, therefore, both as a logical extension of democratic practice and as the indispensable foundation of a genuinely active and fulfilled citizenry. Moreover, in tune with this emphasis, the Guildsmen were not so sure as most of their fellow Socialists were that political struggle was the correct line of advance. They tended to think more of direct action through economic warfare in industry itself. Not least this was because they were dissatisfied with the rate of reform so far achieved by normal constitutional means and felt, in particular, that the Labour Party was not really radical enough. For instance, it maintained too close a contact with the bourgeois Liberals and, after the outbreak of war, actually became a partner in government and condoned the loss of the right to strike under wartime controls.

In a nutshell, then, rather than stressing the political, the state, whether in the form of central or municipal government, the Guildsmen emphasized economic action instead and similarly urged the need for industrial democracy, control by workers as groups focused on their workplace because this was, in a real sense, the hub of a working man's life. Invariably Socialists had been concerned above all with effecting a change in the ownership of industry by its transfer to public hands; the Guildsmen wished instead to bring to the fore questions of its administration and democratic control.[26] During the Great War the National Guilds League issued a pamphlet in which the general aims of the movement were outlined. Its supporters (it was stated) had the intention to

> substitute the national service of the Guilds for the profiteering of the few; substitute responsible labour for a saleable commodity; substitute self-government and decentralisation for the bureaucracy and demoralising hugeness of the modern State and modern joint stock company; and then it may be just once more to speak of a 'joy in labour' and once more to hope that men may be proud of quality and not only of quantity in their work. There is a cant of the Middle Ages, and a cant of 'joy in labour', but it were better, perhaps, to risk that cant than to reconcile ourselves for ever to the philosophy of Capitalism and of Collectivism, which declares that work is a necessary evil never to be made pleasant, and that the workers' only hope is a leisure which shall be longer, richer, and well adorned with municipal amenities.[27]

In the remainder of this section, the Guild Socialist movement will be

26 Cf. N. Carpenter, *Guild Socialism: an Historical and Critical Analysis* (New York, 1922), ch.1.
27 National Guilds League, *The Guild Idea: an Appeal to the Public* (NGL pamphlet no.2; London, n.d.), p.17.

reviewed in a little more detail in particular in respect of the formative factors at work in its creation; the various principles, purposes, and methods it explored and advocated; and finally its decline after the Great War.

Formative factors and growth

The Guild movement emerged in the period immediately before 1914 from a flux of various forces which may conveniently be categorized as either situational or intellectual.

The main circumstantial factor was undoubtedly the period of intense labour unrest of the time. This arose out of the depression of 1907–9 and the unemployment and decline in real wages accompanying it and culminated in a great wave of strikes affecting many basic industries. The intensity of the situation is baldly reflected in the statistics. Between 1901 and 1909 the average number of working days lost each year through industrial action was 3.54 million. But the annual average for 1910 and the subsequent two years was 20.3 million reaching a peak of 40.89 million in 1912.[28] With this notable degree of industrial instability there was coupled a sense of political dissatisfaction. Towards the end of the nineteenth century the Labour movement had begun to bring political as well as industrial pressure to bear in the attempt to secure its members' interests. Among the reasons for this switch of emphasis was the failure of the great strike of 1897–8 undertaken by the Amalgamated Engineers then the most powerful union in the country. There was a growing appreciation, too, of the possibilities to be exploited not only by the organization of the recently enlarged Parliamentary electorate but also through the newly reformed local councils, not least in respect of housing, sanitation, and other such important amenities. Nationally a political alliance with the Liberal Party grew up. But then a reaction set in, some people, like the MP Victor Grayson, feeling that Labour was in danger of becoming a mere ancillary shackled to the Liberals when it should have been marking out a path of its own. Moreover (it was urged once more) this independent course ought to involve increased pressure in the economic sphere where the main strength of the movement lay. Such suggestions seemed especially cogent, too, after the Osborne judgement of 1909 by which the courts held that trade union grants to the Labour Party were illegal. This strengthened the case for eschewing the political front in favour of exerting the Labour movement's undoubtedly greater industrial power. In 1912 Alfred Orage's journal *The New Age* commented, 'since 1906 Trade Unionism has been giving political action

---

28 Figures based on table in D. Butler and J. Freeman, *British Political Facts, 1900–1967*, 2nd edn (London, 1968), p.219.

a trial, but with the failure . . . of political action, Trade Unionism may be expected to resume its industrialism'.[29] The formation in 1914 of the great 'Triple Alliance' of mining, transport, and railway workers seemed at the time to create a basis for such industrial action of very substantial strength indeed. In addition the growth of the shop stewards' movement during the war provided an appropriate rank and file organization on the factory floor to lend colour to the notion of workers' control. Such tendencies were reinforced, too, by exotic influences in the trade union field. Important here was the example provided by the federalized nature of the French union movement which emphasized local organization and control and suggested the possibility of a whole politico-economic system based on the *syndicats* and brought about by united action in a general strike. Of equal significance was the industrial unionism that had developed in the USA and which stood in contrast to the craft organization more common in Britain. There was a direct influence in that the pamphlets of Eugene Debs and Daniel de Leon were widely read in trade union circles in this country at that time. As well, Tom Mann and Ben Tillett were key figures through whom such ideas, especially influential in some areas, such as Clydeside and South Wales, were brought to bear on the British scene. It was not, of course, that Guild Socialism was simply based on these movements – Guild supporters often differed very sharply from the Syndicalists – but it did derive some impulse from them.

Yet the Guildsmen themselves were largely middle-class intellectuals outside the trade union movement and open to a wide range of other, more academic, influences that were rather more important in the formation of specific programmes and policies. Perhaps the key perspective of this more abstract kind is provided by the contemporary tendency of thought called pluralism with its emphasis on the 'group', 'corporation', or 'association'.[30] This doctrine was a reaction against two related ideas: that society was atomistic, simply a collection of discrete individuals; and that it was ruled by an absolute state power by which alone those individuals were welded together in a community. As against such views pluralists saw the state as one association among many and as having, too, only a restricted authority and range of functions. Thus Figgis, one of the leading exponents of pluralist theory, argued that the idea of absolute sovereignty, 'whether proclaimed by John Austin or Justinian, or shouted in conflict by Pope Innocent or Thomas Hobbes', is 'in reality no more than a venerable superstition' rarely true to the facts

29 *The New Age* (29 February 1912), p.411.
30 The best general surveys of pluralist thought are still K. C. Hsaio, *Political Pluralism* (London, 1927) and H. Magid, *English Political Pluralism: the Problem of Freedom and Organization* (New York, 1941).

of any given political situation. Rather 'it is as a series of groups that our social life presents itself' to individuals. And these associations, or most of them, show 'clear signs of a life of their own, inherent and not derived from the concession of the State.' It is the case that the 'State may recognize and guarantee . . . the life of these societies – the family, the club, the union, the college, the Church; but it no more creates that life than it creates the individual. . . .'[31] Of course, Figgis was arguing a special case about the independent functional life of churches as a way of defending religious autonomy; but as well the point has more general application. It could be suggested that in Britain these associations had always bulked largest in the experience of most persons moulding their lives more intimately than 'the great collectivity'.[32] What followed from this was important. As Figgis suggested, in an earlier paper on a similar theme, given the growth in the ambit of the centralized state which had been occurring over the years, it was now all the more necessary 'to secure . . . the liberty and power of self-development of *Societies* other than the State, as a counter to this collectivist enlargement.[33] Another leading theorist of pluralism, Harold Laski, similarly argued that it was essential to start political discussion with an admission that 'the allegiance of man is diverse', relating to 'a variety of interests, functional and territorial', and that the way these concerns are linked with one another 'suggests the necessarily federal character of all government.' Unless the individual has such 'fellowship to guard him' he is 'lost in a big world'. So much is this the case that the kind of polyarchy represented by group theory becomes in effect 'the real salvation for democracy.'[34]

The pluralists maintained, therefore, that the isolated individual did not exist in reality; nor did the concept of state sovereignty have any intrinsic being. It was not in 'a sand-heap' of undifferentiated individuals unrelated except to the state, but only in an 'ascending hierarchy of groups' that the personality could grow and flourish, that is, be free.[35] And the Guild Socialist easily moulded these themes to his own purpose. For example, an article published in *The Guildsman* in 1917 said that the 'economic man of the Victorian theorist was little more than an

31 J. N. Figgis, *Churches in the Modern State* (1913; 2nd edn, London, 1914), p.224. Cf. ibid., p.70. Also Figgis's *Political Thought from Gerson to Grotius, 1414–1625* (1907; Harper Torchbooks, 1960), pp.232ff.
32 Figgis, *Churches in the Modern State*, pp.47–8.
33 J. N. Figgis, 'The Church and the Secular Theory of the State' (1905), in D. Nicholls, *The Pluralist State* (London, 1975), app.A, p.139, italics in original.
34 H. J. Laski, *The Foundations of Sovereignty and Other Essays* (London, 1921), p. viii; *Authority in the Modern State* (New Haven, Conn., 1919), p.85; Laski to Holmes (22 July 1916), M. de W. Howe (ed.), *Holmes-Laski Letters: the Correspondence of Mr. Justice Holmes and Harold J. Laski, 1916–1935* (London, 1953), i.7.
35 Figgis, *Churches in the Modern State*, pp.52, 71–3, 87–9.

economic myth: the economic State of the Collectivist is a most inhuman possibility. But the economic group is an obvious reality; – and that is the measure of the hopefulness of the Group Idea.'[36] The notion may reasonably be described as libertarian in nature, resting as it did on the diffusion of authority, on the belief that freedom from centralized political control was a fundamental value that could (in Figgis's words) 'only be secured by a careful distribution of power among different bodies checking each other.'[37]

This sort of attitude was equally sustained by other recent or contemporary expressions of similar ideas expressive of the prominence of the group rather than the state. There was, for instance, the historical sense that, in the past, corporations in Britain had been supremely important, a view which found voice in commentators as varied as Toulmin Smith and Maitland; there was in particular the latter's domestication of von Gierke's analysis of the crucial legal role of the corporation as an entity as real as an individual and as having, therefore, a life and will of its own independent of the state. The concept of the group also emerged as central to certain kinds of sociology then coming into favour, as with the works of Emile Durkheim in France or A. F. Bentley in the United States. In such terms, the entire social and political process was interpreted as a matter of the interaction of groups and their interests. Likewise, associations were given a vital role in the writings of such theorists as Mary Parker Follett in the USA and Bernard Bosanquet in this country, the pluralism of the latter being married to Idealist philosophy. It is not suggested here that these specific tendencies of thought explicitly influenced the Guildsmen (though this may have been the case with some of them). Rather these indications suggest that an emphasis on the group was one of some contemporary moment. However one tendency that did have a direct impact was the so-called 'Distributist' theory associated with Belloc and the two Chesterton brothers (and which has already been referred to in an earlier chapter). Other arrays of ideas helping to form the ethos of Guild Socialism derived from the Owenite and Co-operative traditions with their stress on the self-governing workshop, factory, or store.[38]

Nor, of course, was the Guild idea unassociated with the various radical critiques of capitalism current at the time. Guildsmen usually stressed their fundamental antipathy to 'Bolshevism', though Marx's analysis of the conventional wage-system had some impact.[39] And, given

36 H. Read, 'The World and the Guild Idea', *The Guildsman* (April 1917), p.6.
37 J. N. Figgis, 'Lecture on Aquinas', notebook no.2, Mirfield MSS, cited in D. Nicholls, *Three Varieties of Pluralism* (London, 1974), p.6.
38 See the summary in H. Perkin, *The Origins of Modern English Society, 1780–1880* (1969; London, 1972), pp.384–7.
39 See e.g. M. B. Reckitt and C. E. Bechhofer, *The Meaning of National Guilds* (1918; 2nd rev. edn, London, 1920), ch.II, esp. p.8 and n.1. Also ibid., pp.212–30.

the generally pluralist emphasis of Guild theories, of all the continental Socialists, Proudhon would be the one regarded as most noteworthy because of the federalist bias of his thought; just as the Paris Commune would be seen as a precedent for or model of the small-scale co-operative commonwealth that must be reared inside the industrial system in order to reform it.[40] But more important by far in their contribution to the ethos of Guild Socialism were the aesthetic or romanticist criticisms of capitalism associated with such writers as Carlyle, Morris, and Ruskin, specifically the point made about the soullessness of modern technology, the need to emancipate man from being a drudge to the machine, and to restore proper ideals of craftsmanship. In this last connexion the medievalist reaction was of prime importance. As early as 1882, for example, Arnold Toynbee had urged that the innumerable associations created by the modern age (especially co-operative societies) ought, ideally, to be 'like mediaeval guilds, living groups of men animated by common principles of religious and industrial faith, and united for the satisfaction of the great permanent needs of human life . . . where capital and labour were associated, and competition held in abhorrence.'[41] Ruskin's Guild of St George – a sort of agricultural self-supporting commune dedicated to the simple life without machines – is a very good example of just such an attempt to renew the English promised land which, in fact, acted as a spur to the idea of communities of craftsmen. Ruskin fervently believed that 'the only proper school for workmen is of the work their fathers bred them to, under masters able to do better than any of their men, and with common principles of honesty and the fear of God, to guide the firm.'[42]

Nor were other early expressions of the Guild idea wanting. One such rather odd exposition of this alternative to state Socialism appeared in 1891.[43] But the main surge occurred over a decade after this, associated with a group of writers more effective in creating, from the array of influence described, a reasonable ideological *mélange*. Many well-known names were associated at one time or another with the Guild movement including Norman Angell, H. N. Brailsford, George Lansbury, Edwin Muir, Herbert Read, B. Russell, and R. H. Tawney. However, the writers most influential in its development were A. J.

40 For contemporary reference, see e.g. H. J. Laski, *Karl Marx: an Essay* (London, 1922), pp.11–13; J. Leatham, *The Commune of Paris: its Story and Meaning* (c.1890; 5th edn, Turriff, Aberdeenshire, n.d.), esp. pp.13–16.

41 T. S. Ashton (ed.), *Toynbee's Industrial Revolution* (1884; Newton Abbot, 1969), pp.222, 224.

42 J. Ruskin, *Praeterita* (1885–9; Oxford, 1978), pp.453–4. For discussion, see P. L. Sawyer, 'Ruskin and St. George: the Dragon-Killing Myth in "Fors Clavigera"', *Victorian Studies*, xxiii (1979–80), esp. pp.7, 11, 13.

43 See 'B.C.S.', *How to Avoid State Socialism* (London, 1891). I am indebted to Dr D. Manning of the University of Durham for drawing my attention to this curious little book.

Penty, A. R. Orage, S. G. Hobson, and G. D. H. Cole. Each showed in varying degree the influence of a medieval-inspired reformism, a dalliance with and then a rejection of Fabian collectivism, and a belief in industrial co-partnership or some scheme of functional representation and workers' control of industry. In 1906 Penty published a book *The Restoration of the Gild System* which anticipated many of the characteristic Guild Socialist theories. He subsequently said his main intention was 'to demonstrate that Collectivism is based upon a succession of fallacies' and was, therefore, 'incapable of providing a solution of our social difficulties'.[44] The following year, Orage became editor of an almost defunct journal, *The New Age*, and in due course turned it into a vehicle of radical anti-collectivist thought of the Guild kind; Hobson, despairing that the Labour Party and the Fabian Society could be used as a basis for Socialist development, began to think in other terms based on the Guild idea; and Cole became interested in Syndicalism and anti-statist political thought as an undergraduate and was converted to Guild Socialism in 1913, coming to see it as a possible middle way between Syndicalism and collectivism. Publishing profusely, Cole became perhaps the school's most prolific if not most interesting propagandist.

The first attempt to create an organization for propagating the doctrine is perhaps best seen as an offshoot of the Arts and Crafts Movement. It occurred in 1906, the year Penty's book appeared, when the Gilds Restoration League was founded. The object was to oppose commercialism in all its forms and to argue that workmen should, in matters relating to their jobs, be subject to the control of the craft to which they belonged. The same sort of idea lay behind the Fabian Arts Group which came into being the following year: it conducted discussions on such matters as 'The Limits of Collectivism' but was inevitably opposed by many other Fabians and soon abandoned. Something of the ground was prepared in this way but with no really lasting impact, and in time this early movement lost momentum and fell away.

Many leading supporters such as Penty, Reckitt, and Cole, became members of the Fabian Society and tried to use it to pursue Guild objectives. They criticized its policies and those of the Labour Party, objecting in particular to the idea of constitutional tactics as a means of achieving reform and to the strong tendency to collectivism.[45] An attempt to change the society's direction, in effect to take it over, was soundly defeated in 1915. As a result a completely separate organization, the National Guilds League, was founded on the basis of the so-called 'Storrington Document', an agreed statement of principles.[46] Like the

---

44 A. J. Penty, letter in *The New Age* (16 November 1911), p. 69.
45 Cf. *The Guildsman* (December 1916), p. 3.
46 This is reprinted in A. Briggs and J. Saville (eds), *Essays in Labour History 1886–1923* (London, 1971), pp. 332–49.

Fabian Society, the NGL was never very large, its membership in 1921 being only a little over 500. Most of these lived in London – there were otherwise only eight small provincial groups – and this proved a substantial handicap to the League's declared policy of trying to permeate with its beliefs, not so much the influential middle and professional classes, but rather the general world of trade unionism. There is, however, evidence that the Guild idea did have a certain influence on some radical members of the Labour movement. For example, a prominent Glasgow shop steward, J. M. Paton, was an active associate. In 1917 he collaborated with W. Gallacher (later a leading member of the Communist Party) in publishing, under the aegis of the Paisley Trades and Labour Council, a booklet on industrial democracy and workers' control.[47] Paton was also a prime mover in the publication of the NGL monthly magazine, *The Guildsman*, which appeared from the end of 1916 until 1923 (when, transformed by the Coles into *New Standards* and similarly dedicated to the cause of workers' control, it ran for a further year before withering from lack of support). Another union convert was Frank Hodges, secretary of the Miners' Federation, which in fact committed itself to a system of public ownership and control explicitly modelled on Guild lines.[48] William Straker, another miners' leader, was also a convinced Guild Socialist.[49] In 1921 the Union of Post Office Workers specifically adopted, as official union policy, a scheme for the postal service to be managed as a National Guild.[50] There was, too, the interesting practical trial of the doctrine in the creation of the Building Guilds after the Great War. These had some initial success both in Manchester and London where, too, a National Guild of Builders was set up. But the experiment was short-lived: changes in government policy, diffidence, difficulties in raising capital, and the like led to its demise in 1923 – and, in effect, this failure spelled the end of Guild Socialism as an organized and practical movement.[51] At the time much

47 J. Paton and W. Gallacher, *Towards Industrial Democracy: a Memorandum on Workers' Control* (1917): for an extract, see K. Coates and A. J. Topham (eds), *Workers' Control: a Book of Readings and Witnesses for Workers' Control* (1968; Panther, 1970), pp.108–11.
48 F. Hodges, 'Workers' Control', A. Gleason, *What the Workers Want: A Study of British Labor* (London, 1920), pp.169–83. Cf. Hodges's *Nationalisation of the Mines* (London, 1920), ch.viii 'Self Government'.
49 See Coates and Topham, op. cit., p.263 n.1.
50 See e.g. 'Guilds at Home and Abroad', *The Guildsman* (May, 1921), p.7; ibid., (June, 1921), p.9.
51 For the building guilds, see N. Carpenter, *Guild Socialism*, pp.118–25, 329–35; Glass, *The Responsible Society*, pp.54–6; and F. Matthews, 'The Building Guilds', in Briggs and Saville, op. cit., ch.11. Contemporary accounts include R. W. Postgate, *The Builders' History* (London, 1923), ch.18; Reckitt and Bechhofer, *The Meaning of National Guilds*, pp.278–87; A. E. Smith, 'Building Self-Government', *The Guildsman* (January 1920); and S. G. Hobson, 'The Building Guild Movement', ibid. (March 1920), pp.3–4.

was (wrongly as it happened) expected of the sort of development which had occurred in the building industry.[52] But the Guild movement probably had little general impact at the grass-roots level. I can, for instance, recall finding little or no Guild material in the collections of the South Wales Miners' Library, though there is plenty of stuff of Syndicalist or IWW provenance dating from the period concerned.

Nevertheless a great deal of effort and time was spent in propagating Guild ideas, warning against the servile state (which was seen to be fast developing), calling on all lovers of liberty to aid the overthrow of capitalism, and, generally, urging 'a constructive plan' for the creation of 'a stable Democracy, founded upon a system of National Guilds.'[53] Like the Fabians, League members organized lectures and discussions, issued propaganda leaflets and pamphlets, and sponsored the magazine already cited, *The Guildsman*. Related groups with similar ideas, like the Church Socialist League, also sprang up and not only in this country.[54] As already mentioned, *The New Age* (which had become one of the most important cultural journals of the day) devoted itself to analysis and exposition of various aspects of Guild doctrine; and while not always orthodox in this respect (for instance in its later advocacy of the Orage-Douglas credit scheme) it was undoubtedly an important agency for disseminating the movement's ideas. But the most significant means in this respect was the substantial literary output of the leading Guildsmen themselves which was extensively read.[55]

Yet, apart from common hostility to state Socialism and collectivism and formal agreement over the need for self-government in industry, there was no necessary uniformity of viewpoint expressed. Indeed a great variety of Guild opinion existed, as a self-deprecating and humorous reference in *The Guildsman* showed. In 1920 a Conservative publicist, Harold Begbie, had produced a book called *The Mirrors of Downing Street* under the pseudonym 'A Gentleman with a Duster'. Margaret Cole, suitably disguised as 'The Lady with a Dish Cloth', wrote an article for the Guild journal (then being edited by her husband and herself) entitled 'The Mirrors of Queer Street'. In it the following passage occurred with reference to the factions of the movement:

> There is not one Guild Socialism, but many Guild Socialisms. Collectivism we know and Capitalism we know. But Guild Socialism is a very Proteus. Its phases are legion, its Guilds of infinite variety. There are the all handwoven Guilds of the Middle Ages Union, the Glory-be-to-God Guilds of Mr. Reckitt, the Glory-be-to-Trotsky

52 See e.g. Carpenter, op. cit., p.110.
53 *The Guildsman* (December 1916), p.1.
54 See Carpenter, op. cit., pp.111–17.
55 See the bibliographies in Carpenter, op. cit., and Glass, op. cit.

Guilds of the new N.G.L. Executive, the esoteric bank-on-me Guilds of Major Douglas, the Guilds-and-water of Mr. Stirling Taylor. Not to mention the functional jig-saws of Mr. Cole. There is also Hobson's Choice.[56]

The NGL did indeed split on a number of issues in the period after the Great War, not least the attitude to be adopted to the social credit policy urged by Orage and to the Russian Revolution and its aftermath.[57] Similarly a range of not always wholly uniform considerations was used to sustain the movement's support for industrial democracy and its opposition to the collectivist state.

Principles, purposes, and methods

As already intimated, the array of Guild publications was considerable.[58] But the main kinds of argument adduced invariably took either an economic or political form.

There was usually accord in launching an all-out attack on capitalism and 'wagery'. The economic analysis was rather similar to that of the Fabians and based on the usual theory of rent and surplus value.[59] And although opinions later differed over the cogency and value of Major Douglas's 'social credit' scheme, one invariable point of agreement lay in the crucial argument about the freedom of the worker. In recent times he had usually been regarded as a tool subject to 'the intolerable degradation of wage-slavery': labour was simply a commodity to be bought and sold like any other article of commerce; and thus the worker was dehumanized, the more so because of modern processes of mass production.[60] In addition he had little or no control over his conditions of work and, in this and other crucial respects, was the subject of an industrial autocracy. Loss of craftsmanship and a sense of frustration and unrest alike derived from these circumstances. Similarly this sense was intensified by the pursuit of private profit in terms of which industry is carried on. Hence what was needed was a radical change in the economic structure to create an environment morally and psychologi-

56 The Guildsman (March 1921), p.3.
57 Carpenter, op. cit., pp.125–37.
58 In addition to sources subsequently cited see, for a summary view, National Guilds League, The Policy of Guild Socialism: a Statement Prepared and Issued in Accordance with the Instructions of the Annual Conference of the National Guilds League (London, 1921); and A Short Statement of the Principles and Objects of the National Guilds League (London, n.d. [1922]). Something may also be gleaned from Guild Socialism: a Syllabus for Class and Study Circles (London, n.d. [1923]).
59 A Short Statement of the Principles and Objects of the National Guilds League (an extract is cited in Reckitt and Bechhofer, pp.14–15 n.1).
60 NGL, The Guild Idea, p.7; National Guilds, p.4.

cally more acceptable and which will lead in the direction of a
functionally organized industry based on workers' control and self-
government. A cognate argument of an aesthetic kind is that good work
can never be accomplished in conditions that give no or little scope to
quality of product, taste, or pride in workmanship as opposed to
profitability.

The political case made to this general end starts from the belief that
freedom is woefully incomplete, an illusion even, so long as industrial
autocracy remains. There are two main reasons. The first is that the
political situation simply registers a given distribution of economic
power and, therefore, the pre-eminence of the industrial ruling class. 'To
talk of democratic control, either of domestic or of foreign policy, will
remain a vanity so long as the possessing few can by their economic grip
throttle the political activities of the many.'[61] The second is that any
person is substantially affected or moulded by his conditions of
employment; and so long as these remain servile, so will his political
status as citizen remain passive. Citizenship, it was said, is 'the privilege
of the free man' and 'impossible for the wage slave.'[62] It is in this context
that the Guildsman elaborates his hostility to collectivist, Webbian-type
Socialism. For this, he believes, far from freeing the worker in any real
sense, will simply place him in subjection to the 'servile state' and its
bureaucracy. And this will constitute, indeed, an autocracy all the more
powerful and effective because it is the agent of what is formally a
popular democracy. Moreover the establishment of a collectivist state –
the 'mere substitution of a public for a private master' – would not
destroy wage-slavery itself.[63] It was too little remembered that

> the largest part of a man's life is devoted to his work, and consequently
> a system of democracy which left man's working hours bureaucrati-
> cally controlled from above would give him but a partial and
> inadequate freedom. Indeed, external collective control might go far
> to stereotype production and to bind the worker in shackles of
> wrought iron.[64]

Nationalization as such, then, presents no effective solution to the basic
problem but may even worsen it.[65] So, although the traditional Socialist

---

61 NGL, *The Guild Idea*, p.9.
62 *The Guildsman*, (December 1916), p.3.
63 NGL, *The Guild Idea*, pp.10–11, 12; *National Guilds*, pp.7–8, 19; Cole and Mellor,
    op. cit., pp.3–4, 25–6 and ch.x; *The Guildsman*, (February 1917), pp.3–4; W. N.
    Ewer, 'L'état c'est l'ennemi', ibid. (March 1917), p.9; J. L. Sabisten, 'Last Notes on
    the State', ibid. (November 1917), pp.7–8. Also B. Russell, 'Why I am a Guildsman',
    ibid. (September 1919), p.3.
64 NGL, *The Guild Idea*, pp.12–13.
65 NGL, *National Guilds*, p.19.

reaction to social evil has been to invoke state action and protection, such a policy was not likely to result in any real or effective emancipation of labour.[66] If the object is 'the abolition of wagedom' (as it is) then the 'ideal' must be a society 'in which the worker shall be in a position to control the industrial forces that now enslave him.' Consequently the Guildsman seeks the destruction of the capitalist oligarchy

> which to-day controls labour, and . . . dominates society. He aims at the democratic organisation of industry as opposed to State beaurocratic [sic] control. State Control, with our present so-called representative institutions, would only be a change of masters; there would be no alteration in status. Better fed and better housed he might be, but the status of slavery would still remain. To become a free man he must win direct responsibility and control in industry. Without economic freedom political democracy is a sham.[67]

Real democracy in modern society, therefore, could not begin and end with the election of representatives to political bodies only but must also embrace effective participation in as many associations as affect the individual not least those that concern his working life. Industry like politics must be democratically governed 'from within and from below.'[68] The worker must select the managers and foremen under whom he works as he does the councillors of the town in which he lives.

The conclusions to which Guild Socialists were led by these various considerations rested on a vision of a better order of society preferable to that created by capitalism and mass technology and which, it was hoped, it would replace. One general summary of purpose ran as follows:

> . . . the industrial needs of modern England cannot be satisfied, with either justice or efficiency, unless the connection with Capitalism is cut deliberately and for ever. In its place, there is put forward the programme of National Guilds – not, however, as a Utopian panacea, but as a practical solution of the industrial problem.
>
> The idea of National Guilds is essentially constructive. It is so at the expense of the assumptions which have, for the most part, been held alike by those who accepted the present industrial system and by those who sought to reform it. It is a challenge both to the capitalist and to the Collectivist. It denies that a man's labour can justly be hired at a 'standard rate,' however high; it denies that his industrial life must be regulated by superior authority, from above or from outside; and it denies that society can be saved, or the worker set free, by the initiative in industrial affairs being transferred to the State. The establishment of

66 'Are We All Socialists Nowadays?', *The Guildsman* (December 1916), pp.6–7.
67 'Industrial Notes', ibid. (December 1916), p.8.
68 NGL, *The Guild Idea*, p.12.

National Guilds involves the abolition of the wage-system, the attainment of self-government in industry, and the modification of State sovereignty.[69]

The central feature of the new society would be the guild itself. Orage defined this as 'a self-governing association of mutually dependent people organised for the responsible discharge of a particular function of society.'[70] It would include all workers involved in any given industry whether their task ·was managerial, technical or manual, skilled or unskilled.[71] In its own sphere each guild would be autonomous and have a virtual monopoly. There would be 'industrial' guilds engaged in the various branches of transport, manufacture, and agriculture. 'Civic' (or 'civil') guilds would embrace the professions and cognate occupations. And (according to some of the Guildsmen) there would also be 'distributive' guilds to organize and oversee the retail aspects of trade.[72] Mostly these guilds, it was assumed, would be organized on a national basis though with as high a degree of decentralization as possible to regional and local levels.[73] As well, running (so to say) horizontally through a guild, there would be a 'craft' organization of those in a given trade. Throughout, 'the guiding principle must be that of industrial democracy.'[74] Each guild would be self-governing its leaders being elected by and responsible to all the personnel of the guild, except – surely a significant omission? – in the case of highly technical posts. There would be a system of indirect representation, workshop committees electing representatives to the district committee, and so upwards. Pay and other such matters would be decided – views varied – either by the guild itself or by a national congress of guilds. It was recognized in this respect that inequalities were likely to subsist for some time though the ultimate objective was to eliminate them. Disputes between guilds and matters of common interest would, it was envisaged, be settled by 'liaison' or by a system of guild congresses.[75]

Here, of course, the question of political authority and its functions emerged. The Guildsman instinctively regarded the state as a major enemy. In the pluralist way he refused to accept that it is or should be the locus of sovereignty, the overriding authority in a community of individuals. It cannot claim primacy over other groups each of which is

69 Reckitt and Bechhofer, op. cit., p.xii.
70 A. R. Orage, *An Alphabet of Economics* (London, 1917), p.53.
71 Reckitt and Bechhofer, op. cit., p.1.
72 Cf. Reckitt and Bechhofer, op. cit., pp.202–3; NGL, *National Guilds*, pp.14–15. For the application of the idea of the 'self-directing group' to the specific field of education, see NGL, *Education and the Guild Idea* (London, 1921).
73 NGL, *National Guilds*, p.9; Cole and Mellor, op. cit., p.42.
74 NGL, *National Guilds*, p.10.
75 ibid., pp.10–11: 'Notes of the Month', *The Guildsman* (March 1917), p.1.

dominant in its own sphere. In a society based on Guild principles, all would work together as partners in a functional whole under the superintendence, not too clearly defined, of some central co-ordinating agency. But what of such traditional communal functions as law and order, defence, foreign policy, the issue of currency, public health, and so forth? In fact the role conceded to a political authority varied. The NGL itself officially often spoke of working in conjunction with the state and acknowledged its general tasks in achieving the common welfare.[76] Some supporters, A. Orage and S. G. Hobson for instance, accepted the idea that there must be a supreme authority as the source of ultimate policy and co-ordination.[77] G. D. H. Cole, of course, changed his mind on this point in a well-publicized parade of vacillation.[78] One authoritative exposition thought the following, very broad, rule would be adequate to decide the details of the matter:

> *The Guilds (through the Guild Congress) shall be the final authority in all purely industrial matters, while the State (through its Parliament) is to be the final authority in all purely political affairs; matters of both political and industrial importance are to be determined by joint committees of the Guild Congress and Parliament.*[79]

Should there be a state at all? What should be the extent of its specific functions? How should it be organized? Or should it be replaced by a hierarchical series of communes which would represent producers and consumers alike? Clearly there might in the latter case be numerous occasions for clashes of interest and authority. But the problem of machinery for effective co-ordination was a vital one and could hardly be avoided. In fact the concept of the state and its sovereignty would not go away and tended to creep back into consideration. However firmly anti-statist in principle the Guildsmen were, they found it difficult to exclude an active general authority of some kind from their vision of future society.[80]

There was also a division of opinion about the precise tactics or means to be adopted to bring about the changes in society which were sought.

There was a broad measure of agreement about the initial steps which

76 e.g. NGL, 'Rules and Constitution', §2 'Objects'; *National Guilds*, p. 5.
77 e.g. A. Orage (ed.), *National Guilds: an Inquiry into the Wage System and the Way Out* (London, 1914), ch. xvi; S. G. Hobson, *Functional Socialism* (London, 1936), p. 154.
78 See the account in A. W. Wright, *G. D. H. Cole and Socialist Democracy* (Oxford, 1979), ch. iii.
79 Reckitt and Bechhofer, op. cit., p. 199, italics in original.
80 For an early comment on the monistic elements remaining in Guild theory, see E. D. Ellis, 'Guild Socialism and Pluralism', *American Political Science Review*, xvii (1923), pp. 584–96.

should be taken concerning trade unions. Their nature and purpose were in need of radical redefinition. From being simply mutual benefit societies or agencies for wage-bargaining they should explicitly become class instruments dedicated to the complete transformation of the economic and social order: 'To Revolutionary Trade Unionism the Guild Idea looks.'[81] Specifically the wider aims they should adopt were the abolition of the wage system and securing the democratic control of industry.[82] With this in mind the unions ought very substantially to increase their membership so as to include all workers in an industry or service whatever their task, thereby establishing a solid front. Equally their structure should be rationalized on industrial lines; and amalgamation and co-ordination should be encouraged to this end.[83] Again it was urged that workshop organization was crucial and needed to be greatly strengthened.[84] Reformed in these ways, the trades unions could become the basis of the new Guild society. 'The realisation of Industrial Unionism, the building-up of the whole body of Labour into one fighting force, and the utilisation of the machine so created for the securing of control are the "next steps" that the Trade Union movement must take.'[85] A resolution passed in 1920 by the National Guilds League summed up this basic policy:

> This Conference urges the workers, in order to fit Trade Unionism for the control of industry, so to proceed with the amalgamation and consolidation of Trade Unions as to link up all Unions into a single body with internally autonomous sections for the various industries and services, with provision for the full representation of various classes of workers by hand and brain, and with the workshop, or similar economic unit, as the basis of the whole system of administration and direction of policy.[86]

But beyond this more or less common ground there were very different lines of policy and action urged by varied Guild Socialist groups.

81 NGL, The Guild Idea, p.14; National Guilds, pp.4–6; Cole and Mellor, op. cit., pp.8ff.
82 Reckitt and Bechhofer, op. cit., pp.59–60; The Guildsman, (December 1916), p.8; ibid. (January 1917), p.3.
83 Reckitt and Bechhofer, op. cit., ch.IV and pp.162–3; National Guilds, pp.5–6, 16–17; Cole and Mellor, op. cit., chsIV–V and pp.40–2.
84 Reckitt and Bechhofer, op. cit., pp.96–102, esp. pp.101–2, citing J. T. Murphy, The Workers' Committee.
85 NGL, National Guilds, pp.19–20. Here, as in earlier references to 'The Miners' Next Step', ibid. p.16, there is clear reference and appeal to the nascent Syndicalism of e.g. the coal workers. Cf. too the specific appeal of another NGL pamphlet Towards a Miners' Guild (NGL pamphlet no. 3; London, n.d. [1922]), esp. pp.6–9 to the kind of belief and policy leading to self-government in the industry.
86 The Guildsman, supplement (June 1920), cited in Carpenter, op. cit., pp.199–200. Cf. The Guildsman (December 1916), p.1.

First of all there were the advocates of what was called a policy of 'supersession', that is, the complete and immediate replacement of the machinery of the capitalist state by workers' organizations.[87] This was no less than a call for the revolutionary seizure of power by the workers. Though perhaps harking back to the old Owenite and Chartist idea of a general strike or 'sacred holiday month' which (it was anticipated) would transfer the powers of government into the workers' hands, the idea was perhaps more manifestly influenced by the Communist theory of the day and modelled on Russian revolutionary practice. In contrast, more moderate and constitutionally minded Guildsmen put forward a programme of 'encroaching control', the piecemeal but cumulative invasion of the capitalist autocracy, involving the gradual dispossession of the present owners of the instruments of production with the consequent long-term undermining of their status and prestige.[88] Several phases to this process were envisaged. The trade unions (which would be the sole representatives of the workers) would first demand and strike for, not the usual goals, but a share in control.[89] The functions of shop stewards and workshop committees would be extended, foremen would be elected, and collective or group (instead of individual) arrangements for the wage contract would be established.[90] Subsequently the unions would begin – in ways that were not fully explicit – to encroach on other managerial prerogatives; and then expropriation would indicate the final transition to 'direct management' as Cole and Mellor called the objective.[91] This might involve increasing union demands on profits. It might mean nationalization, though this was put forward in some cases only, Guildsmen being naturally rather diffident about increasing collectivist elements in society. There was, of course, insistence on workers' control as an essential element of the take-over. Possibly, too, direct action might be called for and here the general strike was usually envisaged as the key weapon, though it was also recognized that a great deal of unrest would be prevented by avoiding complete confiscation and conceding some degree of compensation for assets taken over.

Thirdly there was the tactic of 'propaganda by experimentation', that is, by the setting up of guilds (like those in the building trade) which would function effectively within the framework of the existing economic system and thus demonstrate the practical feasibility of the Guild idea. It was not generally thought, however, that this particular

87 e.g. the resolution proposed at the 1920 conference of the NGL cited in Carpenter, op. cit., pp.129, 203.
88 e.g. G. D. H. Cole, *Self-Government in Industry* (1917; London, 1928), p.97; Reckitt and Bechhofer, op. cit., p.124.
89 NGL, *National Guilds*, p.18.
90 For the advantages to Guild policy of the 'collective contract' etc., see Reckitt and Bechhofer, op. cit., pp.124–8, 168–74.
91 Cole and Mellor, op. cit., pp.22.

process would by itself be adequate to transform capitalism into Guild Socialism. Local guilds of this sort were really no more than bases of propaganda and laboratories for experimentation in industrial democracy. Finally, there was the policy of credit control advocated by the Douglas-Orage group. 'Douglasism' was very different from the other Guild Socialist tactics of achievement. It envisaged the use of the funds and economic power of the unions to take over financial control of various industries, a process called 'the communalization of credit'. A 'producers' bank' would be the mechanism of the transfer of control. It would issue credit-currency based on labour power and use this to 'buy into' control of the industries concerned. Prices would also be regulated so as to be in conformity with effective demand and thus an important element in business policy would come under public regulation. Control of credit would also be the key to industrial development policy.

The main points or issues involved in Guild doctrine are thus summarized by two exponents:

> Trade Unionists are constitutional today in politics, because they are democrats; but they ought to be revolutionary in industry, also because they are democrats. There cannot be peace in industry while the undemocratic system of Capitalism remains. . . . Only when the control of industry is in the hands of public-spirited National Guilds can there be industrial peace. . . . Guild principles of social order have been generally understood to demand decentralisation and a high degree of local initiative; independence of control from the central political authority for movements and associations of a spontaneous and democratic origin; suppression of capitalist systems of wage remuneration; repudiation of systems of 'scientific management' based on a regimentation from above of the 'human machine' by alleged experts; an effort to escape from a purely quantitative production in the direction of subordinating the machine to the man who is at present its slave; and, most [central] of all, the attempt to found an industrial democracy on a Labour discipline self-imposed and a wide area of choice and control for the individual worker through his own associations, independent of outside interference. Guildsmen may have differed about the stress they thought fit to throw upon these various elements of their 'idea,' but they would scarcely have denied the vital importance of all of them.[92]

Decline

During the wartime years and after, conditions were quite favourable to

92 Reckitt and Bechhofer, op. cit., pp.152, 217–18.

the reception of these Guild ideas. The young intellectual of the day often found them appealing.[93] Certainly contemporary Conservative literature, too, often treated Guild Socialism as a political phenomenon worthy of serious examination and careful criticism.[94] And, of course, the Syndicalist agitation of pre-war days had had some effect; the shop stewards' movement had flourished during the war and many workers' committees had developed, especially in the engineering industry. As well the Whitley Council scheme was worked out and applied though in a rather patchy way. The idea of joint control or workers' participation of some kind was being canvassed as part of proposals for publicly-owned industries such as the railways and mines. The Guildsmen were often critical in detail of all these developments which were nevertheless part of an environment in which their ideas could flourish and expect to have some influence. Penty thus ascribed the contemporary appeal of the Guild point of view not so much to the detailed theories themselves but rather to their appropriateness. In 1919, for instance, he wrote that the

> Guild idea is successful because it is in harmony with the popular psychology. It attacks the wage system and directs attention to the danger of the Servile State – evils with which every working man is familiar – while it presents him with a vision of a new social order in which he may take pleasure in his work.[95]

The contemporary outcry against profiteering and a demand for just price and wage levels were, Penty believed, equally the instinctive cry of the working man for what is, in effect, the Guild ethos. In fact 'the Trade Union Movement and the movement against profiteering are the upper and nether millstones between which capitalism is going to be ground and the Guilds restored.'[96]

But there were (as already intimated) diversities of opinion and attitudes within the movement which were ultimately destructive, differences about the Russian Revolution, social credit, and the proper tactics to be adopted by the trade unions. There were further factors, too, that weakened the position of the NGL as a whole. It had suffered a series of domestic financial difficulties. The failure of the Building Guilds experiment dealt a shattering blow; as did, in effect, the political success of the Labour Party with its Fabian-based programme in the 1922 election and after. Moreover the traditional trade union movement

93 See e.g. L. Robbins, *Autobiography of an Economist* (London, 1971), pp. 56–8, 65–6; C. H. Rolph, *Kingsley: the Life, Letters and Diaries of Kingsley Martin* (London, 1973), pp. 69–71.
94 e.g. M. G. Cowan, *Guild Socialism Popularly Stated and Examined* (NUA no. 2155; London, 1923).
95 A. J. Penty, *A Guildsman's Interpretation of History* (London, 1920), p. 299.
96 ibid., p. 300.

proved very resistant to change along the industrial lines envisaged. For one thing the old craft unions were very strong, and for another the tendency to amalgamation into general unions (as with the TGWU and the NUGMW) indicated a crucial development along non-industrial lines; in fact, the idea of an all-inclusive industrial union has all along been strongly resisted in particular by clerical, technical, and similar workers. Again, the General Strike of 1926 showed the substantial limitations which then existed on the power of the unions and how far short they fell in their ability to impose their will on the territorial government. An obvious implication was that reform would have to be fought for in the political way. There was also the realization that the attempt to achieve the industrial arrangements desired might have an untoward effect on economic efficiency and so on living standards.[97] Moreover, was the argument in favour of industrial self-government as watertight as the Guildsmen assumed? Given the nature of modern industry, its large and often very technical problems, would workers be as interested or as capable as usually supposed? Further, would not key decisions have to be taken at several removes from the shop floor thereby severely limiting the scope for self-government at local or grass-roots level? Would workers mind this? Are they not more interested in their leisure, say, than in irksome participation? How far is such self-government really possible when national planning of income and investment requires highly centralized control? Would not worker participation prove in practice to be just as distant and passive as the elector's role in the political field? And would not the real power fall, as there, into the hands of a few representatives and officials? This sort of considerations suggests the likelihood of a state of affairs a long way from the active democracy the Guildsmen anticipated.[98] There was, too, a lot of hostility in the Labour movement itself which the Webbs summed up in their remark that the 'plain truth is that Democracies of Producers cannot be trusted with the ownership of the instruments of production in their own vocations' not least because they will tend to become sectional vested interests.[99] As well the development of the public corporation with no representational element, and which was accepted by the Labour Party as the appropriate means of nationalized control, further diminished the relevance of the Guild appeal. The TUC asserted the need for unions to maintain their independence of these nationalized executives thus paralleling the position in private industry. Joint consultation is the most that was anticipated or, usually, demanded in practice.

97 Cf. Glass, op. cit., pp. 59–60, 65.
98 ibid., pp. 62–3, 65.
99 S. and B. Webb, *A Constitution for the Socialist Commonwealth of Great Britain* (London, 1920), p. 156. Cf. B. Webb, *My Apprenticeship* (1926; Penguin, 1938), ii. 427; *Diaries 1924–1932* (London, 1956), pp. 92–3.

Perhaps, as Dr Glass suggests, Guild Socialism was as much a protest (in the spirit of Morris and Ruskin) against the scale and nature of modern industry as it was against its form of organization whether capitalist or state controlled. 'In their innermost hearts many of the guild socialists disliked modern industry and modern life' as such.[100] Hence, perhaps, the movement's failure and the apparently anachronistic nature of its ideas, looking to the recurrence of an impossible local, small-scale, medieval past free from the nightmare of modern technology – or at least something as close to the older ideal as possible?[101]

And yet, is the Guild vision really so outmoded or its analysis entirely irrelevant today? If the practical impact of the movement was small, it created an ambitious ideal: 'that of a decentralized social structure embodying industrial as well as political democracy, which had as its purpose the diffusion of social responsibility over as many people as possible.'[102] It necessarily involves the acceptance of a high sense of duty. As Tawney had said in *The Acquisitive Society*: 'The workers cannot have it both ways. They must choose whether to assume the responsibility for industrial discipline and become free, or to repudiate it and continue to be serfs.'[103]

THE CHRISTIAN SOCIALISM OF R. H. TAWNEY

> I always think of him as *the* Democratic Socialist *par excellence*. . . . 'The most distinguished economic historian of his generation', by far the greatest force in adult education in the twentieth century, the leading socialist philosopher of our time. . . .
> H. GAITSKELL in TAWNEY, *The Radical Tradition*, Penguin, 1966, pp. 221, 223

Tawney was indeed much admired in all wings of the Labour movement, and, I believe, still is. So, even allowing for the inevitable hyperbole of the occasion, the sort of assessment cited in the above epigraph is at least prima facie evidence that his name must find a place in the pantheon of British Socialism.[104] This remains the case even though Tawney was

100 Glass, op. cit., pp. 64–5.
101 Cf. the account by A. Quinton of other contemporary rejections of mass urban industrialism in favour of the simple rural life, in C. B. Cox and A. E. Dyson (eds), *The Twentieth-Century Mind: History, Ideas, and Literature in Britain* (London, 1972), i.129. See also the similar strains in certain forms of nationalism, referred to in vol. iii, *A Much-Governed Nation*, ch. 3.
102 Glass, op. cit., p. 69.
103 R. H. Tawney, *The Acquisitive Society* (1921; London, 1943), p. 201.
104 Cf. M. Cole's judgement that *The Acquisitive Society* was probably the most powerful of all post-war appeals for Socialism, *The Story of Fabian Socialism* (London, 1961), p. 187; and H. Daltons praise of Tawney's *Equality* in his *Practical Socialism for Britain* (1935; London, 1936), ch. xxxi esp. p. 320 n. 1. Also the comments of T. Parsons, 'In Memoriam: Richard Henry Tawney (1880–1962)',

obviously not, in any but the vulgar sense, a philosopher; and even though, on an impartial consideration, his title to doctrinal pre-eminence might easily be challenged by others. His biographer, R. Terrill, concedes that Tawney 'was not an abstract thinker of high quality'; and an ideological critic like Ernest Benn regarded him as 'a wholly unpractical and inexperienced visionary'.[105] I suppose I should confess at once that I have never myself found Tawney a particularly attractive figure or his writings as impressive as they are usually held to be, believing indeed that they are derivative in important points. But I never had the good fortune to meet him or even hear him lecture; and my opinion (or prejudice) is thus derived solely from his books and articles and what has been written about him. In this regard I was most intrigued by a recent correspondence in the *Times Literary Supplement* on his character and reputation, arising from a comment that had been made to the effect that his work was much overpraised and contained a notable element of meanness. After a plunge into Tawney's writings, I had resurfaced with a definite sense of this myself: and still retain it *pace* the defence offered by his supporters.[106]

Like so many of his fellow Radicals, Tawney's background was conventional and prosperous enough.[107] Born in India he later went to Rugby and, in 1899, to Balliol where the influence of philosophical idealism was still strong. Tawney specifically acknowledged the effect of this intellectual *ambiance*.[108] Of particular importance in this regard were the theological and social doctrines of Bishop Gore who had been a student of T. H. Green and whose notion of a socially conscious Christianity became the guiding theme of Tawney's practical and intellectual career.[109] On the advice of Edward Caird (also a friend and

---

American Sociological Review, xxvii (1962), p.890; P. Foot, *The Politics of Harold Wilson* (Penguin, 1968), p.33; and S. Williams, *Politics is for People* (Penguin, 1981), pp.23–4. Tawney's considerable influence on Gaitskell is indicated in P. M. Williams, *Hugh Gaitskell: a Political Biography* (London, 1979), pp.21, 42, 71–2, etc.

105 R. Terrill, *R. H. Tawney and His Times: Socialism as Fellowship* (Cambridge, Mass., 1973), p.10; E. Benn, *The Confessions of a Capitalist* (1925; 12th edn, London, 1932), pp.176–7.

106 See the comment and letters in the *TLS* (21 January–18 March 1977); also the even more extreme opinion of E. Welbourne, cited in M. Cowling, *Religion and Public Doctrine in Modern England* (Cambridge, 1980), pp.67, 69.

107 The biographical details which follow are based on T. S. Ashton, 'Richard Henry Tawney, 1880–1962', *Proc. Brit. Acad.*, xlviii (1962), pp.461–82; J. R. Williams *et al.*, *R. H. Tawney: a Portrait by Several Hands* (London, 1960); and Terrill, op. cit., part one.

108 M. Richter, *The Politics of Conscience: T. H. Green and His Age* (London, 1964), p.294 and n.4 (p.400).

109 For a specific acknowledgement of this influence and that of William Temple, see Tawney's 'A Note on Christianity and the Social Order' (1937), in *The Attack and Other Papers* (London, 1953), p.167 n.1.

apostle of Green's, and then Master of Balliol), Tawney and his friend
Beveridge went, on leaving Oxford, to the Toynbee Hall University
Settlement, a sort of social studies and educational centre in the East End
of London.[110] The Warden at the time, Canon S. A. Barnett, was devoted
to the practical application of Christian principles in the cause of moral
and social reform. He was the author of a work on *Practicable Socialism*
and active in promoting the provision of educational facilities for the
poor, the improvement of working-class housing, and suchlike causes. It
was he who reinforced Tawney's propensity in this respect and
influenced his choice of a career. So a little later Tawney began work as a
teacher in the field of adult education and at the University of London.
He was long one of the stalwarts of the WEA and a pioneer of the extra-
mural class; and in the other context had a most distinguished record as
an economic historian. He also became increasingly involved in public
and political affairs. For example, he served as a member of the Sankey
Commission on the coal industry (1919) and the Hadow Committee on
secondary education (1926); he helped formulate the Education Act of
1918 and had a major effect on the development of Labour Party
educational policy.[111] He was involved, too, in various Church organizations concerned to revitalize Christianity for new social tasks. Thus
while still in the army during the Great War, he became a member, with
Bishop Gore, of a committee set up by the Archbishop of Canterbury to
explore the application of Christian principles to industrial problems.[112]
He had joined the Fabian Society in 1906 and, three years later, the ILP.
Several times he stood, unsuccessfully, as a Parliamentary candidate in
the Labour interest. His position in the movement generally was such
that in 1928 he was largely responsible for drafting the Labour Party's
new programme presented in *Labour and the Nation*.[113] He visited China
and was much concerned with that country's problems. During the
Second World War he briefly served as a Labour attaché at the British
embassy in Washington. He had a successful secondary career as a
journalist with the *Manchester Guardian* as his main forum. Overall the
amount of writing of various kinds that he produced up to his death in
1962 was very considerable indeed.[114]

110 J. M. Winter, *Socialism and the Challenge of War: Ideas and Politics in Britain,
    1912–18* (London, 1974), p.69. On Toynbee Hall, see A. Toynbee, *Acquaintances*
    (London, 1967), pp.22–3.
111 See R. S. Barker, *Education and Politics, 1900–1951: a Study of the Labour Party*
    (Oxford, 1972), index *sub* 'Tawney'.
112 Report of Archbishop's Fifth Committee of Inquiry, *Christianity and Industrial
    Problems* (1918): this radical document and the associated Life and Liberty Move-
    ment are discussed by Winter, op. cit., pp.172–5; cf. Terrill, op. cit., p.58. The goal
    was reform of the Church, disestablishment, and a fundamental shift in social
    attitudes.
113 C. L. Mowat, *Britain Between the Wars, 1918–1940* (1955; London, 1968), p.350;
    Terrill, op. cit., p.63.
114 See the bibliography of over 570 published items in Terrill, op. cit., pp.287–313.

Tawney was sure that the basic impulse behind the British Socialist movement had been moral and spiritual. And the ethos of his own political writings was in fact closely related to his Christian beliefs. Talcott Parsons correctly noted, in his memorial tribute, that Tawney 'was above all a moralist' and that the grounding of his moralism 'was directly and self-consciously religious.'[115] Indeed, Tawney's own continued insistence on this intimate connexion between religiosity and Socialism estranged many of his fellow ideologists.[116] But he bluntly refused to accept that the character of Socialism was summed up in the pages of the *Communist Manifesto* and *Das Kapital* – or in the Fabian tracts for that matter. Indeed his early political thought constitutes nothing so much as a powerful critique of both these streams of Socialist thinking. Late in his life Tawney himself provided a view of the tradition of Christian ideas to which he was then so indebted. In an essay on 'Religion and Economic Life', written in 1956, he asserted that Christian thinkers have been unable to exclude daily life from the purview of their faith and so have always tried 'to formulate its doctrines in terms designed to bring not only personal character and conduct but counting-house, market-place and workshop within its all-embracing scope.' This was certainly true, he thought, of the 'formidable edifice of speculation, precept, and law' developed by the anti-capitalist religious theorists of the Middle Ages. It was true also of other similar instances of Christian protest:

> the agreeably intemperate fulminations launched by the Reforming children of light against usury, land-grabbing and extortionate prices; the campaign of the followers of Calvin to repress the sin of covetousness by a discipline more remorseless than that which they had overthrown; the disquisitions on commercial morality with which, far into the next century, Puritan theologians continued to edify the elect; the rules for wary walking in business Vanity Fairs enjoined by certain sects – such, in their different styles, are cases in point. The efforts, after the great divide of the Industrial Revolution, of the spokesmen of different denominations to indicate principles of social justice relevant to the new environment created by it are younger members of the same prolific family.

He agreed that the significance to be attached to all this is fair matter for debate. But, he concludes, 'a literature so extensive, and sometimes so learned and acute, cannot be summarily dismissed.' For, whatever 'its aberrations and *lacunae*, it forms a characteristic chapter of religious and political thought.'[117] Seen in this context, Tawney's view of Socialism

115 T. Parsons, loc. cit., p.888. Cf. Williams, op. cit., p.25.
116 Ashton, art. cit., p.479.
117 Tawney, 'Religion and Economic Life', *TLS* (6 January 1956), p.xiv. Cf. the

could never be one which primarily stressed efficiency, the symmetry of a perfect social machine, or even abundance. Rather its emphasis was inevitably spiritual or ethical, emphasizing instead a right order of social relationships based on human fellowship. It involved the demonstration of that social purpose which was 'inherent in the Christian conception of life and of man's duty.'[118] Not, of course, that this was a new emphasis in the context of British Socialism but Tawney helped to give it an academic imprimatur and an historical foundation and so a powerful contemporary stimulus.[119]

The nature of his thought as a whole is best explored by looking, first, at the journal he wrote before the Great War when he was in his early thirties and in which the religious basis of his political creed is manifest: certainly no discussion of his ideas which ignores this dimension can be adequate or complete. Then, secondly, by reviewing in this framework his major and explicitly political tracts and statements. In this sense his ideas occur in two phases though, as Dr Winter has quite correctly said, the 'stability of Tawney's outlook is its most striking characteristic.' His writings after 1918 'bear the same distinctive marks of the moral approach to socialism which he had outlined a decade earlier'.[120]

The spiritual basis

In the diary or 'Commonplace Book' which Tawney kept in the years before the outbreak of the Great War, he reflected on that social ferment and industrial unrest which (as noted in the preceding section) was so serious a feature of the time. It was always evident, even on the basis of his published work, that his ideas were founded on a sincere and fervent acceptance of the essential truth of Christian doctrine. The new data made available by the recent publication of this pre-war journal considerably reinforce this understanding and, as well, make clearer the particular nature of Tawney's beliefs in this regard. It never was appropriate to see, say, his case for equality in merely secular terms: it is now quite unreasonable.

The main thrust of the analysis in this diarial record is that social and political problems are the outcome of a moral deficiency in individuals. These difficulties cannot simply be attributed, therefore, to such forces as class division or political antagonism. Equally they cannot be effectively

---

exploration of a 'distinctively Christian way of life' and its relation to 'capitalist civilisation' in *The Attack*, ch.12.

118 M. Shock, 'R. H. Tawney', *The Listener* (3 November 1960), p.777.

119 Cf. A. J. Penty's stress that all the great social and political principles are to be found in the Gospels, as in his *Towards a Christian Sociology* (London, 1923), pp.15–16, 27, 35, 39–40, 45, etc.

120 Winter, *Socialism and the Challenge of War*, p.284.

overcome merely by the application of some administrative device, the extension of state control, or the passage of a new law. It was not that Tawney regarded these practical possibilities as unimportant. On the contrary, he paid a great deal of attention to them. He certainly believed that social and industrial arrangements were by no means beyond the reach of improvement which should without doubt be sought in all feasible ways. However, in the last resort, all this was simply palliative, a merely external expedient, and could not in itself achieve a fundamental cure which depended on prior ethical advance. Always, therefore, genuine social progress and the proper and ultimate context of political judgement alike rest on the spiritual insight of Christian morality.[121]

These themes are easily exemplified from the entries in this journal.

It is manifest throughout its pages that Tawney accepted implicitly and without question the existence of God whose immanence was vividly real and personally revealed. The 'consciousness of contact' with a divine being Tawney wrote,

> is a fact of direct experience infinitely more immediate than reflection on an absent but existing person, and analogous to the consciousness of the presence of a person in the same room as oneself, whom one is not a[t] the moment looking at, and with whom one communicates nonetheless easily on that account.[122]

Coupled with this belief in an omnipresent power was an acute sense of personal sin, of 'wickedness in oneself' that could not be overcome by willing. It was the feeling that whatever state of 'goodness' individuals have reached 'is a house built on piles driven into black slime and always slipping down into it unless we are building day and night.'[123] The image is vivid if unpleasant, not to say morbid; but in fact the sense of a permanent element of sin in human life never left Tawney.[124] Always he saw mankind as perpetually involved in an intense struggle for regeneration and salvation. And it was because this endeavour is essentially internal and spiritual in nature that the outcome could only be affected in a limited, even superficial, way by political manipulation or social engineering. Ethical disorders required ethical remedies so that the administrative tinkering or even legislatively induced revolution of the sort beloved by state Socialists would not necessarily help at all.[125]

121 Cf. J. M. Winter and D. M. Joslin (eds), R. H. Tawney's Commonplace Book (Cambridge, 1972), intro., pp.xix–xx (subsequently referred to in this section as Commonplace Book); Winter, Socialism and the Challenge of War, p.75.
122 Commonplace Book, pp.78–9 (12 July 1914). It is interesting to compare the strikingly similar passage in H. G. Wells, Mr. Britling Sees It Through (1916; London, 1933), pp.266–7.
123 Commonplace Book, p.15 (10 June 1912).
124 See e.g. The Attack, p.175.
125 Cf. Commonplace Book, pp.17–19 (22 June 1912), pp.62–7 (29 July 1913).

Given this point of view, it is not surprising that – whatever degree of agreement there might be on particular proposals for change – Tawney could never be wholly at one with the Fabians or Marxists. He would inevitably feel that they were too materialistic, too morally glib and superficial. He admired the Webbs greatly in many ways but also feared the implications of their sort of opinions. One thing that long worried him, in an echo of Belloc's concept of the 'Servile State', was the possibly autocratic consequence of welfare reforms: 'However the socialist ideal may be expressed, few things could be more remote from it than a herd of tame animals with wise rulers in command.'[126] Again, he said in 1954 (at a Fabian dinner, no less) that he could not understand the pundits who expected people to live happily 'in the paralytic paradise promised by' Fabians. He thought too many of them were enamoured of their political system for its own sake; and added, with a touch of *lèse-majesté*, 'One whom I revere, Beatrice Webb, once froze my blood by remarking casually that what she most desired was to establish for the benefit of her long-suffering fellow countrymen what she called "a regimen of mental and moral hygiene."' He could not agree either with Sidney Webb that political society was only a sort of machine to be adjusted.[127] This indicated another point of concern that had been with him from the beginning. Tawney felt that under Fabian influence, British Socialism had (in the period prior to the Great War) become merely 'a series of minute readjustments of social arrangements in the interests of the working classes' instead of what was really needed, 'a new conception of social justice'.[128] They 'tidy the room, but they open no windows in the soul.'[129] Being concerned with 'the manipulation of forces and interest', the reforms usually envisaged could have no profound effect, the real disorder, of course, being 'the absence of a moral ideal.' To try to cure this merely by politics is like making a 'surgical experiment on a man who is dying of starvation or who is poisoned by foul air.' Again he remarked that

> Too much time is spent today upon outworks, by writers who pile up statistics and facts, but never get to the heart of the problem. That heart is not economic. It is a question of *moral relationships*. This is the citadel which must be attacked – the immoral philosophy which underlies much of modern industry.[130]

126 Speeches given on various occasions, Tawney MSS, LSE, cited in Terrill, op. cit., p.155. Cf. Tawney, *The Radical Tradition: Twelve Essays on Politics, Education and Literature* (1964; Penguin, 1966), p.176.
127 Tawney MSS, cited in Terrill, op. cit., p.191.
128 Winter, *Socialism and the Challenge of War*, pp.83–4; and, citing the Tawney-Vivian papers f.26, ibid., p.85.
129 *Commonplace Book*, p.51 (6 February 1913).
130 ibid., p.9 (6 May 1912), p.56 (26 March 1913), italics in original.

Even if all industry were collectively owned, as the Fabian type of reformer urges, selfishness and the concern with money and with the power it brings would remain: 'supposing unearned incomes, rents, etc. are pooled, will . . . the world, with its present philosophy, do anything but gobble them up and look up with an impatient grunt for more? That is the real question.'[131] No social change, therefore, can be basically worthwhile without a prior advance in people's attitudes, a new philosophy. 'A good law', he wrote, 'is a rule which makes binding objectively conduct which most individuals already recognize to be binding subjectively.'[132] He elaborated the point as follows:

> What I mean by society needing a philosophy is this. No machinery, whether of the state or minor corporation, can apply ideas which do not exist in society. They must always act at second hand. They must always be fed from without. All that a statute can do is to reduce a philosophy (important or trivial) into sections which are sufficiently clear to be understood even by lawyers. Hence the great days of a Parliament are when there is outside Parliament and in society a general body of ideas which Parl[iamen]t can apply. It has no *creative force*. There *is* no creative force outside the ideas which control men in their ordinary actions. There is no *deus ex machina* who can be invoked though men are always trying to discover one. Nor is the modern futility of Parliament due to mechanical difficulties, which can be removed by mechanical remedies, such as revolution. It is due to the absence of any general accepted philosophy of life. Our principal task is to create one.[133]

The ideological question becomes one, therefore, of making people realize their ethical inadequacy and showing them how to 'objectify' morality.[134] And, as part of his general nexus of religious belief, Tawney held that there existed a real and absolute standard of truth and conduct, a sort of divine or natural law premeditated on a 'transcendental, religious, or mystical' basis. It was by this criterion that not only personal conduct was to be judged, but social injustice and political oppression discerned. And the crucial task of the social reformer was to 'deepen' the 'individual sense of sin' as a step towards the objectification of morality. This sentiment is to be related to the passage in the *Commonplace Book* in which Tawney suggested that the world should be brought to an understanding of its moral duty like 'a miserable sinner, flying from the city of Destruction' and to establish '"rules of life which are approved as

131 ibid., p.61 (22 July 1913).
132 ibid., p.66 (29 July 1913). Cf. ibid., p.46 (2 December 1912), pp.58–9 (6 July 1913).
133 ibid., p.76 (16 June 1914), italics in original.
134 Cf. 'Plan of a Book', ibid., p.9 (6 May 1912).

just by the conscience of mankind".' So, 'the first step towards an improvement in social life is to judge our social conduct by strict moral standards.'[135] Nor are these standards merely abstract but to be seen in fact in a concrete and rather Burkeian way as 'the common property' of Christian countries, as implicit in 'the experience of life in all the principal nations of Western Europe'.[136]

To come to the particular point, therefore, capitalist society stood accused not because it was inefficient or wasteful (though it was in important respects) but because its arrangements were, by the standard Tawney had in mind, morally wrong.[137] It was impugned because it used men as means instead of regarding them as ends; it left so many people ignorant, poor, distressed, and thus unable to lead full lives or, as the jargon went, to fulfil their personality; it placed a premium on selfishness and the pursuit of gain thereby condoning all sorts of untoward conduct; and it led to a hierarchical social structure based on class differences and wage slavery.[138] And for Tawney, the gravamen of the charge against such inequality was that it was sinful: 'economic privileges must be abolished, not, primarily, because they hinder the production of wealth, but because they produce wickedness.' Functionless differences of treatment must always be denied as evil. But such a view could ultimately only be sustained on the basis of belief in a God in whose eyes all men were equally insignificant and alike the children of sin. Tawney is quite blunt about this: 'In order to believe in human equality it is necessary to believe in God.'[139] An effective ethic is just as impossible without the same foundation:

> The essence of all morality is this: to believe that every human being is of infinite importance, and therefore that no consideration of expediency can justify the oppression of one by another. But to believe this it is necessary to believe in God. To estimate men simply by their place in a social order is to sanction the sacrifice of man to that order. It is only when we realize that each individual soul is related to a power above other men, that we are able to regard each as an end in itself. . . . The social order is judged and condemned by a power transcending it.[140]

Given this sort of emphasis it is obvious that, for Tawney, Socialism

135 ibid., p.9 (6 May 1912), p.18 (22 June 1912), pp.30–1 (18 September 1912), and pp.64–5 (29 July 1913).
136 ibid., p.31 (18 September 1912).
137 ibid., pp.70–1 (3 December 1913).
138 ibid., p. 10 (6 May 1912). Cf. ibid., p.13 (10 June 1912), pp.34–5 (6 June 1912).
139 ibid., p.53 (6 March 1913), p.61 (22 July 1913). Cf. ibid., p.43 (30 October 1912), and Winter, *Socialism and the Challenge of War*, pp.88–9.
140 *Commonplace Book*, pp.67–8 (13 August 1913).

must be a doctrine founded on a sense of the need for a moral regeneration in the individual and thereby on the radical reconstruction of human relationships. Nor, of course, was this merely an early view not sustained in the more mature phases of life. In 1952 he was still of opinion that the basic impulse behind British Socialism had thus been 'obstinately and unashamedly ethical.'[141]

This, then, was broadly the Christian- and morality-based approach to political and social change that Tawney was working out in the years immediately before the Great War. Tawney served in that war, and was wounded in action on the Somme: he was never a mere pacifist (though typically he chose to serve as what might be called a gentleman-ranker). Nor was the period of hostilities without effect on the emphasis of his political ideas. As one result, while the ultimate purpose of moral regeneration remained the same for him, was indeed strengthened, his recognition of the importance of specific social reform engineered by state action became more explicit and positive. Of course, this element had always been present, as his long-standing interest in educational matters witnesses. But the war widened the possibilities and the importance he attached to them, preparing him to accept a very substantial measure indeed of government control and thus to go a long way in a collectivist direction to aid the nation's aims and its survival.[142] Nor could he overlook the needs of social reconstruction which, along with the defeat of German militarism, was the other side of the coin of war purpose. For instance, the war effort could not be optimized without engaging the support and loyalties of the Labour movement and this would only be achieved if the working classes could be persuaded that the war could be a powerful vehicle for social change.[143] As the fighting dragged on, Tawney, like so many, felt a disenchantment with its course and prospects. But the general impact remained: social and political relationships could never be the same again. In a contribution to a symposium published in 1918, he wrote:

> The England of 1920 will differ from that of 1914, not merely because it has passed through a new Industrial Revolution, but because of a new quality in its moral and intellectual atmosphere. Partly as the culmination of movements at work in all European countries before 1914, partly as the result of the development of

141 'British Socialism Today' (1952) in The Radical Tradition, p.176. Cf. 'Social Democracy in Britain', ibid., p.146. This piece originally appeared as a chapter in a symposium edited by Bishop W. Scarlett, The Christian Demand for Social Justice (New York, 1949).

142 Winter, Socialism and the Challenge of War, pp.167–9, citing a memorandum Tawney helped to write late in 1916 for submission to D. L. George (which is printed in Tom Jones, Whitehall Diary, ed. K. Middlemass [London, 1969–71], i.3–5).

143 Winter, op. cit., p.169.

thought in the forcing-house of war, the world has been prepared, side by side with the practical innovations in its industrial organization, for a revolution in the standards by which industrial and social life are judged. Not merely the facts, but the minds which appraise them, have been profoundly modified. . . .[144]

The war, therefore, encouraged the view that social reform might be, must be, most radical. It was in this spirit that Tawney now accepted 'the tactical primacy of parliamentary socialism', and, for instance, played a crucial role in formulating the Labour Party's educational policy.[145]

Yet despite this increasing political and practical involvement, Tawney's purpose or end was always a moral, indeed religious, one and this is clearly reflected in his post-war writings. Of course, there is an important difference of emphasis between the style and content of the pre-war *Commonplace Book* and the major works appearing in the decades after 1918. The former is self-searching, introspective, concerned fundamentally with sin and morality; the latter are analyses of specific passages in modern economic and social history or of certain aspects of contemporary arrangements that, in Tawney's view, demand reform. Nevertheless the later studies presuppose, and may be seen to exemplify in particular and important aspects, the conceptions of morality and divine justice in which he had come to believe and which are, often so starkly, reflected in the pages of the diary.

The point may be developed, first, by showing how Tawney himself placed the argument of his published works of history and theory on a broad moral and religious basis. Then, secondly, by indicating the way he explored the major themes deriving from this foundation.

Exemplification

A crucial part of the case Tawney makes in *The Acquisitive Society*, first published in book form in 1921, is that adequate discussion of social issues and political arrangements must have recourse to principles of an ethical, indeed Christian, kind, and that, if they are to be stable and satisfactory, institutions must reflect such a proper scale of values.[146] The kind of political doctrine he is interested in implies that society is not just an 'economic mechanism' but rather a community of wills capable of being inspired by devotion to common ends: it is, therefore, a 'religious' doctrine.[147] It follows that the Christian Church must be urged to

144 Tawney, 'The Conditions of Economic Liberty', *The Radical Tradition*, pp.101–2. This essay originally appeared in S. J. Chapman (ed.), *Labour and Capital after the War* (London, 1918).
145 Winter, op. cit., pp.175–6; Barker, *Education and Politics*, e.g. pp.36–7, 41–5.
146 R. H. Tawney, *The Acquisitive Society* (1921; London, 1943), e.g. pp. 3, 93, 225–6, 241.
147 ibid., p.227.

rediscover and reassert its responsibilities in the application of its principles to the conduct of life, in particular in respect of the need to impose limits on ruthless economic egotism.[148] One of the main troubles of the modern age, Tawney argued, was precisely the common supposition that religion was irrelevant to questions concerning the organization of society. This assumption led to all sorts of untoward consequences. It meant that if human affairs were conducted 'in the light of no end other than the temporary appetites of individuals' then the inevitable result would be 'oppression', 'the unreasoning and morbid pursuit of pecuniary gain' (that is, the 'sin of avarice'), and in effect 'civil war'. On the other hand, so far as

> Christianity is taken seriously, it destroys alike the arbitrary power of the few and the slavery of many, since it maintains a standard by which both are condemned – a standard which men did not create and which is independent of their convenience or desires. By affirming that all men are the children of God, it insists that the rights of all men are equal. By affirming that men are men and nothing more, it is a warning that those rights are conditional and derivative – a commission of service, not a property. To such a faith nothing is common or unclean, and in a Christian society social institutions, economic activity, industrial organization cease to be either indifferent or merely means for the satisfaction of human appetites. They are judged, not merely by their convenience, but by standards of right and wrong. They become stages in the progress of mankind to perfection, and derive a certain sacramental significance from the spiritual end to which, if only as a kind of squalid scaffolding, they are ultimately related.[149]

Tawney makes the same kind of point in his *Equality* which came out ten years later and in which he is quite explicit about the key issue. It is whether the externals of life assist or hinder 'the life of the spirit' and 'the growth towards perfection of individual human beings.' What is crucial here, he says, is whether there is 'faith' in the 'common humanity' of all men. In this light, social arrangements are 'a matter of ethical judgement.'[150] Again, in a number of papers on Christianity and society which Tawney published in the 1920s, in the interval between the two major works of political theory, he is critically concerned with the practical and moral implications of Christian teaching and the need for Churches to deal directly and specifically with the social and economic problems of the day in the context of the spiritual and moral values they

148 ibid., ch. xi.
149 ibid., pp.234–5. Cf. ibid., pp.238–40.
150 Tawney *Equality* (1931; 4th edn rev., London, 1964), pp.49, 85–6.

expound. He calls for (what in fact Penty had already attempted) the elaboration of 'nothing less than a Christian sociology'.[151] A not dissimilar link between Christian principles and the practice of society is to be discerned, too, in Tawney's professional studies of economic history. This is partly a matter of the subjects he chooses for attention, most of which related more or less centrally to the emergence of capitalism and its system of entrepreneurial competition, that is to say, to the origins of the social ethic and arrangements he was elsewhere concerned to criticize. But partly, too, it is a matter of explicit statement in these studies. For instance, in the preface to one of the later editions of *Religion and the Rise of Capitalism*, Tawney makes clear his disapproval of the idea that religious considerations cannot be brought to bear on the business of trade, and that, on the contrary, he rather looks back to the older view which insists that 'Christianity has no more deadly foe than the *appetitus divitiarum infinitus*, the unbridled indulgence of the acquisitive appetite.' And right at the beginning of the text itself he observes:

> Rightly or wrongly, with wisdom or with its opposite, . . . an attempt is being made to restate the practical implications of the social ethics of the Christian faith, in a form sufficiently comprehensive to provide a standard by which to judge the collective actions and institutions of mankind, in the sphere both of international politics and of social organization.[152]

Or, again, he asserts that a 'religious philosophy, unless it is frankly to abandon nine-tenths of conduct to the powers of darkness, cannot admit the doctrine of a world of business and economic relations self-sufficient and divorced from ethics and religion.'[153] In the concluding chapter, too, his personal viewpoint emerges most clearly.

> . . . the assumption . . . that the attainment of material riches is the supreme object of human endeavour and the final criterion of human success . . . is the negation of any system of thought or morals which can . . . be described as Christian. Compromise is . . . impossible between the Church of Christ and the idolatry of wealth, which is the practical religion of capitalist societies. . . .[154]

Tawney's stress on what he believed to be the great moral issue of his

151 Tawney, 'The Churches and Social Ethics', *New Republic*, xxxviii (1924), pp.332–3. Cf. 'The Church and Industry', ibid., xxvi (1921), pp.255–7.
152 Tawney, *Religion and the Rise of Capitalism: a Historical Study* (1926; Penguin, 1942), pp.vi, 16.
153 ibid., pp.31–2. Cf. ibid., p.36.
154 ibid., ch.v, esp. pp.217–20, citation at pp.219–20. Cf. ibid., p.120.

own day was also, therefore, embedded in the writings on economic history.[155]

It is most surprising, therefore, that in esposition or appraisal of Tawney's work, due attention is not always given to the continuous formative influence of his Christian moralism. It is, for instance, a major weakness of Professor Terrill's long study of Tawney's life and ideas that this dimension is neglected.[156] It is very much the case that the heart of his attack on capitalism hinges on an accusation of moral deficiency and its incompatibility with Christian principle. The basic significance of this theme has to be accepted by the student of Tawney's works even if its cogency is not admitted, a position forcefully adopted by Professor A. MacIntyre in a perceptive and all too brief analysis of Tawney's Socialism. This is, MacIntyre rightly asserts, a moral doctrine; but he adds that it is, in his (surely correct) view, characterized by 'cliche-ridden high-mindedness' and a merely 'banal earnestness'.[157]

The question that now arises is how the 'bloodless abstractions' of this religious moralism may be concretely discerned in the 'large outlines of history' and its principles applied to the actual process of political and social affairs.[158] Tawney in fact pursues the implications of his spiritual premises through the exploration of four related themes. First, the defects and inequities of the prevailing arrangements, the 'acquisitive society'; secondly, the character of a better alternative, a 'functional society' based on due recognition of equality; thirdly, the mode of transformation envisaged; and, finally, the importance of education as a specific and crucial aspect of what is, for Tawney, involved in this reformed state of things.

Defects of the 'acquisitive society'

Tawney's numerous monographs in the special field of economic history dealt with various aspects of the way in which the individualist, bourgeois, or capitalist system had emerged from the more static, hierarchical framework of medieval feudalism. This acquisitive society is so called because its 'whole tendency and interest and preoccupation is to promote the acquisition of wealth.'[159] The secret of its triumph is obvious. It fixes men's minds not on restrictive social obligations but on their right to pursue their own self-interest, thus offering great scope for

155 See also Tawney, *The Agrarian Problem in the Sixteenth Century* (London, 1912), p.44.
156 Cf. the discerning remarks of the late H. R. G. Greaves in *Political Studies*, xxii (1974), pp.499–500.
157 A. MacIntyre, 'The Socialism of R. H. Tawney' (1964), in *Against the Self-Images of the Age: Essays on Ideology and Philosophy* (London, 1971), pp.38–41.
158 Cf. Tawney, *The Acquisitive Society*, p.6.
159 ibid., p.32.

money-making and free play to one of the most powerful human instincts.

To the strong it promises unfettered freedom for the exercise of their strength; to the weak the hope that they too one day may be strong. Before the eyes of both it suspends a golden prize, which not all can attain, but for which each may strive, the enchanting vision of infinite expansion. It assures men that there are no ends other than their ends, no law other than their desires, no limit other than that which they think advisable. Thus it makes the individual the centre of his own universe, and dissolves moral principles into a choice of expediencies. And it immensely simplifies the problems of social life in complex communities. For it relieves them of the necessity of discriminating between different types of economic activity and different sources of wealth, between enterprise and avarice, energy and unscrupulous greed, property which is legitimate and property which is theft, the just enjoyment of the fruits of labour and the idle parasitism of birth or fortune, because it treats all economic activities as standing upon the same level, and suggests that excess or defect, waste or superfluity, require no conscious effort of the social will to avert them, but are corrected almost automatically by the mechanical play of economic forces.[160]

Passages of this sort also intimate the type of defects Tawney finds in a society premeditated on a principle of free competition and a reverence for the possession of wealth. There is a 'degradation of those who labour' resulting in an unwholesome perversion of attitude; human energies are systematically underdeveloped from birth to maturity; waste and misapplication of productive power occurs in, for instance, the multiplication of luxuries and the like; reward is divorced from service through, say, the creation of a class of pensioners or *rentiers*; industrial warfare is rife; vested interests are created which resist reform of the economic system on more just and rational lines; and perhaps above all, an irrational and immoral, indeed unchristian, inequality among men emerges.[161]

Instead there must be recognition that individual rights and property should be seen not as in any sense absolute but as limited and directed by a principle. This rule is embodied in Tawney's conception of function and purpose which was crucial to his thought.[162] It was the weakening of

160 ibid., pp. 33–4.
161 ibid., ch. iv 'The Nemesis of Industrialism', esp. pp. 36–44; *Equality*, preface to 1938 edn, p. 27.
162 Cf. Shock, art. cit., p. 777.

the sense of social responsibility entailed by this principle and the effects of the decline which above all he deplored in the acquisitive society.[163]

A 'functional society'

Tawney undoubtedly put the notion of function to good use. He may, of course, have derived the idea directly from Ruskin.[164] Equally it could have been imbibed simply from the study of medieval society: at least one contemporary with similar Christian and radical interests says that (while an undergraduate at Oxford) he was introduced to these themes by Professor Ernest Barker.[165] But it seems most likely Tawney was influenced in this respect by the Guild Socialist circles with which he had associated. The most probable source is a book by the Spanish expatriate Ramiro de Maeztu which had appeared only three years before Tawney's analysis of the acquisitive society and which had made a notable impact.[166] This affinity has been briefly noted by some commentators. But so far as I know Tawney himself never mentions any indebtedness.[167]

Tawney defines a function as 'an activity which embodies and expresses the idea of social purpose.'[168] Consequently a functional society is one in which this notion is given 'pre-eminence over all subsidiary issues' so that all rights, including those derived from wealth, are contingent upon the discharge of obligations to the public. Remuneration, for instance, might be proportioned to service.[169] In such

163 Tawney, *The Acquisitive Society*, pp.9–14.
164 For Ruskin's use of the concept, see R. Williams, *Culture and Society 1780–1950* (1958; Penguin, 1961), pp.148–52.
165 M. B. Reckitt, *As It Happened: an Autobiography* (London, 1941), pp.105, 110.
166 R. de Maeztu, *Authority, Liberty and Function in the Light of the War: a Critique of Authority and Liberty as the Foundations of the Modern State and an Attempt to Base Societies on the Principle of Function* (London, 1916). The book was based on articles which had previously appeared in *The New Age*. Maeztu's considerable influence on English radical thought has been too little noted, but see e.g. S. G. Hobson, *Pilgrim to the Left: Memoirs of a Modern Revolutionist* (London, 1938), pp.179–82. The standard Spanish study is V. Marrero, *Maeztu* (Madrid, 1955). See also D. L. Shaw, *The Generation of 1898 in Spain* (London, 1975), ch.4 and M. Nozick, 'An Examination of Ramiro de Maeztu', *PMLA*, lxix (1954), pp.719–40.
167 On the general affinity with Guild ideas, see e.g. the contemporary comments in *The Guildsman* (April 1917), p.6 and (May 1920), pp.7–8; M. B. Reckitt and C. E. Bechhofer, *The Meaning of National Guilds* (1918; 2nd edn, London 1920), p.237; also F. Bealey's suggestion in *The Social and Political Thought of the British Labour Party* (London, 1970), intro., p.25. For the specific similarity, see N. Carpenter, *Guild Socialism: an Historical and Critical Analysis* (New York, 1922), p.98; P. Mairet, *A. R. Orage: a Memoir* (London, 1936), p.71; S. T. Glass, *The Responsible Society: the Ideas of the English Guild Socialist*, pp.66 n.1; W. Martin, '*The New Age*' under Orage: Chapters in English Cultural History* (New York, 1967), p.229; and R. Brown, *Guild Socialism and the Idea of Function* (unpublished MA thesis, University College, Swansea, 1977), esp. ch.1.
168 Tawney, *The Acquisitive Society*, p.9. Cf. ibid., p.49.
169 ibid., pp.31–2, 44, 96, 223.

a healthy community, Tawney urges, men would regard themselves not as 'owners of rights' (as they do in an acquisitive society) but as 'trustees for the discharge of functions' and 'instruments' of a general purpose.[170] The effect of applying this principle to the distribution of wealth would not, however, necessarily entail a complete levelling or the abolition of private property as such. But it would mean the elimination of indefensible differences of income, circumstances, and opportunity, and so of ownership divorced from obligation. The enemy was not privilege or property in themselves but their functionless existence.[171] And advance in the direction of such objectives requires reform along two lines:

> It involves, in the first place, the resolute elimination of all forms of special privilege, which favour some groups and depress others, whether their source be differences of environment, of education, or of pecuniary income. It involves, in the second place, the conversion of economic power, now often an irresponsible tyrant, into the servant of society, working within clearly defined limits, and accountable for its action to a public authority.[172]

In this way plutocracy is destroyed and 'an equalitarian society' set in its place, one in which the basic conditions of the good life are shared as uniformly as possible, though differentiation beyond this level of provision will be permitted where necessary.[173]

Seen in such a context, industry would have to be 'liberated' and reorganized as a 'profession'. It would cease to be conducted by property-owners for their own gain and would instead be carried on 'for the service of the public', responsibility for this lying upon the shoulders of all those doing the work 'from organizer and scientist to labourer'.[174] Tawney is sure, too (for reasons not wholly clear), that this elimination of the capitalist will not mean inefficiency.[175] The general spirit of what he has in view is revealed in the following summary passage:

> The collective responsibility of the workers for the maintenance of the standards of their profession is, then, the alternative to the discipline which Capitalism exercised in the past, and which is now breaking down. It involves a fundamental change in the position both of employers and of trade unions. As long as the direction of industry is in the hands of property-owners or their agents, who are concerned

170 ibid., p.54.
171 ibid., pp.93–5, 98–101; Equality, pp.49–50, 71–2.
172 Tawney, Equality, preface to 1938 edn, p.30.
173 ibid., pp.31, 49–50; The Radical Tradition, p.92.
174 Tawney, The Acquisitive Society, pp.106ff., 111, 139, 162, 182, 184ff.
175 ibid., pp.105–6, 167.

to extract from it the maximum profit for themselves, a trade union is necessarily a defensive organization. Absorbed, on the one hand, in the struggle to resist the downward thrust of Capitalism upon the workers' standard of life, and denounced, on the other, if it presumes to 'interfere with management,' even when management is most obviously inefficient, it is an opposition which never becomes a government, and which has neither the will nor the power to assume responsibility for the quality of the service offered to the consumer. If the abolition of functionless property transferred the control of production to bodies representing those who performed constructive work and those who consumed the goods produced, the relation of the worker to the public would no longer be indirect but immediate. Associations which are now purely defensive would be in a position, not merely to criticize and oppose, but to advise, to initiate and to enforce upon their own members the obligations of the craft.[176]

A crucial role is envisaged, therefore, for reformed trade unions organized on industrial lines with a self-imposed code of professional conduct.[177] The broad similarity to the ideas of the Guildsmen is manifest.[178] Tawney himself wrote of the building guild experiment as indicating a possible alternative to nationalization and sometimes stressed, too, the importance of the Guild analysis of producer democracy. He was indeed quite sympathetic to much of Penty's own argument in particular because of his belief that economic considerations need to be subordinated to a moral ideal.[179] It should be noted, however, that Penty himself thought Tawney's analysis of these matters and his prescriptions quite inadequate because he failed to grasp or tackle the problems posed by such features of the modern industrial scene as mass production and the division of labour, as well, of course, as of the use of machinery itself.[180]

There is, too, a certain difficulty about Tawney's own treatment of the questions he deals with: that is, that he may be somewhat over-sanguine about the prospects of industrial improvement he envisages because these may seem incompatible with the rather black view of human nature to which he subscribes. He certainly concedes that no change of system or institutions can of themselves avert those causes of social malaise

176 ibid., pp.190–1. Cf. ibid., pp.200–1.
177 ibid., pp.6–8, 222.
178 e.g. on the crucial nature of the professional ethic, see Reckitt and Bechhofer, op. cit., ch.III.
179 Tawney, The Acquisitive Society, pp.119–27, 195; The British Labor Movement (New Haven, Conn., 1925), pp.159–62; review of Penty's Guilds and the Social Crisis in the Daily News (21 March 1919), Penty Collection, University of Hull Library, microtext 795.
180 Penty, Post-Industrialism (London, 1922), pp.73–4.

which consist in the egotism, greed, or quarrelsomeness of human nature. Nevertheless much, he feels, may be hoped from the creation of an environment in which such characteristics are not encouraged.[181] The new 'economic psychology' will not come automatically; it has to be worked for. And the problem of the transition is, therefore, crucial.

The mode of transformation

How was this sea-change in the nature of society in general and industry in particular to be brought about?

This was basically a question of attitude or morale but a great deal could be done by appropriate institutional reform to help create the conditions in which the improvement in attitudes could best be achieved. Here there is a certain difference of emphasis to be discerned in Tawney's discussion. As time moves on he envisages in greater detail a wider panoply of reform with a corresponding increase in the role of government so that on some occasions later in life he presented a prospectus of a rather Fabian kind.[182] Yet it was not his purpose, he insisted, to urge the creation of a collectivist despotism; the kind of state activity he envisaged would always avoid the evils of bureaucracy and pursue a moral purpose.[183] Perhaps this was very naïve of him; but at least his intention was clear. Crossman confided to his diary that what he learned above all from Tawney (and Lindsay) was that the essence of social democracy 'consists of giving people a chance to decide for themselves'. He added that he found his Cabinet colleagues did not seem to share this view believing rather that they should take decisions and then get the people affected to agree.[184]

The basic principle of institutional change that Tawney had in mind was a common one among radicals and is to be found in Laski's writings, too, and in those of Guild Socialists and Syndicalists. It is that the democratic idea should be extended into spheres of life that had hitherto escaped its influence.[185] One aspect of this is that, just as political power had been made responsible to the community, so (as already intimated) must the direction of industry and economic policy similarly be transferred from the hands of capitalists and their agents. This may be achieved in a number of ways and it is certainly a mistake, Tawney feels, to stress nationalization only, let alone to make this device an end in

---

181 Tawney, *The Acquisitive Society*, pp.222–3.
182 See e.g. Tawney's wartime lecture 'We Mean Freedom' (1944), in *The Attack*, pp.92–3.
183 ibid., pp.94–9; *The Radical Tradition*, pp.125, 133–4, 139–40.
184 R. H. S. Crossman, *The Diaries of a Cabinet Minister* (London, 1975–7), ii.50. Cf. ibid., ii.190–1, 626–7.
185 Tawney, *The Radical Tradition*, p.148.

itself.[186] There must, too, be a concomitant spread of industrial democracy. This does not mean the absence of a class of managers, for subordination, authority, and discipline will remain vital for the efficient conduct of a factory or office. It does mean that control should be based on recognized ability and esteem and, too, limited to the extent required by the duties involved.[187] Equally, proper forms of representation, participation, and consultation will have to be created and, along with this, as much decentralization as possible.[188] In all this there is one point that Tawney himself invariably stresses that constitutes a crucial difference of emphasis between him and the generality of Fabians. He knows that the pursuit of industrial efficiency is not enough.[189] What must be sought is a new psychology, an improved morale among workers of all kinds.[190] Unless there is a full sense of responsibility and service on the part of employees they will simply use their strategic position to get as much for themselves as they can at the expense of others: and this, Tawney bluntly says, is as immoral as the functionless exploitation of the *rentier*.[191] But he believes the change desired can be brought about. In an obvious reference to the contemporary guild experiment in the construction industry he said:

> The psychology of a vocation can in fact be changed; new motives can be elicited, provided steps are taken to allow them free expression. It is as feasible to turn building into an organized profession, with a relatively high code of public honour, as it was to do the same for medicine or teaching.[192]

Hence the need for alteration in industrial organization and control, for proper training, selection, esteem, pecuniary incentive, and all the other means to create the proper discipline and responsibility of professional behaviour.[193] But this industrial reformation cannot proceed in isolation. It has to be accompanied by similarly radical changes of a democratic kind in the general social environment. In *Equality* and elsewhere Tawney wrote of the social and economic changes already

186 Tawney, *The Acquisitive Society*, pp.117–19, 139ff., 161–2, 185–8. On the need to recognize 'a diversity of expedients' in this regard, cf. *Equality*, p.187; 'British Socialism Today' (1952) in *The Radical Tradition*, pp.182–4; 'What British Labor Wants', *The New Republic*, xxxvii (1923–4), p.16.

187 Tawney, *The Acquisitive Society*, pp.202–7; *Equality*, pp.112–14.

188 Tawney, *The Acquisitive Society*, pp.210–11; *The Radical Tradition*, pp.107, 109, 185–7.

189 Cf. Tawney's 'Conditions of Economic Liberty', S. J. Chapman (ed.), *Labour and Capital after the War*, pp.124, 127. These passages are partly reprinted in *The Radical Tradition*, p.120.

190 Tawney, *Equality*, p.188; *The Radical Tradition*, p.110.

191 Tawney, *The Acquisitive Society*, pp.162, 167–8, 201.

192 ibid., p.195.

193 ibid., pp.193–6, 201.

under way and which should be extended: the redistribution of wealth especially that which has been inherited; as well the extension of common provision and the like, intended to produce not an identical levelling but a broad similarity of environment based on minimum standards. But the key to Tawney's position here lies in his scornful distaste for the class structure of British society and its effect on people's attitudes. It was a prime cause of inefficiency and unhappiness and was, he said, 'particularly detestable to Christians.'[194] It was by far the most notable instance of the contrast between the political democracy which had been achieved on the one hand and the continued existence of economic and social privilege on the other.[195] In a pungent passage Tawney reflects on the reaction of foreign observers to 'the element of stratification in English social arrangements':

> They come to the conclusion that Englishmen are born with *la mentalité hiérarchique*, and that England, though politically a democracy, is still liable to be plagued, in her social and economic life, by the mischievous ghost of an obsolete tradition of class superiority and class subordination. They find in the sharpness of English social divisions, and in the habit of mind which regards them as natural and inevitable, a quality which strikes them . . . as amusing or barbarous, or grotesque.
>
> Here are these people, they say, who, more than any other nation, need a common culture, for, more than any other, they depend on an economic system which at every turn involves mutual understanding and continuous co-operation, and who, more than any other, possess, as a result of their history, the materials by which such a common culture might be inspired. Yet, so far from desiring it, there is nothing, it seems, which they desire less. They spend their energies in making it impossible, in behaving like the public schoolboys of the universe. *Das Gentlemanideal* has them by the throat; they frisk politely into obsolescence on the playing-fields of Eton. It is all very characteristic, and traditional, and picturesque. But it is neither good business nor good manners. It is out of tune with realities of today. What a magnificent past Great Britain has had![196]

And it is not enough to be satisfied with what he called 'the Tadpole Philosophy', the belief that because a few are able to escape their environment (and rise to be frogs) this justifies the situation (the 'social evils') that some are thus able to evade.[197] Similarly, the 'day when a

194 Tawney, *The Attack*, p.181.
195 e.g. Tawney, *Equality*, pp.33–6.
196 ibid., p.37. Cf. ibid., ch.11 *passim*.
197 ibid., p.105.

thousand donkeys could be induced to sweat by the prospect of a carrot that could be eaten by one' was long over by the time the twentieth century dawned.[198] A more substantial minimizing of inequality than this must take place and again what stands in its way is a state of mind:

> . . . to criticize inequality and to desire equality is not . . . to cherish the romantic illusion that men are equal in character and intelligence. It is to hold that, while their natural endowments differ profoundly, it is the mark of a civilized society to aim at eliminating such inequalities as have their source, not in individual differences, but in its own organization, and that individual differences, which are a source of social energy, are more likely to ripen and find expression if social inequalities are, as far as practicable, diminished. And the obstacle to the progress of equality is something simpler and more potent than finds expression in the familiar truism that men vary in their mental and moral, as well as in their physical characteristics, important and valuable though that truism is as a reminder that different individuals require different types of provision. It is the habit of mind which thinks it, not regrettable, but natural and desirable, that different sections of a community should be distinguished from each other by sharp differences of economic status, of environment, of education and culture and habit of life. It is the temper which regards with approval the social institutions and economic arrangements by which such differences are emphasized and enhanced, and feels distrust and apprehension at all attempts to diminish them.[199]

The various social and economic changes Tawney wishes to see implemented all tend to focus on changing this attitude and, therefore, on eliminating the class structure it reflects. The business of a Socialist party, he suggested,

> is not the passage of a series of reforms in the interest of different sections of the working classes. It is to abolish all advantages and disabilities which have their source, not in differences of personal quality, but in disparities of wealth, opportunity, social position, and economic power. It is, in short . . . a classless society, which does not mean a society without differentiated groups, but one in which varieties of individual endowment, not contrasts of property, income and access to education, are the basis of differentiation.[200]

And of all these nostrums, 'access to education' was perhaps the most vital of all.

198 ibid., p.111.
199 ibid., p.57.
200 Tawney, 'The Choice Before the Labour Party' (1934), in *The Attack*, p.60.

Education

As the list of Tawney's writings makes obvious, he devoted a great deal of time and attention to this matter.[201] There were two reasons for this. One was that diversities of schooling and its quality played a substantial role in sustaining the class distinctions Tawney criticized so vehemently. The other was that if society was to be transformed in the way Tawney desired it would involve a radical change of heart on the part of all sections of the community, a transformation of the acquisitive and competitive attitude into one characterized by fellowship, co-operation, and mutual understanding so that an assertion of rights would be accommodated to a realization of duties. And in respect of each consideration education was vital. Hence Tawney's whole-hearted commitment to school reform and to such work as that which he undertook in helping to formulate Labour Party education policy and at Toynbee Hall and with the WEA. In particular the classes he ran for this last organization were always particularly important to him. They represented a microcosm of the sort of community of belief and common work which was so vital, voluntary groupings of people dedicated to a moral principle: the pursuit of knowledge, one of God's gifts.[202] In this sphere, if anywhere, 'it should be possible to forget the tedious vulgarities of income and social position' in common affection for the qualities which belong to man as such.[203] But, in contrast, the 'hereditary curse upon English education is its organization upon lines of social class.'[204] And, he goes on to argue, the 'English educational system will never be one worthy of a civilized society until the children of all classes in the nation attend the same schools.'[205] If a society's schools 'are sordid', he asks, 'will its life be generous?'[206] Hence the many detailed proposals for reform that in themselves entail a formidable range of government activity: nursery schools in all areas; a proper school medical service; adequate school meals; staffing and equipping primary schools on an imaginative scale; the provision of a variety of secondary education on a free basis at least to sixteen years of age with maintenance assistance where required and without unnecessary distinctions between different

201 See Terrill, op. cit., p.287ff. For instance, out of a total of 335 articles on a wide range of subjects, 205 are on education.
202 Winter, op. cit., p.71. Cf. Tawney's 'An Experiment in Democratic Education' (1914) and 'The W.E.A. and Adult Education' (1953), both in *The Radical Tradition*, chs 6 and 7.
203 *Equality*, p.141. Cf. *The Radical Tradition*, pp.62–3, 72–3, 74, 76, 78.
204 *Equality*, p.142. Cf. 'A National College of All Souls', *The Attack*, p.34.
205 *Equality*, p.144. He is naturally, therefore, very hostile to the public schools, ibid., p.145. Cf. 'The Problem of the Public Schools' (1943), in *The Radical Tradition*, ch.5.
206 *Equality*, p.145.

sorts of school.[207] His general view is summed up in the following passage (taken from a discussion of the educational goals and policies of the Labour movement):

> The social aspirations, which have created the industrial and political labor movements, have in fact had as their counterpart the growth of an educational idealism which regards the widest possible extension of educational facilities as the indispensable condition of realizing the type of social order which it is the purpose of those movements to bring into existence.[208]

*   *   *

Dr Maurice Shock wrote a couple of decades ago that there were many Socialist doctrines, some inconsistent with Tawney's, but that few have laid as much stress as his on the moral roots of Socialism.[209] Perhaps the general thrust of Tawney's argument is revealed in the following peroration:

> A society is free in so far, and only in so far, as, within the limits set by nature, knowledge and resources, its institutions and policies are such as to enable all its members to grow to their full stature, to do their duty as they see it, and – since liberty should not be too austere – to have their fling when they feel like it. In so far as the opportunity to lead a life worthy of human beings is needlessly confined to a minority, not a few of the conditions applauded as freedom would more properly be denounced as privilege. Action which causes such opportunities to be more widely shared is, therefore, twice blessed. It not only subtracts from inequality, but adds to freedom.[210]

His ideal was fellowship, participating citizenship, a process of growing individual self-development in a richer and less privileged social environment than that which he criticized. He was concerned, not so much to build a tidy social system, as to release people's energies and potentialities in a proper nexus of social relationships based on genuine moral principle. In a speech he once made on 'A Christian World Order' he defined Christianity as

> a body of doctrine which affirms that the nature of God and man is such that only insofar as men endeavour to order their lives in accordance with the principles expressed in the life and teaching of our

207 e.g. ibid., p.146.
208 *The British Labor Movement*, p.121.
209 Shock, art. cit., p.778.
210 *Equality*, 'Epilogue, 1938–1950', p.235.

Lord will they realize the highest values of which human beings are capable.[211]

Not unnaturally Tawney was most concerned in his later years about the direction British Socialism had taken. He was not unmindful of the great changes brought about by the welfare state; but nevertheless in his last public address he said that Socialism had 'become dehumanised'.[212] It was failing to achieve that sense of moral inspiration in daily life which was the crucial transformation to be desired: neither affluence nor collectivist control was enough. He was naturally not indifferent to the great importance of increasing the output of material wealth, of avoiding waste of natural resources and human capacity; but the main note of criticism of the existing order was (in terms he had used earlier) 'ethical rather than purely economic.'[213] And he had long been concerned that the paternalistic goal of authority to secure the welfare of the masses might turn the individual citizen into a mere 'sleeping partner' of the state with no active role to play in political and social life.[214] He feared, that is, that the 'Servile State' might be well on the way to becoming firmly established. What then would be the prospect of creating the Kingdom of God upon earth?

211 Speeches on Various Occasions, Tawney MSS, cited in Terrill, op. cit., p.246.
212 Speeches Given on Various Occasions, Tawney MSS, cited ibid., p.260.
213 Tawney, *The British Labor Movement*, p.153.
214 Tawney, *The Agrarian Problem in the Sixteenth Century*, p.342.

13

SOCIALISM AND THE GREAT
LEVIATHAN: LATER PHASES

The hon. Member has not explained whether he wants State socialism or
guild socialism, or what form of socialism. It is very fundamental.
161 H. C. DEB. 5s., 20 March 1923, col. 2495 (Sir A. Mond)

CONTINUING AMBIVALENCE

British socialists have been broadly of two kinds – the Fabians with their
emphasis on efficiency and social justice, and their devotion to facts, and
the idealistic socialists, inspired by such men as Robert Owen and
William Morris, with their emphasis on the dignity of man and of
labour.
M. YOUNG, *Small Man: Big World. A Discussion of Socialist
Democracy*, 1949, p.13

THE BASIC antithesis in British Socialism between, on the one hand, a
stress on the role and power of the state and, on the other, fear of it or at
least unease about its growth, has persisted and been clearly observable
since the end of the second war. Indeed these years were such as to
stimulate fundamental debate about the means and purposes of Socialist
policy in this respect. Attitudes were inevitably affected by the Labour
Party's participation in the wartime coalition government and by the
experience after 1945 of its first majority administration, a period which
witnessed a substantial enlargement of the public sphere. Beyond this, it
was not simply that its senior personalities were tired, even exhausted, by
the stress of ten years' responsibility of office in the most trying
circumstances; it was as well that, inevitably, a new generation of leaders
was emerging, representing different views and priorities. In addition,
the extensive legislative programme which had been implemented during
both the war and post-war years saw the passage to the statute book of a
good many of the proposals with which radicalism had long been
associated: the extension of public ownership, the establishment of a
National Health Service and other welfare schemes, a new Education Act,

the transformation of the Empire, and the like. How to maintain this reforming impetus seemed an urgent question. Further, there had emerged substantial disagreement over not only domestic affairs but also the 'cold war' and the conduct of foreign and defence policy. These differences, which reached an early culmination in the resignations of Bevan and Wilson in 1951, provided leadership of a kind previously lacking to the left-wing critics in the party and hardened or exacerbated these internal divergences. Then, and by no means least, there was the loss of three consecutive general elections in 1951, 1955, and 1959 which meant the party was out of office for well over a decade and which led naturally to a great inquest. Given all this, it is hardly surprising that during the 1950s and after there arose a notable concern or even bewilderment about the proper course for the Labour movement to follow, and a great deal of discussion took place of its policy and doctrine and what need there might be to reformulate them. So much had been achieved but: what was to be done next? What should be the direction, pace, and nature of future advance?

In fact the tension has continued in various forms to the present day and some part of its many domestic aspects and implications is reviewed in this chapter.[1] The matters arising may all be seen to focus on questions relating to the proper role and office of government in a Socialist society. And the debate is exemplified in two phases. The first was a controversy about the place of public ownership in Labour policy. There were those who believed it was central and others who were convinced it should either be played down or even cast aside as no longer so relevant or crucial as it had once been. This quarrel reached its climax in the fight over clause four of the Labour Party constitution, the outcome being an uneasy compromise. The second, more recent, phase is in some respects simply an extension of the first though there are also important new elements. The latter relate to a widespread concern about, on the one hand, what is often called 'corporatism' (that is, the development of large-scale organization and concentrated control in both government and industry) and the consequential need for decentralization and more effective means of accountability; and, on the other, to the considerable success of radical left elements within the party and the trade unions and what this might portend. The manifestations of all this that receive attention below relate in particular to the revival of Syndicalist ideas, the emergence of the 'new left' (in its diverse forms), and the attitudes associated with the recent creation of a separate Social Democratic Party.

Naturally these are complex tendencies with many dimensions. What is fascinating, however, is the manifest way in which the main trends of

---

1 Cognate issues arising in respect of external affairs will be examined in vol. iv, *The World Outside*.

thought involved reflect the basic tension in our modern political life between libertarian and collectivist proclivities and, therefore, that fundamental Socialist ambivalence which is the theme of this part of *The Ideological Heritage*.

THE NATIONALIZATION CONTROVERSY

To secure for the producers by hand or by brain the full fruits of their industry, and the most equitable distribution thereof that may be possible, upon the basis of the common ownership of the means of production. . . .
The Constitution of the Labour Party, 1918, §3(d)

A central feature of the quarrels that shook the Labour Party between the late 1940s and early 1960s concerned the role of the state in economic affairs, focusing on the policy of nationalization and to what extent it should be emphasized in the party programme. There was a continuing see-saw of decision and emphasis as the argument was swayed by the habitual forces of intra-party strife: the claims of ideology and the pressures of particular interests, personalities, and expediencies of one sort or another. The orthodox case for public ownership was invariably formally acknowledged and rehearsed in a parade of conventional rhetoric: as the late C. A. R. Crosland observed, the Labour Party is unique among European Socialist parties in the doctrinal stress it gives to public ownership.[2] However, crucial differences emerged over questions of timing and of the precise list of industries and services (if any) deemed ripe for take-over. The contrast of attitudes involved was well reflected in what happened at the 1957 conference. A large majority there accepted an official policy statement *Industry and Society* which put forward a very diminished version of public ownership seeing it simply as one way among many of achieving Socialism and urging alternatives to outright nationalization, in particular the achievement of economic control by other means such as fiscal policy. At the same time the traditional view was urged strongly during the debate. For instance, J. Campbell of the National Union of Railwaymen, speaking as 'an old-fashioned Socialist', deplored the tone of the official document and moved a resolution affirming belief 'in the common ownership of all the basic industries and means of production'. He completely rejected 'the present tendency to deviate from these accepted Socialist principles' and asked that the statement be referred back so that a more satisfactory policy could be formulated, one indicating quite clearly a detailed commitment, to be assumed by the next Labour government, to nationalize a whole range of

2 C. A. R. Crosland, *Social Democracy in Europe* (Fabian tract no.438; London, 1975), p.10.

specifically named industries. This move failed after a debate that was lengthy and often heated.[3]

What, then, were the various points of view revealed in these intra-party discords? They will be indicated in what follows here by reference to the positions adopted by those called 'fundamentalists', 'consolidators', and 'revisionists'. Of course, it is not intended to suggest that these names reflect either unchanging and cohesive groups of persons or, necessarily, any fully worked-out doctrine. But each reflects, in broad terms, a recognizable attitude to questions about the role of the state in general and public ownership in particular.

Fundamentalism: Bevan and his associates

Fundamentalism was (or is) not simply an acceptance of the traditional and formal commitment of the Labour Party to the public ownership of the instruments of production, distribution, and exchange: it was the belief that this policy was in an important sense the essential and basic part of any Socialist programme. As Crossman put it in one of his diaries: 'the two most important emotions of the Labour Party are a doctrinaire faith in nationalization . . . and . . . in pacifism' (though he added that it did not know what the former meant and refused to face the consequences of the latter).[4]

Radical indictment of existing arrangements had always stressed their failure adequately to utilize natural resources, take full advantage of technological progress, and secure a proper distribution of wealth and standard of life for the people. And the consequent prescription was that private ownership and control should be replaced by that of the community.[5] This diagnosis gathered strength as more and more economic and social difficulties emerged leading to that process of cumulative state intervention already described in *The Rise of Collectivism*.[6] The Socialist remedy could thus be presented as entailing no more than hastening and regularizing what was already under way. As Philip Snowden said in the House of Commons in 1923, in supporting his famous motion on the 'Capitalist System', the whole business of Parliament had in effect come to centre on dealing with 'the failures of private enterprise' and all the Labour Party asked was that this fact or tendency be recognized and become 'the conscious policy of government'.[7] And nationalization was naturally always a most crucial aspect

3 *KCA* (1957–8), p.15891A(15892).
4 J. Morgan (ed.), *The Backbench Diaries of Richard Crossman* (London, 1981), p.615.
5 For a typical instance, see 'Nunquam' [R. Blatchford], *Merrie England* (1893; London, 1976), pp.44–5.
6 loc. cit., ch.3.
7 161 H.C. Deb. 5s., 20 March 1923, cols 2483–4.

of this matter because it touched basic issues of industrial organization and was seen as 'the leading question' in the class struggle, at least for those not afraid of what A. J. Penty (describing Snowden's speech) called 'orthodox collectivism'.[8] It was this ethos which strongly persisted on the traditional or fundamentalist left of the Labour movement and which, for the 1940s and 1950s, may be conveniently exemplified by an examination of the domestic aspects of Bevanism. Aneurin Bevan's biographer said that the three strongest strands which 'interwove perpetually' in his political creed were 'his detestation of a class-ridden society, his belief in the collectivist cure, and his dream (he would never dare call it a certainty) that democratic processes . . . and vigour, intrepidly unleashed, could accomplish revolutionary ends.'[9]

The one formal and more or less systematic statement of his views that Bevan published was a book called *In Place of Fear* which appeared in 1952. The main question he addresses is: where does power in Britain lie and how may it be attained by the workers? The collectivist emphasis of his answer is clear.

Under the influence of Marxist and Syndicalist notions, he had in his early days believed that desirable change would be achieved only by revolutionary action based on the industrial power of the trade unions. But, not least because of the failure of the General Strike in 1926, he came instead to accept the efficacy of a political road to change, a view he confirmed in this tract. It was, he stated, one of the weaknesses of 'classic Marxism' that it underestimated the potential for change to be achieved by Parliamentary democracy under a universal franchise as 'a sword pointed at the heart of property-power.'[10] But constitutional action was not to be merely ameliorative, concerned with abating the difficulties of capitalism. It must have as its aim control of the economy and the total transformation of social structure: 'to the Socialist, Parliamentary power is to be used progressively until the main streams of economic activity are brought under public direction.' He thus asserts 'the efficacy of State action and of collective policies.'[11] One of the central chapters of the book deals with 'Modern Man and Modern Society' and its burden is, similarly, the need to reject any tendency away from the considerable degree of direction required by contemporary problems.[12] This supervision of social and economic life to mitigate 'the gaunt austerity of *laissez-*

---

8 A. E. Davies, *The Case for Nationalization* (London, 1920), p.11; A. J. Penty, *Towards a Christian Sociology* (London, 1923), p.13.

9 M. Foot, *Aneurin Bevan: a Biography* (London, 1962–73), ii.104. (For a scathing and damaging analysis of some aspects of this book, see P. M. Williams, 'Foot-Faults in the Gaitskell-Bevan Match', *Political Studies*, xxvii [1979], pp.129–40.)

10 A. Bevan, *In Place of Fear* (London, 1952), pp.5, 19, 21, 26, 28.

11 ibid., pp.29–32.

12 ibid., ch.3.

faire principles' has been long under way. It is, he said, 'the central fact of our day' and no amount of clamour against 'Statism' can conceal this.[13] Bevan's survey in this little book is not, of course, intended to be comprehensive but he gives numerous examples of areas in which state action is appropriate or necessary: the attack on poverty, ill-health, and inequality; education; a national wages policy which is 'an inevitable corollary of full employment'; and an increasing public role in industry which is seen as vital because the state is now a permanent instrument of intervention in economic affairs.[14] And specifically, as the debate in the party became more intense, Bevan increasingly recurred to the identity between Socialism and the extension of public ownership, government control, and planning.[15] In particular, he asserted the need for more nationalization not on any piecemeal basis but as the result of set and systematic policy so that the community would own and operate the commanding positions in the economy. In his last major speech, made to conference in 1959 and in specific rebuttal of proposals to change the party constitution in this respect, he spoke of Britain's task as the custodian of democratic representative government:

> The job is that we must try and organise our economic life intelligently and rationally in accordance with some order of priorities and a representative government; but we must not abandon our main case. Our main case is and must remain that in modern complex society it is impossible to get rational order by leaving things to private economic adventure. Therefore I am a Socialist. I believe in public ownership.

He went on, in consequence, to urge that the party should not turn its back on the traditional doctrine.[16] Shortly afterwards he wrote an article in *Tribune* which contained the following passage, a kind of valedictory summary of his beliefs:

> Those described as fundamentalists are people who believe that there are certain principles that have held good and are likely to hold good so long as British society is based in the main on the institutions of private ownership. They take the view that if the Labour Party was to abandon its main thesis of public ownership it would not differ in any important respect from the Tory Party. The only conflict would be about nuances, about semi-tones and half-tints. . . . If the Labour Party decided to adjust its policy in accordance with these ideas, it would be practically certain to wreck itself. The Party has been

13 ibid., pp.149–51.
14 For the phrase cited, see ibid., p.112.
15 Cf. the comments of K. O. Morgan, 'In the Pursuit of Power', *TLS* (24 December 1976), p.1615.
16 Labour Party Annual Report, 1959, pp.151–5 (citation at p.153).

nurtured in the belief that its *raison d'être* is a transformation of society. . . . [The] controversy is between those who want the mainsprings of economic power transferred to the community and those who believe that private enterprise should still remain supreme but that its worst characteristics should be modified by liberal ideas of justice and equality. It is . . . a classic conflict. It has been going on in Western European society right throughout the first half of the twentieth century. It is hardly likely to be settled in the Labour Party by an absolute victory of one side or the other, but what is quite certain is that the overwhelming majority of the Labour Party will not acquiesce in the jettisoning of the concept of progressive public ownership.[17]

This is a clear recognition of the development of interventionist tendencies in modern society and of the ambivalence of Labour Party attitudes. It is also a resolute affirmation on Bevan's part of his stand on the corporatist side.[18] It is merely absurd, of course, to suggest that the case Bevan put constituted 'a coherent political philosophy'.[19] But in his day, he was undoubtedly one of the most skilful advocates of the collectivist cause in the political market-place.

This cause was also associated in particular with the stance adopted by the so-called Bevanites, a group within the Parliamentary Labour Party which really began in April 1951.[20] There were, of course, very similar conclaves before and after (such as Keep Left and Victory for Socialism), their degree of organization and cohesiveness undoubtedly varying from time to time; they also had a notable following in the party outside Parliament often representing the 'pure' Socialism of constituency activists.[21] Bevan's own association with these factions was not always close or constant partly perhaps because of a certain waywardness or even dilettantism in his character which kept him ultimately aloof but also because of the divergences of view continually being revealed. There was indeed no consistent or coherent Bevanite policy, a matter that R. H. S. Crossman for one was always bewailing.[22] And for a good part of the time the main preoccupation was, of course, with foreign and defence policy, issues such as German re-armament, aid to the Third World, attitudes to Russia and the USA, nuclear weapons, and so forth. This

17 A. Bevan, 'How to Avoid Shipwreck', *Tribune* (11 December 1959), p.5.
18 Cf. Foot, op. cit., ii.498, 650–2; also K. O. Morgan's comment on Bevan's 'unreflecting commitment to bureaucratic forms of public ownership', 'Adding Freedom to Freedom', *TLS* (14 November 1980), p.1277.
19 The suggestion is made in Foot, op. cit., i.302–3.
20 M. Jenkins, *Bevanism: Labour's High Tide. The Cold War and the Democratic Mass Movement* (Nottingham, 1979), pp.152–3.
21 These matters are discussed, ibid., *passim*, but see pp.147, 164, 167, 169. See also P. M. Williams, *Hugh Gaitskell: a Political Biography* (London, 1979), pp.302ff.
22 J. Morgan (ed.), *The Backbench Diaries of Richard Crossman*, e.g. pp.47, 53, 206.

concentration of attention was indeed possible largely because commitment to the traditional domestic programme of the Labour Party was undoubted. In such good Socialist circles it could in a sense be accepted as given (until, that is, it came to be challenged in various ways). But what references there were took the usual collectivist form. Thus the eponymous pamphlet *Keep Left* published in 1947 applauded the nationalization programme to which the Labour Party was committed by its 1945 election pledges and asserted the necessity of continuing and extending it so that the public sector would 'embrace every industry which has a hold over our national economy or which cannot be made efficient in private hands.' Similarly the later *Keeping Left* (1950) advocated an extensive schedule of industries to be nationalized.[23] The magazine *Tribune* was one of the main outlets for Bevanite opinion and, again, it was there that Bevan himself in 1952 attacked those who wanted to dilute the traditional programme of the movement and to substitute 'novel remedies' in the struggle for power in the state. It is, he claimed, 'essential that we should keep clear before us that one of the central principles of Socialism is the substitution of public for private ownership. There is no way around this.'[24] Similarly Bevan stressed the need for effective central planning and control in a Fabian pamphlet he had brought out a couple of years before. He conceded there would for the foreseeable future still remain a private sector – we do not, he said, intend to nationalize the barber shops – and, therefore, a mixed economy; but a people's government must have its hands 'on the levers of economic power' and so there would also be a major public element.[25]

In this way, therefore, nationalization was, for Bevan and those like him, absolutely vital if property relations were to be transformed: it was a shibboleth of the left. Hence, of course, the hostility (which continued unabated after Bevan's death in 1959) towards those in the movement who believed otherwise, the consolidators and revisionists who held that such extensive enhancement of the public sector was unnecessary, undesirable, and irrelevant.

Morrison and consolidation

With not too much proprietorial exaggeration Beatrice Webb claimed in her diary in 1934, on the occasion of the Labour Party winning control of the LCC, that the credit for the victory belonged to Herbert Morrison.

23 R. H. S. Crossman *et al.*, *Keep Left* (London, 1947), p.11; Sir R. Acland *et al.*, *Keeping Left* (London, 1950).
24 Bevan, 'The Fatuity of Coalition', *Tribune* (13 June 1952), p.2.
25 Bevan, *Democratic Values* (Fabian tract no.282; London, 1951), pp.6–9. Cf. N. I. Gelman, 'Bevanism: a Philosophy for British Labour ?', *The Journal of Politics*, xvi (1954), p.658 on the basic purpose and policy involved.

'He is a Fabian of Fabians, a direct disciple of Sidney Webb's', she wrote, 'the very quintessence of Fabianism in policy and outlook.'[26] This remark implies three things. First it meant that, with due formal regard to the democratic process, Morrison believed efficient administration was the highest political virtue. He once said, in fact, that his supreme ambition was 'the achievement of tidiness'.[27] Socialism meant clearing up muddles. As he later told the House of Commons (during the second reading debate on the Coal Nationalization Bill in 1946):

> Nationalisation, socialisation, public ownership are not ends in themselves; and the Socialist . . . has to think about a lot more. . . . The object is to make possible the organisation of a more efficient industry, rendering more public service, and because of its efficiency and increased productivity is enabled to do progressively better for its workers.[28]

Mrs Webb's remark meant secondly that Morrison believed in collective ownership and control of major economic assets and services though with something of a municipal bias in this regard. Finally it suggested that he was above all a political pragmatist concerned with achievement rather than purist and impractical adherence to principle. But if Mrs Webb saw these qualities as virtues not all observers agreed. Sir Oswald Mosley, for instance, who had once been Morrison's senior in the party, described him in his autobiography as 'a narrow, rigid, vain little bureaucrat devoid of vision and incapable of movement beyond his office stool.'[29] Even remembering that Morrison had kept Mosley in unpleasant conditions of detention for a long time during the war, it is possible to discern through the bitterness a certain justice and something of what Morrison's latter-day colleagues of the left also felt about him. Specifically, in the context of concern here, he was someone who, to a degree, was prepared to sacrifice the policy of nationalization on the altar of electoral survival and, therefore, to dilute the traditional and long-standing party commitment in this respect. And because he was, for over two decades, in many ways one of the most important figures in the political wing of the Labour movement, he was able to have a crucial influence in forming in this direction his party's programme and tactics.

Morrison's pragmatism, his acute eye for the best political chance or solution, showed itself throughout his career: it was what made him one of the ablest public men of his day. Early on he had been a fiery

26 Mrs Webb's diary (14 March 1934), cited in B. Donoghue and G. W. Jones, *Herbert Morrison: Portrait of a Politician* (London, 1973), pp.190–1.
27 As cited ibid., p.176.
28 418 H.C. Deb. 5s., 30 January 1946, col.967.
29 O. Mosley, *My Life* (1968; London, 1970), p.235.

revolutionary, always citing *Das Kapital*, but fairly quickly realized that this sort of approach was unlikely to achieve much in Britain. So he turned to the ILP and the better prospects of constitutional reform, realizing that if his sort of radicalism was to succeed it had to appeal to a wider audience than the industrial working class and to demonstrate manifest practical advantages. Similarly while he had long accepted that basic social change required community control of the system of production and distribution, he was prepared to be flexible about timing and means. He had an exemplary record in this respect so far as the politics and administration of London were concerned and supported an extensive programme of municipal enterprise.[30] He naturally also paid some attention to the wider issues of what was then usually called 'socialization' and, for instance, had organized rallies calling for the state to take over the mines. But his central interest in this regard continued to be the affairs of the capital and, when he was Minister of Transport in the second Labour government of 1929–31, his main legislative preoccupation was with a scheme to acquire control of London transport. Ever ready to adapt his previous views when shown a better practical alternative, he was persuaded that it would be better, instead of administration by the LCC itself, to follow the precedents established not long before and to create a body on the lines of the BBC and the Central Electricity Generating Board (or of the even earlier Port of London Authority). And in 1933 just such a new public corporation was established, the London Passenger Transport Board. And this experience became an important factor in determining the design of post-1945 schemes of public ownership. Probably the idea of nationalization through the public corporation owes more to Morrison than to any other single person. The book he wrote in 1933 *Socialization and Transport* deals with the principles and application of this idea and is, in the British context, one of the fundamental texts dealing with the theory and practice of these matters.[31] Of course, there was opposition to his views. During the 1930s, for instance, the left wing of the day thought his obsession with the public corporation would in many ways leave the essentials of the existing system untouched, would in fact simply bolster capitalism with bureaucracy.[32] But because he was very active and extremely influential in the councils of the Labour Party Morrison's ideas played a crucial role in determining policy in these matters. Thus he stood out as a champion of the public ownership of major industries and of the planned economy.

Yet as later became apparent he was not really a collectivist on

30 Donoghue and Jones, op. cit., e.g. pp. 33–4, 56 and n. 46, 83, 86–7, 89, 111.
31 Cf. vol. iii, *A Much-Governed Nation*, ch. 7.
32 Donoghue and Jones, op. cit., p. 239.

principle in the sense that nationalization was not to him the be-all and end-all of Socialism. It was rather a device, one means among many, to be used or not as seemed appropriate to the service or industry being considered or as was deemed prudent in a given political situation.[33] This flexible attitude emerged very clearly in the intra-party squabbles of the 1950s. As party manager after 1945 Morrison was much concerned with preparing for the next electoral test and he was quite clear that the key problem in this regard was how Labour could retain the support or win over more of the uncommitted vote from the middle ground of society and politics. It was essential, as he often used to say, to appeal to 'all the useful people'.[34] He set out, therefore, to fashion a programme which, he hoped, would not alienate this crucial vote arguing, in effect, that it was all very well to talk about going full speed ahead for Socialism (whatever that was) but what good would this do if the only result was to put the Tories back in office?

It was in this context that Morrison became associated with the idea of 'consolidation'. An opponent from within the party later described the position in this way:

> Morrison at the Party Conference in June 1948 had first spoken the word which was taken to epitomize the controversy. 'Whilst in the next programme it will be right – and I can promise you that the Executive will do it – to give proper consideration to further propositions for public ownership, do not ignore the need, not merely for considering further public ownership, but for allowing ministers to *consolidate*. . . .' Thenceforward Morrison directed his inexhaustible energies to ensure that the consolidation of past achievements should dominate Labour's thinking: here was the best way to make the nationalization measures already taken administratively successful, to liberate the parliamentary timetable for other less controversial measures, to dissipate middle-class resentment, to hook the floating voter.[35]

Tribune took a different view, believing that such pragmatism and the stress on piecemeal reform it entailed were not enough. The need was rather for a direct attack on capital and the ruling classes in the orthodox way.[36] Morrison simply feared that a Labour programme fervently committed to more extensive nationalization was a recipe for electoral disaster. While not against the idea of public ownership as such, therefore, he opposed proceeding with steel nationalization and disliked

33 Cf. his speeches reported in *The Times* (29 April, 9 June 1950) and cited in Donoghue and Jones, op. cit., pp.457, 458.
34 ibid., pp.441–4; Lord Morrison of Lambeth, *Herbert Morrison: an Autobiography* (London, 1960), p.239.
35 M. Foot, *Aneurin Bevan: a Biography*, ii.258, italics in original.
36 Editorial, 'Herbert Steps Out', *Tribune* (16 June 1950), pp.3–4.

the shopping-list approach: he wanted a much more open-ended commitment as a sort of doctor's mandate.[37] Naturally, when, in 1950 and 1951, the Labour Party did suffer electoral reverses and was driven from office, this consolidationist policy was regarded by the left as one of the main causes of defeat: Labour had lost support because it had thus weakened its genuine Socialist objectives. On the other hand Morrison continued to urge that the failure was due to the drifting away of the middle-class vote which was horrified at the thought of more nationalization and at the poor performance of existing public industries and services.

In this way the battles of the ensuing decade were heralded. Morrison invited the Labour movement to look again at its traditional emphasis on, even obsession with, nationalization, urging it to think its position out carefully in the political circumstances of the day, and to ask itself whether what seemed vital in 1918 or even 1933 was still so central. But he never really took this cool, new look himself, and simply urged caution. Partly perhaps this was for reasons of a personal political kind; and as well it was probably because, a little oddly, he was himself too old-fashioned to realize how much the total situation had altered. If this demanded a revision of Socialist thinking, he was still wedded to the Webbism of yesteryear albeit in a cautious, modified form. Later, after the clause four controversy, he said he did not think 'the row was worth while' and that, for his taste, the new principles suggested were much too right wing.[38]

What, then, were these new principles that went beyond Morrison's consolidationist position to suggest a radical examination and re-statement of party ideology and policy?

The revisionists

Revisionism is a term long familiar in a Marxist context, one synonymous with some form of reinterpretation of doctrine so critical as to amount (in the eyes of orthodoxy) to heresy or deviation. Thus it was originally applied in the latter part of the nineteenth century to the ideas of Eduard Bernstein who was associated with the view that a transformation of society might well not follow a political catastrophe or require a revolution led by a party autocracy, but be achieved rather by means of democratic, constitutional reform based on the power of the newly-enfranchised working classes. Bernstein argued that, in the light of historical experience, analysis of social problems and prospects had to be radically altered from that which had been found adequate years before in the days of, say, The Communist Manifesto.[39] In the present context

37 Cf. Morrison, Herbert Morrison, pp. 287-8, 312, 329-30.
38 ibid., p. 329; Donoghue and Jones, Herbert Morrison, p. 552.
39 See e.g. E. Bernstein, Evolutionary Socialism: a Criticism and Affirmation (1899, 1st English edn, 1909; Schocken Books, 1972) with a useful introduction by S. Hook.

the concept is applied (in a not dissimilar way) to the recent tendency in the Labour Party to accept that the capitalist enemy is not what it was a couple of generations ago, that the economic and social state of affairs has been so altered since the beginning of the century that it is no good continuing to apply automatically perceptions based on the old analysis but necessary rather to think out a new programme relevant to the radically changed circumstances. To do otherwise is to be merely anachronistic and so either utopian or reactionary.

A clear sense that the traditional doctrines, policies, and even language of Socialism needed to be rethought because conditions had altered so much since the Labour Party's pioneer days is to be detected as long as forty or more years ago. Certain studies by Labour politicians, appearing in the late 1930s, were the equivalent in the Labour Party of the search for a new middle way reflected elsewhere in the work of the Liberal industrial inquiry and that of Macmillan and the Next Five Years Group. The party mainstream was represented by Hugh Dalton's *Practical Socialism for Britain* published in 1935 with its conventional stress on the need for 'socialization' in its various forms and on full-scale economic planning as a means crucial to the achievement of Socialist aims.[40] There is, for instance, the usual shopping-list of industries ripe for nationalization.[41] However, as against this established view, Douglas Jay's statement of the Socialist case, which appeared three years later, specifically repudiated any argument simply because it was traditional.[42] And in fact the specific question of public ownership receives in this work very short shrift, the main concern being with the possibilities revealed by policies of the type based on the writings of J. M. Keynes.[43] In addition there was E. F. M. Durbin's most significant essay on social policy which came out in 1940. It was ambitious in scope, endeavouring to relate questions of theory and practice to considerations based on psychological analysis of human co-operation and conflict. But the book's most important theme, and that which has had most influence, was the account given of 'Capitalism in Transition'.[44] The point was that the 'classical' capitalist system had been so transformed by various changes in economic and social life that it was necessary for Socialist diagnosis and prescription to be radically readjusted.[45] Because of these developments, Durbin argued, '*laisser-faire* capitalism' as a whole or in its pure form could no longer be said to exist and was giving way to a new

40 H. Dalton, *Practical Socialism for Britain* (1935; London, 1936), esp. parts III and V.
41 e.g. ibid., pp.140ff. Cf. ibid., pp.27, 93 on the need to extend the socialized sector.
42 D. Jay, *The Socialist Case* (1938; rev. edn, London, 1947), preface, p.ix.
43 ibid., esp. part III 'Money and the Trade Cycle'.
44 E. F. M. Durbin, *The Politics of Democratic Socialism: an Essay on Social Policy* (London, 1940), part II.
45 See e.g. the summary, ibid., pp.133–4. Cf. p.480 below.

economic order under a notable degree of state control albeit with a substantial continuing element of private enterprise, even that organized monopolistically.[46] The specific significant point is that in his prescription Durbin gives no great emphasis to nationalization as such though an extension of public ownership or control in some form is, he believes, to be expected.[47]

One further set of influences must be mentioned in this context. A major factor in forming the analysis Durbin had presented was the publication in 1932 in America of a classic survey entitled *The Modern Corporation and Private Property*. Its authors A. Berle and G. Means described a fundamental shift in power and form that was occurring in the capitalist system: the entrepreneur had a diminishing role and was being replaced by the professional executive in the larger corporate units which were coming increasingly to dominate economic life.[48] This theme was given wider point and more directly polemical power by the first appearance in Britain ten years later of *The Managerial Revolution* by the ex-Trotskyite James Burnham. This book had a considerable impact in intellectual circles, even those where its message was found unpalatable. The argument was that, though traditional capitalism was breaking down, it was being replaced, not by Socialism, but by a kind of society dominated in all spheres of life by 'managers'. These were a sort of professional élite composed of scientists, technologists, executives, bureaucrats, military leaders, and so on, a group not unlike that envisaged by the cameralists from Bacon to St-Simon and Wells. Burnham urged that this transition was happening in the world as he wrote and in all advanced industrialized countries whatever their formal political arrangements. What was thus emerging was a planned, centralized society of a hierarchical kind, neither capitalist nor democratic (at least in the usual sense of the words). In some respects Burnham painted an awesome, apocalyptic vision that was bound to sustain or create fears of centralized autocracy. And, of course, this is precisely what a further substantial extension of state ownership and control might seem to invite.

To many people important questions seemed thus to arise. Was the conventional Socialist anathema, 'capitalism', a real and present enemy, or was this rather the growth of managerial power? And so, was the usual solution to capitalist deficiencies – public ownership and control – a

46 Durbin, op. cit., pp.134–6, 147, 325–7.
47 ibid., pp.294, 301, 314–16.
48 A. A. Berle and G. Means, *The Modern Corporation and Private Property* (New York, 1933). Of course, others had discerned this development long before e.g. W. Clarke in the original *Fabian Essays* (1889; Jubilee edn, London, 1950) pp.78–9; what was new was its systematic empirical confirmation.

desirable or appropriate remedy? Consequently was a new analysis of the situation and a fresh prescription required?[49]

The Second World War, already under way when Durbin's and Burnham's studies appeared, only intensified most of the changes in traditional capitalism that had been thus detected. But the contrast of opinion with conventional Labour attitudes that their diagnosis implied did not become significant, or come to a head, until the 1950s. The substantial completion of the post-war programme, the electoral defeat of 1951, the emerging rivalries over the party leadership and future direction, in particular about public ownership, conspired to bring the whole matter into the open.[50] Of course, the ground had in many ways already been prepared, too, by Morrison's consolidationist approach and by the canvassing of various alternatives to nationalization (competitive public enterprise; state share-buying; control over investment decisions, location of industry, availability of foreign exchange, and the like). There was a growing and widespread acceptance of the idea of the mixed economy; and, as well, criticisms of existing nationalized industries were heard in respect of, for instance, over-centralization, lack of effective worker consultation, inefficiency of service, and so forth. The result was in general a fluid situation in which a reappraisal of the whole concept of nationalization and its relevance in prevailing circumstances seemed to many to be not simply possible but required. Yet what other theme could cement together the different parts of the Labour movement or provide the basis of a persuasive and effective domestic policy?

Various manifestations of the revisionist point of view appeared. There was the long series of articles and books by the late C. A. R. Crosland which commanded attention not simply because of their intellectual force but because of his position in the Parliamentary Labour Party.[51] There were also, interestingly enough, the later writings of John Strachey who before the war had been an ardent Marxist but who subsequently mellowed and, in the late 1940s and after, was thinking of a *rapprochement* with 'contemporary capitalism', a kind of constitutional middle way of reform.[52] Then there were the publications of a group

49 J. Burnham, *The Managerial Revolution, or What Is Happening In the World Now* (1941; London, 1944). Burnham's second study, *The Machiavellians*, appeared in 1943 and was followed four years later by *The Struggle for the World*. For a critical Socialist reaction, see e.g. G. Orwell, *James Burnham and the Managerial Revolution* (London, 1946).

50 See the interesting account by V. Bogdanor, 'The Labour Party in Opposition, 1951–1964', in V. Bogdanor and R. Skidelsky, *The Age of Affluence, 1951–1964* (London, 1970), ch. 3.

51 See in particular the following titles: *The Future of Socialism* (London, 1956); *The Conservative Enemy: a Programme of Radical Reform for the 1960s* (London, 1962); and *Socialism Now and Other Essays* (London, 1974).

52 As in his *Contemporary Capitalism* (London, 1956).

called Socialist Union formed after the defeat in 1951 by a number of Labour Party intellectuals specifically to assert the need to state anew the principles of Socialism and to elaborate them in policies relevant to the new circumstances of the contemporary world.[53] Finally there was the collection of *New Fabian Essays* that appeared in 1952 with the same sort of message. *The Times* newspaper described these essays and the publications of Socialist Union as together contributing to 'an open rejection of both the collectivism of the early Fabians and the commonly accepted definition of Socialism as "the nationalisation of the means of production, distribution and exchange." '[54]

Naturally there were many different nuances and emphases within the revisionist fold but there was a common point of departure which was the need 'to refine – even to revise – the apparent certainties of the past'; it could not be enough merely to repeat 'the creed of yesterday'.[55] The British Labour movement had long lived on the intellectual capital and policies provided by the original Fabians. And it was clear (at least to the revisionists) that to a great extent the welfare state of the present day was the outcome of this influence. But, partly as a result of this success, times had radically changed and the old analyses and views were no longer so appealing or appropriate.[56] As M. Cole and R. Crossman put it in their introduction to the *New Fabian Essays*, indicating the context of the discussions to follow:

> For two generations, socialist thought had been largely concentrated on the techniques for carrying out the programme envisaged in the original Essays and the expedients required to adapt that programme to the emergencies which had arisen. Comparatively little attention had been given to the structural changes in society which had been taking place and the new social sciences which were emerging. As a result, the election of the Labour Government in 1945, and the rapid completion of the Fabian programme, had been followed by a dangerous hiatus both of thought and action. It was not merely new expedients which were required, or new planks in an election programme, but a new analysis of the political, economic and social scene as a basis for reformulating socialist principles.[57]

The nature of the change that the revisionists thought had occurred

53 *Socialism: a New Statement of Principles* (1952; 3rd edn, London, 1954); *Twentieth Century Socialism: The Economy of Tomorrow* (Penguin, 1956). The latter was drafted by Allan Flanders and Rita Hinden (editor of *Socialist Commentary*).
54 'Labour Thinking', *The Times* (27 June 1952), p.7.
55 Socialist Union, *Socialism: a New Statement of Principles*, pp.12, 13.
56 C. R. Attlee's preface in R. H. S. Crossman (ed.), *New Fabian Essays* (1952; London, 1953), p.vii.
57 ibid., p.xi.

was described in detail by C. A. R. Crosland, whose discussion, and indeed that of the school as a whole, shows a very great indebtedness to the earlier analysis represented by Durbin's book.[58] Crosland argued that traditional Socialist policies were directed against 'capitalism'. But this no longer existed because the economic and social system had been transformed in various crucial ways. For example, personal ownership and control of business enterprise had, partly through the establishment of joint-stock arrangements, been replaced by large-scale organizations characterized by passive shareholding and the emergence of a managerial class. There had, too, been an enormous growth in the role of the state so that economic life was no longer autonomous; substantial welfare services had been developed; the policy of full employment was accepted by all parties; notable improvements in the general standard of living had occurred; partly because of progressive taxation the class structure was more varied than it had been; the power of trade unions had grown enormously; and so on, in the way Durbin had indicated. As a result of all these changes, a completely new kind of society had emerged which Crosland called a 'statist' or 'post-capitalist' society and which presented new problems requiring fresh answers not simply the reiteration of old and now irrelevant slogans. For its part Socialist Union, while accepting that a substantial role for the state was indispensable, specifically warned of the dangers involved. In libertarian fashion, what was feared was the prospect of a

> managerial society . . . run by administrators out of reach of popular control. By virtue of their role and responsibility – in government, in industry, in the social services – these rulers can easily come to treat ordinary folk not as persons but as means to an end. So many of the forces at work conspire to bring this about. Mass production and the growth of large-scale organisation, the centralisation of power, the spreading intervention of the state in our daily lives, the complexity of modern civilisation, have all helped to create this leading problem of our age . . . accentuated by the preoccupation with defence and industrial efficiency.[59]

Clearly if this sort of analysis is correct and the tendency discerned was indeed afoot, a radical revision of Socialist beliefs and policies was invited because the problem faced had altered fundamentally. It was no longer a matter of controlling or replacing 'capitalism' for that system (as traditionally understood) had disappeared. It was rather a question of

58 Crosland, 'The Transition from Capitalism', ibid., pp.33–68; *The Future of Socialism*, part one 'The Transformation of Capitalism'. The echo in these titles of Durbin's analysis is obvious.

59 Socialist Union, *Socialism: a New Statement of Principles*, pp.55–6. Cf. ibid., p.19 and, on the specific question of centralization, ibid., pp.22–3.

dealing with the problems of 'statism' and the dangers of managerial society. The goal was not simply the seizure of total economic power and thus the achievement of a centralized Socialist efficiency but of finding a proper place for the individual in modern society which so often dwarfs him to littleness, condemns him to frustration, and makes him no more than the state's 'helpless victim'.[60] 'A socialist programme should now aim at deliberately shaping all the institutions of our society in the light of their effects on the individual.'[61] Of course, the remaining evils of class division have to be eradicated but a new attack must be developed 'to arouse *responsible participation*' and prevent apathy and to do this (in Tawneyan manner) with less emphasis on forms of organization and more on changing people's attitudes.[62]

The issues became concentrated on the question of public ownership which the revisionists saw as no longer the only effective response to the problems of industry and as being in some ways a positive bar to the achievement of social justice. The fundamentalist doctrine was that 'through some form of collectivism the just and good society would be established' and that this meant the idea of the common ownership of land and capital and 'some sort of planning'.[63] But this simplistic viewpoint could no longer be accepted. Nationalization will not straightforwardly 'usher in the millenium' or by itself alter industrial and social relationships; it might well bring above all a dangerous centralization of power.[64]

> The theories . . . which asserted that complete common ownership was the gateway to the promised land, no longer carry conviction. Because socialism has become identified exclusively with common ownership, loss of faith in common ownership as the great panacea often means loss of faith in socialism itself. There is an obvious way out of this dilemma if socialists have the courage to take it. The whole problem of ownership, and of how the power it confers can be socially controlled, must be examined afresh.[65]

It was not that there must be no further public ownership at all, say in the field of utilities, monopolies on the large-scale, where there had been consistent under-investment, or a need to plan a vital material resource,

---

60 Socialist Union, *Twentieth Century Socialism*, p.15. Among many such references, cf. ibid., pp.124–6, 135, 138–41, 146–7.
61 Socialist Union, *Socialism: a New Statement of Principles*, p.60.
62 ibid., pp.58–9, italics in original, 61. This emphasis occurred too in *Socialist Commentary*: see the articles cited by S. Haseler, *The Gaitskellites: Revisionism in the British Labour Party 1951–64* (London, 1969), p.74.
63 Socialist Union, *Socialism: a New Statement of Principles*, pp.14–15 *et seq.*
64 ibid., pp.21–3.
65 Socialist Union, *Twentieth Century Socialism*, pp.124–5.

but that new methods were often required, for example, on the lines of 'the competitive public enterprise approach' taking over not whole industries but selected firms or setting up new government owned plants as rivals to private industry.[66] Even so, following the Keynesian argument that extensive state Socialism is not required, Crosland for one never expected public enterprise to be a major element in Socialist planning: government could effectively impose its strategic will on the economy without this. These matters, he said astringently, cannot be settled by evoking 'the spirit of Keir Hardie'. And he did 'not want a steadily extending chain of State monopolies' which would be both 'bad for liberty' and 'wholly irrelevant' to Socialism as he understood it. 'State ownership of all industrial capital is not now a condition of creating a socialist society, establishing social equality, increasing social welfare, or eliminating class distinctions.'[67]

The revisionists accepted that the fundamental ethical goals of Socialism had not altered: the basic trinity of objectives – equality, freedom, and fellowship – remained and were indeed notably stressed in their publicity.[68] The epigraph to Socialist Union's first pamphlet indicated its stance. It was a citation from the pioneer Socialist Robert Blatchford which began 'We should take to socialism because it is ethically right', but added 'otherwise we shall stop short at collectivism.'[69] The real problem was thus one of 'applied ethics'.[70] Conditions had been so changed by a century or more of social advance, war, and so on, that the specific problems faced by Socialism in the 1950s were quite different from those of the time of Robert Owen, Keir Hardie, and even Sidney Webb. New tactics, new programmes, new means were required to move more effectively towards the Socialist goals; and the fundamentalists in the party were in error – and a politically dangerous liability – because they could not see this: they had stopped short at collectivism.

The whole debate on domestic issues came to a climax with the revisionist assault on the formal commitment to common ownership which is enshrined in the Labour Party constitution itself.

The fight over clause four

The revisionists appeared to be in a dominant position after the election

66 Crosland, *The Future of Socialism*, pp.476, 487ff.
67 ibid., pp.496–7. For Keynes's view that state ownership of the instruments of production is irrelevant to economic control, see *The General Theory of Employment, Interest and Money* (1936; London, 1942), p.378.
68 Socialist Union, *Twentieth Century Socialism*, chs 3–5 and p.61; *Socialism: a New Statement of Principles*, pp.26–37.
69 Socialist Union, *Socialism: a New Statement of Principles*, p.[3].
70 Socialist Union, *Twentieth Century Socialism*, p.7 and ch.1 *passim*.

of H. Gaitskell to the party leadership in 1955. The range of policy statements issued not long afterwards and, despite some opposition, subsequently accepted by conference, by and large reflected the revisionist point of view.[71] Then, after the party's third electoral defeat in succession in 1959, the revisionists initiated a further debate on party policy and doctrine that constituted a direct challenge to traditional opinion.[72] There were two major focuses of conflict: in foreign affairs, the issue of unilateral nuclear disarmament; and in the domestic context, the controversy over clause four of the Labour Party constitution. As part of the process of refurbishing the Labour image, Gaitskell determined to erase the connexion in the public mind between the party and nationalization. Having already achieved some success in respect of the party programme and conference decisions, he turned his attention to this formal statement as the key embodiment of the style and attitude he wished to displace or at least modify.[73] The debate that ensued went beyond the quarrel over consolidation because it was concerned not with whether this or that list of nationalization proposals was desirable, should be shortened, or the like. The issue for the party assumed instead an acutely embarrassing constitutional dimension: whether one of its main objectives, indeed the major, traditional aim, was relevant to the conditions obtaining in the mid-twentieth century. Moreover the leader of the party himself was directly and closely embroiled in what was in effect a power struggle with fundamentalists of all sorts about not only the strategic purpose of the party but also immediate electoral tactics. For Gaitskell was convinced that Labour was unlikely to regain office unless it recovered the 'middle ground' and thus improved its popular appeal. In the outcome he failed to win a complete victory in the fight over these matters. Basically this was because he did not foresee the strong reaction that arose and, in particular, was unable to carry the trade union movement along with him. So the revisionist cause suffered a setback.[74]

Clause IV of the Labour Party constitution deals with 'Party Objects' and had seven sub-clauses, the fourth of which (by itself often referred to as clause four) was widely regarded as 'the basic national object of the Party'.[75] It reads:

4.   To secure for the workers by hand or by brain the full fruits of

71 Cf. Gaitskell, *Socialism and Nationalisation* (Fabian tract no. 300; London, 1956); and the policy statement *Industry and Society* (London, 1956). Gaitskell's role in the clause four controversy is reviewed in Williams, *Hugh Gaitskell*, ch. 21.

72 Haseler, op. cit., pp. 142, 158.

73 ibid., p. 148.

74 ibid., pp. 159, 166, 170–6; Williams, op. cit., pp. 549, 552. On the variation in union support, see also *KCA* (1959–60), p. 17518A (17520–1).

75 H. Tracey (ed.), *The British Labour Party: its History, Growth, Policy and Leaders* (1948; London, 1948), i. 6.

their industry and the most equitable distribution thereof that may be possible, upon the basis of the common ownership of the means of production, distribution, and exchange, and the best obtainable system of popular administration and control of each industry or service.[76]

At no time did Gaitskell ask for the removal of this passage from the party constitution; indeed he had never been opposed to nationalization as such.[77] Instead he suggested the clause might be amplified and so brought up to date to make it more applicable to modern conditions. This could be done by placing alongside it a new declaration of aims; though without doubt the effect of this would have been tantamount to the dilution or nullification of the original clause.[78]

The controversy between what Crossman called 'these yelping ideological phalanxes' was sparked off afresh in the immediate aftermath of the 1959 election by an article, written by D. Jay, in the periodical *Forward*. He urged there that Labour was failing to win electorally because it lacked a wide appeal; and the reason was it suffered from 'two fatal handicaps – the class "image" and the myth of "nationalisation".' He urged, therefore, that the party should divest itself of its working-class image, as by changing its name, and should drop all further plans for nationalization (including the renationalization of the steel industry). Similar views were also expressed a little while afterwards by P. G. Walker.[79] Naturally these views drew an immediate ripost from *Tribune* which declared that, on the contrary, the nationalization policy must not be abandoned but made a reality. Crossman urged at this time that 'what really distinguishes a Socialist is the belief in public ownership and State trading.'[80] The lines thus drawn were taken up at the impending party conference.

A shorter conference than usual was held in November 1959 and, in

76 Cited from the 1950 version in G. H. L. Le May, *British Government, 1914–1953: Select Documents* (London, 1955), p.381. In the original formulation of 1918, the word 'producers' was used instead of 'workers', and the terms 'distribution and exchange' were not included, ibid., p.353 (cited as epigraph to this section, p.466 above).
77 See Williams, op. cit., pp.68–9, 354, 356–7, 387, 446–52, 545–7, 553–5, 562–3, 565, 658–62, etc.
78 Haseler, op. cit., pp.166–7, 169–70.
79 D. Jay, 'Are We Downhearted? Yes!', *Forward* (16 October 1959), pp.1–12. For Jay's reaction to the electoral defeat in the terms stated, see also Williams, op. cit., pp.538–9; P. Gordon Walker, 'Slam the Door on the Liberals', *Forward* (23 October 1959), pp.1, 12. Crossman's remark is in J. Morgan (ed.), *The Backbench Diaries of Richard Crossman*, p.880.
80 'What are We Going to Do?', *Tribune* (16 October 1959), pp.1, 6; Morgan (ed.), op. cit., p.797; cf. ibid., p.839 and n.

effect, took the form of an inquest on the party's electoral defeat.[81] The central issue, on which contrasting views were expressed, was whether the policy of nationalization had played any part in that defeat and what role public ownership should play in the future programme of the party. The chairman, B. Castle, in her opening address strongly opposed abandoning the attempt to take over more industries and make them more publicly responsible. In this she was supported by a number of speakers including M. Foot, F. Cousins, and members of the Victory For Socialism group. For instance, Cousins said there could be no Socialism without nationalization and that he was a 'bit disturbed' at the suggestion the party's constitution needed revising. In his reply as party leader, Gaitskell made a major plea for change in revisionist terms that harked back to Durbin's analysis, now two decades old. He urged that the Labour Party was operating in a social and economic context that had radically changed from that which had been faced a generation before in the party's pioneering days. He wanted to secure some recognition of this altered situation and he listed a long series of reforms he would like to see adopted. These ranged from stressing more issues that would appeal to younger people to improved behaviour by some Labour councils. It was then he turned to the question of nationalization and public ownership, a major factor, he believed, in the party's contemporary unpopularity. He did not at all rule out further extension of the public sector in the future though he wondered (as Durbin, Tawney, and many others had done before) whether these might not perhaps take some other form than the conventional public corporation. What he could not accept was that 'nationalization or even public ownership is the be-all and end-all, the ultimate first principle and aim of Socialism.' Rather it was one means among many — and not necessarily the most important means — of implementing certain basic Socialist principles such as equality, social justice, the pre-eminence of the public interest, help for the needy, and so forth. 'Our goal', he said, 'is not 100 per cent State ownership. Our goal is a society in which Socialist ideals are realized.' This led Gaitskell to the specific issue of constitutional reform.

We should try to express in the most simple and comprehensive fashion our ultimate ideals. The only official document which now attempts to do this is the party constitution, written over 40 years ago. It seems to me that this needs to be brought up to date. For instance, can we really be satisfied today with a statement of fundamentals which makes no reference to colonial freedom, race relations, disarmament, full employment, or planning?

81 The following account is based on the detailed report in *KCA* (1959–60), p.17181 A. Crossman gives a sketch of the debate at a slightly earlier meeting of the PLP, Morgan (ed.), op. cit., pp.793–5, 796.

He then referred to the famous clause four and said that, standing on its own he thought it 'misleading': 'It implies that we propose to nationalize everything, but do we? Everything? The whole of light industry, the whole of agriculture, all the shops, every little pub and garage? Of course not! We have long ago come to accept a mixed economy. . . .'

This speech, and Gaitskell's subsequent reiteration of the position therein adopted, led to a major split in the party, controversy, and much mutual recrimination, each faction claiming to represent the true spirit of Socialism. A detailed narrative of this parade of fervour and animosity is not possible or necessary here, fascinating though the topic is.[82] The upshot was that clause four itself remained unamended (much party and union opinion was too wedded to it for this to be possible) but its meaning was glossed by the NEC in such a way as to concede something crucial to the revisionist point of view.[83] This recognized in particular that old-fashioned nationalization was only one policy among a number that might be pursued, along with various other forms of planning and social reform, as a means of changing society and achieving scientific efficiency and growth and the welfare this would make possible. As Haseler put it in his crucial study of these matters, 'No longer did the debate revolve around . . . "Socialist versus Capitalist" controversies but instead became concerned with how best to manage and work the mixed economy and to use the new technology in the interests of social justice.'[84]

When I ponder this revisionist attack on the centrality to Socialism of the doctrine of public ownership, I am always reminded of Carlyle's sarcastic verses in *Past and Present* about another fundamentalist dogma:

> The Builder of this Universe was wise,
> He plann'd all souls, all systems, planets, particles:
> The Plan He shap'd all Worlds and Æons by,
> Was – Heavens! – Was thy small Nine-and-thirty Articles?

But basic beliefs are impervious to such scathing, impregnable even against rational or empirical assault. However much they might seem beyond resuscitation, to attempt their modification or replacement invites the most tenacious resistance.[85] Consequently since the heady days of turmoil released by the fight over clause four, the power of the fundamentalist creed has in no whit abated and for many Socialists public ownership remains the most crucial part of the ideology and its

82   See Williams, op. cit., pp. 549ff.
83   ibid., ch. 21, app., pp. 572–3.
84   Haseler, op. cit., p. 248.
85   T. Carlyle, 'Past and Present' (1843), *The Works* (People's edn, London, 1871–4), xiv. 101. Cf. the same parallel with the Anglican articles in D. Taverne, *The Future of the Left: Lincoln and After* (London, 1974), p. 18.

programme. Yet there have been not uninteresting or insignificant changes of viewpoint in the interim. One result of the controversy and the re-emphasis of policy which followed, of the apparent diminution of enthusiasm for the direct and militant crusade against the capitalist enemy, was that some people on the left became disenchanted – or more so than before – with the way the Labour Party seemed to be going and began to anticipate alternative political channels. At the same time, if the central point itself about nationalization has continued to be sustained, it is increasingly in the context of a much greater concern with avoiding the deficiencies of centralization and the large scale and of securing greater participation by individuals than the traditional doctrine of the public corporation allowed. Something of all this is reviewed in the remaining section of this chapter.

MARXISM, SYNDICALISM, AND SOCIAL DEMOCRACY

The Labour leaders are men whose doctrine requires them to make the
state stronger, and whose good British instinct is to make the state as
weak as possible.
E. HALÉVY, *The Era of Tyrannies*, 1938, trans. edn 1967, p.198

Like all large political movements the Labour Party has always been a coalition of diverse elements and ideas. Naturally, therefore, it has invariably manifested fissiparous tendencies of varying strength and importance and latterly these have (for the first time in half a century) assumed a major practical significance creating for Socialism in this country a fundamental crisis. Manifestly the predicament has arisen because of a particular conjuncture of circumstances.[86] The lack of success of recent Labour governments in the search for solutions to contemporary economic problems, coupled with a failure to pursue policies of really fundamental social reform, led to increasing dissatisfaction with the Parliamentary establishment and its traditional views. This seemed to indicate, too, the collapse of that revisionism which has dominated the mainstream of Labour thinking since the mid-1950s; and the radical left has moved to fill the ideological vacuum thus created. All this has to be seen as well in the context of a sharp decline in popular support for the Labour Party and, presumably, its policies. From a post-war peak of nearly 14 million votes in 1951, its support had by 1979 (and in an increasing total electorate) fallen to $11\frac{1}{2}$ million, a figure which represented only a very little over 28 per cent of those entitled to vote.[87] Individual membership of the party has also fallen dramatically by some

86 Cf. P. Shipley, *Extremism and the Left* (CRD Politics Today Series no.13 [20 July 1981]), pp.234–7.
87 The Conservatives did only marginally better receiving the support of a third of the electorate.

two-thirds over the same period. To this extent, therefore, there has been a clear erosion of that general working-class basis on which the party has traditionally been supposed to rely for its electoral strength. This state of affairs, coupled with the effects of economic depression, youth frust-ration, inner city decline, and other social tensions, has intensified pressures for reconsideration and change from all quarters of the Labour movement: it has led both to a marked shift to the left and the departure of the social democrats. But, of course, a wider context than that provided by the immediate situation is necessary to appreciate properly the range of ideas and policies now clamouring for dominance in the Socialist ring. This is true in particular of assessment of the various radical tendencies which have recently sprung to the fore. It may be rather misleading to see them simply as reflecting a fierce revival of old-style Socialism, a reassertion of the fundamentalist faith against any continuing revision. Certainly there is in those circles a resolute opposition to the abandonment of further experiments in common ownership. Yet it is not just more of the Morrisonian public corporation which is demanded; for a much greater role is proposed for democratic influence and worker participation as envisaged indeed in the strict terms of the Labour Party constitution itself. For clause four has always referred to common ownership in a context of 'popular administration and control of each industry or service'.[88] Alongside the Marxism and the collectivism, therefore, a certain libertarian concern is also to be observed; and it appears in many quarters. Some aspects of this contemporary Socialism will now be reviewed.

The new left

The intellectual basis of the new left as it has emerged over the past two decades or so has rested on a kind of Marxist revival. The numerous (and often mutually hostile) groups concerned all reflected this.[89] However their variety is such that I can pretend to no more than a fleeting acquaintance with the many organizations and ideas, so the sketch that follows is only a very patchy and selective account of the themes they espouse though it is not, I think, misleading.

One aspect of this revival was the considerable disquiet increasingly felt about the Soviet Union and traditional Moscow-oriented Commun-ism. By the mid-1950s things had moved a long way from the pre-war

88 See above p.484.
89 These groupings are described in e.g. Shipley, op. cit.; *idem*, *Revolutionaries in Modern Britain* (London, 1976), esp. pp.207–11; D. Webster, *The Labour Party and the New Left* (Fabian tract no.477; London, 1981), esp. §4; B. Baker, *The Far Left: an Exposé of the Extreme Left in Britain* (London, 1981); and D. and M. Kogan, *The Battle for the Labour Party* (Fontana, 1982).

adulation represented by the Webbs and their fellow members of the radical intelligentsia and from the euphoria of the wartime alliance. Khrushchev's speech in 1956 to the 20th Party Congress made plain to the Communist sympathizer, what others had long known or feared: the truth about the unpleasant and unacceptable face of Stalinism and Russian state capitalism. The Soviet persecution of Yugoslavia and the invasion of Hungary in 1956 seemed to demonstrate beyond doubt the hard intolerance of Russian imperialism, a manifestation confirmed, too, by similar treatment of Czechoslovakia some years later. There were other things also, such as the cynical manipulation for political advantage by Russia and the Communists of the plight of the Rosenbergs in the USA. Such matters led a number of intellectuals to look closely at their ideological and party affiliations. One recalls the traumatic heart-searchings caused to some academic colleagues by the case of Hungary in particular. I remember, too, the late Harry Hanson telling me it was the Rosenberg affair which led finally to his resignation from the Communist Party.[90] Many of these people began to ask, as Trotsky had done years before, what had gone wrong with the Russian experiment and how Marxist doctrine, long used to sustain the dictatorship of a one-party state, had thus become debased. There was a feeling that Marx's ideas had to be dissevered from what Russian Communists had made of them: and a search began for the real or pure Marx. Partly, too, this tendency was aided by a certain recognition that classical or orthodox Marxism needed re-examination. It had been supposed to reveal the inherent contradictions of capitalism, to foretell the necessary intensification of the class struggle, and all the rest of it. On this basis certain predictions had been made about the inevitable demise of the capitalist system and its replacement by a classless Socialism. If hierarchical and autocratic Russia was to be the prototype of this development then something was amiss. Moreover, at that time of emerging affluence, prophecies of the destruction of the acquisitive society in a chaos of class warfare seemed sadly in error. It could not be, of course, that Marx was wrong; but he had been woefully misinterpreted. What better than to re-examine the canon with a view to resurrecting the real truth that must lie hidden there. And this propensity was strongly reinforced by the appearance in English (if not, strictly, for the first time then in a newly accessible form) of some of Marx's early writings, in particular the *Economic and Philosophic Manuscripts* of 1844. The worried intellectuals of the left fell on these bits and pieces of Hegelian musing with avidity and made much of them, a performance repeated some years later with the publication of the *Grundrisse* when, the 1844 papers not proving (hardly

90 Something of all this acute concern is reflected in D. Widgery (ed.), *The Left in Britain, 1956–1968* (Penguin, 1976), pp. 66ff.

surprisingly) all that had been anticipated, this other hitherto unknown work was received with similar éclat by those in search of further pristine authority. Another dimension was given to all this by the emergence of the Third World. There was a gross contradiction between the interests of the affluent and the undeveloped countries; and Marxist analysis seemed to provide a means both of exploring this antithesis and of intimating how it might be overcome. Nor was the exposition of new Marxist-based doctrines in Africa, the nether Americas, and China without similar influence.

All this intimated the possibility of a Marxism outside the framework provided by the traditional Communist parties of western Europe. Trotsky became newly fashionable; so did other unorthodox Marxists of the older generation such as the members of the Frankfurt School, the Italian theorist Gramsci, and R. Luxemburg. The outcome was a heated debate and the usual fragmentation, the emergence from this welter of a series of Marxist based groups with different interpretations of doctrine and policy based on a critical reading of the tradition and concerned at the tendencies revealed by modern industry and technology whether in capitalist or other forms.

Initially, during the late 1950s, a number of the British dissidents concerned wrote about working-class history, social communication, and literary and cognate aspects of politics: what G. Watson, in his cutting way, describes as 'a sort of latter-day Stalinism with a gloss of cultural analysis.'[91] Of course, not all the writers involved in the new left thus stimulated were Marxists let alone Communists; early, and most popular, works characteristic of their concerns included R. Hoggart's *The Uses of Literacy* (1957), R. Williams's *Culture and Society* (1958), and E. Thompson's *The Making of the English Working Class* (1963). There were also more direct expressions of political opinion in, for instance, *Out of Apathy* (1960) and *May Day Manifesto* (1967) as well as in the journals of the movement such as the *New Left Review* (which appeared from 1960 onwards). There was sometimes a propensity to urge the claims of state monopoly but it was usually done with a certain diffidence arising from recognition of the dangers of bureaucracy and centralized control involved. And much of it was never really systematic in the manner of traditional political theory being rather in the style of pamphleteering instead. Yet a typical theoretical case was presented in the writings of Ralph Miliband who expounds an anti-Labourist version of the new left position. In effect Professor Miliband provides a modified and updated version of the later views of Harold Laski whose student and colleague he had been during Laski's so-called Marxist phase. These views are presented in a number of places but their main expression is in

91 G. Watson, *Politics and Literature in Modern Britain* (London, 1977), p.26.

two books *Parliamentary Socialism* (1961) and *The State in Capitalist Society* (1969): the latter presents a general perspective while the earlier work undertakes within this context a specific analysis of the Labour Party and its ideas and policies.

The strategic theme is a rebuttal (from a Marxist point of view) of the revisionism presented by Crosland and others, specifically of the basic point that advanced western societies have entered a 'post-capitalist' phase that makes traditional Socialist analysis and criticism irrelevant. It is urged, on the contrary, that despite various changes of form these societies continue to show crucial capitalist characteristics. In particular they still contain an economically dominant class, the emergence of a meritocracy of managers notwithstanding. Similarly the degree of the redistribution of wealth that has occurred is much exaggerated and substantial differences of income and property ownership remain. And even though a 'consumer revolution' has taken place, there is still a large group in the community subject to varying degrees of poverty and deprivation.[92] Miliband concedes there is a plurality of élites in advanced capitalist society, a variety that constitutes distinct associations and interests that compete with one another. Yet over and above such differences these various groups possess a high degree of cohesion and solidarity and have common purposes transcending any specific disagreements.[93] And the relationship between the people who are economically dominant and those who control the political machine is very close. The point is put firmly and unambiguously:

> What the evidence conclusively suggests is that in terms of social origin, education and class situation, the men who have manned *all* command positions in the state system have largely, and in many cases overwhelmingly, been drawn from the world of business and property, or from the professional middle classes. Here as in every other field, men and women born into the subordinate classes, which form of course the vast majority of the population, have fared very poorly – and not only, it must be stressed, in those parts of the state system, such as administration, the military and the judiciary, which depend on appointment, but also in those parts of it which are exposed or which appear to be exposed to the vagaries of universal suffrage and the fortunes of competitive politics. In an epoch when so much is made of democracy, equality, social mobility, classlessness and the rest, it has remained a basic fact of life in advanced capitalist countries that the vast majority of men and women in these countries has been governed, represented, administered, judged, and commanded in war

92 R. Miliband, *The State in Capitalist Society* (1969; Quartet Books, 1973), chs 1–2 *passim*.

93 ibid., pp. 44–5.

by people drawn from other, economically and socially superior and relatively distant classes.[94]

There is thus, in Miliband's view, an interlocking network of select minorities the purpose and interest of which is to sustain capitalism. And in this they are aided by a powerful process of 'political socialization' operating through parties, churches, the education system, the cultural influence of business in favour of free enterprise, the media, and so on and so forth. This is obviously a theme very difficult to sustain in terms of hard evidence and it must be admitted that Miliband's case is often rather slight in this respect. But the perspective or viewpoint it is intended to establish is clear enough; and it constitutes the context in which the specific analysis of the political state of affairs in Britain is to be seen.

The main argument of the earlier book on *Parliamentary Socialism* is that, despite any political rhetoric to the contrary, the Labour Party has in fact done little, since it began three-quarters of a century ago, to transform this capitalist system into a Socialist one. It has indeed never been a genuinely Socialist party. Its creed has been not Socialism but 'Labourism'. Its leaders and its dominant sections have stood for moderation and compromise, for social reform rather than social revolution. They have in effect accepted that their task, through various forms of state intervention, has been to make capitalism more efficient, to regulate and humanize it rather than to replace it. Moreover by emphasizing the constitutional and Parliamentary road to such change they have sapped the strength of the Labour movement whose main potential for political ends has lain outside Parliament in the form of industrial action and mass demonstration which have almost always been eschewed. Both the essential goal and the most effective means to it have thus been renounced in what Miliband sees as a betrayal. At the same time he believes that the real faith has always been sustained: first by what he usually calls 'the Labour left', variously represented by the ILP, the Socialist League, Victory for Socialism, and suchlike groups which have stood for a more radical and militant attitude; and secondly by the 'extra-parliamentary left' as embodied in, say, the SDF and the Communist Party. An internal battle about these matters has in fact gone on 'uninterruptedly' since the Labour Party itself was founded but the fight has (unfortunately as he sees it) almost always gone in favour of the Labourist right and centre. And if, in the early 1960s, the changes in union leadership and policy under way seemed possibly to presage a turn for the better, then ten years later his customary pessimism had reasserted itself.[95] This is the general framework in which he reviews,

94 ibid., pp. 61–2, italics in original.
95 R. Miliband, *Parliamentary Socialism: a Study in the Politics of Labour* (1961; 2nd edn, London, 1972), pp. 345–6, 350ff.

critically, the Labour attitude to the many problems which it has faced from its 'Lib-Lab' days in the last century right down to the present era of the mixed economy. He does not think it can ever be 'a socialist party, genuinely committed to the creation of a radically different social order'. Its leaders may make 'radical-sounding noises' but they will always ensure that the party 'remains, in practice, what it has always been – a party of modest social reform in a capitalist system within whose confines it is ever more firmly and by now irrevocably rooted.' It follows that, for Miliband, what is really needed is preparation of the ground for the emergence of a properly Socialist alternative to the Labour Party and its doctrine.[96]

In some respects Miliband seems to reach this conclusion rather reluctantly. He appears more than a little unwilling to give the Labour Party up for lost, hoping, as it were against the record, that it might be revivified in a properly Socialist form. A like ambivalence appears in some other recent writings of the left which have, however, in the end often been rather more hopeful of what the Labour Party might achieve. For instance, K. Coates, at one time a Communist, was vehemently critical of the 'neo-capitalist' policies pursued by the Labour governments of 1964–70, but nevertheless seemed to feel that the course of the party might be properly modified by contact with the 'hard' left and the influence of union militancy. 'There is still some time', he wrote, 'in which to save the Labour party from the shame of its recent past. But not much.'[97] Personally, too, he was very anxious to be reinstated as a member of the Labour Party after having been expelled, no doubt to assist from within the process of ideological transformation. Similarly M. B. Brown, writing in 1972, does not totally despair of the possibilities the Labour Party presents to the genuine Socialist. Of course, he believes the Crosland thesis about the changed nature of capitalism to be quite erroneous and misleading: 'Capitalism has not been reformed and still contains . . . nearly all . . . its old anti-social and anarchic tendencies.'[98] But the Labour Party should not be completely rejected as a vehicle of change. It can still help forward the process of radical reform especially if it can be forced to press very hard questions of social ownership and control of the economy and if it does this in conjunction with an increasingly militant union movement 'right up and beyond the limits of what capitalism is capable of' [sic].[99] Another who shares this qualified optimism about the possibility of the Labour Party effectively helping the

96 ibid., pp. 372, 376, 377.
97 K. Coates, *The Crisis of British Socialism: Essays on the Rise of Harold Wilson and the Fall of the Labour Party* (Nottingham, 1971), p. 243.
98 M. B. Brown, *From Labourism to Socialism: the Political Economy of Labour in the 1970s* (Nottingham, 1972), p. [12].
99 ibid., pp. [13], 238–9. Cf. ibid., pp. 148, 229.

working class is E. Roberts of the AUEW (and later an MP).[100] But there are others who cleave more closely to the more despairing aspects of Miliband's type of analysis. For instance, one discussion, written from the point of view of International Socialism, urges that the Labour Party has always failed and must of its nature fail to create 'a genuinely socialist society'; it is, indeed, a positive impediment to that achievement.[101] It is necessary, therefore, if one is a Socialist, to commit one's loyalty and effort to the 'revolutionary' alternative, to an apocalyptic upheaval based on 'a radicalised working class'. This class must be mobilized on a mass basis for open war with capitalist society. The conflict will doubtless be 'bitter and bloody' but this alone can transcend 'the irrationalities of capitalist production and the alienation of human labour that is at that system's core.' There is a crying need for a powerful new movement of this sort, 'a mass revolutionary socialist party in Britain'. Consequently mere 'activity within the Labour Party is pointless.'[102] From the same camp, P. Foot wrote that today 'Intelligible socialist theory is impossible without the recognition of class society and of the impotence of Parliamentary institutions' − and therefore the Labour Party − 'to change it.'[103]

Much of all this critical diatribe is naturally merely negative, concerned to analyse the dominant Labour Party and its tradition, hoping either to shake it up and make it genuinely Socialist or to point out that it is bankrupt and that little or nothing can really be hoped from it. This is the focus of the debate about 'entryism' or 'non-entryism' that has taken place among those on the extreme left.[104] And certainly since the abolition in 1973 of the Labour Party's list of proscribed organizations, Trotskyite and similar infiltration has notably increased as indicated, for instance, by the growing influence of the so-called 'Militant Tendency'.[105] The actual ideas deployed seem often to be rather imprecise. There is usually a conviction that capitalism must in the end be destroyed by revolutionary violence so that involvement in any existing constitutional process is only pursued for the tactical advantage it may bring. There is, too, a considerable emphasis on the need for a fully planned economy and for state ownership and control which, it is assumed, must be massively extended quickly, through enabling legis-

---

100 E. Roberts, *Workers' Control* (London, 1973), pp. 56, 224–5, 227–9.
101 D. Coates, *The Labour Party and the Struggle for Socialism* (London, 1975), pp. v–vi, 130–44, 218–19.
102 ibid., pp. vi, xii, 219, 227–8.
103 P. Foot, *The Politics of Harold Wilson* (Penguin, 1968), p. 340.
104 See e.g. Widgery, op. cit., pp. 202, 209–11, 440–1; Shipley, *Revolutionaries in Modern Britain*, index *sub* 'Entryism'.
105 See e.g. Shipley, *Extremism and the Left*, pp. 232–3.

lation, and without compensation for the assets acquired.[106] At the same time there is also a wish in principle to avoid the evils and deficiencies of large-scale corporatism and to ensure that democratic participation is widespread and effective. Yet it is not by any means clear how these two goals may be jointly achieved. Miliband urges that there has not been anywhere near enough state intervention and nationalization; but he is equally very clear that what there has been so far is of the wrong sort creating bureaucratic paternalism rather than industrial democracy.[107] D. Coates polishes one criticism of Parliamentarianism by urging that because of its 'limited potential' it must necessarily fail 'to confront the problem of class power *within* industry'. It has offered as a panacea mere officialism.[108] Specifically it proved incapable of conveying a view of Socialism 'that was conterminous with the establishment of workers' control at the point of production' and which would involve dismantling 'the managerial hierarchies and authority structures' generated by capitalism.[109] M. B. Brown has also argued that the new dynamic needed comes from a demand for the extension of workers' control, rank and file participation to avoid autocratic management or bureaucracy. In other words, the development of a new 'grass roots' politics.[110]

This is indeed the interesting libertarian or anti-statist element enmeshed in the most all-embracing collectivism, the assertion of the crucial importance of decentralization and of popular participation of various sorts and at different levels of political and social activity. It is in this context that notions of industrial democracy or workers' control have latterly assumed a fresh significance in the thinking of the left (and indeed not only there). And here at least there is a considerable link with a dormant tradition of Socialist ideas of very notable significance indeed: for there is at work a re-awakened Syndicalism.[111]

The Syndicalist revival

On the whole the Labour Party, in its programme and achievements, has

---

106 For one instance, see the policy document issued by the National Committee of the Labour Party Young Socialists as reported in the *Daily Telegraph* (6 March 1978).
107 e.g. Miliband, *Parliamentary Socialism*, pp.204, 350 and n.1.
108 D. Coates, op. cit., pp.197, italics in original, 205; cf. ibid., pp.213–14 and ch.7 *passim*.
109 ibid., p.219.
110 Brown, op. cit., pp.183–8, 230–1.
111 Cf. K. Coates and A. Topham (eds), *Workers' Control: a Book of Readings and Witnesses for Workers' Control* (1968; Panther, 1970), p.350. This is a most useful collection of sources on which, in what follows, I have drawn substantially as a guide to the original literature.

reflected a collectivist and centralizing ethos, one associated as well with an emphasis on the primacy of political and Parliamentary action as a means of achieving its goals. But it is important to recall that this has not been the sole constituent of the British Socialist tradition which has also manifested lines of thought and policy hostile to state control and bureaucracy and which has been concerned to stress the significance of trade union militancy and the strike weapon rather than constitutional reform and this both as a means of conducting the class war and securing change and as the basis of post-revolutionary society. The inaugural edition of *Solidarity*, the journal of the Industrial Democracy League, affirmed (before the Great War) that the objective was to prepare 'the workers for their economic emancipation by taking possession of the means of production and distribution through an economic organisation outside the control of any parliamentary party' – a clear rebuff to the Labour Party itself.[112] The specific aim here is not simply public ownership but some form of industrial democracy or workers' control as a means of self-government and development. This latter form of Socialism is usually called Syndicalism and has from time to time and in different forms appeared (or erupted) on the Labour scene in this country. It has not, however, been much apparent since the failure of the General Strike in 1926 and the confirmation at about the same time of the Labour Party itself as a major political force which led to the complete rehabilitation of constitutional methods of securing change. Labour participation in the wartime coalition and its subsequent independent electoral success seemed to confirm the Syndicalist decline. Reflecting the general party opinion, Morrison in 1932 completely rejected the idea of workers' control as mere middle-class romanticism (a reference perhaps to the Guildsmen) and not Socialism at all.[113] Equally, the revisionists of the 1950s hardly gave much attention to the possibility of such arrangements.[114] Yet recently there has occurred a resurgence of these notions in certain quarters, some of them intellectually sophisticated, some of them politically influential, and in a way that seems to cast a degree of doubt on the value of half a century of political reform and even of the Labour Party itself.[115] In the present context, the significance of

112　*Solidarity* (September 1913), cited in R. J. Holton, *British Syndicalism, 1900–1914: Myths and Realities* (London, 1976), p.145.

113　H. Morrison, in *The New Clarion* (17 September 1932), cited in E. E. Barry, *Nationalisation in British Politics: the Historical Background* (London, 1965), p.315.

114　See e.g. Socialist Union, *Twentieth Century Socialism: The Economy of Tomorrow* (Penguin, 1956), ch.10; C. A. R. Crosland, *The Future of Socialism* (London, 1956), pp.93–4, 343–50. For Gaitskell's hostility, see P. M. Williams, *Hugh Gaitskell: a Political Biography* (London, 1979), pp.171–2.

115　See e.g. R. S. Barker, 'Guild Socialism Revisited?', *Political Quarterly*, xlvi (1975), pp.246–54. For an international perspective, there is C. Levinson (ed.), *Industry's*

these ideas lies, of course, in their often overt hostility to the growth of centralized state power and in their counter-assertion of the need to find other forms of more democratic and participatory methods of communal ownership and control than have so far been developed. It constitutes a kind of quasi-libertarianism of the extreme left, the prefix being appropriate because it seems uncertain in the end how far exponents of these views would permit any effective degree of dissent, of individual as opposed to group choice and decision. Their workers' communes would operate closed shops and would somehow have to conform to the demands of a planned economy. But at least the explicit and formal hostility to statist collectivism in the conventional, centralized style is very clear.

The idea of workers' control: early stages

Workers' control is a form of industrial democracy; its exponents would say, the only proper such form. For industrial democracy can mean a number of different things.[116] The term has been used simply to describe a state of affairs in which industries are publicly owned and their operation by a board of appointed directors is in some way responsible to the community. The nationalized industries in Britain obviously fall into this category. Alternatively it would be possible for the labour interests concerned to be directly represented as such on the controlling body having the power to nominate certain of its members. This is the course of action that Bevin continually, and unavailingly, pressed Morrison to adopt when the London Transport and later socialization schemes were being considered.[117] Then, of course, there are the numerous ways of securing some form of joint consultation or participation in management decisions. But much beyond any of these possibilities is workers' control in a more fundamental sense by which those responsible for operating an industry or service are elected or appointed by, and accountable to, all the workers involved; or, going even further still, there is a utopian vision of direct industrial democracy in which any vestige of delegation is dispensed with. Workers' control in anything like the full degree entails, therefore, not only the abolition of private ownership in industry (which could be achieved by state collectivism) but the creation of a completely new 'industrial order' in which the industries of a country 'will be controlled (partly or completely) by associations of the workers

Democratic Revolution (London, 1974) ch.1, esp. pp.72ff. on 'The Gathering Momentum' where examples are given of various worker-participation and co-ownership schemes established in recent years.

116 Cf. R. A. Dahl, 'Workers' Control of Industry and the British Labor Party', _American Political Science Review_, xli (1947), pp.890–3.

117 B. Donoghue and G. W. Jones, _Herbert Morrison: Portrait of a Politician_ (London, 1973), pp.185–7.

employed in those industries.'[118] Workers' control thus conceived has two main objects. The first is to complete the process of democratization by extending to the economic sphere the same popular dominance that has broadly become established in the world of politics. The second, more specifically libertarian, is to avoid any kind of official paternalism. It is easy initially to exemplify these points by reference to a pamphlet produced before the Great War by James Connolly, the Irish Socialist (who was later executed for his part in the Easter Rising). Entitled *Socialism Made Easy*, its publication was sponsored by the Socialist Labour Party, a Marxist group (mainly centred on the Clyde) which broke away from the SDF in 1903 and which was, under the influence of the American Socialist Daniel de Leon, dedicated to industrial insurrection.[119] Connolly urged the first aim mentioned above by demanding 'the application to industry, or to the social life of the nation, of the fundamental principles of democracy. Such application', he went on, 'will necessarily have to begin in the workshop, and proceed logically and consecutively upward through all the grades of industrial organisation'. This conception also meets the second point, allaying 'all the fears of a bureaucratic state, ruling and ordering the lives of every individual from above'.[120] The danger to working-class interests that would arise from a centralized collectivism was widely recognized, even by opponents of Syndicalism.[121] *A fortiori* people like Connolly wanted above all to ensure that the future social order envisaged would 'be an extension of the freedom of the individual and not a suppression of it.' This was why it was essential that 'the administration of affairs' should be 'in the hands of representatives of the various industries of the nation' and that the workshop life of each industry should be democratically controlled by a union of all workers, all those in authority over others from foremen upward being elected.[122]

Of course, such views were neither unprecedented nor wholly unique. Something has already been said in an earlier chapter about the cognate ideas of Guild Socialism. Similarly there were the various instances of working-class co-operation which had occurred. Beatrice Webb describes, for instance, what were called 'Working Class Limiteds', that is, the joint-stock companies formed by wage-earners in the cotton industry; also the activity of the Co-operative Aid Society, an organiz-

118 B. Pribićević, *The Shop Stewards' Movement and Workers' Control, 1910–1922* (Oxford, 1959), p.1.
119 See Holton, *British Syndicalism*, pp.40ff.; R. Challinor, *The Origins of British Bolshevism* (London, 1977), pp.23–6.
120 J. Connolly, *Socialism Made Easy* (1908; Glasgow, n.d. [1917]), p.17.
121 e.g. Sir A. Clay, *Syndicalism and Labour: Notes Upon Some Aspects of Social and Industrial Questions of the Day* (London, 1911), pp.123–4, 134.
122 Connolly, op. cit., p.17.

ation established to help groups of working men start self-governing workshops.[123] However, one of the distinguishing features of the Syndicalist movement proper was that it derived from the zeal of trade unionists themselves.

It must be recalled that in Britain, after the collapse of Chartism, it was the trade unions that emerged as by far the strongest embodiment of organized proletarian sentiment and demand and that when a Parliamentary wing finally emerged it was for long seen as an ancillary to the main industrial movement (as for many on the left it still is). In Britain effective action to assert workers' control began in the summer of 1910 when Tom Mann founded *The Industrial Syndicalist* and its associated Education League which brought together and thus gave focus to previously rather isolated if not fissiparous activities. Writing in that journal in 1910, E. J. B. Allen, one of the principal leaders of the Industrialist League, urged that workers must obtain 'the full proceeds of their labour' and 'this necessarily means the taking into possession of the mines, railways, factories, and mills by those who operate them'; for the 'men and women who actually work in the various industries should be the persons best capable of organizing them.'[124] Later, after the Russian Revolution in 1917, these notions were often intermingled with the idea of the 'soviet'. Those associated with *The Workers' Dreadnought*, for instance, urged that the first step in achieving the revolution was for workers to take direct control through workers' committees or soviets, the idea of delegation to representatives being firmly rejected.[125] And, of course, the development of industrial unionism was seen as a basis for the leap to complete control of the management of factories.[126] At this time, too, the pamphlets of such exotic pioneers of Syndicalism as Eugene Debs and Daniel de Leon were often reprinted and their authority frequently invoked in the radical behalf.

The nature of Syndicalist doctrine and the idea of the industrial union on which it was based meant that it had a special appeal in places where a particular heavy industry was found (as with coal in South Wales, shipbuilding on the Clyde, or steel in Sheffield) or in industries that were large, important, and easily differentiated such as the railways. Thus these views had early been expressed by the railwaymen whose main union was the first to declare in favour of the Syndicalist demand for some degree of workers' control. The feeling was expressed that nationalization itself would not be enough and would not change their status and lot. This was, as one railway activist put it, because the 'State

123 B. Webb, *My Apprenticeship* (1926; Penguin, 1938), ii.418–19 and nn.
124 Allen, 'Working Class Socialism', *The Industrial Syndicalist* (1910) cited in Coates and Topham, *Workers' Control*, p.7.
125 e.g. L. A. Motler, *The Revolution Tomorrow* (London, n.d.), pp.2–4.
126 e.g. E. L. Pratt, *Industrial Unionism* (London, n.d. [1917]), p.5.

is essentially a ruling-class organisation' with chiefly coercive functions. It was necessary rather for railwaymen to take over 'entire control and management' of the railways 'by themselves in the common interest' and an aggressive industrial unionism was required to achieve this.[127] Again, W. W. Craik, writing for the Plebs League, and similarly from the point of view of the railway workers, said that the working class must, through the organization of industrial unions, fight for the democratic control of industry.[128]

Similar views were expressed in the mining industry, for instance by the Unofficial Reform Committee, a rank and file body which sprang up in South Wales.[129] A number of its members, probably including N. Ablett, W. F. Hay, W. H. Mainwairing, and N. Rees, drafted a very famous – and, in my view, somewhat overpraised – pamphlet called *The Miners' Next Step* which was brought out in Tonypandy in 1912. It rejected mere nationalization as no solution at all to the problems and aspirations of the miners and demanded 'industrial democracy' instead:

> To have a vote in determining who shall be your foreman, manager, inspector, etc., is to have a vote in determining the conditions which shall rule your working life. . . . [That] vote . . . would give you . . . control over your conditions of work. To vote for a man to represent you in Parliament, to make rules for, and assist in appointing officials to rule you, is a different proposition altogether.

So the objective is: 'Every industry thoroughly organized . . . to fight, to gain control of, and then to administer, that industry. . . . This would mean real democracy in real life. . . . Any other form of democracy is a delusion and a snare.'[130] The idea was that all the industries of the country would be covered by a series of industrial unions so as to centralize and maximize fighting power and that this arrangement, aggressively pursued, would become the basis of a completely new social structure. The same issues were also canvassed in a sort of sequel to *The Miners' Next Step* produced by the South Wales Socialist Society, the then President of which, W. F. Hay, had been part author of the earlier pamphlet. The issue was put, again, as one between 'bureaucracy' and

127 C. Watkins, 'Conciliation or Emancipation', *Industrial Syndicalist* (May 1911), cited in Holton, *British Syndicalism*, pp.106–7. Cf. Pribićević, *The Shop Stewards' Movement and Workers' Control*, pp.4–7.
128 W. W. Craik, *A Short History of the Modern British Working-Class Movement*, 3rd edn (London, 1919), pp.112–13, 115. At the same time this particular statement was not, as were so many, overtly anti-Parliamentarian, cf. ibid., pp.116–18.
129 An informative, brief note on the background is D. Egan, 'The Miners' Next Step', *Bulletin of the Society for the Study of Labour History* (no.38, Spring 1979), pp.10–11.
130 Unofficial Reform Committee, *The Miners' Next Step: Being a Suggested Scheme for the Reorganisation of the Federation* (1912; London, 1973), p.32.

'democracy'. Quite a number of ideas have been put forward, it was said, to achieve collective ownership and control. They have

> mostly centred on the proposal to nationalise the mines and to administer them under a Ministry of Mines controlled by Parliament. Such schemes offer no attraction to the miner, who sees in them only a proposal to nationalise **him** together with the mines. Practically every advocate of such schemes endorse [*sic*], under the term 'nationalisation', **officialisation** of the mining industry, i.e., the establishment of a bureaucratic control. . . .

But this is simply 'a change of masters'.[131] Whereas from the miners' point of view the scheme needs to be modified

> by the introduction of **democratic local and departmental autonomy,** in order that each person may retain as large a measure of control as may be over his own working condition. . . . The . . . principle of democratic control affords the miner the necessary guarantee of personal freedom, of limitation of effort and of increased remuneration, as an inducement to produce his maximum output, while at the same time assuring him of an adequate participation in the results of his efforts. . . .[132]

For some time indeed a controversy was going on among the mining trade unionists in South Wales about the relative merits of state Socialism and Syndicalism. Naturally there was a substantial difference of view about the relevance and desirability of a nationalization law.[133] In the Welsh miners' debate of 1912, Ablett, the main Syndicalist speaker, said that 'the roadway to emancipation' did not 'lie in the direction of bureaucracy' or the 'offices of a Minister of Mines' but 'in the democratic organization, and eventually control, of the industries by the workers themselves'.[134] In this vein the secretary of the Northumberland Miners' Association introduced his evidence to the Sankey Commission in 1919 by saying:

> The root of the matter is the straining of the spirit of man to be free. . . . Any administration of the mines, under nationalisation,

131 South Wales Socialist Society, *Industrial Democracy for Miners: a Plan for the Democratic Control of the Mining Industry* (Porth, Rhondda Valley, n.d. [1919?], pp. 5, 8, emphasis in original.

132 ibid., pp. 5–6, emphasis in original. Overall supervision of all industry would be exercised by 'a Central Board of Control', ibid., p. 13.

133 For one incident in this controversy, see K. O. Morgan, 'Socialism and Syndicalism: the Welsh Miners' Debate, 1912', *Bulletin of the Society for the Study of Labour History* (no. 30, Spring 1975), pp. 22–37 where a contemporary transcript of the discussion is reprinted.

134 ibid., p. 31.

must not leave the mine worker in the position of a mere wage-earner, whose sole energies are directed by the will of another. He must have a share in the management of the industry in which he is engaged. . . . Just as we are making political democracy world-wide, so we must have industrial democracy, in order that men may be free.[135]

The same skein of ideas was also to be found in other parts of the country. For instance, in Scotland working-class publicists urged the claims of direct action completely to transform the social and economic system. The workers were thus beginning to struggle against the 'industrial degradation' that system entailed for them:

They are realizing that the right to vote for Parliament, once in five years, is of little value compared with the right to vote on the way industry should be carried on. Consequently, the demand is arising that the brain and manual workers in industry shall by electing their own controlling bodies and their own officials, democratically manage the industry in which they work. . . . The problem of attaining Self-Government in industry can only be solved by the development of workers' power in industry. . . . The Servile State or Industrial and Social Democracy ? That is the choice that circumstances are presenting to the workers.[136]

Similarly on behalf of the ILP it was urged that to fight capitalism effectively the trades unions must 'assume control of production with a view to self-government in industry.'[137] Nor did the British Socialist Party fail to discuss the importance of the 'social-democratic ownership and control of industry'.[138] As has been noted, too, a phrase about popular administration and control as a crucial aspect of common ownership was included in 1918 in the Labour Party constitution.[139]

Nevertheless ideas such as those described would tend to keep politics in a subordinate place and give primacy to revolutionary goals pursued by an industrial policy of direct action. It was only thus, through an aggressive trade unionism independent of Parliament, that capitalism could be destroyed. As James Connolly wrote, 'the fight for the conquest of the political state is not the battle, it is only the echo of the battle. The real battle is the battle being fought out every day for the power to

135 The Coal Industry. R. Com. Rep., 1919 (vol.xi), vol.1, Reports and Minutes of Evidence, Cmd.359, p.324.
136 J. S. Clarke, Direct Action (Glasgow, n.d. [1919]), pp.7, [28].
137 R. P. Arnot, Trade Unionism: a New Model (ILP pamphlet, n.s., no.19; London, 1919), p.3. Cf. H. N. Brailsford, Socialism for Today (London, 1925), pp.88–9, 91.
138 Report of the Seventh Annual Conference of the British Socialist Party (London, 1918), pp.17–21.
139 See above p.484.

control industry'.[140] G. D. H. Cole said in 1917, albeit from a Guild viewpoint, that the 'new revolutionaries' knew that 'only by means of Trade Unionism can Capitalism be transformed'; so the aim must be to consolidate trade union forces.[141] And, of course, the crucial weapon in the industrial struggle was the general strike. It was in this climax that the unions manifested the extreme pressure that could be brought to bear to paralyse capitalist society.[142] It was this sort of policies, too, that caused concern and led to criticism on the part of other Socialists, as with the Webbs and such Fabian acolytes as L. Woolf who objected to Syndicalism because it failed to take sufficient or any note of the interests of the consumer and put a premium on industrial self-interest.[143] Some of the more extreme Syndicalist statements even spoke, in almost anarchist fashion, of the complete elimination of political institutions as normally conceived. Thus Tom Mann wrote:

> Syndicalism implies a condition of society where industry will be controlled by those engaged therein on the basis of free societies, these to co-operate for the production of all the requirements of life in the most efficient manner, and the distribution of the same with the truest equity, a society in which Parliaments and Governments will have disappeared, having served their purpose with the capitalist system.[144]

Not that this radical huff and bluster, the frequent loss of confidence in union leadership on the part of ordinary members, or the accompanying industrial unrest, led the government of the day to feel that Syndicalism as such had acquired any real hold in the country.[145] But it was a strand of some interest and effect if not in the Labour Party then in certain sections of the Labour movement as a whole. And it meant a number of specific things. First it sought the rejection of traditional trade unionism, with its varied forms of organization often on a small craft basis, and pursued instead the large-scale industrial union. It spurned, too, the orthodox union emphasis on careful bargaining and compromise, on conciliation and respectability. Equally it was concerned about the centralized bureaucratic control implied by Fabian-type collectivism. And it empha-

140 Connolly, op. cit., p.24. At the same time Connolly did not deny the important effect on the working class of 'action at the Ballot Box', ibid.
141 G. D. H. Cole, *Self-Government in Industry* (1917; 5th edn, rev., London, 1920), p.41.
142 See e.g. the citation from E. J. B. Allen, 'Working Class Socialism', *Industrial Syndicalist* (November 1910), in Holton, op. cit., p.62.
143 L. S. Woolf, *Co-operation & the Future of Industry* (London, 1918), pp.124.
144 T. Mann, *From the Single Tax to Syndicalism*, p.xv, cited in Pribićević, op. cit., p.19.
145 See the memorandum (13 April 1912) of S. Buxton, then President of the Board of Trade, in PRO, CAB 37/110 item 62, pp.3–4.

sized not so much constitutional reform through political and electoral means as direct action by the application of industrial strength.[146]

These Syndicalist ideas were indeed kept alive even during the inter-war period (when most of the earlier impetus was lost) mainly, though not entirely, in more extreme political quarters. It was always a matter of interest to those represented by the Fourth International. The doctrine of industrial action was promulgated, for instance, in 1938 in Trotsky's 'transitional programme' which urged, amid much else, the need to bolster mass unions, to establish a wide range of factory committees, to demand the opening of the books, and so forth: a statement which has not been uninfluential, too, in more recent years.[147] The orthodox Communist Party also asserted workers' control as the basis of industrial reorganization.[148] So did the Communist-inspired 'minority movement' which consciously followed in the footsteps of the earlier South Wales Syndicalists.[149] In other traditional Syndicalist centres as well, the stress on the primacy of economic rather than political action continued to be heard.[150] The largely middle-class Socialist League of the late 1930s espoused the idea of workers' control as part of its ideological *mélange* though without doing much at all to create links with the trade union movement. Similarly the Socialist Labour Party still kept alive in the early 1940s the memory of de Leon whose writings rejecting state reformism in favour of economic take-over through Industrial Unions had been so influential in this respect earlier in the century. Thus was sustained the old slogan: 'The workshops to the workers'.[151] The ILP, too, often argued that workers' control was the only way to avoid state capitalism and union bureaucracy. In 1941, for instance, it was urged in its behalf, somewhat in the old Syndicalist fashion, that unionism should be developed on industrial lines as the basis for workers' control of industry in the future Socialist state and that as part of this process workshop committees must be created and the shop stewards' movement de-veloped.[152] So did the SPGB, though in its usual negative way this party

146 Cf. R. Miliband, *Parliamentary Socialism*, p.33.
147 L. Trotsky, *The Death Agony of Capitalism and the Tasks of the Working Class* (1938; London, n.d. [1942?]), pp.11–16. On the recent influence of this document, see e.g. P. Shipley, *Revolutionaries in Modern Britain*, chs III–IV, esp. pp.64, 75.
148 e.g. R. Palme Dutt, *Capitalism or Socialism in Britain?* (London, 1931), pp.24–5.
149 e.g. National Miners' Minority Movement, *The Miners' Fight* (London, n.d. [1924?]), pp.3, 11–12.
150 e.g. G. A. Aldred, *Socialism and Parliament*, part I 'Socialism or Parliament' (1923; 2nd edn, Glasgow, 1934), pp.4, 9, 63–4; also his *Pioneers of Anti-Parliamentarism* (Glasgow, 1940).
151 SLP, *Socialism and the State* (Edinburgh, n.d. [1942]), pp.4–6, 25–6, 27.
152 R. Edwards, *Freedom or Servitude* (London, 1941), p.4, 11, 20. For a later, more

tended rather to reject the alternatives on offer (such as nationalization) as state capitalism merely, than reveal the details of the alternative society based on workers' control that it envisaged.[153] The Labour Party and the TUC also discussed these questions from time to time. There was even occasional official consideration given to the possibility of extending co-partnership, including an element of control, as a means of achieving greater industrial efficiency and of palliating unrest. During the Great War, the Whitley Committee had proposed the establishment of joint bodies at all levels with functions going much beyond normal collective bargaining. A few such Joint Industrial Committees were created. But government interest was intermittent.[154] Similarly wartime concern with the need to expand production involved examining the role that could be played by the development of joint committees; and both Churchill and Bevin agreed the matter should be pressed. The occasion was used by the Clyde shipbuilders, in conformity with their Communist and Syndicalist tradition, to demand 'a say in the control of things'. The Prime Minister (no doubt recalling the intenser days of the Great War and before) minuted the report that went to him, 'I don't see much harm in it. It is very ordinary stuff'.[155] Nor was it completely unusual for Conservatives to advocate industrial democracy and urge the claims of labour to share an important degree of influence in the conduct of industry.[156]

But perhaps the most important practical prospect for the idea of workers' control was intimated by the shop stewards' movement.

The shop stewards' movement

A shop steward has been defined as 'a local union representative who has definite responsibility for the first stage of local negotiations, but is neither a full-time officer nor a branch secretary with recognized negotiating rights in that capacity.'[157] Today there are over 250,000 of them and their relation to the full-time union officials is a matter of some

---

specific, ILP expression of similar views, see the *Jubilee Conference of the I.L.P.* (London, 1943), pp.19–21; and A. Pannekoek, *The Way to Workers' Control* (London, n.d. [1953/4?]), pp.1–4.

153 SPGB, *Is Labour Government the Way to Socialism?* (London, 1946), p.18.
154 On the Whitley proposals, see H. Parris, *Staff Relations in the Civil Service: Fifty Years of Whitleyism* (London, 1973), pp.25–31. An example of later government discussion is in CAB 27/314 at the PRO.
155 PRO, PREM 4, 40/8.
156 e.g. P. Loftus, *The Creed of a Tory* (London, 1926), part II, ch.III. Tory Reform Committee, *Forward – By the Right!* (London, 1943), pp.2–3; C. Hollis, *Can Parliament Survive?* (London, 1949), p.98 and chs viii–ix *passim;* H. Macmillan, *Tides of Fortune: 1945–1955* (London, 1969), p.301.
157 H. A. Clegg *et al., Trade Union Officers: a Study of Full-Time Officers, Branch Secretaries and Shop Stewards in British Trade Unions* (Oxford, 1961), p.180.

delicacy and difficulty especially when they take unilateral action as in leading an 'unofficial' strike. The influence of a good many shop stewards is undoubted. As one left-wing commentator lately put it, the shop steward is much closer to the worker than his MP and can do more for him. He can be removed or at least checked the moment he fails to represent the workers' views fully; and he reflects the instinct to exert control over the workplace which is (it is said) much more deeply felt than participation in the quinquennial ritual of voting for Parliament.[158]

The shop stewards' movement can be traced back as far as the early 1850s in some of the militant areas of the engineering industry; and by the last decade of the century the engineering shop committees had increasing functions and influence.[159] But it was not until the Great War that it achieved any real degree of widespread organization and recognition: it is not insignificant that the first use of the term 'shop-steward' so far recorded by the OED occurred in 1915.[160] Certainly the movement developed strongly at that time for a number of reasons. One was that there emerged an array of problems (those concerned with dilution of labour, for instance) which could only effectively be tackled at workshop level. In addition, there occurred a shift towards industrial action because of the decline in real wages since 1910 and a certain disillusion with the performance and effectiveness of the Labour Party in defence of workers' interests. Moreover increased government action during the war in the sphere of labour relations aroused many suspicions which helped sustain the view that it would not be possible to trust the state with complete industrial control in an era assumed to herald a growing degree of public ownership. Also the habit of consulting trade unions made it easy to believe that workers generally should have some say in the running of industry. Nor was the initial impact of the Russian Revolution unimportant in stimulating the idea of the 'soviet' which in this context took the form of an elected workshop committee.[161] In fact in the early stages the movement was for the most part largely confined to the engineering industry where, too, Guild influences had not been insignificant.[162] Nevertheless all this prepared the ground for a wider penetration of the idea of workers' control than would otherwise have been likely. By 1917 it was possible to hold the first national conference of

158 D. Widgery (ed.), *The Left in Britain, 1956–1968*, p.161.
159 E. A. Roberts, *Workers' Control*, pp.69, 72, 79; H. A. Clegg *et al.*, *A History of British Trade Unions Since 1889* (Oxford, 1964), i.431–2.
160 *OED*, ii.4061 (1933 supplement).
161 On this particular point, see S. R. Graubard, *British Labour and the Russian Revolution, 1917–1924* (London, 1956); and R. Miliband, *Parliamentary Socialism*, ch.III, esp. p.86.
162 Pribićević, *The Shop Stewards' Movement and Workers' Control*, pp.85, 164–5, and ch.vi *passim*.

the Shop Stewards' and Workers' Committee Movement and to see it as constituting a leadership of country-wide authority. In the same year, J. T. Murphy, a leading member of the Sheffield Committee, wrote a pamphlet *The Workshop Committee – an Outline of its Principles and Structure* which was quickly and generally adopted as a kind of textbook or guide.[163] The following is a good contemporary summary (written in 1919) of this development:

> The shop steward, who has become so important in the developments of the last few years, was originally a minor official appointed from the men in a particular workshop and charged with the duty of seeing that all the Trade Union contributions were paid. He had other small duties. But gradually, as the branch got more and more out of touch with the men in the shop, these men came to look to the official who was on the spot to represent their grievances. During the War the development of the shop-steward movement was very rapid, particularly in the engineering industry. In some big industrial concerns, composed of a large number of workshops, the committee of stewards from the various shops very largely took over the whole conduct of negotiations and arrangement of shop conditions. Further, a national organisation of shop stewards was formed, at first mainly for propagandist purposes. The existing unions have considered some of the activities of the shop stewards to be unofficial, and there has been a good deal of dissension within the unions on this score.[164]

The connexion of this movement with control as a political objective was clear from the beginning, at least in the minds of some partisans:

> the movement for the overthrow of capitalism by an abolition of the wages system must begin, not at Westminster, not in the trade union executive, nor yet in the trade union branches, but in the workshops. And it should take the form of the assumption by the workers of an ever-increasing share in control. . . . The first step should be to establish in every industrial area, and for each industry, a system of Workshop Committees . . . to undertake . . . the entire business of production. . . .[165]

Again, the 'Constitution' of the Federation of the Amalgamation Committees (a Syndicalist body concerned to bring unions together on an

163 E. E. Barry, *Nationalisation in British Politics: the Historical Background* (London, 1965), p.209.
164 R. P. Arnot, *Trade Unionism: a New Model*, pp.5–6 n.
165 W. Gallacher and J. Paton, *Towards Industrial Democracy: a Memorandum on Workers' Control* (Glasgow, 1917), cited in Coates and Topham, *Workers' Control*, pp.108–9. Cf. the summary of shop stewards' rules during the war, cited ibid., pp.113–14.

industrial basis and closely connected with the shop stewards' movement) declared that its 'ultimate functions' were: 'To prepare the workers for their economic emancipation by their *taking possession* of the means of production and distribution through an economic organization outside the control of any parliamentary party or religious sect.' It was made very clear that the workers, through their industrial unions, would control the new society, not simply operating but owning productive units.[166]

But though the shop stewards' movement developed strongly during the war, its role diminished afterwards. Partly this was a matter of the dogmatic and often unrealistic militancy of some stewards which tended to lose support (and, often, cause their dismissal); much more, it was the changed economic conditions of growing unemployment and the like which made the unions and their officials, as the larger organizations, seem likely to be more effective in protecting their members' interests. So by the early 1930s, while shop stewards still existed, few were linked in factory committees and fewer still had any idea of constituting a national movement, though this was often suggested. In 1934, for instance, the Socialist League urged that 'The workers should be organised at the point of production; workshop and factory-committees should be built up' on the basis of industrial unions.[167] But beyond the plea or the vision little that was effective in this way actually occurred.[168] However, the situation then began to alter as pockets of stability in employment emerged and especially after the coming of the second war. As before, the shop stewards became much involved, through joint works councils and workshop committees, in the process of increasing war production, acquiring once again a definite place in industrial organization with important if limited functions. It was a strong basis on which further developments could occur. In fact the numbers of stewards have notably increased in the subsequent period and, since 1945, stewards have on the whole found their local, workshop power has grown in respect both of wage-bargaining and negotiations about conditions of work.

Obviously this movement has as a whole not necessarily reflected any widespread or systematic demand for workers' control – perhaps not until the past ten years or so – but it has embodied the nucleus of workshop organization and contained at least an implicit (and sometimes overt) demand for more consultation about or participation in the exercise of managerial authority. It was and is a basis or example, therefore, on which more systematic and radical political claims might be formed.

166 Pribićević, op. cit., pp.73–4, italics in original, citing the Constitution of the Federation of Amalgamation Committees.
167 Socialist League, *Problems of the Socialist Transition* (1934), pp.204–5, 215, cited in Barry, op. cit., p.330.
168 Coates and Topham, op. cit., p.139.

Experience of public enterprise

Another aspect of the matter that requires special mention is the place of the idea of industrial democracy in the public sector, specifically the nationalized industries and the trading activities of local authorities. Nearly half a century ago Herbert Morrison wrote that 'the position of the workers in socialised industries' is 'a matter of which much will be heard as socialisation proceeds.'[169]

Not unnaturally it was in the field of public enterprise, actual or proposed, that the notion of guild or union control made most headway, for it had long been urged, in some Socialist circles at least, that the goal could not be 'mere Governmental ownership or management.'[170] In 1917 G. D. H. Cole asked, 'is not nationalised industry a good seeding-ground' for the idea of industrial self-government?'[171] The Union of Post Office Workers had officially stressed this policy since the previous year and still does.[172] It is built into the Union's constitution as its major objective and has resulted in the issue of even such recent publications as *The U.P.W. and Workers' Control* (1942) and *The Business of Workers' Control: the U.P.W. Members' Introduction to Industrial Democracy* (1961). The nature of the commitment involved is indicated by a UPW pamphlet published in 1942 when the prospect of a post-war extension of public ownership was beginning to emerge. 'Corporations are but nationalised capitalism. . . . Their Boards display the worst features of the Civil Service. . . . Democratic they certainly are not, since, in no instance known to us, do they provide for the constructive mind of the organised workers to play its part.' In fact, the argument went on, even departmental responsibility was undesirable because 'Bureaucratic nationalisation' was as bad as 'the Public Utility Corporation' being equally remote from popular control.[173] The Union never tired of stressing the need for the whole Labour movement to revive understanding of 'the social philosophy that finds its expression in the demand for control by the workers'.[174] Other early proposals for nationalization

169 H. Morrison, *Socialisation and Transport: the Organisation of Socialised Industries with Particular Reference to the London Passenger Transport Bill* (London, 1933), p. viii.

170 E. B. Bax and H. Quelch, *A New Catechism of Socialism*, 6th edn (London, 1909), p. 8.

171 Cole, *Self-Government in Industry*, p. 164. Cf. E. Davies, *The State in Business or the Collectivist State in the Making* (1914; 2nd edn, London, 1920), p. xxxii.

172 For the reaction of the National Guilds League, see W. Milne-Bailey, *Towards a Postal Guild* (London, 1921).

173 Union of Post Office Workers, *People's Ownership or Public Corporation: the U.P.W. Explains a Scheme* (London, 1942), pp. [2], [4]. Cf. the interesting analysis on Guild Socialist lines (the anonymous author was a member of the NGL), in UPW, *Postal Trade Unionism Against Pioneering: an Examination of the Implications of the U.P.W. Report on Workers' Control* (London, n.d. [1942/3?]).

174 UPW, *Postal Trade Unionism Against Pioneering*, pp. 11–12.

often (though by no means always) included schemes for union participation in management in some way or other. The reasons lying behind such suggestions were clearly brought out in a Guild discussion of railway nationalization in which it was affirmed that the organized workers in the industry had come to understand that, even under state ownership they would still be 'wage-slaves, subject to the dictates of a power over which they would have no direct control. . . . Where they are crying out for freedom and self-government, State control would give them only a further dose of officialism.' Workers do not want to be controlled by 'the cold-blooded bureaucrats of Whitehall'; they are fit to govern themselves by choosing their own officers and administrators.[175] But nothing much came of this early agitation. For instance, the 1921 Railways Act stopped far short of the nationalization demanded and offered, in the particular respect here concerned, only an improved conciliation scheme.[176] And though they had at first been diffident about ideas seeming to smack of Syndicalism, the miners' leaders were won over at least to the extent that, by the time of the Sankey Inquiry, they included joint control as part of the package of ideas about nationalization which they urged, unsuccessfully, on that Royal Commission.[177]

During the inter-war period, such discussion of nationalization as there was in the Labour movement was largely conducted in Morrisonian terms. That is to say, the prime objects were industrial efficiency on the one hand and responsibility to Parliament on the other. Without the first, Socialism in the form of public ownership, would be discredited; with the latter, direct union representation would be an irrelevance. So on both counts, the idea of workers' control in state-owned industries or services tended to be at a discount or even specifically repudiated. Moreover, it would (it was argued) inhibit freedom of action by the trade unions concerned as well as invite claims to similar representation for other interests.[178] This is not to say the idea of workers' control in nationalized industries was not canvassed or, in the Labour Party, officially acknowledged. For instance, at about the time of the General Strike, a group of London left-wingers urged a programme of extensive nationalization, a concurrent rationalizing of industrial structure, and the establishment of factory committees as the basis of control.[179] The TUC discussed these matters as did the political

175 National Guilds League, *Towards a National Railway Guild* (NGL pamphlet no. 4; London, n.d. [1917 ?]), pp. 4–5.
176 Cf. P. Bagwell, *The Railwaymen: the History of the National Union of Railwaymen* (London, 1963), pp. 408–10.
177 Cf. the citation at pp. 501–2 above; and C. L. Mowat, *Britain Between the Wars 1918–1940* (1955; London, 1968), p. 34.
178 The debate about these matters is reviewed in R. A. Dahl, 'Workers' Control of Industry and the British Labor Party', loc. cit., pp. 887–90.
179 The Greater London Left Wing Committee, *The Left Wing and its Programme* (London, n.d. [1926 ?]), p. 7.

wing of the movement.[180] For instance, the statement of policy accepted at the Labour Party conference in 1934 promised that employees of publicly owned industries should have an effective and fair share in their direction and control.[181] The following year Hugh Dalton reviewed the question and accepted that in some form or other an increasing degree of workers' consultation and control was inevitable in both private and public sectors and would, in fact, go further and faster in the latter.[182] But on the whole, a Morrisonian diffidence predominated. And when, before the last war and after, specific schemes of nationalization were implemented, deliberately no provision was made for specific worker representation at board level, let alone was any heed paid to any more extreme notion of workers' control, on the ground that the industries involved would best be served by appointments made solely on the basis of ability wherever this might be found. Someone so radical as Sir Stafford Cripps doubted whether, even if full workers' control were in principle desirable, there were enough workers capable of undertaking the task.[183] Subsequently the revisionist view of these matters was quite clear: the idea of joint control, let alone anything more radical, was quite unconvincing. All such suggestions rested on a false analogy between politics and economic life. Just because voting was crucial in the former did not mean it was appropriate to the running of industry.[184]

Despite this dominant tendency of opinion, which was indeed reflected in government policy, the principle of workers' control in state enterprises continued to be canvassed by some unions and Socialist groups. For example, in 1945 and after, the National Union of Railwaymen urged that no public industry could be a success without it. Similarly the demand for complete workers' control in the nationalized steel industry was heard at the Labour Party conference in 1948 and again a few years later.[185] The appearance of various party pamphlets indicated that the issue was coming alive again, at least in the sense of requiring some discussion.[186] At the same time various critics of existing

180 See E. E. Barry, op. cit., pp. 319–24; Dahl, art. cit., pp. 883–7.
181 Labour Party, For Socialism and Peace: the Labour Party's Programme of Action (1934; London, 1935), pp. 5, 15.
182 H. Dalton, Practical Socialism for Britain (1935; London, 1936), ch. XVII. Advocacy of workers' control is to be found, too, in A. J. Cook and J. Maxton, Our Case for a Socialist Revival (London, n.d. [1928]), pp. 2, 19; and F. Brockway, The Next Step: Towards Working Class Unity (London, 1933), p. 4.
183 The Times (28 October 1946), p. 2.
184 Socialist Union, Twentieth Century Socialism, ch. 10, esp. pp. 103–4.
185 Bagwell, The Railwaymen, pp. 623–6; conference proceedings, cited in Coates and Topham, op. cit., pp. 318–22, 329–30.
186 Labour Party, 'Towards Tomorrow' discussion series (London, n.d. [1948?]); E. White, Workers' Control? (Fabian tract no. 271; London, 1949); M. Young, Small Man: Big World. A Discussion of Socialist Democracy (London, 1949), parts III–IV; J. M. Chalmers et al., Consultation or Joint Management? a Contribution to the Discussion of Industrial Democracy (Fabian tract no. 277; London, 1949).

arrangements for joint consultation, as in the Bevanite pamphlet *Keeping Left*, demanded a much more effective and extensive array of procedures to this end.[187] The Communists equally stressed the need to see that nationalization meant workers' and technicians' control of the managing boards together with a very substantial degree of participation in the discussion of plans.[188] Equally, from his idiosyncratic Socialist point of view, Sir Oswald Mosley stressed his continuing belief in the need to avoid detailed regulation and the large scale. He always, he claimed, favoured the Guild rather than the state Socialists; and, so far as industry was concerned, nationalized and other, he thought workers' ownership was desirable.[189]

There were several reasons for continuing interest in this particular context. One was a certain sense of dissatisfaction on the part of employees in nationalized industries. The euphoria of take-over quickly dissipated; there was no significant alteration in conditions, status, or responsibility; one employer had simply been exchanged for another and the consultation machinery which had been created hardly produced any real sense of worker involvement. At the 1948 TUC conference several union members spoke of their grave concern about such matters.[190] How else, it was often felt, was this sense of disenchantment or alienation to be dissipated save by some radical reform in the direction of industrial democracy? This feeling was often recognized. For instance, in 1959, Crosland accepted that to overcome it worker participation was necessary, if not in the reaches of higher management then, at the level of the primary work group.[191] Of course, those associated with the Institute for Workers' Control have stressed the importance of changing in this direction the traditional structure of management in the entire public sector.[192] The second reason was the specific reflection in the field of nationalized industries of a nagging general concern that was being aroused by the growing collectivization of society as a whole. A couple of Fabian tracts constituted signs of the times in this regard, one entitled *Socialism and Bureaucracy*, the other *Socialism and the New Despotism*.[193] The latter stated, for instance, that the first task of

187 Sir R. Acland *et al.*, *Keeping Left* (London, 1950), pp. 30–1.
188 See e.g. J. Gollan, *People's Democracy for Britain* (London, 1952), p. 22. Cf. also his later *The Case for Socialism in the Sixties* (London, 1966), pp. 86–8; and J. Mahon, *The Party of Socialism* (London, n.d. [1955?]).
189 Sir O. Mosley, *My Life* (1968; London, 1970), pp. 136, 172–3.
190 TUC Report, 1948, pp. 371–8. For similar references, see K. L. Shell, 'Industrial Democracy and the British Labor Movement', *Political Science Quarterly*, lxxii (1957), p. 521 n. 11.
191 C. A. R. Crosland, 'What Does the Worker Want?', *Encounter*, xii (February 1959), pp. 10–17.
192 See e.g. M. B. Brown and S. Holland, *Public Ownership and Democracy* (IWC pamphlet no. 38; Nottingham, n.d. [1973?]), pp. 5–6.
193 W. H. Morris Jones, *Socialism and Bureaucracy* (Fabian tract no. 277; London,

Socialism in the contemporary context was to challenge the power of the new managerial oligarchy and to recognize that the growth of a vast state bureaucracy constituted a grave threat to social democracy.[194] Nor, thirdly, did the increasing complexity of modern technology, the monotony of mass production processes, and a tendency for the size of industrial units to get larger mitigate these concerns; on the contrary they were exacerbated as a result. Moreover there was often a sense that, however 'mixed' the economy might have become, however much the state dominated the system, the old owning class was still pre-eminent or, where not, had been replaced by a new managerial élite equally distant and autocratic. Also more than three decades of nearly full employment had placed the trade unions in a very strong position. It was perhaps inevitable, given the British context and history, that they should have moved in due course further to consolidate the position of their members in terms not of wages or jobs simply but status, involvement in managerial decisions, and cognate matters. What were called 'control bargains' thus became matters for discussion. And this tendency to stress the workers' position has been heightened by the development of wage freezes, incomes policy, and so forth: a counter-strategy was the natural response.

Renaissance

Thus the old path of workers' control came to offer, or so it seemed, new opportunities. It was almost a case of the members of the leftist *avant-garde* putting their steps in the tracks of their forefathers where they felt they could neither wander nor stumble. The shades of long-forgotten Syndicalists and Guild Socialists seem to be stalking the land again.[195] In his old age Bertrand Russell was in various ways, not least in terms of practical support, a major influence in this sort of revival. In a book published at the end of the Great War he had recorded, albeit with some criticism, the very favourable impression made on him by Guild and Syndicalist doctrines. He had, too, been a member of the NGL. This sort of sympathy never left him and, half a century later, he welcomed the growing importance of the concept of workers' control because, he said, its demands went to the heart of what he had always understood Socialism to require.[196] There seemed indeed to be a growing demand for

1949); R. H. S. Crossman, *Socialism and the New Despotism* (Fabian tract no.298; London, 1956).

194 Crossman, op. cit., pp.5–6. Cf. his 'Towards a Philosophy of Socialism', R. H. S. Crossman (ed.), *New Fabian Essays* (1952; London, 1953), p.27.

195 Cf. A. W. Wright, 'Guild Socialism Revisited', *Journal of Contemporary History*, ix, no.1 (1974), pp.165–80; R. S. Barker, 'Guild Socialism Revisited?', loc. cit., pp.246–54.

196 B. Russell, *Roads to Freedom: Socialism, Anarchism, and Syndicalism* (London, 1918), esp. chsIII, VIII; Foreword to H. Scanlon, *The Way Forward for Workers' Control* (IWC pamphlet no.1; Nottingham, 1968), p.[1].

some form of effective industrial democracy as a means of securing a radical shift in the balance of economic power in favour of the working class. And this tendency was accompanied by a gradually increasing amount of attention of a varied academic and activist provenance, and, most important of all, by a renaissance of interest in the unions themselves.

After 1950 a certain amount of discussion had been directed to study of experiments in workers' councils abroad, in both Yugoslavia and Algeria for instance, and also of the West German system of *Mitbestimmung* (co-determination).[197] In 1957 the trendy and influential *Universities and Left Review* brought out a pamphlet on the interlocking structure of the establishment and demanded its break-up and the democratization of economic power; in the same year Raymond Williams referred to the emphasis of Guild Socialist ideas as constituting a 'creative and indispensable' part of Socialist thinking.[198] However, a couple of years later Professor Hugh Clegg of Nuffield College, Oxford, and a leading Fabian, reviewed the whole question of industrial democracy and suggested that, on the contrary, Syndicalism and the like were undesirable. This was in part because democracy depended on opposition and a distrust of power so that in industry trade unions ought always to maintain their independence of management and thus constitute a force ultimately hostile to it. If they become involved with it, as opposed to limiting and checking it through the process of collective bargaining, they would undermine 'the existing institutions of industrial democracy, already developed under capitalism.'[199] Royden Harrison of Sheffield University responded to this argument with the counter-assertion that democracy always involves effective accountability and the possibility of replacing leaders; opposition is also important but only as a means to this end. In this sense democracy has hardly begun to exist in industry and Socialists must argue ever more strongly for opportunities for the workers, as electorate, to replace management; they must press for such workers' control in a widening range of social ownership.[200] This flurry of academic controversy was not the cause, naturally, but a preliminary symptom of the wider discussion that ensued. Other left-wing writers looked at the issue; it was raised at the Labour Party, TUC,

197   See the discussion and references given in K. Coates and A. J. Topham, *The New Unionism: the Case for Workers' Control* (1972; Penguin, 1974), ch.15. For an early example of academic interest, see D. J. R. Scott, 'Producers' Representation in Yugoslavia', *Political Studies*, ii (1954), pp.210–26.

198   Stuart Hall *et al.*, *The Insiders* (London, 1957), esp. pp.38–41; R. Williams, *Culture and Society, 1780–1950* (1958; Penguin, 1961), p.191.

199   H. A. Clegg, *A New Approach to Industrial Democracy* (Oxford, 1960), p.29.

200   R. Harrison, 'Retreat from Industrial Democracy', *New Left Review* (no.4, July–August 1960), pp.32–8.

and similar conferences; in trade union journals, broadsheets, and the like.[201]

Something of the general flavour of the increasingly voluble advocacy of workers' control involved may be given by reference to some of its specific manifestations. One of the main departure points is indicated, for instance, by Ness Edwards, the Welsh miners' leader who had held minor office in the Attlee government. In the mid-1950s he published a kind of valedictory warning about the dangers of drifting into a bureaucratic or managerial society in which democracy would be weakened by centralized planning and the absence of participation in the vast new public corporations being created. He did not specifically urge the idea of workers' control but the sort of concern he expressed was part of the basis on which the renaissance of the idea might occur.[202] Similarly the following passage, from an editorial in the Marxist journal *International Socialism* in 1967, provides a general perspective and gives a good indication of the anti-collectivist attitude involved:

> It was a central thesis of social democracy that each extension of state power by the Labour Party, given effective parliamentary democracy, was an extension of popular power, and took place at local and national levels as well as in industry through the trade unions. But if the basic condition for this extension – namely a popular movement behind the Labour Party, acting through the electoral machinery – fails, what is left? Merely the extension of the state, the purposes of which can no longer be identified automatically with popular interests. The state has become autonomous, not merely the instrument of the popular will, nor even 'bodies of armed men', but the supreme expression of the *status quo* and independent of the ritual of party politics. Each past crisis of socialist thought has embodied an immense change of gear in the nature of capitalism, and the current crisis arises from the emergence of state capitalism within the formerly private capitalist countries. Thus, the slogans of the past – extension of state power, nationalization, planning and so on – have two meanings: the first, when such slogans were pitched against the greed and anarchy of private capitalism; the second, when such slogans become the declared aims of a developing state capitalist regime. The first embodied popular revolt. The second embodies the new *status quo*, for it lacks any popular basis to make it meaningful in socialist terms, it lacks at the national level, decisive democratic determination, and at the industrial level, workers' control. . . . Nationalization without workers' control means, not socialism, but state capitalism.[203]

201 Perhaps the fullest recent account of the ideas and tactics involved is Coates and Topham, *The New Unionism*.
202 N. Edwards, *Is This the Road?* (Wrexham, n.d. [1955]), esp. pp. 5–6.
203 N. Harris, in *International Socialism* (Summer 1967) cited in D. Widgery (ed.), *The*

The sense of dissatisfaction with the panacea of state ownership as such was elsewhere brought out in this way:

> The 1960s are a telling time for socialism. Pits, railways, electricity in Britain have been nationalized for twenty years. Yet whilst as in coal, industrial relations have sometimes improved, the status of the worker, as a 'hired hand', has in no way changed. Faceless bureaucracy has replaced the private employer, at best well-meaning paternalism has replaced bare-faced ruthless exploitation.

Neither material prosperity nor state ownership is enough to create 'a fuller life', as the experience of modern Russia and America shows. In Britain workers' control is required in addition to nationalization, not least as a complement to political democratization:

> it proposes self-administration of the work-place instead of control from above; to give men *in the plant* the civil rights and privileges he [sic] enjoys outside. . . . Socialism requires workers' rule and this must begin at the work-place if it is to exist through society as a whole. . . .
>
> Workers' control plans to put the flesh and blood into the economic structure of socialism; it is nothing more or less than socialism with its working clothes on.[204]

It was quite clear to the new Syndicalists, then, that the old Socialist idea that working-class power would be extended by the mere act of state take-over was no longer acceptable; it was indeed 'destroyed by workers' experience of the Attlee nationalization.'[205] In fact, on this sort of view, workers' control was the only way to achieve the genuine proletarian state for this depended not on the existence of planning or on the form of property ownership involved by itself – whether the factory is owned by government or by ICI is not crucial – but on the relations of production existing at the workplace.[206] Hence all the demands for '*really* democratic' workers' councils or committees.[207]

Of course, some of these statements are of little practical account, interesting only by virtue of the shrill and naïve extremism of their

---

Left in Britain, pp.232–3. Cf. P. Sedgwick on the importance of workers' control, in the same journal (no.17; August 1964) cited ibid., pp.133, 136; also M. Kidron, loc. cit. (no.14, Autumn 1963) cited ibid., p.213.

204 W. Kendall in *October*, magazine of the Brighton May Day Manifesto Group, 2nd issue, cited in Widgery, op. cit., pp.300–1, italics in original.

205 ibid., p.205.

206 See e.g. extracts from a speech by an IS speaker in 1967 and from a leaflet produced by the industrial sub-committee of the Committee of 100, cited ibid., pp.94–5, 122.

207 Cf. passages cited ibid., pp.172, 335–6; also R. Rosewall, *The Struggle for Workers' Power* (IS pamphlet, 1973), cited in Shipley, *Revolutionaries in Modern Britain*, pp.149–50; and the similar views of the 'Black Cross' anarchists and the Anarchist Workers Association cited ibid., pp.190, 196.

expression or by the way in which, without apparently realizing it, they simply repeat the diatribe of Penty and that ilk against modern mass technology and in favour of some form of post-industrial society. Equally others have been of direct political significance. This has been true of some of the Trotskyite inspired themes and groups. The so-called Militant Tendency is of importance here. This is one of a number of such groupings that formed the Revolutionary Socialist League which believed in a policy of 'deep entryism', that is, of operating widely within the Labour Party by infiltrating its branches and organizations. In 1972, for instance, it gained formal control of the Young Socialists, having since had a co-opted representative on the party NEC; and one member was appointed National Youth Organizer of the Labour Party. The achievement of democratic workers' control through the nationalization of the 'top 250 monopolies' is the main plank of its programme. The success of this group undoubtedly accounts in some part at least for the recent growth of a leftist tendency in the Labour Party.[208]

There is another significant aspect of this tendency of relevance here.[209] In 1963 a newspaper called *The Voice of the Unions* was founded (or re-founded, accounts differ) to campaign for workers' control and union democracy. Its first editor was F. Allaun, Labour MP for Salford East. The following year another such journal, *The Week*, was launched largely by a coterie of Marxists of various kinds in the Nottingham Labour Party and under the sponsorship of a range of sympathetic academics, trade unionists, and Labour MPs. In 1964 these two papers promoted a conference on workers' control of industry and attracted a similarly mixed and wide-ranging group of participants. This included A. Greenwood and F. Cousins (both shortly to become Cabinet ministers in Wilson's government), J. Jones, H. Scanlon, and C. Jenkins from the trade union movement, a number of university teachers, and representatives of various Syndicalist, Anarchist, and left-wing groups. This meeting was extremely successful and was subsequently repeated, leading in 1968 to the creation of the Institute for Workers' Control a body which has concentrated its efforts, and with some success, on influencing opinion within the Labour Party. A close observer of these affairs has noted:

> Within six years of its foundation, the Institute for Workers' Control progressed from the obscurity of the Trotskyist-connected fringe to a prominent position on Labour's left wing, supported by government

208 Shipley, op. cit., pp.96–7; Widgery, op. cit., pp.211, 496–7; D. Webster, *The Labour Party and the New Left*, pp.18–20; P. Shipley, *Extremism and the Left*, pp.232–3.
209 The account which follows is based on Widgery, op. cit., pp.201, 486, 503; and Shipley, *Revolutionaries in Modern Britain*, pp.105–8.

ministers and a dozen backbench Members of Parliament. Its growth reflects both the increasing interest in the subject of workers' participation in the management of industry across the whole of the political spectrum and, more particularly, the steady resurgence of radical socialism in the Labour Party.[210]

The IWC's main source of financial support was the Bertrand Russell Peace Foundation and it had a quite substantial range of backing from 'several hundred activists'. Its aim was to be an intellectual pressure group, somewhat in the Fabian style: 'to act as a research and educational body, to co-ordinate discussion and communication between workers' control groups, and trade unions, to provide lists of speakers and publish important materials on the subject of industrial democracy and workers' control.'[211] It was hoped by this propaganda to increase the practical impetus towards workers' control in industry and to spread the idea in the unions and the Socialist movement generally. The Institute has produced an impressive output of books and pamphlets to which there has been a substantial trade union contribution. It has organized annual conferences some of which have been attended by over 1000 delegates. The sort of direct political influence it has had on the Labour Party is indicated by the fact that in 1974, A. W. Benn, then Secretary of State for Industry, invited the Institute to submit recommendations on industrial democracy for official consideration. If at the present time, Benn is seen as playing a part filled a generation ago by A. Bevan then his supporters in the IWC have aptly been called 'Benn's Tribunites'.[212] As well, prominent supporters included a dozen or so left-wing Labour MPs such as S. Orme, N. G. Kinnock, E. S. Heffer, R. G. Thomas, and E. G. Varley whose participation is alone ample evidence of the IWC's tangible advance in the political sphere: three of those named are, for instance, front-bench spokesmen for the Opposition.[213] K. Coates, a former Communist and Trotskyite sympathizer who regained membership of the Labour Party in 1969, is the central figure in the Institute's activities and has published a number of interesting papers and books on workers' control. The IWC itself has not stated its collective aims precisely, preferring not to adopt a dogmatic line of policy but to keep itself open to an eclectic range of influences and ideas on the subject of workers' self-management. It seems clear, however, that the Institute's impact, and that of *Voice of the Unions*, on the Labour movement has

210 Shipley, *Revolutionaries in Modern Britain*, p.125.
211 K. Coates, *What Is the I.W.C.?* (IWC pamphlet no.14; Nottingham, 1969), pp. [6]–[7].
212 Widgery, op. cit., p.486. On Benn's sympathy, see also pp. 523–5 below.
213 Also Varley has written *The Case for Workers' Control in the Mining Industry* (IWC pamphlet no.40; Nottingham, 1974).

been not insubstantial. It has helped make the radical ideas propounded more acceptable especially as, on the whole, any cataclysmic revolutionary emphasis has been sedulously avoided.

If the idea of workers' control has recently undergone a renaissance of practical significance, then, this is due to its acceptance by a number of left-wing Labour politicians including a few of some seniority but, above all, by the commitment to industrial democracy of influential trade union leaders. The TUC itself stressed a growing interest too.[214] In 1963 Sidney Hill, then General Secretary of the National Union of Public Employees, wrote that in future trade unions should be concerned not simply with making pay packets bigger but with transforming workers' surroundings and relationships at 'the point of production', in particular with securing 'a continually increasing share in determining the organization and operation of jobs they are doing.' He commented on the various signs of renewed interest in these matters and continued with an indication of the anti-collectivist feeling involved: 'The developing tendency towards monopolistic structure and large scale organization in industry and business and the extension of State intervention in economic affairs . . . are prompting the realization that unions must turn more of their attention to a serious discussion of industrial democracy.'[215] In various industries indeed some groups of workers themselves put forward proposals for increasing democratization at the workplace, 'opening the books', and such like, aided by some of the intelligentsia of the left.[216] But not the least significant of developments in this regard was the acceptance of these goals by very such senior and powerful union leaders as H. Scanlon of the AUEW and J. Jones of the TGWU. When the IWC was founded in 1968 Scanlon stressed the need for democratic self-management in industry through a network of elected workers' committees; and the same year Jones commended a similar course to the Labour Party conference during a debate on industrial democracy.[217] Nor did their advocacy of these matters flag; rather the contrary in fact. In a subsequent symposium, for instance, they gave a nice conspectus of their opinions: the need to extend collective bargaining from wages and conditions into areas hitherto regarded as

214 See the TUC Annual Reports for 1963, pp.494–5; and 1964, pp.446–7, both cited in Coates and Topham, *Workers' Control*, pp.367–8. For the IWC reaction to the 1973 report on co-determination, see K. Coates and A. J. Topham, *Catching Up with the Times: How Far the TUC Get the Message about Workers' Control* (IWC pamphlet no.37; Nottingham, 1973).

215 S. Hill, *Public Employees Journal* (no.6, 1963), cited in Coates and Topham, *Workers' Control*, p.369.

216 See the varied range of citation and reference, ibid., pp.375ff.

217 H. Scanlon, *The Way Forward for Workers' Control*; Labour Party Annual Conference Report, 1968, pp.157–9. Cf. R. H. S. Crossman, *The Diaries of a Cabinet Minister* (London, 1975–7), ii.375.

managerial prerogatives; the importance of the growing shop stewards'
movement (there are now something over a quarter of a million of them);
the desirability of institutional experiment in placing workers' representatives on the boards of both public and private industry; and, as all
this implied free debate on the widest range of policy issues and
decisions, it was vital for there to be a full disclosure of information.[218]
Jones thought a great deal of practical progress had latterly been made:

> On the one hand there is the move towards the decentralization and
> 'democratization' of decision making within the union itself, while on
> the other there is an extension and a widening of the range of subjects
> being opened up for *joint* agreement, or even *joint* control, instead of
> remaining a purely unilateral management decision.
>
> This is the most practical contribution that can be made. If we can
> bring *most* workers into making decisions about many things
> previously regarded as being the sole prerogative of management, then
> a major step will have been taken towards industrial democracy. We
> shall have laid the basis for a more open and democratic industry and
> society.[219]

And this is all the more necessary as industry becomes larger and more
complex.[220]

A more extensive statement of interest and intent by a senior union
official (who later became an MP) was E. Roberts's volume on workers'
control which appeared in 1973. Roberts was assistant general secretary
of the AUEW with a long experience in the Labour Party and as a shop
steward in the engineering industry. He is also associated with the IWC.
His book is an interesting polemic, often more rhetorical than realistic
and sometimes downright misleading, but clear on the major ideological
issue that not only is workers' control 'the very essence . . . of socialism'
but an idea whose time has come.[221] The goal is not simply nationalization because the public corporations are ridden with bureaucracy and
the workers' position in public industries has shown no change. Rather
the aim is nationalization plus workers' control.[222] The spirit at work in
Roberts's survey is clearly anti-statist, hostile to centralization and
élitism, and fervent in the belief that any authority in the community
whatsoever must be democratically appointed and responsible. This
applies not only to national politics and to industry, but also to trade
unions themselves and to the Labour Party as well. He carries these
notions indeed to a considerable extreme seeming to envisage in almost

218 C. Levinson (ed.), *Industry's Democratic Revolution*, chs 9–10.
219 Jones, ibid., p.257, italics in original.
220 ibid., pp.259–61.
221 E. Roberts, *Workers' Control*, p.8.
222 ibid., *passim*, but esp. chs 3–4.

anarchic fashion that with the coming of full workers' control the state will wither away and man's inhumanity to man will be banished for ever. He cites with firm approval a (crassly naïve, Trotskyite inspired) statement of aim in the Young Socialists' *Fighting Programme for Labour* (1971):

> The simple facts and figures, the stranglehold exercised by the handful of exploiters, if hammered home would generate overwhelming support for the demand for nationalisation with minimum compensation on the basis of proven need of the 250 major monopolies. On the basis of a planned nationalised economy, democratically operated by the Trade Unions, the housewives, the shop-stewards, the small businessmen and the working class as a whole, it would be possible to begin to organise society in a way that would guarantee that poverty, hunger and war would be something of the dim and distant past. Such is the programme, such is the battle cry of the Labour Movement.[223]

The general tactic envisaged in all this is what the Guild Socialists used to call 'encroaching control', the incremental advance towards complete industrial democracy.[224] The point of view was well summarized in 1967 by the May Day Manifesto Committee:

> Workers already 'participate' in industry, but on terms set by capital. A socialist policy on industrial democracy begins from this fact, and from a principled rejection of the structures it creates. The socialist aim is to substitute publicly accountable ownership and control for the present system with its 'managerial (in fact, capitalist) prerogatives'. As first steps, it demands definite controls, by trade unions, over such matters as dismissals, discipline and safety. In wider questions of policy, it insists, in the case of joint discussion within any particular firm, on all the facts being made available – 'opening the books' – and further, on the extension of such discussions to the level of the whole industry, so that cost and market questions can be brought to a rational plane – a plan for the whole industry – instead of being left within the irrationalities of competition. That is to say, a socialist trade union policy envisages a step-by-step extension of workers' control to the point where it engages with the policies emerging from the wider democratic process, at which point the power of capital can be isolated and ended. . . . Further, it is absolutely essential, as the unions enlarge their functions, that their internal democracy should be radically overhauled and extended.[225]

223 ibid., p.20.
224 Acknowledgement of indebtedness to Guild Socialist ideas is not common, but on this particular policy, see K. Coates, *The Crisis of British Socialism*, p.136.
225 Stuart Hall *et al.*, *New Left May Day Manifesto, 1967* (London, 1967), p.40. Cf. the

Certainly a good many strikes have in recent times been concerned not with wage increases but with working arrangements. Scanlon claimed a few years ago that these grounds of industrial action nowadays comprised the goals of some three-quarters of all strikes (as compared with only a third a few years before).[226] Workers' control, then, is seen as 'an important form of immediate local democracy', but it is also, by extension, 'a part of a general democratic process.'[227]

The Labour Party began to pay vague attention: after all this objective could be said to be implied in its constitution. For instance, its 1966 election manifesto promised to 'an effort to stimulate industrial de-mocracy.'[228] A more or less contemporary entry in R. H. S. Crossman's diary is revealing. The context is specific but the purport general enough to be relevant here. Addressing a regional conference of the party, an audience which contained, it seems, a number of trade union activists, he wrote:

> At the last moment I ended with a passionate appeal for the Party to participate actively in working out the new prices and incomes policy . . . , working it out on the shop-floor level. It's only if the Government works with the Party at all levels, I told them, that we have any chance of achieving a real, workable prices and incomes policy.
>
> All that goes down marvellously well with our Party workers but I'm afraid very few members of the Cabinet believe in participation. I learnt the philosophy from Tawney and Lindsay who taught me that social democracy consists of giving people a chance to decide for themselves – that's the essence of it. This philosophy is extremely unpopular, I find, with most members of the Cabinet. They believe in getting power, making decisions and getting people to agree with the decisions after they've been made. They have the routine politician's attitude to public opinion that the politician must take decisions and then get the public to acquiesce. The notion of creating the extra burden of a live and articulate public opinion able to criticize actively and make its own choices is something which most socialist politicians keenly resent.[229]

In 1967 a working party, which had been chaired by J. Jones, issued a report on industrial democracy which argued the urgency of extending workers' participation and generally government by consent in indus-

parallel passage in R. Williams (ed.), *May Day Manifesto* (Penguin, 1968), pp.136–7.
226 H. Scanlon, *The Way Forward for Workers' Control*, p.[3].
227 Williams (ed.), *May Day Manifesto*, p.137.
228 Cited in F. W. S. Craig (ed.), *British General Election Manifestos, 1918–1966* (Chichester, 1970), p.270.
229 R. H. S. Crossman, *The Diaries of a Cabinet Minister*, ii.49–50 (24 September 1966).

try.[230] The left wing of the Parliamentary Labour Party naturally tended to plead for more workers' participation through, for instance, representation on managing boards.[231] After the mid-1960s the NEC industrial policy committee did further work on these matters under the chairmanship of A. W. Benn.[232] For his own part, Benn has frequently and increasingly stressed the importance of developing means of worker participation and control: Mrs Castle describes in her diaries how he pressed on a ministerial committee the view that industrial democracy was a much more important means than devolution of bringing power nearer to the people.[233]

Benn goes out of his way to stress the important connexion that has always subsisted between Christianity and the British Socialist tradition.[234] And his manner itself has been portrayed as that of a lay preacher or Old Testament prophet (a description with which, it seems, he was himself hugely pleased).[235] He accepts as, say, Tawney did before him the necessity on this basis for the considerable extension of 'common ownership'; but he does not believe that nationalization in the conventional form is adequate. This will simply enlarge state capitalism and increase the prospect of a 'corporatist nightmare permitting the worst forms of managerial authoritarianism' whereas a major object must be to 'transform the role of the workers in the industries concerned.'[236] The growth of large-scale organization and the implications of the new technology make it necessary to consider human relationships in the context of greater decentralization and more openness, participation, and accountability in government and industry alike. And workers' control is specifically urged as a most vital aspect of this process.[237] As he put it in one place, indicating clearly the context of Labour Party policy involved:

---

230 Report of the Labour Party Working Party on Industrial Democracy (London, 1967), p.6.
231 e.g. R. Kerr et al., Beyond the Freeze: a Socialist Policy for Economic Growth (London, n.d., [1966]), p.31.
232 See the account of the committee's work in A. W. Benn et al., Workers' Control: How Far Can the Structure Meet Our Demands (IWC pamphlet no.36; Nottingham, 1973), pp.2ff.
233 B. Castle, The Castle Diaries 1974–76 (London, 1980), pp.282–3.
234 A. W. Benn, Arguments for Socialism (1979; Penguin, 1980), pp.13, 23–9, 146; idem, Arguments for Democracy (London, 1981), pp.123–41.
235 Castle, op. cit., pp.312, 421–2.
236 Benn, Arguments for Socialism, pp.42–3, 53, 57–64, 70–1, 140, 145–7 (the phrases cited are at pp.42, 59). Cf. idem, A New Course for Labour (IWC pamphlet no.51; Nottingham, 1976), p.17.
237 idem, The New Politics: a Socialist Reconnaissance (Fabian tract no.402; London, 1970), pp.16–18. I owe this reference to Dr J. Hart of the Australian National University, Canberra.

Herbert Morrison's achievement in establishing our main public industries was a formidable one and history will record it as such. But it is now equally important that the Labour Movement should turn its mind to the transformation of those public corporations into expressions of our socialist purpose. Namely, that policies and institutions must serve the people and not become the masters.[238]

Benn was able himself, when in office after 1964, to initiate and support some experiments in co-operative enterprise.[239] Nor has his enthusiasm been abated by their failure. Equally his admiration for the role of the shop stewards in aiding the cause of industrial self-management is considerable: he regards them (in the terms of a rather far-fetched analogy) as a sort of present-day equivalent of the civil war 'agitators'.[240] In fact Benn sees the whole economy being run (or planned) by a tripartite consortium of government, industry, and workers.[241] Exactly how this will be done is not wholly clear but he stresses the substantial role that will be played by compulsory planning agreements with particular industries and firms.[242] Of course, Benn is a very busy politician but it is a very great pity he has not felt the need or had the opportunity to present us with a study in depth of his wide-ranging views.[243] But it is obvious from what has been published that there is an intriguing libertarian air about a great deal of it. Certainly in abstract terms, it is a pluralistic and democratic rather than a centralized Socialism that Benn explicitly espouses; authoritarianism in either politics or industry simply will not work any more.[244] Naturally there are self-deceptions and obvious omissions. Awkward trade union issues like that of the closed shop are, for instance, largely disregarded; and on the face of it the welcome accorded to a whole range of extreme left support (on the doubtful basis that Marxism has always played a legitimate and inspirational role in the Labour movement) appears not a little disingenuous.[245] But there is throughout it all the emphasis on more people wanting to do more for themselves, the belief that they are capable of this if only the conditions could be created to make it possible. If one ignores the populist stridency of tone, there is more than a passing affinity to the bourgeois themes of J. S. Mill or Green than to any trendy

238 Benn, *Arguments for Socialism*, p.64.
239 ibid., pp.66–70, 158–60.
240 Benn, *The Levellers and the English Democratic Tradition* (IWC pamphlet no.54; Nottingham, 1976), p.13. Cf. *Arguments for Socialism*, pp.29–32.
241 Benn, *Arguments for Socialism*, pp.152ff.
242 ibid., pp.47–8, 56, 157.
243 Even so the judgement of W. Waldegrave, 'The Brave New Bennite World', *TLS* (18 July 1980), p.816 is surely too harsh.
244 Benn, *Arguments for Socialism*, pp.17, 110.
245 For the supposed role of Marxism, see ibid., pp.33–9.

Trotskyite Marxism.[246] In any event, Benn currently pursues what the left always yearns for: 'a new socialist politics, with roots deep down in the Labour rank and file', a 'new, . . . libertarian socialism' to be born out of the ashes of Parliamentary pragmatism.[247]

So far perhaps the most elaborate and sophisticated analysis of these matters to appear is the work of another MP, S. Holland's *The Socialist Challenge* which is a deliberate attempt to provide a systematic critique of the revisionist view and of the idea of regulated capitalism on which it rested. The key argument (as I understand the book's case) is that it is no longer possible to think of a controlled economy managed by Keynesian policies and, through the growth achieved, supporting a substantial degree of reform. This is not simply because of the intrinsic limitations of Keynesianism but is the result, further, of the rise of the multinationals, the 'new mesoeconomic power' (as Holland calls it) which is able to inhibit the degree of control a national government can exercise over its own economy. The gradualism of conventional social democracy has thus been compromised. This situation has

> made imperative a programme of fundamental and effectively re-
> volutionary reforms, transforming the injustice, inequality and inef-
> ficiency of modern capitalism. This includes not only a major
> extension of new public enterprise through the mesoeconomic sector,
> but also socialist planning in which new patterns of ownership and
> control are made possible.[248]

With a nice touch of irony Holland argues that, with the development of 'monopoly-multinational capital', conditions have radically altered since the revisionists recognized that classical capitalism had been trans-formed and that thus conventional Socialist policy was out-of-date. The new circumstances rather make that traditional policy all the more relevant.[249] But if, as a way to ensure the 'socialist harnessing of mesoeconomic power', extended public enterprise and strategic plan-ning are essential, Holland does not urge the mere reassertion of the old fundamentalist point of view. For he believes that there are certain conditions which must be observed about the way the process of

246 Cf. the comment of J. R. Vincent, 'A Manifesto for Marginals', *TLS* (11 September 1981), pp.1023–4 that the 'true Benn' is a Liberal idealist of the period before the Great War. K. O. Morgan sees Benn as 'a *déclassé* populist with Tory Democrat overtones', 'Dimensions of Dissent', ibid., (25 September 1981), p.1090. Whoever is right, there is clearly something old-fashioned about him.

247 P. Foot, *The Politics of Harold Wilson*, pp.21, 347.

248 S. Holland, *The Socialist Challenge* (1975; Quartet, 1976), p.9. For further discussion of the problems created by the multinationals, see *idem, The UnCom-mon Market: Capital, Class and Power in the European Community* (London, 1980), esp. pp.66–71.

249 Holland, *The Socialist Challenge*, pp.28–30, 154.

transition is achieved. It must be non-violent and democratic; it must be 'backed by the economic and social force of the organized working class', that is the trade unions; and – crucially – it must entail the widespread application of new means of ensuring a wider scope for 'the effective control of working people'. This last consideration is a vital one and may mean either 'outright' workers' control of individual firms or taking part in 'national bargaining'.[250] As with most of these analyses that admit a Marxist rather than a Guild or Ruskinian provenance, the workers' sense of alienation or 'anomie' is regarded as being caused by that break-up of traditional society due to the development of the capitalist mode of production.[251] The machine and technology are not regarded as crucial in themselves (surely a major oversight?). But the problem posed is that of how to secure an effective degree of involvement in economic decision-making at all levels given the necessity for 'socialist planning'. A crucial safeguard against 'central state bureaucracy' in this respect must be that workers within the companies concerned should take part in the negotiation of planning agreements, probably through shop stewards' committees and the like.[252] There should also be a substantial extension of workers' self-management in individual companies.[253] Views about the cogency or importance of Holland's case may reasonably differ. One harsh critic believes that while it has little intellectual merit in itself, it is significant as providing a plausible rationalization of left-wing Labour views which for so long they have lacked.[254] Certainly it is the most wide-ranging justification of both planning and industrial democracy, and their attempted conflation, to have appeared recently in this country.

In 1975 as part of the same sort of tendency, the then Labour government appointed a committee of inquiry under the chairmanship of Lord Bullock 'to advise on questions relating to representation at board level in the private sector'.[255] Its reports appeared in January 1977, the majority recommending that trade unions should be given, by statute, the right to appoint employee directors to the boards of larger enterprises with a view to moving towards an effective transfer of power in industry. This suggestion was, however, widely criticized, and not only by employers.[256] In addition, there were, under the aegis of recent Labour

250 ibid., pp.38, 155, 162–4, 246.
251 ibid., pp.258–9.
252 ibid., p.271 and ch.10 passim.
253 ibid., pp.284ff. and ch.11.
254 D. Marquand, 'Clause Four Rides Again', TLS (26 September 1975), p.1095.
255 Industrial Democracy. Cttee of Inquiry Rep., 1976–7 (vol.xvi), Cmnd. 6706, p.v. For the Cabinet discussion of the proposal to set up this committee, see Castle, The Castle Diaries, pp.422–4.
256 See e.g. B. C. Roberts, 'Participation by Agreement', Lloyds Bank Review (July, 1977), pp.12–23; and C. Hanson, 'The Bullock Report and the West German System of Co-Determination', Three Banks Review (December 1977), pp.30–51. J. R.

governments, some practical experiments in the same direction (not altogether happy) such as the workers' co-operatives at the Meriden motor cycle factory, Kirkby Manufacturing and Engineering, and the *Scottish Daily News*. Nor is the idea of industrial (as opposed to simply consumer) co-operatives without exemplification or advocacy; and in 1978 a Co-operative Development Agency was established to aid and promote the growth of such organizations.[257] The Labour election manifesto of 1979 committed the party 'to a major extension of industrial democracy' as part of a wider programme of democratic 'protection and enhancement'.[258] The Conservatives welcomed the prospect of closer participation but refused to provide for it by law; much more positively the Liberals saw it 'as the key to reversing Britain's economic decline' and which as such must be firmly aided and advanced.[259] Of course, these are only election promises or possibilities.

In any event, it is manifest that ideas at least about these matters have been and are stirring. For over half a century the doctrine of the Labour movement has been largely dominated by centralist, Fabian ideas and policies, the goal of workers' control being substantially though never completely abandoned.[260] Now what has hitherto been an undercurrent is, perhaps through actual experience of collectivism, surfacing again and in some important places. And in one perspective at least what is happening may be simply a further stage in a process that began in 1832 or even before. The achievement of popular democracy in the political arena is being followed by similar pressures in economic life for an extension of the democratic ideal to the sphere of production. Just as traditional authorities in the state were made representative and accountable, so now the tide may be making in the same direction in industry and commerce whether publicly or privately owned.[261] The equivalent of 1832 yet alone of 1867 is yet to come, but the possible line of pressure is clear even though it is difficult to see how far the tendency can go because, inevitably, there is a certain ambivalence about the prospect. For if a government or a country is committed to the rational allocation of resources, the idea of a planned or managed economy, and all the rest of it, then the extent to which any great degree of autonomy may be permitted in specific sectors of economic life (especially when these are

---

Shackleton, 'Is Workers' Self-Management the Answer?', *National Westminster Bank Quarterly Review* (February 1976), pp. 45–57.
257 See e.g. R. Oakeshott, 'Industrial Co-operatives: the Middle Way', *Lloyds Bank Review* (January 1978), pp. 44–58, and the sources and examples there cited. For the CDA, see *KCA* (1978), p. 29180A.
258 *KCA* (1978), p. 29629A (29631).
259 ibid., pp. 29634, 29639.
260 Dahl, art. cit., pp. 875–8.
261 Cf. Benn, *Arguments for Socialism*, p. 43.

crucial to the whole) is obviously limited and a very substantial role must remain for central government and its agencies.[262] Equally this is true in so far as decentralization, worker participation, and the like may entail a less than optimum efficiency in the purely material terms of output and financial return. Moreover a productive unit in industry is not like a democratic society. It does not have an open-ended series of goals, being faced with 'imperatives of production' which may not permit much range of choice or decentralization in decision-making to the level of the shop or plant.[263] In itself the economic price involved might be worth paying for the social and political advantages anticipated; but the extent to which this is so will inevitably be limited by the economic needs of the nation. Nor is it really adequate to argue (as the IWC does) that centralization is not required by modern technology and that 'direct planning' is (somehow) wholly compatible with decentralized human communities. It is not enough simply to say that 'the movement for "workers' control" is . . . the standard bearer of "Plan" against the "Market".'[264] It is necessary to show in some detail what mode of organization is involved and this is not done effectively, any more than it was by the Guildsmen all those years ago. One would have thought that, paradoxically enough, the possibilities of effective decentralization and worker control might be greater when the state shows less propensity than hitherto to plan the economy or otherwise to play a substantive part in industry and commercial affairs. The practical achievement of industrial democracy may, oddly enough, rest on the success of the Thatcherite revolution or something like it. This apart, it is likely, therefore, that the most that can be expected is a growing degree of consultation or limited participation simply, based, of course, on adequate provision of information and opportunities for debate. In any case, will much be achieved if the trade union system is not itself altered a great deal more (as by organization on industrial lines, the development of comprehensive workshop arrangements, being less committed to uniformity and centralization as expressed, for example, in national wage negotiations)? Will there not be some conflict, too, in the trade union position? And is not a mistake made when it is supposed that denial of status, dignity, and responsibility to the worker is implicit in *capitalism*? May his subordinate role and sense of alienation not be due rather to the nature and large scale of modern industrial technology, mass production processes, and the like, and an interdependent economy as such? Can more be done than to offer sufficient economic satisfaction

262 Cf. Shackleton, art. cit., pp. 52–6.
263 Cf. Shell, art. cit., p. 528.
264 J. Eaton, *The New Society: Planning and Workers' Control* (IWC pamphlet no. 33; Nottingham, 1972), p. 15.

to make this position acceptable? Can it be palliated adequately by a necessarily limited degree of consultation?

Whatever the anticipations eagerly fostered in some sections of the Labour movement, such questions as these necessarily occur to the disinterested observer; and the nature and course of the old Guild Socialist movement may provide a salutary study: perhaps Penty on post-industrialism has said it all before anyway; and perhaps his inability to halt the march of the machine age is indicative of further failure to come. But, in the present context, the revival of these ideas is relevant and interesting, and may even be significant. Some have appeared, too, in the context of the recent developments leading to the establishment of the Social Democratic Party.

Social Democracy

In face of an earlier phase of left-wing activism, H. Gaitskell (then leader of the Labour Party in opposition) pledged himself to fight, fight, and fight again to save the party he loved from the unilateralist fate that then threatened it (and the country itself). Some time later, more defeatist or, it may be, simply more realistic in the face of a still stronger challenge from the left, a number of Labour MPs seceded and formed the Social Democratic Party. One of them, S. Williams (presumably in echo of Gaitskell) said, on resigning from the NEC, that the party she had 'loved and worked for over so many years no longer exists'. It had ceased to be the democratic Socialist party she had joined.[265] With hindsight it is now possible to discern signs of disaffection going back some years and thus to see, too, how some of the characteristic themes of the Social Democratic point of view (as these have so far emerged) bear a close resemblance both to the revisionism of the 1950s and to the libertarian concern about participation and decentralization that has more recently moved to the fore.

Straws in the wind
Perhaps the first firm portent was the creation in 1960 of the short-lived Campaign for Democratic Socialism (which was wound up three years later). Its object was to combat the intra-party groups of the left and it had some success in this. One of its founder members wrote: 'We were determined . . . to prevent the Party becoming a neo-Marxist Party dedicated to large-scale nationalization at home and neutralism abroad, a Party without hope of recapturing power except in the event of a

265 In a letter to R. Hayward, General Secretary of the Labour Party (10 February 1981), cited in I. Bradley, *Breaking the Mould? The Birth and Prospects of the Social Democratic Party* (Oxford, 1981), p.97.

national catastrophe.'[266] A further indication was the Taverne affair of the early 1970s. D. Taverne had been Labour Member for Lincoln for ten years when in 1972 he resigned because of differences which had arisen with his local party over entry to the EEC. He was, too, very critical of constituency caucuses and the way in which Labour affairs were dominated by the block vote system. A subsequent electoral success for his breakaway movement proved only temporary. What is relevant here are the ideas and policies expounded on the occasion to help mould the future of the left in a congenial image.[267]

Taverne starts from the premiss that the Labour Party is a coalition of two main groups with conflicting political doctrines. One of these is the revisionists, the other reflects the fundamentalist position; and he describes the fight over clause four (and unilateralism) in which they had been involved.[268] Nor was this rift merely a temporary bad patch; it suggested rather something more radical, no less than the imminence of a period when 'existing party alignments' would 'break up and re-form.'[269] What Taverne wanted to do was to give a preliminary sketch of the policies and ideas which a new social democratic party should embody. These were outlined in the statement of aims issued by the Campaign for Social Democracy, the group Taverne founded to this end.[270] There was, of course, the ritual recognition of social justice as the general goal to be achieved through democracy. A mixed economy was accepted though with notable collectivist elements, a continuing prices and incomes policy, the more close statutory regulation of collective bargaining, the redistribution of wealth, a high level of public spending, and so forth. Wholesale nationalization was rejected, however, though a central body was proposed as a means of channelling the flow of investment in the public interest. And greater democracy at work was envisaged. Obviously this is all rather general and also, in some ways, simply the Labour mixture as before (or one brand of it). But an interesting emphasis that was in this respect a little ahead of its time was the stress on decentralization, the need to reform our organizations and our technology in the direction of smallness and simplicity: 'Variety is more important to human beings than efficiency.'[271] The argument is very brief

266 D. Taverne, *The Future of the Left: Lincoln and After* (London, 1974), p.21.
267 On the Taverne affair, see *KCA* (1973), pp.25777A, 25961A (25962); ibid., (1974), pp.26381A, 26757A. Also Taverne's own *The Future of the Left*, part 1.
268 Taverne, *The Future of the Left*, pp.13–20.
269 ibid., p.98.
270 App. B, pp.171–5. The Campaign for Social Democracy is obviously ideologically similar to, but must not be confused with, the earlier Campaign for Democratic Socialism.
271 ibid., pp.144–7. The sentence cited is at p.147. Cf. the preliminary discussion about limiting economic growth, ibid., pp.139–44.

but in certain passages bears a clear affinity both to Spencer's evolutionary themes and to the case made long before by the Guildsmen and Distributists. The ghosts of the Chesterbelloc and of Adam Wayne were beginning to stalk the land again.

Further squabbles followed, those associated, for example, with C. Mayhew's defection to the Liberals and R. Prentice's to the Conservatives. The points of objection varied, of course, but included such issues as Labour's dependence on the trade unions and its vulnerability to the left. There was also a notable disenchantment with the economic policies espoused. Both men looked to a realignment of British politics and the possibility of a centre party emerging.[272] A few other like-minded Labour MPs (such as R. Jenkins, B. Walden, and D. Marquand) left politics completely, an indication presumably not simply of dissatisfaction with Labour but also with the prospects of a separate Social Democratic organization. However the formation in 1975 of the Social Democratic Alliance (dedicated again to combating dogmatic and alien elements in the Labour Party) was a sign that the idea remained albeit on the small scale. Similar later developments were the establishment of the Manifesto Group of Labour MPs in 1974 and of the Campaign for Labour Victory in 1977. The latter was supported among others by S. Williams, W. Rodgers, and D. Owen.[273]

But these events were just preliminary straws in the wind of discontent and (as the above brief summary indicates) they were blown hither and yon. The shift to the left, changing the traditional balance of power in the party, showed itself in various ways over the following decade and which may be indiscriminately listed. Among MPs the Tribune Group doubled from thirty-five to seventy so that it came to comprise nearly a third of the PLP. The effects of entryism in the constituencies showed in the increasing number of local parties that fell under the sway of Trotskyite and other activists. A concerted effort was made to influence in a leftward direction union attitudes to Labour Party debates. The political complexion of some of the trade unions changed. The larger ones used on the whole to be fairly solidly right-wing or of the centre but now the movement is more evenly poised which means that at party and TUC conferences (both of which are dominated in important respects by the block vote) it cannot be assumed that left-wing proposals will in the end be defeated. The left has also come to occupy a dominant position in the NEC since 1975 when it won an overall majority there. The consequences of this have been manifest as by the abolition of the list of proscribed organizations (which used to be strictly enforced); the development of

272 These matters are summarized in *KCA* (1974), p.26634B; ibid. (1977), pp.28190A, 28674A.
273 On these groups and their activities, see e.g. Bradley, op. cit., pp. 58–63.

friendly relations with foreign Communist Parties; but above all by the use of NEC sub-committees to produce a whole range of new policies involving, for instance, a neutralist stance in foreign affairs and a programme of large-scale nationalization in the domestic sphere. The defeat of Labour in the 1979 election, the subsequent retirement of J. Callaghan and his replacement by M. Foot of impeccable radical lineage naturally strengthened the determination of the left to ensure that the party enters the next election committed to an acceptably Socialist programme and that a future Labour goverment will be mandated to carry these policies through Parliament. Hence the series of amendments (actual or proposed) to the party's constitution the better to secure this end, changes concerning the method of choosing the leader, the final responsibility for drawing up the election manifesto, and the reselection of MPs as Parliamentary candidates. All this entailed prolonged and often bitter discussion and caused severe strains in the party.[274]

This continual and successful pressure by the extreme Socialists and their allies led to a consolidation of opposing opinion that the current (and accelerating) tendency to the left was unacceptable not least because it would place the PLP under the control of the extra-Parliamentary forces, that is, the trade unions and the constituency organizations, the latter in particular being seen as coming more and more under the influence of extremist elements such as the Militant Tendency. This resistance to the left-wing advance has taken a number of forms including the launching of a Labour Solidarity Campaign representing a broad cross-section of the PLP and dedicated *inter alia* to the reversal of 'narrow and intolerant decisions and views' which 'unrepresentative minorities' have been able to impose and intend to carry further.[275] But the most interesting and perhaps important development has been the major series of defections after 1979 and the emergence of a separate Social Democratic Party.

The sign of four
In an 'open letter' published in *The Guardian* newspaper on 1 August 1980, D. Owen, W. Rodgers, and S. Williams urged that the Labour Party would only regain electoral support for progressive policies if it was firmly committed to Parliamentary democracy, rejected the idea of class war, accepted the mixed economy and the need to manage it efficiently, and attached real significance to traditional ideas of freedom, equality, and social justice. At the end of the year the SDA was proscribed by the NEC (quite correctly in accordance with traditional party

274 There is a full factual summary in *KCA* (1981), pp. 30757A, 30911A (30912–13), and ibid. (1982), p. 31307A.
275 ibid. (1981), p. 30911A (30912).

practice) after it had decided to establish a separate programme and organization to promote candidates in opposition to the Labour Party. A little later, immediately after the special conference in January 1981, the three MPs mentioned above together with R. Jenkins (who had just relinquished his appointment as President of the European Commission) issued the so-called 'Limehouse Declaration' with its proposal to set up an organization to 'rally all those who are committed to the values, principles and policies of social democracy' and thus to face 'a realignment of British politics'.[276] The premiss for defection was bluntly stated:

> The calamitous outcome of the [rules revision] conference demands a new start in British politics. A handful of trade union leaders can now dictate the choice of a future Prime Minister. The conference disaster is the culmination of a long process by which the Labour Party has moved steadily away from its roots in the people of this country and its commitment to parliamentary government.

Consequently, the Declaration went on, 'We propose to set up a Council for Social Democracy' with the object of trying to reverse Britain's economic decline, and 'to create an open, classless and more equal society'. The drift to extremism and the pendulum shifts of adversary politics were alike condemned; and the need for a radical reformation of British politics asserted.

Following statements of political and public support (mainly from Labour and ex-Labour Members), the Social Democratic Party was formally launched in March 1981 by which time the SDP group in the House of Commons numbered fourteen (thirteen ex-Labour and one ex-Conservative Members). By the following month, membership in the country at large had risen to over 43,000. While some Liberals were diffident about the prospects, overtures for a closer connexion were made from the outset and, after establishing a Parliamentary co-ordinating committee in May and issuing a joint statement the following month, a working electoral alliance was proclaimed at the Liberal Party conference in September 1981.

What all this means in terms of ideas and policies (as they apply to our domestic affairs) and what is implied about the role of government is revealed in two ways: first by the general SDP statements issued for public consumption; and secondly by the more elaborate reviews of policy and principle published by leading SDP supporters.

The major statements have been three in number: the original Limehouse Declaration (January 1981), the document called *Twelve*

276 The Declaration is reprinted ibid., pp. 30759–60, from which the following citations are taken.

Tasks for Social Democrats (issued on the formal announcement of the creation of the SDP in March), and *A Fresh Start for Britain* jointly proclaimed in June 1981 by both wings of the Alliance.[277] What these proposals come down to is a middle-of-the-road mixture with some inclination to a libertarian tendency wherever opportunity offers. Thus there is a commitment to a stable and healthy mixed economy. The superior wealth-creating possibilities of competitive enterprise are accepted but so is the need for some regulation and control as with a flexible incomes policy, the need to ensure a fair distribution of rewards, the elimination of mass unemployment; and a properly thought-out investment programme is urged to use the temporary oil wealth to the best effect. Poverty must be eliminated and greater equality secured. There must be improved welfare and cognate services. And this improved provision must somehow be achieved without stifling enterprise or imposing bureaucratic control from London. Thus the dangers of excessive substantive intervention or control are recognized. The necessity of greater decentralization of decision-making in both industry and government is strongly stressed as is the corollary importance of increased public participation through (say) various forms of industrial democracy, profit-sharing, or co-operative enterprise. Constitutionally this tendency must lead, on the one hand, to an improvement of the position and authority of Parliament *vis-à-vis* parties and the executive and, on the other, to plans for effective devolution. A basic prerequisite is, of course, electoral reform.

The specific demand for proportional representation apart, little is particularized: there is no indication, for instance, of the detail of anti-inflation or incomes policy or (say) how far Keynesian programmes are deemed necessary. This sort of thing presumably will come in due course. It will certainly have to if practical credibility is to be secured. Meanwhile the other sources must provide the only detailed guidance we have so far. These are up to now three in number: E. Luard, *Socialism Without the State* (1979), published in fact before the actual formation of the SDP; S. Williams, *Politics is for People* (1981); and D. Owen, *Face the Future* (1981). The first is the most articulate statement in abstract theoretical terms of the position involved; the second is oddly naïve and simplistic, even elementary, in its approach, without doubt the least satisfactory of the three books; the last is by far the most mature and full (even in its abridged version).

Luard grasps at once the ambivalence of Socialist doctrine leading as it may either to the omnipresence of the state or to liberation from it and its apparatus of oppression. He is clear, too, that the former tendency has been easily the stronger: 'the idea of socialism came everywhere to be

277 For the last, see ibid., p. 30980A.

identified with the expansion and strengthening of state power.' And the prime instrument for achieving the Socialist aims was a policy of nationalization.[278] But he believes that this collectivist trend has had many untoward consequences not least in the 'dehumanisation' and 'alienation' or sense of remoteness entailed, caused by the scale of organization necessarily involved:

> The greater the numbers employed, the more complex will be the hierarchy, the more remote and impersonal the system of command and communication. The more advanced the technology, the more elaborate the division of labour. And this will in itself make difficult the creation of the wholly new, more human, more equal relationships which many have demanded from a socialist economy.[279]

Or again:

> The growing concentration of authority in the state and state institutions, the dominance of the bureaucracy and other elites, the complex system of organisation, the inability of the vast mass of the population to affect decisions reached by their leaders, the increase in scale, the impersonal character of city life,

these are characteristic features of the modern world. There is, too, its 'anonymity', 'the sense that the individual is lost in a vast crowd, few of whose members he knows personally', and the 'otherness' of a growing and increasingly concentrated authority.[280] Nor will these problems be solved – indeed they are likely to be exacerbated – by any reform of the private ownership of the means of production achieved by the transfer of these assets to the state or some other public agency.[281] That desirable sense of social cohesion, of group loyalty and activity, which has been lost, is (on the contrary) only to be recovered by breaking up the large and complex organizations which have been created and by avoiding the assumption that, crudely, Socialism simply means nationalization in the traditional style. The creed thus needs to be seen 'as a principle for organising individual communities rather than for building ever more centralised national states.'[282] What is required, therefore, is a prescrip-

---

278 E. Luard, *Socialism Without the State* (London, 1979), pp.1–3. On the equation of Socialism with the extension of the state, cf. ibid., pp.9, 27, 29, 34, 41, 127–8, 145–8. Also *idem, Socialism at the Grass Roots* (Fabian tract no.468; London, 1980), pp.1, 4–5, 19.
279 Luard, *Socialism Without the State*, p.44.
280 ibid., p.47. Cf. ibid., pp.88–93. For the decentralist emphasis, see also D. Owen, *Face the Future* (1981; abr. edn, Oxford, 1981), ch.2; and Bradley, *Breaking the Mould?*, pp.130–6. Owen, op. cit., pp.8–9 clearly distinguishes the statist and anti-statist forms of British Socialism.
281 Luard, op. cit., pp.45, 47.
282 ibid., p.59. Cf. ibid., pp.27, 148–59.

tion which envisages a smaller, simpler, and more decentralized set of arrangements in which people will feel more at home and be fulfilled in a way which is not now possible. The consciousness of the individual must be enhanced; he must be self-directed in his work; the rewards of effort must be justly, more equally, shared; and the whole character of society must be transformed (as by repudiation of the assumptions of 'a selfish commercialism'.)[283] The spirit is clearly that of Tawney and of Penty and the Guildsmen of yore; though there are equally similarities with other protests against the scale of modern society and the alienation of the age. Luard is, too, refreshingly frank about the need to secure effective and wide involvement, not just the creation of more and more bodies that will be dominated by small cliques and oligarchies.[284]

What is disappointing (after the persuasive fervour of this basic analysis) is the paucity of specific prescription. the mere generality of the proposals in view to secure greater equality, participation, less alienation, more decentralized organization, and so forth. Drawing on foreign and domestic experience of the recent past, there is a certain amount of detail in the discussion of how to achieve greater industrial democracy.[285] But otherwise specific ideas about how exactly the spiral may be reversed are disappointingly few, apart from a few brief references to 'neighbourhood' enterprises, shared decision-making in schools, and the like. The need in principle to encourage decentralization and diversity is, however, continuously stressed.[286] The general spirit of these pages is most reminiscent of the old-fashioned romanticism (or utopianism) of Carpenter, Penty, Wells, and Ruskin. All important enough, of course, as a driving force but needing, not least for purposes of the hustings, to be particularized and made concrete. Nor is the suspicion wholly avoided of a radical contradiction of policies. For it is not easy to see, for example, how the effective pursuit of greater equality through a permanent incomes policy imposed by the state or the need for a system of national planning and a wide-ranging array of social services are objectives easily compatible with a dilution or diminution of centralized power.[287] Nor is greater equality necessarily achieved by more decentralization which is likely to result in more diversity.

On the whole, the same is true of the other two major expositions of SDP thinking: at least they stress the significance of a new emphasis on 'micro-socialism', the need for the doctrine to be rooted in the smaller,

283 ibid., pp.29–32.
284 See e.g. *Socialism at the Grass Roots*, p.5.
285 Luard, *Socialism Without the State*, pp.117–28.
286 e.g. ibid., pp.148ff.
287 For the particular objectives mentioned, see Luard, *Socialism at the Grass Roots*, pp.1–4. Cf. ibid., p.5 for reference to this particular issue.

living communities; but notable elements of 'macro-socialism', the stress on the organization of things by the central state, remain.[288]

In contrast to Luard's review, S. Williams's book is better on the details of various problems than on the general framework or approach which is indeed particularly lacking. It is noticeable, too, that even on the specifics she avoids dealing with what might be called the 'moral' social issues of our day, about abortion and drugs, and so forth. Perhaps not unreasonably, however, she concentrates on questions relating to the crisis of industrialism and the corporate system. None the less the ambivalence of Socialism (and other ideologies) is recognized and may be taken as the theoretical starting point of the exposition.[289] And she opts unhesitatingly for an emphasis which is formally libertarian: 'If politics is to be for people, then the first requirement is that the powers of government must be limited, ... Socialism without liberty is not worth having, for [it] will in time create a new and arrogant ruling class.'[290] This stance emerges from a context provided by the recent development of anti-collectivist sentiment and a hostility to the growth of public intervention:

> Many socialist policies have depended upon the state as their instrument; they have required an expansion in the role of central government. Socialists need to recognize the force of the antipathy that now exists towards 'big government': the multiplication of bureaucracy, the increase in cost, the feeling that government already has too large an influence over people's individual lives. . . . [There] is felt to be a disturbing degree of dependence, both psychological and economic, on government agencies.[291]

Yet this does not mean that the frontiers of intervention must be rolled back. It is not weak government or the undermining of welfare provision that is advocated. Rather is the problem one of devolution to regional and local communities and of ensuring greater participation.[292] It is 'a new romanticism' compounded of concern with the environment, suspicion of centralization and bureaucracy, and recognition of the need to improve the quality of life.[293] The main thrust of the argument is thus clear and takes the form of urging, for instance, the need for industrial deconcentration, for greater democracy in economic life, for more

288 The terms are Luard's: see ibid., p.19.
289 For the recognition, see e.g. S. Williams, *Politics is for People* (Penguin, 1981), pp.21, 32–5.
290 ibid., p.204. Cf. the invocation of Tawney, ibid., p.42.
291 ibid., pp.28–9. Cf. ibid., pp.63, 69. For the specific attack on high public expenditure, ibid., pp.30–1, 141–6.
292 ibid., pp.37–8.
293 ibid., pp.42, 43–5.

participation in the welfare state, for more open government, for enhanced Parliamentary powers *vis-à-vis* the executive, and so on. But again, as with the case urged by Luard, one ponders the question of internal consistency. For Williams sustains also a passion for equality and social justice. Government has, she believes, a clear responsibility to find work for those who want it and to cope with the varied array of problems involved (and some very interesting things are proposed in this regard). Yet it is difficult to see how, in the last resort, these objectives of full employment, retraining, and the like, can be pursued without a notable centralist control (even if the idea of a siege economy is firmly repudiated). And when the chips are down Williams sides (albeit with expressions of reluctance) for command in the name of equality and social justice rather than with freedom of choice for the citizen: as in the crucial case of the independent schools.[294] Yet as Williams explicitly recognizes decentralization may mean the emergence of greater distinctions and differences than might be palatable on other grounds: 'It is a difficult balance to get right.'[295] Indeed. But one comes away from a study of her book with the feeling that inside the libertarian Social Democrat there is perhaps a statist-minded Socialist still struggling to get out, one who is quite prepared to use the power of government to see people are made more alike in housing, education, and many other social benefits and attributes.[296]

D. Owen's *Face the Future* is fuller and more carefully worked-out in the detail: in this sense a much more sophisticated, systematic and satisfactory review of the Social Democratic possibilities (though it is, of course, not an official programme). Basically it, too, is about the justification of, and means appropriate to, the establishment of a more decentralized and participatory society in an age of increasing collectivist tendency. It is, in fact, the nearest approach to (as it were) a revised revisionism, an adaptation of Crosland's argument to the new circumstances of the 1980s. After what has been said already of recent Social Democratic writing, it is perhaps not necessary to examine this work closely. But I shall cite, in summary of its theme, a passage from one of Crosland's own last papers in which he warns against 'being in the business of creating endless giant Leviathans manned by armies of bureaucrats'; and as well that

> the contradictions of capitalism are not now those which Marx analysed 100 years ago. The need today is for the development of a more profound industrial democracy; for more democratic control

294 ibid., pp.157–8, 208. Interestingly D. Owen adopts a different view: see *Face the Future*, p.259.
295 Williams, op. cit., pp.207–8.
296 See e.g., ibid., pp.208–9. Cf. the perceptive comments in Bradley, op. cit., p.102.

over our private and public bureaucracies; for the fostering of a greater sense of community and spirit of co-operation – all combined with the ever present, everlasting need for vigilance in the defence of liberty.[297]

Thus what the Social Democrats seem to be envisaging is what Owen calls the 'Enabling State', seeing government not as a centralized controlling force but as one with the vital role of creating the conditions of individual fulfilment through the devolved agencies of a pluralist society and the encouragement of participation.[298] Whatever the outcome it is manifestly a repudiation of statism, a ditching of clause four Socialism, and an interesting revival of the libertarian tradition at least to some degree. That strand of the ideology takes two forms. It may either wish to roll back the frontiers of the state as such (as with the case of the Guildsmen); or it may wish not so much to do this as to disperse the power of the state rather than to reduce it. To judge from the documents so far available, the SDP's position is more nearly the latter.

297 C. A. R. Crosland, *Social Democracy in Europe* (Fabian tract no. 438; London, 1975), pp. 5, 14.

298 Owen, op. cit., ch. 12. For a summary of SDP views on the need to tame Leviathan, see Bradley, op. cit., pp. 130–6.

CODA

OF COURSE, the advice not to repeat a story comes from one of the oldest and most august of literary authorities.[1] And one more recent urges, too, that a theory is not proved even if the evidence in its favour looks well at first sight. There is, he says, 'an old proverb, very homely in expression, but well deserving to be had in constant remembrance by all men, engaged either in action or in speculation – "One story is good till another is told!" '[2] Yes, indeed. And one is aware as well of the danger of giving a theme an air of authenticity which is based simply upon a selective attitude to documents and facts, those alone being arrayed which sustain the point of view in question.[3] All the same, the plot of the ideological story which has been told is here a cogent (I do not say valid) one and may at this point be very shortly reviewed if only as a preliminary to what still lies ahead.

It is suggested that, of all the great changes which have overtaken this country in the past century and a half, the crucial political fact is the growth of government, the considerable extension of its intervention and control over the life of a community itself increasingly complex. In this process many factors and occasions have been at work.[4] It is a development which has, too, been aided by and reflected in our political ideologies. There have been opinions applauding this assumption of wider communal responsibilities while others have deplored and resisted the extension of the public sphere at the expense of the private or at least have wished to mitigate the more untoward of its consequences. As this volume has tried to indicate, both reactions are manifest in each of the major political creeds none of which reveals an essential, exclusive, or unchanging view of the role and office of government. As also suggested this is simply intrinsic to the nature of ideology which is necessarily ambivalent and rests not on a constant nucleus of aims, arguments, and assumptions but on a wide range of possibilities any of which may be deployed as need and circumstances dictate.[5] A quirk of human nature or

1 Cf. Homer, *The Odyssey* (Penguin, 1948), p.207 (xii.452–3).
2 Macaulay, 'Sadler's Refutation Refuted' (1831), in *The Miscellaneous Writings and Speeches* (Popular edn, London, 1889), p.254.
3 Cf. ibid., p.253.
4 See vol.i, *The Rise of Collectivism, passim.*
5 See above ch.1, pp.7ff.

logic or even of national psychology may also be at work. '"We're not a thorough people"', says a friend of Mr Britling's in H. G. Wells's novel, and goes on in (a surely unconscious) Hegelian fashion: '"When we think of anything, we also think of its opposite. When we adopt an opinion we also take in a provisional idea that it is probably nearly as wrong as it is right."'[6]

What this volume of case-studies has aimed to achieve, therefore, is to present a picture of the varied and even contrary aspects of modern political doctrine as carefully (and I hope as impartially) as possible; to give an account that is compatible with the documents and the historical record; and better at least than the usual misleading polarities of a sundered right and left. Perhaps, too, it makes clear for those interested the nature and tradition of the partisan contrasts at present on offer in the political market place, contrasts which are, in many respects, starker and clearer than they have been for a long time. The review of these matters has been very long; though it is hardly so lengthy that it might not have been fuller in many desirable ways. At least, as the old saw Macaulay had in mind suggested, it will perhaps do until a better story comes along. It may also make it difficult in the future for British politics to be considered without close reference to ideas as has so often been done hitherto.

Thus the story so far, then. What has now to be told is not what will happen in the ideological future – the owl of Minerva takes wing only with the coming of the dusk – but something which, if related, is different. For, of course, it is not only in arguments of state, in the field of doctrine and in party controversy over both creed and policy, that the development of the collectivist tendency and the rearguard action of libertarianism have been apparent. These have also been manifest in the way our political institutions and other public agencies have expanded and altered in recent times. And this will be shown in the next volume, *A Much-Governed Nation*: now read on.[7]

---

6 H. G. Wells, *Mr. Britling Sees It Through* (1916; London, 1933), p.172. For a similar view, see G. B. Shaw, *Socialism for Millionaires* (Fabian tract no.107; London, 1901), pp.11–12.
7 This volume will appear in 1984.

INDEX

I found this index difficult (and time-consuming) to compile. Many important topics cropped up so often that to give all the references would have meant some very long strings of page numbers indeed, while to categorize these effectively would have taken impossibly long (given the publisher's deadline), would have extended the total length even more, and would probably have been of only marginal extra use. What follows is the best compromise I can offer in listing and cross-referencing the numerous subjects covered. There is no entry for either 'collectivism' or 'libertarianism' which, of course, are reviewed throughout. But something of the treatment of such general themes may be discerned by looking, for instance, at the sub-headings given under under individual political doctrines. I have thus tried to make the entries relating to the ideologies themselves, their key concepts, and major exponents as complete as possible. As well, references are given to other persons, book titles, institutions, events, and the like where these are mentioned in the text itself.

'Marney, *Lord*' (*Sybil*) 207
Marquand, D. 531
Marriott, *Sir* John 281
Martin, B.K. 365
Marx, K. 5, 119, 120, 199, 349, 539
  influence in Britain 355, 357, 366, 424, 468,
    498, 526
  Labour Party 524
  rejected by
    Fabians 372–3, 378, 386–7 n.123
    Blatchford, R. 413
Marxism 168, 488
  agitation and propaganda 9 n.14
  Benthamism 356 n.23
  re-examined 488–90
  revisionism 475
  Trotskyite 15
  Webbs, the 404–5
Mass production 429
Mass uniformity 93
  individuality 298–9
Masses
  character 114–15
  equity for 160, 230–1, 232, 241–2
  significance 106–7, 142, 379
  supervision 113, 114, 142–3
Masterman, C.F.G. 171, 252, 391
  collectivist Liberalism 155–6, 172
Maude, *Sir* Angus 313, 327
Maurice, F.D. 352
Maxwell Fyfe, D.P. (later *1st Earl*
    Kilmuir) 311
May Day Manifesto (R. Williams *et al.*) 490
May Day Manifesto Committee 521
Mayhew, C.P. (later *Baron*) 531
Meaning of Liberalism, The (J.M.
    Robertson) 160
Meaning of Socialism, The (J.B.
    Glasier) 414–15
Means, G. 477
Media, the
  and socialization 492
Melchett, *1st Baron see* Mond, *Sir* Alfred
Mellor, W. 435
Mercantilism *see also* Cameralism
  reversion to 240, 259, 260
  spirit 235
  state action 361–2
Meriden Motor Cycle Co-operative 527
Meritocracy 363
Mesoeconomic power 525
Metaphysical Theory of the State, The (L.T.
    Hobhouse) 162
Methodism 353, 357 *see also* Nonconformity
Methods of Social Study (S. and B.
    Webb) 395
Metropolitan Board of Works 211
Meyer, *Sir* Anthony 326

Middle Ages 91, 420, 428, 442
  ideal 425, 454
Middle Class Defence League 273, 286
Middle way, a
  Conservatism 233, 238, 245, 249, 250,
    251–3, 255, 257, 258, 260, 261, 315–16,
    326, 341, 476
  Liberalism 172–3, 177, 178–9, 251–2
  Social Democracy 534
  Socialism 252, 476, 478, 486, 513, 530, 532
Middle Way, The (H. Macmillan) 250, 253,
    258
Miliband, R. 490–3, 495
Militancy *see also* Spencer, H.
  in Britain 68, 80–1
  in external policy opposed 32, 37, 39, 98
Militant Tendency, the 15, 350, 494, 517, 532
Mill, James 104, 115, 356 n.23
Mill, J.S. 47, 49, 137, 306, 328, 350, 353, 524
  ambiguous language 109–11
  anti-Malthusianism 117
  bridge, the 109–10
  collectivist inclinations 104, 105 and n.5,
    109–24
  democracy
    consequences 106–7
    defects 115–16, 368
    institutional remedies 116
  despotic rule 111, 116, 117
  early life 104
  economic ideas
    influence of 373
  élitism 114–17, 122–3, 363
  Fabianism 114, 373
  facts and ideas 4
  freedom defended 104, 105, 107–8, 109,
    109–10, 111, 114, 123
  government
    and the economy 108, 113, 118
    functions 105, 109, 111–14
    restrictions on 108, 111, 112
    umpire 108
  ideological contrasts 15
  individuality sustained 104–9, 120, 121, 123
  industrial co-operatives 120–1
  influence 103, 105, 114, 119, 284, 386
  laissez faire
    qualified support 112
  land nationalization 373
  London's water supply 112
  masses, the
    character 114–15
    need supervision 113–14
    political significance growing 106–7
  names and ideas 7
  peasant proprietorship 120–1
  philosophical necessity 122
  property distribution 119–21